BUSINESS ACCOUNTING

Second Irish Edition

BUSINESS ACCOUNTING

Second Irish Edition

Tommy Robinson

Frank Wood

FT Prentice Hall

FINANCIAL TIMES

An imprint of **Pearson Education**

Harlow, England • London • New York • Boston • San Francisco • Toronto • Sydney • Singapore • Hong Kong
Tokyo • Seoul • Taipei • New Delhi • Cape Town • Madrid • Mexico City • Amsterdam • Munich • Paris • Milan

Pearson Education Limited
Edinburgh Gate
Harlow
Essex CM20 2JE
England

and Associated Companies throughout the world

Visit us on the World Wide Web at:
http://www.pearsoned.co.uk

First published in 1994
Second edition published in 1999

© Frank Wood 1967
© Longman Group UK Limited 1972, 1979, 1984, 1989, 1993
© Tommy Robinson 1994, 1999

ISBN 978-0-273-63153-8

A catalogue record for this book is available from the British Library.

657 ROB

10
07

£56.91

All names of individuals and businesses used in this book are fictitious.
Any resemblance to real people or businesses is purely coincidental.

While both the authors and KPMG have taken great care to ensure that all
material in this book is correct, it should be borne in mind that it may not
provide all the information required to deal directly with a particular situation.
The references and examples given should, therefore, not necessarily be
considered to be sufficient for making decisions.

Typeset by Land & Unwin (Data Sciences) Limited
Printed and bound in Great Britain by Ashford Colour Press Ltd. Gosport, Hants

Contents

A Companion Web Site accompanies The Frank Wood series of books

Visit the Frank Wood Companion Web Site at www.booksites.net/wood

to find valuable teaching and learning material including:

For Students:
- Study material designed to help you improve your results
- Exam tips
- Accounting Standards Updates
- Glossary for difficult terms

For Lecturers:
- A secure, password protected site with material to help you teach your course
- Solutions manual
- OHPs for download
- Syllabus manager that allows you to create a course homepage with no technical knowledge

Preface

This textbook has been written so as to provide Irish students with a thorough introduction to accounting. It should be useful to third level students undertaking courses in business or accounting, both as part of a business/accounting degree or as part of a broader degree, or other qualification. As much of the Leaving Certificate Accounting course is covered it should also be of use to students studying that subject. In addition, it is ideal for any person who wants to obtain a good grounding in accounting, for whatever purpose.

The text is recommended reading for students preparing for the following professional examinations:

The Institute of Chartered Accountants in Ireland – Professional One – Introduction to Accounting
The Institute of Accounting Technicians in Ireland – Foundation Examination – Accounts I
The Institute of Taxation in Ireland
The Institute of Certified Public Accountants in Ireland – Formation I – Accounting
The Association of Chartered Certified Accountants – Paper 1 – The Accounting Framework

Past examination questions from all of the above bodies, for the papers listed above and other papers, are included throughout the book. We thank them, and also the Institute of Bankers in Ireland, the Association of Accounting Technicians, the Chartered Institute of Management Accountants and the Institute of Chartered Secretaries and Administrators for granting us permission to reproduce questions from their examination papers. We accept full responsibility for any errors, whether in the suggested solutions to these questions, to other questions, or in the text.

We thank our friends, colleagues and others, too numerous to mention, for their advice and assistance. We trust that they will not be offended by our inability to list them all here. We thank, also, the Irish Accountancy Educational Trust for its support and the many students who, through their insightful questions, have contributed to the book.

We have attempted to make this difficult subject easy to understand. Consequently, throughout the text the figures and amounts used are relatively small. Although the figures used may, in some cases, seem unrealistic, we believe that keeping matters simple is more important. We focus on the principles of accounting, which are the same regardless of the amounts concerned, rather than tedious calculations. A *Solutions Manual* for those questions not answered in this book is available free of charge to lecturers and teachers upon application to the publishers. It may also be used as a source of overhead transparency masters.

Suggestions or any other comments as to how to improve this book are welcome and should be sent to the publishers who will forward them to us.

Tommy Robinson and Frank Wood

How to get the most from this book

To learn accounting requires lots of practice. Therefore, in addition to reading the chapters in this book, you should attempt as many questions as possible which test your knowledge of those chapters.

At the end of each chapter

At the end of most chapters there are 'Review questions' to test your knowledge of that chapter. These are carefully ordered so as to build up from relatively simple questions to more complicated ones.

To help you with your private study suggested solutions to some of these questions are given in Appendix I. The questions for which suggested solutions are provided have the letter 'A' after the question number.

It is important that you attempt the questions to which solutions are provided. Check the suggested solution to a question only AFTER you have attempted to answer it. If you don't know how to do a particular question you should first revise the chapter and then attempt the question. If you are still unable to do it you should look at the suggested solution to learn from it, not simply to find the answer. We do not recommend that you look at the suggested solutions without first attempting the questions and have deliberately had the answers printed using a different page layout to try to stop you doing this.

At the end of groups of related chapters

This book is divided into eight parts. This is done in order to group related chapters together and also to allow students to leave out one or more complete parts where certain areas are not on their syllabus.

At the end of parts four to eight inclusive there are 'Revision questions'. Most of these questions test knowledge gained from more than one chapter. Again, suggested solutions to some of these questions are provided, this time in Appendix II. Attempting the revision questions should prove to be an efficient way of revising topics shortly before exams.

Multiple-choice questions

As it is the practice of many examining bodies (for example, the Institute of Chartered Accountants in Ireland and the Institute of Accounting Technicians in Ireland), and of many lecturers, to set multiple-choice questions on their examination papers, a separate accompanying book of these questions is available (see back cover for details). Many of the questions in that book are drawn from the past examination papers of the above bodies.

In total, there are four hundred questions covering every topic covered in the main text. It is important that you attempt the multiple-choice questions, as well as the review and revision questions in this book. Multiple-choice questions may test your knowledge in far greater detail than the longer questions may do.

Some students may find it useful, as they progress through this book, to do the multiple-choice questions in blocks, for example, at the end of each part, so as to test their power of recall. Others will prefer to do them at the end of each chapter. Others will attempt them only as part of their revision. When you do these questions is not so important; what is important is that you do them sometime.

Sources of questions in this book

In common with the accompanying book of multiple-choice questions, many of the review and revision questions in this book have been drawn from past examination papers of accounting and other professional bodies. The source of such questions is given at the end of each question. Some of these questions have an asterisk after the source of the question. This means that the dates referred to in the original exam paper have been changed but ALL other details are as originally shown.

The names of some of the professional bodies from which questions have been drawn are abbreviated when listed. These abbreviations are as follows:

ICAI   The Institute of Chartered Accountants in Ireland
IATI   The Institute of Accounting Technicians in Ireland
ICPAI   The Institute of Certified Public Accountants in Ireland

Accounting terminology

Students learning accounting for the first time frequently experience difficulty with accounting 'jargon'. In an effort to overcome this problem, every time a new term is encountered in the text it is shown in **bold** print. In addition, there is an extensive glossary of accounting and financial terms at the end of the book.

The need for practice

As was stated at the outset, to learn accounting requires lots of practice. You should try to find the time to answer as many review, revision and multiple-choice questions as possible. The reasons for this are as follows:

1 Even though you may think you understand the text, when you come to answer the questions you may often find that your understanding is incomplete. The real test of understanding is whether you can answer the questions correctly.
2 For examination purposes, you need to be able, not only to answer questions correctly, but also to do this quickly and still present your answers neatly. You will not be able to do this without practice. When answering the review and revision questions in this book you should get into the habit of making sure that your answers are well laid out. Once you have mastered the basics and get to the level of actual examination questions you should do your answers 'against the clock'.

Good luck in your exams!

Abbreviations

Explanations of the abbreviations listed below are given in the glossary (*see* pp. 699–718). Most are listed there under their full title. 'PAYE' and 'PRSI' however, are listed in their abbreviated form.

AGM   Annual General Meeting
ASB   Accounting Standards Board
ASC   Accounting Standards Committee
AVCO   Average Cost Method of Stock Valuation
b/d   Balance Brought Down
b/f   Balance Brought Forward
CCAB   Consultative Committee of the Accountancy Bodies
c/d   Balance Carried Down
c/f   Balance Carried Forward
ED   Exposure Draft
EGM   Extraordinary General Meeting
EPS   Earnings per Share
FIFO   First-in, First-out Method of Stock Valuation
FRC   Financial Reporting Council
FRED   Financial Reporting Exposure Draft
FRS   Financial Reporting Standards
GAAP   Generally Accepted Accounting Practices
LIFO   Last-in, First-out Method of Stock Valuation
NBV   Net Book Value
NRV   Net Realisable Value
PAYE   Pay-As-You-Earn (taxation)
PRSI   Pay Related Social Insurance
SSAP   Statement of Standard Accounting Practice
UITF   Urgent Issues Task Force
VAT   Value Added Tax

1

Introduction to accounting

This chapter introduces the subject of accounting. It explains what accounting is, provides a general overview of the business environment in which accounting operates and explains the role of accounting in helping to produce the information which businesses need.

In this way, before accounting is examined in detail, you will have a broad picture of how the subject fits into the business world as a whole.

1.1 The nature of accounting

Many people think of accounting as being the work which accountants do, but do not fully understand what this entails. It is a widely held view that accountants deal exclusively with figures all day, every day. Figures do represent a significant proportion of the work of accountants but where do these figures come from and what do they mean?

In general, the figures that accountants deal with are the result of business transactions. For example, if a business which sells computers buys a computer from the manufacturer for £1,000 and subsequently sells it to a customer for £1,500 two transactions giving rise to figures have taken place. The first transaction is that the business has bought a computer for £1,000 and the second is that the business has sold the same computer for £1,500. An accountant could 'deal' with these figures to produce the result that the business has earned a profit of £500. He could then communicate this information, either verbally or in the form of a report, to the owner of the business.

Obviously, in most businesses there will be hundreds, or even thousands, of transactions such as the above every week or month. Because of this volume of transactions it makes sense (and is necessary as one could not keep all this data in one's mind) to firstly, record all of them individually, then summarise them and only then produce the result of the business's trading.

For example, if, in a given month, the above business bought 20 computers for £1,000 each and subsequently sold all of them for £1,500 each the result could be arrived at in two ways. Firstly, one could say that the business earned a profit of £500 on the sale of each computer and, since it sold 20 of them it earned a profit of 20 times £500, which is £10,000. Alternatively, this same figure could be arrived at by saying that the business purchased 20 computers for £1,000 each and therefore purchased £20,000 worth of computers in total. It sold 20 computers for £1,500 each and therefore sold £30,000 worth of computers. Having sold the computers which it had purchased for £20,000 for £30,000 the business earned a profit of £10,000.

The second method of calculating the profit is the one used in practice. This method provides better information than the first as, in addition to showing how much profit was earned by the business for a month, it also shows the total value of the business's sales and purchases for that month and involves calculating profit once only.

The above example illustrates some of the more important aspects of accounting. The first of these is that accounting involves the recording of data. It was seen that each

transaction, whether it was a purchase or a sale, was recorded by the business. The second aspect is that accounting involves classifying and summarising data. Again, it was seen that each transaction was classified as being either a purchase or a sale and, at the end of the month, all of the sales transactions were summarised into a total figure for sales and the purchase transactions into a total figure for purchases. The third aspect is that accounting involves the communication of information to those who are entitled to receive such information.

Accounting is, therefore, concerned with:

1 The *recording* of data;
2 *Classifying and summarising* data, and
3 *Communicating* what has been learned from the data.

1.2 What is bookkeeping?

The part of accounting that is concerned with recording data is often known as **bookkeeping**. Before the advent of computers, accounting data was recorded on paper, the separate sheets of paper being bound to form 'books'. It can be seen, therefore, that the term bookkeeping literally means the keeping of books or the maintenance of a record of business transactions. Nowadays, although books may be used to keep a record of business transactions, quite obviously a lot of accounting data is recorded using computers. Most of the recording of data is undertaken by clerical staff rather than by accountants.

A business needs to keep accounting records or records of its business transactions for reasons other than to help its own accountant in preparing reports. Most businesses are required by law to keep specified accounting records. These records must be made available to auditors and/or the Revenue Commissioners, if requested, so that they can verify the figures given to them by the business. Firms also need to keep records to assist in the day-to-day management and control of the business.

For example, if the business above sold one of its computers to a customer who agreed to pay for it at a later date the business should record the fact that it is owed money so that if the customer does not pay on time the business won't forget to remind the customer. Furthermore, the keeping of records facilitates the provision of information to those who manage businesses and allows them to make decisions and plan for the future.

1.3 Different types of business organisation

Different types of organisation, whether business organisations or other types of organisation, may be treated differently in terms of accounting.

For example, wholesalers buy goods at one price from a manufacturer and sell them at a higher price, and usually in smaller quantities, to a number of retailers thereby making a profit. Retailers do the same except that they may buy directly from a manufacturer or wholesaler and sell to customers who buy the goods for themselves rather than to re-sell.

The accounting for these firms is like that in the example of the computer dealer above, itself a retail business.

Service businesses, on the other hand, such as a bank or a firm of accountants, do not purchase goods for re-sale because what they sell are their services rather than a physical product. Their profit is therefore the difference between the cost of providing their services and the amount they sell those services for.

Manufacturing businesses buy in materials, subject them to a production process and ultimately sell the goods they thus manufacture. Their profit is the difference between the

amount they receive when they sell their products and the cost of those products, which is made up of the cost of the materials purchased and the cost of converting those materials into saleable goods.

Non-business organisations such as universities, hospitals and sports clubs, which exist for reasons other than to make a profit, need to keep a record of their income and expenses in order to effectively and efficiently run the organisation.

The amount and type of accounting information which any business will keep may also depend upon the legal structure of the business. For example, if an individual decides to set up business on his own then he need only keep records to satisfy himself and the Revenue Commissioners. If two or more individuals enter into business together as partners then whoever keeps the accounting records must keep them in sufficient detail to satisfy both partners. If the two partners had set up a company then they would be obliged by law to keep detailed accounting records and have these records independently examined by an auditor each year. Some accounting data would also have to be sent to the Companies Registration Office where anyone could examine it.

1.4 Accounting conventions

Irrespective of the nature of a business or its legal form, accounting reports will be prepared, usually annually, to show how much profit (or loss) the business has earned (or incurred) in that year and the value of the business's resources as well as how much has been invested in it and how much it owes at the end of that period.

The above paragraph illustrates three conventions fundamental to accounting. It is important that you are aware of these conventions at this stage so that you will be better able to appreciate many of the later chapters.

The Entity Convention means that the accounting reports mentioned above show the profit or loss earned or incurred by the business during a particular period and the resources and debts of the firm at the end of the period *as distinct from* the profit, loss, resources and debts of the owner(s) of the business. For example, if the owner of a business has taken out a mortgage to buy his home and the business which he owns owes money to a supplier for goods purchased then only the money owed to the supplier will appear in the accounting report which lists the debts of the business. This is because the mortgage is owed by the owner in his personal capacity and personal debts (and resources and income, etc.) must be kept separate from those of the business entity.

The Money Measurement Convention means that only items capable of being measured reasonably accurately in money terms are reflected in accounting reports. This means that whilst sales, purchases, debts, etc. can be shown in accounting reports other facts relevant to a business, such as the fact that the business has much better management personnel than its competitors, or the fact that the employees are about to go on strike, or the fact that a new product is about to be launched by a competitor thus eroding the business's market share, cannot be shown because they are not capable of being quantified with reasonable accuracy.

The effect of this is that if you compare the accounting reports of two businesses and they show, for example, that both businesses earned the same amount of profit last year, this does not mean that they will do so next year because of reasons such as the above which are not reflected in the figures. Therefore, accounting reports present a limited picture only of a business.

The Accounting Period Convention means that accounting reports are prepared at regular intervals to show the profit earned or the loss incurred by a business for the period of time elapsed since either the business was set up in the case of the first accounting period or, more frequently, since the last day of the preceding accounting period.

The management of the business can choose the length of the accounting period. Most businesses choose a period of one year for convenience. This is frequently the calendar year but need not be. For example, if a person commenced business on July 1st, 1998 he would probably have his accounting reports prepared for the years ending June 30th, 1999, 2000 and so on. Alternatively, if he wanted to follow the calendar year he could have his first accounting reports prepared for the six months ended December 31st, 1998 and have subsequent reports prepared for the years ending on December 31st, 1999 and so on.

Companies must report their results for tax purposes for periods not exceeding one year and therefore, to avoid having to prepare one set of results for tax purposes and another set for accounting purposes, they choose to report for accounting purposes for the same period as they use for tax purposes. Accounting reports are usually prepared monthly for the management of a business but only annually for tax and legal purposes.

Accounting conventions (or concepts) are considered in greater detail in Chapter 11.

1.5 Users of accounting information

The accounting or financial reports referred to may be read by a wide variety of people. Many different people may want different information about a business depending on their relationship with it.

As well as the owners or managers of a business those who want information about a business include investors in the business, people who are owed money by the business, the employees of the business and government bodies such as the Revenue Commissioners.

An important objective of accounting reports is to provide information to these people to assist them in making informed decisions about the business.

1.6 Desirable qualities of accounting information

In order for this information to be useful to these people it must be relevant to their needs and presented to them in a way which they can understand. They must also receive the information in time to make their decision.

Accountants should strive to produce financial information which meets these standards.

Part I

RECORDING BUSINESS TRANSACTIONS 1: Introduction to double entry accounting

2

The accounting equation and the balance sheet

2.1 The accounting equation

The whole of financial accounting is based upon a very simple idea called the *accounting equation*. This can best be explained by way of example.

For example, in order for a firm to set up, and start trading, it needs resources. Assume that initially it is the owner(s) of the business who have supplied all of the resources. This can be shown as:

> **The resources in the business = The resources supplied by the owner(s)**

In accounting, terms are used to describe things. The amount of the resources supplied by the owner is called **capital**. The actual resources that are then in the business are called **assets**. This means that the accounting equation above, when the owner(s) have supplied all of the resources, can be shown as:

> **Assets = Capital**

Usually, however, people other than the owner(s) have supplied some of the assets. **Liabilities** is the name given to the amounts owing to these people for these assets. The equation now becomes:

> **Assets = Capital + Liabilities**

It can be seen that the two sides of the equation will have the same totals. This is because we are dealing with the same thing from two different points of view. It is:

> **Resources: what they are = Resources: who supplied them**
> **(Assets)   (Capital + Liabilities)**

It is a fact that the totals of each side will always equal one another, and that this will always be true no matter how many transactions there may be. The actual assets, capital and liabilities may change, but the total of the assets will always equal the total of capital + liabilities.

Assets consist of property of all kinds, such as buildings, machinery, stocks of goods and vehicles. Also benefits such as debts owed by customers and the amount of money in the bank account are included.

Liabilities consist of money owing for goods supplied to the firm and for expenses. Loans made to the firm are also included.

Capital is often called the owner's **equity** or **net worth**.

2.2 The balance sheet and the effects of business transactions

The accounting equation is expressed in a financial position statement called the **Balance Sheet**. It is not the first accounting record to be made, but it is a convenient place to start to consider accounting. We will do this by examining the effects of a number of business transactions.

Transaction 1 – The introduction of capital

Suppose that on 1 May 1998 B Blake started in business and deposited £5,000 into a bank account opened specially for the business. After this transaction has taken place, the Balance Sheet of his business would appear as follows:

B Blake

Balance Sheet as at 1 May 1998

	£
Assets	
Cash at bank	5,000
Capital	5,000

Transaction 2 – The purchase of an asset by cheque

On 3 May 1998 Blake bought a building worth £3,000 and paid for it by cheque. The effect of this transaction is that the amount in the business's bank account has decreased and a new asset, i.e. buildings, appears. After these two transactions, the Balance Sheet would appear as:

B Blake

Balance Sheet as at 3 May 1998

	£
Assets	
Buildings	3,000
Cash at bank (£5,000 – £3,000)*	2,000
	5,000
Capital	5,000

* The explanations shown in brackets would not normally be shown in a Balance Sheet. They are shown here to aid understanding.

Transaction 3 – The purchase of an asset and the incurring of a liability

On 6 May 1998 Blake bought some goods for £500 from D Smith, and agreed to pay for them within two weeks. The effect of this transaction is that a new asset, **stock** of goods, is acquired, and a liability for the goods is incurred. A person to whom money is owed for goods is known in accounting language as a **creditor**. After these three transactions, the balance sheet of the business would appear as:

B Blake
Balance Sheet as at 6 May 1998

	£
Assets	
Buildings	3,000
Stock of goods	500
Cash at bank	2,000
	5,500
Liability	
Creditors	500
	5,000
Capital	5,000

Transaction 4 – The sale of an asset on credit

On 10 May 1998 goods which had cost B Blake £100 were sold to J Brown for the same amount, the money to be paid later. The effect of this sale is a reduction in the stock of goods and the creation of a new asset. A person who owes a firm money is known, in accounting language, as a **debtor** of that firm. After these four transactions the balance sheet of the business would appear as:

B Blake
Balance Sheet as at 10 May 1998

	£
Assets	
Buildings	3,000
Stock of goods (£500 – £100)	400
Debtor	100
Cash at bank	2,000
	5,500
Liability	
Creditor	500
	5,000
Capital	5,000

Transaction 5 – The sale of an asset for immediate payment

On 13 May 1998 goods which had cost B Blake £50 were sold to D Daley for the same amount. Daley paid for them immediately by cheque. Here one asset, stock of goods, is reduced, while another asset, the amount in the bank account, is increased. The balance sheet would now appear as:

B Blake

Balance Sheet as at 13 May 1998

	£
Assets	
Buildings	3,000
Stock of goods (£400 – £50)	350
Debtor	100
Cash at bank (£2,000 + £50)	2,050
	5,500
Liability	
Creditor	500
	5,000
Capital	5,000

Transaction 6 – The payment of a liability

On 15 May 1998 Blake wrote a cheque for £200 to D Smith in part payment of the amount owing to him. Blake's bank balance is therefore reduced, and the liability of the creditor is also reduced. The balance sheet now appears as:

B Blake

Balance Sheet as at 15 May 1998

	£
Assets	
Buildings	3,000
Stock of goods	350
Debtor	100
Cash at bank (£2,050 – £200)*	1,850
	5,300
Liability	
Creditor (£500 – £200)	300
	5,000
Capital	5,000

* Although a cheque may not be 'cashed' for a few days it is conventional in accounting to reduce the bank balance figure as soon as cheques are written. This convention is explained further in Chapter 11.

Transaction 7 – The collection of an asset

J Brown, the debtor who owed Blake's business £100, paid £75 by cheque on 31 May 1998. The effect of this is to reduce one asset, the debtor, and to increase another asset, the bank balance. This results in a balance sheet as follows:

B Blake

Balance Sheet as at 31 May 1998

	£
Assets	
Buildings	3,000
Stock of goods	350
Debtor (£100 – £75)	25
Cash at bank (£1,850 + £75)	1,925
	5,300
Liability	
Creditor	300
	5,000
Capital	5,000

2.3 Equality of the accounting equation

It can be seen that every transaction has affected two items. Sometimes the effect of a transaction is to change two assets by reducing one and increasing the other. Other times both assets and liabilities may be affected. A summary of the effect of some transactions upon assets, liabilities and capital is shown below.

No.	Nature of transaction	Effects of transaction on the Balance Sheet			
1	Buy goods on credit	↑	Increase asset (Stock of goods)	↑	Increase liability (Creditors)
2	Buy goods and pay by cheque	↑	Increase asset (Stock of goods)	↓	Decrease asset (Bank)
3	Pay creditor by cheque	↓	Decrease asset (Bank)	↓	Decrease liability (Creditors)
4	Owner pays more capital into the bank	↑	Increase asset (Bank)	↑	Increase capital
5	Owner takes money out of the business bank account for his own use	↓	Decrease asset (Bank)	↓	Decrease capital
6	Owner pays creditor from private money outside the firm	↓	Decrease liability (Creditors)	↑	Increase capital

Each transaction has, therefore, maintained the same total for assets as that of capital + liabilities as illustrated in the following table:

Transaction Number (per previous table)	Effect upon assets	Effect upon liabilities	Effect upon capital	Net effect on balance sheet totals
1	+	+		Both top and bottom halves added to equally
2	+ −			A + and a − **both** in the assets section cancelling out each other
3	−	−		Top and bottom halves have equal deductions
4	+		+	Top and bottom halves have equal additions
5	−		−	Top and bottom halves have equal deductions
6		−	+	Both top and bottom halves added to equally

Review questions

In addition to the questions below, you should attempt questions 1–6 in the accompanying book of multiple-choice questions (see back cover for further details).

Suggested solutions to review questions with the letter 'A' after the question number are given in Appendix I (page 601).

2.1A Complete the gaps in the table below:

	Assets	Liabilities	Capital
	£	£	£
(a)	12,500	1,800	?
(b)	28,000	4,900	?
(c)	16,800	?	12,500
(d)	19,600	?	16,450
(e)	?	6,300	19,200
(f)	?	11,650	39,750

2.2 Complete the gaps in the following table:

	Assets	Liabilities	Capital
	£	£	£
(a)	55,000	16,900	?
(b)	?	17,200	34,400
(c)	36,100	?	28,500
(d)	119,500	15,400	?
(e)	88,000	?	62,000
(f)	?	49,000	110,000

2.3A   Classify the items (a) to (f) below as either assets or liabilities of J Ryan.

(*a*) Office machinery
(*b*) Loan from C Shirley
(*c*) Fixtures and fittings

(*d*) Vehicles
(*e*) Money owed for goods purchased
(*f*) Bank balance

2.4   Classify the following items into liabilities and assets:

(*a*) Vehicles
(*b*) Premises
(*c*) Creditors for goods
(*d*) Stock of goods
(*e*) Debtors

(*f*) Money owed to bank
(*g*) Cash in hand
(*h*) Loan from D Jones
(*i*) Machinery

2.5A   State which of the following is/are shown under the wrong heading for J White's business:

Assets	*Liabilities*
Loan from C Smith	Stock of goods
Cash on hand	Debtors
Machinery	Money owing to a bank
Creditors	
Premises	
Vehicles	

2.6   Which of the following is/are shown under the wrong heading for P Kelly's business?

Assets	*Liabilities*
Cash at bank	Loan from J Graham
Fixtures	Machinery
Creditors	Vehicles
Building	
Stock of goods	
Debtors	
Capital	

2.7A   A Smart set up a new business. Before he actually sold anything, he bought a vehicle for £2,000, premises for £5,000 and a stock of goods for £1,000. He did not pay in full for his stock and still owes £400 in respect of it. He borrowed £3,000 from D Bevan. After the events just described, and before trading started, he had £100 cash in hand and £700 in the bank. Calculate the amount of his capital at that point in time.

2.8   T Charles started a business. Before he actually sold anything, he bought fixtures for £2,000, a vehicle for £5,000 and a stock of goods for £3,500. Although he paid in full for the fixtures and the vehicle, he still owes £1,400 for some of the goods. J Preston lent him £3,000. Charles, after the above, had £2,800 in the business bank account and £100 cash in hand. Calculate his capital.

2.9A Draw up A Foster's balance sheet as at 31 December 1997, from the following:

	£
Capital	23,750
Debtors	4,950
Vehicles	5,700
Creditors	2,450
Fixtures	5,500
Stock of goods	8,800
Cash at bank	1,250

2.10 Draw up Kelly's balance sheet as at 30 June 1998 from the following items:

	£
Capital	13,000
Office machinery	9,000
Creditors	900
Stock of goods	1,550
Debtors	275
Cash at bank	5,075
Loan from C Smith	2,000

2.11A Complete the columns to the right of the list of transactions below to show the effects of each transaction on the assets, liabilities and capital of a firm:

Transactions	Effect upon		
	Assets	Liabilities	Capital
(a) The firm pays a creditor £70 in cash.			
(b) Bought fixtures for £200 paying by cheque.			
(c) Bought goods on credit for £275.			
(d) The proprietor introduces £500 cash into the firm.			
(e) J Walker lends the firm £200 in cash.			
(f) A debtor pays the firm £50 by cheque.			
(g) The firm returns goods costing £60 to a supplier whose bill the firm had not yet paid.			
(h) The firm bought additional shop premises paying £5,000 by cheque.			

2.12   As for question 2.11 complete the columns to show the effects of the following transactions:

Transactions	Effect upon		
	Assets	Liabilities	Capital
(a) Bought a used van on credit for £500.			
(b) Repaid a loan of £1,000 owed to P Smith.			
(c) Bought goods for £150 paying by cheque.			
(d) The owner lodges £5,000 cash into the business.			
(e) A debtor returns goods sold to him for £80. It is agreed to make an allowance for them.			
(f) Bought goods on credit for £220.			
(g) The owner takes out £100 cash for his personal use.			
(h) The firm pays a creditor £190 by cheque.			

2.13A   C Sangster had the following items in his balance sheet as at 30 April 1998:

Capital £18,900; Loan from T Sharples £2,000; Creditors £1,600; Fixtures £3,500; Vehicle £4,200; Stock of goods £4,950; Debtors £3,280; Cash at bank £6,450; Cash in hand £120.

During the first week of May:

(a) Sangster bought extra stock of goods £770 on credit.
(b) One of the debtors paid Sangster £280 in cash.
(c) Sangster bought extra fixtures by cheque £1,000.

Draw up a balance sheet as at 7 May 1998 after the above transactions have been completed.

2.14   F Dale had the following assets and liabilities as at 30 November 1997:

Creditors £3,950; Equipment £11,500; Vehicle £6,290; Stock of goods £6,150; Debtors £5,770; Cash at bank £7,280; Cash in hand £40.

The capital at that date is to be deduced by you.
During the first week of December:

(a) Dale bought more equipment on credit for £1,380.
(b) Dale bought more stock by cheque £570.
(c) Dale paid creditors by cheque £790.
(d) Debtors paid Dale £840 by cheque and £60 by cash.
(e) D Terry lent Dale £250 cash.

Draw up a balance sheet as at 7 December 1997 after the above transactions have been completed.

3

The double entry system for assets, liabilities and capital

3.1 The double entry system

We have seen that every transaction affects two items. If we want to show the effect of every transaction when we are doing our bookkeeping, we will have to show the effect of a transaction on each of the two items. For each transaction this means that a bookkeeping entry will have to be made to show an increase or decrease in that item, and another entry to show the increase or decrease in the other item. From this you will probably be able to see that the term **double entry system** of bookkeeping is a good one, as each entry is made twice.

It may be thought that drawing up a new balance sheet after each transaction would provide all the information required. However, a balance sheet does not give enough information about a business. It does not, for instance, tell who the debtors are and how much each one of them owes the firm, or who the creditors are and the details of money owing to each of them. Also, the task of drawing up a new balance sheet after each transaction becomes an impossibility when there are many hundreds of transactions each day, as this would mean drawing up hundreds of balance sheets daily. Because of the work involved, balance sheets are in fact only drawn up periodically, at least annually, but frequently half-yearly, quarterly, or monthly.

The double entry system has an **account** (meaning details of transactions relating to a particular item) for every asset, every liability and for capital. Thus, there will be a shop premises account (for transactions involving shop premises), a vehicles account (for transactions involving vehicles), and so on for every asset, liability and for capital.

3.2 The accounts for double entry

In a paper-based (as opposed to a computerised) bookkeeping system each account should be shown on a separate page. The double entry system divides each page into two halves. The left-hand side of each page is called the **debit** side, while the right-hand side is called the **credit** side. The title of each account is written across the top of the account.

You must not think that the words 'debit' and 'credit' in bookkeeping mean the same as the words 'debit' or 'credit' in normal language usage. If you do, you may become confused.

A page of an accounts book would look like the following:

The title of the account (on that page)	
Left-hand side of the page. This is the 'debit' side.	Right-hand side of the page. This is the 'credit' side.

If you have to make an entry of £10 on the debit side of the account, the instructions given to you as bookkeeper could say 'debit the account with £10' or 'the account needs to be debited with £10'.

In Chapter 2 we saw transactions that increased and/or decreased assets, liabilities or capital. The double entry rules for these three classes of accounts are:

Accounts	To record	Entry in the account
Assets	an increase a decrease	Debit Credit
Liabilities	an increase a decrease	Credit Debit
Capital	an increase a decrease	Credit Debit

Let us look once again at the accounting equation:

	Assets =	Liabilities +	Capital
To increase each item	Debit	Credit	Credit
To decrease each item	Credit	Debit	Debit

The double entry rules for both liabilities and capital are the same, but they are the opposite of those for assets. This is because assets are on the opposite side of the equation and, therefore, follow opposite rules. Looking at the accounts the rules will appear as:

Any asset account		*Any liability account*		*Capital account*	
Increases +	*Decreases* −	*Decreases* −	*Increases* +	*Decreases* −	*Increases* +

We have not enough space in this book to put each account on a separate page, so we will have to show the accounts under each other. In a real firm (using a manual bookkeeping system) at least one full page would be used for each account.

3.3 Examples of double entry bookkeeping

The double entry for a few transactions will now be illustrated:

Transaction 1 A person started a firm with £10,000 in cash on 1 August.

Effect	Action
1 Increases the *asset* of cash	Debit the cash account
2 Increases the capital	Credit the capital account

These are shown as:

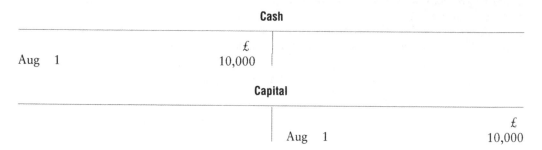

Cash

		£	
Aug 1		10,000	

Capital

			£
		Aug 1	10,000

The date of the transaction has already been entered. Now there remains the description which is to be entered alongside the amount. This is completed by a cross-reference to the title of the other account in which double entry is completed. The double entry to the item in the cash account is completed by an entry in the capital account, therefore the word 'Capital' will appear in the cash account. Similarly, the double entry to the item in the capital account is completed by an entry in the cash account, therefore the word 'Cash' will appear in the capital account.

The finally completed accounts are therefore:

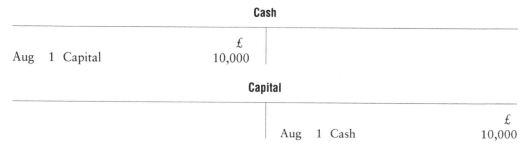

Cash

		£	
Aug 1 Capital		10,000	

Capital

			£
		Aug 1 Cash	10,000

Transaction 2 A used van is bought for £2,750 cash on 2 August.

Effect	Action
1 Decreases the *asset* of cash	Credit the cash account
2 Increases the *asset* of vans	Debit the van account

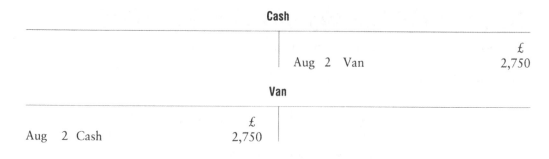

Cash

			£
		Aug 2 Van	2,750

Van

		£	
Aug 2 Cash		2,750	

Transaction 3 Fixtures are bought on credit from Shop Fitters Ltd for £115 on 3 August.

Effect	Action
1 Increases the *asset* of fixtures	Debit the fixtures account
2 Increases the *liability* to Shop Fitters Ltd	Credit the Shop Fitters Ltd account

Fixtures

	£	
Aug 3 Shop Fitters Ltd	115	

Shop Fitters Ltd

			£
		Aug 3 Fixtures	115

Transaction 4 Paid the amount owing in cash to Shop Fitters Ltd on 17 August.

Effect	Action
1 Decreases the *asset* of cash	Credit the cash account
2 Decreases the *liability* to Shop Fitters Ltd	Debit the Shop Fitters Ltd account

Cash

			£
		Aug 17 Shop Fitters Ltd	115

Shop Fitters Ltd

	£	
Aug 17 Cash	115	

Transactions to date.
Taking the transactions numbered **1** to **4** above, the records will now appear:

Cash

	£		£
Aug 1 Capital	10,000	Aug 2 Van	2,750
		„ 17 Shop Fitters Ltd	115

Capital

			£
		Aug 1 Cash	10,000

Van

	£	
Aug 2 Cash	2,750	

Shop Fitters Ltd

	£			£
Aug 17 Cash	115	Aug 3 Fixtures		115

Fixtures

	£	
Aug 3 Shop Fitters Ltd	115	

Before you read further you should work through questions 3.1 and 3.2.

3.4 Another example of double entry accounting

Now that you have actually made some entries in accounts you should go through the example in the table below. Make certain that you understand every entry.

Transactions		Effects	Action
May 1	Started an engineering business putting £10,000 into a business bank account.	↑ Increases the *asset* of bank. ↑ Increases *capital* of the owner.	Debit the bank account. Credit the capital account.
„ 3	Bought works machinery on credit from 'Unique Machines' for £2,750.	↑ Increases the *asset* of machinery. ↑ Increases the *liability* to Unique Machines.	Debit the machinery account. Credit the Unique Machines account.
„ 4	Withdrew £200 cash from the bank and placed it in the cash box.	↓ Decreases the *asset* of bank. ↑ Increases the *asset* of cash.	Credit the bank account. Debit the cash account.
„ 7	Bought a used van paying in cash £1,800.	↓ Decreases the *asset* of cash. ↑ Increases the *asset* of vans.	Credit the cash account. Debit the vans account.
„ 10	Sold some of the machinery for £150 on credit to B Barnes.	↓ Decreases the *asset* of machinery. ↑ Increases the *asset* of money owing from B Barnes.	Credit the machinery account. Debit B Barnes' account.

	Transactions	Effects	Action
May 21	Returned some of the machinery, value £270 to Unique Machines.	↓ Decreases the *asset* of machinery.	Credit the machinery account.
		↓ Decreases the *liability* to Unique Machines.	Debit Unique Machines' account.
„ 28	B Barnes pays the firm the amount owing, £150, by cheque.	↑ Increases the *asset* of bank.	Debit the bank account.
		↓ Decreases the *asset* of money owing by B Barnes.	Credit B Barnes' account.
„ 30	Bought another van paying by cheque £4,200.	↓ Decreases the *asset* of bank.	Credit the bank account.
		↑ Increases the *asset* of vans.	Debit the vans account.
„ 31	Paid the £2,480 owed, to Unique Machines by cheque.	↓ Decreases the *asset* of bank.	Credit the bank account.
		↓ Decreases the *liability* to Unique Machines.	Debit Unique Machines' account.

In account form the transactions in the above table are shown as:

Bank

		£			£
May 1	Capital	10,000	May 4	Cash	200
„ 28	B Barnes	150	„ 30	Vans	4,200
			„ 31	Unique Machines	2,480

Cash

		£			£
May 4	Bank	200	May 7	Vans	1,800

Capital

				£
		May 1	Bank	10,000

Machinery

		£			£
May 3	Unique Machines	2,750	May 10	B Barnes	150
			„ 21	Unique Machines	270

Vans

	£		
May 7 Cash	1,800		
„ 30 Bank	4,200		

Unique Machines

	£		£
May 21 Machines	270	May 3 Machinery	2,750
„ 31 Bank	2,480		

B Barnes

	£		£
May 10 Machinery	150	May 28 Bank	150

3.5 Abbreviation of 'limited'

In this book when we come across transactions with limited companies the use of the letters 'Ltd' is used as the abbreviation for 'Limited Company'. Thus we will know that, if we see the name of a firm as P Kelly Ltd, then that firm will be a limited company. In our books the transactions with P Kelly Ltd will be entered the same as for any other customer or supplier. It will be seen later that some limited companies use 'plc' instead of 'Ltd'.

Review questions

In addition to the questions below, you should attempt questions 7–9 in the accompanying book of multiple-choice questions (see back cover for further details).

Suggested solutions to review questions with the letter 'A' after the question number are given in Appendix I (page 602).

3.1A   Complete the following table:

Transactions	Account to be debited	Account to be credited
(a) Bought office machinery on credit from D Isaacs Ltd.		
(b) The proprietor paid a creditor, C Jones, from his private funds.		
(c) A debtor, N Fox, paid us in cash.		
(d) Repaid part of a loan from P Exeter by cheque.		
(e) Returned some office machinery to D Isaacs Ltd.		
(f) A debtor, N Lyn, pays us by cheque.		
(g) Bought a used van and paid in cash.		

3.2   Complete the following table showing which accounts are to be debited and which to be credited in the accounts of C Smiley & Co, a firm of builders' providers.

Transactions	Account to be debited	Account to be credited
(a) Bought a lorry for cash.		
(b) Paid a creditor, T Lake, by cheque.		
(c) Repaid P Logan's loan in cash.		
(d) Sold the lorry for cash.		
(e) Bought office machinery on credit from Ultra Ltd.		
(f) A debtor, A Hill, pays us by cash.		
(g) A debtor, J Cross, pays us by cheque.		
(h) The proprietor puts a further amount into the business by cheque.		
(i) A loan of £200 in cash is received from L Lowe.		
(j) Paid a creditor, D Lord, in cash.		

3.3A   Write up the asset, liability and capital accounts to record the following transactions in the records of G Powell, a carpenter.

July	1	Started business with £2,500 in the bank.
,,	2	Bought office furniture by cheque £150.
,,	3	Bought machinery £750 on credit from Planers Ltd.
,,	8	Sold some of the office furniture – not suitable for the firm – for £60 on credit to J Walker & Sons.
,,	15	Paid the amount owing to Planers Ltd £750 by cheque.
,,	23	Received the amount due from J Walker £60 in cash.
,,	31	Bought more machinery by cheque £280.

3.4A   Open the asset, liability and capital accounts and record the following transactions in the records of C Williams.

June	1	Started business with £2,000 in cash.
,,	2	Paid £1,800 of the opening cash into a bank account for the business.
,,	5	Bought office furniture on credit from Betta-Built Ltd for £120.
,,	12	Bought works machinery from Evans & Sons on credit for £560.
,,	18	Returned faulty office furniture costing £62 to Betta-Built Ltd.
,,	25	Sold some of the works machinery for £75 cash.
,,	26	Paid the amount owing to Betta-Built Ltd, £58 by cheque.
,,	28	Withdrew £100 out of the bank and put it in the cash till.
,,	30	J Smith lent us £500 – giving us the money by cheque.

3.5 Write up the asset, capital and liability accounts in the books of C Walsh to record the following transactions:

June 1   Started business with £5,000 in the bank.

,,   2   Bought a used van from Super Motors for £2,000, paying £1,200 by cheque, the balance to be paid later.

,,   5   Bought office fixtures £400 on credit from Young Ltd.

,,   12   Withdrew £100 out of the bank and put it into the cash till.

,,   15   Bought office fixtures paying by cash £60.

,,   19   Paid Super Motors a cheque for £800.

,,   21   A loan of £1,000 cash is received from J Jarvis.

,,   25   Lodged £800 of the cash in hand into the bank account.

,,   30   Bought more office fixtures paying by cheque £300.

3.6 Write up the accounts to record the following transactions:

March 1   Started business with £1,000 cash.

,,   2   Received a loan of £5,000 from M Chow by cheque, a bank account being opened and the cheque paid into it.

,,   3   Bought machinery for cash £600.

,,   5   Bought display equipment on credit from Better-View Machines £550.

,,   8   Withdrew £300 out of the bank and put it into the cash till.

,,   15   Repaid part of Chow's loan by cheque £800.

,,   17   Paid the amount owing to Better-View Machines £550 by cheque.

,,   24   Repaid part of Chow's loan by cash £100.

,,   31   Bought additional machinery, this time on credit from D Smith for £500.

4

The asset of stock

4.1 Stock movements

Goods are sometimes sold at the same price at which they are bought, but this is not usually the case. Normally they are sold above cost price, the difference being **profit**; sometimes however they are sold at less than cost price, the difference being a **loss**.

If all sales were at cost price, it would be possible to have a stock account, the goods sold being shown as a decrease of an asset, i.e. on the credit side. The purchase of stock could be shown on the debit side as it would be an increase of an asset. The difference between the two sides would then represent the cost of the goods unsold at that date, if wastages and losses of stock are ignored. However, most sales are not at cost price, and therefore the sales figures include elements of profit or loss. Because of this, the difference between the two sides would not represent the stock of goods. Such a stock account would therefore serve no useful purpose.

The **Stock Account** is accordingly divided into several accounts, each one showing a movement of stock. These can be said to be:

1 **Increases in stock.** These can be due to one of two causes:

(*a*) By the purchase of additional goods.

(*b*) By the return in to the firm of goods previously sold. The reasons for this are numerous. The goods may have been the wrong type, they may have been surplus to requirements, have been faulty and so on.

To distinguish the two aspects of the increase of stocks of goods two accounts are opened. These are:

(*i*) A **Purchases Account** – in which purchases of goods are entered.

(*ii*) A **Returns Inwards Account** – in which goods being returned in to the firm are entered. The alternative name for this account is the **Sales Returns Account**.

2 **Decreases in the stock of goods.** These can also be due to one of two causes if wastages and losses of stock are ignored.

(*a*) By the sale of goods.

(*b*) Goods previously bought by the firm now being returned out of the firm to the supplier.

To distinguish the two aspects of the decrease of stocks of goods two accounts are opened. These are:

(*i*) A **Sales Account** – in which sales of goods are entered.

(*ii*) A **Returns Outwards Account** – in which goods being returned out to a supplier are entered. The alternative name for this is the **Purchases Returns Account**.

As stock is an asset, and these four accounts are all connected with this asset, the double entry rules are those used for assets. We shall now look at some entries in the following sections.

4.2 The purchase of stock on credit

Example: On 1 August, goods costing £165 were bought on credit from D Henry. First, the twofold effect of the transaction must be considered so that the bookkeeping entries can be worked out.

1   The asset of stock is increased. An increase in an asset needs a debit entry in an account. Here the account is a stock account showing the particular movement of stock, in this case it is the 'purchases' movement so that the account must be the purchases account.

2   An increase in a liability. This is the liability of the firm to D Henry because the goods bought have not yet been paid for. An increase in a liability needs a credit entry, so that to enter this part of the transaction a credit entry is made in D Henry's account.

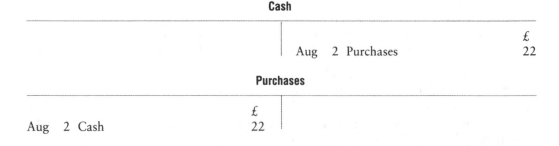

Purchases

	£		
Aug 1 D Henry	165		

D Henry

			£
		Aug 1 Purchases	165

4.3 The purchase of stock for cash

On 2 August, goods costing £22 were bought and paid for in cash.

1   The asset of stock is increased, so that a debit entry will be needed. The movement of stock is that of a purchase, so that it is the purchases account which needs to be debited.

2   The asset of cash is decreased. To reduce an asset a credit entry is called for, and the asset is that of cash so that the cash account needs to be credited.

Cash

			£
		Aug 2 Purchases	22

Purchases

	£		
Aug 2 Cash	22		

4.4 The sale of stock on credit

On 3 August, goods worth £250 are sold on credit to J Lee.

1   The asset of stock is decreased. For this a credit entry to reduce an asset is needed. The movement of stock is that of a 'Sale' so the account credited is the sales account.

2   An asset account is increased. This is the account showing that J Lee is a debtor for the goods. The increase in the asset of debtors requires a debit and the debtor is J Lee, so that the account concerned is that of J Lee.

Sales

		£
	Aug 3 J Lee	250

J Lee

	£	
Aug 3 Sales	250	

4.5 The sale of stock for cash

On 4 August, goods were sold for £55 cash.

1 The asset of cash is increased. A debit entry is required in the cash account to show this.
2 The asset of stock is reduced. The reduction of an asset requires a credit and the movement of stock is represented by 'Sales'. Thus the entry needed is a credit in the sales account.

Sales

		£
	Aug 4 Cash	55

Cash

	£	
Aug 4 Sales	55	

4.6 Returns inwards

On 5 August, goods which had been previously sold to F Lowe for £29 were returned by him.

1 The asset of stock is increased by the goods returned. Thus a debit representing an increase of an asset is needed, and this time the movement of stock is that of **Returns Inwards**. Therefore, the entry required is a debit in the returns inwards account.
2 A decrease in an asset. The debt of F Lowe to the firm is now reduced, and to record this a credit is needed in F Lowe's account.

Returns Inwards

	£	
Aug 5 F Lowe	29	

F Lowe

		£
	Aug 5 Returns inwards	29

An alternative name for a Returns Inwards Account is a **Sales Returns Account**.

4.7 Returns outwards

On 6 August, goods previously bought for £96 were returned by the firm to K Howe.

1   The asset of stock is decreased by the goods sent out. Thus, a credit representing a reduction in an asset is needed, and the movement of stock is that of **Returns Outwards** so that the entry will be a credit in the returns outwards account.

2   The liability of the firm to K Howe is decreased by the value of the goods returned to him. The decrease in a liability needs a debit, this time in K Howe's account.

Returns Outwards

			£
	Aug 6 K Howe		96

K Howe

	£		
Aug 6 Returns outwards	96		

An alternative name for a Returns Outwards Account is a **Purchases Returns Account**.

4.8 Example of double entry accounting for stock movements

May	1	Bought goods on credit £68 from D Small.
,,	2	Bought goods on credit £77 from A Lyon & Son.
,,	5	Sold goods on credit to D Hughes for £60.
,,	6	Sold goods on credit to M Spencer for £45.
,,	10	Returned goods £15 to D Small.
,,	12	Goods bought for cash £100.
,,	19	M Spencer returned £16 goods to us.
,,	21	Goods sold for cash £150.
,,	22	Paid cash to D Small £53.
,,	30	D Hughes paid the amount owing by him, £60 in cash.
,,	31	Bought goods on credit £64 from A Lyon & Son.

Purchases

	£		
May 1 D Small	68		
,, 2 A Lyon & Son	77		
,, 12 Cash	100		
,, 31 Lyon & Son	64		

Sales

		£
	May 5 D Hughes	60
	,, 6 M Spencer	45
	,, 21 Cash	150

Returns Outwards

		£
	May 10 D Small	15

Returns Inwards

	£		
May 19 M Spencer	16		

D Small

	£		£
May 10 Returns outwards	15	May 1 Purchases	68
„ 22 Cash	53		

A Lyon & Son

		£
	May 2 Purchases	77
	„ 31 Purchases	64

D Hughes

	£		£
May 5 Sales	60	May 30 Cash	60

M Spencer

	£		£
May 6 Sales	45	May 19 Returns inwards	16

Cash

	£		£
May 21 Sales	150	May 12 Purchases	100
„ 30 D Hughes	60	„ 22 D Small	53

4.9 Specific meaning of 'sales' and 'purchases' in accounting

The terms 'Sales' and 'Purchases' have a very specific meaning in accounting when compared to ordinary language usage.

'Purchases' in accounting means the *purchase of those goods which the firm buys with the prime intention of selling*. Obviously, sometimes the goods are altered, added to, or used in the manufacture of something else, but it is the element of resale that is important. To a firm that deals in typewriters for instance, typewriters constitute purchases. If something else is bought, such as a van, such an item cannot be called purchases, even though in ordinary language it may be said that a van has been purchased. The prime intention of buying the van is for usage and not for resale.

Similarly, 'Sales' means the *sale of those goods in which the firm normally deals and were bought with the prime intention of resale*. The word 'Sales' must never be used in relation to the disposal of other items.

If we did not keep to these meanings, it would result in the different kinds of stock accounts containing something other than goods sold or for resale.

4.10 Comparison of cash and credit transactions for purchases and sales

The difference between the records needed for cash and credit transactions can now be seen.

The complete set of entries for purchases of goods where they are paid for immediately by cash would be:

1 Credit the cash account.
2 Debit the purchases account.

On the other hand the complete set of entries for the purchase of goods on credit can be broken down into two stages: (i) the purchase of the goods and (ii) the payment for them.

The first part is:

1 Debit the purchases account.
2 Credit the supplier's account.

The second part is:

1 Credit the cash account.
2 Debit the supplier's account.

The difference can now be seen; with the cash purchase no record is kept of the supplier's account. This is because cash passes immediately and therefore there is no need to keep a check of indebtedness (money owing) to a supplier. On the other hand, in the credit purchase the records should show to whom money is owed until payment is made.

A study of cash sales and credit sales will reveal a similar difference.

Cash Sales	Credit Sales

Complete entry:
    Debit the cash account
    Credit the sales account
	First part:
	    Debit the customer's account
	    Credit the sales account
	 Second part:
	    Debit the cash account
	    Credit the customer's account

Review questions

In addition to the questions below, you should attempt questions 10–12 in the accompanying book of multiple-choice questions (see back cover for further details).

Suggested solutions to review questions with the letter 'A' after the question number are given in Appendix I (pages 602–3).

4.1A Complete the following table showing which accounts are to be credited and which are to be debited:

Transactions	Account to be debited	Account to be credited
(a) Goods bought on credit from J Reid.		
(b) Goods sold on credit to B Perkins.		
(c) Van bought on credit from H Thomas.		
(d) Goods sold, a cheque being received immediately.		
(e) Goods sold for cash.		
(f) Goods we returned to H Hardy.		
(g) Machinery sold for cash.		
(h) Goods returned to us by J Nelson.		
(i) Goods bought on credit from D Simpson.		
(j) Goods we returned to H Forbes.		

4.2 Complete the following table:

Transactions	Account to be debited	Account to be credited
(a) Goods bought on credit from T Morgan.		
(b) Goods returned to us by J Thomas.		
(c) Machinery returned to L Jones Ltd.		
(d) Goods bought for cash.		
(e) Van bought on credit from D Davies Ltd.		
(f) Goods returned by us to I Prince.		
(g) D Picton paid us his account by cheque.		
(h) Goods bought by cheque.		
(i) We paid a creditor, B Henry, by cheque.		
(j) Goods sold on credit to J Mullings.		

4.3A Write up the following transactions:

July	1	Started business with £500 cash.
,,	3	Bought goods for cash £85.
,,	7	Bought goods on credit £116 from E Morgan.
,,	10	Sold goods for cash £42.
,,	14	Returned goods to E Morgan £28.
,,	18	Bought goods on credit £98 from A Moses.
,,	21	Returned goods to A Moses £19.
,,	24	Sold goods to A Knight £55 on credit.
,,	25	Paid E Morgan's account by cash £88.
,,	31	A Knight paid his account in cash £55.

4.4A Enter the following transactions in the relevant accounts:

Aug	1	Started business with £1,000 cash.
,,	2	Paid £900 of the opening cash into the bank.
,,	4	Bought goods on credit £78 from S Holmes.
,,	7	Bought goods for cash £55.
,,	10	Sold goods on credit £98 to D Moore.
,,	12	Returned goods to S Holmes £18.
,,	19	Sold goods for cash £28.
,,	22	Bought fixtures on credit from Kingston Equipment Co £150.
,,	24	D Watson lent us £100 paying us the money by cheque.
,,	29	We paid S Holmes his account by cheque £60.
,,	31	We paid Kingston Equipment Co by cheque £150.

4.5A Enter the following transactions in the accounting records of E Sangster, a supermarket owner:

July	1	Started business with £10,000 in the bank.
,,	2	T Cooper lent us £400 in cash.
,,	3	Bought goods on credit from F Jones £840 and S Charles £3,600.
,,	4	Sold goods for cash £200.
,,	6	Took £250 of the cash and lodged it at the bank.
,,	8	Sold goods on credit to C Moody £180.
,,	10	Sold goods on credit to J Newman £220.
,,	11	Bought goods on credit from F Jones £370.
,,	12	C Moody returned goods to us £40.
,,	14	Sold goods on credit to H Morgan £190 and J Peat £320.
,,	15	We returned goods to F Jones £140.
,,	17	Bought a used van on credit from Mid-west Motors £2,600.
,,	18	Bought office furniture on credit from Faster Supplies Ltd £600.
,,	19	We returned goods to S Charles £110.
,,	20	Bought goods for cash £220.
,,	24	Goods sold for cash £70.
,,	25	Paid money owing to F Jones by cheque £1,070.
,,	26	Goods returned to us by H Morgan £30.
,,	27	Returned some office furniture costing £160 to Faster Supplies Ltd.
,,	28	E Sangster put a further £500 into the business in the form of cash.
,,	29	Paid Mid-west Motors £2,600 by cheque.
,,	31	Bought office furniture for cash £100.

4.6 Enter the following transactions in the accounting records:

May	1	Started business with £2,000 in the bank.
,,	2	Bought goods on credit from C Shaw £900.
,,	3	Bought goods on credit from F Hughes £250.
,,	5	Sold goods for cash £180.
,,	6	We returned goods to C Shaw £40.
,,	8	Bought goods on credit from F Hughes £190.
,,	10	Sold goods on credit to G Wood £390.
,,	12	Sold goods for cash £210.
,,	18	Lodged £300 of the cash in hand at the bank.
,,	21	Bought machinery by cheque £550.
,,	22	Sold goods on credit to L Moore £220.
,,	23	G Wood returned goods to us £140.
,,	25	L Moore returned goods to us £10.
,,	28	We returned goods to F Hughes £30.
,,	29	We paid Shaw by cheque £860.
,,	31	Bought machinery on credit from D Lee £270.

4.7 Enter the following in the relevant accounts:

July	1	Started business with £1,000 cash.
,,	2	Paid £800 of the opening cash into a bank account for the firm.
,,	3	Bought goods on credit from H Grant £330.
,,	4	Bought goods on credit from D Clark £140.
,,	8	Sold goods on credit to B Miller £90.
,,	8	Bought office furniture on credit from Barrett's Ltd £400.
,,	10	Sold goods for cash £120.
,,	13	Bought goods on credit from H Grant £200.
,,	14	Bought goods for cash £60.
,,	15	Sold goods on credit to H Sharples £180.
,,	16	We returned goods £50 to H Grant.
,,	17	We returned some of the office furniture £30 to Barrett's Ltd.
,,	18	Sold goods on credit to B Miller £400.
,,	21	Paid H Grant's account by cheque £480.
,,	23	B Miller paid us the amount owing in cash £490.
,,	24	Sharples returned to us £50 goods.
,,	25	Goods sold for cash £150.
,,	28	Bought goods for cash £370.

5

The effect of profit or loss on capital: The double entry system for expenses and revenues

5.1 The effect of profit or loss on capital

In Chapters 2, 3 and 4 we have been concerned with the accounting need to record changes in assets and liabilities. We have not looked at how the capital is affected when a profit is made by the business. This must now be considered.

When we talk about profit we mean the excess of revenues over expenses for a set of transactions. The revenues consist of the monetary value of goods and services that have been supplied to customers. The expenses consist of the monetary values of the assets used up to obtain those revenues.

We can now look at the effect of profit upon capital by the use of an example:

On 1 January the assets and liabilities of a firm are:

Assets: Fixtures £10,000, Stock £7,000, Cash at the bank £3,000.

Liabilities: Creditors £2,000.

The capital at that date is found by re-arranging the accounting equation to become:

> **Assets – Liabilities = Capital**

In this case capital works out at (£10,000 + £7,000 + £3,000) – £2,000 = £18,000. During January the whole of the £7,000 stock is sold for £11,000 cash. On 31 January the assets and liabilities have become:

Assets: Fixtures £10,000, Stock nil, Cash at the bank £14,000 (£3,000 + £11,000).
Liabilities: Creditors £2,000.

The capital at the end of January can be calculated as:

Assets (£10,000 + £14,000) – Liabilities £2,000 = £22,000

It can be seen that capital has increased from £18,000 to £22,000 = £4,000 increase because the £7,000 stock was sold for £11,000, a profit of £4,000. Profit, therefore, increases capital.

> **Old Capital + Profit = New Capital**

£18,000 + £4,000 = £22,000

On the other hand a loss would reduce the capital so that the formula would become:

$$\boxed{\text{Old Capital} - \text{Loss} = \text{New Capital}}$$

5.2 Profit or loss and sales

A **profit** will be made when goods or services are sold at more than cost price, while the opposite will mean a **loss**.

5.3 Profit or loss and expenses

To alter the capital account it will be necessary to calculate profits or losses. How often this will be done will depend on the firm. Some firms calculate their profits and losses only once a year. Others do it at much more frequent intervals.

What it does mean is that accounts will be needed to collect together the expenses and revenues pending the calculation of profits for a period. All the expenses could be charged to one Expenses Account, but you would be able to understand the calculations better if full details of each type of expense are shown in profit and loss calculations. The same applies to each type of revenue.

To serve this purpose a separate account is opened for each type of expense and for each type of revenue. For instance there may be accounts as follows:

Rent Account	Postage Account
Wages Account	Stationery Account
Salaries Account	Insurance Account
Telephone Account	Motor Expenses Account
Rent Receivable Account	General Expenses Account

It is purely a matter of choice in a firm as to the title of each expense or revenue account. For example, an account for postage stamps could be called 'Postage Stamps Account', 'Postage Account', 'Communication Expenses Account', and so on. Also, different firms amalgamate expenses, some having a 'Rent and Telephone Account', others a 'Rent, Telephone and Insurance Account', etc. Infrequent or small items of expense are usually put into a 'Sundry', 'Miscellaneous' or 'General' expenses account.

5.4 Debit or credit

We have to decide whether expense accounts are to be debited or credited with the costs involved. Assets involve expenditure by the firm and are shown as debit entries. Expenses also involve expenditure by the firm and therefore should also be debit entries.

An alternative explanation may also be used for expenses. Every expense results in a decrease in an asset or an increase in a liability, and because of the accounting equation this means that the capital is reduced by each expense. The decrease of capital needs a debit entry and therefore expense accounts contain debit entries for expenses.

Revenue is the opposite of expenses and therefore appears on the opposite side to expenses, that is, revenue accounts appear on the credit side of the books. Pending the periodic calculation of profit therefore, revenue is collected together in appropriately named accounts, and until it is transferred to the profit calculations it will therefore need to be shown as a credit.

Consider too that expenditure of money pays for expenses, which are used up in the short term, or assets, which are used up in the long term, both for the purpose of earning

revenue. Both of these are shown on the debit side of the accounts, while the revenue which has been earned is shown on the credit side of the accounts.

5.5 The effects of transactions

A few illustrations will demonstrate the double entry required.

1   Rent of £200 is paid in cash.
    Here the twofold effect is:

   (*a*) The asset of cash is decreased. This necessitates crediting the cash account to show the decrease of the asset.

   (*b*) The total of the rent expense is increased. As expense entries are shown as debits, and the expense is rent, the action required is to debit the rent account.

   Summary: Credit the cash account with £200.
   Debit the rent account with £200.

2   Motor expenses are paid by cheque £355.
    The twofold effect is:

   (*a*) The asset of money in the bank is decreased. Therefore credit the bank account to show the decrease of the asset.

   (*b*) The total of the motor expenses paid is increased. To increase an expense account that account must be debited, so the action required is to debit the motor expenses account.

   Summary: Credit the bank account with £355.
   Debit the motor expenses account with £355.

3   £60 cash is received for commission earned by the firm.
    The twofold effect is:

   (*a*) The asset of cash is increased. A debit in the cash account will increase the asset.

   (*b*) The revenue of commissions received is increased. Revenue is shown by a credit entry, therefore to increase the revenue account in question the Commissions Received Account is credited.

   Summary: Debit the cash account with £60.
   Credit the commissions received account with £60.

It is now possible to study the effects of some more transactions showing the results in the form of a table:

		Increase	**Action**	**Decrease**	**Action**
June	1 Paid for postage stamps by cash £50	Expense of postage	Debit the postage account	Asset of cash	Credit the cash account
„	2 Paid for electricity by cheque £229	Expense of electricity	Debit the electricity account	Asset of bank	Credit the bank account
„	3 Received rent in cash £138	Asset of cash	Debit the cash account		
		Revenue of rent	Credit the rent received account		
„	4 Paid insurance by cheque £142	Expense of insurance	Debit the insurance account	Asset of bank	Credit the bank account

The above four examples can now be shown in account form:

Cash

	£		£
June 3 Rent received	138	June 1 Postage	50

Bank

			£
		June 2 Electricity	229
		„ 4 Insurance	142

Electricity

	£	
June 2 Bank	229	

Insurance

	£	
June 4 Bank	142	

Postage

	£	
June 1 Cash	50	

Rent Received

			£
		June 3 Cash	138

5.6 Drawings

Sometimes the owner of a business will want to take cash out of the business for his private use. This is known as **drawings**. Any money taken out as drawings will reduce capital.

The capital account is a very important account. To help to stop it getting full of small details, each item of drawings is not entered in the capital account. Instead a drawings account is opened, and the debits are entered there.

The following example illustrates the entries for drawings.

On 25 August, the proprietor took £50 cash out of the business for his own use.

Effects	Actions
1 Capital is decreased by £50	Debit the drawings account £50
2 Cash is decreased by £50	Credit the cash account £50

Cash

				£
		Aug 25 Drawings		50

Drawings

	£		
Aug 25 Cash	50		

Sometimes goods are also taken for private use. These are also known as drawings. Entries for such transactions will be described later in the book (Section 27.8).

Review questions

In addition to the questions below, you should attempt questions 13 and 14 in the accompanying book of multiple-choice questions (see back cover for further details).

Suggested solutions to review questions with the letter 'A' after the question number are given in Appendix I (pages 603–4).

5.1A   Complete the following table for a newsagent, showing the accounts to be debited and those to be credited:

Transactions	Account to be debited	Account to be credited
(a) Paid insurance by cheque.		
(b) Paid motor expenses in cash.		
(c) Rent received in cash.		
(d) Paid rates by cheque.		
(e) Received refund of rates by cheque.		
(f) Paid for stationery expenses in cash.		
(g) Paid wages in cash.		
(h) Sold surplus stationery, receiving the proceeds by cheque.		
(i) Received sales commission by cheque.		
(j) Bought a van and paid by cheque.		

5.2A Enter the following transactions in the relevant accounts following the rules of double entry accounting.

May 1 Started business with £20,000 in the bank.
,,   2 Purchased goods £175 on credit from M Mills.
,,   3 Bought fixtures and fittings £150 paying by cheque.
,,   5 Sold goods for cash £275.
,,   6 Bought goods on credit £114 from S Waites.
,, 10 Paid rent by cash £150.
,, 12 Bought stationery £27, paying in cash.
,, 18 Goods returned to M Mills £23.
,, 21 Let part of the premises receiving rent by cheque £50.
,, 23 Sold goods on credit to U Henry for £77.
,, 24 Bought a used van paying by cheque £3,000.
,, 30 Paid wages by cash £117.
,, 31 The proprietor took cash for himself £44.

5.3A Write up the following transactions in the books of L Thompson:

March 1 Started business with cash £1,500.
,,   2 Bought goods on credit from A Hanson £296.
,,   3 Paid rent by cash £280.
,,   4 Paid £1,000 of the cash of the firm into a bank account.
,,   5 Sold goods on credit to E Linton £54.
,,   7 Bought stationery £15 paying by cheque.
,, 11 Cash Sales £49.
,, 14 Goods returned by us to A Hanson £17.
,, 17 Sold goods on credit to S Morgan £29.
,, 20 Paid for repairs to the building by cash £18.
,, 22 E Linton returned goods to us £14.
,, 27 Paid Hanson by cheque £279.
,, 28 Cash purchases £125.
,, 30 Paid cleaning expenses in cash £15.
,, 31 Bought fixtures £120 on credit from A Webster.

5.4 Enter the following transactions in double entry accounts:

July 1 Started business with £8,000 in the bank.
,,   2 Bought stationery by cheque £30.
,,   3 Bought goods on credit from I Walsh £900.
,,   4 Sold goods for cash £180.
,,   5 Paid insurance by cash £40.
,,   7 Bought machinery on credit from H Morgan £500.
,,   8 Paid for machinery expenses by cheque £50.
,, 10 Sold goods on credit to D Small £320.
,, 11 Returned goods to I Walsh £70.
,, 14 Paid wages by cash £70.
,, 17 Paid rent by cheque £100.
,, 20 Received cheque £200 from D Small.
,, 21 Paid H Morgan by cheque £500.
,, 23 Bought stationery on credit from Express Ltd £80.
,, 25 Sold goods on credit to N Thomas £230.
,, 28 Received rent £20 in cash for part of premises sub-let.
,, 31 Paid Express Ltd by cheque £80.

5.5   Write up the following transactions in the records of C Haughey:

Feb	1	Started business with £3,000 in the bank and £500 cash.
„	2	Bought goods on credit from: T Small £250; C Todd £190; V Ryan £180.
„	3	Bought goods for cash £230.
„	4	Paid rent in cash £100.
„	5	Bought stationery paying by cheque £49.
„	6	Sold goods on credit to: C Crooks £140; R Rogers £100; B Grant £240.
„	7	Paid wages in cash £80.
„	10	Returned goods to C Todd £60.
„	11	Paid rent in cash £100.
„	13	R Rogers returns goods to us £20.
„	15	Sold goods on credit to: J Burns £90; J Smart £130; N Thorn £170.
„	16	Paid rates by cheque £130.
„	18	Paid insurance in cash £40.
„	19	Paid rent by cheque £100.
„	21	Paid motor expenses in cash £6.
„	23	Paid wages in cash £90.
„	24	Received part of amount owing from B Grant by cheque £200.
„	28	Received refund of rates £10 by cheque.
„	28	Paid by cheque: T Small £250; C Todd £130.

5.6A   From the following table, which gives the cumulative effects of individual transactions, you are required to state as fully as possible what transaction has taken place in each of the cases 'A' to 'I' inclusive. There is no need to copy out the table.

Transaction:	A	B	C	D	E	F	G	H	I
Assets	£000	£000	£000	£000	£000	£000	£000	£000	£000
Land and buildings	450	450	450	450	575	575	275	275	275	275
Vehicles	95	100	100	100	100	100	100	100	100	100
Office equipment	48	48	48	48	48	48	48	48	48	48
Stock	110	110	110	110	110	110	110	110	110	93
Debtors	188	188	188	188	188	108	108	108	108	120
Bank	27	22	22	172	47	127	427	77	77	77
Cash	15	15	11	11	11	11	11	11	3	3
	933	933	929	1,079	1,079	1,079	1,079	729	721	716
Liabilities										
Capital	621	621	621	621	621	621	621	621	621	616
Loan from Lee	200	200	200	350	350	350	350	–	–	–
Creditors	112	112	108	108	108	108	108	108	100	100
	933	933	929	1,079	1,079	1,079	1,079	729	721	716

5.7   The following table shows the cumulative effects of a succession of separate transactions on the assets and liabilities of a business.

Transaction:		A	B	C	D	E	F	G	H	I
Assets	£000	£000	£000	£000	£000	£000	£000	£000	£000	£000
Land and buildings	500	500	535	535	535	535	535	535	535	535
Equipment	230	230	230	230	230	230	230	200	200	200
Stocks	113	140	140	120	120	120	120	120	119	119
Trade debtors	143	143	143	173	160	158	158	158	158	158
Prepaid expenses	27	27	27	27	27	27	27	27	27	27
Cash at bank	37	37	37	37	50	50	42	63	63	63
Cash on hand	9	9	9	9	9	9	9	9	9	3
	1,059	1,086	1,121	1,131	1,131	1,129	1,121	1,112	1,111	1,105
Liabilities										
Capital	730	730	730	740	740	738	733	724	723	717
Loan	120	120	155	155	155	155	155	155	155	155
Trade creditors	168	195	195	195	195	195	195	195	195	195
Accrued expenses	41	41	41	41	41	41	38	38	38	38
	1,059	1,086	1,121	1,131	1,131	1,129	1,121	1,112	1,111	1,105

Required:

Identify clearly and as fully as you can what transaction has taken place in each case. Give two possible explanations for transaction 'I'. Do not copy out the table but use the reference letter for each transaction.

(*Association of Accounting Technicians*)

Note by authors: We have not yet come across the term 'accrued expenses'. It means the same as expenses owing, so in F obviously £3,000 was paid off expenses owing as well as another £5,000 being used for something else.

6

Balancing off double entry accounts

Where debtors have paid their accounts

What you have been reading so far is the recording of transactions in the books by means of debit and credit entries. At the end of each period we will have to look at each account to see what is shown by the entries.

Probably the most obvious reason for this is to find out how much our customers owe us for goods we have sold to them. In most firms this is done at the end of each month. Let us look at the account of one of our customers, K Tandy, for transactions in August:

K Tandy

	£			£
Aug 1 Sales	144	Aug 22 Bank		144
Aug 19 Sales	300	Aug 28 Bank		300

This shows that during the month we sold a total of £444 goods to Tandy, and have been paid a total of £444 by him. At the close of business at the end of August he therefore owes us nothing. His account can be closed off on 31 August by inserting the totals on each side, as follows:

K Tandy

	£			£
Aug 1 Sales	144	Aug 22 Bank		144
Aug 19 Sales	300	Aug 28 Bank		300
	444			444

Notice that totals in accounting are shown with a single line above them, and a double line underneath. Totals on accounts at the end of a period are always shown on a level with one another, as shown in the following completed account for C Lee.

C Lee

	£			£
Aug 11 Sales	177	Aug 30 Bank		480
Aug 19 Sales	203			
Aug 22 Sales	100			
	480			480

In this account, C Lee also owed us nothing at the end of August, as he had paid us for all sales to him.

If an account contains only one entry on each side and they are equal, totals are unnecessary. For example:

K Wood

	£			£
Aug 6 Sales	214	Aug 12 Bank		214

Where debtors still owe for goods at the end of an accounting period

On the other hand, some of our customers will still owe us something at the end of a month. In these cases the totals of each side would not equal one another. Let us look at the account of D Knight for August:

D Knight

	£		£
Aug 1 Sales	158	Aug 28 Bank	158
Aug 15 Sales	206		
Aug 30 Sales	118		

If you add the figures you will see that the debit side adds up to £482 and the credit side adds up to £158. You should be able to see what the difference of £324 (i.e. £482 – £158) represents. It consists of sales of £206 and £118 not paid for and therefore owing to us on 31 August.

In double entry we only enter figures as totals if the totals on both sides of the account agree. We do, however, want to close off the account for August, but showing that Knight owes us £324. If he owes £324 at close of business on 31 August, then he will still owe us that same figure when the business opens on 1 September. We show this by **balancing the account**. This is done in five stages:

1   Add up both sides to find out their totals. Do not write anything in the account at this stage.
2   Deduct the smaller total from the larger total to find the balance.
3   Now enter the balance on the side with the smallest total. This now means the totals will be equal.
4   Enter totals on a level with each other.
5   Now enter the balance on the line below the totals. The balance below the totals should be on the opposite side to the balance shown above the totals.

Against the balance above the totals, complete the date column by showing the last day of that period. Below the totals show the first day of the next period against the balance. The balance above the totals is described as a balance *carried down*. The balance below the total is described as a balance *brought down*.

Knight's account when 'balanced off' will appear as follows:

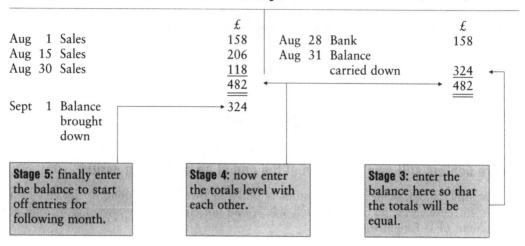

D Knight

	£		£
Aug 1 Sales	158	Aug 28 Bank	158
Aug 15 Sales	206	Aug 31 Balance	
Aug 30 Sales	118	carried down	324
	482		482
Sept 1 Balance brought down	324		

Stage 5: finally enter the balance to start off entries for following month.

Stage 4: now enter the totals level with each other.

Stage 3: enter the balance here so that the totals will be equal.

Notes:

- In future we will abbreviate 'carried down' to c/d, and 'brought down' to b/d.
- The date given to balance c/d is the last day of the period which is finishing, and the balance b/d is given the opening date of the next period.
- As the total of the debit side originally exceeded the total of the credit side, the balance is said to be a debit balance. This being a personal account (an account for a person), the person concerned is said to be a debtor – the accounting term for anyone who owes money to a firm. Therefore, the term debtor refers to a person whose account has a debit balance.

If accounts contain only one entry it is unnecessary to enter the total. A double line ruled under the entry will mean that the entry is its own total. For example:

B Walters

	£		£
Aug 18 Sales	51	Aug 31 Balance c/d	51
Sept 1 Balance b/d	51		

6.2 Accounts for creditors

Exactly the same principles apply when the balances are carried down to the credit side. We can look at two accounts of our suppliers which are to be balanced off.

E Williams

	£		£
Aug 21 Bank	100	Aug 2 Purchases	248
		Aug 18 Purchases	116

K Patterson

	£		£
Aug 14 Returns outwards	20	Aug 8 Purchases	620
Aug 28 Bank	600	Aug 15 Purchases	200

We now add up the totals and find the balance, i.e. stages 1 and 2.

When balanced these will appear as:

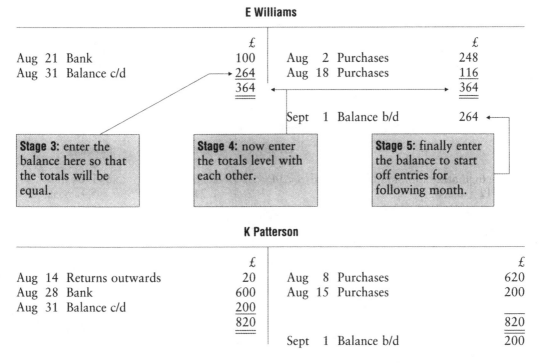

E Williams

		£			£
Aug 21 Bank		100	Aug 2 Purchases		248
Aug 31 Balance c/d		264	Aug 18 Purchases		116
		364			364
			Sept 1 Balance b/d		264

Stage 3: enter the balance here so that the totals will be equal.

Stage 4: now enter the totals level with each other.

Stage 5: finally enter the balance to start off entries for following month.

K Patterson

		£			£
Aug 14 Returns outwards		20	Aug 8 Purchases		620
Aug 28 Bank		600	Aug 15 Purchases		200
Aug 31 Balance c/d		200			
		820			820
			Sept 1 Balance b/d		200

The type of accounts which have been demonstrated so far, properly known as ledger accounts, are often known as *T accounts*. This is because the accounts are in the shape of a T, as has already been seen.

Before you read further attempt exercises 6.1 and 6.2 at the end of the chapter.

6.3 Computers and accounts

Throughout this book the type of account used shows the left-hand side of the account as the debit side, and the right-hand side as the credit side. However, when most computers are used the style of the ledger account is different. It appears as three columns of figures, there being one column for debit entries, another column for credit entries, and the last column for the balance. If you have an account at a bank your bank statements will normally be shown using this method.

The accounts used in this chapter will now be redrafted to show the ledger accounts drawn up in this way.

K Tandy

Date	Details	Debit	Credit	Balance (and whether debit or credit)
		£	£	£
Aug 1	Sales	144		144 Dr
Aug 19	Sales	300		444 Dr
Aug 22	Bank		144	300 Dr
Aug 28	Bank		300	0

C Lee

		Debit £	Credit £	Balance £
Aug 11	Sales	177		177 Dr
Aug 19	Sales	203		380 Dr
Aug 22	Sales	100		480 Dr
Aug 30	Bank		480	0

K Wood

		Debit £	Credit £	Balance £
Aug 6	Sales	214		214 Dr
Aug 12	Bank		214	0

D Knight

		Debit £	Credit £	Balance £
Aug 1	Sales	158		158 Dr
Aug 15	Sales	206		364 Dr
Aug 28	Cash		158	206 Dr
Aug 31	Sales	118		324 Dr

H Henry

		Debit £	Credit £	Balance £
Aug 5	Sales	300		300 Dr
Aug 24	Returns		50	250 Dr
Aug 28	Sales	540		790 Dr
Aug 29	Bank		250	540 Dr

B Walters

		Debit £	Credit £	Balance £
Aug 18	Sales	51		51 Dr

E Williams

		Debit £	Credit £	Balance £
Aug 2	Purchases		248	248 Cr
Aug 18	Purchases		116	364 Cr
Aug 21	Bank	100		264 Cr

K Patterson

		Debit £	Credit £	Balance £
Aug 8	Purchases		620	620 Cr
Aug 14	Returns	20		600 Cr
Aug 15	Purchases		200	800 Cr
Aug 28	Bank	600		200 Cr

It will be noticed that the balance is calculated again after every entry. This can be done quite simply when using a computer because it is the machine which calculates the new balance.

However, when manual methods are being used it is often too much work to have to calculate a new balance after each entry. It also means that the greater the number of calculations the greater the possibility of errors. For these reasons it is usual for students to use two-sided accounts. However, it is important to note that there is no difference in principle, the final balances are the same using both methods.

Review questions

In addition to the questions below, you should attempt questions 15–18 in the accompanying book of multiple-choice questions (see back cover for further details).

Suggested solutions to review questions with the letter 'A' after the question number are given in Appendix I (pages 604–5).

6.1A Enter the following transactions in the necessary debtors accounts only, do *not* write up other accounts. Then balance off each personal account at the end of the month. (Keep your answer, it will be used as a basis for question 6.3.)

May	1	Sales on credit to H Harvey £690, N Morgan £153, J Lindo £420.
„	4	Sales on credit to L Masters £418, H Harvey £66.
„	10	Returns inwards from H Harvey £40, J Lindo £20.
„	18	N Morgan paid us by cheque £153.
„	20	J Lindo paid us £400 by cheque.
„	24	H Harvey paid us £300 in cash.
„	31	Sales on credit to L Masters £203.

6.2A Enter the following transactions in the personal accounts only. Do *not* write up the other accounts. Then balance off each personal account at the end of the month. (Keep your answer, it will be used as the basis for question 6.4.)

June	1	Purchases on credit from J Young £458, L Williams £120, G Norman £708.
„	3	Purchases on credit from L Williams £77, T Harris £880.
„	10	We returned goods to G Norman £22, J Young £55.
„	15	Purchases on credit from J Young £80.
„	19	We paid T Harris by cheque £880.
„	28	We paid J Young £250 in cash.
„	30	We returned goods to L Williams £17.

6.3A Redraft each of the accounts given in your answer to question 6.1 in three-column computer-style accounts.

6.4A Redraft each of the accounts given in your answer to question 6.2 in three-column computer-style accounts.

6.5A   Enter the following transactions in the personal accounts only, do *not* write up the other accounts. Balance off each personal account at the end of the month. After completing this state which of the balances represent debtors and which are creditors.

Sept 1   Sales on credit to D Williams £458, J Moore £235, G Grant £98.
„   2   Purchases on credit A White £77, H Samuels £231, P Owen £65.
„   8   Sales on credit to J Moore £444, F Franklin £249.
„   10   Purchases on credit from H Samuels £12, O Oliver £222.
„   12   Returns Inwards from G Grant £9, J Moore £26.
„   17   We returned goods to H Samuels £24, O Oliver £12.
„   20   We paid A White by cheque £77.
„   24   D Williams paid us by cheque £300.
„   26   We paid O Oliver by cash £210.
„   28   D Williams paid us by cash £100.
„   30   F Franklin paid us by cheque £249.

6.6   Enter the following transactions in the relevant personal accounts only. Bring down balances at the end of the month. After completing this state which of the balances represent debtors and which are creditors.

May 1   Credit sales B Flynn £241, R Kelly £29, J Long £887, T Fryer £124.
„   2   Credit purchases from S Wood £148, T Thumb £27, R Johnson £77, G Glitter £108.
„   8   Credit sales to R Kelly £74, J Long £132.
„   9   Credit purchases from T Thumb £142, G Glitter £44.
„   10   Goods returned to us by J Long £17, T Fryer £44.
„   12   Cash paid to us by T Fryer £80.
„   15   We returned goods to S Wood £8, G Glitter £18.
„   19   We received cheques from J Long £500, B Flynn £241.
„   21   We sold goods on credit to B Flynn £44, R Kelly £280.
„   28   We paid by cheque the following: S Wood £140; G Glitter £50; R Johnson £60.
„   31   We returned goods to G Glitter £4.

6.7   Redraft each of the accounts given in your answer to question 6.6 in three-column computer-style accounts.

6.8   On 2 November Fred Bilding set up in business on his own account as an Estate Agent. The following transactions occurred during the month of November:

Nov 2   Fred Bilding paid £10,000 into a bank account for the business and immediately withdrew £200 in cash.
Nov 3   An office was rented for the business and the rent of £750 for November was paid by cheque.
Nov 4   Office furniture costing £2,400 was purchased from Grumwicks plc under their 'interest-free' credit scheme. A down payment of £600 was paid immediately by cheque. The balance is to be paid in three equal monthly instalments.
Nov 5   A wordprocessor costing £525 was purchased for the office and paid for by cheque.
Nov 6   Office supplies of £155 were purchased and paid for by cheque.
Nov 13   Fred Bilding received a cheque for £600 as commission in respect of the sale of a client's home.
Nov 19   The home of another client, Jacob Podmore, was sold. The commission on this sale was £875 but it will not be received in cash until December.
Nov 25   Advertising bills totalling £410 were paid by cheque, of which £110 was incurred advertising the home of Jacob Podmore. This amount is recoverable from the client.
Nov 26   Further office supplies costing £97 were purchased and paid for in cash.

Nov 28   Fred Bilding transferred £604 from his business bank account to his private bank account, £84 of which was to reimburse himself for motor expenses incurred on business use. The remaining £520 was withdrawn for private purposes.

Required:

(a) Show by means of ledger accounts how the above transactions would be recorded in the books of Fred Bilding, and

(b) Balance off those ledger accounts containing more than one entry as at 30 November entering the correct balances in the accounts.

(*Association of Accounting Technicians*)

7

The trial balance

7.1 Total debit entries = total credit entries

You have already seen that the most common method of bookkeeping in use is the double entry method. This means:

- For each debit entry there is a credit entry
- For each credit entry there is a debit entry

All the items recorded in all the accounts on the debit side should equal in *total* all the items recorded on the credit side of the books. We need to check that for each debit entry there is also a credit entry. To see if the two totals are equal, usually known as seeing if the two sides of the books 'balance', a **trial balance** may be drawn up at the end of a period.

A form of a trial balance could be drawn up by listing all the accounts and adding together all the debit entries and at the same time adding together all the credit entries. Using the worked example in section 4.8 such a trial balance would appear as below. Note that it could not be drawn up until after all the entries have been made. It will therefore be dated 'as at' 31 May 19XX.

Trial Balance as at 31 May 19XX		
	Dr £	Cr £
Purchases	309	
Sales		255
Returns outwards		15
Returns inwards	16	
D Small	68	68
A Lyon & Son		141
D Hughes	60	60
M Spencer	45	16
Cash	210	153
	708	708

7.2 Total debit balances = total credit balances

The above is not the normal method of drawing up a trial balance, but it is the easiest to understand at first. Usually, a trial balance is a list of balances only, arranged according to whether they are debit balances or credit balances. If the trial balance above had been drawn up using the normal balances method it would appear as follows:

Trial Balance as at 31 May 19XX		
	Dr £	Cr £
Purchases	309	
Sales		255
Returns outwards		15
Returns inwards	16	
A Lyon & Son		141
M Spencer	29	
Cash	57	
	411	411

Here the two sides also 'balance'. The sums of £68 in D Small's account, £60 in D Hughes' account, £16 in M Spencer's account and £153 in the cash account have, however, been cancelled out from each side of these accounts by taking only the *balances* instead of *totals*. As equal amounts have been cancelled from each side, £297 in all, the new totals should still equal one another, as in fact they do at £411.

This form of trial balance is the easiest to extract when there are more than a few transactions during the period. Also the balances are either used later when the profit is being calculated, or else appear in a balance sheet. Trial balances, therefore, are prepared for reasons other than to find errors.

7.3 Trial balances and errors

It may at first sight appear that the balancing of a trial balance proves that the books are correct. This, however, is quite wrong. It means that certain types of errors have not been made, but there are several types of errors that will not affect the balancing of a trial balance. Examples of the errors which would be revealed, provided there are no compensating errors which cancel them out, are errors in additions, using one figure for the debit entry and another figure for the credit entry, entering only one aspect of a transaction and so on.

7.4 Types of errors which do not affect trial balance agreement

Suppose that a bookkeeper correctly entered cash sales of £70 on the debit side of the cash book, but did not enter the £70 on the credit side of the sales account. If this was the only error in the books, the trial balance totals would differ by £70.

However, there are certain kinds of error which would not affect the agreement of the trial balance totals. These are discussed below:

1 Errors of omission

An error of omission refers to a situation where a bookkeeper 'omits' to record a transaction. For example, if goods were sold to a customer, but the bookkeeper did not make an entry in either the sales account or the customer's personal account, the trial balance would still 'balance', because effectively there has been a zero debit entry and a zero credit entry.

2 Errors of commission

An error of commission arises when the correct amount is entered but in the wrong person's account, e.g. where a sale to C Green is entered in the account of K Green. It will be noted that the correct class of account was used, both of the accounts concerned being personal accounts.

3 Errors of principle

This is where a transaction is entered in the wrong class of account, e.g. if a fixed asset such as a van is debited in error to an expense account such as the motor expenses account.

4 Compensating errors

Errors which cancel each other out are known as compensating errors. If the sales account was added up to be £10 too much and the purchases account was also added up to be £10 too much, then these two errors would cancel out in the trial balance. This is because the totals of both the debit side and the credit side of the trial balance will be £10 too much.

5 Errors of original entry

An error of original entry occurs when an incorrect figure is posted to the correct sides of the correct accounts. For example, if the total of a sales invoice for £150 was accidentally misread by the bookkeeper as £130 who then proceeded to post £130 to the credit side of the sales account and the debit side of the customer's personal account, the trial balance would still 'balance', albeit at a figure £20 less than the correct balance.

6 Complete reversal of entries

This is where the correct accounts are used but each item is shown on the wrong side of the account. Suppose we had paid a cheque to D Williams for £200. The double entry is to credit Bank £200 and debit D Williams £200. If this transaction was entered in error as credit D Williams £200 and debit Bank £200 the trial balance totals will still be equal.

Review questions

In addition to the questions below, you should attempt questions 19–25 in the accompanying book of multiple-choice questions (see back cover for further details).

Suggested solutions to review questions with the letter 'A' after the question number are given in Appendix I (see pages 605–6).

7.1A   Draw up the necessary accounts for the month of May from the following details, and then balance off the accounts and extract a trial balance as at 31 May 1998.

May   1   Started a firm with capital in cash of £250.
  „   2   Bought goods on credit from the following persons: D Ellis £54; C Murphy £87; K Gibson £25; D Booth £76; L Lowe £64.
  „   4   Sold goods on credit to: C Bailey £43; B Hughes £62; H Spencer £176.
  „   6   Paid rent by cash £12.

May 9 Bailey paid us his account by cheque £43.
  „ 10 H Spencer paid us £150 by cheque.
  „ 12 We paid the following by cheque: K Gibson £25; D Ellis £54.
  „ 15 Paid carriage by cash £23.
  „ 18 Bought goods on credit from C Murphy £43; D Booth £110.
  „ 21 Sold goods on credit to B Hughes £67.
  „ 31 Paid rent by cheque £18.

7.2A Write up the books of E Power from the following details for the month of March, and extract a trial balance as at 31 March 1998.

March 1 Started business with £800 in the bank.
  „   2 Bought goods on credit from the following persons: K Henry £76; M Hyatt £27; T Braham £56.
  „   5 Cash sales £87.
  „   6 Paid wages in cash £14.
  „   7 Sold goods on credit to: H Elliott £35; L Lane £42; J Carlton £72.
  „   9 Bought goods for cash £46.
  „ 10 Bought goods on credit from: M Hyatt £57; T Braham £98.
  „ 12 Paid wages in cash £14.
  „ 13 Sold goods on credit to: L Lane £32; J Carlton £23.
  „ 15 Bought shop fixtures on credit from Betta Ltd £50.
  „ 17 Paid M Hyatt by cheque £84.
  „ 18 We returned goods to T Braham £20.
  „ 21 Paid Betta Ltd a cheque for £50.
  „ 24 J Carlton paid us his account by cheque £95.
  „ 27 We returned goods to K Henry £24.
  „ 30 J King lent us £60 in cash.

7.3 Record the following details relating to the business of M Fenton for the month of November and extract a trial balance as at 30 November:

Nov 1 Started with £5,000 in the bank.
  „   3 Bought goods on credit from: T Henry £160; J Smith £230; W Rogers £400; P Boone £310.
  „   5 Cash sales £240.
  „   6 Paid rent by cheque £200.
  „   7 Paid rates by cheque £190.
  „ 11 Sold goods on credit to: L Matthews £48; K Allen £32; R Hall £1,170.
  „ 17 Paid wages by cash £40.
  „ 18 We returned goods to: T Henry £14; P Boone £20.
  „ 19 Bought goods on credit from: P Boone £80; W Rogers £270; D O'Connor £130.
  „ 20 Goods were returned to us by K Allen £2; L Matthews £4.
  „ 21 Bought a van on credit from U Z Motors £5,000.
  „ 23 We paid the following by cheque: T Henry £146; J Smith £230; W Rogers £300.
  „ 26 Received a loan of £400 cash from A Williams.
  „ 28 Received cheques from: L Matthews £44; K Allen £30.
  „ 30 Proprietor brings a further £300 into the business, by a payment into the business bank account.

7.4   Record the following for the month of January, balance off all the accounts, and then extract a trial balance as at 31 January:

Jan 1   Started business with £3,500 cash.
   „   2   Put £2,800 of the cash into a bank account.
   „   3   Bought goods for cash £150.
   „   4   Bought goods on credit from L Coke £360; M Burton £490; T Hill £110; C Small £340.
   „   5   Bought stationery on credit from Swift Ltd £170.
   „   6   Sold goods on credit to: S Walters £90; T Binns £150; C Howard £190; P Peart £160.
   „   8   Paid rent by cheque £55.
   „   10   Bought fixtures on credit from Matalon Ltd £480.
   „   11   Paid salary in cash £120 to a new employee.
   „   14   Returned goods to M Burton £40; T Hill £60.
   „   15   Bought a van on credit £7,000 from Cork Garages.
   „   16   Received a loan from J Henry by cheque £600.
   „   18   Goods returned to us by: S Walters £20; C Howard £40.
   „   21   Cash sales £90.
   „   24   Sold goods on credit to: T Binns £100; P Peart £340; J Smart £115.
   „   26   We paid the following by cheque: M Burton £450; T Hill £50.
   „   29   Received cheques from: J Smart £115; T Binns £250.
   „   30   Received a further loan from J Henry by cash £200.
   „   30   Received £500 cash from P Peart.

7.5   Your client, Mr Kelly, has informed you that his bookkeeper has extracted a balanced Trial Balance from his books. Because the Trial Balance has balanced he believes that there cannot be any errors in his books.

Requirement:
Draft a brief note to Mr Kelly outlining possible errors that might remain in his books notwithstanding the fact that the Trial Balance balanced.
(*IATI Foundation Examination*)

Part II

AN INTRODUCTION TO THE FINAL ACCOUNTS OF SOLE TRADERS

8

Trading accounts and profit and loss accounts: an introduction

8.1 The purpose of trading accounts and profit and loss accounts

The main reason why people set up businesses is to make profit. Of course, if they are not successful they may well incur losses instead. The calculation of such profits and losses is probably the most important objective of the accounting function. The owner of a business will want to know how the profit he has actually made compares with the profit he had hoped to make. He may also want to know his profits for reasons such as: to assist him to plan ahead, to help him to obtain a loan from a bank or from a private individual, to show to a prospective partner or to a person to whom he hopes to sell the business, or maybe he will need to know his profits for tax purposes.

Chapter 5 dealt with the grouping of revenue and expenses prior to bringing them together to compute profit. In the case of a trader, meaning someone who is mainly concerned with buying and selling, the profits are calculated by drawing up special accounts called **Trading Accounts and Profit and Loss Accounts**. For a manufacturer, it is useful to prepare a **Manufacturing Account** as well. Manufacturing Accounts are dealt with in Chapter 48.

8.2 The format of trading accounts and profit and loss accounts

One of the most important uses of trading and profit and loss accounts is that of comparing the results obtained with the results expected. In a trading organisation a lot of attention is paid to how much profit is made, before deducting expenses, for every £100 of sales. So that this can easily be seen in the profit calculations, the account in which profit is calculated is split into two sections – one in which the **Gross Profit** is found, and the next section in which the **Net Profit** is calculated.

Gross Profit (calculated in the **trading account**)	This is the excess of sales over the cost of goods sold in a period.
Net Profit (calculated in the **profit and loss account**)	This is what is left of the gross profit after all other expenses have been deducted.

The gross profit, calculated in the **Trading Account,** is the excess of sales over the cost of goods sold. The net profit, found when the **Profit and Loss Account** is prepared, consists of the gross profit plus any revenue other than that from sales, such as discounts received or commissions earned, less the total costs incurred during the period. Where the cost of goods sold is greater than the sales the result would be a **Gross Loss,** but this is a

relatively rare occurrence. Where other costs incurred exceed the total of gross profit plus other revenue then the result is said to be a **Net Loss**. By taking the figure of sales less the cost of goods sold, it can be seen that the accounting custom is to calculate a trader's profits only when the goods have been disposed of and not before.

8.3 Information needed to prepare trading and profit and loss accounts

Before drawing up a trading and profit and loss account you should get out the trial balance. This contains nearly all the information needed. (Later on in this book you will see that certain adjustments have to be made, but we will ignore these at this stage.)

Exhibit 8.1 shows the trial balance of B Swift, drawn up as at 31 December 1997 after the completion of his first year in business.

Exhibit 8.1

B Swift Trial Balance as at 31 December 1997	Debit	Credit
	£	£
Sales		3,850
Purchases	2,900	
Rent	240	
Lighting expenses	150	
General expenses	60	
Fixtures and fittings	500	
Debtors	680	
Creditors		910
Bank	1,510	
Cash	20	
Drawings	700	
Capital		2,000
	6,760	6,760

Usually some of the goods bought (purchases) have not been sold by the end of the accounting period. We have already seen that gross profit is calculated as follows:

> **Sales – Cost of Goods Sold = Gross Profit**

However, purchases equals the cost of goods sold only if there is no stock at the end of a period. Where there is stock at the end of a period we can calculate cost of goods sold as follows:

What we bought in the period: Purchases
Less goods bought but not sold in the period: Closing stock
= Cost of goods sold

However, there is no record in the books of the value of the unsold stock on 31 December for B Swift. The only way that Swift can find this figure is by stock-taking on 31 December at the close of business. To do this he would have to make a list of all the unsold goods and then find out their value. The value he would normally place on them would be the cost price of the goods. Let us assume that this works out to be £300.

The cost of goods sold figure will be:

	£
Purchases	2,900
less Closing stock	300
= Cost of goods sold	2,600

Given sales of £3,850, the gross profit can be calculated as:

Sales – Cost of Goods Sold = Gross Profit
£3,850 – £2,600 = £1,250

This, however, is not performing the task by using double entry accounts. In double entry the following entries must be made.

The balance on the sales account is transferred to the trading account by:

1 Debiting the sales account (with the amount necessary to balance it).
2 Crediting the trading account (with the same amount).

The balance on the purchases account is transferred to the trading account by:

1 Debiting the trading account.
2 Crediting the purchases account (thus closing it).

There is, as yet, no entry for the closing stock in the double entry accounts. This is achieved as follows:

1 Debit a stock account with the value of the closing stock.
2 Credit the trading account (thus completing the double entry).

It is usual for both the trading account and the profit and loss account to be shown under one combined heading, the trading account being the top section and the profit and loss account being the lower section of this combined account. The trading account portion is shown below:

B Swift
Trading and Profit and Loss Account for the year ended 31 December 1997

		£
Sales		3,850
Purchases	2,900	
Closing stock	300	2,600
Gross profit		1,250

The balance shown on the trading account is shown as gross profit rather than being described as a balance. When found, the gross profit is 'carried down' to the profit and loss section of the account. The double entry accounts used so far appear as follows:

Sales

	£		£
Dec 31 Trading account	3,850	Dec 31 Balance b/d	3,850

Purchases

	£		£
Dec 31 Balance b/d	2,900	Dec 31 Trading account	2,900

Stock

	£	
Dec 31 Trading account	300	

The entry of the closing stock on the credit side of the trading and profit and loss account is, in effect, a deduction from the purchases on the debit side. In accounting practice it is usual to find the closing stock shown as a deduction from the purchases, and the figure then disclosed being described as 'cost of goods sold'. This is illustrated in Exhibit 8.2.

The profit and loss account can now be drawn up. Any revenue accounts, other than sales, which has already been dealt with, would be transferred to the credit section of the profit and loss account. Typical examples are commissions received and rent received. In the case of B Swift there are no such revenue accounts.

The costs incurred in the year, in other words the expenses for the year, are transferred to the debit section of the profit and loss account. It may also be thought, quite rightly so, that, as the fixtures and fittings have been used during the year with the subsequent deterioration of the asset, an amount should be charged for this use. This is dealt with in Chapters 24 and 25.

The revised trading account with the addition of the profit and loss account (below it) will now appear as follows:

Exhibit 8.2

B Swift

Trading and Profit and Loss Account for the year ended 31 December 1997

	£	£
Sales		3,850
Purchases	2,900	
Closing stock	300	2,600
Gross profit		1,250
Expenses		
Rent	240	
Lighting expenses	150	
General expenses	60	450
Net profit		800

The expense accounts closed off will now appear as:

Rent

	£		£
Dec 31 Balance b/d	240	Dec 31 Profit and loss account	240

Lighting Expenses

	£		£
Dec 31 Balance b/d	150	Dec 31 Profit and loss account	150

General Expenses

	£		£
Dec 31 Balance b/d	60	Dec 31 Profit and loss account	60

8.4 The effect of profits and losses on the capital account

Although the net profit has been calculated at £800, and is shown as a debit entry in the profit and loss account, no corresponding credit entry has yet been made. This now needs to be done. As net profit increases the capital of the proprietor the credit entry must be made in the capital account.

The trading and profit and loss account, and indeed all the revenue and expense accounts can thus be seen to be devices whereby the capital account is saved from being concerned with unnecessary detail. Every sale of a good at a profit increases the capital of the proprietor as does each item of revenue such as rent received. On the other hand each sale of a good at a loss, or each item of expense, decreases the capital of the proprietor. Instead of altering the capital account after each transaction the respective items of profit and loss and of revenue and expense are collected together using suitably described accounts. Then, the whole of the details are brought together in one set of accounts, the trading and profit and loss account, and the increase to the capital, i.e. the net profit, is determined. Alternatively, the decrease in the capital, as represented by the net loss, is ascertained.

The fact that a separate drawings account has been in use can now also be seen to have been in keeping with the policy of avoiding unnecessary detail in the capital account. There will thus be one figure for drawings which will be the total of the drawings for the whole of the period, and will be transferred to the debit of the capital account.

The capital account, showing these transfers, and the drawings account now closed is as follows:

Capital

1997		£	1997			£
Dec 31	Drawings	700	Jan 1	Cash		2,000
„ 31	Balance c/d	2,100	Dec 31	Net profit from		
				Profit and loss account		800
		2,800				2,800
			1998			
			Jan 1	Balance b/d		2,100

Drawings

		£			£
Dec 31	Balance b/d	700	Dec 31	Capital	700

8.5 The balances remaining in the double entry accounts after the trading and profit and loss account has been prepared

It should be noticed that not all the items in the trial balance have been used in the trading and profit and loss account. The remaining balances are assets, liabilities or capital; they are not expenses or revenue. These will be dealt with later when a balance sheet is drawn up, for, as has been shown in Chapter 2, assets, liabilities and capital are shown in balance sheets.

In Exhibit 8.3, although it is not necessary to redraft the trial balance after the trading and profit and loss accounts have been prepared, it is useful at this stage to do so in order

to establish which balances still remain. The first thing to notice is that the stock account, not originally in the trial balance, is in the redrafted trial balance, as the item was not created as a balance in the books until the trading account was prepared. These balances will be used by us in the next chapter, when we start to look at balance sheets.

Exhibit 8.3

B Swift Redrafted Trial Balance as at 31 December 1997 (after the Trading and Profit and Loss Account has been completed)	Debit	Credit
	£	£
Fixtures and fittings	500	
Debtors	680	
Creditors		910
Stock	300	
Bank	1,510	
Cash	20	
Capital		2,100
	3,010	3,010

Review questions

In addition to the questions below, you should attempt questions 26–29 in the accompanying book of multiple-choice questions (see back cover for further details).

Suggested solutions to review questions with the letter 'A' after the question number are given in Appendix I (page 606).

8.1A From the following trial balance of B Webb, extracted after one year's trading, prepare a trading and profit and loss account for the year ended 31 December 1997.

Trial Balance as at 31 December	Dr	Cr
	£	£
Sales		18,462
Purchases	14,629	
Salaries	2,150	
Motor expenses	520	
Rent	670	
Insurance	111	
General expenses	105	
Premises	1,500	
Vehicles	1,200	
Debtors	1,950	
Creditors		1,538
Cash at bank	1,654	
Cash in hand	40	
Drawings	895	
Capital		5,424
	25,424	25,424

Stock at 31 December was £2,548.

(Keep your answer; it will be used later in question 9.1.)

8.2A From the following trial balance of C Worth after his first year's trading, you are required to draw up a trading and profit and loss account for the year ended 30 June 1998.

Trial Balance as at 30 June	Dr	Cr
	£	£
Sales		28,794
Purchases	23,803	
Rent	854	
Lighting and heating expenses	422	
Salaries and wages	3,164	
Insurance	105	
Buildings	50,000	
Fixtures	1,000	
Debtors	3,166	
Sundry expenses	506	
Creditors		1,206
Cash at bank	3,847	
Drawings	2,400	
Vans	5,500	
Motor running expenses	1,133	
Capital		65,900
	95,900	95,900

Stock at 30 June was £4,166.

(Keep your answer; it will be used later in question 9.2.)

8.3 From the following trial balance of F Chaplin drawn up on conclusion of his first year in business, prepare a trading and profit and loss account for the year ended 31 December 1997.

Trial Balance as at 31 December	Dr	Cr
	£	£
General expenses	210	
Rent	400	
Motor expenses	735	
Salaries	3,560	
Insurance	392	
Purchases	18,385	
Sales		26,815
Vehicle	2,800	
Creditors		5,160
Debtors	4,090	
Premises	20,000	
Cash at bank	1,375	
Cash in hand	25	
Capital		24,347
Drawings	4,350	
	56,322	56,322

Stock at 31 December was £4,960.

(Keep your answer; it will be used later in question 9.3.)

8.4   Extract a trading and profit and loss account for the year ended 30 June 1998 for F Kidd. The trial balance at that date after his first year of trading, was as follows:

Trial Balance as at 30 June	Dr	Cr
	£	£
Rent..	1,560	
Insurance...	305	
Lighting and heating expenses..	516	
Motor expenses..	1,960	
Salaries and wages..	4,850	
Sales		35,600
Purchases...	30,970	
Sundry expenses	806	
Vans	3,500	
Creditors		3,250
Debtors..	6,810	
Fixtures	3,960	
Buildings..	28,000	
Cash at bank..	1,134	
Drawings..	6,278	
Capital..		51,799
	90,649	90,649

Stock at 30 June was £9,960.

(Keep your answer; it will be used later in question 9.4.)

9

Balance sheets

9.1 Contents of the balance sheet

It was seen in Chapter 2 that balance sheets contain details of assets, capital and liabilities. These details have to be found in our records and then written out as a balance sheet.

It is easy to find these details. They consist of all the balances remaining in our records once the trading and profit and loss account for the period has been completed. All balances remaining have to be assets, capital or liabilities. All the other balances should have been closed off when the trading and profit and loss account was completed.

9.2 Drawing up a balance sheet

Let us now look at Exhibit 9.1, the trial balance of B Swift (from Exhibit 8.3) as at 31 December 1997 *after* the trading and profit and loss account had been prepared.

Exhibit 9.1

B Swift Trial Balance as at 31 December 1997 (after Trading and Profit and Loss Account completed)	Dr £	Cr £
Fixtures and fittings	500	
Debtors	680	
Creditors		910
Stock	300	
Bank	1,510	
Cash	20	
Capital		2,100
	3,010	3,010

We can now draw up a balance sheet as at the date of the trial balance, Exhibit 9.2. You have already seen examples of balance sheets in Chapter 2 and may need to refer to that chapter to refresh your memory before continuing.

Exhibit 9.2

B Swift
Balance Sheet as at 31 December 1997

Assets	£
Fixtures and fittings	500
Stock	300
Debtors	680
Bank	1,510
Cash	20
	3,010
Liabilities	
Creditors	910
	2,100
Capital	2,100

9.3 No double entry in balance sheets

It may seem very strange to you to learn that balance sheets are *not* part of the double entry system.

When we draw up accounts such as the cash account, rent account, sales account, trading and profit and loss account and so on, we are writing up part of the double entry system. We make entries on the debit sides and the credit sides of these accounts.

In drawing up a balance sheet we do not enter anything in the various accounts. We do not actually transfer the fixtures balance or the stock balance, or any of the others, to the balance sheet.

All we do is to *list* the asset, capital and liabilities balances so as to form a balance sheet. This means that none of these accounts have been closed off. *Nothing is entered in the accounts.*

When the next accounting period starts, these accounts are still open containing balances. Entries are then made in them to add to, or deduct from, the amounts shown in the accounts using normal double entry.

If you see the word 'account', you will know that it is part of the double entry system and will include debit and credit entries. If the word 'account' is not used, it is not part of double entry. For instance, these are not part of the double entry system.

Trial balance: A list of balances to see if the records are correct.

Balance sheet: A list of balances arranged according to whether they are assets, capital or liabilities.

9.4 The layout of the balance sheet

All of the items shown in balance sheets should be shown in an ordered fashion to permit those who read them to more easily understand and interpret them.

For people such as bank managers, accountants and investors who look at a lot of different balance sheets, we want to keep to one method so as to make a comparison of balance sheets easier. The following is a good method for showing items in balance sheets.

Assets

Assets should be shown under two headings, **Fixed Assets** and **Current Assets**.

Assets are called fixed assets when they:

1 are of long life;
2 are to be used in the business; and
3 were not bought only for the purposes of resale.

Examples: buildings, machinery, vehicles, fixtures and fittings.

Fixed assets are listed starting with those we will keep the longest, down to those which will not be kept so long. For instance:

Fixed Assets
1 Land and buildings
2 Fixtures and fittings
3 Machinery
4 Vehicles

Current assets are, for example, cash in hand, cash at bank, items held for resale at a profit or other items that have a short life.

These are listed starting with the asset furthest away from being turned into cash, finishing with cash itself. For instance:

Current Assets
1 Stock
2 Debtors
3 Cash at bank
4 Cash in hand

The order with which most students would disagree is that stock has appeared before debtors. On first sight it would appear that stock can be more readily converted into cash than debtors. In fact, however, debtors could normally be more quickly turned into cash by factoring them, i.e. selling the rights to the amounts owing to a finance company for an agreed amount. On the other hand, to dispose of all the stock of a business is often a long and difficult task. Also, before any sale takes place there must be a stock of goods, which, when sold on credit turns into debtors, and, when payment is made by the debtors, turns into cash.

Liabilities

● Long-term liabilities: for instance, loans which do not have to be repaid in the near future.
● Current liabilities: items to be paid for in the near future.

9.5 A properly drawn up balance sheet

Exhibit 9.3 shows the same data as Exhibit 9.2 but is better laid out.

Exhibit 9.3

B Swift
Balance Sheet as at 31 December 1997

		£
Fixed assets		
Fixtures and fittings		500
Current assets		
Stock	300	
Debtors	680	
Bank	1,510	
Cash	20	
	2,510	
Current liabilities		
Creditors	910	1,600
		2,100
Capital		
Cash introduced		2,000
Net profit for the year		800
		2,800
Drawings		700
		2,100

Notes to Exhibit 9.3

(*a*) A total for capital and for each class of asset and liability should be shown. An example of this is the £2,510 total of current assets. To do this the figures for each asset are listed, and only the total is shown in the end column.

(*b*) You should not write the word 'account' after each item.

(*c*) The owner will be most interested in his capital. To show only the final balance of £2,100 means that the owner will not know how it was calculated. Therefore, we show the full details of his capital account.

(*d*) Look at the date on the balance sheet. Now compare it with the dates put on the top of the trading and profit and loss account. The balance sheet is a **position statement**, it is shown as being at one point in time, e.g. as at 31 December 1997. The trading and profit and loss account is different. It is for a period of time, in this case for a whole year.

Review questions

In addition to the questions below, you should attempt questions 30–43 in the accompanying book of multiple-choice questions (see back cover for further details).

Suggested solutions to review questions with the letter 'A' after the question number are given in Appendix I (page 607).

9.1A Complete question 8.1A by drawing up a balance sheet as at 31 December 1997.

9.2A Complete question 8.2A by drawing up a balance sheet as at 30 June 1998.

9.3 Complete question 8.3 by drawing up a balance sheet as at 31 December 1997.

9.4 Complete question 8.4 by drawing up a balance sheet as at 30 June 1998.

10

Trading and profit and loss accounts and balance sheets: further considerations

10.1 Returns inwards and returns outwards

In Chapter 4 the idea of different accounts for different movements of stock was introduced. Accordingly there were sales, purchases, returns inwards and returns outwards accounts. In our first look at the preparation of a trading account in Chapter 8, returns inwards and returns outwards were omitted. This was done deliberately so that the first sight of trading and profit and loss accounts would not be a difficult one.

However, a large number of firms will return goods to their suppliers (returns outwards), and will have goods returned to them by their customers (returns inwards). Thus, when the gross profit is calculated these returns will have to enter into the calculations. Suppose that in Exhibit 8.1, the trial balance of B Swift, the balances showing stock movements had instead been as follows:

Trial Balance as at 31 December 1997 (Extract only)	Debit	Credit
	£	£
Sales		4,000
Purchases	3,120	
Returns inwards	150	
Returns outwards		220

Looking back at Exhibit 8.1 it can be seen that originally the example used was of Sales £3,850 and Purchases £2,900. Using the figures in the trial balance above a new Trading Account can be prepared. This is shown in Exhibit 10.1 below.

Exhibit 10.1 Trading account with returns

Trading and Profit and Loss Account for the year ended 31 December 1997

		£
Sales		4,000
Less Returns inwards		150
		3,850
Purchases	3,120	
Less Returns outwards	220	
	2,900	
Closing stock	300	2,600
Gross profit		1,250

Note: Sales less Returns inwards is often called 'Turnover'. In Exhibit 10.1 above, turnover is £3,850.

Comparing Exhibit 10.1 above to Exhibit 8.1 it can be seen that they do, in fact, amount to the same thing as far as gross profit is concerned. Sales were £3,850 in the original example. In the new example returns inwards should be deducted to get the correct figure for goods sold to customers and *kept* by them, i.e. £4,000 – £150 = £3,850. Purchases originally were £2,900; in the new example returns outwards should be deducted to get the correct figure of purchases *kept* by Swift. The gross profit remains at £1,250 as per Exhibit 8.1.

10.2 Carriage

Carriage (the cost of transporting goods) from suppliers into a firm is called **carriage inwards**. Carriage of goods out of a firm to its customers is called **carriage outwards**.

When goods are bought the cost of carriage inwards may either be included as part of the price, or else the firm may have to pay separately for it. Suppose the firm was buying exactly the same goods from two different suppliers. One supplier might sell them for £100, and he would deliver the goods and not send you a bill for carriage. Another supplier might sell the goods for £95, but you would have to pay £5 to a haulage firm for carriage inwards, i.e. a total cost of £100.

To ensure that the cost of buying goods is always shown on the same basis, carriage inwards is always added to purchases in the trading account.

Carriage outwards to customers is not part of our firm's expenses in buying goods, and is always entered in the profit and loss account.

Suppose that, in the example shown in Exhibit 10.1, the goods had been bought for the same total figure of £3,120, but in fact £2,920 was the figure for purchases and £200 for carriage inwards. The related trial balance and trading account appear as Exhibit 10.2.

Exhibit 10.2

Trial Balance as at 31 December 1997 (Extract only)	Debit	Credit
	£	£
Sales		4,000
Purchases	2,920	
Returns inwards	150	
Returns outwards		220
Carriage inwards	200	

Trading and Profit and Loss Account for the year ended 31 December 1997

		£
Sales		4,000
less Returns inwards		150
		3,850
Purchases	2,920	
less Returns outwards	220	
	2,700	
Carriage inwards	200	
	2,900	
Closing stock	300	2,600
Gross profit		1,250

It can be seen that Exhibits 8.1, 10.1 and 10.2 have been concerned with the same overall amount of goods bought and sold by the firm, at the same overall prices. Therefore, as shown, in each case the same gross profit of £1,250 is shown.

Before you proceed further you should attempt Review Questions 10.1 and 10.2.

10.3 The second year of a business

At the end of his second year of trading, on 31 December 1998, B Swift extracts another trial balance.

Exhibit 10.3

B Swift Trial Balance as at 31 December 1998	Debit	Credit
	£	£
Sales		6,700
Purchases	4,260	
Lighting and heating expenses	190	
Rent	240	
Shop assistant's wages	520	
General expenses	70	
Carriage outwards	110	
Buildings	2,000	
Fixtures and fittings	750	
Debtors	1,200	
Creditors		900
Bank	120	
Cash	40	
Loan from J Marsh		1,000
Drawings	900	
Capital		2,100
Stock (at 31 December 1997)	300	
	10,700	10,700

Adjustments needed for stock

Previously we have done the accounts for new businesses only. They started without stock and therefore had closing stock only, as we were doing the first trading and profit and loss account.

When we prepare the trading and profit and loss account for the second year we can now see the difference. Looking at Exhibits 9.1 and 10.3 for B Swift we can see the stock figures needed for the trading accounts:

Trading Account for period	Year to 31 December 1997	Year to 31 December 1998
Opening stock 1.1.1997	None	
Closing stock 31.12.1997	£300	
Opening stock 1.1.1998		£300
Closing stock 31.12.1998		£550

This means that calculations for the first year of trading, to 31 December 1997, had only one stock figure included in them. This was the closing stock. For the second year of trading, to 31 December 1998, both opening and closing stock figures will be in the calculations.

The stock shown in the trial balance, Exhibit 10.3, is that brought forward from the previous year on 31 December 1997; it is, therefore, the opening stock of 1998. The closing stock at 31 December 1998 can only be found by stock-taking. Assume it amounts, at cost, to £550.

Let us first of all calculate the cost of goods sold for 1998:

	£
Stock of goods at start of year	300
Add Purchases	4,260
Total goods available for sale	4,560
Less What remains at the end of the year:	
i.e. stock of goods at close	550
Therefore cost of goods that have been sold	4,010

We can look at a diagram to illustrate this, *see* Exhibit 10.4.

Exhibit 10.4

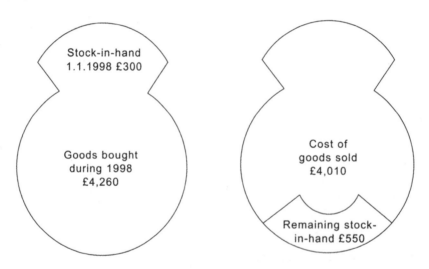

The sales were £6,700, so Sales £6,700 – Cost of Goods Sold £4,010 = Gross Profit £2,690.

Now the trading and profit and loss accounts can be drawn up, *see* Exhibit 10.5.

Exhibit 10.5

B Swift
Trading and Profit and Loss Account for the year ended 31 December 1998

		£
Sales		6,700
Opening stock	300	
Add Purchases	4,260	
	4,560	
Less Closing stock	550	
Cost of goods sold		4,010
Gross profit		2,690
Expenses		
Wages	520	
Lighting and heating	190	
Rent	240	
General expenses	70	
Carriage outwards	110	1,130
Net profit		1,560

The balances now remaining in the books, including the new balance on the stock account, are now drawn up in the form of a balance sheet. *See* Exhibit 10.6.

Exhibit 10.6

B Swift
Balance Sheet as at 31 December 1998

		£
Fixed assets		
Buildings		2,000
Fixtures and fittings		750
		2,750
Current assets		
Stock	550	
Debtors	1,200	
Bank	120	
Cash	40	
	1,910	
Current liabilities		
Creditors	900	1,010
		3,760
Long-term liability		
Loan from J Marsh		1,000
		2,760
Capital		
Balance at 1 January		2,100
Net profit for the year		1,560
		3,660
Drawings		900
		2,760

Stock account

It is perhaps helpful if the stock account covering both years can now be seen:

Stock

1997	£			£
Dec 31 Trading A/c	300			
1998		1998		£
Dec 31 Trading A/c	550	Jan 1 Trading A/c		300

Final accounts

The term **Final Accounts** is often used to mean collectively the trading and profit and loss account and the balance sheet. The term can be misleading as the balance sheet is not an account.

Other expenses in the trading account

All costs of putting goods into a saleable condition should be charged in the Trading Account. In the case of a trader these are relatively few. An example could be a trader who sells clocks packed in boxes. If he bought the clocks from one source, and the boxes from another source, both of these items would be charged in the Trading Account as Purchases. In addition, if someone is paid to pack the clocks, then such wages would be charged in the Trading Account. The wages of shop assistants who sold the clocks would be charged in the Profit and Loss Account. The wages of the person packing the clocks would be the only wages in this instance concerned with 'putting the goods into a saleable condition'.

Review questions

In addition to the questions which follow you should attempt questions 44–53 in the accompanying book of multiple-choice questions (see back cover for further details).

Suggested solutions to review questions with the letter 'A' after the question number are given in Appendix I (pages 607–8).

10.1A From the following details draw up the trading account of T Clarke for the year ended 31 December 1997, which was his first year in business:

	£
Carriage inwards	670
Returns outwards	495
Returns inwards	890
Sales	38,742
Purchases	33,333
Stocks of goods at 31 December	7,489

10.2 The following details for K Taylor for the year ended 31 March 1998 are available. Draw up the trading account for that year.

	£
Stocks at the end of the accounting period	18,504
Returns inwards	1,372
Returns outwards	2,896
Purchases	53,397
Carriage inwards	1,122
Sales	54,600

10.3A From the following trial balance of R Graham draw up a trading and profit and loss account for the year ended 30 September 1998, and a balance sheet as at that date.

	Dr	Cr
	£	£
Stock at 1 October 1997	2,368	
Carriage outwards	200	
Carriage inwards	310	
Returns inwards	205	
Returns outwards		322
Purchases	11,874	
Sales		18,600
Salaries and wages	3,862	
Rent	304	
Insurance	78	
Motor expenses	664	
Office expenses	216	
Lighting and heating expenses	166	
General expenses	314	
Premises	5,000	
Vehicles	1,800	
Fixtures and fittings	350	
Debtors	3,896	
Creditors		1,731
Cash at bank	482	
Drawings	1,200	
Capital		12,636
	33,289	33,289

Stock at 30 September 1998 was £2,946.

10.4A The following trial balance was extracted from the books of B Jackson on 30 April 1998. From it, and the note below it, prepare his trading and profit and loss account for the year ended 30 April 1998, and a balance sheet as at that date.

	Dr	Cr
	£	£
Sales		18,600
Purchases	11,556	
Stock at 1 May 1997	3,776	
Carriage outwards	326	
Carriage inwards	234	
Returns inwards	440	
Returns outwards		355
Salaries and wages	2,447	
Motor expenses	664	
Rent	576	
Sundry expenses	1,202	
Vehicles	2,400	
Fixtures and fittings	600	
Debtors	4,577	
Creditors		3,045
Cash at bank	3,876	
Cash in hand	120	
Drawings	2,050	
Capital		12,844
	34,844	34,844

Stock at 30 April 1998 was £4,998.

10.5 The following is the trial balance of J Smailes as at 31 March 1998. Draw up a set of final accounts for the year ended 31 March 1998.

	Dr £	Cr £
Stock at 1 April 1997	18,160	
Sales		92,340
Purchases	69,185	
Carriage inwards	420	
Carriage outwards	1,570	
Returns outwards		640
Wages and salaries	10,240	
Rent and rates	3,015	
Communication expenses	624	
Commission paid	216	
Insurance	405	
Sundry expenses	318	
Buildings	20,000	
Debtors	14,320	
Creditors		8,160
Fixtures	2,850	
Cash at bank	2,970	
Cash in hand	115	
Loan from K Ball (repayable 1999)		10,000
Drawings	7,620	
Capital		40,888
	152,028	152,028

Stock at 31 March 1998 was £22,390.

10.6 L Stokes drew up the following trial balance as at 30 September 1998. You are to draft the trading and profit and loss account for the year to 30 September 1998 and a balance sheet as at that date.

	Dr £	Cr £
Loan from P Owens (repayable 2002)		5,000
Capital		25,955
Drawings	8,420	
Cash at bank	3,115	
Cash in hand	295	
Debtors	12,300	
Creditors		9,370
Stock at 30 September 1997	23,910	
Van	4,100	
Office equipment	6,250	
Sales		130,900
Purchases	92,100	
Returns inwards	550	
Carriage inwards	215	
Returns outwards		307
Carriage outwards	309	
Motor expenses	1,630	
Rent	2,970	
Telephone charges	405	
Wages and salaries	12,810	
Insurance	492	
Office expenses	1,377	
Sundry expenses	284	
	171,532	171,532

Stock at 30 September 1998 was £27,475.

11

Accounting concepts

What you have been reading about so far has been concerned with the recording of transactions in the books. Such recording has been based on certain assumptions. Quite deliberately these assumptions were not discussed in detail at the time. This is because it is much easier to look at them with a greater understanding *after* basic double entry has been covered. These assumptions are known as the *concepts of accounting*.

The trading and profit and loss accounts and balance sheets shown in the previous chapters were drawn up for the owner of the business. As shown later in the book, businesses are often owned by more than just one person and these accounting statements are for the use of all of the owners.

An owner of a business may not be the only person to see his final accounts. He may have to show them to his bank manager if he wants to borrow money. The Revenue Commissioners will want to see them for the calculation of taxes. He may also need them to show to someone when he sells his business. Similarly, a new partner or investor would want to see them.

11.2 One set of final accounts for all purposes

If it had always been the custom to draft different kinds of final accounts for different purposes, so that one type was given to a banker, another type to someone wishing to buy the business, etc., then accounting would be different than it is today. However, copies of the same set of final accounts are given to all of the different people.

This means that the banker, the prospective buyer of the business, the owner and the other people all see the same trading and profit and loss account and balance sheet. This is not an ideal situation as the interests of each party are different and each party needs different kinds of information from that wanted by the others. For instance, the bank manager would really like to know how much the assets would sell for if the firm ceased trading. He could then see what the possibility would be of the bank obtaining repayment of its loan. Other people would also like to see the information in the way that is most useful to them. Yet normally only one sort of final accounts is available for these different people.

This means that trading and profit and loss accounts have to be used for different needs, and to be of any use, the different parties have to agree to the way in which they are drawn up.

Assume that you are in a class of students and that you have the problem of valuing your assets, which consist of 10 textbooks. The first value you decide is that of how much you could sell them for. Your own guess is £30, but the other members of the class may give figures from £15 to £50.

Suppose that you now decide to put a value on their use to you. You may well think that the use of these books will enable you to pass your examinations and so you will get a good job. Another person may have the opposite idea concerning the use of the books to him/her. The use value placed on the books by others in the class will be quite different.

Finally you decide to value them by reference to cost. You take out of your pocket the receipts for the books, which show that you paid a total of £60 for the books. If the rest of the class do not think that you have altered the receipts, then they also can all agree that the value expressed as cost is £60. As this is the only value that you can all agree to, then each of you decides to use the idea of showing the value of his asset of books at the cost price.

11.3 Objectivity and subjectivity

The use of a method which all can agree to, instead of everyone using their own different method, is said to be **objective**. To use cost for the value of an asset is therefore a way to be objective.

When you are **subjective**, it means that you want to use your own method, even though no one else may agree to it.

The desire to provide the same set of accounts for many different parties, and thus to provide a measure that gains their consensus of opinion, means that objectivity is sought in accounting. If you are able to understand this desire for objectivity, then many of the apparent contradictions can be understood because it is often at the heart of the accounting methods in use at the present time.

Accounting seeks objectivity, and of course it must have rules which lay down the way in which the activities of the business are recorded. These rules are known as concepts.

11.4 Basic accounting concepts

The cost concept

The need for this has already been described. It means that assets are normally shown at cost price, and that this is the basis for valuation of the asset.

The money measurement concept

Accounting is concerned only with those facts covered by (a) and (b) which follow:

(a) it can be measured in money, and
(b) most people will agree to the money value of the transaction.

This means that accounting can never tell you everything about a business. For example, accounting does not show the following:

(a) whether the firm has good or bad managers,
(b) that there are serious problems with the workforce,
(c) that a rival product is about to take away many of our best customers,
(d) that the government is about to pass a law which will cost us a lot of extra expense in future.

The reason that (a) to (d) or similar items are not recorded is that it would be impossible to work out a money value for them which most people would agree to.

Some people think that accounting tells you everything you want to know. The above shows that this is not true.

The going concern concept

Normally we assume that a business will continue for a long time. Only if the business was going to be sold or closed down would we show how much the assets would sell for. This is because we use the cost concept. If businesses were not assumed to be **going concerns**, the cost concept could not be used. If firms were to be treated as if they were going to be sold immediately, then the saleable value of assets would be used instead of cost.

The entity concept

The items recorded in a firm's books are limited to the transactions which affect the firm as a business entity. Suppose that a proprietor of a firm, from his personal monies outside the firm, buys a diamond necklace for his wife. As the money spent was not out of the firm's bank account or cash box, then this item will not be entered in the firm's books.

The only time that the personal resources of the proprietor affect the firm's accounting records is when he brings new capital into the firm, or takes drawings out of the firm.

The realisation concept

Normally, profit is said to be earned at the time when:

(*a*) goods or services are passed to the customer, and
(*b*) he then incurs liability for them.

This concept of profit is known as the **realisation** concept. Notice that is *not*

(*a*) when the order is received, or
(*b*) when the customer pays for the goods.

It can mean that profit is brought into account in one period, and it is found to have been incorrectly taken as such when the goods are returned in a later period because of some deficiency. Also the services can turn out to be subject to an allowance being given in a later period owing to poor performance. If the allowances or returns can be reasonably estimated an adjustment may be made to the calculated profit in the period when they passed to the customer.

The dual aspect concept

This states that there are two aspects of accounting, one represented by the assets of the business and the other by the claims against them. The concept states that these two aspects are always equal to each other. In other words:

$$\text{Assets} = \text{Capital} + \text{Liabilities}$$

Double entry is the name given to the method of recording the transactions for the **dual aspect concept**.

The accruals concept

The **accruals concept** says that net profit is the difference between revenues and expenses, i.e.

$$\text{Revenues} - \text{Expenses} = \text{Net Profit}$$

Determining the expenses used up to obtain the revenues is referred to as *matching* expenses against revenues.

This concept is particularly misunderstood by people who have not studied accounting. To many of them, actual payment of an item in a period is taken as being matched against the revenue of the period when the net profit is calculated. The fact that expenses consist of the assets used up in a particular period in obtaining the revenues of that period, and that cash paid in a period and expenses of a period are usually different as you will see later, comes as a surprise to a great number of them.

The time interval concept

One of the underlying principles of accounting is that final accounts are prepared at regular intervals of one year. For internal management purposes they may be prepared far more frequently, possibly as frequent as on a monthly basis.

11.5 Further overriding concepts

The concepts of accounting already discussed have become accepted in the business world, their assimilation having taken place over many years. These concepts, however, are capable of being interpreted in many ways. What has therefore grown up in accounting are generally accepted approaches to the application of the earlier concepts. The main ones in these further concepts may be said to be: materiality, prudence, consistency and substance over form.

Materiality

Accounting does not serve a useful purpose if the effort of recording a transaction in a certain way is not worthwhile. Thus, if a box of paper-clips was bought it would be used up over a period of time, and this cost is used up every time someone uses a paper-clip. It is possible to record this as an expense every time it happens, but obviously the price of a box of paper-clips is so little that it is not worth recording it in this fashion. The box of paper-clips is not a material item, and therefore would be charged as an expense in the period it was bought, irrespective of the fact that it could last for more than one accounting period. In other words do not waste your time in the elaborate recording of trivial items.

Similarly, the purchase of a cheap metal ashtray would also be charged as an expense in the period it was bought because it is not a material item, even though it may in fact last for twenty years. A lorry would, however, be deemed to be a material item, and so, as will be seen in Chapter 24 on depreciation, an attempt is made to charge each period with the cost consumed in each period of its use.

Firms fix all sorts of arbitrary rules to determine what is material and what is not. There is no law that lays down what these should be, the decision as to what is material and what is not is dependent upon judgement. A firm may well decide that all items under £100 should be treated as expenses in the period in which they were bought even though they may well be in use in the firm for the following ten years. Another firm, especially a large one, may fix the limit of £1,000. Different limits may be set for different types of item.

It can be seen that the size and the type of firm will affect the decisions as to which items are material. With individuals, an amount of £1,000 may well be more than you, as a student, possess. For a multi-millionaire as to what is a material item and what is not will almost certainly not be comparable. Just as individuals vary then so do firms. Some

firms have a great deal of machinery and may well treat all items of machinery costing less than £1,000 as not being material, whereas another firm which makes about the same amount of profits, but has very little machinery, may well treat a £600 machine as being a material item as they have fixed their limit at £250.

The prudence concept

Very often an accountant has to use his judgement to decide which figure he will take for an item. Suppose a debt has been owing for quite a long time, and no one knows whether it will ever be paid. Should the accountant be an optimist in thinking that it will be paid, or should he be more pessimistic?

It is the accountant's duty to see that people get the proper facts about a business. He should make certain that assets are not valued too highly. Similarly, liabilities should not be shown at values too low. Otherwise, people might inadvisedly lend money to a firm, which they would not do if they had the proper facts.

The accountant should always be on the side of safety, and this is known as prudence. The prudence concept means that normally he will take the figure which will understate rather than overstate the profit. Thus, he should choose the figure which will cause the capital of the firm to be shown at a lower amount rather than at a higher one. He will also normally make sure that all losses are recorded in the books, but profits should not be anticipated by recording them before they should be.

The consistency concept

Even if we do everything already listed under concepts, there will still be quite a few different ways in which items could be recorded. This is because there can be different interpretations as to the exact meaning of the concept.

Each firm should try to choose the method which gives the most reliable picture of the business.

This cannot be done if one method is used in one year and another method in the next year and so on. Constantly changing the methods would lead to misleading profits being calculated from the accounting records. Therefore the convention of consistency is used. This convention says that when a firm has once fixed a method for the accounting treatment of an item, it will enter all similar items that follow in exactly the same way.

However, it does not mean that the firm has to follow the method until the firm closes down. A firm can change the method used, but such a change is not taken without a lot of consideration. When such a change occurs and the profits calculated in that year are affected by a material amount, then either in the profit and loss account itself or in one of the reports with it, the effect of the change should be stated.

Substance over form

It can happen that the legal form of a transaction can differ from its real substance. Where this happens accounting should show the transaction in accordance with its real substance, which is basically how the transaction affects the economic situation of the firm. This means that accounting in this instance will not reflect the exact legal position concerning that transaction.

You have not yet come across the best and easiest illustration of this concept. Later in your studies you may have to learn about accounting for fixed assets being bought on hire-purchase. We will take a car as an example.

- From a legal point of view the car does not belong to the firm until all the hire-purchase instalments have been paid, and an option taken up whereby you take over legal possession of the car.
- From an economic point of view you have used the car for business purposes, just as any other car owned by the business which was paid for immediately has been used. In this case the business will show the car being bought on hire-purchase in its accounts and balance sheet as though it were legally owned by the business, but also showing separately the amount still owed for it.

In this way, therefore, the substance of the transaction has taken precedence over the legal form of the transaction.

11.6 The assumption of the stability of currency

One does not have to be very old to remember that a few years ago many goods could be bought with less money than today. If one listens to one's parents or grandparents then many stories will be heard of how little this item or the other could be bought for x years ago. The currencies of the countries of the world are not stable in terms of what each unit of currency can buy over the years.

Accounting, however, uses the cost concept, this stating that the asset is normally shown at its cost price. This means that accounting statements will be distorted because assets will be bought at different points in time at the price then ruling, and the figures totalled up to show the value of the assets in cost terms. For instance, suppose that you had bought a building 20 years ago for £20,000. You now decide to buy an identical additional building, but the price has now risen to £40,000. You buy it, and the buildings account now shows buildings at a figure of £60,000. One building is measured cost-wise in terms of the currency of 20 years ago, while the other is taken at today's currency value. The figure of a total of £60,000 is historically correct, but, other than that, the total figure cannot be said to be particularly valid for any other use.

This means that to make a correct assessment of accounting statements one must bear in mind the distorting effects of changing price levels upon the accounting entries as recorded. There are techniques of adjusting accounts so as to try and eliminate these distortions. These are dealt with later.

11.7 Accounting standards and financial reporting standards

At one time there used to be quite wide differences in the ways that accountants calculated profits. In the late 1960s a number of cases led to a widespread outcry against the lack of uniformity in accounting.

To reduce the possibility of very large variations in reported profits under different methods, the accounting bodies formed an Accounting Standards Committee. This committee over a period of about 20 years issued 25 Statements of Standard Accounting Practice, abbreviated as SSAPs. Accountants and auditors were expected to comply with the SSAPs. If they were not complied with, then the audit report had to give the reasons why the SSAP had been ignored.

The use of the SSAPs did not mean that two identical businesses would show exactly the same profits year by year. It did, however, considerably reduce the possibilities of very large variations in such profit reporting.

In 1990 the accountancy bodies set up a new board, called The Accounting Standards Board Limited. This board took over the SSAPs which were still in use; 22 of them. These continue to be known as SSAPs. New standards developed by the board are called Financial Reporting Standards, abbreviated as FRSs.

The Accounting Standards Board may issue pronouncements other than FRSs. As each one appears, the board will state what authority, scope and application it will have.

11.8 Accounting standards and the legal framework

The FRSs are drafted so that they comply with the laws of the Republic of Ireland. They also fit in with the European Community Directives. This is to ensure that there is no conflict between the law and accounting standards.

11.9 SSAP 2

It is rather unfortunate that this SSAP mentions 'four fundamental concepts', and to a student it could be misunderstood to mean that there are *only* four concepts. In fact it has simply limited its investigations to the ones it considered most important, i.e. accruals, consistency, going concern and prudence. The academic world does not limit its concern with concepts to these four concepts only.

Review questions

Questions 54–64 in the accompanying book of multiple-choice questions examine the material covered in this chapter (see the back cover of this book for further details).

Part III

RECORDING BUSINESS TRANSACTIONS 2:
Books of original entry

12

Books of original entry and ledgers

12.1 The accounting consequences of growth

While a firm is very small, all the double entry accounts can be kept in one book, called a ledger. As firms grow it is not practical to use only one book, as the number of pages needed to deal with the volume of transactions means that the book would be too big to handle. Also, suppose there are several bookkeepers. They could not all do their work properly if there was only one ledger.

The answer to this problem is for us to use more books. When we do this we put similar types of transactions together and have a book for that type. In each book we will not mix together transactions which are different from each other.

12.2 Books of original entry

These are the books in which transactions are first recorded. We have a separate book for each different kind of transaction. The nature of the transaction determines which book it is entered into. Sales will be entered in one book, purchases in another book, cash in another book, and so on. We enter the transactions in these books giving the following details:

- The date of the transaction. (Transactions should be shown in chronological order.)
- Details of the transaction.
- The amount of money involved in the transaction.

12.3 Types of books of original entry

These are:

- **The Sales Journal** – for credit sales.
- **The Purchases Journal** – for credit purchases.
- **The Returns Inwards Journal** – for returns inwards.
- **The Returns Outwards Journal** – for returns outwards.
- **The Cash Book** – for receipts and payments of cash.
- **The General Journal** – for other items.

12.4 Using more than one ledger

Although we have now made lists of transactions in the books of original entry, we still have more work to do. We have got to show the effect of the transactions by putting them into double entry accounts. Instead of keeping all the double entry accounts in one ledger, we have several ledgers. This again makes it easier to divide the work between different bookkeepers.

12.5 Types of ledgers

The different types of ledgers are:

- **The Sales Ledger.** This is kept just for customers' personal accounts.
- **The Purchases Ledger.** This is kept just for suppliers' personal accounts.
- **The General Ledger.** This contains the remaining double entry accounts such as expenses, fixed assets, capital etc.

12.6 Diagram of books used

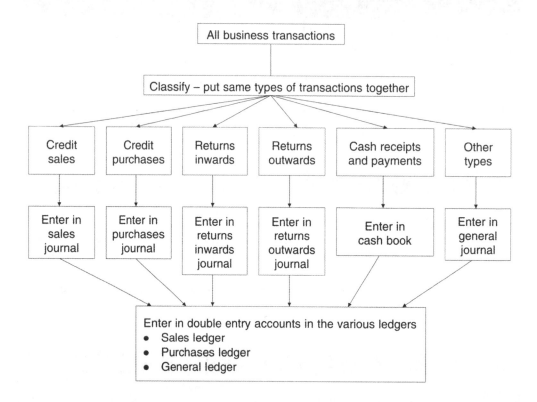

12.7 Description of books used

In the next few chapters we will look at the books used in more detail, except for the general journal which will be dealt with at a later stage.

12.8 Types of accounts

Some people describe all accounts as **personal** accounts or as **impersonal** accounts.

- **Personal Accounts** – These are for debtors and creditors.
- **Impersonal Accounts** – Divided between real accounts and nominal accounts.
- **Real Accounts** – Accounts in which property is recorded. Examples are buildings, machinery, fixtures and stock.
- **Nominal Accounts** – Accounts in which expenses, income and capital are recorded.

The following diagram may enable you to understand it better:

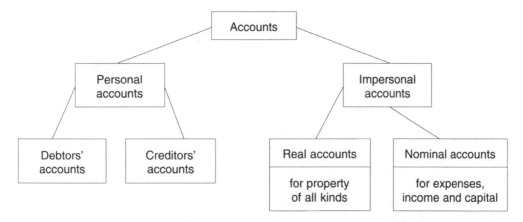

12.9 Nominal and private ledgers

The ledger in which the impersonal accounts are kept is known as the **nominal** (or general) **ledger**. Very often, to ensure privacy for the proprietor(s), the capital and drawing accounts and similar accounts are kept in a **private ledger**. By doing this office staff cannot see details of items which the proprietors want to keep a secret.

12.10 Computers and accounting

At this point it might be thought that the authors had never heard of computers, as the text has been discussing 'books' of various sorts.

In fact the term 'book' or 'journal' is simply a convenient way of describing what is, in effect, a 'collection point' for a particular type of information. The principles of accounting can therefore be more easily discussed if the authors keep to standard terms. The principles remain exactly the same whether manual or computerised methods are in use.

12.11 The accountant as a communicator

Quite often the impression is given that all that the accountant does is to produce figures, arranged in various ways. Naturally, such forms of computation do take up quite a lot of the accountant's time, but what then takes up the rest of his time is exactly how he communicates these figures to other people.

First of all, he can obviously arrange the figures in such a way as to present the information in as meaningful a way as possible. Suppose, for instance, that the figures he has produced are to be given to several people all of whom are very knowledgeable about accounting. He could, in such an instance, present the figures in a normal accounting way, knowing full well that the recipients of the information will understand it.

On the other hand, the accounting figures may well be needed by people who have absolutely no knowledge at all of accounting. In such a case a normal accounting statement would be of no use to them, as they would not understand it. In this case he might set out the figures in a completely different way to try to make it easy for them to grasp. For instance, instead of preparing a normal trading and profit and loss account he might show it as follows:

	£	£
During 1998 you sold goods for		50,000
Now how much had those goods cost you to buy?		
At the start of the year you had stock costing	6,000	
+ You bought some more goods in the year costing	28,000	
So altogether you had goods available to sell of	34,000	
− At the end of the year you had stock of goods unsold of	3,000	
So the goods you had sold in the year had cost you	31,000	
Let us deduct this from what you had sold the goods for		31,000
This means that you had made a profit on buying and selling goods, before any other expenses had been paid, amounting to		19,000
(We call this sort of profit the gross profit)		
But you suffered other expenses such as wages, rent, lighting and so on, and during the year the amount of these expenses, not including anything taken for yourself, amounted to		9,000
So, this year your sales value exceeded all the cost involved in running the business, so that the sales could be made, by		£10,000
(We call this sort of profit the net profit)		

If an accountant cannot arrange the figures to make them meaningful to the recipient then he is failing in his task. His job is not just to produce figures for himself to look at, his job is to communicate these results to other people.

Very often the accountant will have to talk to people to explain the figures, or send a letter or write a report concerning them. He will also have to talk or write to people to find out exactly what sort of accounting information is needed by them or explain to them what sort of information he could provide. This means that if accounting examinations consist simply of computational type questions then they will not test the ability of the candidate to communicate in any other way than by writing down accounting figures. In recent years more attention has been paid by examining boards to these aspects of an accountant's work.

Review questions

Questions 65–69 in the accompanying book of multiple-choice questions examine the material covered in this chapter (see the back cover of this book for further details).

13

Two-column cash books

13.1 Introduction

The cash book consists of the cash account and the bank account put together in one book. Initially we showed these two accounts on different pages of the ledger. Now it is easier to put the two sets of account columns together. This means that we can record all money received and paid out on a particular date on the same page.

In the cash book the debit column for cash is put next to the debit column for bank. The credit column for cash is put next to the credit column for bank.

13.2 Drawing up a cash book

We can now look at a cash account and a bank account in Exhibit 13.1 as they would appear if they had been kept separately. Then in Exhibit 13.2 they are shown as if the transactions had instead been kept in a cash book.

The bank column contains details of the payments made by cheque and of the money received and paid into the bank account. The bank will have a copy of the account in its own books.

The bank will send a copy of the account in its books to the firm, a bank statement. When the firm receives the bank statement, it will check it against the bank column in its own cash book to ensure that there are no errors.

Exhibit 13.1

Cash

			£				£
Aug	2	T Moore	33	Aug	8	Rent	20
,,	5	K Charles	25	,,	12	C Potts	19
,,	15	F Hughes	37	,,	28	Wages	25
,,	30	H Howe	18	,,	31	Balance c/d	49
			113				113
Sept	1	Balance b/d	49				

Bank

			£				£
Aug	1	Capital	1,000	Aug	7	Rates	105
,,	3	W P Ltd	244	,,	12	F Small Ltd	95
,,	16	K Noone	408	,,	26	K French	268
,,	30	H Sanders	20	,,	31	Balance c/d	1,204
			1,672				1,672
Sept	1	Balance b/d	1,204				

Exhibit 13.2

			Cash £	Bank £				Cash £	Bank £
		Cash Book							
Aug	1	Capital		1,000	Aug	17	Rates		105
„	2	T Moore	33		„	8	Rent	20	
„	3	W P Ltd		244	„	12	C Potts	19	
„	5	K Charles	25		„	12	F Small Ltd		95
„	15	F Hughes	37		„	26	K French		268
„	16	K Noone		408	„	28	Wages	25	
„	30	H Sanders		20	„	31	Balances c/d	49	1,204
„	30	H Howe	18						
			113	1,672				113	1,672
Sept	1	Balances b/d	49	1,204					

13.3 Cash lodged into the bank

In Exhibit 13.2, the payments into the bank have been cheques received by the firm which have been banked immediately. We must now consider cash being paid into the bank.

1 Let us look at the position when a customer pays his account in cash, and later a part of this cash is paid into the bank. The receipt of the cash is debited to the cash column on the date received, the credit entry being in the customer's personal account. The cash banked has the following effect needing action as shown:

	Effect	**Action**
1	Asset of cash is decreased	Credit the asset account, i.e the cash account which is represented by the cash column in the cash book.
2	Asset of bank is increased	Debit the asset account, i.e. the bank account which is represented by the bank column in the cash book.

Example:

A cash receipt of £100 from M Davies on 1 August, later followed by the lodgement on 3 August of £80 of this amount would appear in the cash book as follows:

			Cash £	Bank £				Cash £	Bank £
		Cash Book							
Aug	1	M Davies	100		Aug	3	Bank	80	
„	3	Cash		80					

The details column shows entries against each item stating the name of the account in which the completion of double entry has taken place. Against the cash payment of £80

appears the word 'bank', meaning that the debit £80 is to be found in the bank column, and the opposite applies.

2 Where the whole of the cash received is banked immediately the receipt can be treated in exactly the same manner as a cheque received, i.e. it can be entered directly in the bank column.

3 If the firm requires cash it may withdraw cash from the bank. This is done by making out a cheque to pay itself a certain amount in cash. The bank will give cash in exchange for the cheque.

The twofold effect and the action required may be shown:

Effect	Action
1 Asset of bank is decreased	Credit the asset account, i.e the bank column in the cash book.
2 Asset of cash is increased	Debit the asset account, i.e. the cash column in the cash book.

A withdrawal of £75 cash on 1 September from the bank would appear in the cash book thus:

Cash Book					
	Cash £	*Bank* £		*Cash* £	*Bank* £
Sept 1 Bank	75		Sept 1 Cash		75

Both the debit and credit entries for this item are in the same book. When this happens it is known as a **contra** item.

13.4 The use of folio columns

As has already been seen, the details column in an account contains the name of the other account in which double entry has been completed. Anyone looking through the books would therefore be able to find where the other half of the double entry was.

However, when many books are being used, just to mention the name of the other account would not be enough information to find the other account quickly. More information is needed, and this is given by using **folio columns**.

In each account and in each book being used, a folio column is added, always shown on the left of the money columns. In this column the name of the other book, in abbreviated form, and the number of the page in the other book where double entry is completed is stated against each and every entry in the books.

An entry of a receipt of cash from C Kelly whose account was on page 45 of the sales ledger, and the cash recorded on page 37 of the cash book, would use the folio column thus:

In the cash book. In the folio column would appear SL 45.
In the sales ledger. In the folio column would appear CB 37.

By this method full cross-reference would be given. Each of the contra items, being shown on the same page of the cash book, would use the letter 'C' in the folio column.

13.5 Advantages of folio columns

These are:

● As described in section 13.4 it speeds up reference to the other book where double entry for the item is completed.
● The folio column is filled in when double entry has been completed. If it has not been filled in, double entry will not have been made.

Looking through the folio columns to ensure they have all been filled in will help us to detect such errors.

13.6 Example of a cash book with folio columns

The following transactions are written up in the form of a cash book. The folio columns are filled in as though double entry had been completed to other accounts.

			£
Sept	1	Proprietor puts capital into a bank account for the business.	940
,,	2	Received cheque from M Boon.	115
,,	4	Cash sales.	102
,,	6	Paid rent by cash.	35
,,	7	Banked £50 of the cash held by the firm.	50
,,	15	Cash sales paid direct into the bank.	40
,,	23	Paid cheque to S Wills.	277
,,	29	Withdrew cash from bank for business use.	120
,,	30	Paid wages in cash.	118

			Folio	Cash £	Bank £				Folio	Cash £	Bank £
Sept	1	Capital	GL1		940	Sept	6	Rent	GL65	35	
,,	2	M Boon	SL98		115	,,	7	Bank	C	50	
,,	4	Sales	GL87	102		,,	23	S Wills	PL23		277
,,	7	Cash	C		50	,,	29	Cash	C		120
,,	15	Sales	GL87		40	,,	30	Wages	GL39	118	
,,	29	Bank	C	120		,,	30	Balances	c/d	19	748
				222	1,145					222	1,145
Oct	1	Balances	b/d	19	748						

Cash Book (table title)

The abbreviations used in the folio column are as follows:
GL = General Ledger: SL = Sales Ledger: C = Contra: PL = Purchases Ledger.

Review questions

In addition to the questions which follow, you should attempt questions 70–72 in the accompanying book of multiple-choice questions (see back cover for further details).

Suggested solutions to review questions with the letter 'A' after the question number are given in Appendix I (pages 608–9).

13.1A Write up a two-column cash book from the following details, and balance it off as at the end of the month:

May	1	Started business with capital in cash £100.
,,	2	Paid rent by cash £10.
,,	3	F Lake lent us £500, paid by cheque.
,,	4	We paid B McKenzie by cheque £65.
,,	5	Cash sales £98.
,,	7	N Miller paid us by cheque £62.
,,	9	We paid B Burton in cash £22.
,,	11	Cash sales paid directly into the bank £53.
,,	15	G Moores paid us in cash £65.
,,	16	We took £50 out of the cash till and paid it into the bank account.
,,	19	We repaid F Lake £100 by cheque.
,,	22	Cash sales paid directly into the bank £66.
,,	26	Paid motor expenses by cheque £12.
,,	30	Withdrew £100 cash from the bank for business use.
,,	31	Paid wages in cash £97.

13.2A Write up a two-column cash book from the following details, and balance it off as at the end of the month:

Mar	1	Balances brought down from the previous month: Cash in hand £56; Cash in Bank £2,356.
,,	2	Paid rates by cheque £156.
,,	3	Paid for postage stamps in cash £5.
,,	5	Cash sales £74.
,,	7	Cash paid into the bank £60.
,,	8	We paid T Lee by cheque £75: We paid C Brooks in cash £2.
,,	12	J Moores pays us £150, £50 being in cash and £100 by cheque.
,,	17	Cash drawings by the proprietor £20.
,,	20	P Jones pays us by cheque £79.
,,	22	Withdrew £200 from the bank for business use.
,,	24	Bought a used van for £1,950 and paid by cheque.
,,	28	Paid rent by cheque £40.
,,	31	Cash sales paid directly into the bank £105.

13.3   Write up a two-column cash book from the following:

Nov 1   Balances brought forward from the previous month: Cash £105; Bank £2,164.
,,   2   Cash Sales £605.
,,   3   Took £500 out of the cash till and paid it into the bank.
,,   4   J Matthews paid us by cheque £217.
,,   5   We paid for postage stamps in cash £60.
,,   6   Bought office equipment by cheque £189.
,,   7   We paid J Lucas by cheque £50.
,,   9   Received rates refund by cheque £72.
,,   11   Withdrew £250 from the bank for business use.
,,   12   Paid wages in cash £239.
,,   14   Paid motor expenses by cheque £57.
,,   16   L Levy lent us £200 in cash.
,,   20   R Norman paid us by cheque £112.
,,   28   We paid general expenses in cash £22.
,,   30   Paid insurance by cheque £74.

14

Cash discounts and three-column cash books

14.1 Cash discounts

It is better for businesses if their customers pay them quickly. A firm may accept a smaller sum in full settlement if payment is made within a certain period of time. The amount of the reduction of the sum to be paid is known as a *cash discount*. The term 'cash discount' thus refers to the allowance given for prompt payment. It is still called cash discount, even if the account is paid by cheque.

The rate of cash discount is usually stated as a percentage. Full details of the percentage allowed, and the period within which payment is to be made, are quoted on all sales documents by the selling company. A typical period during which discount may be allowed is one month from the date of the original transaction.

14.2 Discounts allowed and discounts received

A firm may have two types of cash discounts in its books. These are:

1 **Discounts allowed.** Cash discounts allowed by a firm to its customers when they pay their accounts quickly.
2 **Discounts received.** Received by a firm from its suppliers when it pays their accounts quickly.

We can see the effect of discounts by looking at two examples.

Example 1

W Clarke owed us £100. He paid on 2 September by cash within the time limit laid down, and was allowed 5% cash discount. Therefore, he paid £100 – £5 = £95 in full settlement of his account.

Effect	Action
1 Of cash: Cash is increased by £95. Asset of debtors is decreased by £95.	Debit cash account, i.e. enter £95 in debit column of cash book. Credit W Clarke £95.
2 Of discounts: Asset of debtors is decreased by £5. (After the cash was paid the balance of £5 still appeared. As the account has been paid this asset must now be cancelled.) Expenses of discounts allowed increased by £5.	Credit W Clarke £5. Debit discounts allowed account £5.

Example 2

A firm owed S Small £400. It paid him on 3 September by cheque within the time limit laid down by him and he allowed 2½% cash discount. Thus, the firm paid £400 – £10 = £390 in full settlement of the account.

Effect	Action
1 Of cheque: Asset of bank is reduced by £390. Liability of creditors is reduced by £390.	Credit bank, i.e. enter in credit bank column, £390. Debit S Small's account £390.
2 Of discounts: Liability of creditors is reduced by £10. (After the cheque was paid the balance of £10 remained. As the account has been paid the liability must now be cancelled.) Revenue of discounts received increased by £10.	Debit S Small's account £10. Credit discounts received account £10.

The accounts in the firm's books would appear:

Cash Book (*page 32*)

	Cash	Bank		Cash	Bank
	£	£		£	£
Sept 2 W Clarke SL12	95		Sept 3 S Small PL75		390

Discounts Received (General Ledger *page 18*)

			£
	Sept 2 S Small PL75		10

Discounts Allowed (General Ledger *page 17*)

	£	
Sept 2 W Clarke SL12	5	

W Clarke (Sales Ledger *page 12*)

	£		£
Sept 1 Balance b/d	100	Sept 2 Cash CB32	95
		,, 2 Discount GL17	5
	100		100

S Small (Purchases Ledger *page 75*)

	£		£
Sept 3 Bank CB32	390	Sept 1 Balance b/d	400
,, 3 Discounts GL18	10		
	400		400

It is an accounting custom to enter the word 'Discount' in the personal accounts, not stating whether it is a discount received or a discount allowed.

14.3 Discount columns in the cash book

The discounts allowed account and the discounts received account are in the general ledger along with all the other revenue and expense accounts. As has already been stated, every effort should be made to avoid too much reference to the general ledger. In the case of discounts this is done by adding an extra column on each side of the cash book in which the amounts of discounts are entered. Discounts received are entered in the discount column on the credit side of the cash book, and discounts allowed in the discount column on the debit side of the cash book.

The cash book, if completed for the two examples so far dealt with, would appear:

Cash Book

	Discount	Cash	Bank		Discount	Cash	Bank
	£	£	£		£	£	£
Sept 2 W Clarke SL12	5	95		Sept 3 S Small PL75	10		390

There is no alteration to the method of showing discounts in the personal accounts.

To make entries in the discounts accounts

Total of discounts column on receipts side of cash book $\Big\}$ Enter on debit side of discounts allowed account

Total of discounts column on payments side of cash book $\Big\}$ Enter on credit side of discounts received account

14.4 Example of accounting for cash discounts

		£
May 1	Balances brought down from April:	
	Cash Balance	29
	Bank Balance	654
	Debtors accounts:	
	B King	120
	N Campbell	280
	D Shand	40
	Creditors accounts:	
	U Barrow	60
	A Allen	440
	R Long	100
„ 2	B King pays us by cheque, having deducted 2½% cash discount £3.	117
„ 8	We pay R Long his account by cheque, deducting 5% cash discount £5.	95
„ 11	We withdrew £100 cash from the bank for business use.	100
„ 16	N Campbell pays us his account by cheque, deducting 2½% discount £7.	273
„ 25	We paid wages in cash.	92

May 28   D Shand pays us in cash after having deducted 2½% cash discount.   38
  „   29   We pay U Barrow by cheque less 5% cash discount £3.   57
  „   30   We pay A Allen by cheque less 2½% cash discount £11.   429

Cash Book   *page 64*

	Folio	Discount	Cash	Bank		Folio	Discount	Cash	Bank
		£	£	£			£	£	£
May 1 Balances	b/d		29	654	May 8 R Long	PL58	5		95
May 2 B King	SL13	3		117	May 11 Cash	C			100
May 11 Bank	C		100		May 25 Wages	GL77		92	
May 16					May 29				
N Campbell	SL84	7		273	U Barrow	PL15	3		57
May 28 D Shand	SL91	2	38		May 30 A Allen	PL98	11		429
					May 31 Balances	c/d		75	363
		12	167	1,044			19	167	1,044
Jun 1 Balances	b/d		75	363					

Sales Ledger

B King   *(page 13)*

		£				£
May 1 Balance b/d		120	May 2 Bank	CB 64		117
			„ 2 Discount	CB 64		3
		120				120

N Campbell   *(page 84)*

		£				£
May 1 Balance b/d		280	May 16 Bank	CB 64		273
			„ 16 Discount	CB 64		7
		280				280

D Shand   *(page 91)*

		£				£
May 1 Balance b/d		40	May 28 Cash	CB 64		38
			„ 28 Discount	CB 64		2
		40				40

Purchases Ledger

U Barrow   *(page 15)*

		£			£
May 29 Bank	CB 64	57	May 1 Balance b/d		60
„ 29 Discount	CB 64	3			
		60			60

R Long *(page 58)*

			£				£
May 8	Bank	CB 64	95	May 1	Balance b/d		100
„ 8	Discount	CB 64	5				
			100				100

A Allen *(page 98)*

			£				£
May 30	Bank	CB 64	429	May 1	Balance b/d		440
„ 30	Discount	CB 64	11				
			440				440

General Ledger

Wages *(page 77)*

			£	
May 25	Cash	CB 64	92	

Discount Received *(page 88)*

			£
May 31 Total for the month	CB 64	19

Discount Allowed

			£	
May 31 Total for the month	CB 64	12		

Is the above method of entering discounts correct?
You can easily check. See the following:

Discounts in Ledger Accounts	Debits		Credits	
		£		
Discounts Received	U Barrow	3	Discounts	
	R Long	5	received	
	A Allen	11	account	£19
		19		
				£
Discounts Allowed	Discounts		B King	3
	allowed		N Campbell	7
	account	£12	D Shand	2
				12

You can see that proper double entry has been carried out. Equal amounts, in total, have been entered on each side of the accounts.

14.5 Bank overdrafts

A firm may borrow money from a bank by means of a bank overdraft. This means that the firm is allowed to pay more out of the bank account, by paying out cheques, than the total amount which is placed in the account.

Up to this point the bank balances have all been money at the bank, so they have all been assets, i.e. debit balances. When the account is overdrawn the firm owes money to the bank, so the account is a liability and the balance becomes a credit one.

Taking the cash book last shown, suppose that the amount payable to A Allen was £1,429 instead of £429. Thus the amount in the bank account, £1,044, is exceeded by the amount paid out. We will take the discount as being £11. The cash book would appear as follows:

Cash Book

	Discount	Cash	Bank		Discount	Cash	Bank
	£	£	£		£	£	£
May 1 Balances b/d		29	654	May 8 R Long	5		95
„ 2 B King	3		117	„ 11 Cash			100
„ 11 Bank		100		„ 25 Wages		92	
„ 16 N Campbell	7		273	„ 29 U Barrow	3		57
„ 28 D Shand	2	38		„ 30 A Allen	11		1,429
„ 31 Balance c/d			637	„ 31 Balance c/d		75	
	12	167	1,681		19	167	1,681
Jun 1 Balance b/d		75		Jun 1 Balance b/d			637

On a balance sheet, a bank overdraft will be shown as an item included under the heading of current liabilities.

14.6 Cash receipts books and cheque payments books

Except for in very small organisations, three-column cash books will not often be found. All receipts, whether of cash or cheques, will be entered in a **Cash Receipts Book** and lodged daily. A **petty cash book** (covered in Chapter 19) will be used for payments of cash. This means that there will not be a need for cash columns in the cash book itself. All payments by cheque are entered in a **Cheque Payments Book**.

In addition to the questions which follow, you should attempt questions 73–75 in the accompanying book of multiple-choice questions (see back cover for further details).

Suggested solutions to review questions with the letter 'A' after the question number are given in Appendix I (page 609).

14.1A Draw up a three-column cash book and record the transactions below in it. Balance it off at the end of the month, and show the relevant discount accounts as they would appear in the general ledger.

May	1	Started business with £6,000 in the bank.
"	1	Bought fixtures paying by cheque £950.
"	2	Bought goods paying by cheque £1,240.
"	3	Cash Sales £407.
"	4	Paid rent in cash £200.
"	5	N Morgan paid us his account of £220 by a cheque for £210; we allowed him £10 discount.
"	7	Paid S Thompson & Co £80 owing to them by means of a cheque £76; they allowed us £4 discount.
"	9	We received a cheque for £380 from S Cooper, discount having been allowed £20.
"	12	Paid rates by cheque £410.
"	14	L Curtis pays us a cheque for £115.
"	16	Paid M Monroe his account of £120 by cash £114, having deducted £6 cash discount.
"	20	P Exeter pays us a cheque for £78, having deducted £2 cash discount.
"	31	Cash Sales paid directly into the bank £88.

14.2A A three-column cash book is to be written up from the following details, it is to be balanced off and the relevant discount accounts in the general ledger shown.

Mar	1	Balances brought forward: Cash £230; Bank £4,756.
"	2	The following paid their accounts by cheque, in each case deducting 5% cash discounts; Accounts: R Burton £140; E Taylor £220; R Harris £300.
"	4	Paid rent by cheque £120.
"	6	J Cotton lent us £1,000 paying by cheque.
"	8	We paid the following accounts by cheque in each case deducting a 2½% cash discount; N Black £360; P Towers £480; C Rowse £800.
"	10	Paid motor expenses in cash £44.
"	12	H Hankins pays his account of £77 by cheque £74, deducting £3 cash discount.
"	15	Paid wages in cash £160.
"	18	The following paid their accounts by cheque, in each case deducting 5% cash discount: Accounts: C Winston £260; R Wilson & Son £340; H Winter £460.
"	21	Cash withdrawn from the bank £350 for business use.
"	24	Cash Drawings £120.
"	25	Paid T Briers his account of £140, by cash £133, having deducted £7 cash discount.
"	29	Bought fixtures paying by cheque £650.
"	31	Received commission by cheque £88.

14.3   Enter the following in a three-column cash book. Balance off the cash book at the end of the month and show the discount accounts in the general ledger.

June 1   Balances brought forward: Cash £97; Bank £2,186.
  „   2   The following paid us by cheque in each case deducting 5% cash discount; R Harris £1,000; C White £280; P Peers £180; O Hardy £600.
  „   3   Cash Sales paid directly into the bank £134.
  „   5   Paid rent by cash £88.
  „   6   We paid the following accounts by cheque, in each case deducting 2½% cash discount: J Charlton £400; H Sobers £640; D Shallcross £200.
  „   8   Withdrew cash from the bank for business use £250.
  „   10   Cash Sales £206.
  „   12   D Deeds paid us their account of £89 by cheque less £2 cash discount.
  „   14   Paid wages by cash £250.
  „   16   We paid the following accounts by cheque: L Lucas £117 less cash discount £6; D Fisher £206 less cash discount £8.
  „   20   Bought fixtures by cheque £8,000.
  „   24   Bought lorry paying by cheque £7,166.
  „   29   Received £169 cheque from D Steel.
  „   30   Cash Sales £116.
  „   30   Bought stationery paying by cash £60.

15

The sales journal and the sales ledger

15.1 Introduction

In Chapter 12 we saw that the ledger had been split up into a set of journals and ledgers. This chapter explains sales journals and sales ledgers in detail.

15.2 Cash sales

When goods sold are paid for immediately in cash there is no need to enter these sales in the sales journal. In such cases we do not need to know the names and addresses of customers and what has been sold to them as we don't have to keep a record of money owing to us.

15.3 Credit sales

In many businesses most of the sales will be made on credit rather than for cash. In fact, the sales of some businesses will consist entirely of credit sales.

For each credit sale the selling firm will send a document to the buyer showing full details of the goods sold and the prices of the goods. This document is known as an **invoice**, and to the seller it is known as a **sales invoice**. The seller will keep one or more copies of each sales invoice for his own use. Exhibit 15.1 is an example of an invoice.

Exhibit 15.1

		Per unit	Total
To: D Poole Charles Street Dublin	**INVOICE No. 16554** J Blake 7 The Elms Waterford 1 September 1998		
		£	£
21 cases McBrand Pears		20	420
5 cartons Kay's Flour		4	20
6 cases Joy's Vinegar		20	120
			560
Terms 1¼% cash discount if paid within one month			

You must not think that all invoices will look exactly like the one chosen as Exhibit 15.1. Each business will have its own design. All invoices will be numbered, and they will contain the names and addresses both of the supplier and of the customer. In this case the supplier is J Blake and the customer is D Poole.

15.4 Copies of sales invoices

As soon as the sales invoices for the goods being sent have been made out, they are sent to the customer. The selling firm will keep copies of all these sales invoices.

15.5 Entering credit sales into the sales journal

From the copy of the sales invoice the seller enters up his sales journal. This book is merely a list, showing the following:

- The date of the sale
- The name of customer to whom the goods were sold
- The number of the invoice relating to the sale
- The value of the invoice

There is no need to show details of the goods sold in the sales journal. These can be found by looking at copy invoices.

We can now look at Exhibit 15.2, an example of a sales journal, starting with the record of the sales invoice already shown in Exhibit 15.1. Let us assume that the entries are on page 26 of the journal.

Exhibit 15.2

Sales Journal		(page 26)
	Invoice No.	£
Sept 1 D Poole	16554	560
„ 8 T Cockburn	16555	1,640
„ 28 C Carter	16556	220
„ 30 D Stevens & Co	16557	1,100
		3,520

15.6 'Posting' credit sales to the sales ledger

Instead of having only one ledger for all accounts, we now have a sales ledger solely for credit sale transactions.

1 The credit sales are now posted, one by one, to the debit side of each customer's account in the sales ledger.
2 At the end of each period the total of the credit sales is posted to the credit of the sales account in the general ledger. This is illustrated in Exhibit 15.3.

Exhibit 15.3: Posting credit sales

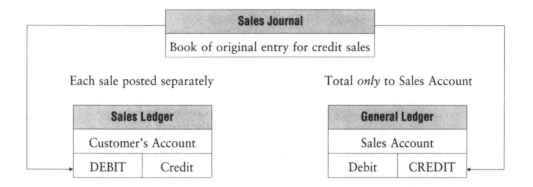

15.7 An example of posting credit sales

The sales journal in Exhibit 15.2 is now shown again. This time posting is made to the sales ledger and the general ledger. Notice the completion of the folio columns with the reference numbers.

Sales Journal			*(page 26)*
	Invoice No.	*Folio*	£
Sept 1 D Poole	16554	SL 12	560
„ 8 T Cockburn	16555	SL 39	1,640
„ 28 C Carter	16556	SL 125	220
„ 30 D Stevens & Co	16557	SL 249	1,100
Transferred to the Sales Account		GL 44	3,520

Sales Ledger

D Poole   *(page 12)*

		£	
Sept 1 Sales	SJ 26	560	

T Cockburn   *(page 39)*

		£	
Sept 8 Sales	SJ 26	1,640	

C Carter   *(page 125)*

		£	
Sept 28 Sales	SJ 26	220	

D Stevens & Co *(page 249)*

			£
Sept 30 Sales		SJ 26	1,100

General Ledger
Sales *(page 44)*

		£
	Sept 30 Credit Sales for	
	the month SJ 26	3,520

Alternative names for the sales journal are the **sales book** and the **sales day book**. Before you continue you should attempt Review Question 15.1.

15.8 Trade discounts

Suppose you are the proprietor of a business. You are selling to three different kinds of customer:

1 Traders who buy a lot of goods from you.
2 Traders who buy only a few items from you.
3 Direct to the general public.

The traders themselves have to sell the goods to the general public in their own areas. They have to make a profit, so they will want to pay you less than retail price.

The traders who buy in large quantities will not want to pay as much as the traders who buy in small quantities. You want to attract large customers, and so you are happy to sell to them at a lower price.

This means that your selling prices are at three levels: **1** to traders buying large quantities, **2** to traders buying small quantities, and **3** to the general public.

So that your staff do not need three different price lists, all goods are shown on your price lists at the same price. However, a reduction (discount), called a **trade discount**, is given to both types of trader. An example of this is given below.

Example

You are selling a make of food mixing machine. The retail price is £200. Traders **1** are given 25% trade discount, traders **2**, 20% and the general public pay the full retail price. The prices paid by each type of customer would be:

		Trader 1		Trader 2	General Public 3
		£		£	£
Retail price		200		200	200
Less Trade discount	(25%)	50	(20%)	40	nil
Price to be paid by the customer		150		160	200

Exhibit 15.4 is an invoice for goods sold to D Poole. It is for the same items as were shown in Exhibit 15.1, but this time the seller is R Grant and he uses trade discounts to arrive at the price paid by his customers.

Exhibit 15.4

		R Grant
		Dublin Road
		Sligo
To: D Poole	INVOICE No. 30756	2 September 1998
Charles Street		Tel (071) 123456
Dublin		Fax (071) 456789

	Per unit	Total
	£	£
21 cases McBrand Pears	25	525
5 cartons Kay's Flour	5	25
6 cases Joy's Vinegar	25	150
		700
Less 20% Trade discount		140
		560

By comparing Exhibits 15.1 and 15.3 you can see that the final price paid by D Poole is the same in both cases. It is simply the method of calculating the price that is different.

15.9 No double entry for trade discounts

As trade discount is simply a way of calculating sales prices, no entry for trade discount should be made in the double entry records or in the sales journal. The recording of Exhibit 15.4 in R Grant's Sales Journal and D Poole's personal account will appear:

Sales Journal			*(page 87)*
	Invoice No.	*Folio*	
			£
Sept 2 D Poole	30756	SL 32	560

Sales Ledger
D Poole   *(page 32)*

		£	
Sept 2 Sales	SJ 87	560	

To compare trade discounts with cash discounts:
Trade discounts: are not shown in double entry accounts.
Cash discounts: are shown in double entry accounts.

15.10 Manufacturer's recommended retail price

Looking at an item displayed in a shop window, you will frequently see something like the following:

Nicam Stereo TV:	Manufacturer's Recommended Retail Price	£500
	less discount of 20%	£100
	You pay	£400

Very often the manufacturer's recommended retail price is a figure above what the manufacturer would expect the public to pay for its product. Probably, in the case shown the manufacturer would have expected the public to pay around £400 for its product.

The inflated figure used for the 'manufacturer's recommended retail price' is often only a sales gimmick. Most people like to feel they are getting a bargain. Sales staff know that someone usually would prefer to get '20% discount' and pay £400, rather than the price simply be shown as £400 with no mention of a discount.

15.11 Credit control

Any organisation which sells goods on credit should keep a close check to ensure that debtors pay their accounts on time. If this is not done properly, the amount of debtors can grow to an amount that will cripple the business. The following procedures should be carried out:

1 For each debtor a limit should be set and the debtor should not be allowed to owe more than this limit. The amount of the limit will depend on the circumstances. Such things as the size of the customer's firm and the amount of business done with it, as well as its past record of payments, will help in choosing the limit figure.
2 As soon as the payment date has been reached check to see whether payment has been made or not. Failure to pay on time may mean you refusing to supply any more goods unless payment is made quickly.
3 Where payment is not forthcoming, after investigation, it may be necessary to take legal action to sue the customer for the debt. This will depend on the circumstances.
4 It is important that the customer is aware of what will happen if he does not pay his account by the due date.

Review questions

In addition to the questions which follow, you should attempt questions 76–78 in the accompanying book of multiple-choice questions (see back cover for further details).

Suggested solutions to review questions with the letter 'A' after the question number are given in Appendix I (pages 609–10).

15.1A Prepare the sales journal from the following details. Post the items to the relevant accounts in the sales ledger and then show the transfer to the sales account in the general ledger.

Mar	1	Credit sales to J Gordon	£187
,,	3	Credit sales to G Abrahams	£166
,,	6	Credit sales to V White	£12
,,	10	Credit sales to J Gordon	£55
,,	17	Credit sales to F Williams	£289
,,	19	Credit sales to U Richards	£66
,,	27	Credit sales to V Wood	£28
,,	31	Credit sales to L Simes	£78

15.2   Draw up the sales journal from the following, post the items to the relevant accounts in the sales ledger and show the transfer to the sales account in the general ledger.

Mar	1	Credit sales to J Johnson	£305
„	3	Credit sales to T Royes	£164
„	5	Credit sales to B Howe	£45
„	7	Credit sales to M Lee	£100
„	16	Credit sales to J Jakes	£308
„	23	Credit sales to A Vinden	£212
„	30	Credit sales to J Samuels	£1,296

15.3A   F Benjamin of 10 Lower Street, Castlebar, is selling the following items, the recommended retail prices as shown: white tape at £10 per roll, green baize at £4 per metre, blue cotton at £6 per sheet, black silk at £20 per dress length. He makes the following sales:

May 1 To F Gray, Newport Road, Westport: 3 rolls white tape, 5 sheets blue cotton, 1 dress length black silk. Less 25% trade discount.

„ 4 To A Gray, Killala Road, Ballina: 6 rolls white tape, 30 metres green baize. Less 33⅓% trade discount.

„ 8 To E Hines, High Road, Balla: 1 dress length black silk. No trade discount.

„ 20 To M Allen, Knock Road, Swinford: 10 rolls white tape, 6 sheets blue cotton, 3 dress lengths black silk, 11 metres green baize. Less 25% trade discount.

„ 31 To B Cooper, Top Lane, Castlebar: 12 rolls white tape, 14 sheets blue cotton, 9 metres green baize. Less 33⅓% trade discount.

Required:
(a) Draw up a sales invoice for each of the above sales;
(b) enter the sales in the sales journal and post them to the personal accounts; and
(c) transfer the total to the sales account in the general ledger.

15.4   J Fisher, White House, Cork, is selling the following items, the retail prices as shown: plastic tubing at £1 per metre, polythene sheeting at £2 per length, vinyl padding at £5 per box, foam rubber at £3 per sheet. He makes the following sales:

June 1 To A Cotter, Kilkenny Road, Waterford: 22 metres plastic tubing, 6 sheets foam rubber, 4 boxes vinyl padding. Less 25% trade discount.

„ 5 To B Butler, Model Farm Road, Cork: 50 lengths polythene sheeting, 8 boxes vinyl padding, 20 sheets foam rubber. Less 20% trade discount.

„ 11 To A Gate, Ballincollig, Cork: 4 metres plastic tubing, 33 lengths of polythene sheeting, 30 sheets foam rubber. Less 25% trade discount.

„ 21 To L Mackeson, Main Road, Cobh: 29 metres plastic tubing. No trade discount is given.

„ 30 To M Alison, Lakes Road, Killarney: 32 metres plastic tubing, 24 lengths polythene sheeting, 20 boxes vinyl padding. Less 33⅓% trade discount.

Required:
(a) Draw up a sales invoice for each of the above sales;
(b) enter each sale in the sales journal and post to the personal accounts; and
(c) transfer the total to the sales account in the general ledger.

16

The purchases journal and the purchases ledger

16.1 Purchase invoices

An invoice is a **purchase invoice** when it is entered in the books of the firm purchasing the goods. The same invoice, in the books of the seller, would be a sales invoice. For example: Exhibit 15.1, an invoice,

1 In the books of D Poole: it is a purchase invoice.
2 In the books of J Blake: it is a sales invoice.

16.2 Entering purchase invoices into the purchases journal

From the purchase invoices, for goods bought on credit, the purchaser enters the details in his purchases journal. This book is merely a list, showing the following:

- the date of the purchase
- the name of the supplier from whom goods were purchased
- the reference number of the invoice
- the final amount of the invoice

There is no need to show details of the goods bought in the purchases journal. This can be found by looking at the invoices themselves. Exhibit 16.1 is an example of a purchases journal.

Exhibit 16.1

Purchases Journal			(page 49)
	Invoice No.	*Folio*	£
Sept 2 R Simpson	9/101		670
„ 8 B Hamilton	9/102		1,380
„ 19 C Brown	9/103		120
„ 30 K Gabriel	9/104		510
			2,680

16.3 Posting credit purchases to the purchases ledger

We now have a separate purchases ledger. The double entry for purchases made on credit is as follows:

1 The credit purchases are posted one by one, to the credit of each supplier's account in the purchases ledger.

2   At the end of each period the total of the credit purchases is posted to the debit of the purchases account in the general ledger. This is now illustrated in Exhibit 16.2.

Exhibit 16.2: *Posting Credit Purchases*

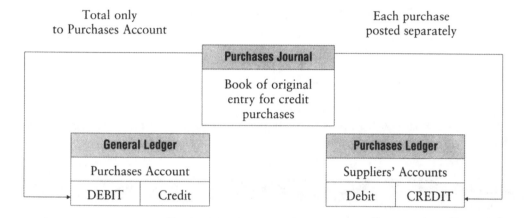

Total only
to Purchases Account

Each purchase
posted separately

Purchases Journal

Book of original
entry for credit
purchases

General Ledger		**Purchases Ledger**	
Purchases Account		Suppliers' Accounts	
DEBIT	Credit	Debit	CREDIT

16.4 An example of posting credit purchases

The purchases journal in Exhibit 16.1 is now shown again. This time posting is made to the purchases ledger and the general ledger. Notice the completion of the folio columns.

Purchases Journal			*(page 49)*
	Invoice No.	Folio	
			£
Sept 2 R Simpson	9/101	PL 16	670
„ 8 B Hamilton	9/102	PL 29	1,380
„ 19 C Brown	9/103	PL 55	120
„ 30 K Gabriel	9/104	PL 89	510
Transferred to purchases account		GL 63	2,680

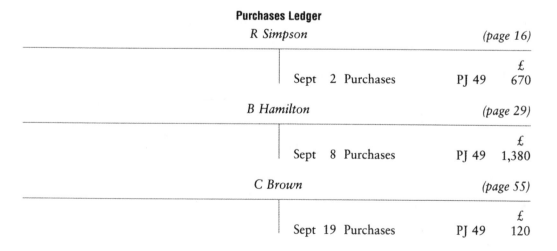

Purchases Ledger

R Simpson   *(page 16)*

			£
	Sept 2 Purchases	PJ 49	670

B Hamilton   *(page 29)*

			£
	Sept 8 Purchases	PJ 49	1,380

C Brown   *(page 55)*

			£
	Sept 19 Purchases	PJ 49	120

K Gabriel *(page 89)*

			£
	Sept 30 Purchases	PJ 49	510

General Ledger

Purchases *(page 63)*

	£	
Sept 30 Credit purchases for the month	PJ 49	2,680

The purchases journal is often known also as the **purchases book** or as the **purchases day book**.

Review questions

In addition to the questions which follow, you should attempt questions 79–81 in the accompanying book of multiple-choice questions (see back cover for further details).

Suggested solutions to review questions with the letter 'A' after the question number are given in Appendix I (page 610).

16.1A B Mann has the following purchases for the month of May.

May 1 From K King: 4 radios at £30 each, 3 music centres at £160 each. Less 25% trade discount.

„ 3 From A Bell: 2 washing machines at £200 each, 5 vacuum cleaners at £60 each, 2 dishwashers at £150 each. Less 20% trade discount.

„ 15 From J Kelly: 1 music centre at £300, 2 washing machines at £250 each. Less 25% trade discount.

„ 20 From B Powell: 6 radios at £70 each. Less 33⅓% trade discount.

„ 30 From B Lewis: 4 dishwashers at £200 each. Less 20% trade discount.

Required:
(a) Enter the above in the purchases journal for the month.
(b) Post the transactions to the suppliers' accounts.
(c) Transfer the total to the purchases account.

16.2 A Rowland has the following purchases for the month of June.

June 2 From C Lee: 2 sets of golf clubs at £250 each. 5 footballs at £20 each. Less 25% trade discount.

„ 11 From M Elliott: 6 cricket bats at £20 each, 6 ice skates at £30 each, 4 rugby balls at £25 each. Less 25% trade discount.

„ 18 From B Wood: 6 golf trophies at £100 each, 4 sets of golf clubs at £300 each. Less 33⅓% trade discount.

„ 25 From B Parkinson: 5 cricket bats at £40 each. Less 25% trade discount.

„ 30 From N Francis: 8 goal posts at £70 each. Less 25% trade discount.

Required:
(a) Enter the above in the purchases journal for the month.
(b) Post the items to the suppliers' accounts.
(c) Transfer the total to the purchases account.

16.3A C Phillips, a sole trader, has the following purchases and sales for the month of March.

Mar 1 Bought from Smith Stores: silk £40, cotton £80. Both less 25% trade discount.
„ 8 Sold to Grantley: linen goods £28, woollen items £44. No trade discount.
„ 15 Sold to A Henry: silk £36, linen £144, cotton goods £120. All less 20% trade discount.
„ 23 Bought from C Kelly: cotton £88, linen £52. Both less 25% trade discount.
„ 24 Sold to D Sangster: linen goods £42, cotton £48. Both less 10% trade discount.
„ 31 Bought from J Hamilton: Linen goods £270. Less 33⅓% trade discount.

Required:
(a) Prepare the purchases and sales journals of C Phillips from the above.
(b) Post the items to the personal accounts.
(c) Post the totals of the journals to the sales and purchases accounts.

16.4 A Henry has the following purchases and sales for the month of May.

May 1 Sold to M Marshall: brass goods £24, bronze items £36. Less 25% trade discount.
„ 7 Sold to R Richards: tin goods £70, lead items £230. Less 33⅓% trade discount.
„ 9 Bought from C Clarke: tin goods £400. Less 40% trade discount.
„ 16 Bought from A Charles: copper goods £320. Less 50% trade discount.
„ 23 Sold to T Young: tin goods £50, brass items £70, lead figures £80. All less 20% trade discount.
„ 31 Bought from M Nelson: brass figures £100. Less 50% trade discount.

Required:
(a) Write up the sales and purchases journals.
(b) Post the transactions to the personal accounts.
(c) Post the totals of the journals to the sales and purchases accounts.

17

The returns journals

Sometimes customers will return goods to us and we will give them an allowance. This might be for reasons such as the following:

- The goods delivered were of the wrong type
- They were the wrong colour
- They were faulty
- The customer bought more than he needed

Customers might return the goods or agree to keep the goods if an allowance is made to reduce the price of the goods.

In each of these cases a document known as a **credit note** will be sent to the customer, showing the amount of the allowance given by us for the returns or the faulty goods. It is called a credit note because the customer's account will be credited with the amount of the allowance, to show the reduction in the amount he owes. Exhibit 17.1 shows an example of a credit note.

Exhibit 17.1

		R Grant Dublin Road Sligo 8 September 1998
To: D Poole Charles Street Dublin		
CREDIT NOTE No. 9/37		
	Per Unit	Total
2 cases McBrand Pears *Less* 20% Trade Discount	£ 25	£ 50 10 40

To stop them being mistaken for invoices, credit notes are often printed in red.

17.2 Returns inwards journal

The credit notes are listed in a returns inwards journal. This is then used for posting the items, as follows:

1 Sales ledger. Credit the amount of credit notes, one by one, to the accounts of the customers in the sales ledger.
2 General ledger. At the end of the period the total of the returns inwards journal is posted to the debit of the returns inwards account.

17.3 Example of a returns inwards journal

An example of a returns inwards journal showing the items posted to the sales ledger and the general ledger is shown below:

Returns Inwards Journal			(page 10)
	Credit Note No.	Folio	£
Sept 2 D Poole	9/37	SL 12	40
,, 17 A Brewster	9/38	SL 58	120
,, 19 C Vickers	9/39	SL 99	290
,, 29 M Nelson	9/40	SL 112	160
Transferred to returns inwards account		GL 114	610

Sales Ledger

D Poole (page 12)

				£
	Sept 2 Returns inwards	RI 10		40

A Brewster (page 58)

				£
	Sept 17 Returns inwards	RI 10		120

C Vickers (page 99)

				£
	Sept 19 Returns inwards	RI 10		290

M Nelson (page 112)

				£
	Sept 29 Returns inwards	RI 10		160

General Ledger

Returns Inwards   *(page 114)*

		£	
Sept 30	Returns for the month	RI 10	610

Alternative names in use for the returns inwards journal are the **returns inwards book** or the **sales returns book**.

17.4 Returns outwards and debit notes

If the supplier agrees, goods bought previously may be returned. When this happens a **debit note** is sent to the supplier giving details of the goods and the reason for their return.

Also, an allowance might be given by the supplier for any faults in the goods. Here also, a debit note should be sent to the supplier. Exhibit 17.2 shows an example of a debit note.

Exhibit 17.2: Example of a debit note

To: B Hamilton Athlone Road Longford		R Grant Dublin Road Sligo 11 September 1998
DEBIT NOTE No. 9/34		
	Per Unit	Total
4 cases Lot's salt *Less* 25% Trade Discount	£ 60	£ 240 60 180

17.5 Returns outwards journals

The debit notes are listed in a returns outwards journal. This is then used for posting the items, as follows:

1 Purchases ledger. Debit the amounts of debit notes, one by one, to the accounts of the suppliers in the purchases ledger.
2 General ledger. At the end of the period, the total of the returns outwards journal is posted to the credit of the returns outwards account.

17.6 Example of a returns outwards journal

An example of a returns outwards journal, showing the items posted to the purchases ledger and the general ledger, is shown below:

Returns Outwards Journal			*(page 7)*
	Debit Note No.	*Folio*	£
Sept 11 B Hamilton	9/34	PL 29	180
” 16 B Rose	9/35	PL 46	100
” 28 C Blake	9/36	PL 55	30
” 30 S Saunders	9/37	PL 87	360
Transferred to returns outwards account		GL 116	670

Purchases Ledger

B Hamilton   *(page 29)*

		£	
Sept 11 Returns outwards	RO 7	180	

B Rose   *(page 46)*

		£	
Sept 16 Returns outwards	RO 7	100	

C Blake   *(page 55)*

		£	
Sept 28 Returns outwards	RO 7	30	

S Saunders   *(page 87)*

		£	
Sept 30 Returns outwards	RO 7	360	

General Ledger

Returns outwards   *(page 116)*

			£
	Sept 30 Returns for the month	RO 7	670

Other names in use for the returns outwards journal are the **returns outwards book** or the **purchases returns book**.

17.7 Double entry and returns

Exhibit 17.3 shows the double entries which are made for both returns inwards and returns outwards.

Exhibit 17.3: Posting returns inwards and returns outwards

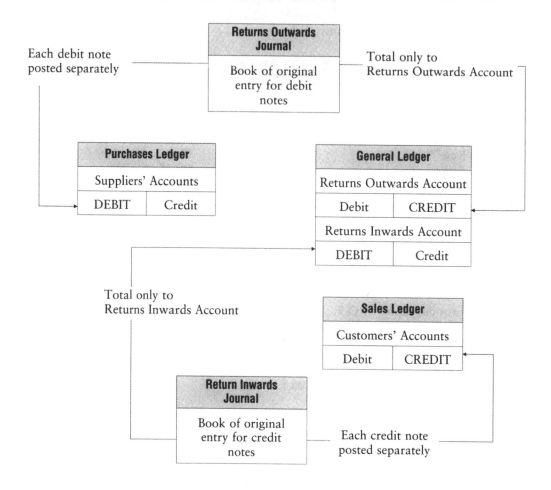

17.8 Statements

At the end of each month a **statement** (or statement of account) should be sent to each debtor who owes money on the last day of each month. It is really a copy of his account in our books. It should show:

1 the amount owing at the start of the month;
2 the amount of each sales invoice sent to him during the month;
3 the amounts of any credit notes sent to him during the month;
4 all cash and cheques received from him during the month;
5 the amount due from him at the end of the month; and
6 the date by which payment of the amount owed is due.

The debtor will use this to see if the account in his accounting records agrees with his account in our records. If in our books he is shown as owing £798, then, depending on items in transit between us, his books should show us as a creditor for £798. The statement also acts as a reminder to the debtor that he owes us money.

An example of a statement follows:

STATEMENT OF ACCOUNT

R GRANT
Dublin Road
Sligo
Tel (071) 123 456
Fax (071) 456 789

D Poole
Charles Street
Dublin

Statement Date: 30 September 1998

Date	Details	Debit	Credit	Balance
		£	£	£
Sept 1	Balance brought forward			880
Sept 2	Invoice 30756	560		1,440
Sept 8	Credit note 9/37		40	1,400
Sept 25	Payment received		880	520
Sept 30	Amount due			520

All accounts are due and payable within 1 month of the invoice date

17.9 Sales and purchases via credit cards

Various banks, building societies and other financial organisations issue credit cards to their customers. Examples are Visa, Access, and American Express. The holder of the credit card purchases items or services without giving cash or cheques, but simply signs a special voucher used by the store or selling organisation. Later on, usually several weeks later, the credit card holder pays the organisation for which he holds the card, e.g. Visa, for all of his previous month's outgoings.

The sellers of the goods or services present the vouchers to the credit card company and the total of the vouchers less commission is paid to them by that credit card company.

In effect the sales are 'cash sales' for as far as the purchaser is concerned he has seen goods (or obtained services) and has received them, and in his eyes he has paid for them by using his credit card. Such sales are very rarely sales to anyone other than the general public, as compared with professionals in a specific trade.

Once the customer has departed with his goods, or had the necessary services, he does not become a debtor needing an entry for him in a sales ledger. All the selling company is then interested in, from a recording point of view, is collecting the money from the credit card company.

The double entry needed is:

Sale of items via credit cards:	Dr: Credit card company
	Cr: Cash sales
Receipt of money from credit card company:	Dr: Bank
	Cr: Credit card company
Commission charged by credit card company:	Dr: Selling expenses
	Cr: Credit card company

17.10 Internal control

When sales invoices are being made out they should be scrutinised very carefully. A system is usually set up so that each stage of the preparation of the invoice is checked by someone other than the person whose job it is to send out the invoice. If this was not done then it would be possible for someone inside a firm to send out an invoice, for example, at a price less than the true price. Any difference could then be split between that person and the outside firm. If an invoice should have been sent to Ivor Twister & Co for £2,000, but the invoice clerk made it out deliberately for £200, then, if there was no cross-check, the difference of £1,800 could be split between the invoice clerk and Ivor Twister & Co.

Similarly, outside firms could send invoices for goods which were never received by the firm. This might be in collaboration with an employee within the firm, but there are firms sending false invoices which rely on the firms receiving them being inefficient and paying for items never received. There have been firms sending invoices for such items as advertisements which have never been published. The cashier of the firm receiving the invoice, if the firm is an inefficient one, might possibly think that someone in the firm had authorised the advertisements and would pay the bill.

Besides these there are, of course, genuine errors, and these should also be detected. A system is, therefore, set up whereby the invoices have to be subject to scrutiny, at each stage, by someone other than the person who sends out the invoices or is responsible for paying them. Incoming invoices will be stamped with a rubber stamp, with spaces for each stage of the check.

The spaces in the stamp will be filled in by the people responsible for making the checks. For instance:

- The person certifying that the goods were actually received.
- The person certifying that the goods were ordered.
- The person certifying that the prices and calculations on the invoice are correct, and in accordance with the order originally placed and agreed.
- The person certifying that the goods are in good condition and suitable for the purpose for which ordered.

Naturally in a small firm, simply because the office staff might be quite small, this cross-check may be in the hands of only one person other than the person who will pay the invoice. A similar sort of check will be made in respect of sales invoices being sent out.

17.11 Factoring

One of the problems that face many businesses is the time taken by debtors to pay their accounts. Few businesses have so much cash available to them that they do not mind how long the debtor takes to pay. It is a fact that a lot of businesses which become bankrupt, do so, not because the business is not making profits, but because the business has run out of cash. Once that happens, the confidence factor in business evaporates, and the business then finds that very few people will supply it with goods, and it also cannot pay its employees. Closure of the firm then happens fairly quickly in many cases.

In the case of debtors, the cash problem may be alleviated by using the services of a financial intermediary called a **factor**.

Factoring is a financial service designed to improve the cash flow of healthy, growing companies, enabling them to make better use of management time and the money tied up in trade credit to customers.

In essence, factors provide their clients with three closely integrated services covering sales accounting and collection, credit management, which can include protection against bad debts, and the availability of finance against sales invoices.

Review questions

In addition to the questions which follow, you should attempt questions 82–86 in the accompanying book of multiple-choice questions (see back cover for further details).

Suggested solutions to review questions with the letter 'A' after the question number are given in Appendix I (page 611).

17.1A Draw up the purchases journal and the returns outwards journal from the following details, post the items to the relevant accounts in the purchases ledger and show the transfers to the general ledger at the end of the month.

May	1	Credit purchase from H Lloyd £119.
„	4	Credit purchases from the following: D Scott £98; A Simpson £114; A Williams £25; S Wood £56.
„	7	Goods returned by us to the following: H Lloyd £16; D Scott £14.
„	10	Credit purchase from A Simpson £59.
„	18	Credit purchases from the following: M White £89; J Wong £67; H Miller £196; H Lewis £119.
„	25	Goods returned by us to the following: J Wong £5; A Simpson £11.
„	31	Credit purchases from: A Williams £56; C Cooper £98.

17.2 Draw up the sales journal and the returns inwards journal from the following details. Then post the transactions to the customers' accounts and show the transfers to the general ledger.

June	1	Credit sales to: A Simes £188; P Tulloch £60; J Flynn £77; B Lopez £88.
„	6	Credit sales to: M Howells £114; S Thompson £118; J Flynn £66.
„	10	Goods returned to us by: A Simes £12; B Lopez £17.
„	20	Credit sales to M Barrow £970.
„	24	Goods returned to us by S Thompson £5.
„	30	Credit sales to M Parkin £91.

17.3A Draw up the sales, purchases, returns inwards and returns outwards journals from the following details and post the items to the relevant accounts in the sales and purchase ledgers. The total of the journals are then to be transferred to the accounts in the general ledger.

May	1	Credit sales: T Thompson £56; L Rogers £148; K Barton £145.
„	3	Credit purchases: P Potter £144; H Harris £25; B Spencer £76.
„	7	Credit sales: K Kelly £89; N Mendes £78; N Lee £257.
„	9	Credit purchases: B Perkins £24; H Harris £58; H Miles £123.
„	11	Goods returned by us to: P Potter £12; B Spencer £22.
„	14	Goods returned to us by: T Thompson £5; K Barton £11; K Kelly £14.
„	17	Credit purchases: H Harris £54; B Perkins £65: L Nixon £75.
„	20	Goods returned by us to B Spencer £14.
„	24	Credit sales: K Molloy £57; K Kelly £65; O Green £112.
„	28	Goods returned to us by N Mendes £24.
„	31	Credit sales: N Lee £55.

17.4 Enter the following items in the relevant journals, post to the personal accounts, and show the transfers to the general ledger.

July 1 Credit purchases from: K Hill £380; M Norman £500; N Senior £106.

„ 3 Credit sales to: E Rigby £510; E Phillips £246; F Thompson £356.

„ 5 Credit purchases from: R Morton £200; J Cook £180; D Edwards £410; C Davies £66.

„ 8 Credit sales to: A Green £307; H George £250; J Ferguson £185.

„ 12 Returns outwards to: M Norman £30; N Senior £16.

„ 14 Returns inwards from: E Phillips £18; F Thompson £22.

„ 20 Credit sales to: E Phillips £188; F Powell £310; E Lee £420.

„ 24 Credit purchases from: C Ferguson £550; K Walsh £900.

„ 31 Returns inwards from: E Phillips £27, E Rigby £30.

„ 31 Returns outwards to: J Cook £13; C Davies £11.

18

The journal

We have seen in earlier chapters that most transactions are entered in one of the following books of original entry:

- Cash book
- Sales journal
- Purchases journal
- Returns inwards journal
- Returns outwards journal

These books have grouped together similar things, e.g. all credit sales are in the sales journal. To trace any transaction would be relatively easy, as we know which book it will be in.

18.2 The journal: the other book of original entry

The other items which do not pass through the above books are much less common, and sometimes much more complicated. It would be easy for a bookkeeper to forget the details of these transactions.

If the bookkeeper left the firm it could be impossible to understand such bookkeeping entries.

What is needed is a form of diary to record such transactions, before the entries are made in the double entry accounts. This book is called **the journal**. It will contain, for each transaction:

- The date of the transaction.
- The name of the account(s) to be debited and the amount(s).
- The name of the account(s) to be credited and the amount(s).
- A description of the transaction (this is called a 'narrative').
- A reference number should be given for the documents giving proof of the transaction.

The use of the journal makes fraud by bookkeepers more difficult. It also reduces the risk of entering the item once only instead of having double entry. Despite these advantages there are many firms which do not have such a book.

18.3 Typical uses of the journal

Some of the main uses of the journal are listed below. It must not be thought that this list is a fully detailed one.

- The purchase and sale of fixed assets on credit.
- The correction of errors.

● Writing off 'bad' debts.*
● Opening entries. These are the entries needed to open a new set of books.

* A 'bad' debt is an amount receivable from a debtor which, in the opinion of the management of the business to which it is owed, will not be received. It is 'written off', i.e. the total of debtors as shown in the ledger is reduced so that the ledger reflects only amounts that are likely to be received.

The layout of the journal is as follows:

The Journal

Date		Folio	Dr	Cr
			£	£
The name of the account to be debited.			x	
	The name of the account to be credited.			x
The narrative.				

You can see that we put on the first line the account to be debited. The second line gives the account to be credited. We do not write the name of the account to be credited directly under the name of the account to be debited. This makes it easier to see which is the debit and which is the credit.

It should be remembered that the journal is not a double entry account. It is a form of diary, and entering an item in the journal is not the same as recording an item in an account. Once the journal entry is made, the entry in the double entry accounts can then be made. Examples of the uses of the journal are now given.

The purchase and sale of fixed assets on credit

1 A milling machine is bought on credit from Toolmakers for £550 on 1 July.

		Dr	Cr
		£	£
July 1	Machinery	550	
	Toolmakers		550
	Purchase of milling machine on credit, Capital		
	Purchases invoice No 7/159		

2 Sale of a vehicle for £3,000 on credit to K Lamb on 2 July.

		Dr	Cr
		£	£
July 2	K Lamb	3,000	
	Vehicles disposal		3,000
	Sale of vehicle per Capital		
	Sales invoice No 7/43		

The correction of errors

This is explained in detail in Chapters 31 and 32.

Writing off bad debts

A debt of £78 owing to us from H Mander is written off as a bad debt on 31 August.

		Dr	Cr
		£	£
Aug 31	Bad debts	78	
	H Mander		78
	Debt written off as bad. See letter in file 7/8906		

Posting opening entries

J Brew, after being in business for some years without keeping proper records, now decides to keep a double entry set of books. On 1 July he establishes that his assets and liabilities are as follows:

Assets: Used van £840, Fixtures £700, Stock £390,
              Debtors – B Young £95, D Blake £45, Bank £80, Cash £20.
Liabilities: Creditors – M Quinn £129, C Walters £41.

The Assets therefore total £840 + £700 + £390 + £95 + £45 + £80 + £20 = £2,170; and the Liabilities total £129 + £41 = £170.

The Capital consists of Assets – Liabilities, £2,170 – £170 = £2,000.

We must start the writing up of the books on 1 July. To do this we:

1 Open asset accounts, one for each asset. Each opening asset is shown as a debit balance.
2 Open liability accounts, one for each liability. Each opening liability is shown as a credit balance.
3 Open an account for the capital. Show it as a credit balance.

The journal, as shown in Exhibit 18.1, records what you are doing, and why.

Exhibit 18.1

		The Journal	Folio	Dr	(page 5) Cr
				£	£
July 1	Van		GL 1	840	
	Fixtures		GL 2	700	
	Stock		GL 3	390	
	Debtors	– B Young	SL 1	95	
		– D Blake	SL 2	45	
	Bank		CB 1	80	
	Cash		CB 1	20	
	Creditors	– M Quinn	PL 1		129
		– C Walters	PL 2		41
	Capital		GL 4		2,000
				2,170	2,170

Assets and liabilities at this date entered to open the books.

The opening entries in the double entry accounts

General Ledger

Van   *(page 1)*

			£	
July	1	Balance	J 5	840

Fixtures   *(page 2)*

			£	
July	1	Balance	J 5	700

Stock   *(page 3)*

			£	
July	1	Balance	J 5	390

Capital   *(page 4)*

				£
July	1	Balance	J 5	2,000

Sales Ledger

B Young   *(page 1)*

			£	
July	1	Balance	J 5	95

D Blake   *(page 2)*

			£	
July	1	Balance	J 5	45

Purchases Ledger

M Quinn   *(page 1)*

				£
July	1	Balance	J 5	129

C Walters   *(page 2)*

				£
July	1	Balance	J 5	41

Cash Book

				Cash	*Bank*	*(page 1)*
				£	£	
July	1	Balances	J 5	20	80	

Once these opening balances have been recorded in the books the day-to-day transactions can be entered in the normal manner. The need for opening entries will not occur very

often. They will not be needed each year as the balances from last year will have been brought forward.

Other items entered in the journal

These can be of many kinds and it is impossible to write out a complete list. Several examples are now shown:

1 K Young, a debtor, owed £2,000 on 1 July. He was unable to pay his account in cash, but offers a used car in full settlement of the debt. The offer is accepted on 5 July.

 The debt shown in the personal account is, therefore, not now owed and the account needs to be credited. On the other hand the firm now has an extra asset, a car, therefore the car account needs to be debited.

The Journal		Dr	Cr
		£	£
July 5	Car	2,000	
	K Young		2,000
	Accepted car in full settlement of debt		
	per letter dated 5 July		

2 T Jones is a creditor. On 10 July his business is taken over by A Lee to whom the debt is now to be paid.

 Here it is just one creditor being substituted for another one. The action needed is to cancel the amount owing to T Jones by debiting his account, and to show it owing to Lee by opening an account for Lee and crediting it.

The Journal		Dr	Cr
		£	£
July 10	T Jones	150	
	A Lee		150
	Transfer of indebtedness as per		
	letter ref G/1335		

3 We had previously bought an office typewriter for £310. It is faulty. On 12 July we return it to the supplier, RS Ltd. An allowance of £310 is agreed, so that we will not have to pay for it.

The Journal		Dr	Cr
		£	£
July 12	RS Ltd	310	
	Office equipment		310
	Faulty typewriter returned to supplier		
	Full allowance given. See letter dated 10 July		

18.4 The basic structure of bookkeeping and accounting

Now that we have covered all aspects of bookkeeping entries, we can see the whole structure in the form of a diagram.

Where original information is to be found	• Sales and purchases invoices • Debit and credit notes for returns • Bank lodgement slips and cheque counterfoils • Receipts for cash paid and received • Correspondence containing other financial information

What happens to it	Classified and then entered in books of prime entry: • Sales and purchases journals • Returns inwards and outwards journals • Cash books* • The journal

Double entry accounts

How the dual aspect of each transaction is recorded	

General ledger	Sales ledger	Purchases ledger	Cash books*
Real and nominal accounts	Debtors' accounts	Creditors' accounts	Cash book and petty cash book

(*Note: Cash books fulfil both the roles of books of prime entry and double entry accounts. The petty cash book is covered in Chapter 19)

Check of arithmetical accuracy of double entry accounts	Trial Balance

Calculation of profit or loss for the accounting period	Trading and Profit and Loss Account

Financial statement showing assets, liabilities and capital at the end of the accounting period	Balance Sheet

Review questions

In addition to the questions which follow, you should attempt questions 87 and 88 in the accompanying book of multiple-choice questions (see back cover for further details).

Suggested solutions to review questions with the letter 'A' after the question number are given in Appendix I (pages 612–13).

18.1A Open the books of K Mullings, a trader, using the journal to record the assets and liabilities. Record the daily transactions for the month of May, and prepare a trial balance as at 31 May.

May	1	*Assets:* Premises £2,000; Used Van £450; Fixtures £600; Stock £1,289. Debtors: N Hardy £40; M Nelson £180. Cash at bank £1,254; Cash in hand £45. *Liabilities:* Creditors: B Blake £60; V Reagan £200.
May	1	Paid rent by cheque £15.
„	2	Goods bought on credit from: B Blake £20; C Harris £56; H Gordon £38; N Lee £69.
„	3	Goods sold on credit to: K O'Connor £56; M Benjamin £78; L Staines £98; N Duffy £48; B Green £118; M Nelson £40.
„	4	Paid for motor expenses in cash £13.
„	7	Cash drawings by the proprietor £20.
„	9	Goods sold on credit to: M Benjamin £22; L Pearson £67.
„	11	Goods returned to Mullings by: K O'Connor £16; L Staines £18.
„	14	Bought another used van on credit from Better Motors Ltd for £300.
„	16	The following paid Mullings their accounts by cheque less 5% cash discount: N Hardy; M Nelson; K O'Connor; L Staines.
„	19	Goods returned by Mullings to N Lee £9.
„	22	Goods bought on credit from: J Johnson £89; T Best £72.
„	24	The following accounts were settled by Mullings by cheque less 5% cash discount: B Blake; V Reagan; N Lee.
„	27	Wages paid by cheque £56.
„	30	Paid rates by cheque £66.
„	31	Paid Better Motors Ltd a cheque for £300.

18.2A   Show the journal entries necessary to record the following transactions:

(a)	May	1	Bought a vehicle on credit from Kingston's Garage for £6,790.
(b)	„	3	A debt of £34 owing from H Newman was written off as a bad debt.
(c)	„	8	Office furniture bought by us for £490 was returned to the supplier Unique Offices, as it was unsuitable. Full allowance will be given to us.
(d)	„	12	We are owed £150 by W Charles. He is declared bankrupt and we received £39 in full settlement of the debt.
(e)	„	14	The proprietor takes £45 worth of goods out of the business stock without paying for them.
(f)	„	28	Some time ago we paid an insurance bill thinking that it was all in respect of the business. We now discover that £76 of the amount paid was in fact insurance of the proprietor's private house.
(g)	„	28	Bought machinery for £980 on credit from Systems Accelerated.

18.3 Show the journal entries necessary to record the following:

Apr 1   Bought fixtures on credit from J Harper £1,809.
  „   4   The proprietor takes £500 worth of the business stock without paying for it.
  „   9   £28 of the goods taken on 4 April are returned back into stock. No money is taken for the return of the goods.
  „ 12   K Lamb owes us £500. He is unable to pay his debt. We agree to take some office equipment worth £500 from him and cancel the debt.
  „ 18   £65 worth of the fixtures bought from J Harper are found to be unsuitable and are returned to him for full allowance.
  „ 24   A debt owing to us by J Brown of £68 is written off as a bad debt.
  „ 30   Office equipment bought on credit from Super Offices for £2,190.

19

The analytical petty cash book and the imprest system

19.1 Division of the cash book

With the growth of the firm it has been seen that it becomes necessary to have several books instead of just one ledger.

This idea can be extended to the cash book. It is obvious that in almost any firm there will be many small cash payments to be made. It would be an advantage if the records of these payments could be kept separate from the main cash book. Where a separate book is kept it is known as a **petty cash book**.

The advantages of keeping a separate petty cash book include:

- The task of handling and recording the small cash payments could be given by the cashier (the person who handles cash and maintains the cash book) to a junior member of staff. This person would then be known as the petty cashier. The cashier, who is a higher paid member of staff, would be saved from routine work which would be done by the petty cashier who is a junior and lower paid member of staff.

- If small cash payments were entered into the main cash book, these items would then need posting one by one to the ledgers. If travelling expenses were paid to staff on a daily basis, this could mean over 250 postings to the staff travelling expenses account during the year, i.e. 5 days per week × 50 working weeks per year. However, if a special form of petty cash book is kept, it would only be the monthly totals for each period that need to be posted to the general ledger. If this was done, only 12 entries would be needed in the staff travelling expenses account instead of over 250.

When the petty cashier makes a payment to someone, then that person will have to fill in a voucher showing exactly what the payment was for. He may have to attach bills – e.g. bills for petrol – to the petty cash voucher. He would sign the voucher to certify that his expenses had been paid to him by the petty cashier.

19.2 The imprest system

The **imprest system** is a system whereby the cashier gives the petty cashier enough cash to meet his needs for the following period. At the end of the period the cashier finds out the amounts spent by the petty cashier, and gives him an amount equal to that spent. The petty cash in hand should then be equal to the *original* amount with which the period was started. Exhibit 19.1 shows an example of this method.

Exhibit 19.1

		£
Period 1	The cashier gives the petty cashier	100
	The petty cashier pays out in the period	78
	Petty cash now in hand	22
	The cashier now gives the petty cashier the amount spent	78
	Petty cash in hand at the end of period 1	100
Period 2	The petty cashier pays out in the period	84
	Petty cash now in hand	16
	The cashier now gives the petty cashier the amount spent	84
	Petty cash in hand end of period 2	100

It may be necessary to increase the fixed sum, often called the cash 'float', to be held at the start of each period. In the above case, if we had wanted to increase the 'float' at the end of the second period to £120, then the cashier would have given the petty cashier an extra £20, i.e. £84 + £20 = £104.

19.3 Illustration of an analytical petty cash book

An analytical petty cash book is often used. One of these is shown as Exhibit 19.2.

The receipts column is the debit side of the petty cash book. On giving £50 to the petty cashier on 1 September the credit entry is made in the cash book while the debit entry is made in the petty cash book. A similar entry is made on 30 September for the £44 paid by the chief cashier to the petty cashier. This amount covers all expenses paid by the petty cashier. On the credit side:

1 Enter the date and details of each payment. Put the amount in the total column.
2 For 1 also put the amount in the column for the type of expense.
3 At the end of each period, add up the totals column.
4 Now add up each of the expense columns. The total of 3 should equal the total of all the expense columns. In Exhibit 19.2 this is £44.

To complete the double entry for petty cash expenses paid:

1 The total of each expense column is debited to the expense account in the general ledger.
2 Enter the folio number of each general ledger page under each of the expense columns in the petty cash book.
3 The last column in the petty cash book is a ledger column. In this column items paid out of petty cash which need posting to a ledger other than the general ledger are shown. This would happen if a purchases ledger account was settled out of petty cash or if a refund was made out of the petty cash to a customer who had overpaid his account.

The double entry for all the items in Exhibit 19.2 appears as Exhibit 19.3.

£

Sept	1	The cashier gives £50 as float to the petty cashier	
		Payments out of petty cash during September:	
,,	2	Tea and biscuits	6
,,	3	J Green – lunch	3
,,	3	Postage	2
,,	4	D Davies – lunch	2
,,	7	Cleaning fluids	1
,,	9	Biscuits	1
,,	12	K Jones – lunch	3
,,	14	Coffee and milk	3
,,	15	L Black – lunch	5
,,	16	Cleaning cloths	1
,,	18	Biscuits	2
,,	20	Postage	2
,,	22	Cleaning fluids	1
,,	24	G Wood – lunch	7
,,	27	Settlement of C Brown's account in the Purchases Ledger	3
,,	29	Postage	2
,,	30	The cashier reimburses the petty cashier the amount spent during the month.	

Exhibit 19.2

PETTY CASH BOOK (page 31)

Receipts	Folio	Date	Details	Voucher No	Total	Office Expenses	Staff Lunch Expenses	Postage	Cleaning	Ledger Folio	Ledger Accounts
£					£	£	£	£	£		£
50	CB19	Sept 1	Cash								
		,, 2	Tea	1	6	6					
		,, 3	J Green	2	3		3				
		,, 3	Postage	3	2			2			
		,, 4	D Davies	4	2		2				
		,, 7	Cleaning	5	1				1		
		,, 9	Biscuits	6	1	1					
		,, 12	K Jones	7	3		3				
		,, 14	Coffee	8	3	3					
		,, 15	L Black	9	5		5				
		,, 16	Cleaning	10	1				1		
		,, 18	Biscuits	11	2	2					
		,, 20	Postage	12	2			2			
		,, 22	Cleaning	13	1				1		
		,, 24	G Wood	14	7		7				
		,, 27	C Brown	15	3					PL 18	3
		,, 29	Postage	16	2			2			
					44	12	20	6	3		3
						GL 17	GL 29	GL 44	GL 64		
44	CB 22	,, 30	Cash								
		,, 30	Balance	c/d	50						
94					94						
50		Oct 1	Balance	b/d							

Exhibit 19.3

Cash Book (Bank Column only)   *(page 19)*

		£
	Sept 1 Petty cash PCB 31	50
	„ 30 Petty cash PCB 31	44

General Ledger

Office Expenses   *(page 17)*

	£	
Sept 30 Petty cash PCB 31	12	

Staff Lunch Expenses   *(page 29)*

	£	
Sept 30 Petty cash PCB 31	20	

Postage   *(page 44)*

	£	
Sept 30 Petty cash PCB 31	6	

Cleaning   *(page 64)*

	£	
Sept 30 Petty cash PCB 31	3	

Purchases Ledger

C Brown   *(page 18)*

	£		£
Sept 30 Petty cash PCB 31	3	Sept 1 Balance b/d	3

19.4 Bank cash book

In a firm with both a cash book and a petty cash book, the cash book is often known as a bank cash book. This means that *all* cash payments are entered in the petty cash book, and the bank cash book will contain *only* bank columns and discount columns. In this type of firm any cash sales will be paid directly into the bank.

In such a cash book, as in fact could happen in an ordinary cash book, an extra column could be added. In this details of the cheques lodged would be shown with just the total of the lodgements being shown in the total column.

Exhibit 19.4 shows the receipts side of the Bank Cash Book. The totals of the lodgements made on the three days were £192, £381 and £1,218. The details column shows what the lodgements are made up of.

Exhibit 19.4

Bank Cash Book (Receipts side)

Date	Details	Discount £	Items £	Total Lodged £
May 14	G Archer	5	95	
„ 14	P Watts	3	57	
„ 14	C King		40	192
„ 20	K Dooley	6	114	
„ 20	Cash Sales		55	
„ 20	R Jones		60	
„ 20	P Mackie	8	152	381
„ 31	J Young		19	
„ 31	T Broome	50	950	
„ 31	Cash Sales		116	
„ 31	H Tiller	7	133	1,218

Review questions

In addition to the questions which follow, you should attempt questions 89 and 90 in the accompanying book of multiple-choice questions (see back cover for further details).

Suggested solutions to review questions with the letter 'A' after the question number are given in Appendix I (page 613).

19.1A   The following is a summary of the petty cash transactions of Jockfield Ltd for the month of May.

May   1   Received from Cashier £300 as petty cash float

		£
„ 2	Postage	18
„ 3	Travelling	12
„ 4	Cleaning	15
„ 7	Petrol for delivery van	22
„ 8	Travelling	25
„ 9	Stationery	17
„ 11	Cleaning	18
„ 14	Postage	5
„ 15	Travelling	8
„ 18	Stationery	9
„ 18	Cleaning	23
„ 20	Postage	13
„ 24	Delivery van 5,000 mile service	43
„ 26	Petrol	18
„ 27	Cleaning	21
„ 29	Postage	5
„ 30	Petrol	14

You are required to:

(a) Rule up a suitable petty cash book with analysis columns for expenditure on cleaning, motor expenses, postage, stationery, travelling;

(b) Enter the month's transactions;

(*c*)   Enter the receipt of the amount necessary to restore the imprest and carry down the balance for the commencement of the following month;

(*d*)   State how the double entry for the expenditure is completed.

(*Association of Accounting Technicians*)

19.2

(*a*)   Why do some businesses keep a petty cash book as well as a cash book?

(*b*)   Paul Kelly keeps his petty cash book using the imprest system, the imprest being £100. For the month of October his petty cash transactions were as follows.

				£
Oct	1	Petty cash balance		12
„	1	Petty cashier presented vouchers to cashier and obtained cash to restore the imprest		88
„	5	Bought stamps		6
„	8	Paid to John Donohoe, a creditor		27
„	10	Paid bus fares		3
„	16	Bought envelopes		4
„	24	Received cash for personal telephone call		1
„	28	Bought petrol		20

(i)   Enter the above transactions in the petty cash book and balance the petty cash book at 31 October, bringing down the balance on 1 November.

(ii)   On 1 November Paul Kelly received an amount of cash from the cashier to restore the imprest. Enter this transaction in the petty cash book.

(*c*)   Complete the double entry for the following:

(i)   The petty cash analysis columns headed '*Postage and Stationery*' and '*Travelling Expenses*';

(ii)   The transactions dated 8 and 24 October.

19.3   The Oakhill Printing Co Ltd operates its petty cash account on the imprest system. It is maintained at a figure of £80 on the first day of each month.

At 30 April 19X7 the petty cash box held £19.37 in cash.

During May 19X7, the following petty cash transactions arose:

Date			Amount
19X7			£
May	1	Cash received to restore imprest	to be derived
„	1	Bus fares	0.41
„	2	Stationery	2.35
„	4	Bus fares	0.30
„	7	Postage stamps	1.70
„	7	Trade journal	0.95
„	8	Bus fares	0.64
„	11	Correcting fluid	1.29
„	12	Typewriter ribbons	5.42
„	14	Parcel postage	3.45
„	15	Paper-clips	0.42
„	15	Newspapers	2.00
„	16	Photocopier repair	16.80

Date			Amount
19X7			£
May	19	Postage stamps	1.50
„	20	Drawing pins	0.38
„	21	Train fare	5.40
„	22	Photocopier paper	5.63
„	23	Display decorations	3.07
„	23	Correcting fluid	1.14
„	25	Wrapping paper	0.78
„	27	String	0.61
„	27	Sellotape	0.75
„	27	Biro pens	0.46
„	28	Typewriter repair	13.66
„	30	Bus fares	2.09
June	1	Cash received to restore imprest	to be derived

Required:

Open and post the company's petty cash account for the period 1 May to 1 June 19X7 inclusive and balance the account at 30 May 19X7.

In order to facilitate the subsequent double entry postings, all items of expense appearing in the 'payments' column should be analysed individually into suitably labelled expense columns.

(*Association of Chartered Certified Accountants*)

20

Value Added Tax

20.1 Introduction

Value Added Tax is a tax charged on the supply of most goods and services. Some goods and services are not taxable and some persons and firms are exempted. Value Added Tax is usually abbreviated as VAT.

20.2 Rates of Value Added Tax

The various rates of VAT in force at any given time are decided upon by the Government. At the time of writing there are three principal rates of VAT applicable to various types of goods and services. These are the standard rate of 21% (by far the most common) and other rates of 12.5% and 3.6%. A rate of 10% is used in the examples in this chapter. This is simply because it is easy to calculate. Most examining bodies have set VAT questions assuming a rate of 10% to make the calculations easier for examination candidates.

The Collector-General is responsible for the collection of VAT on behalf of the Government.

20.3 Taxable firms

Suppose that a firm sells raw materials which it has grown both to the general public and to traders who, in turn, sell to the general public.

1 **Sale to the general public**
   The firm sells goods to Jones for £100 + VAT.

		£	
The sales invoice is for:	Price excl. VAT	100	
	+ VAT 10%	10	= Total price £110

The firm will then pay the £10 it has collected to the Collector-General.

2 **Sale to another trader, who then sells to the general public**
   The firm sells goods to another firm for £100 + VAT.

		£	
The sales invoice is for:	Price excl. VAT	100	
	+ VAT 10%	10	= Total price £110

The second firm alters the goods in some way, and then sells them to a member of the general public for £140 + VAT.

		£	
The sales invoice is for:	Price excl. VAT	140	
	+ VAT 10%	14	= Total price £154

In this case the first firm will pay the £10 to the Collector-General for VAT collected. The second firm will pay £4, being the amount collected of £14 less the VAT paid to the first firm of £10.

In the above cases you can see that the full amount of VAT has fallen on the person who finally buys the goods. The two firms have merely acted as collectors of the tax.

The value of goods sold by us or of services supplied by us is known as our **outputs**. Thus VAT on such items may be called **output tax**. The value of goods bought by us or of services supplied to us is known as **inputs**. The VAT on these items is, therefore, **input tax**.

20.4 Exempted firms

Some firms do not have to add VAT on to the price at which they sell their products or services. Some firms will not get a refund of the VAT they have themselves paid on goods and services bought by them. The types of firms exempted can be listed under two headings:

1 **Nature of business**. Various types of business do not have to add VAT to charges for goods or services. For example, educational services provided by recognised institutions, medical services provided by hospitals and postal services provided by An Post are exempt from VAT.
2 **Small firms**. Firms with a turnover of less than a certain amount do not have to register for VAT if they do not want to. The turnover limit is changed from time to time. With effect from 1 July 1994 persons or firms selling goods valued at less than £40,000 in a year do not have to register. In the case of services the limit is £20,000 per annum. This means that if they do not register they do not have to add VAT to the value of their sales invoices.

If small firms do register for VAT then they will have to keep full VAT records in addition to charging out VAT. To save very small businesses the costs and effort of keeping such records the Government, therefore, allows them not to register unless they want to.

20.5 Zero-rated goods and services

A firm which sells only goods which are zero rated:

1 does not have to add VAT on to the selling price of products, and
2 can obtain a refund of all VAT paid on the purchase of goods or services.

If, therefore, £100,000 of goods are sold by the firm, nothing has to be added for VAT but, if £8,000 VAT had been paid by it on goods or services bought, then the firm would be able to claim a full refund of the £8,000 paid.

It is 2 above which distinguishes it from an exempted firm. A zero rated firm is, therefore, in a better position than an exempted firm. Examples of zero rated goods and services are goods which are exported, children's clothing and footwear, many medicines, books and most food.

20.6 Traders selling goods or services taxable at different rates

Some traders will find that they are selling some goods which are exempt and some which are zero rated and others which are standard rated. These traders will have to apportion their turnover accordingly, and follow the rules already described for each separate part of their turnover.

20.7 Different methods of accounting for VAT

It can be seen from what has been said already that VAT complicates the recording of business transactions. For example, there will be a difference between:

1 **Firms which can recover VAT paid.** All firms except exempted firms do not suffer VAT as an expense. They either:

- Get a refund of whatever VAT they have paid, as in the case of a zero rated firm, or
- Collect VAT from their customers, deduct the VAT paid on goods and services bought by them, and simply remit the difference to the Collector-General.

2 **Firms which cannot recover VAT paid.** This applies to all firms which are treated as exempted firms, and, therefore, suffer the tax as they cannot get refunds from it. The following discussion of the accounting entries needed will, therefore, distinguish between those two types of firms, those which do not suffer VAT as an expense, and those firms to whom VAT is an expense.

20.8 Firms which can recover VAT paid

1 Taxable firms

Value added tax and sales invoices

A taxable firm will have to add VAT to the value of the sales invoices. It must be pointed out that this is based on the amount of the invoice *after* any trade discount has been deducted. Exhibit 20.1 is an invoice drawn up from the following details:

On 2 March, W Frank & Co, Galway Road, Limerick, sold the following goods to R Bainbridge Ltd, Star Road, Donegal: Bainbridge's order was for the following items:

200 Rolls T56 Black Tape at £6 per 10 rolls
600 Sheets R64 Polythene at £10 per 100 sheets
7,000 Blank Perspex B49 Markers at £20 per 1,000

All of these goods are subject to VAT at the rate of 10%. A trade discount of 25% is given by Frank & Co. The sales invoice is numbered 8851.

Exhibit 20.1

	W Frank & Co **Galway Road** **Limerick**	
To: R Bainbridge Star Road Donegal	**INVOICE No. 8851**	Date: 2 March 1998 VAT Registration No. 1/1234567/X

	£
200 Rolls T56 Black Tape @ £6 per 10 rolls	120
600 Sheets R64 Polythene @ £10 per 100 sheets	60
7,000 Blank Perspex B49 Markers @ £20 per 1,000	140
	320
Less Trade Discount 25%	80
	240
Add VAT 10%	24
	264

The sales journal will normally have an extra column for the VAT content of sales. This makes it easier to account for VAT. The entry of several sales invoices in the sales journal and in the ledger accounts can now be examined:

W Frank & Co sold the following goods during March:

			Total of invoice, after trade discount deducted but before VAT added	VAT 10%
			£	£
March	2	R Bainbridge Ltd (*see* Exhibit 20.1)	240	24
,,	10	S Lange & Son	300	30
,,	17	K Bishop	160	16
,,	31	R Andrews	100	10

Sales Book					*page 58*
	Invoice No	Folio	Net	VAT	Gross
			£	£	£
March 2 R Bainbridge Ltd	8851	SL 77	240	24	264
,, 10 S Lange & Son	8852	SL 119	300	30	330
,, 17 K Bishop	8853	SL 185	160	16	176
,, 31 R Andrews	8854	SL 221	100	10	110
Transferred to general ledger			800	80	880
			GL 76	GL 90	

Now that the sales book has been written up, the next task is to enter the amounts of the invoices in the individual customers' accounts in the sales ledger. These are simply charged with the full amounts of the invoices including VAT.

For example, K Bishop will be shown as owing £176. When he pays his account he will pay £176. It will then be the responsibility of W Frank & Co to ensure that the figure of £16 VAT in respect of this item is included in the total cheque payable to the Collector-General.

Sales Ledger

R Bainbridge Ltd   (*page 77*)

	£	
Mar 2 Sales SB 58	264	

S Lange & Son   (*page 119*)

	£	
Mar 10 Sales SB 58	330	

K Bishop		(page 185)
	£	
Mar 17 Sales SB 58	176	

R Andrews		(page 221)
	£	
Mar 31 Sales SB 58	110	

In total, therefore, the personal accounts have been debited with £880, this being the total of the amounts which the customers will have to pay. The actual sales of the firm are not £880, the amount which is actually sales is £800, the other £80 being simply the VAT that W Frank & Co is collecting on behalf of the Government. The double entry that is made in the general ledger (having already posted £880 to the individual debtors accounts) is:

1 Credit the sales account with the sales content only, i.e. £800
2 Credit the Value Added Tax account with the VAT content only, i.e. £80

These are shown as follows:

General Ledger

Sales		(page 76)
		£
	Mar 31 Debtors accounts SB 58	800

Value Added Tax		(page 90)
		£
	Mar 31 Debtors accounts SB 58	80

Value Added Tax and Purchases

In the case of a taxable firm, the firm will have to add VAT to its sales invoices, but it will *also* be able to get a refund of the VAT which it pays on its purchases.

Instead of paying VAT to the Collector-General, and then claiming a refund of the VAT on purchases, the firm can set off the amount paid as VAT on purchases against the amount payable as VAT on sales. This means that only the difference has to be paid to the Collector-General. It is shown as:

	£
(a) VAT charged on sales invoices	xxx
(b) Less VAT on purchases	xxx
(c) Net amount to be paid to the Collector-General	xxx

Sometimes (a) may be less than (b). If that was the case, then it would be the Collector-General that would refund the difference (c) to the firm. Such a settlement between the firm and the Collector-General will take place every two months.

The recording of purchases in the purchases book and purchases ledger follows a similar method to that of sales, but with the personal accounts being credited instead of debited. We can now look at the records of purchases for the same firm whose sales have been dealt with, W Frank & Co. The firm made the following purchases during March:

			Total of invoice, after trade discount deducted but before VAT added	VAT 10%
			£	£
Mar	1	E Lyal Ltd (*see* Exhibit 20.2)	180	18
„	11	P Potter & Co	120	12
„	24	J Davidson	40	4
„	29	B Cuffe & Son Ltd	70	7

Before looking at the recording of these in the purchases records, compare the first entry for E Lyal Ltd with Exhibit 20.2, to ensure that the correct amounts have been shown.

Exhibit 20.2

E Lyal Ltd
College Avenue
Waterford

Date: 1/3/1998   **INVOICE No. K453/A**

To: W Frank & Co   Terms: Strictly net 30 days
Galway Road
Limerick   VAT Registration No. IE 9/7654321/Y

	£
50 metres of BYC plastic 1 metre wide × £3 per metre	150
1,200 metal tags 500 mm × 10p each	120
	270
Less Trade discount at 33⅓%	90
	180
Add VAT 10%	18
	198

The purchases book can now be drawn up.

Purchases Book				*page 38*
	Folio	Net £	VAT £	Gross £
March 1 E Lyal Ltd	PL 15	180	18	198
„ 11 P Potter	PL 70	120	12	132
„ 24 J Davidson	PL 114	40	4	44
„ 29 B Cuffe Ltd	PL 166	70	7	77
Transferred to general ledger		410	41	451
		GL 54	GL 90	

These are entered in the purchases ledger. Once again there is no need for the VAT to be shown as separate amounts in the accounts of the suppliers.

Purchases Ledger

E Lyal Ltd   (page 15)

			£
	Mar 1 Purchases PB 38		198

P Potter   (page 70)

			£
	Mar 11 Purchases PB 38		132

J Davidson   (page 114)

			£
	Mar 24 Purchases PB 38		44

B Cuffe Ltd   (page 166)

			£
	Mar 29 Purchases PB 38		77

The personal accounts have been credited with a total of £451, this being the total of the amounts which W Frank & Co will have to pay to them.

The actual cost of purchases is not, however, £451. You can see that the correct amount is £410. The other £41 is the VAT which the various firms are collecting for the Collector-General. This amount is also the figure for VAT which is reclaimable from the Collector-General by W Frank & Co. The debit entry in the purchases account is, therefore, £410, as this is the actual cost of the goods to the firm. The other £41 is entered on the debit side of the VAT account.

Notice that there is already a credit of £80 in the VAT account in respect of the VAT added to Sales.

General Ledger

Purchases   (page 54)

	£		
Mar 31 Creditors accounts PB 38	410		

Value Added Tax   (page 90)

	£		£
Mar 31 Creditors accounts PB 38	41	Mar 31 Debtors accounts SB 58	80
„ 31 Balance c/d	39		
	80		80
		April 1 Balance b/d	39

In the final accounts of W Frank & Co, the following entries would be made:

Trading Account for the month of March:
   Debited with £410 as a transfer from the Purchases account
   Credited with £800 as a transfer from the Sales account

Balance Sheet as at 31 March:
   Balance of £39 (credit) on the VAT account would be shown as a current liability, as it represents the amount owing to the Collector-General for VAT.

2 Firms selling only zero-rated goods or services

These firms:

1 Do not have to add VAT on to their sales invoices, as their rate of VAT is zero or nil.
2 They can however reclaim from the Collector-General any VAT paid on goods or services bought.

Accordingly, because of **1** no VAT is entered in the Sales Book. VAT on sales does not exist. Because of **2** the Purchases Book and Purchases Ledger will appear exactly in the same manner as for other firms, as already shown in the case of W Frank & Co.

The VAT account will only have debits in it, being the VAT on Purchases. Any balance on this account will be shown in the balance sheet as a debtor, i.e. an amount receivable from the Collector-General.

20.9 Firms which cannot get refunds of VAT paid (exempt firms)

As these firms do not add VAT on to the value of their Sales Invoices there is obviously no entry for VAT in the Sales Book or the Sales Ledger. They do not get a refund of VAT on Purchases. This means that there will not be a VAT account. All that will happen is that VAT paid is included as part of the cost of the goods bought.

A purchase of goods for £120 + VAT £12 from D Oswald Ltd will appear as:

Purchases Book

		£
May 16 D Oswald Ltd		132

Purchases Ledger

D Oswald Ltd

		£
	May 16 Purchases	132

General Ledger

Purchases

	£			£
May 31 Credit Purchases for		May 31 Transfer to Trading		
the month	132	Account		132

Trading Account for the month ended 31 May (extract)

	£
Purchases	132

20.10 Calculation of the amount of VAT

You will often know only the gross amount of an item. This figure will in fact be made up of the net amount plus VAT. To find the amount of VAT which has been added to the net amount, a formula capable of being used with any rate of VAT can be used. It is:

$$\frac{\%\ \text{rate of VAT}}{100 + \%\ \text{rate of VAT}} \times \text{Gross Amount} = \text{VAT in £}$$

Suppose that the gross amount of sales was £1,650 and the rate of VAT was 10%. Find the amount of VAT and the net amount before VAT was added. Using the formula:

$$\frac{10}{100 + 10} \times £1,650 = \frac{10}{110} \times £1,650 = £150.$$

Therefore the net amount was £1,500, which with VAT £150 added, becomes £1,650 gross.

Given a rate of 21% VAT, to find the amount of VAT in a gross price of £605, the calculation is:

$$\frac{21}{100 + 21} \times £605 = \frac{21}{121} \times £605 = £105.$$

20.11 VAT on items other than sales and purchases

VAT is not just paid on purchases. It is also payable on many items of expense and on the purchase of certain fixed assets (see 20.13 below).

Firms which *can* get refunds of VAT paid will not include VAT as part of the cost of the expense or fixed asset. Firms which *cannot* get refunds of VAT paid will include the VAT cost as part of the expense or fixed asset. For example, two firms buying similar items would treat the following items as shown:

Transaction	Firm which can reclaim VAT		Firm which cannot reclaim VAT	
Buys Machinery £200 + VAT £20	Debit Machinery Debit VAT Account	£200 £20	Debit Machinery	£220
Buys Stationery £150 + VAT £15	Debit Stationery Debit VAT Account	£150 £15	Debit Stationery	£165

20.12 Relief from VAT on bad debts

It is possible to claim relief for debts which have become bad. Should the debt later be paid, the VAT refunded will then have to be paid back to the Collector-General.

20.13 The purchase of cars

The VAT paid on a car bought as a fixed asset for a business is not reclaimable. A garage which buys a car as stock for resale can reclaim VAT on the purchase (and will pay VAT when it sells the car to a customer).

20.14 VAT and the balance sheet

At the end of an accounting period if a firm owes VAT to the Collector-General this liability will be shown as a current liability in the firm's balance sheet. If money is receivable from the Collector-General this should be shown as a current asset.

20.15 Columnar day books and VAT

The use of columns for VAT in both Sales and Purchases Analysis Books is shown in Chapter 22.

20.16 Value Added Tax returns and payment

Details of VAT suffered by a firm and of VAT collected by it on behalf of the Collector-General must be sent to the Collector-General every two months. The details are shown on form VAT3. This form must be submitted by the 19th of the month following each two-month VAT period. These periods are January/February, March/April and so on. Small firms have the option of submitting one annual return instead of six bi-monthly ones.

An additional return showing the value of sales and purchases is required once annually for each year ending 31 August.

Payment of any tax due, as shown by the bi-monthly returns, is due at the same time as the return form itself.

There are penalties of up to five years' imprisonment and a fine of £10,000 for failure to make a return or pay tax due on time.

Review questions

In addition to the questions which follow, you should attempt questions 91–111 in the accompanying book of multiple-choice questions (see back cover for further details).

Suggested solutions to review questions with the letter 'A' after the question number are given in Appendix I (page 614).

20.1A On 1 May, D Wilson Ltd, Waterford Road, Cork, sold the following goods on credit to G Christie & Son, The Golf Shop, Killarney:

3 sets 'Boy Michael' golf clubs at £270 per set.
150 Watson golf balls at £8 per 10 balls.
4 Faldo golf bags at £30 per bag.

Trade discount is given at the rate of 33⅓%.
All goods are subject to VAT at 10%.

(a) Prepare the Sales Invoice to be sent to G Christie & Son. The invoice number will be 10586. D Wilson's VAT Registration number is 9/4445555/P.
(b) Show the entries in the Personal Ledgers of D Wilson Ltd and G Christie & Son.

20.2 On 1 March, C Black, Cork Road, Limerick, sold the following goods on credit to J Booth, Main Street, Thurles.

20,000 Coils Sealing Tape @ £4.40 per 1,000 coils
40,000 Sheets Bank A5   @ £4.50 per 1,000 sheets
24,000 Sheets Bank A4   @ £4.25 per 1,000 sheets

All goods are subject to VAT at 10%.

(a) Prepare the Sales Invoice to be sent to J Booth.
(b) Show the entries in the Personal Ledgers of J Booth, and C Black.

20.3A   The following sales and purchases were made by R Colman Ltd during May.

			Net	VAT added
			£	£
May	1	Sold goods on credit to B Davies & Co	150	15
„	4	Sold goods on credit to C Grant Ltd	220	22
„	10	Bought goods on credit from:		
		G Cooper & Son	400	40
		J Wayne Ltd	190	19
„	14	Bought goods on credit from B Lemon	50	5
„	16	Sold goods on credit to C Grant Ltd	140	14
„	23	Bought goods on credit from S Hayward	60	6
„	31	Sold goods on credit to B Kelly	80	8

Draw up the Sales and Purchases Books, the Sales and Purchases Ledgers and the General Ledger for the month of May. Carry the balance down on the VAT account.

20.4   The credit sales and purchases for December in respect of C Dennis & Son Ltd were:

			Net, after trade discount	VAT 10%
			£	£
Dec	1	Sales to M O'Pell	140	14
„	4	Sales to G Ford Ltd	290	29
„	5	Purchases from P Daimler & Son	70	7
„	8	Purchases from J Lancia	110	11
„	14	Sales to R Volvo Ltd	180	18
„	18	Purchases from T Honda & Co	160	16
„	28	Sales to G Ford Ltd	100	10
„	30	Purchases from J Lancia	90	9

Write up all of the relevant books and ledger accounts for the month.

20.5   Mudgee Ltd issued the following invoices to customers in respect of credit sales made during the last week of May 19X7. The amounts stated are all net of Value Added Tax. All sales made by Mudgee Ltd are subject to VAT at 15%.

Invoice No.	Date	Customer	Amount
			£
3045	25 May	Laira Brand	1,060.00
3046	27 May	Brown Bros	2,200.00
3047	28 May	Penfold's	170.00
3048	29 May	T Tyrrell	460.00
3049	30 May	Laira Brand	1,450.00
			£5,340.00

On 29 May Laira Brand returned half the goods (in value) purchased on 25 May. An allowance was made the same day to this customer for the appropriate amount.

On 1 May 19X7 Laira Brand owed Mudgee Ltd £2,100.47. Other than the purchases detailed above Laira Brand made credit purchases (including VAT) of £680.23 from Mudgee Ltd on 15 May. On 21 May Mudgee Ltd received a cheque for £2,500 from Laira Brand.

Required:
(a) Show how the above transactions would be recorded in Mudgee Ltd's Sales Book for the week ended 30 May 19X7.
(b) Describe how the information in the Sales Book would be incorporated into Mudgee Ltd's double entry system.
(c) Reconstruct the personal account of Laira Brand as it would appear in Mudgee Ltd's ledger for May 19X7.

(*Association of Accounting Technicians*)

21

Employees' pay

21.1 Introduction

In this chapter we will consider the calculation of employees' pay and the deductions that are made from it by employers.

There is no exact definition of 'wages' and 'salaries'. In general it is accepted that wages are earnings paid on a weekly basis, whilst salaries are paid monthly.

The employer will have to make various deductions so that a distinction is made between:

- Gross pay: This is the amount of wages or salary *before* deductions are made.
- Net pay: This is the amount of wages or salary *after* deductions (also known as 'take-home' pay).

21.2 Methods of calculating gross pay

The methods can vary widely between employers and also as regards different employees in the same organisation. The main methods are :

- Fixed amount salaries or wages: these are an agreed annual amount.
- Piece rate: based on the number of units produced by the employee.
- Commission: a percentage based on the amount of sales made by the employee.
- Basic rate per hour: a fixed rate multiplied by number of hours worked.

Arrangements for rewarding people for working overtime (time exceeding normal hours worked) will vary widely. The rate will usually be in excess of that paid during normal working hours. People being paid salaries will often not be paid for overtime.

In addition bonuses may be paid on top of the above earnings. Bonus schemes will also vary widely, and may depend on the amount of net profit made by the company, or on the amount of work performed or production achieved, either by the whole company or else the department in which the employee works.

21.3 Income tax deductions

Wages and salaries of all employees are liable to have income tax deducted from them. This does not mean that everyone will pay income tax, but that if income tax is found to be payable then the employer will deduct the tax from the employee's wages or salary. The office of the Collector-General, a branch of the Revenue Commissioners, is responsible for the collection of Income Tax.

Each employee is allowed to subtract various amounts from his/her earnings to see if he/she is liable to pay income tax. The amounts allowed to be deducted for each person depend upon his or her personal circumstances. An extra amount can be deducted by a

married person as compared to a single person. The total of these for a person is known as his or her tax-free allowance (TFA). An individual's taxable pay is income tax on their gross pay less their tax-free allowances, that is:

	£
Gross pay	xxx
less tax-free allowance	xxx
Equals pay which is taxable	xxx

A person is also entitled to make a number of 'deductions' from their taxable pay. The principal deductions are as follows:

Type of deduction	Amount
	£
Personal allowance	4,200 (single person)
	8,400 (married couple)
PAYE allowance	1,000

The actual amount deducted from taxable pay is the relevant amount above multiplied by the current standard rate of income tax.

There are also deductions for mortgage interest and VHI premiums paid.

Two people may, therefore, earn the same wages, but if one of them has a higher tax-free allowance than the other then he/she will have less taxable pay, and will pay less income tax than the other person.

Each year in his budget, the Minister for Finance announces what the rates of income tax are going to be for the following year, and also how tax-free allowances are to be calculated. Because of the annual changes the rates of income tax shown below will *not necessarily* be the actual rates of income tax at the time you are reading this book.

Tax rates apply to a 'tax year'. Each tax year begins on the 6th of April and ends on the following 5th April. For the tax year 1999/2000, that is for the period 6 April 1999 to 5 April 2000, the rates of income tax and the amount of income liable to those rates were as follows:

for a single person:
on the first £14,000 of income in excess of one's TFA	24%
on the balance of one's income	46%

for a married person:
on the first £28,000 of income in excess of one's TFA	24%
on the balance of one's income	46%

The income tax payable by each of four persons can now be looked at. (All examples relate to the tax year 1999/2000.)

1 Miss Brown earned £3,800. Her tax liability is calculated as follows:

		£
Taxable pay		3,800
Tax at 24%		912
Less deductions	£	
Personal allowance (single person)	4,200	
PAYE allowance	1,000	
	5,200	
At 24%		(1,248)
Tax payable		Nil*

* This same result could have been arrived at without any calculations as Miss Brown's taxable pay is less than her deductions.

2   Mr Green, who is single, earned £8,760. His tax liability is calculated as follows:

		£
Taxable pay		8,760
Tax at 24%		2,102.40

	£	
Less deductions		
Personal allowance (single person)	4,200	
PAYE allowance	1,000	
	5,200	
At 24%		(1,248.00)
Tax payable		854.40

3   Mr Black, who is single, earned £20,000. The amount of income tax he has to pay is calculated as follows:

		£
Taxable pay		20,000
First £14,000 taxable at 24%		3,360
Balance (£6,000) taxable at 46%		2,760
		6,120

	£	
Less deductions		
Personal allowance (single person)	4,200	
PAYE allowance	1,000	
	5,200	
At 24%		(1,248)
Tax payable		4,872

4   Mr and Mrs White earned £39,700 between them. Mrs White's income tax is calculated as follows

		£
Taxable pay		39,700
First £28,000 taxable at 24%		6,720
Balance (£11,700) taxable at 46%		5,382
		12,102

	£	
Less deductions		
Personal allowance (married couple)	8,400	
PAYE allowance (two employees)		2,000
	10,400	
At 24%		(2,496)
Tax payable		9,606

Most employees pay their income tax under the PAYE (Pay As You Earn) system. This means that the correct amount of tax is deducted from their gross pay by their employer and they can keep the amount of net pay which they receive. Other people, who are not taxed under the PAYE system, have to pay their own income tax to the Revenue Commissioners rather than having it deducted from their gross pay and paid to the Revenue Commissioners on their behalf by their employer.

Let us assume that Miss Brown and Mr Green are paid weekly, and Mr Black and Mrs White are paid monthly. If each payment to them during the year was of an equal amount, then we can calculate the amount of PAYE deducted from each payment of earnings.

PAYE deducted on a weekly basis:

1 Miss Brown. Tax for year = nil. Tax each week = nil.
2 Mr Green. Tax for year = £854.40. Tax each week £854.40 ÷ 52 = £16.43.

PAYE deducted on a monthly basis:

3 Mr Black. Tax for year = £4,872. Tax each month £4,872 ÷ 12 = £406.
4 Mrs White. Tax for year = £9,606. Tax each month £9,606 ÷ 12 = £800.50.

The examples above were deliberately made easy to understand. In real life, earnings will change part way through a tax year, the amounts paid in each period may be different, and so on. To help employers to calculate PAYE tax under all circumstances the Revenue Commissioners issue tax tables to all employers for this purpose. As different employees have different tax-free allowances and deductions and as it is necessary to know these to calculate his/her net pay and tax, the Revenue Commissioners notify each employer of each of their employees' allowances and deductions at the beginning of each tax year.

21.4 Pay Related Social Insurance (PRSI)

Most employees have to pay PRSI in addition to paying PAYE. The payment of such contributions is so that the employee will be able to claim benefits from the State, if and when he or she is in a position to claim, e.g. for retirement or health benefits. The contributions are split into two parts:

1 The part that the employee has to suffer by it being deducted from his pay.
2 The part that the employer has to suffer. This is not deductible from pay.

For the tax year 1999/2000, in respect of most private sector employees, employers had to pay PRSI of 12% of gross pay and employees had to pay 6.5% (including the 2% 'Health Levy').

21.5 Other deductions from gross pay

1 Pension contributions

An employee may contribute to a pension fund. The money paid into the fund may be paid partly by the firm and partly by the employee, e.g. the employee's contribution might be (say) 6% of gross pay, with the firm paying whatever is necessary to give the employee the agreed amount of pension.

The amount of the contribution payable by the employee will therefore be deducted in calculating the net pay due to him. The term 'superannuation' is often used instead of 'pension'.

2 Voluntary contributions

These may include items such as Voluntary Health Insurance (VHI) contributions, subscriptions to the firm's social club and union subscriptions.

21.6 Calculation of net pay

Two examples of the calculation of net pay are given below. The percentages used are for illustrative purposes only.

		£
(A) G Jarvis:	Gross earnings for the week ended 26 August	100
	Income tax: found by reference to G Jarvis' tax-free allowances, deductions and total pay to date this tax year	12
	Employee's PRSI = 9% of gross pay	

G Jarvis: Payslip for the week ended 26 August	£	£
Gross pay for the week		100
Less Income tax	12	
" PRSI	9	21
Net pay		79

		£
(B) H Reddish:	Gross earnings for the month of September	800
	Income tax (found as above)	150
	Superannuation: 6% of gross pay	
	Employee's PRSI 9% of gross pay	

H Reddish: Payslip for the month ended 30 September	£	£
Gross pay for the month		800
Less Income tax	150	
" Superannuation	48	
" PRSI	72	270
Net pay		530

The total costs to the employer in each of the above cases will be as follows, *assuming* the employer's PRSI contribution to be £10 for Jarvis and £81 for Reddish:

	G Jarvis	H Reddish
	£	£
Gross pay	100	800
Employer's share of PRSI	10	81
Total cost to the employer	110	881

It will be the figures of £110 and £881 that will be incorporated in the profit and loss account as expenses shown under wages and salaries headings.

Review questions

In addition to the questions which follow, you should attempt questions 112–116 in the accompanying book of multiple-choice questions (see back cover for details).

Suggested solutions to review questions with the letter 'A' after the question number are given in Appendix I (pages 614–15).

Note: The questions below are for general use only. They have been designed to be able to be worked out without the use of tax or PRSI tables. The PRSI given is the employee's part only.

21.1A H Smith is employed at a rate of £5 per hour. During the week to 16 September he worked his basic week of 40 hours. The income tax due on his wages was £27, and his PRSI was £16. Calculate his net wages.

21.2A B Charles has a basic working week of 40 hours, paid at the rate of £4 per hour. For hours worked in excess of this he is paid 1½ times basic rate. In the week to 19 August he worked 45 hours. His tax amounted to £27.50. His PRSI amounted to £17. Calculate his net wages.

21.3A B Croft has a job as a car salesman. He is paid a basic salary of £200 per month, and commission of 2% on the value of his car sales. During the month of April he sells £30,000 worth of cars. His income tax for the month is £87.50. He also pays PRSI for the month of £66. Calculate his net pay for the month.

21.4A T Penketh is an accountant with a salary of £2,000 per month plus bonus, which, for the month of May, was £400. He pays superannuation contributions of 5% of gross pay and his tax for the month totalled £830.50. In addition, he pays PRSI of £190. Calculate his net pay for the month.

21.5 K Blake is employed at the rate of £6 per hour. During the week to 25 May he works 35 hours. For that week he should pay income tax of £28 and PRSI of £18. Calculate his net wages.

21.6 R Kennedy is a security van driver. He has a wage of £200 per week, plus danger money of £2 per hour extra spent in transporting gold bullion. During the week ended 15 June he spends 20 hours taking gold bullion to the Airport. His tax for the week is £40. He pays PRSI for the week of £19. Calculate his net pay for the week.

22

Columnar day books

Some firms use only one book to record all items obtained on credit. This will include purchases, stationery, fixed assets, motor expenses and so on. All credit invoices for any expense will be entered in this book.

However, all of the various types of items are not simply lumped together, as the firm needs to know how much of the items were for purchases, how much for stationery, how much for motor expenses, etc., so that the relevant expense accounts can have the correct amount of expenses entered in them. This is achieved by having a set of analysis columns in the book, all of the items are entered in a total column, but then they are analysed as between the different sorts of expenses, etc.

Exhibit 22.1 shows such a Purchases Analysis Book (or analysed Purchases Journal) drawn up for a month from the following list of items obtained on credit:

			£
May	1	Bought goods from D Watson Ltd on credit	296
„	3	Bought goods on credit from W Donachie & Son	76
„	5	Van repaired, received invoice from Barnes Motors Ltd	112
„	6	Bought stationery from J Corrigan & Co on credit	65
„	8	Bought goods on credit from C Bell Ltd	212
„	14	Lorry serviced, received invoice from Barnes Motors Ltd	39
„	23	Bought stationery on credit from A Hartford & Co	35
„	26	Bought goods on credit from M Doyle Ltd	243
„	30	Received invoice for carriage inwards on goods from G Owen	58

Exhibit 22.1

Purchases Analysis Book

(page 105)

Date	Name of firm	PL Folio	Total	Purchases	Stationery	Motor expenses	Carriage inwards
			£	£	£	£	£
May 1	D Watson Ltd	129	296	296			
„ 3	W Donachie & Son	27	76	76			
„ 5	Barnes Motors Ltd	55	112			112	
„ 6	J Corrigan & Co	88	65		65		
„ 8	C Bell Ltd	99	212	212			
„ 14	Barnes Motors Ltd	55	39			39	
„ 23	A Hartford & Co	298	35		35		
„ 26	M Doyle Ltd	187	243	243			
„ 30	G Owen	222	58				58
			1,136	827	100	151	58
				GL77	GL97	GL156	GL198

Exhibit 22.1 shows that the figure for each item is entered in the Total column, and is then also entered in the column for the particular type of expense. At the end of the month the arithmetical accuracy of the additions can be checked by comparing the total of the Total column with the sum of totals of all of the other columns.

It can be seen that the total of purchases for the month of May was £827 and therefore this can be debited to the Purchases Account in the General Ledger; similarly the total of stationery bought on credit in the month can be debited to the Stationery Account in the General Ledger and so on. The folio number of the page to which the relevant total has been debited is shown immediately under the total figure for each column, e.g. under the column for purchases is GL77, meaning that the item has been entered in the General Ledger page 77.

The entries can now be shown:

General Ledger

Purchases *(page 77)*

	£
May 31 Purchases analysis 105	827

Stationery *(page 97)*

	£
May 31 Purchases analysis 105	100

Motor Expenses *(page 156)*

	£
May 31 Purchases analysis 105	151

Carriage Inwards *(page 198)*

	£
May 31 Purchases analysis 105	58

The individual accounts of the creditors, whether they be for goods or for expenses such as stationery or motor expenses, can be kept together in a single Purchases Ledger. There is no need for the Purchases Ledger to have accounts only for creditors for purchases. Perhaps there is a slight misuse of the name Purchases Ledger where this happens. However, most firms use the title **Creditors Ledger** to mean what is referred to above as the Purchases Ledger.

To carry through the double entry involved with Exhibit 22.1 the Purchases Ledger is now shown.

Purchases Ledger

W Donachie & Son *(page 27)*

			£
May 3 Purchases analysis	105	76

Barnes Motors Ltd   *(page 55)*

			£
May 5	Purchases Analysis	105	112
„ 14	„	105	39

J Corrigan & Co   *(page 88)*

			£
May 6	Purchases Analysis	105	65

C Bell Ltd   *(page 99)*

			£
May 8	Purchases Analysis	105	212

D Watson Ltd   *(page 129)*

			£
May 1	Purchases Analysis	105	296

M Doyle Ltd   *(page 187)*

			£
May 26	Purchases Analysis	105	243

G Owen   *(page 222)*

			£
May 20	Purchases Analysis	105	58

A Hartford & Co   *(page 298)*

			£
May 13	Purchases Analysis	105	35

If the business was split up into departments or sections, instead of having one *Purchases* column it would be possible to have one column for *each* of the departments. By this means the total purchases for each department for the accounting period could be ascertained. (The preparation of accounts for departmental businesses is discussed in more detail in Chapter 49.)

22.2 Sales analysis books

Where, instead of knowing only the total of sales for the accounting period, it would be preferable to know the sales for each section or department of the business, a sales analysis book (or analysed Sales Journal) could be kept. For a firm selling sports goods, household goods and electrical items, it might appear as in Exhibit 22.2.

Exhibit 22.2

Sales Analysis Book

Date	Name of firm	SL Folio	Total	Sports Dept	Household Dept	Electrical Dept
			£	£	£	£
May 1	N Coward Ltd	87	190		190	
„ 5	L Oliver	76	200	200		
„ 8	R Colman & Co	157	300	102		198
„ 16	Aubrey Smith Ltd	209	480			480
„ 27	H Marshall	123	220	110	45	65
„ 31	W Pratt	66	1,800		800	1,000
			3,190	412	1,035	1,743

22.3 Sales analysis books and VAT

If a firm was not registered for VAT then it would not have to add VAT on to the value of its sales invoices. This could have been the case in Exhibit 22.2 where there is no mention of VAT. Suppose instead that the same firm was registered then it might have had to add VAT.

All that is needed is an extra column for VAT. In Exhibit 22.3 below, the debtors would be charged with gross amounts, e.g. N Coward Ltd with £209. The VAT account would be credited with £319 being the total of the VAT column. The sales account would be credited with the sales figures of £412, £1,035 and £1,743. (Assumed VAT rate of 10%.)

Exhibit 22.3

Sales Analysis Book

Date	Name of firm	SL Folio	Total	VAT	Sports Dept	Household Dept	Electrical Dept
			£	£	£	£	£
May 1	N Coward Ltd	87	209	19		190	
„ 5	L Oliver	76	220	20	200		
„ 8	R Colman & Co	157	330	30	102		198
„ 16	Aubrey Smith Ltd	209	528	48			480
„ 27	H Marshall	123	242	22	110	45	65
„ 31	W Pratt	66	1,980	180		800	1,000
			3,509	319	412	1,035	1,743

Similarly, a purchases analysis book could have a VAT column included. In this case the total of the VAT column would be debited to the VAT account. The total of the purchases column would be debited to the purchases account with the total of each expense column debited to the various expense accounts. Remember that VAT is not payable on some items, e.g. rent.

22.4 Journals as collection points for information

We can see that the various sales and purchases journals, and the ones for returns, are simply collection points for the data to be entered in the accounts of the double entry system. There is nothing by law that says that, for instance, a sales journal has to be written up. What we could do is to look at the sales invoices and enter debits in the

customers' personal accounts from them. Then we could keep all the sales invoices together in a file. At the end of the month we could add up the amounts of the sales invoices, and then enter that total to the credit of the sales account in the general ledger.

That means that we would have done without the sales journal. Such a system could lead to more errors being made and not being detected. It could also mean that bookkeepers could more easily commit fraud as it would be more difficult for proprietors to see what was going on. This system could also be used for purchases and for returns.

Review questions

Suggested solutions to review questions with the letter 'A' after the question number are given in Appendix I (page 615).

22.1A C Taylor, a wholesale dealer in electrical goods, has three departments: (a) Hi Fi, (b) TV, and (c) Sundries. The following is a summary of Taylor's Sales Invoices during the period 1 to 7 February:

	Customer	Invoice No	Depart- ment	List price less trade discount	VAT	Total invoice price
				£	£	£
Feb 1	P Small	586	TV	2,600	260	2,860
2	L Goode	587	Hi Fi	1,800	180	1,980
3	R Daye	588	TV	1,600	160	1,760
5	B May	589	Sundries	320	Nil	320
7	L Goode	590	TV	900	90	990
7	P Small	591	Hi Fi	3,400	340	3,740

(a) Record the above transactions in a columnar book of original entry and post to the general ledger in columnar form.

(b) Write up the personal accounts in the appropriate ledger.
NB Do not balance off any of your ledger accounts. VAT is charged at 10% on TV and Hi Fi goods.

22.2A Draw up a purchases analysis book with columns for the various expenses for M Barber for the month of July from the following information on credit items.

			£
July	1	Bought goods from L Ogden	220
„	3	Bought goods from E Evans	390
„	4	Received ESB bill (lighting & heating)	88
„	5	Bought goods from H Noone	110
„	6	Lorry repaired, received bill from Kirk Motors	136
„	8	Bought stationery from Avon Enterprises	77
„	10	Van serviced, bill from Kirk Motors	55
„	12	Gas bill received from Bord Gais (lighting & heating)	134
„	15	Bought goods from A Dodds	200
„	17	Bought light bulbs (lighting & heating) from O Smith	24
„	18	Goods bought from J Kelly	310
„	19	Invoice for carriage inwards from D Adams	85
„	21	Bought stationery from J Moore	60
„	23	Goods bought from H Noone	116
„	27	Received invoice for carriage inwards from D Flynn	62
„	31	Invoice for vehicle parts supplied during the month received from Kirk Motors	185

22.3A Draw up the relevant accounts in the purchases and general ledgers from the purchases analysis book you have completed for question 22.2.

Part IV

ADJUSTMENTS REQUIRED BEFORE PREPARING FINAL ACCOUNTS

23

Capital and revenue expenditure and receipts

23.1 Capital expenditure

Money spent to either:

1 buy fixed assets, or
2 add to the value of an existing fixed asset

is **capital expenditure**. Money spent to add to the value of fixed assets includes:

1 The cost of transporting the asset to the firm, if borne by the purchaser.
2 Legal costs associated with buying buildings.
3 Any other cost needed to get the fixed asset ready for use.

23.2 Revenue expenditure

Expenditure which does not increase the value of fixed assets, but is for running the business on a day-to-day basis, is known as **revenue expenditure**.

The difference can be seen clearly with the total cost of using a van for a firm. To buy a van is capital expenditure. The van will be in use for several years and is, therefore, a fixed asset.

To pay for petrol to use in the van for the next few days is revenue expenditure. This is because the expenditure is used up in a few days and does not add to the value of fixed assets.

23.3 Differences between capital expenditure and revenue expenditure

A few instances listed on the next page demonstrate the difference.

It can be seen that revenue expenditure is that chargeable to the trading or profit and loss account, while capital expenditure will result in increased figures for fixed assets in the balance sheet.

Item of Expenditure	Type of Expenditure
1 Buying a van	Capital
2 Petrol costs for the van	Revenue
3 Repairs to the van	Revenue
4 Putting extra spotlights on the van	Capital
5 Buying machinery	Capital
6 Electricity costs of using machinery	Revenue
7 We spent £1,500 on machinery. £1,000 was for an item added to the machine: £500 for repairs	Capital £1,000 Revenue £500
8 Painting the outside of a new building	Capital
9 Three years later – repainting the outside of the above building	Revenue

23.4 Capital expenditure: further analysis

Capital expenditure consists of not only the cost of purchasing fixed assets, but also includes other costs necessary to get those fixed assets operational. Some of the possible additional costs are now given:

(a) Delivery cost;
(b) Installation costs;
(c) Inspection and testing the fixed asset before use;
(d) Legal costs in purchasing property and land;
(e) Architects' fees for building plans and for supervising construction of buildings;
(f) Demolition costs to remove something before new building can begin.

23.5 Joint expenditure

Sometimes one item of expenditure constitutes both capital and revenue expenditure. An example is given below:

A builder was engaged to tackle some work on your premises, the total bill being for £3,000. If one-third of this was for repair work and two-thirds for improvements, £1,000 should be charged in the profit and loss account as revenue expenditure, and £2,000 identified as capital expenditure and, therefore, added to the value of premises and shown as such in the balance sheet.

23.6 Incorrect treatment of expenditure

If one of the following occurs:

1 Capital expenditure is incorrectly treated as revenue expenditure, or
2 Revenue expenditure is incorrectly treated as capital expenditure, then both the balance sheet figures and the trading and profit and loss account figures will be incorrect.

This means that the net profit figure will also be incorrect. If the expenditure affects items in the trading account, then the gross profit figure will also be incorrect.

23.7 Treatment of loan interest

If money is borrowed to finance the purchase of a fixed asset then interest will have to be paid on the loan. The loan interest however is *not* a cost of acquiring the asset, but is simply a cost of financing it. This means that loan interest is revenue expenditure and *not* capital expenditure.

23.8 Capital and revenue receipts

When an item of capital expenditure is sold, the receipt is called a capital receipt. Suppose that a van is bought for £5,000, and sold five years later for £750. The £5,000 was treated as capital expenditure. The £750 received is treated as a capital receipt.

Revenue receipts are sales or other revenue items, such as rent receivable or commissions receivable.

Review questions

In addition to the questions which follow, you should attempt questions 117–123 in the accompanying book of multiple-choice questions (see back cover for details).

Suggested solutions to review questions with the letter 'A' after the question number are given in Appendix I (page 616).

23.1A Some of the following items should be treated as capital and some as revenue. For each of them state which classification applies:

(i)   The purchase of machinery for use in the business.
(ii) Carriage paid to bring the machinery in (i) above to the works.
(iii) Complete redecoration of the premises at a cost of £1,500.
(iv) A quarterly account for heating.
(v)   The purchase of a soft drinks vending machine for the canteen with a stock of soft drinks.
(vi) Wages paid by a building contractor to his own workmen for the construction of an office in the builder's stockyard.

23.2 Indicate which of the following would be revenue items and which would be capital items in a wholesale bakery.

(*a*) Purchase of a new van.
(*b*) Purchase of a replacement engine for an existing van.
(*c*) Cost of altering the interior of the new van to increase its carrying capacity.
(*d*) Cost of road tax for the new van.
(*e*) Cost of road tax for an existing van.
(*f*) Cost of painting the firm's name on the new van.
(*g*) Repair and maintenance of an existing van.

23.3A For the business of J Charles, a wholesale chemist, classify the following between 'capital' and 'revenue' expenditure:

(*a*) Purchase of a new van.
(*b*) Cost of rebuilding a warehouse wall which had fallen down.
(*c*) Building an extension to the warehouse.
(*d*) Painting the extension to the above warehouse when it is first built.
(*e*) Repainting the extension to the warehouse three years later than that done in (*d*).
(*f*) Carriage costs on bricks for the new warehouse extension.
(*g*) Carriage costs on purchases.

(*h*) Carriage costs on sales.
(*i*) Legal costs of collecting debts.
(*j*) Legal costs related to acquiring a new office premises.
(*k*) Fire insurance premium.
(*l*) Costs of installing a new machine.

23.4 For the business of H Ward, a food merchant, classify the following between 'capital' and 'revenue' expenditure:

(*a*) Repairs to a meat slicer.
(*b*) New tyre for a van.
(*c*) Additional shop counter.
(*d*) Renewing signwriting on the shop.
(*e*) Fitting partitions in the shop.
(*f*) Roof repairs.
(*g*) Installing security equipment.
(*h*) Wages of a shop assistant.
(*i*) Carriage on returns outwards.
(*j*) New cash register.
(*k*) Repairs to the office safe.
(*l*) Installing an extra toilet.

23.5A
(*a*) Distinguish between capital and revenue expenditure.
(*b*) Napa Ltd took delivery of a microcomputer and printer on 1 July 19X6, the beginning of its financial year. The list price of the equipment was £4,999 but Napa Ltd was able to negotiate a price of £4,000 with the supplier. However, the supplier charged an additional £340 to install and test the equipment. The supplier offered a 5% discount if Napa Ltd paid for the equipment and the additional installation costs within seven days. Napa Ltd was able to take advantage of this additional discount. The installation of special electrical wiring for the computer cost £110. After initial testing certain modifications costing £199 proved necessary. Staff were sent on special training courses to operate the microcomputer and this cost £990. Napa Ltd insured the machine against fire and theft at a cost of £49 per annum. A maintenance agreement was entered into with Sonoma plc. Under this agreement Sonoma plc promised to provide 24 hour breakdown cover for one year. The cost of the maintenance agreement was £350.

Required:
Calculate the acquisition cost of the microcomputer to Napa Ltd.

(*c*) The following costs were also incurred by Napa Ltd during the financial year ended 30 June 19X7:

(1) Interest on loan to purchase microcomputer.
(2) Cost of software for use with the microcomputer.
(3) Cost of customising the software for use in Napa Ltd's business.
(4) Cost of paper used by the computer printer.
(5) Wages of computer operators.
(6) Cost of ribbons used by the computer printer.
(7) Cost of adding extra memory to the microcomputer.
(8) Cost of floppy discs used during the year.
(9) Costs of adding a manufacturer's upgrade to the microcomputer equipment.
(10) Cost of adding air conditioning to the computer room.

Required:
Classify each of the above as either capital expenditure or revenue expenditure.

(*Association of Accounting Technicians*)

23.6 Declan McGrath, a new client of your firm, has asked you to send him a brief letter to explain why capital expenditure and revenue expenditure are distinguished from each other.

Required:
Draft a *brief* letter to Mr McGrath explaining the distinction between capital expenditure and revenue expenditure and the reasons for the distinction, and outlining how each type of expenditure will be dealt with in his accounts.

(IATI Foundation Examination)

23.7 Sema plc, a company in the heavy engineering industry, carried out an expansion programme in the 19X6 financial year, in order to meet a permanent increase in contracts.

The company selected a suitable site and commissioned a survey and valuation report, for which the fee was £1,500. On the basis of the report the site was acquired for £90,000.

Solicitor's fees for drawing up the contract and conveyancing were £3,000.

Fees of £8,700 were paid to the architects for preparing the building plans and overseeing the building work. This was carried out partly by the company's own workforce (at a wages cost of £11,600), using company building materials (cost £76,800) and partly by sub-contractors who charged £69,400, of which £4,700 related to the demolition of an existing building on the same site.

The completed building housed two hydraulic presses.

The cost of press A was £97,000 (ex works), payable in a single lump sum two months after installation. Sema was given a trade discount of 10% and a cash discount for prompt payment of 2%. Hire of a transporter to collect the press and to convey it to the new building was £2,900. Installation costs were £2,310, including hire of lifting gear, £1,400.

Press B would have cost £105,800 (delivered) if it had been paid in one lump sum. However, Sema opted to pay three equal annual instalments of £40,000, starting on the date of acquisition. Installation costs were £2,550, including hire of lifting gear, £1,750.

The whole of the above expenditure was financed by the issue of £500,000 7% Debentures (on which the annual interest payable was £35,000).

Before the above acquisitions were taken into account, the balances (at cost) on the fixed asset accounts for premises and plant were £521,100 and £407,500 respectively.

Required:
(a) Using such of the above information as is relevant, post and balance the premises and plant accounts for the 19X6 financial year.
(b) State, with reasons, which of the given information you have not used in your answer to (a) above.

(Association of Chartered Certified Accountants)

Authors' note: The issue of 7% debentures is similar to the raising of a loan at an annual interest rate of 7%.

24

Depreciation of fixed assets I: Nature and calculations

24.1 The nature of fixed assets

As already seen in section 9.4, fixed assets are those assets of significant value which:
- are of long life, and
- are to be used in the business, and
- are not bought with the intention of being re-sold.

24.2 Depreciation of fixed assets

However, fixed assets such as machinery, vans, fixtures and even buildings, do not last for ever. If the amount received (if any) when they are disposed of is deducted from the cost of buying them, the difference is called **depreciation**.

The only time that depreciation can be calculated accurately is when the fixed asset is disposed of, and the difference between the cost to its owner and the amount received on disposal is then calculated. If a van was bought for £10,000 and sold five years later for £2,000, then the amount of depreciation is £10,000 – £2,000 = £8,000.

24.3 Depreciation is an expense

Depreciation is the part of the cost of the fixed asset consumed during its period of use by the firm. It is an expense for services consumed in the same way as expenses for items such as wages, rent or electricity. Because it is an expense, depreciation will have to be charged to the profit and loss account, and will therefore reduce net profit.

You can see that the only real difference between the cost of depreciation for a motor vehicle and the cost of petrol for the motor vehicle is that the petrol cost is used up in a day or two, whereas the cost for the motor vehicle is spread over several years. Both costs are costs of the business.

24.4 Causes of depreciation

The principal causes of deprecation are physical deterioration, economic factors, the time factor and depletion. Let us look at these in more detail.

Physical deterioration

1 **Wear and tear.** When a vehicle, machinery or fixtures and fittings are used they eventually wear out. Some last many years, others last only a few years. This is also true of buildings, although some may last for a long time.
2 **Erosion, rust, rot and decay.** Land may be eroded or wasted away by the action of wind, rain, sun and other elements of nature. Similarly, the metals in vehicles or machinery will rust away. Wood will rot eventually. Decay is a process which will also be present due to the elements of nature and the lack of proper attention.

Economic factors

These may be said to be the reasons for an asset being put out of use even though it is in good physical condition. The two main factors are usually **obsolescence** and **inadequacy**.

1 **Obsolescence.** This is the process of becoming obsolete or out of date. For example, propeller-driven aeroplanes, which, although in good physical condition, were made obsolete by the introduction of jet aircraft. The propeller-driven aircraft were put out of use by large airlines when they still had quite a few more years of potential use, because the newer aircraft were more suited to the needs of the airlines.
2 **Inadequacy.** This is when an asset is no longer used because of the growth and changes in the size of the firm. For instance, a small ferryboat that is operated by a firm at a seaside resort is entirely inadequate when the resort becomes more popular. It is found that it would be more efficient and economical to operate a large ferryboat, and so the smaller boat is put out of use by the firm.

Both obsolescence and inadequacy do not necessarily mean that the asset is destroyed. It is merely put out of use by the firm. Another firm will often buy it. For example, many of the aeroplanes no longer used by large airlines are bought by smaller firms.

The time factor

Wear and tear, erosion, obsolescence and inadequacy take time. However, there are fixed assets to which the time factor is connected in a different way. These are assets which have a legal life fixed in terms of years.

For instance, you may agree to rent some buildings for 10 years. This is normally called a lease. When the years are finished the lease is worth nothing to you, as it has finished. Whatever you paid for the lease is now of no value.

A similar asset is where you buy a patent with complete rights so that only you are able to produce something. When the patent's life has finished it has no value.

Instead of using the term depreciation, the term *amortisation* is often used for these assets.

Depletion

Some assets are of a 'wasting' character, perhaps due to the extraction of raw materials from them. These materials are then either used by the firm to make something else, or are sold in their raw state to other firms. Natural resources such as mines, quarries and oil wells come under this heading. **Depletion** is the term used to describe the consumption of an asset of a wasting character.

24.5 Land and buildings

Statement of Standard Accounting Practice No. 12 (SSAP 12) contains the rules which accountants must follow in relation to depreciation. It states that all property, except freehold land (i.e. land owned outright rather than leased), must be depreciated. This is because land does not normally fall in value over time. Buildings, however, do eventually fall into disrepair and therefore should be subject to a charge for depreciation each year over their expected useful economic life.

24.6 Appreciation

At this stage of the chapter readers may well begin to ask themselves about the assets that increase (appreciate) in value. The answer to this is that normal accounting procedure would be to ignore any such appreciation, as to bring appreciation into account would be to contravene both the cost concept and the prudence concept as discussed in Chapter 11. Nevertheless, in certain circumstances appreciation is taken into account in partnership and limited company accounts, but this is left until partnerships and limited companies are considered in Parts V and VI respectively.

24.7 Provision for depreciation as an allocation of cost

Depreciation in total over the life of an asset can be calculated quite simply as cost less any amount receivable when the asset is put out of use by the firm. If the item is bought and sold within the one accounting period, then the depreciation for that period is charged as a revenue expense in arriving at that period's Net Profit. The difficulties start when the asset is used for more than one accounting period, and an attempt has to be made to charge each period with an amount of depreciation appropriate to that period.

Even though depreciation provisions are generally regarded as allocating the cost of fixed assets over each accounting period benefiting from their use, it does not follow that there is any single correct method of doing this. All that can be said is that the cost should be allocated over the life of the asset in such a way as to charge it as equitably as possible to the periods in which the asset is used. The difficulties involved, some of which are listed below, are considerable.

1 How can a firm accurately assess the useful economic life of most assets?
2 How is 'use' measured? For example, a car owned by a firm for two years may have been driven one year by a very careful driver and another year by a reckless driver. The standard of driving will affect the car and also the amount which it can be sold for. How should such a firm apportion the car's depreciation costs?
3 There are other expenses besides depreciation such as repairs and maintenance of fixed assets. As both of these affect the rate and amount of depreciation should they not also affect the depreciation provision calculations?
4 How should a firm estimate the amount it will receive when it sells an asset when it doesn't know with certainty when this will be?

These are only some of the difficulties. Therefore, the methods of calculating provisions for depreciation are mainly accounting conventions rather than scientifically correct formulae.

24.8 Principal methods of calculating depreciation charges

The two main methods of calculating depreciation are the **straight line method** and the **reducing balance method**. The straight line method is the one which is the most widely used in practice.

The straight line method of calculating depreciation

Using this method, estimates are made both of the number of years for which each fixed asset is likely to be used and of the amount for which each asset is likely to be sold at the end of that period. The cost of the asset less the estimated **residual value** (the amount for which it is likely to be sold) is then divided by the estimated useful economic life of the asset to get the annual depreciation charge.

For example, if a delivery van was bought for £22,000, we thought we would keep it for four years and then sell it for £2,000, the depreciation to be charged would be:

$$\frac{\text{Cost (£22,000)} - \text{Estimated disposal value (£2,000)}}{\text{Estimated number of years of use (4)}} = \frac{£20,000}{4}$$

= £5,000 each year for four years.

If, after four years, the van would have had no disposal value, the charge for depreciation would have been:

$$\frac{\text{Cost (£22,000)}}{\text{Number of years use (4)}} = \frac{£22,000}{4}$$

= £5,500 each year for four years.

The reducing balance method of calculating depreciation

Using this method the depreciation charge is a fixed percentage of the cost of the asset in the first year. In the second or later years the same percentage is taken of the reduced balance (i.e. the cost *less* depreciation already charged).

For example, if a machine is bought for £10,000, and depreciation is to be charged at 20 per cent per annum using the reducing balance method, the calculations for the first three years would be as follows:

	£
Cost	10,000
First year: depreciation (20%)	2,000
	8,000
Second year: depreciation (20% of £8,000)	1,600
	6,400
Third year: depreciation (20% of £6,400)	1,280
	5,120

The formula used to find the percentage which must be used to fully depreciate an asset over a specified number of years using the reducing balance method is:

$$r = 1 - \sqrt[n]{\frac{s}{c}}$$

where
$r =$ the rate of depreciation to be applied
$n =$ the number of years which the asset is expected to be used for
$s =$ the net residual value (this must be a significant amount or the answers will be absurd, since the depreciation rate would amount to nearly one)
$c =$ the cost of the asset

For example, for an asset which cost £10,000, is expected to be used for 4 years and has an estimated residual value of £256 the percentage rate of depreciation which has to be applied in order to charge £9,744 depreciation (£10,000 – £256) over 4 years using the reducing balance method is:

$$r = 1 - \sqrt[4]{\frac{256}{£10,000}} = 1 - \frac{4}{10} = 0.6 \ or \ 60\%$$

The depreciation calculation applied to each of the four years of use would be:

	£
Cost	10,000
Year 1: Depreciation provision 60% of £10,000	6,000
Cost not yet apportioned, end of Year 1 (= Net book value)	4,000
Year 2: Depreciation provision 60% of £4,000	2,400
Cost not yet apportioned, end of Year 2 (= Net book value)	1,600
Year 3: Depreciation provision 60% of £1,600	960
Cost not yet apportioned, end of Year 3 (= Net book value)	640
Year 4: Depreciation provision 60% of £640	384
Cost not yet apportioned, end of Year 4 (= Estimated Residual Value).	256

In this case the percentage to be applied worked out conveniently to a round figure. However, the answer will often come out to several places of decimals. In this case it would be usual to take the nearest integer as the percentage to be applied.

The percentage to be applied, assuming a significant amount for residual value, is usually between two to three times greater for the reducing balance method than for the straight line method.

The advocates of this method usually argue that it helps to even out the total amount charged as expenses for the use of the asset each year. They state that provisions for depreciation are not the only costs charged, there are the running costs in addition and that the repairs and maintenance element of running costs usually increase with age. Therefore, to equate total usage costs for each year of use the depreciation provisions should fall as the repairs and maintenance element increases. However, as can be seen from the figures of the example already given, the repairs and maintenance element would have to be comparatively large to bring about an equal total charge for each year of use.

To summarise, the people who favour this method argue that:

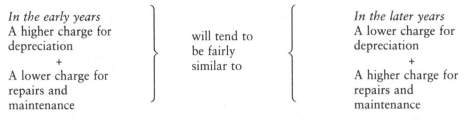

In the early years A higher charge for depreciation + A lower charge for repairs and maintenance	will tend to be fairly similar to	*In the later years* A lower charge for depreciation + A higher charge for repairs and maintenance

24.9 Choice of method of charging depreciation

No particular method of calculating depreciation is specified either by SSAP 12 or by law. Therefore, a business can choose whichever method it prefers.

The purpose of depreciation is to spread the total cost of an asset over the periods in which it is available to be used. The method chosen should be that which allocates the cost to each period in accordance with the amount of benefit gained from the use of the asset in that period.

If, therefore, the main value is to be obtained from the asset in its earliest years, it may be appropriate to use the reducing balance method which charges more in the early years. If, on the other hand, the benefits are to be gained evenly over the years, then the straight line method would be more appropriate.

The repairs and maintenance factor also has to be taken into account. One argument has already been mentioned in the last section.

Exhibit 24.1 gives a comparison of the calculations using the two methods, using the same initial cost.

Exhibit 24.1

A firm has just bought a machine for £8,000. It will be kept in use for four years, then it will be disposed of for an estimated amount of £500.

Using the straight line method depreciation of (£8,000 – £500) ÷ 4 = £1,875 per annum will be charged. For the reducing balance method a rate of 50%, calculated by applying the formula in section 24.8, will be used.

	Method 1 Straight Line £		Method 2 Reducing Balance £
Cost	8,000		8,000
Depreciation: year 1	1,875	(50% of £8,000)	4,000
	6,125		4,000
Depreciation: year 2	1,875	(50% of £4,000)	2,000
	4,250		2,000
Depreciation: year 3	1,875	(50% of £2,000)	1,000
	2,375		1,000
Depreciation: year 4	1,875	(50% of £1,000)	500
Estimated residual value	500		500

This illustrates the fact that using the reducing balance method has a much higher charge for depreciation in the early years, and lower charges in the later years.

Another name for the reducing balance method is the **diminishing balance method.**

24.10 Depreciation provisions and assets bought or sold

There are two main methods of calculating depreciation provisions for assets bought or sold during an accounting period.

1 To ignore the dates during the year in which the assets were bought or sold, merely calculating a full period's depreciation on the assets in use at the end of the period. Thus, assets sold during the accounting period will have had no provision for depreciation made for that last period irrespective of how many months they were in use. Conversely, assets bought during the period will have a full period of depreciation provision calculated even though they may not have been owned throughout the whole of the period.

2 Provision for depreciation made on the basis of one month's ownership, one month's provision for depreciation. Fractions of months are usually ignored. This is obviously a more scientific method than that described in 1 above.

For examination purposes, where the dates on which assets are bought and sold are shown, then Method 2 is the method expected by the examiner. If no such dates are given, then obviously Method 1 will have to be used. Sometimes, however, you may be given the dates of purchases and sales but also told only to depreciate assets owned at the end of the period. In this case, Method 1 should be used.

24.11 Other methods of calculating depreciation

There are many more methods of calculating depreciation but they are beyond the scope of this chapter. These are fully considered in Chapter 48. You will find the revaluation method, the depletion unit method, the machine hour method, the sum of the year's digits method and the units of output method there.

Review questions

In addition to the questions which follow, you should attempt questions 124–139 in the accompanying book of multiple-choice questions (see back cover for details).

Suggested solutions to review questions with the letter 'A' after the question number are given in Appendix I (page 616).

24.1A D Sankey, a manufacturer, purchases a lathe for £4,000. It has an estimated life of five years and an estimated scrap value of £500.

Sankey is not certain whether he should use the straight line method or the reducing balance method for the purpose of calculating depreciation on the machine.

You are required to calculate the depreciation on the lathe using both methods, showing clearly the cost less the accumulated depreciation at the end of each of the five years for both methods. (Assume that 40% per annum is to be used for the reducing balance method.)

24.2A A machine costs £12,500. It will be kept for four years, and then sold for an estimated figure of £5,120. Show the calculations of the figures for depreciation (to the nearest £) for each of the four years using (*a*) the straight line method, (*b*) the reducing balance method, using a depreciation rate of 20% for (*b*).

24.3A A vehicle costs £6,400. It will be kept for five years, and then sold for £200. Calculate the depreciation for each year using (*a*) the reducing balance method, using a depreciation rate of 50%, (*b*) the straight line method.

24.4 A machine costs £5,120. It will be kept for five years, and then sold for an estimated £1,215. Show the calculations of the figures for depreciation for each year using (*a*) the straight line method, (*b*) the reducing balance method, for this method using a depreciation rate of 25%.

24.5 A bulldozer costs £12,150. It will be kept for five years. At the end of that time agreement has already been made that it will be sold for £1,600. Show your calculations of the amount of depreciation each year (*a*) if the reducing balance method at a rate of 33⅓% was used, and (*b*) the straight line method was used.

24.6 A tractor is bought for £6,000. It will be used for three years, and then sold back to the supplier for £3,072. Show the depreciation calculations for each year using (*a*) the reducing balance method using a rate of 20%, and (*b*) the straight line method.

24.7A A company, which prepares its accounts annually to 31 December, provides for depreciation of its machinery at the rate of 10% per annum using the diminishing balance method.

On 31 December 1997, the machinery consisted of the following three items.

Date purchased	Item	Cost (£)
1 January 1995	Machine A	3,000
1 April 1996	Machine B	2,000
1 July 1997	Machine C	1,000

Required:
Your calculations showing the depreciation provision for 1997.

24.8

(i)   What is the purpose of the depreciation charge in accounts?

(ii) Critically evaluate the statement that the purpose of depreciation is to provide for the replacement of fixed assets.

(iii) Explain why it was considered necessary to introduce an accounting standard concerning depreciation.

24.9

(a) Explain what is meant by the term depreciation.

(b) Why should buildings be depreciated even though they may be appreciating (increasing) in value?

(c) Why should the cost of leasehold land be depreciated but the cost of freehold land not be depreciated?

(d) Which of the following costs, incurred in the acquisition and maintenance of plant and machinery, should be included in the capital cost of the plant and machinery and which should not?

  (i)   Original cost of plant and machinery

  (ii) Delivery costs of plant and machinery

  (iii) Installation costs of plant and machinery

  (iv) Repairs to plant and machinery

  (v)   Wages of maintenance staff

  (vi) Recoverable VAT paid on the acquisition of plant and machinery

(*IATI Admission Examination*)

24.10 Jackal Ltd, a manufacturing company, stated its accounting policy in respect of depreciation of fixed assets in its draft accounts as follows:

"*Depreciation:* Freehold land, leasehold land and freehold buildings are not depreciated. All other tangible fixed assets are depreciated by equal annual instalments over their estimated useful lives."

Required:
Draft a letter to the Managing Director of Jackal Ltd in which you should:

(a) define depreciation;

(b) comment on whether the above accounting policy adopted by Jackal Ltd complies with the requirements of SSAP 12 'Accounting for Depreciation', and, if not, in what respects it does not comply; and

(c) set out the principal disclosure requirements of SSAP 12 'Accounting for Depreciation'.

(*IATI Admission Examination*)

25

Depreciation of fixed assets II: Double entry records

Fixed asset accounts are always kept for showing the assets at cost price. The depreciation is shown accumulating in a separate 'provision for depreciation' account.

Example

In a business with financial years ended 31 December a machine is bought for £2,000 on 1 January 1995. It is to be depreciated at the rate of 20% per annum using the reducing balance method. The records for the first three years are now shown.

No entry is made in the asset account for depreciation. Instead, the depreciation is shown accumulating in a separate account.

The double entry is:
  Debit the profit and loss account
  Credit the provision for depreciation account

Machinery

1995	£		
Jan 1 Bank	2,000		

Provision for Depreciation – Machinery

1995		£	1995		£
Dec 31 Balance c/d		400	Dec 31 Profit and Loss		400
1996			1996		
Dec 31 Balance c/d		720	Jan 1 Balance b/d		400
			Dec 31 Profit and Loss		320
		720			720
1997			1997		
Dec 31 Balance c/d		976	Jan 1 Balance b/d		720
			Dec 31 Profit and Loss		256
		976			976
			1998		
			Jan 1 Balance b/d		976

Profit and Loss Account for the years ended 31 December

		£
1995	Depreciation	400
1996	Depreciation	320
1997	Depreciation	256

Now the balance on the Machinery Account is shown on the balance sheet at the end of each year less the balance on the Provision for Depreciation Account.

Balance Sheets

	£	£
As at 31 December 1995		
Machinery at cost	2,000	
less Depreciation to date	400	
		1,600
As at 31 December 1996		
Machinery at cost	2,000	
less Depreciation to date	720	
		1,280
As at 31 December 1997		
Machinery at cost	2,000	
less Depreciation to date	976	
		1,024

25.2 The disposal of a fixed asset

When we charge depreciation on a fixed asset we are having to make guesses. We cannot be absolutely certain how long we will keep the asset in use, nor can we be certain at the date of purchase how much cash will be received for the asset when we dispose of it. To get our guesses absolutely correct would be quite rare. This means that when we dispose of an asset, the cash received for it is usually different from our original guess.

This can be shown by looking back at the illustration already shown in this chapter. At the end of 1997 the value of the machinery on the balance sheet is shown as £1,024. We can now see the entries needed if (1) the machinery was sold on 2 January 1998 for £1,070 and then (2) if instead it had been sold for £950.

(a)	Transfer the cost price of the asset sold to an Asset Disposal Account (in this case a Machinery Disposals Account).	(Dr) (Cr)	Machinery Disposals Account Machinery Account
(b)	Transfer the depreciation already charged to the Asset Disposal Account.	(Dr) (Cr)	Provisions for Depreciation – Machinery Machinery Disposals Account
(c)	For remittance received on disposal.	(Dr) (Cr)	Cash Book Machinery Disposals Account
(d)	Transfer the balance (difference) on Machinery Disposals Account to the Profit and Loss Account.		
	If the difference is on the debit side of the disposal account, it is a profit on sale.	(Dr) (Cr)	Machinery Disposals Account Profit and Loss Account
	If the difference is on the credit side of the disposal account, it is a loss on sale.	(Dr) (Cr)	Profit and Loss Account Machinery Disposals Account

1 Asset sold at a profit

Machinery

1995			£	1995			£
Jan	1	Bank	2,000	Dec	31	Balance c/d	2,000
1996				1996			
Jan	1	Balance b/d	2,000	Dec	31	Balance c/d	2,000
1997				1997			
Jan	1	Balance b/d	2,000	Dec	31	Balance c/d	2,000
1998				1998			
Jan	1	Balance b/d	2,000	Jan	2	Machinery disposals *(a)*	2,000

Provision for Depreciation: Machinery

1998				£	1998			£
Jan	2	Machinery disposals	*(b)*	976	Jan	1	Balance b/d	976

Machinery Disposals

1998				£	1998				£
Jan	2	Machinery	*(a)*	2,000	Jan	2	Bank	*(c)*	1,070
Dec	31	Profit and loss	*(d)*	46	Jan	2	Provision for depreciation	*(b)*	976
				2,046					2,046

Profit and Loss Account for the year ended 31 December 1998

		£
Profit on sale of machinery	*(d)*	46

2 Asset sold at a loss

Machinery

1995			£	1995			£
Jan	1	Bank	2,000	Dec	31	Balance c/d	2,000
1996				1996			
Jan	1	Balance b/d	2,000	Dec	31	Balance c/d	2,000
1997				1997			
Jan	1	Balance b/d	2,000	Dec	31	Balance c/d	2,000
1998				1998			
Jan	1	Balance b/d	2,000	Jan	2	Machinery disposals *(a)*	2,000

Provision for Depreciation: Machinery

1998				£	1998			£
Jan	2	Machinery disposals	*(b)*	976	Jan	1	Balance b/d	976

Machinery Disposals

1998			£	1998				£
Jan	2	Machinery	(a) 2,000	Jan	2	Bank	(c)	950
				Jan	2	Provision for depreciation	(b)	976
				Dec	31	Profit and loss	(d)	74
			2,000					2,000

Profit and Loss Account for the year ended 31 December 1994

		£
Loss on sale of machinery	(d)	74

In many cases the disposal of an asset will mean that we have sold it. This will not always be the case. An existing car may be traded in against the purchase of a new car. Here the disposal value is the exchange value. If a new car costing £10,000 was to be paid for by £6,000 in cash and £4,000 for the old car, then the disposal value of the old car is £4,000.

Similarly a car may have been in an accident and now be worthless. If insured, the disposal value will be the amount received from the insurance company. If an asset is scrapped, the disposal value is that received from the sale of the scrap, which may be nil.

25.3 Change of depreciation method

It is possible to change the method of calculating depreciation. This should not be done frequently, and it should only be undertaken after a thorough review. Where the method is changed the effect, if material (*see* Chapter 11 on materiality), should be shown as a note to the final accounts in the year of change.

Further examples

So far the examples shown have deliberately been kept simple. Only one item of an asset has been shown in each case. Exhibits 25.1 and 25.2 give examples of more complicated cases.

Exhibit 25.1

A machine is bought on 1 January 1995 for £1,000 and another one on 1 October 1996 for £1,200. The first machine is sold on 30 June 1997 for £720. The firm's financial year ends on 31 December. The machinery is to be depreciated at 10%, using the straight line method and based on assets in existence at the end of each year ignoring items sold during the year.

Machinery

1995		£	1995		£
Jan 1 Bank		1,000	Dec 31 Balance c/d		1,000
1996			1996		
Jan 1 Balance b/d		1,000			
Oct 1 Bank		1,200	Dec 31 Balance c/d		2,200
		2,200			2,200
1997			1997		
Jan 1 Balance b/d		2,200	Jun 30 Machinery disposals		1,000
			Dec 31 Balance c/d		1,200
		2,200			2,200
1994					
Jan 1 Balance b/d		1,200			

Provision for Depreciation – Machinery

		£	1995		£
			Dec 31 Profit and Loss		100
1996			1996		
Dec 31 Balance c/d		320	Dec 31 Profit and loss		220
		320			320
1997			1997		
Jun 30 Disposals			Jan 1 Balance b/d		320
(2 years × 10%			Dec 31 Profit and loss		120
× £1,000)		200			
Dec 31 Balance c/d		240			
		440			440
			1998		
			Jan 1 Balance b/d		240

Disposals of Machinery

1997		£	1997		£
Jun 30 Machinery		1,000	Jun 30 Bank		720
			Jun 30 Provision for		
			depreciation		200
			Dec 31 Profit and loss		80
		1,000			1,000

Profit and Loss Account for the years ended 31 December

		£
1995	Provision for depreciation	100
1996	Provision for depreciation	220
1997	Provision for depreciation	120
	Loss on machinery sold	80

Balance Sheet (extracts) as at 31 December

		£	£
1995	Machinery at cost price	1,000	
	less Depreciation to date	100	
			900
1996	Machinery at cost	2,200	
	less Depreciation to date	320	
			1,880
1997	Machinery at cost	1,200	
	less Depreciation to date	240	
			960

Another example can now be given. This is somewhat more complicated owing first to a greater number of items, and second because the depreciation provisions are calculated on a proportionate basis, i.e. one month's depreciation for every one month's ownership.

Exhibit 25.2

A business with its financial year end being 31 December buys two items of office equipment, No 1 for £800 and No 2 for £500, both on 1 January 1993. It also buys another, No 3, on 1 July 1995 for £900 and another, No 4, on 1 October 1995 for £720. The first two items are sold, No 1 for £229 on 30 September 1996, and the other No 2, was sold for scrap £5 on 30 June 1997.

Depreciation is on the straight line basis, 20% per annum, ignoring scrap value in this particular case when calculating depreciation per annum. Show the extracts from the assets account, provision for depreciation account, disposal account, profit and loss account for the years ended 31 December 1993, 1994, 1995, 1996, and 1997, and the balance sheets as at those dates.

Office Equipment

1993			£	1993			£
Jan	1	Bank	1,300	Dec	31	Balance c/d	1,300
1994				1994			
Jan	1	Balance b/d	1,300	Dec	31	Balance c/d	1,300
1995				1995			
Jan	1	Balance b/d	1,300				
July	1	Bank	900				
Oct	1	Bank	720	Dec	31	Balance c/d	2,920
			2,920				2,920
1996				1996			
Jan	1	Balance b/d	2,920	Sept	30	Disposals	800
				Dec	31	Balance c/d	2,120
			2,920				2,920
1997				1997			
Jan	1	Balance b/d	2,120	June	30	Disposals	500
				Dec	31	Balance c/d	1,620
			2,120				2,120
1998							
Jan	1	Balance b/d	1,620				

Provision for Depreciation – Office Equipment

1993		£	1993		£
Dec 31	Balance c/d	260	Dec 31	Profit and loss	260
1994			1994		
			Jan 1	Balance b/d	260
Dec 31	Balance c/d	520	Dec 31	Profit and loss	260
		520			520
1995			1995		
			Jan 1	Balance b/d	520
Dec 31	Balance c/d	906	Dec 31	Profit and loss	386
		906			906
1996			1996		
Sept 30	Disposals	600	Jan 1	Balance b/d	906
Dec 31	Balance c/d	850	Dec 31	Profit and loss	544
		1,450			1,450
1997			1997		
June 30	Disposals	450	Jan 1	Balance b/d	850
Dec 31	Balance c/d	774	Dec 31	Profit and loss	374
		1,224			1,224
			1998		
			Jan 1	Balance b/d	774

Workings – depreciation provisions

		£	£
1993	20% of £1,300		260
1994	20% of £1,300		260
1995	20% of £1,300 × 12 months	260	
	20% of £900 × 6 months	90	
	20% of £720 × 3 months	36	386
1996	20% of £2,120 × 12 months	424	
	20% of £800 × 9 months	120	544
1997	20% of £1,620 × 12 months	324	
	20% of £500 × 6 months	50	374

Workings – transfers of depreciation provisions to disposal account

Item 1 Bought Jan 1 1993 Cost £800
Sold Sept 30 1996
Period of ownership 3¾ years
Depreciation provisions 3¾ × 20% × £800 = £600

Item 2 Bought Jan 1 1993 Cost £500
Sold June 30 1996
Period of ownership 4½ years
Depreciation provisions 4½ × 20% × £500 = £450

Disposals of Office Equipment

1996		£	1996		£
Sept 30	Office equipment	800	Sept 30	Provision for depreciation	600
Dec 31	Profit and loss	29	„ „	Bank	229
		829			829
1997			1997		
Jun 30	Office equipment	500	Jun 30	Provision for depreciation	450
			„ „	Bank	5
			Dec 31	Profit and loss	45
		500			500

Profit and Loss Account for the years ended 31 December (extracts)

		£
1993	Provision for depreciation	(260)
1994	Provision for depreciation	(260)
1995	Provision for depreciation	(386)
1996	Provision for depreciation	(544)
	Profit on equipment sold	29
1997	Provision for depreciation	(374)
	Loss on equipment sold	(45)

Balance Sheets (extracts) as at 31 December

		£	£
1993	Equipment at cost	1,300	
	less Provision for depreciation	260	
			1,040
1994	Equipment at cost	1,300	
	less Provision for depreciation	520	
			780
1995	Equipment at cost	2,920	
	less Provision for depreciation	906	
			2,014
1996	Equipment at cost	2,120	
	less Provision for depreciation	850	
			1,270
1997	Equipment at cost	1,620	
	less Provision for depreciation	774	
			846

25.4 Depreciation provisions and the replacement of assets

Making a provision for depreciation does not mean that the amount charged is invested somewhere to finance the replacement of the asset when it is put out of use. It is simply a bookkeeping entry, and the end result is that lower net profits are shown because the provisions have been charged to the profit and loss account.

It is not surprising to find that people who have not studied accounting misunderstand the situation. They often think that a provision is the same as money kept somewhere with which to replace the asset eventually.

On the other hand, lower net profits may also mean lower drawings by the proprietor. If this is so, then there will be more money in the bank with which to replace the asset. However, there is no guarantee that lower net profits mean lower drawings.

Review questions

In addition to the questions which follow, you should attempt questions 140–151 in the accompanying book of multiple-choice questions (see back cover for details).

Suggested solutions to review questions with the letter 'A' after the question number are given in Appendix I (pages 617–20).

25.1A A company started in business on 1 January. You are to write up the computers account and the provision for depreciation of computers account for the year ended 31 December from the information given below. Depreciation is at the rate of 20% per annum, using the basis of one month's ownership means one month's depreciation.

> Bought two computers for £1,200 each on 1 January
> Bought one computer for £1,400 on 1 July

25.2A A company started in business on 1 January 1994, its financial year end being 31 December. You are to show:

(a) The machinery account
(b) The provision for depreciation of machinery account
(c) The balance sheet extracts for each of the years 1994, 1995, 1996 and 1997.

The machinery bought was:

1994	1 January	1 machine costing £800
1995	1 July	2 machines costing £500 each
	1 October	1 machine costing £600
1997	1 April	1 machine costing £200

Depreciation is at the rate of 10% per annum, using the straight line method, machines being depreciated for each proportion of a year for which they are owned.

25.3 A company maintains its fixed asset accounts at cost. Depreciation provision accounts, one for each type of asset, are in use. Machinery is to be depreciated at the rate of 12½% per annum, and fixtures at the rate of 10% per annum, using the reducing balance method. Depreciation is to be calculated on assets in existence at the end of each year, charging a full year's depreciation even though the asset was bought part of the way through the year. The following transactions in assets have taken place:

1996	1 January	Bought machinery £640, Fixtures £100
	1 July	Bought fixtures £200
1997	1 October	Bought machinery £720
	1 December	Bought fixtures £50

The financial year end of the business is 31 December.

You are to show:

(a) The machinery account.
(b) The fixtures account.
(c) The two separate provision for depreciation accounts.
(d) The fixed assets section of the balance sheet at the end of each year, for the years ended 31 December 1996 and 1997.

25.4
(a) List some reasons why depreciation may occur.
(b) Illustrate how depreciation provisions are an application of the consistency concept.
(c) Explain why depreciation provisions are based on estimates as well as facts rather than facts alone.
(d) Illustrate the effects which depreciation has on the final accounts of businesses.

25.5A A company maintains its fixed asset accounts at cost. Depreciation provision accounts for each asset are kept.

At 31 December 1996 the position was as follows:

	Total cost to date	Total depreciation to date
	£	£
Machinery	52,590	25,670
Office Furniture	2,860	1,490

The following additions were made during 1997:

Machinery £2,480, office furniture £320
Some old machines bought in 1993 for £2,800 were sold for £800 during the year.
The rates of depreciation are:
Machinery 10%, office furniture 5%, both using the straight line basis and calculated on the assets in existence at the end of each financial year irrespective of the date of purchase.

You are required to show the asset and depreciation accounts for the year ended 31 December 1997 and the related balance sheet entries at that date.

25.6A
(a) Identify four factors which cause fixed assets to depreciate.
(b) Which one of these factors is the most important for each of the following assets?

(i) a gold mine,
(ii) a motor lorry,
(iii) a 50 year lease on a building,
(iv) land,
(v) a ship used to ferry passengers and vehicles across a river following the building of a bridge across the river,
(vi) a franchise to market a new computer software package in a certain country.

(c) The financial year of Ochre Ltd will end on 31 December 19X6. At 1 January 19X6 the company had in use equipment with a total accumulated cost of £135,620 which had been depreciated by a total of £81,374. During the year ended 31 December 19X6 Ochre Ltd purchased new equipment costing £47,800 and sold off equipment which had originally cost £36,000 and which had been depreciated by £28,224 for £5,700. No further purchases or sales of equipment are planned for December. The policy of the company is to depreciate equipment at 40% using the diminishing balance method. A full year's depreciation is provided for on all equipment in use by the company at the end of each year.

Required:
Show the following ledger accounts for the year ended 31 December 19X6:

(i) the Equipment Account.
(ii) the Provision for Depreciation on Equipment Account.
(iii) the Assets Disposals Account.

(*Association of Accounting Technicians*)

25.7 Mavron plc owned the following vehicles as at 1 April 19X6:

Vehicle	Date acquired	Cost	Estimated residual value	Estimated life (years)
		£	£	
AAT 101	1 October 19X3	8,500	2,500	5
DJH 202	1 April 19X4	12,000	2,000	8

Mavron plc's policy is to provide at the end of each financial year depreciation using the straight line method applied on a month-by-month basis on all motor vehicles used during the year.

During the financial year ended 31 March 19X7 the following occurred:

(a) On 30 June 19X6 AAT101 was traded in and replaced with KGC303. The trade-in allowance was £5,000. KGC303 cost £15,000 and the balance due (after deducting the trade-in allowance) was paid partly in cash and partly by a loan of £6,000 from Pinot Finance. KGC303 is expected to have a residual value of £4,000 after an estimated economic life of 5 years.

(b) The estimated remaining economic life of DJH202 was reduced from 6 years to 4 years with no change in the estimated residual value.

Required:

(a) Show any Journal entries necessary to give effect to the above.

(b) Show the Journal entry necessary to record depreciation on Vehicles for the year ended 31 March 19X7.

(c) Reconstruct the Vehicles Account and the Provision for Depreciation Account for the year ended 31 March 19X7.

Show the necessary calculations clearly.

(*Association of Accounting Technicians*)

25.8A A firm buys a fixed asset for £10,000. The firm estimates that the asset will be used for 5 years. After exactly 2½ years, however, the asset is suddenly sold for £5,000. The firm always provides a full year's depreciation in the year of purchase and no depreciation in the year of disposal.

Required:

(a) Write up the relevant accounts (including disposal account but not profit and loss account) for each of Years 1, 2 and 3:
   (i) Using the straight line depreciation method (assume 20% pa);
   (ii) Using the reducing balance depreciation method (assume 40% pa).

(b) (i) What is the purpose of depreciation? In what circumstances would each of the two methods you have used be preferable?
   (ii) What is the meaning of the net figure for the fixed asset in the balance sheet at the end of Year 2?

(c) If the asset was bought at the beginning of Year 1, but was not used at all until Year 2 (and it is confidently anticipated to last until Year 6), state under each method the appropriate depreciation charge in Year 1, and briefly justify your answer.

(*Association of Chartered Certified Accountants*)

25.9   Your firm's client, Thompson Ltd, has provided you with the following information in relation to its fixed assets. The company's accounting period ended on 31st December, 1997.

Balances as at 1st January, 1997	Plant	Vehicles	Total
Cost	£194,000	£58,000	£252,000
Accumulated depreciation	£82,000	£30,000	£112,000
Depreciation rates (Straight line)	20%	20%	
Additions during 1997	£38,000	£20,000	
Assets disposed of during 1997			
Cost	£21,000	£25,000	
Proceeds of sale	£8,000	£7,200	
Year of Acquisition	1995	1993	

A full year's depreciation is provided in the year of purchase and none in the year of sale.

You are required to calculate:
(a) the cost of fixed assets at 31st December, 1997;
(b) the accumulated depreciation on fixed assets at 31st December, 1997; and
(c) the profit and / or loss on the disposals of fixed assets.

(*IATI Foundation Examination*)

25.10A At the beginning of its financial year on 1st June, 1996 a firm had a balance on its Plant Account of £84,000 and on its Provision for Depreciation of Plant Account of £32,000. The firm provides for depreciation, using the reducing balance method, on fixed assets held at the end of its financial year at 20% per annum.

On 31st December, 1996 the firm sold a machine which, on 1st February, 1993 had cost £16,000 and on which installation charges had totalled £1,000. The cost of transporting this machine to the premises had been £3,000. The proceeds of sale were £10,000. In August 1995, substantial repairs to this machine had cost £3,500. In September 1995 an additional part costing £5,000 had been fitted to this machine in order to improve its performance.

On 1st January, 1997 the firm bought second-hand plant costing £24,000, installation costs of which were £4,000 and the cost of repairs to put the machine into working order were £6,000.

Prepare, for the year ended 31st May, 1997:
(a) the Plant Account;
(b) the Provision for Depreciation of Plant Account; and
(c) the Profit and Loss on Disposal of Plant Account.

(*ICPAI Formation I*)

25.11A At the beginning of its financial year on 1st January, 1996 J Sedgewick & Co had a balance on its Machinery Account of £150,000 and on its Provision for Depreciation of Machinery Account of £30,000. The firm provides for depreciation at the rate of 10% per annum on fixed assets held at the end of its financial year, using the reducing balance method.

On 31st March, 1996 the firm sold a machine which had cost £24,000 on 30th September, 1992. Installation charges on this machine were £4,000 and the cost of transporting it to the premises was £2,000. In April 1994 substantial repairs to this machine had cost £5,000. In May 1994 an additional part was fitted to the machine in order to improve its performance. This cost £6,000. The sale proceeds were £29,000.

On 30th June, 1997 the firm bought a second-hand machine for £10,000. Installation costs were £2,000 and transport costs were £1,000. It was discovered that this machine was unsuitable for its intended purpose and, on 30th September, 1997 it was sold for £8,000. The cost of dismantling it and transporting it to the buyer was £2,000.

Required: Prepare for the years ended 31st December, 1996 and 1997:
(a) the Machinery Account;
(b) the Provision for Depreciation of Machinery Account; and
(c) the Disposal of Machinery Account.

(*ICPAI Formation I*)

25.12 Steel Ltd commenced business on 1st July 1994, on which date it purchased a rolling machine for £10,000 and a milling machine for £15,000. Each machine had an estimated useful life of 5 years and no scrap value.

On 30th June 1996 Steel Ltd traded in the milling machine against a new milling machine the list price of which was £24,000. The company was given a trade-in allowance of £6,000 on its old machine. The new machine had an estimated useful life of 5 years.

On 1st July 1997 the company purchased a new machine which could do the work of its two existing machines. The list price of the new machine was £25,000 and Steel Ltd was given a trade-in allowance of £15,000 against its old machines. The estimated useful life of the new machine was 5 years.

The financial year of Steel Ltd ends on 30th June each year. It is the policy of the company to depreciate its fixed assets on a straight line basis.

Required: Show how the above transactions would be recorded in the books of Steel Ltd. for the period 1st July, 1994 to 30th June, 1998.

(*ICAI Professional Examination One*)

25.13 The following information relates to the fixed assets of Axel Ltd:

Asset	Date purchased	Cost
Premises	1st January, 1994	£200,000
Plant and Equipment	1st May, 1995	£80,000
Vehicles	1st June, 1996	£20,000

Additional information:
(1) Premises are depreciated at 2% per annum on the straight line basis.
(2) Plant and equipment is depreciated at 20% per annum on the reducing balance basis.
(3) Vehicles are depreciated at 20% per annum on the straight line basis.
(4) All Vehicles were disposed of for £12,000 during the year ended 31st December 1997.
(5) The policy of the company is to provide a full year's depreciation in the year of purchase and none in the year of sale.

Required: Prepare and balance the following accounts for the year ended 31st December, 1997:
(a) Premises at Cost;
(b) Plant and Equipment at Cost;
(c) Vehicles at Cost;
(d) Provision for Depreciation of Premises;
(e) Provision for Depreciation of Plant and Equipment;
(f) Provision for Depreciation of Vehicles; and
(g) Vehicles Disposal Account.

(*IATI Foundation Examination*)

25.14A
(1) What factors should be considered in the assessment of depreciation and its allocation to accounting periods?
(2) In what circumstances does SSAP 12 'Accounting for Depreciation' permit a change in the method of providing for depreciation?
(3) In the context of SSAP 12 how should a permanent diminution in the value of a fixed asset be treated?
(4) How should re-valued fixed assets be depreciated?
(5) What are the disclosure requirements of SSAP 12?

(*ICPAI Formation I*)

26

Bad debts, provisions for bad debts and provisions for discounts on debtors

26.1 Bad debts

With many businesses, a large proportion, if not all, of the sales are made on credit. The business is therefore taking the risk that some of the customers may never pay for the goods sold to them. This is a normal business risk and therefore **bad debts** as they are called are a normal business expense, and must be charged as such when calculating the profit or loss for the period.

When a debt is found to be 'bad', the asset, as shown by the debtor's account, is worthless, and must accordingly be eliminated as an asset account. This is done by crediting the debtor's account to cancel the asset and increasing the expenses account of bad debts by debiting it. Sometimes the debtor will have paid part of the debt, leaving the remainder to be 'written off' as a bad debt. The total of the bad debts account is later transferred to the profit and loss account.

An example of debts being written off as bad can now be shown:

Exhibit 26.1

C Bloom

		£			£
Jan 8	Sales	50	Dec 31	Bad debts	50

R Shaw

		£			£
Feb 16	Sales	240	Aug 17	Bank	200
			Dec 31	Bad debts	40
		240			240

Bad Debts

		£			£
Dec 31	C Bloom	50	Dec 31	Profit and loss	90
„ „	R Shaw	40			
		90			90

Profit and Loss Account for the year ended 31 December

	£
Bad debts	90

26.2 Provision for bad or doubtful debts

Why provisions are needed

In addition to accounting for the bad debts that occur during an accounting period, we also need to make a provision in respect of debts owing at the end of the accounting period which may eventually turn out to be bad debts.

The total of the debtors appears in the balance sheet as an asset. If they all paid their accounts then this would mean that the debtors figure was a correct figure. If some of the debtors do not pay, the figure for debtors has been overstated in the balance sheet. To try to get as accurate a figure as possible for debtors, a firm will make the best estimate it can of the amount due from debtors which may never be received. This estimate can be made:

1 by looking at each debt, and estimating which ones are likely to be bad debts;
2 by estimating, on the basis of experience, what percentage of the debts will prove to be bad debts.

It is well known that the longer a debt is owing the more likely it is that it will become a bad debt. Some firms draw up an ageing schedule, showing for how long debts have been owing. Older debtors need higher percentage estimates of bad debts than do newer debts. Exhibit 26.2 gives an example of such an ageing schedule.

Exhibit 26.2

Ageing Schedule for Doubtful Debts			
Period for which debt is owing	*Amount of debt*	*Estimated percentage doubtful*	*Estimated provision for doubtful debts*
	£	%	£
Less than one month	5,000	1	50
1 month to 2 months	3,000	3	90
2 months to 3 months	800	4	32
3 months to 1 year	200	5	10
Over 1 year	160	20	32
	9,160		214

Accounting entries for provisions for doubtful debts

When the decision has been taken as to the amount of the provision to be made, then the accounting entries needed for the provision are:

In the year in which a *provision is first made*:

1 Debit the profit and loss account with the amount of the provision.
2 Credit the provision for bad debts account (or provision for doubtful debts account if this title is preferred).

Exhibit 26.3 shows the entries needed for a provision for bad or doubtful debts.

Exhibit 26.3

At 31 December 1995 the debtors figure amounted to £10,000. It is estimated that 2% of debts (i.e. £200) are likely to become bad debts, and it is decided to make a provision for these. The accounts will appear as follows:

Profit and Loss Account for the year ended 31 December 1995

	£
Provision for bad debts	200

Provision for Bad Debts

		1995	£
		Dec 31 Profit and loss	200

In the balance sheet the balance on the provision for bad debts account will be deducted from the total of debtors:

Balance Sheet (extracts) as at 31 December 1995

Current Assets	£
Debtors	10,000
Less Provision for bad debts	200
	9,800

26.3 Increasing the provision for bad or doubtful debts

Let us suppose that for the same firm as in Exhibit 26.3, at the end of the following year (31 December 1996), the bad debts provision needed to be increased. This was because the provision was kept at 2%, but the debtors had risen to £12,000. A provision of £200 had been brought forward from the *previous* year, but we now want a total provision of £240 (i.e. 2% of £12,000). All that is needed is a provision for an extra £40. The double entry will be:

1 Debit the profit and loss account.
2 Credit the provision for bad debts account.

Profit and Loss Account for the year ended 31 December 1996

	£
Provision for bad debts	(40)

Provision for Bad Debts

1996		£	1996		£
Dec 31 Balance c/d		240	Jan 1 Balance b/d		200
			Dec 31 Profit and loss		40
		240			240
			1997		
			Jan 1 Balance b/d		240

The balance sheet as at 31 December 1996 will appear as:

Balance Sheet (extract) as at 31 December 1996

	£
Current assets	
Debtors	12,000
Less Provision for bad debts	240
	11,760

26.4 Reducing the provision for bad or doubtful debts

The provision is shown as a credit balance. Therefore to reduce it we would need a debit entry in the provision account. The credit would be in the profit and loss account. Let us assume that at 31 December 1997, in the firm already examined, the debtors figure had fallen to £10,500 but the provision remained at 2%, i.e. £210 (2% of £10,500). Thus the provision needs a reduction of £30. The double entry is:

1 Debit the provision for bad debts account.
2 Credit the profit and loss account.

Profit and Loss Account for the year ended 31 December 1997

	£
Provision for bad debts: Reduction	30

Provision for Bad Debts

1997		£	1997		£
Dec 31	Profit and loss	30	Jan 1 Balance b/d		240
„ 31	Balance c/d	210			
		240			240
			1998		
			Jan 1 Balance b/d		210

The balance sheet will appear:

Balance Sheet (extracts) as at 31 December 1997

	£
Current assets	
Debtors	10,500
Less Provision for bad debts	210
	10,290

Let us now look at a comprehensive example, Exhibit 26.4:

Exhibit 26.4

A business started on 1 January 1994 and its financial year end is 31 December. A table of the debtors, the bad debts written off and the estimated bad debts at the rate of 2% of debtors at the end of each year is now given. The double entry accounts, and the extracts from the final accounts follow.

Year to 31 December	Debtors at end of year (after bad debts written off)	Bad debts written off during year	Debts thought at end of year to be impossible to collect: 2% of debtors
	£	£	£
1994	6,000	423	120 (2% of £6,000)
1995	7,000	510	140 (2% of £7,000)
1996	7,750	604	155 (2% of £7,750)
1997	6,500	610	130 (2% of £6,500)

Profit and Loss accounts for the years ended 31 December (extracts)

			£
1994	Bad debts		(423)
	Provision for bad debts		(120)
1995	Bad debts		(510)
	Increase in provision for bad debts		(20)
1996	Bad debts		(604)
	Increase in provision for bad debts		(15)
1997	Bad debts		(610)
	Reduction in provision for bad debts		25

Provision for Bad Debts

	£		£
		1994	
		Dec 31 Profit and loss	120
1995		1995	
Dec 31 Balance c/d	140	Dec 31 Profit and loss	20
	140		140
1996		1996	
Dec 31 Balance c/d	155	Jan 1 Balance b/d	140
		Dec 31 Profit and loss	15
	155		155
1997		1997	
Dec 31 Profit and loss	25	Jan 1 Balance b/d	155
Balance c/d	130		
	155		155
		1998	
		Jan 1 Balance b/d	130

Bad Debts

1994		£	1994		£
Dec 31	Various debtors	423	Dec 31	Profit and loss	423
1995			1995		
Dec 31	Various debtors	510	Dec 31	Profit and loss	510
1996			1996		
Dec 31	Various debtors	604	Dec 31	Profit and loss	604
1997			1997		
Dec 31	Various debtors	610	Dec 31	Profit and loss	610

Balance Sheets as at 31 December (extracts)

		£	£
1994	Debtors	6,000	
	Less Provision for bad debts	120	5,880
1995	Debtors	7,000	
	Less Provision for bad debts	140	6,860
1996	Debtors	7,750	
	Less Provision for bad debts	155	7,595
1997	Debtors	6,500	
	Less Provision for bad debts	130	6,370

26.5 Diagram of entries

Students often find it difficult to understand why there should be entries in the profit and loss account for bad debts and also a provision for bad debts. The following example should show why both of the items are needed:

T Kime starts a business. Let us look at some of the figures from his first year's trading:

1 He has sold £50,000 worth of goods on credit.
2 Debtors have paid him £39,600.
3 Two debtors owing him a total of £400 have been declared bankrupt. No money will ever be received from them.
4 In addition to the two debtors above, there was another £10,000 owing to him at the year end.
5 Some of the £10,000 will probably never be paid. Kime does not know exactly how much it would be. He estimates it will be 1% of debtors, i.e. £10,000 × 1% = £100. He decides to make a provision for bad debts.

Extracts from the final accounts are now shown. The numbers in brackets refer to the details given above.

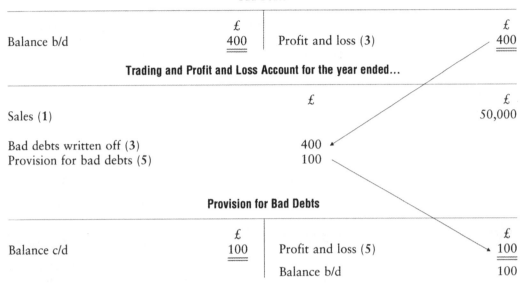

Bad Debts

	£		£
Balance b/d	400	Profit and loss (3)	400

Trading and Profit and Loss Account for the year ended...

	£		£
Sales (1)			50,000
Bad debts written off (3)	400		
Provision for bad debts (5)	100		

Provision for Bad Debts

	£		£
Balance c/d	100	Profit and loss (5)	100
		Balance b/d	100

For the balance sheet, the balances for debtors (4) and the provision for bad debts (5) have to be shown. There is no balance on the bad debts account, and therefore this will not appear.

Balance Sheet as at .....

	£
Current Assets	
Debtors (4)	10,000
less Provision for bad debts (5)	100
	9,900

To summarise:

Sales £50,000. Of this, the amount that would not be paid, £400 (definite) + further £100 (estimated) = £500	recorded in profit and loss account as	Bad debts £400, provision for bad debts £100 = £500 charged against profits
Expected realisable value of debtors: Debtors £10,000 *less* £100 estimated not receivable = £9,900	shown in balance sheet as	Debtors £10,000 *less* Provision for bad debts £100 £9,900

26.6 Bad debts recovered

It is not uncommon for a debt written off at one point in time to be recovered later. When this occurs, the bookkeeping procedures are as follows:

First, reinstate the debt by making the following entries:

    Debit the Debtors Account
    Credit the Bad Debts Recovered Account

The reason for reinstating the debt in the ledger account of the debtor is to have a detailed history of his/her account as a guide for granting credit in future. By the time a debt is written off as bad, it will be recorded in the debtor's ledger account. Therefore when such a debt is recovered, it also must be shown in the debtor's ledger account.

When the cash or cheque is later received from the debtor in settlement of the account or part thereof,

> Debit the cash or bank account
> Credit the Debtor's Account

with the amount received.

At the end of the financial year, the credit balance in the Bad Debts Recovered Account will be transferred to either the Bad Debts Account or directly to the credit side of the Profit and Loss Account. The effect is the same since the Bad Debts Account will itself be transferred to the Profit and Loss Account at the end of the financial year.

26.7 Provisions for discounts on debtors

Some firms create provisions for discounts that may be allowed to customers who owe money at the balance sheet date. This, they maintain, is quite legitimate, as the amount of debtors less any doubtful debt provision is not the best estimate of collectable debts, owing to cash discounts which will be given to debtors if they pay within a given time. The cost of discounts, it is argued, should be charged in the period when the sales were made.

To do this the procedure is similar to the doubtful debts provision. It must be borne in mind that the estimate of discounts to be allowed should be based on the net figure of debtors less bad debts provision, as it is obvious that discounts are not allowed on bad debts!

Example

Year ended 31 December	Debtors	Provision for bad debts	Provision for discounts allowed
	£	£	%
1995	4,000	200	2
1996	5,000	350	2
1997	4,750	250	2

Profit and Loss Account for the years ended 31 December (extracts)

		£
1995	Provision for discounts on debtors (2% of £3,800)	(76)
1996	Increase in provision for discounts on debtors (to 2% of £4,650)	(17)
1997	Reduction in provision for discounts on debtors (to 2% of £4,500)	3

Provision for Discounts on Debtors

	£	1995	£
		Dec 31 Profit and loss	76
1996		1996	
Dec 31 Balance c/d	93	Dec 31 Profit and loss	17
	93		93
1997		1997	
Dec 31 Profit and loss	3	Jan 1 Balance b/d	93
„ „ Balance c/d	90		
	93		93
		1998	
		Jan 1 Balance b/d	90

Balance Sheets as at 31 December (extracts)

	£	£
1995		
Debtors (net of bad debts)		4,000
less Provision for bad debts	200	
„ Provision for discounts on debtors	76	
		276
		3,724
1996		
Debtors (net of bad debts)		5,000
less Provision for bad debts	350	
„ Provision for discounts on debtors	93	
		443
		4,557
1997		
Debtors (net of bad debts)		4,750
less Provision for bad debts	250	
„ Provision for discounts on debtors	90	
		340
		4,410

26.8 An alternative method of accounting for bad and doubtful debts

In accounting there are many ways to the same end result. It would have been possible to amalgamate the Bad Debts Account and the Provision for Bad Debts Account.

Review questions

In addition to the questions which follow, you should attempt questions 152–156 in the accompanying book of multiple-choice questions (see back cover for details).

Suggested solutions to review questions with the letter 'A' after the question number are given in Appendix I (pages 621–3).

26.1A In a new business during 1997 the following debts are found to be bad, and are written off on the dates shown:

30 April	H Gordon	£110
31 August	D Bellamy Ltd	£64
31 October	J Alderton	£12

On 31 December 1997 the schedule of remaining debtors, amounting in total to £6,850, is examined, and it is decided to make a provision for doubtful debts of £220.

You are required to show:
(a) The Bad Debts Account, and the provision for Bad Debts Account.
(b) The charge to the Profit and Loss Account.
(c) The relevant extracts from the Balance Sheet as at 31 December 1997.

26.2A A business started trading on 1 January 1996. During 1996 and 1997 the following debts were written off on the dates stated:

31 August 1996	W Best	£85
30 September 1996	S Avon	£140
28 February 1997	L J Friend	£180
31 August 1997	N Kelly	£60
30 November 1997	A Oliver	£250

On 31 December 1996 there had been a total of debtors remaining of £40,500. It was decided to make a provision for doubtful debts of £550.

On 31 December 1997 there had been a total of debtors remaining of £47,300. It was decided to make a provision for doubtful debts of £600.

You are required to show:
(i) The Bad Debts Account and the Provision for Bad Debts Account for each of the two years.
(ii) The charges to the Profit and Loss Account for each of the two years.
(iii) The relevant extracts from the balance sheets as at 31 December 1996 and 1997.

26.3
(a) The creation of a provision for bad or doubtful debts is an application of one of the four fundamental accounting concepts. Which one? Explain your answer, stating why such a provision is created.
(b) Explain at least two methods of calculating a provision for bad or doubtful debts.
(c) On 1 January 1995 a firm had a balance of £500 in its provision for bad debts account. The provision for bad debts is to be maintained at 5% of debtors at each year end. The firm's debtors over a period of three years were as follows:

Debtors at 31 December	1995	1996	1997
	£12,000	£8,000	£8,000

Show the requisite entries in the provision for bad debts account and the profit and loss account for each of the years ended 31 December 1995, 1996 and 1997.

(d) Explain the difference between bad debts and a provision for bad debts.

26.4 A business, which started trading on 1 January 1995, adjusted its bad debt provisions at the end of each year on a percentage basis, but each year the percentage rate is adjusted in accordance with the current 'economic climate'. The following details are available for the three years 1995, 1996 and 1997.

	Bad Debts written off year to 31 December	Debtors at 31 December	Per cent provision for Bad Debts
	£	£	%
1995	656	22,000	5
1996	1,805	40,000	7
1997	3,847	60,000	6

You are required to show:

(*i*) The Bad Debts Accounts and the Provision for Bad Debts Accounts for each of the three years.

(*ii*) Balance Sheet extracts as at 31 December 1995, 1996 and 1997.

26.5A The balance sheet as at 31 May 19X7 of Forest Traders Limited included a provision for doubtful debts of £2,300. The company's accounts for the year ended 31 May 19X8 are now being prepared. The company's policy now is to relate the provision for doubtful debts to the age of debts outstanding. The debts outstanding at 31 May 19X8 and the required percentage provisions for doubtful debts are as follows:

Debts outstanding	Amount	Provision for doubtful debts
	£	%
Up to 1 month	24,000	1
More than 1 month and up to 2 months	10,000	2
More than 2 months and up to 3 months	8,000	4
More than 3 months	3,000	5

Customers are allowed a cash discount of 2½% for settlement of debts within one month. It is now proposed to make a provision for discounts to be allowed in the company's accounts for the year ended 31 May 19X8.

Required:

Prepare the following accounts for the year ended 31 May 19X8 in the books of Forest Traders Limited to record the above transactions:

(*a*) Provision for doubtful debts;

(*b*) Provision for discounts to be allowed on debtors.

(*Association of Accounting Technicians*)

26.6 A firm makes a provision for bad debts of 5% of debtors and a provision of 2½% for discount on debtors.

On 1 January 1997 the balances brought forward on the relevant accounts were: provision for bad debts £672 and provision for discounts on debtors £631.

You are required to:

(*a*) Enter the balances in the appropriate accounts, using a separate Provision for Bad Debts Account.

(*b*) During 1997 the firm incurred bad debts £2,960 and allowed discounts £6,578. On 31 December 1997 debtors amounted to £25,600. Show the entries in the appropriate accounts for 1997, assuming that the firm's accounting year ends on 31 December, and balance sheet extracts at 31 December 1997.

26.7A   E Chivers commenced business on 1 January 1995 and prepares his accounts to 31 December every year. For the year ended 31 December 1995, bad debts written off amounted to £1,200. It was also found necessary to create a provision for doubtful debts of £2,000.

In 1996, debts amounting to £1,600 proved bad and were written off. Mrs P Iles whose debt of £350 was written off as bad in 1995 settled her account in full on 30 November 1996. As at 31 December 1996 total debts outstanding were £56,000. It was decided to bring the provision up to 5% of this figure on that date.

In 1997, £2,350 debts were written off during the year, and another recovery of £150 was made in respect of debts written off in 1995. As at 31 December 1997, total debts outstanding were £42,000. The provision for doubtful debts is to be maintained at 5% of this figure.

You are required to show for the years ended 31 December 1995, 1996 and 1997, the
(a)   Bad Debts Account.
(b)   Bad Debts Recovered Account.
(c)   Provision for Bad Debts Account.
(d)   Relevant extracts from the Profit and Loss Accounts.

26.8A   C Dickens prepares his accounts up to 31st December each year. Provision for doubtful debts at 31st December, 1994 was £8,750. Bad Debts written off in 1995 totalled £12,500. Debtors at 31st December, 1995 were £135,000. Provision for doubtful debts is to be 4% of this figure. In addition, a provision for discounts on debtors of 2% is to be introduced.

Debtors at 31st December, 1996 were £190,000 of which £5,000 is to be written off in respect of debts considered to be bad. A further £3,200 had already been written off during the year. A specific provision of £2,000 is to be made against one customer's account and a general provision for doubtful debts of 4% of remaining debtors is to be carried. Provision for discounts on debtors is to remain at 2%.

Debtors at 31st December, 1997 were £220,000. Bad Debts written off during the year amounted to £6,500. The account on which the specific provision was previously made is now to be written off as bad to the extent of £1,500. Provision for doubtful debts and discounts on debtors are to be maintained at 4% and 2% respectively.

Required:
Show for the years ended 31 December 1995, 1996 and 1997:
(a)   the Bad Debts account;
(b)   the Provision for Doubtful Debts account;
(c)   the Provision for Discounts on Debtors account;
(d)   relevant extracts from the Profit and Loss Accounts; and
(e)   relevant extracts from the Balance Sheets.

(*ICPAI Formation I*)

26.9   Michael Judge commenced business on 1st April, 1994 and prepares his accounts up to 31st March each year.

At 31st March, 1995 his Debtors Ledger balances totalled £260,000. He decided to write off £7,500 of this figure for bad debts and to make a provision for doubtful debts of 4% of debtors. He also decided to make a provision for discounts on debtors of 2% of debtors.

At 31st March, 1996 debtors were £264,000, of which £15,000 is to be written off in respect of debts considered to be bad. A specific provision of £4,000 is to be made against one customer's account and a general provision of 4% of remaining debtors is to be carried. Provision for discounts on debtors is to remain at 2%.

At 31st March, 1997 debtors were £278,000. The account against which the specific provision was previously made is to be written off as bad at an amount of £4,000. In addition a further £9,000 is to be treated as bad. Provisions for doubtful debts and discounts on debtors are to be maintained at 4% and 2% respectively.

Required:
Show for each of the years ended 31st March, 1995, 1996 and 1997:
(*a*) the Bad Debts Account;
(*b*) the Provision for Doubtful Debts Account;
(*c*) the Provision for Discounts on Debtors Account;
(*d*) relevant extracts from the Profit and Loss Accounts; and
(*e*) relevant extracts from the Balance Sheets.

(*ICPAI Formation I*)

26.10A John Orange has been in business for a number of years. The following is an aged analysis of his debtors ledger at 31st December, 1997.

	Total	Less than 1 month	Over 1 month	Over 2 months	Over 3 months	4 months and over
A. Ash	15,000	10,000	5,000	–	–	–
B. Black	14,900	900	4,000	6,000	4,000	–
C. Crimson	13,600	600	6,000	–	–	7,000
D. Dark	18,400	2,400	6,000	6,000	4,000	–
Ebony Ltd	5,900	–	–	–	–	5,900
	£67,800	£13,900	£21,000	£12,000	£8,000	£12,900

Additional information:
1 (*i*) Provision for bad debts at 1st January, 1997   £4,900
   (*ii*) Bad debts provided for during the year ended 31 December 1997   £5,000
   (*iii*) Bad debts written off during the year   £4,500
2 (*i*) Ebony Ltd. has gone into liquidation and, as none of this debt is recoverable, it is to be written off in full.
   (*ii*) The provision for bad debts at 31st December, 1997, is to be calculated on the following basis:
   Debtors 4 months old and over   30%
   Debtors over 3 months and less than 4 months old   25%
   On all other debtors   5%

Required:
(*a*) You are required, in respect of John Orange, to
   (*i*)   prepare the bad debts provision account for the year ended 31st December, 1997;
   (*ii*)   calculate the bad debts profit and loss entries for the year ended 31st December, 1997; and
   (*iii*) show the entries which will appear in the balance sheet at 31st December, 1997.
(*b*) Explain briefly what you understand by the prudence concept.

(*IATI Foundation Examination*)

27

Adjustments for accrued and prepaid expenses

27.1 Final accounts so far

The trading and profit and loss accounts you have seen up to now have taken the sales for a period and deducted all the expenses for that period, the result being a net profit (or a net loss).

Thus far it has been assumed that expenses paid in a particular period for which a trading and profit and loss account was being drawn up covered all of that period and none of any other period. For example, if the trading and profit and loss account for the year ended 31 December 1997 was being drawn up, then the rent paid as shown in the trial balance was for the calendar year 1997. There was no rent owing at the beginning of 1997 nor any owing at the end of 1997, nor had any rent been paid in advance.

Having kept things relatively simple so far it is now time to consider the effects of amounts paid in advance and amounts due but unpaid at the end of a period.

27.2 Adjustments needed to take account of amounts due or paid in advance

Let us look at two firms who pay rent for buildings in Galway. The rent for each building is £1,200 per annum.

1   Firm A pays £1,000 during the year. At the end of the year it owes £200 for rent.
    Rent expense used up   = £1,200
    Rent paid for   = £1,000

2   Firm B pays £1,300 during the year. This figure includes £100 in advance for the following year.
    Rent expense used up   = £1,200
    Rent paid for   = £1,300

In accordance with the accruals or matching concept (discussed in Chapter 11) a profit and loss account for 12 months must show 12 months' rent as an expense = £1,200.

This means that in both 1 and 2 the double entry accounts showing the amounts paid will have to be adjusted to reflect the amount due or paid in advance at the end of the year.

In all the examples following in this chapter the trading and profit and loss accounts are for the year ended 31 December 1997.

27.3 Accrued expenses

Assume that a premises was rented at an annual rent of £1,000. The rent was supposed to

be paid in four instalments of £250, one at the end of each three month period. Payments were not always made on time. Details are as follows:

Amount	Date rent due	Date rent paid
£250	31 March 1997	31 March 1997
£250	30 June 1997	2 July 1997
£250	30 September 1997	4 October 1997
£250	31 December 1997	5 January 1998

The rent account appeared as:

Rent

1997	£	
Mar 31 Bank	250	
Jul 2 ,,	250	
Oct 4 ,,	250	

The rent paid on 5 January 1998 will appear in the books for 1998 as part of the double entry.

The rent expense for 1997 is obviously £1,000, as that is the year's rent, and this is the amount needed to be transferred to the profit and loss account. But if £1,000 was put on the credit side of the rent account (the debit being in the profit and loss account) the account would not balance. We would have £1,000 on the credit side of the account and only £750 on the debit side.

To make the account balance the £250 rent owing for 1997, but paid in 1998, must be carried down to 1998 as a credit balance because it is a liability on 31 December 1997. Instead of rent owing it could be called rent **accrued** or simply an **accrual**. The completed account can now be shown.

Rent

1997	£	1997	£
Mar 31 Bank	250	Dec 31 Profit and loss	1,000
Jul 2 ,,	250		
Oct 4 ,,	250		
Dec 31 Balance c/d (accrual)	250		
	1,000		1,000
		1998	
		Jan 1 Balance b/d (accrual)	250

27.4 Expenses prepaid

As an example of expenses prepaid assume that insurance for a firm is at the rate of £840 per annum, starting from 1 January 1997. The firm has agreed to pay this at the rate of £210 every three months. However, payments were not made at the correct times. Details were:

Amount	Date insurance due	Insurance paid
£210	31 March 1997	£210 28 February 1997
£210 £210	30 June 1997 30 September 1997	£420 31 August 1997
£210	31 December 1997	£420 18 November 1997

The insurance account will be shown as follows in the books:

Insurance

	£	
Feb 28 Bank	210	
Aug 31 ,,	420	
Nov 18 ,,	420	

The last payment of £420 is not just for 1997, it can be split as £210 for the three months to 31 December 1997 and £210 for the three months ended 31 March 1998. For a period of 12 months the cost of insurance is £840 and this is, therefore, the figure which should be transferred to the profit and loss account.

The amount needed to balance the account will therefore be £210 and at 31 December 1997 this is a benefit paid for but not used up; it is an asset and needs to be carried forward as such to 1998, i.e. as a debit balance. It is a **prepaid expense** or a **prepayment**.

The account can now be completed.

Insurance

1997		£	1997		£
Feb 28 Bank		210	Dec 31 Profit and loss		840
Aug 31 ,,		420			
Nov 18 ,,		420	,, 31 Balance c/d (prepayment)		210
		1,050			1,050
1998					
Jan 1 Balance b/d (prepayment)		210			

A prepayment will also happen when items other than purchases are bought for use in the business, and they are not fully used up in the period.

For instance, stationery is normally not entirely used up over the period in which it is bought, there being a stock of stationery in hand at the end of the period. This stock is, therefore, a form of prepayment and needs to be carried down to the following period in which it will be used.

This can be seen in the following example:

Year ended 31 December 1997.
Stationery bought during the year £2,200.
Stock of stationery in hand at the end of the year £400.

Looking at the example, it can be seen that in 1997 the stationery used up will have been £2,200 – £400 = £1,800. We will still have a stock of £400 worth of stationery at

31 December 1997 to be carried forward to 1998. The £400 stock will be carried forward as an asset (debit balance).

Stationery

1997		£	1997		£
Dec 31 Bank		2,200	Dec 31 Profit and loss		1,800
			Dec 31 Balance c/d (stock)		400
		2,200			2,200
1998					
Jan 1 Balance b/d (stock)		400			

The stock of stationery is **not** added to the stock of unsold goods in hand in the balance sheet, but is added to the other prepayments of expenses.

27.5 Revenue receivable (by the firm) at the end of a period

The revenue due for sales is already shown in the books. These are the debit balances on our customers' accounts, i.e. debtors. There may be other kinds of revenue owed to the firm e.g. rent receivable. An example now follows:

Our warehouse is larger than we need. We rent part of it to another firm for £800 per annum. Details for the year ended 31 December 1997 were as follows:

Amount	Date rent due	Date rent received
£200	31 March 1997	4 April 1997
£200	30 June 1997	6 July 1997
£200	31 September 1997	9 October 1997
£200	31 December 1997	7 January 1998

The account for 1997 appeared:

Rent Receivable

			£
Apr	4	Bank	200
Jul	6	Bank	200
Oct	9	Bank	200

The rent received of £200 on 7 January 1998 will be entered in the books in that year.

Any rent paid by the firm would be charged as a debit to the profit and loss account. Any rent received, being the opposite, is transferred to the credit of the profit and loss account.

The amount to be transferred for 1997 is that earned for the twelve months, i.e. £800. The rent receivable account is completed by carrying down the balance owing as a debit balance to 1998. The £200 owing is an asset at 31 December 1997.

The rent receivable account can now be completed:

Rent Receivable

1997		£	1997			£
Dec 31 Profit and loss		800	Apr 4	Bank		200
			Jul 6	Bank		200
			Oct 9	Bank		200
			Dec 31	Balance c/d (accrual)		200
		800				800
1998						
Jan 1 Balance b/d (accrual)		200				

27.6 Expense and revenue account balances and the balance sheet

In all the cases listed dealing with adjustments in the final accounts, there will still be a balance on each account after the preparation of the trading and profit and loss accounts. All such balances remaining should appear in the balance sheet. The only question left is where and how they shall be shown.

The amounts owing for expenses are usually added together and shown as one figure. These could be called expense creditors, expenses owing, or accrued expenses. The item would appear under the heading of current liabilities as they are expenses which have to be discharged in the near future.

The items prepaid are also added together and called prepayments, prepaid expenses, or payments in advance. Often they are added to the debtors in the balance sheet, otherwise they are shown next under the debtors. Amounts owing for rents receivable or other revenue owing are usually added to debtors.

The balance sheet in respect of the accounts so far seen in this chapter would appear:

Balance Sheet as at 31 December 1997

	£
Current assets	
Stock	x
Debtors	200
Prepayments (400 + 210)	610
Ban	x
Cash	x
Current liabilities	£
Trade creditors	x
Accrued expenses	250

27.7 Expense and revenue accounts covering more than one period

Students are often confused when asked to draw up an expense or revenue account for a full year, when there are amounts owing or prepaid at both the beginning and end of the year. We can now see how this is done.

Example 1

The following details are available:

1 On 31 December 1996 three months' rent of £3,000 was owing.
2 The rent chargeable per year was £12,000.

3 The following payments were made during 1997:
6 January £3,000; 4 April £3,000; 7 July £3,000; 18 October £3,000.
4 The final three months' rent for 1997 is still owing.

Now we can look at the completed rent account. The numbers 1 to 4 refer to the details above.

Rent

1997			£	1997			£
Jan	6	Bank	(3) 3,000	Jan 1	Balance b/d	(1)	3,000
Apr	4	Bank	(3) 3,000	Dec 31	Profit and loss	(2)	12,000
Jul	7	Bank	(3) 3,000				
Oct	18	Bank	(3) 3,000				
Dec	31	Balance c/d (accrual)	(4) 3,000				
			15,000				15,000
				1998			
				Jan 1	Balance b/d (accrual)		3,000

Example 2

The following details are available:

1   On 31 December 1996 packing materials in hand amounted to £1,850.
2   During 1997 £27,480 was paid for packing materials.
3   There was no stock of packing materials on 31 December 1997.
4   On 31 December 1997 we still owed £2,750 for packing materials already received and used.

The packing materials account will appear as:

Packing Materials

1997			£	1997		£
Jan	1	Balance b/d (stock)	(1) 1,850	Dec 31	Profit and loss	32,080
Dec	31	Bank	(2) 27,480			
Dec	31	Balance c/d (accrual)	(4) 2,750			
			32,080			32,080
				1998		
				Jan 1	Balance b/d (accrual)	2,750

The figure of £32,080 is the difference on the account, and is transferred to the profit and loss account. We can prove it is correct:

	£	£
Stock at the start of the year		1,850
Add bought and used:		
Paid for	27,480	
Still owed for	2,750	30,230
Cost of packing materials used during the year		32,080

Example 3

Where different expenses are put together in one account, it can get even more confusing. Let us look at where rent and rates are joined together. Here are the details for 1997:

1 Rent of £6,000 per annum is payable.
2 Rates of £4,000 per annum are payable by instalments.
3 At 1 January 1997 rent of £1,000 had been prepaid in 1996.
4 On 1 January 1997 rates of £400 were owed.
5 During 1997 rent was paid £4,500.
6 During 1997 rates were paid £5,000.
7 On 31 December 1997 rent £500 was owing.
8 On 31 December 1997 rates of £600 had been prepaid.

A combined rent and rates account is to be drawn up for 1997 showing the transfer to the profit and loss account, and balances are to be carried down to 1998.

Rent and Rates

1997			£	1997			£
Jan 1	Balance b/d (rent prepaid) (3)		1,000	Jan 1	Balance b/d (rates owed) (4)		400
Dec 31	Bank: Rent	(5)	4,500	Dec 31	Profit and loss (1 + 2)		10,000
Dec 31	Bank: Rates	(6)	5,000				
Dec 31	Balance c/d (rent owed) (7)		500	Dec 31	Balance c/d (rates prepaid) (8)		600
			11,000				11,000
1998				1998			
Jan 1	Balance b/d (Rates prepaid)	(8)	600	Jan 1	Balance b/d (rent owed) (7)		500

27.8 Adjustment required for goods taken from the business by the proprietor for his own use

A trader will often take items out of his business stocks for his own use, without paying for them. There is nothing wrong about this, but an entry should be made to record the event. The double entry is:

1 Credit the purchases account.
2 Debit the drawings account.

Adjustments may also be needed for other private items. For instance, if a trader's private insurance had been incorrectly charged to the insurance account, then the correction would be:

1 Credit the insurance account.
2 Debit the drawings account.

27.9 Distinctions between various kinds of capital

The capital account represents the claim of the proprietor against the assets of the business at a point in time. The word **Capital** is, however, often used in a specific sense. The main meanings are listed below.

Capital invested

This means the actual amount of money, or money's worth, brought into the business by the proprietor from his outside interests. The amount of capital invested is not affected by the amount of profits made by the business or losses incurred.

Capital employed

This is the effective amount of money that is being used in the business. Thus, if all the assets were added together and the liabilities of the business deducted, the answer would be that the difference is the amount of money employed in the business. You will by now realise that this is the same as the closing balance of the capital account. It is also sometimes called **net assets**.

Working capital

This is a term for the excess of the current assets over the current liabilities of a business.

27.10 Final accounts in the services sector

So far we have looked at accounts for people who traded in some sort of goods. Because we wanted to be able to see what the gross profit on goods was for each firm we drew up a trading account for that purpose.

There are, however, many firms which do not deal in 'goods' but instead supply 'services'. This will include professional firms such as accountants, solicitors, doctors, and estate agents and also firms supplying services such as television maintenance, window-cleaning, gardening, hairdressing, and piano-tuning. As 'goods' are not dealt in there is no need for trading accounts to be drawn up. Instead a profit and loss account and a balance sheet will be drafted.

The first item in the profit and loss account will be the revenue which might be called 'work done', 'fees', 'charges', 'accounts rendered', 'takings', etc., depending on the nature of the organisation. Any other items of income will be added, e.g. rent receivable, and then the expenses will be listed and deducted to arrive at a net profit or net loss.

An example of the profit and loss account of a solicitor is given in Exhibit 27.1.

Exhibit 27.1

J Plunkett, Solicitor
Profit and Loss Account for the year ended 31 December 1997

	£	£
Revenue:		
Fees charged		87,500
Insurance commissions		1,300
		88,800
Less Expenses:		
Wages and salaries	29,470	
Rent and rates	11,290	
Office expenses	3,140	
Motor expenses	2,115	
General expenses	1,975	
Depreciation	2,720	50,710
Net profit		38,090

Exhibit 27.2

JOHN BROWN WORKSHEET

See exercise 27.11

	Trial Balance		Adjustments		Trading Account		Profit & Loss Account		Balance Sheet	
	Dr 1	Cr 2	Dr 3	Cr 4	Dr 5	Cr 6	Dr 7	Cr 8	Dr 9	Cr 10
Sales		400,000				400,000				
Purchases	350,000				350,000					
Sales returns	5,000				5,000					
Purchases returns		6,200				6,200				
Opening stock	100,000				100,000					
Provision for bad debts		800		180 (iv)						980
Wages and salaries	30,000		5,000 (ii)				35,000			
Rates	6,000			500 (iii)			5,500			
Telephone	1,000		220 (v)				1,220			
Shop fittings	40,000			4,000 (vi)					36,000	
Van	30,000			6,000 (vi)					24,000	
Debtors	9,800								9,800	
Creditors		7,000								7,000
Bad debts	200						200			
Capital		179,000								179,000
Bank	3,000								3,000	
Drawings	18,000								18,000	
	593,000	593,000								
Closing stock – Asset			120,000 (i)						120,000	
Closing stock – Cost of goods sold				120,000 (i)		120,000				
Accrued expenses				5,000 (ii) / 220 (v)						5,000 / 220
			135,900	135,900						
Provision for bad debts			180 (iv)				180			
Prepaid expenses			500 (iii)						500	
Depreciation of shop fittings			4,000 (vi)				4,000			
Depreciation of van			6,000 (vi)				6,000			
Gross profit (balancing figure)					71,200			71,200		
					526,200	526,200				
Net profit (balancing figure)							19,100			19,100
							71,200	71,200	211,300	211,300

27.11 Worksheets

Instead of drawing up a set of final accounts in the way already shown, a worksheet could be drawn up. It may provide a useful aid where many adjustments are required.

Worksheets are usually drawn up on specially preprinted stationery with suitable columns.

Exhibit 27.2 shows the worksheet that would be drawn up as an answer to question 27.11 at the end of this chapter. Compare your answer, drawn up in the usual way, with the worksheet. The gross profits and net profits are the same; it is simply the layout that is different.

If you were an accountant working for John Brown, the final account given to him and to anyone else who was an interested party, such as the Revenue Commissioners or a bank, would be the same as the conventional type. They would not be given a worksheet.

Review questions

In addition to the questions which follow, you should attempt questions 157–173 in the accompanying book of multiple-choice questions (see back cover for details).

Suggested solutions to review questions with the letter 'A' after the question number are given in Appendix I (pages 613–15).

27.1A   The financial year of H Saunders ended on 31 December. Show the ledger accounts for the following items including the balance transferred to the necessary part of the final accounts, also the balances carried down to the following year:

(a) Motor expenses: Paid during the year £744; Owing at 31 December £28.
(b) Insurance: Paid during the year £420; Prepaid as at 31 December £35.
(c) Stationery: Paid during the year £1,800; Owing as at 1 January £250; Owing as at 31 December £490.
(d) Rent: Paid during the year £950; Prepaid as at 1 January £220; Prepaid as at 31 December £290.
(e) Saunders sub-lets part of the premises. Receives £550 during the year. Tenant owed Saunders £180 on 1 January and £210 on 31 December.

27.2   J Owen's financial year ended on 30 June 1998. Write up the ledger accounts, showing the transfers to the final accounts and the balances carried down to the next year for the following:

(a) Stationery: Paid during the year £855; Stocks of stationery at the start of the year £290; at the end of the year £345.
(b) General expenses: Paid during the year £590; Owing at the start of the year £64; Owing at the end of the year £90.
(c) Rent and rates (combined account): Paid during the year £3,890; Rent owing at the start of the year £160; Rent paid in advance at the end of the year £250; Rates owing at the start of the year £205; Rates owing at the end of the year £360.
(d) Motor expenses: paid during the year £4,750; Owing at the start of the year £180; Owing at the end of the year £375.
(e) Owen earns commission from the sales of one item. Received during the year £850; Owing at the start of the year £80; Owing at the end of the year £145.

27.3A   Jones Ltd prepares accounts each year to 31st December. The company maintains a combined rent and rates account within its nominal ledger. The company leases its premises on a 35 year lease at an annual rent of £72,000 payable quarterly in advance. The following payments were made by the company during 1997:

Date	Payment	Amount
1st February	Rent	£18,000
31st March	Rates for the 6 months to 31st March, 1997	£12,000
1st May	Rent	£18,000
1st August	Rent	£21,000
30th September	Rates for the 6 months to 30th September, 1997	£12,000
1st November	Rent	£21,000

Additional information

(*i*) Rent of £18,000 was paid on 1st November, 1996, in respect of the quarter to 31st January, 1997.

(*ii*) A rent review took place on 31st July, 1997, and the annual rent increased to £84,000 from 1st August, 1997.

(*iii*) Rates for the year to 30th September, 1997, amounted to £24,000 and for the year to 30th September, 1998 amounted to £30,000.

Required:
Write up the rent and rates account as it would appear in the nominal ledger of Jones Ltd for the year ended 31st December, 1997.

(*IATI Foundation Examination*)

27.4 Andrew Brown prepares accounts to 31st December each year. He maintains a combined Rent and Rates Account in his ledger. At 1st January, 1997 the balances on the Rent and Rates Account were as follows:

Rates Prepaid	(3 months to 31st March, 1997)	£2,000
Rent Accrued	(2 months to 31st December, 1996)	£4,000

Rent is payable quarterly; rates are payable half yearly. The following payments were made during 1997.

1st February	Paid rent for the quarter to 31st January, 1997
1st May	Paid rates for the half year to 30th September, 1997
2nd May	Paid rent for the quarter to 30th April, 1997
14th August	Paid rent for the quarter to 31st July, 1997
12th October	Paid rates for the half year to 31st March, 1998
11th November	Paid rent for the quarter to 31st October, 1997

Rates were increased by £800 per annum with effect from 1st April, 1997. Rent was increased by £2,400 per annum with effect from 1st November, 1997.

Required:
Draw up the Rent and Rates Account for Andrew Brown for the year ended 31st December, 1993.

(*ICAI Professional Examination One*)

27.5A Mr Peter Jones owns a house which is subdivided into 3 flats. He prepares annual accounts to 31st December. There was no rent owing or prepaid at the start of the year on 1st January, 1997. On that date the flats were let at a monthly rent as follows.

Flat 1	Flat 2	Flat 3
£210 per month	£220 per month	£280 per month

He received the following rental income during the year.

Flat 1	Flat 2	Flat 3
£3,402	£1,639	£3,640

Flat 1 was occupied throughout the year. Flat 2 was occupied for the first 4 months and the last 6 months of the year. Flat 3 was occupied for the first month and the last 10 months of the year. The rent of the flats increased as follows during the year.

Flat 1   10% from 1st April, 1997
Flat 2   15% from 1st July, 1997
Flat 3   20% from 1st September, 1997

Required:
Prepare the rent receivable account of Mr Peter Jones for the year ended 31st December, 1997.

(*IATI Foundation Examination*)

27.6   International Airlines Ltd has one large wide bodied jet aircraft. Transport regulations require that the aircraft be subject to a major overhaul after every 10,000 flying hours. The cost of a major overhaul is estimated at £1,500,000.

It is the policy of the company to charge the overhaul expense to accounting periods in proportion to the number of hours flown in each period and, to this end, the company maintains a provision for major overhauls account.

The number of hours flown and the actual overhaul costs paid in each of the years 1994 through 1997 were as follows:

	1994	1995	1996	1997
Hours Flown	5,600	6,200	5,800	6,400
Overhaul Cost Paid	Nil	£1.5m	Nil	£1.5m

Required:
(*a*) Write up the provision for major overhauls account for each of the years ended 31st December, 1994, 1995, 1996 and 1997, and
(*b*) Indicate how any balance on the account would be included in the balance sheet.

(*ICAI Professional Examination One*)

27.7   Paul Remick speculates in property and has asked you to provide him with the overall results of his transactions for the year ended 31st March, 1998, which are as follows:

	£	£	£
Property Held at 1st April, 1997	Capital Cost	Accrued Rent	
Dublin	105,000	520	
Cork	125,000	460	
Limerick	135,000	660	
Property Bought During the Year	Capital Cost	Accrued Rent	Total Cost
Waterford	74,000	150	74,150
Galway	96,000	250	96,250
Sligo	68,000	180	68,180
Property Sold During the Year	Capital	Rent	Total Proceeds
Dublin	120,000	300	120,300
Cork	120,000	500	120,500
Galway	105,000	150	105,150
Sligo (Cost £34,000)	40,000	100	40,100

Rent received during the year and/or accrued as at 31st March, 1998 was as follows:

Property	Rent Received during the Year	Rent Accrued at 31st March, 1998
Dublin	3,600	–
Cork	4,500	–
Limerick	8,400	330
Waterford	1,200	200
Galway	800	–
Sligo	1,600	120

Properties sold have been disposed of in full unless otherwise stated.

Required:
Prepare the accounts necessary to record the above transactions, showing properties held as at 31st March, 1998 at cost, and distinguishing between rent receivable during the year and the profit or loss on the sale of properties.

(*ICPAI Formation I*)

27.8 The owner of a small business selling and repairing cars, which you patronise has just received a copy of his accounts for the current year.

He is rather baffled by some of the items and as he regards you as a financial expert, he has asked you to explain certain points of difficulty to him. This you have readily agreed to do. His questions are as follows:

(*a*) 'What is meant by the term "assets"? My mechanical knowledge and skill is an asset to the business but it does not seem to have been included.'
(*b*) 'The house I live in cost £30,000 five years ago and is now worth £60,000, but that is not included either.'
(*c*) 'What is the difference between "fixed assets" and "current assets"?'
(*d*) 'Why do amounts for "vehicles" appear under both fixed asset and current asset headings?'
(*e*) 'Why is the "bank and cash" figure in the balance sheet different from the profit for the year shown in the profit and loss account?'
(*f*) 'I see the profit and loss account has been charged with depreciation on equipment etc. I bought all these things several years ago and paid for them in cash. Does this mean that I am being charged for them again?'

Required:
Answer each of his questions in terms which he will be able to understand.

(*Association of Chartered Certified Accountants*)

27.9A The following trial balance was extracted from the books of A Scholes at the close of business on 28 February 1998.

	Dr £	Cr £
Purchases and sales	11,280	19,740
Cash at bank	1,140	
Cash in hand	210	
Capital 1 March 1997		9,900
Drawings	2,850	
Office furniture	1,440	
Rent	1,020	
Wages and salaries	2,580	
Discounts	690	360
Debtors and creditors	4,920	2,490
Opening stock	2,970	
Provision for bad and doubtful debts 1 March 1997		270
Delivery van	2,400	
Van running costs	450	
Bad debts written off	810	
	32,760	32,760

Notes:
(*a*) Stock 28 February 1998 £3,510.
(*b*) Wages and salaries accrued at 28 February 1998 £90.
(*c*) Rent prepaid at 28 February 1998 £140.
(*d*) Van running costs owing at 28 February 1998 £60.
(*e*) Increase the provision for Bad and Doubtful Debts by £60.
(*f*) Provide for depreciation as follows: Office furniture £180. Delivery van £480.

Required:
Draw up the trading and profit and loss accounts for the year ended 28 February 1998 together with a balance sheet as at that date.

27.10 T Morgan, a sole trader, extracted the following trial balance from his books at the close of business on 31 March 1998:

	Dr £	Cr £
Purchases and sales	22,860	41,970
Opening stock	5,160	
Capital 1 April 1997		7,200
Bank overdraft		4,350
Cash	90	
Discounts	1,440	930
Returns inwards	810	
Returns outwards		570
Carriage outwards	2,160	
Rent and insurance	1,740	
Provision for bad and doubtful debts		660
Fixtures and fittings	1,200	
Delivery van	2,100	
Debtors and creditors	11,910	6,060
Drawings	2,880	
Wages and salaries	8,940	
General office expenses	450	
	61,740	61,740

Notes:
(a) Stock at 31 March 1998 £4,290.
(b) Wages and salaries accrued at 31 March 1998 £210, Office expenses owing £20.
(c) Rent prepaid at 31 March 1998 £180.
(d) Increase the provision for bad and doubtful debts by £150 to £810.
(e) Provide for depreciation as follows: Fixtures and fittings £120, Delivery van £300.

Required:
Prepare the trading and profit and loss accounts for the year ended 31 March 1998 together with a balance sheet as at that date.

27.11A From the following trial balance of John Brown, a store owner, prepare a trading account and profit and loss account for the year ended 31 December 1997, and a balance sheet as at that date, taking into consideration the additional information given:

Trial Balance as at 31 December 1997

	Dr £	Cr £
Sales		400,000
Purchases	350,000	
Sales returns	5,000	
Purchases returns		6,200
Opening stock	100,000	
Provision for bad debts		800
Wages and salaries	30,000	
Rates	6,000	
Telephone	1,000	
Shop fittings at cost	40,000	
Van at cost	30,000	
Debtors and creditors	9,800	7,000
Bad debts	200	
Capital		179,000
Bank balance	3,000	
Drawings	18,000	
	593,000	593,000

Additional information:
(i) Closing stock £120,000.
(ii) Accrued wages at 31 December 1997, £5,000.
(iii) Rates prepaid at 31 December 1997, £500.
(iv) The provision for bad debts to be increased to 10% of debtors.
(v) Telephone account outstanding at 31 December 1997, £220.
(vi) Depreciate shop fittings at 10% per annum, and the van at 20% per annum, on cost.

27.12 The following trial balance has been extracted from the ledger of Mr Yousef a sole trader.

Trial Balance as at 31 May 19X6

	Dr £	Cr £
Sales		138,078
Purchases	82,350	
Carriage	5,144	
Drawings	7,800	
Rent, rates and insurance	6,622	
Postage and stationery	3,001	
Advertising	1,330	
Salaries and wages	26,420	
Bad debts	877	
Provision for bad debts		130
Debtors	12,120	
Creditors		6,471
Cash on hand	177	
Cash at bank	1,002	
Stock as at 1 June 19X5	11,927	
Equipment		
at cost	58,000	
accumulated depreciation		19,000
Capital		53,091
	216,770	216,770

The following additional information as at 31 May 19X6 is available:

(*a*) Rent is accrued by £210.
(*b*) Rates have been prepaid by £880.
(*c*) £2,211 of carriage represents carriage inwards on purchases.
(*d*) Equipment is to be depreciated at 15% per annum using the straight line method.
(*e*) The provision for bad debts to be increased by £40.
(*f*) Stock at the close of business has been valued at £13,551.

Required:
Prepare a trading and profit and loss account for the year ended 31 May 19X6 and a balance sheet as at that date.

(*Association of Accounting Technicians*)

27.13A   Mr Chai has been trading for some years as a wine merchant. The following list of balances has been extracted from his ledger as at 30 April 19X7, the end of his most recent financial year.

	£
Capital	83,887
Sales	259,870
Trade creditors	19,840
Returns out	13,407
Provision for bad debts	512
Discounts allowed	2,306
Discounts received	1,750
Purchases	135,680
Returns inwards	5,624
Carriage outwards	4,562
Drawings	18,440
Carriage inwards	11,830
Rent, rates and insurance	25,973
Heating and lighting	11,010
Postage, stationery and telephone	2,410
Advertising	5,980
Salaries and wages	38,521
Bad debts	2,008
Cash on hand	534
Cash at bank	4,440
Stock as at 1 May 19X6	15,654
Trade debtors	24,500
Fixtures and fittings – at cost	120,740
Provision for depreciation on fixtures and fittings – as at 30 April 19X7	63,020
Depreciation	12,074

The following additional information as at 30 April 19X7 is available:

(*a*)   Stock at the close of business was valued at £17,750.
(*b*)   Insurances have been prepaid by £1,120.
(*c*)   Heating and lighting is accrued by £1,360.
(*d*)   Rates have been prepaid by £5,435.
(*e*)   The provision for bad debts is to be adjusted so that it is 3% of trade debtors.

Required:
Prepare Mr Chai's trading and profit and loss account for the year ended 30 April 19X7 and a balance sheet as at that date.

(*Association of Accounting Technicians*)

28

The valuation of stock

28.1 Different valuations of stock

Most people would think that there can be only one figure for the valuation of stock. This is not true. We will examine in this chapter how we can calculate different figures for stock.

Assume that a firm has just completed its first financial year and is about to value stock at cost price. It has dealt in only one type of goods. A record of the transactions is shown below.

Exhibit 28.1 Transactions involving stock during the year to 31 December

Bought		£	Sold		£
January	10 units at £30 each	300	May	8 units for £50 each	400
April	10 units at £34 each	340	November	24 units for £60 each	1,440
October	20 units at £40 each	800			
	40	1,440		32	1,840

Still in stock at 31 December, 8 units (40 – 32).

The total figure of purchases is £1,440 and that of sales is £1,840. The trading account for the first year of trading can now be completed if the closing stock is brought into the calculations.

But what value do we put on each of the 8 units left in stock at the end of the year? If all of the units bought during the year had cost £30 each, then the closing stock would be 8 × £30 = £240. However, we have bought goods at different prices. This means that the valuation depends on which goods are taken for this calculation, the units at £30 or at £34, or at £40.

Many firms do not know whether they have sold all the oldest units before they sell the newer units. For instance, a firm selling spanners may not know if the oldest spanners had been sold before the newest spanners.

The stock valuation will therefore be based on an accounting custom, and not on the facts of exactly which units were still in stock at the year end. The three main methods of doing this are now discussed.

28.2 The first in, first out method of valuing stock

This is usually known as FIFO, the first letters of each word. This method values stock on the basis of the assumption that the first goods to be received are the first to be issued. Using the figures in Exhibit 28.1 we can now calculate the closing stock using this method as follows:

	Units Received	Units Issued	Stock after each transaction		
				£	£
January	10 at £30 each		10 at £30 each		300
April	10 at £34 each		10 at £30 each	300	
			10 at £34 each	340	640
May		8 at £30 each	2 at £30 each	60	
			10 at £34 each	340	400
October	20 at £40 each		2 at £30 each	60	
			10 at £34 each	340	
			20 at £40 each	800	1,200
November		2 at £30 each			
		10 at £34 each			
		12 at £40 each			
		24	8 at £40 each		320

The stock on hand at 31 December is therefore valued using the FIFO method at £320.

28.3 The last in, first out method of valuing stock

This is usually known as LIFO. As each issue of goods is made the goods are assumed to be from the last lot of goods received before that date. Where there is not enough left of the last lot of goods, then the balance of goods needed is assumed to come from the previous lot still unsold.

From the information shown in Exhibit 28.1 the calculation of the valuation of closing stock using the LIFO method can now be shown.

	Units Received	Units Issued	Stock after each transaction		
				£	£
January	10 at £30 each		10 at £30 each		300
April	10 at £34 each		10 at £30 each	300	
			10 at £34 each	340	640
May		8 at £34 each	10 at £30 each	300	
			2 at £34 each	68	368
October	20 at £40 each		10 at £30 each	300	
			2 at £34 each	68	
			20 at £40 each	800	1,168
November		20 at £40 each			
		2 at £34 each			
		2 at £30 each			
		24	8 at £30 each		240

The closing stock at 31 December is, therefore, valued using the LIFO method at £240.

28.4 The average cost method of valuing stock

Using the average cost (AVCO) method, upon each receipt of goods the average cost for each item of stock is recalculated. Further issues of goods are then valued at that figure, until another receipt of goods means that another recalculation is needed. From the information in Exhibit 28.1 the calculation can be shown.

Units of Stock Received	Units of Stock Issued	Average cost per unit of stock held	Number of units in stock	Total value of stock
		£		£
January 10 at £30		30	10	300
April 10 at £34		32*	20	640
May	8 at £32	32	12	384
October 20 at £40		37*	32	1,184
November	24 at £37	37	8	296

The closing stock at 31 December is therefore valued using the average cost method at £296.

*In April, the value of stock is calculated as follows: opening stock (10 × £30) = £300 + stock received (10 × £34) £340 = total £640. There are 20 units in stock, so the average cost is £640 ÷ 20 = £32. In October, the value of stock is calculated as follows: opening stock (12 × £32) = £384 + stock received (20 × £40) £800 = £1,184. There are 32 units in stock, so the average cost is £1,184 ÷ 32 = £37.

28.5 Stock valuation and the calculation of profit

Using the figures from Exhibit 28.1 with stock valuations shown by the three methods of FIFO, LIFO, and AVCO, the trading accounts would appear:

Trading Account for the year ended 31 December			
	FIFO	LIFO	AVCO
	£	£	£
Sales	1,840	1,840	1,840
Cost of sales			
Purchases	1,440	1,440	1,440
less Closing stock	320	240	296
	1,120	1,200	1,144
Gross profit	720	640	696

As you can see, different methods of stock valuation will mean that different profits are shown.

28.6 Reduction of stock from cost to net realisable value (NRV)

The net realisable value of stock is calculated as follows :

Sales value – expenses to be incurred prior to sale = net realisable value.

The prudence concept is applied when stock is valued. Stock should not be over-valued, otherwise profits shown will be too high. Therefore, if the net realisable value of stock is less than the cost of the stock, the figure to be taken for the final accounts is that of net realisable value.

A somewhat exaggerated example will show the necessity for this action. Assume that an art dealer has bought only two paintings during the financial year to 31 December. He starts off the year without any stock, and then buys a genuine masterpiece for £6,000, selling this later in the year for £11,500. The other is a fake, but he does not realise this

when he buys it for £5,100, only to discover during the year that in fact he had made a terrible mistake and that the net realisable value is £100. The fake remains unsold at the end of the year. The trading accounts, Exhibit 28.2, would appear as (*a*) if stock is valued at cost, and (*b*) if stock is value at net realisable value.

Exhibit 28.2

Trading Account for the year ended 31 December				
		(*a*) £		(*b*) £
Sales		11,500		11,500
Purchases	11,100		11,100	
Closing stock	5,100	6,000	100	11,000
Gross profit		5,500		500

Method (*a*) ignores the fact that the dealer had a bad trading year owing to his skill being found wanting. If this method was used, then the loss on the fake would reveal itself in the following year's trading account. Method (*b*), however, realises that the loss really occurred at the date of purchase rather than at the date of sale. Following the prudence concept method (*b*) is preferred.

28.7 Effect of stock groups on valuation

If there is only one product in stock, calculating the lower of cost or net realisable value is easy. If we have several products or types of product in stock, we can use one of two methods to calculate the value of stock.

From the information given in Exhibit 28.3 we will calculate the value of stock in two different ways.

Exhibit 28.3

Stock at 31 December			
Article	*Product category*	*Cost*	*Net realisable value*
		£	£
1	A	100	80
2	A	120	150
3	A	300	400
4	B	180	170
5	B	150	130
6	B	260	210
7	C	410	540
8	C	360	410
9	C	420	310
		2,300	2,400

Assume that articles 1, 2 and 3 are televisions, articles 4, 5 and 6 are radios, and articles 7, 8 and 9 are videos.

The category method

Using this method the same sorts of items are put together in categories. Thus, articles 1, 2 and 3 are televisions and shown as category A. Articles 4, 5 and 6 are radios and shown as category B. Articles 7, 8 and 9 are videos and shown as category C.

A calculation of both cost and net realisable value for each category is now shown.

Category	Cost	Net realisable value
A	£100 + £120 + £300 = £520	£80 + £150 + £400 = £630
B	£180 + £150 + £260 = £590	£170 + £130 + £210 = £510
C	£410 + £360 + £420 = £1,190	£540 + £410 + £310 = £1,260

The lower of cost and net realisable value using the category method is, therefore:

		£
Category A: lower of £520 or £630	=	520
Category B: lower of £590 or £510	=	510
Category C: lower of £1,190 or £1,260	=	1,190
Stock is valued in the final accounts at		2,220

The article method

Using this method, the lower of cost or net realisable value for *each article* is compared and the lowest figure taken. From Exhibit 28.3 this gives us the following valuation:

Articles	Valuation (lower of cost and net realisable value)
	£
1	80
2	120
3	300
4	170
5	130
6	210
7	410
8	360
9	310
	£2,090

28.8 Another method of stock valuation

Retail businesses often estimate the cost of stock by calculating its sale value, and then deducting the normal margin of gross profit on such stock. Adjustment is made for items which are to be sold at other than normal selling prices.

28.9 Some factors affecting the stock valuation decision

Obviously, the overriding consideration applicable in all circumstances when valuing stock is the need to give a 'true and fair view' of the state of affairs of the business as at the balance sheet date and of the trend in its trading results. There is, however, no precise definition of 'true and fair view'; it obviously rests on the judgement of the persons concerned. However the judgement of any two persons will not always be the same in the differing circumstances of various firms.

In fact, the only certain thing about stock valuation is that the concept of consistency should be applied, i.e. that once adopted, the same basis should be used in the annual accounts until some good reason occurs to change it. A reference should then be made in the final accounts to the effect of the change on the reported profits, if the amount involved is material.

It will perhaps be useful to look at some of the factors which cause a particular basis to be chosen. The list is intended to be indicative rather than comprehensive, and is merely intended as a first brief look at matters which will have to be studied in depth by those intending to pursue a career in accountancy.

1 Ignorance

The personalities involved may not appreciate the fact that there is more than one possible method of valuing stock.

2 Convenience

The basis chosen may not be the best for the purposes of profit calculation but it may be the easiest to calculate. It must always be borne in mind that the benefits which flow from possessing information should be greater than the costs of obtaining it. The only difficulty with this is actually establishing when the benefits do exceed the cost, but in some circumstances the decision not to adopt a given basis will be obvious.

3 Custom

It may be the particular method used in a certain trade or industry.

4 Taxation

The whole idea may be to defer the payment of tax for as long as possible. Because the stock figures affect the calculation of profit, on which the tax is based, the lowest possible stock figures may be taken to show the lowest profits up to the balance sheet date.

5 The capacity to borrow money or to sell the business at the highest possible price

The higher the stock value shown, then the higher will be the profits calculated to the date of that valuation, and therefore, at first sight, the business looks more attractive to a buyer or lender. Either of these considerations may be more important to the proprietors than anything else. It may be thought that businesspeople are not so gullible, but all businesspeople are not necessarily well acquainted with accounting customs. In fact, many small businesses are bought, or money is lent to them without the expert advice of someone well versed in accounting.

6 Remuneration purposes

Where someone managing a business is paid in whole or in part by reference to the profits earned, then one basis may suit him better than others. He may therefore strive to have that basis used to suit his own ends. The owner, however, may try to follow another course to minimise the remuneration that he will have to pay out.

7 Lack of information

If proper stock records have not been kept, it may not be possible to calculate the value of stock using the average cost method or the LIFO method.

8 Advice of auditors

Many firms use a particular basis following advice from their auditors. If a different auditor is appointed he may well advise that a different basis of stock valuation be used.

28.10 Stock valuation as a compromise between conflicting aims

The above list of some of the factors which affect the stock valuation decision illustrates the fact that stock valuation is usually a compromise. There is usually more than one figure which is 'true and fair'. Therefore the desire to borrow money, and in so doing to present as favourably as possible the financial performance and position of the firm by being reasonably optimistic in valuing stock, will be tempered by the fact that this may increase the tax bill. Stock valuation is therefore a compromise between the various ends for which it is to be used.

28.11 The valuation of work in progress

The valuation of work in progress (items in the course of production in manufacturing firms) is subject to all the various criteria and methods used in valuing stock. Probably the cost element is more strongly pronounced than in stock valuation, as it is very often impossible or irrelevant to say what net realisable value or replacement price would be applicable to partly finished goods. Firms in industries such as those which have contracts covering several years have evolved their own methods.

28.12 Goods on 'sale or return'

Goods received on sale or return

Sometimes we may receive goods from one of our suppliers on a **sale or return** basis. This means that we do not have to pay for the goods until we sell them. If we do not sell them we have to return them to our supplier.

Such goods do not belong to us. If we have some goods which we received on a sale or return basis at the stocktaking date, they should not be included in our stock valuation.

Goods sent to customers on sale or return

We may send goods on a sale or return basis to our customers. The stock will belong to us until it is sold. At our stocktaking date any such goods held by our customers should be included in our stock valuation.

28.13 Stocktaking and the balance sheet date

Students often think that all the counting and valuing of stock is done on the last day of an accounting period. This might be true in a small business, but it is often impossible in larger businesses. There may be too many items of stock to do it so quickly.

This means that stocktaking may take place over a period of days. To get the figure of the stock valuation as on the last day of the accounting period, we will have to make adjustments. An example of this is given below.

Example

Lee Ltd's financial year ended on 31 December. The counting of stock which commenced at the close of business on 31 December was not finished until 8 January. When the items in stock on that date were valued, it was found that the stock amounted to £28,850. The following information is available about transactions between 31 December and 8 January:

1 Purchases since 31 December amounted to £2,370 at cost.
2 Returns inwards since 31 December were £350 at selling price.
3 Sales since 31 December amounted to £3,800 at selling price.
4 The selling price is always cost price + 25%.

Lee Ltd
Computation of stock as at 31 December

	£	£	£
Stock (at cost)			28,850
Add Items which were in stock on 31 December (at cost)			
Sales		3,800	
Less Profit content (20% of selling price)*		760	3,040
			31,890
Less Items which were not in stock on 31 December (at cost)			
Returns inwards	350		
Less Profit content (20% of selling price)*	70	280	
Purchases (at cost)		2,370	2,650
Stock as at 31 December			29,240

*Stock at cost (or net realisable value), and not at selling price. As this calculation has a sales figure in it which includes profit, we must deduct the profit part to get to the cost price. This is true also for returns inwards.

The counting of a firm's stock is usually overseen by the firm's auditors.

28.14 Stock levels

One of the most common faults found in the running of a business is that too much stock is on hand at any given point in time.

A considerable number of firms that have problems relating to a shortage of finance will find that they can help matters by having a sensible look at the amounts of stock they hold. It would be a very rare firm indeed which, if they had not investigated the matter previously, could not manage to let parts of their stock run down. As this would save spending cash on items not really necessary, this cash could be better utilised elsewhere.

Review questions

In addition to the questions which follow, you should attempt questions 174–185 in the accompanying book of multiple-choice questions (see back cover for details).

Suggested solutions to review questions with the letter 'A' after the question number are given in Appendix I (page 626).

28.1A From the following figures calculate the value of the closing stock using each of the following methods: (i) FIFO, (ii) LIFO, (iii) AVCO.

Bought		*Sold*	
January	10 at £30 each	April	8 for £46 each
March	10 at £34 each	December	12 for £56 each
September	20 at £40 each		

28.2A   For question 28.1A draw up the trading account for the year showing the gross profits that would have been reported using each of the three methods.

28.3   From the following figures calculate the value of stock remaining using each of (i) FIFO, (ii) LIFO, (iii) AVCO methods.

Bought		Sold	
January	24 at £10 each	June	30 at £16 each
April	16 at £12.50 each	November	34 at £18 each
October	30 at £13 each		

28.4   Draw up trading accounts using each of the three methods from the details in 28.3.

28.5   A picture framing firm had the following transactions for the 6 months ended 31st December, 1997. The figures are exclusive of VAT.

Purchases		Sales	
25/7/97	Purchased 150 units @ £20 each	15/9/97	Sold 305 units @ £45 each
28/8/97	Purchased 225 units @ £30 each	4/10/97	Sold 50 units @ £45 each
10/11/97	Purchased 410 units @ £40 each	23/12/97	Sold 100 units @ £75 each

Additional information:

1   The Balance Sheet as at 1st July, 1997, was as follows:

Bank Balance	£10,000
Capital Account	£10,000

2   Two months' credit is taken from suppliers.
3   One month's credit is given to debtors.
4   Expenses of £1,400 are paid each month as incurred.
5   Assume that purchases are liable to VAT at 10%. Assume that sales are liable to VAT at 20%.

You are required to:

(*a*)   calculate the value of closing stock at the end of each month during the period 1st July, 1997 to 31st December, 1997, using the first in, first out method (FIFO), and

(*b*)   prepare a Trading and Profit and Loss Account and Balance Sheet for the 6 months ended 31st December, 1997 and a balance sheet as at that date.

(*IATI Foundation Examination*)

28.6   The Managing Director of Enigma Ltd, a client of your firm, has asked you to explain different stock valuation methods.

Required:

Draft a brief letter to the Managing Director explaining each of the following:

(*a*)   First In First Out (FIFO)
(*b*)   Last In First Out (LIFO)
(*c*)   Average Cost
(*d*)   Lower of cost and net realisable value

(*IATI Foundation Examination*)

28.7A Thomas Brown and Partners, a firm of practising accountants, have several clients who are retail distributors of the Allgush Paint Spray guns.

The current price list of Gushing Sprayers Limited, manufacturers, quotes the following wholesale prices for the Allgush Paint Spray guns:

Grade A distributors   £500 each
Grade B distributors   £560 each
Grade C distributors   £600 each

The current normal retail price of the Allgush Paint Spray gun is £750.

Thomas Brown and Partners are currently advising some of their clients concerning the valuation of stock in trade of Allgush Paint Spray guns.

1 Charles Gray – Grade B distributor
On 30 April 19X1, 15 Allgush Paint Spray guns were in stock, including 1 gun which was slightly damaged and expected to sell at half the normal retail price. Charles Gray considers that this gun should remain in stock at cost price until it is sold.

K Peacock, a customer of Charles Gray, was expected to purchase a spray gun on 30 April 19X1, but no agreement was reached owing to the customer being involved in a road accident and expected to remain in hospital until late May 19X1.

Charles Gray argues that he is entitled to regard this as a sale during the year ended 30 April 19X1.

2 Jean Kim – Grade C distributor
On 31 May 19X1, 22 Allgush Paint Spray guns were in stock. Unfortunately Jean Kim's business is suffering a serious cash flow crisis. It is very doubtful that the business will survive and therefore a public auction of the stock in trade is likely. Reliable sources suggest that the spray guns may be auctioned for £510 each, auction fees and expenses are expected to total £300.

Jean Kim has requested advice as to the basis upon which her stock should be valued at 31 May 19X1.

3 Peter Fox – Grade A distributor
Peter Fox now considers that stock valuations should be related to selling prices because of the growing uncertainties of the market for spray guns.

Alternatively, Peter Fox has suggested that he uses the cost prices applicable to Grade C distributors as the basis for stock valuations – 'after all this will establish consistency with Grade C distributors'.

Required:
A brief report to each of Charles Gray, Jean Kim and Peter Fox concerning the valuation of their stocks in trade.

Note: Answers should include references to appropriate accounting concepts.

(*Association of Accounting Technicians*)

28.8 Mary Smith commenced trading on 1 September 19X0 as a distributor of the Straight Cut garden lawn mower, a relatively new product which is now becoming increasingly popular.

Upon commencing trading, Mary Smith transferred £7,000 from her personal savings to open a business bank account.

Mary Smith's purchases and sales of the Straight Cut garden lawn mower during the three months ended 30 November 19X0 are as follows:

19X0	*Bought*	*Sold*
September	12 machines	–
	at £384 each	
October	8 machines	4 machines
	at £450 each	at £560 each
November	16 machines	20 machines
	at £489 each	at £680 each

Assume all purchases are made in the first half of the month and all sales are in the second half of the month.

At the end of October 19X0, Mary Smith decided to take one Straight Cut garden lawn mower out of stock for cutting the lawn outside her showroom. It is estimated that this lawn mower will be used in Mary Smith's business for 8 years and have a nil estimated residual value. Mary Smith wishes to use the straight line basis of depreciation.

Additional information:
1 Overhead expenses paid during the three months ended 30 November 19X0 amounted to £1,520.
2 There were no amounts prepaid on 30 November 19X0, but sales commissions payable of 2½% of the gross profit on sales were accrued due on 30 November 19X0.
3 Upon commencing trading, Mary Smith resigned a business appointment with a salary of £15,000 per annum.
4 Mary Smith is able to obtain interest of 10% per annum on her personal savings.
5 One of the lawn mowers not sold on 30 November 19X0 has been damaged in the showroom and is to be repaired in December 19X0 at a cost of £50 before being sold for an expected £400.
Note: Ignore taxation.

Required:
(*a*) Prepare, in as much detail as possible, Mary Smith's trading and profit and loss account for the quarter ended 30 November 19X0 using:
   (i) the first in first out basis of stock valuation, and
   (ii) the last in first out basis of stock valuation.
(*b*) Using the results in (*a*) (i) above, prepare a statement comparing Mary Smith's income for the quarter ended 30 November 19X0 with that for the quarter ended 31 August 19X0.
(*c*) Give one advantage and one disadvantage of each of the bases of stock valuations used in (*a*) above.

(Association of Accounting Technicians)

28.9A 'The idea that stock should be included in accounts at the lower of historical cost and net realisable value follows the prudence convention but not the consistency convention.'

Required:
(*a*) Do you agree with the quotation?
(*b*) Explain, with reasons, whether you think this idea (that stocks should be included in accounts at the lower of historical cost and net realisable value) is a useful one. Refer to at least two classes of user of financial accounting reports in your answer.

(Association of Chartered Certified Accountants)

28.10 After stocktaking for the year ended 31 May 19X5 had taken place, the closing stock of Cobden Ltd was aggregated to a figure of £87,612.

During the course of the audit which followed, the undernoted facts were discovered:

(a) Some goods stored outside had been included at their normal cost price of £570. They had, however, deteriorated and would require an estimated £120 to be spent to restore them to their original condition, after which they could be sold for £800.

(b) Some goods had been damaged and were now unsaleable. They could, however, be sold for £110 as spares after repairs estimated at £40 had been carried out. They had originally cost £200.

(c) One stock sheet had been over-added by £126 and another under-added by £72.

(d) Cobden Ltd had received goods costing £2,010 during the last week of May 19X5 but because the invoices did not arrive until June 19X5, they have not been included in stock.

(e) A stock sheet total of £1,234 had been transferred to the summary sheet as £1,243.

(f) Invoices totalling £638 arrived during the last week of May 19X5 (and were included in purchases and in creditors) but, because of transport delays, the goods did not arrive until late June 19X5 and were not included in closing stock.

(g) Portable generators on hire from another company at a charge of £347 were included, at this figure, in stock.

(h) Free samples sent to Cobden Ltd by various suppliers had been included in stock at the catalogue price of £63.

(i) Goods costing £418 sent to customers on a sale or return basis had been included in stock by Cobden Ltd at their selling price, £602.

(j) Goods sent on a sale or return basis to Cobden Ltd had been included in stock at the amount payable (£267) if retained. No decision to retain had been made.

Required:
Using such of the above information as is relevant, prepare a schedule amending the stock figure as at 31 May 19X5. State your reason for each amendment or for not making an amendment.

(Association of Chartered Certified Accountants)

28.11 The management of Confused Ltd, a company which manufactures table tennis tables, is unable to decide on how to value raw materials and finished goods at the end of its financial year. (There is no work-in-progress at the company's year-end.)

Raw Materials Stocks:
The management has been considering the following options for valuing raw materials stocks:

1 Stocks of raw materials should be valued at cost on a First In, First Out (FIFO) basis.
2 Stocks of raw materials should be valued at cost on a Last In, First Out (LIFO) basis.
3 Stocks of raw materials should be valued at cost on a First In, First Out basis or a Last In, First Out basis, whichever gives the lower valuation.

Finished Goods Stocks:
The management is undecided over the following point with regard to the valuation of finished goods stocks:

Should finished goods stocks be valued at cost, net realisable value, the lower of cost and net realisable value, or the higher of cost and net realisable value?

Required:
Prepare a memorandum to the management of the company setting out your opinion as to how both raw materials stocks and finished goods stocks should be valued, bearing in mind the requirements of SSAP 9, 'Stocks and Long-Term Contracts'.

(IATI Admission Examination)

29

Bank and creditors' reconciliation statements

29.1 The need for bank reconciliation statements

At the end of each period the cash book will be balanced off. About the same time the firm will receive a bank statement. When the closing balance in the cash book is compared with the balance on that date on the bank statement, the two balances will usually be found to be different.

At this point a **bank reconciliation statement** should be prepared. This will either show:

1 that the reasons for the difference between the two balances are valid ones, showing that it has not been as a result of errors made by us or the bank, or
2 that there is not a good reason for the difference between the balances.

In the case of **2** we will have to find out exactly what the errors are. They can then be corrected.

29.2 An example of a bank reconciliation statement

Let us assume that we have just written up our cash book. We call at the bank on 30 June and get from the bank manager a copy of our bank statement. On our return we tick off in our cash book and on the bank statement the items that are similar. A copy of our cash book (bank columns only) and of our bank statement are shown as Exhibit 29.1.

Exhibit 29.1

Cash Book (bank columns only)

			£				£
June	1 Balance b/d	✓	80	June 27	I Gordon – Cheque 934	✓	35
"	28 D Jones	✓	100	" 29	B Tyrell – Cheque 935		40
				" 30	Balance c/d		105
			180				180
July	1 Balance b/d		105				

Bank Statement

			Dr £	Cr £	Balance £
June 26	Balance	✓			80 Cr
" 28	Lodgement	✓		100	180 Cr
" 30	Cheque No. 934	✓	35		145 Cr

By comparing the cash book and the bank statement, it can be seen that the only item that was not in both of these was the cheque payment to B Tyrell of £40 in the cash book.

The reason this was in the cash book, but not on the bank statement, is simply one of timing. The cheque had been posted to B Tyrell on 29 June, but enough time had not elapsed either for it to be received by him, lodged by him or for the bank to charge our account with it if it was lodged. Such a cheque is called an **unpresented cheque** because it has probably not yet been presented at the bank.

To prove that although they are different figures the balances are not different because of errors, a bank reconciliation statement is drawn up. This is as follows:

Bank Reconciliation Statement as at 30 June

	£
Balance in hand as per cash book	105
Add unpresented cheque: Tyrell – Cheque No. 935	40
Balance in hand as per bank statement	145

It would have been possible for the bank reconciliation statement to have started with the bank statement balance:

Bank Reconciliation Statement as at 30 June

	£
Balance in hand as per bank statement	145
Less unpresented cheque: Tyrell – Cheque No. 935	40
Balance in hand as per cash book	105

You should notice that the bank account is shown as a debit balance in the firm's cash book because to the firm it is an asset. In the bank's books the bank account is shown as a credit balance because this is a liability of the bank to the firm.

29.3 Some reasons for differences between the cash book and the bank statement

We can now look at a more complicated example in Exhibit 29.2. Similar items in both cash book and bank statement are shown ticked.

Exhibit 29.2

Cash Book (bank columns only)

		£			£
Dec 27 Total b/fwd*		2,000	Dec 27 Total b/fwd*		1,600
„ 29 J Potter	✓	60	„ 28 J Jacobs – Cheque 1076 ✓		105
„ 31 M Johnson (b)		220	„ 30 M Chatwood – Cheque 1077(a)		15
			„ 31 Balance c/d		560
		2,280			2,280
Jan 1 Balance b/d		560			

*this means the total of the items for the month of December up to the 27th.

Bank Statement

			Dr £	Cr £	Balance £
Dec 27	Balance				400 Cr
„ 29	Lodgement	✓		60	460 Cr
„ 30	Cheque 1076	✓	105		355 Cr
„ „	Credit transfer: L Shaw (c)			70	425 Cr
„ „	Bank charges (d)		20		405 Cr

The balance brought forward in the bank statement £400 is the same figure as that in the cash book, i.e. totals b/fwd £2,000 – £1,600 = £400. However, items (a) and (b) are in the cash book only, and (c) and (d) are on the bank statement only. We can now examine these in detail:

(a) This is a cheque recently sent by us to Mr Chatwood. It has not yet passed through the banking system and been presented to our bank, and is therefore an 'unpresented cheque'.

(b) This is a cheque lodged by us on our visit to the bank when we collected the copy of our bank statement. As we handed this over the counter at the same time as the bank clerk gave us our bank statement, naturally it has not yet been entered on the statement.

(c) A customer, L Shaw, has paid his account by instructing his bank to pay us direct through the banking system, instead of paying by cheque. Such a transaction is usually called a **credit transfer**.

(d) The bank has charged us for the services given in keeping a bank account for us. It did not send us a bill: it simply takes the money from our account by debiting it and reducing the amount of our balance.

We can show these differences in the form of a table. This is followed by bank reconciliation statements drawn up both ways. This is for illustration only; we do not have to draw up a table or prepare two bank reconciliation statements. All we need in practice is one bank reconciliation statement, drawn up whichever way we prefer.

Items not in both the Cash Book and the Bank Statement	Effect on Cash Book balance	Effect on Bank Statement balance	Adjustment required to one balance to reconcile it with the other	
			To Cash Book balance	To Bank Statement balance
1. Payment M Chatwood £15	reduced by £15	none – not yet entered	add £15	deduct £15
2. Lodgement M Johnson £220	increased by £220	none – not yet entered	deduct £220	add £220
3. Bank charges £20	none – not yet entered	reduced by £20	deduct £20	add £20
4. Credit transfers £70	none – not yet entered	increased by £70	add £70	deduct £70

Bank Reconciliation Statement as at 31 December

		£	£
Balance in hand as per cash book			560
Add	Unpresented cheque no. 1077 to M Chatwood	15	
	Credit transfer	70	
			85
			645
Less	Bank charges	20	
	Lodgement not yet entered on the bank statement	220	
			240
Balance per bank statement			405

Bank Reconciliation Statement as at 31 December

		£	£
Balance per bank statement			405
Add	Bank charges	20	
	Lodgement not yet entered on the bank statement	220	
			240
			645
Less	Unpresented cheque no. 1077 to M Chatwood	15	
	Credit transfer	70	
			85
Balance per cash book			560

29.4 Correction of the cash book before preparing a bank reconciliation

Although the foregoing reconciliations explain the difference between the cash book and the bank statement the cash book may still be wrong after they have been prepared. It is better to correct the cash book first and then prepare a reconciliation statement. All items on the bank statement will then be in the cash book. This means that the only differences will be items in the cash book but not on the bank statement.

If, in Exhibit 29.2, the cash book had been written up before the bank reconciliation statement had been drawn up, then the cash book and reconciliation statement would have appeared as follows.

Exhibit 29.3

Cash Book

			£				£
Dec	27	Total b/fwd	2,000	Dec	27	Total b/fwd	1,600
„	29	J Potter	60	„	28	J Jacobs – cheque 1076	105
„	31	M Johnson	220	„	30	M Chatwood – cheque 1077	15
„	31	Credit transfer –		„	31	Bank charges	20
		L Shaw	70	„	31	Balance c/d	610
			2,350				2,350
Jan	1	Balance b/d	610				

Bank Reconciliation Statement as at 31 December

		£
Balance in hand as per cash book		610
Add Unpresented cheque no. 1077 to M Chatwood		15
		625
Less Lodgement not yet entered on the bank statement		220
Balance in hand as per bank statement		405

29.5 The effect of a bank overdraft on a bank reconciliation statement

When there is a bank overdraft the adjustments required to prepare a bank reconciliation statement will be the opposite to those required when the bank statement shows money in the bank.

Exhibit 29.4 is of a corrected cash book, and a bank statement, showing an overdraft. The only items for which adjustments are required are the cheque from G Cumberbatch (a) £106 and the cheque paid to J Kelly (b) £63. Work through the reconciliation statement and then see the note after it.

Exhibit 29.4

Cash Book (bank columns only)

		£			£
Dec 5	I Howe	308	Dec 1	Balance b/d	709
„ 24	L Mason	120	„ 9	P Davies – cheque 601	140
„ 29	K King – credit transfer	124	„ 27	J Kelly – cheque 602 (b)	63
„ 31	G Cumberbatch (a)	106	„ 29	United Trust – standing order	77
„ „	Balance c/d	380	„ 31	Bank charges	49
		1,038			1,038

Bank Statement

		Dr £	Cr £	Balance £
Dec 1	Balance			709 O/D
„ 5	Lodgement		308	401 O/D
„ 14	Cheque 601	140		541 O/D
„ 24	Lodgement		120	421 O/D
„ 29	K King: Credit transfer		124	297 O/D
„ 29	United Trust: Standing order	77		374 O/D
„ 31	Bank charges	49		423 O/D

Note: on a bank statement an overdraft is shown either with the letters 'O/D' following the amount or else shown as a debit balance, indicated by the letters 'DR' after the amount.

Bank Reconciliation Statement as at 31 December

	£
Overdraft as per cash book	380
Add Lodgement not on bank statement – G Cumberbatch	106
	486
Less Unpresented cheque no. 602 to J Kelly	63
Overdraft per bank statement	423

Note: now compare the reconciliation statements in Exhibits 29.3 and 29.4. This shows:

	Exhibit 29.3 *Balances*	Exhibit 29.4 *Overdrafts*
Balance/Overdraft per cash book	XXXX	XXXX
Adjustments		
Unpresented cheque	PLUS	LESS
Lodgement not entered	LESS	PLUS
Balance/Overdraft per bank statement	XXXX	XXXX

Adjustments are, therefore, made in the opposite way to normal when there is an overdraft.

29.6 Dishonoured cheques

When a cheque, received from a customer, is lodged, it is recorded on the debit side of the cash book. It is also shown on the bank statement as a lodgement. However, at a later date it may be found that the customer's bank will not honour it. They will not let it go through the customer's account. It is called a **dishonoured cheque**.

There are several possible reasons for this. Let us suppose that K King gave us a cheque for £5,000 on 20 May 1998. We lodge it, but a few days later our bank returns the cheque to us. Typical reasons are:

1 King had put £5,000 in figures on the cheque, but had written it in words as five thousand five hundred pounds. You will have to give the cheque back to King for amendment.
2 Normally cheques are considered *stale* six months after the date on the cheque, in other words, the banks will not pay cheques over six months old. If King had put 1997 on the cheque instead of 1998, then the cheque would be returned to us by our bank.
3 King simply did not have sufficient funds in his bank account. Suppose he had previously a balance of only £2,000 and yet he has given us a cheque for £5,000. His bank has not allowed him to have an overdraft. In such a case the cheque would be dishonoured. The bank would write on the cheque *'refer to drawer'*, and we would have to get in touch with King to see what he was going to do about it.

In all of the above cases the bank would show the original lodgement as being cancelled by showing the cheque paid out of our bank account. As soon as this happens they will notify us. We will then also show the receipt of money as being cancelled by a credit in the cash book. We will then debit that amount to King's account.

When King originally paid his account our records would appear as:

K King

	£		£
May 1 Balance b/d	<u>5,000</u>	May 20 Bank	<u>5,000</u>

Bank

	£	
May 20 K King	5,000	

After recording the dishonoured cheque, the records will appear as:

K King

	£		£
May 1 Balance b/d	5,000	May 20 Bank	5,000
May 25 Bank: cheque dishonoured	5,000		

Bank

	£		£
May 20 K King	5,000	May 25 K King: cheque dishonoured	5,000

In other words, King is once again shown as owing us £5,000.

29.7 Some other reasons for differences in balances

1 **Standing Orders**. A firm may instruct its bank to pay regular amounts of money at stated dates to persons or firms. For instance you may ask your bank to pay £600 a month to a building society to repay a mortgage.
2 **Direct Debits**. These are payments which have to be made, such as rates, insurance premiums and similar items. Instead of asking the bank to pay the money, as with standing orders, you give permission to the creditor to obtain the money directly from your bank account. This is particularly useful if the amounts payable may vary from time to time, as it is the creditor who changes the payments, not you. With standing orders, if the amount is ever to be changed then you have to inform the bank. With direct debits it is the creditor who arranges that, not you.

Both of the above types of payment may be shown on the bank statement but will not have been entered in the cash book.

29.8 Reconciliation of our ledger accounts with suppliers' statements

Because of differences in timing, the balance on a supplier's statement on a certain date can differ from the balance on that supplier's account in our purchases ledger. This is similar to the fact that a bank statement balance may differ from the cash book balance. In a similar fashion a reconciliation statement may also be necessary. Such a reconciliation is shown below:

Our Purchases Ledger

C Young

		£				£
Jan	10 Bank	1,550	Jan	1	Balance b/d	1,550
„	29 Returns outwards (1)	116	„	6	Purchases	885
„	31 Balance c/d	1,679	„	18	Purchases	910
		3,345				3,345
			Feb	1	Balance b/d	1,679

Supplier's Statement:

Charlie Young
Patrick Street
Cork

STATEMENT

Account Name: A Hall Ltd.
Account Number: H124

Statement Date: 31 Jan 1998

			Debit £	Credit £	Balance £
Jan	1	Balance			1,550 Dr
„	4	Invoice no. 864	885		2,435 Dr
„	13	Payment received – Thank you		1,550	885 Dr
„	18	Invoice no. 1029	910		1,795 Dr
„	31	Invoice no. 1211	425		2,220 Dr

Comparing our purchases ledger account with the supplier's statement, two differences can be seen.

1 We sent returns £116 to C Young, but they had not received them and recorded them in their books by the end of January.
2 Our supplier has sent goods to us, but we had not received them and therefore not entered the £425 in our books by the end of January.

A reconciliation statement can be drawn up by us as at 31 January.

Reconciliation of Supplier's Statement

C Young as at 31 January

			£	£
Balance per our purchases ledger				1,679
Add Purchases not received by us	(2)		425	
Returns not received by supplier	(1)		116	541
Balance per supplier's statement				2,220

In addition to the questions which follow, you should attempt questions 186–196 in the accompanying book of multiple-choice questions (see back cover for details).

Suggested solutions to review questions with the letter 'A' after the question number are given in Appendix I (pages 627–8).

29.1A   From the following draw up a bank reconciliation statement as at 31 December:

	£
Cash at bank as per bank column of the cash book	678
Unpresented cheques	256
Cheques received and lodged into the bank, but not yet entered on the bank statement	115
Credit transfers shown on the bank statement to have been received but not entered in the cash book	56
Cash at bank as per bank statement	875

29.2   From the following draw up a bank reconciliation statement as at 31 March after correcting the cash book, ascertaining the balance on the bank statement.

	£
Cash at bank at 31 March as per bank column of the cash book (Dr)	3,896
Lodgements made but not yet entered on the bank statement	606
Bank charges on the bank statement but not yet in the cash book	28
Cheque no. 524 sent to C Clarke but not yet presented	117
Standing order to ABC Ltd entered on bank statement, but not in cash book	55
Credit transfer from A Cosgrave entered on bank statement, but not yet in cash book	189

29.3   The following information relating to the bank account of Joseph Brown has been presented to you:

1st June Bank balance per nominal ledger (Debit)	£891

Lodgements	£	Cheque Payments		£
2nd June	24,819	3rd June	Cheque No. 60	3,351
5th June	5,769	5th June	Cheque No. 61	1,314
16th June	7,485	11th June	Cheque No. 62	26,334
16th June	9,126	15th June	Cheque No. 63	9,000
21st June	5,784	19th June	Cheque No. 64	1,770
22nd June	1,386	21st June	Cheque No. 65	2,133
30th June	144	30th June	Cheque No. 66	1,566

Joseph received the following bank statement for the month of June:

Date	Particulars	Debit	Credit	Balance
1st June	Balance			£3,600
2nd June	Lodgement		£900	
2nd June	Lodgement		£24,819	£29,319
4th June	Cheque No. 59	£1,233		£28,086
5th June	Cheque No. 58	£2,376		
5th June	Cheque No. 60	£3,351		
5th June	Lodgement		£5,769	£28,128
16th June	Lodgement		£16,611	£44,739
21st June	Cheque No. 61	£1,314		
21st June	Cheque No. 64	£1,770		
21st June	Lodgement		£5,844	£47,499
22nd June	Cheque No. 65	£2,133		
22nd June	Lodgement		£1,386	£46,752
25th June	Standing Order	£825		£45,927
30th June	Bank Giro		£576	£46,503

You are informed by the bank that all entries on their statement are correct.

Required:

(a) Prepare a statement showing your reconciliation of the closing balance on the bank statement with the corrected nominal ledger balance at 30th June.

(b) Explain briefly which items, if any, in your bank reconciliation statement would require further investigation.

(*ICAI Professional Examination One*)

29.4A A client of your firm, Mr Gerard Knight, has provided you with his Bank Statement showing the following details for the month ended 31st December:

Date	Details	Debit £	Credit £	Balance £
Dec 1	Balance forward			1,500 Dr
Dec 2	Life Assurance DD	45		
	Cheque 8204	125		
	Cheque 8206	138		
	Lodgement		900	908 Dr
Dec 5	Motor Lease DD	287		
	Cheque 8205	185		
	Cheque 8209	142		
	Lodgement		1,500	22 Dr
Dec 9	Cheque 8207	200		222 Dr
Dec 12	Cheque Dishonoured	450		672 Dr
Dec 16	Interest	315		
	Bank Charges	204		1,191 Dr
Dec 19	Lodgement		2,000	809 Cr
	Cheque 8214	309		500 Cr
Dec 31	Cheque 8213	140		
	Cheque 8215	212		
	Bank Charges	3		145 Cr

Mr Knight has also provided you with the bank account in his own records for the month ended 31st December, which shows the following:

Receipts		£	Payments		£
Dec 2	Lodgement	900	Dec 1	Balance b/d	1,810
Dec 9	Lodgement	1,500	Dec 2	Cheque 8206	138
Dec 18	Lodgement	1,890	Dec 4	Cheque 8207	200
			Dec 5	Cheque 8208	350
			Dec 5	Cheque 8209	140
			Dec 6	Cheque 8210	285
			Dec 6	Cheque 8211	487
			Dec 7	Cheque 8212	384
			Dec 16	Cheque 8213	140
			Dec 16	Cheque 8214	390
			Dec 20	Cheque 8215	221
Dec 31	Balance c/d	288	Dec 21	Cheque 8216	33
		4,578			4,578

You are advised that the entries on the Bank Statement are correct.

Required:

(a) Write up the adjustments in the bank account in Mr Knight's books, and

(b) Prepare the Bank Reconciliation Statement as at 31st December.

(*IATI Foundation Examination*)

29.5A The following is an extract of the cash book, bank columns, of Graham Baker and Sons Limited, Northtown, for the last week of May 19X1.

19X1		£	19X1		Cheque number	£
24 May	Balance c/d	540	24 May	L Gates	989	364
24 May	K Lambert	1,844	24 May	Petty cash	990	167
27 May	L Hughes	895	27 May	Stationery – J Gordon	991	198
27 May	T Binder	19	27 May	S Bean	992	39
27 May	Cash sales	941	28 May	Postages – Post Office Counters Ltd	993	134
28 May	T Sumner	1,097	28 May	Motor vehicle expenses – Town Garages Ltd	994	359
28 May	Cash sales	639				
29 May	D Abdul	192	29 May	Smith's Travel Agents Ltd	995	133
29 May	Cash sales	784	29 May	John Page & Co Solicitors – purchase of building land	996	9,360
30 May	B Kemp	366				
30 May	Cash sales	317	30 May	Wages	997	1,390
31 May	L Payne	288	30 May	J Grant	998	337
31 May	Cash sales	420	31 May	M Willow	999	649
		8,342				13,130

The company which banks with the North General Bank plc, Main Street Branch, Westown, has received the following statement of account from the bank:

Graham Baker and Sons, Limited
In account with North General Bank plc, Main Street Branch, Westown

Date	Particulars	Payment	Receipts	Balance
19X1		£	£	£
24 May	Balance b/d			861 O/D
24 May	Bank giro credit		1,494	633
27 May	990	167		466
27 May	937	93		373
27 May	Bank giro credit		1,844	2,217
28 May	991	198		2,019
28 May	Bank giro credit		1,855	3,874
29 May	Div		90	3,964
29 May	Bank giro credit		1,736	5,700
30 May	993	134		5,566
30 May	997	1,390		4,176
30 May	Bank giro credit		976	5,152
30 May	Standing Order – Traders Mutual Support Society	36		5,116
31 May	Cheque referred to drawer (T Binder)	19		5,097
31 May	Charges	110		4,987
31 May	Bank giro credit		683	5,670

The company's managing director has suggested that at each accounting year end, the bank balance in the company's accounts should be amended to that shown in the company's bank statement at that date.

Required:

(a) An accounting statement completing the cash book (bank columns) for May 19X1 and bringing down the balance outstanding at the end of the month.
Note: Commence your statement with the total receipts (£8,342) and total payments (£13,130) given in the extract of the cash book.

(b) A bank reconciliation statement as at 31 May 19X1.
Note: Commence with the cash book balance as at 31 May 19X1.

(c) A report addressed to the company's managing director commenting on his suggestion concerning the year end bank balance.

(Association of Accounting Technicians)

29.6 In the draft accounts for the year ended 31 October 19X9, of Thomas P Lee, garage proprietor, the balance at bank according to the cash book was £894.68 in hand.

Subsequently the following discoveries were made:

(1) Cheque number 176276 dated 3 September 19X9 for £310.84 in favour of G Lowe Limited has been correctly recorded in the bank statement, but included in the cash book payments as £301.84.

(2) Bank commission charged of £169.56 and bank interest charged of £109.10 have been entered in the bank statement on 23 October 19X9, but not included in the cash book.

(3) The recently received bank statement shows that a cheque for £29.31 received from T Andrews and credited in the bank statements on 9 October 19X9 has now been dishonoured and debited in the bank statement on 26 October 19X9. The only entry in the cash book for this cheque records its receipt on 8 October 19X9.

(4) Cheque number 177145 for £15.10 has been recorded twice as a credit in the cash book.

(5) Amounts received in the last few days of October 19X9 totalling £1,895.60 and recorded in the cash book have not been included in the bank statements until 2 November 19X9.

(6) Cheques paid according to the cash book during October 19X9 and totalling £395.80 were not presented for payment to the bank until November 19X9.

(7) Traders' credits totalling £210.10 have been credited in the bank statement on 26 October 19X9, but not yet recorded in the cash book.

(8) A standing order payment of £15.00 on 17 October 19X9 to Countryside Publications has been recorded in the bank statement but is not mentioned in the cash book.

Required:

(a) Prepare a computation of the balance at bank to be included in Thomas P Lee's balance sheet as at 31 October 19X9.

(b) Prepare a bank reconciliation statement as at 31 October 19X9 for Thomas P Lee.

(c) Briefly explain why it is necessary to prepare bank reconciliation statements at accounting year ends.

(*Association of Accounting Technicians*)

29.7A The bank statement for G Greene for the month of March is as follows:

		Dr £	Cr £	Balance £
Mar 1	Balance			5,197 O/D
Mar 8	Cheque 821	122		5,319 O/D
Mar 16	Lodgement		244	5,075 O/D
Mar 20	Cheque 822	208		5,283 O/D
Mar 21	Lodgement		333	4,950 O/D
Mar 31	M Turnbull: trader's credit		57	4,893 O/D
Mar 31	BKS: standing order	49		4,942 O/D
Mar 31	Bank charges	28		4,970 O/D

The cash book for March is:

	£		£
Mar 16 N Marsh	244	Mar 1 Balance b/d	5,197
Mar 21 K Alexander	333	Mar 6 L Tulloch – Cheque 821	122
Mar 31 U Sinclair	160	Mar 30 A Bennett – Cheque 822	208
Mar 31 Balance c/d	5,280	Mar 30 J Shaw – Cheque 823	490
	6,017		6,017

You are to:

(a) Write the cash book up to date, and

(b) Draw up a bank reconciliation statement as at 31 March.

29.8A Included in the creditors' ledger of J Cross, a shopkeeper, is the following account which disclosed that the amount owing to one of his suppliers at 31 May 19X4 was £472.13.

Creditors Ledger
Nala Merchandising Company

19X4		£	19X4		£
May 18	Purchases returns	36.67	May 1	Balance b/d	862.07
27	Purchases returns	18.15	16	Purchases	439.85
„	Adjustment		25	Purchases	464.45
	(overcharge)	5.80	„	Adjustment	
31	Discount received	24.94		(undercharge)	13.48
„	Bank	1,222.16			
„	Balance b/d	472.13			
		1,779.85			1,779.85
			June 1	Balance b/d	472.13

In the first week of June 19X4, J Cross received a statement (shown below) from the supplier which showed an amount owing of £2,424.53.

J Cross in account with
Nala Merchandising Company, Statement of Account

			Debit	Credit	Balance
19X4			£	£	£
May	1	BCE			1,538.70 Dr
	3	DISC		13.40	1,525.30 Dr
		CHQ		634.11	891.19 Dr
	5	ALLCE		29.12	862.07 Dr
	7	GDS	256.72		1,118.79 Dr
	10	GDS	108.33		1,227.12 Dr
	11	GDS	74.80		1,301.92 Dr
	14	ADJ	13.48		1,315.40 Dr
	18	GDS	162.55		1,477.95 Dr
	23	GDS	301.90		1,779.85 Dr
	25	ALLCE		36.67	1,743.18 Dr
	28	GDS	134.07		1,877.25 Dr
	29	GDS	251.12		2,128.37 Dr
	30	GDS	204.80		2,333.17 Dr
	31	GDS	91.36		2,424.53 Dr
	31	BCE			2,424.53 Dr

Abbreviations:
BCE = Balance; CHQ = Cheque; GDS = Goods; ALLCE = Allowance; DISC = Discount; ADJ = Adjustment.

Required:
Prepare a statement reconciling the closing balance on the supplier's account in the creditor's ledger with the closing balance shown on the statement of account submitted by the supplier.

(*Association of Chartered Certified Accountants*)

30

Control accounts

When all the accounts were kept in one ledger a trial balance could be drawn up as a test of the arithmetical accuracy of the accounts. It must be remembered that certain errors were not revealed by such a trial balance. If the trial balance totals disagreed, for a small business the books could easily and quickly be checked so as to find the errors.

However, when the firm has grown and the accounting work has been so divided up that there are several ledgers, any errors could be very difficult to find. We could have to check every item in every ledger. What is required is a type of trial balance for each ledger, and this requirement is met by **control accounts**. Thus, it is only the ledgers whose control accounts do not balance that need detailed checking to find errors.

The principle on which the control account is based is simple and is as follows. If the opening balance of an account is known, together with information of the additions and deductions entered in the account, the closing balance can be calculated.

Applying this to a complete ledger, the total of opening balances together with the additions and deductions during the period should give the total of closing balances. This can be illustrated by reference to a sales ledger for entries for a month.

		£
Total of balances at the beginning of the month		3,000
Add	Total of entries which have increased the balances	9,500
		12,500
Less	Total of entries which have reduced the balances	8,000
Total of balances at the end of the month should be		4,500

Because totals are used, the accounts are often known as *total accounts*. Thus, a control account for a sales ledger could be known as either a *sales ledger control account* or as a *total debtors account*.

Similarly, a control account for a purchases ledger could be known either as a *purchases ledger control account* or as a *total creditors account*.

It must be emphasised that control accounts are *not necessarily* a part of the double entry system. They are merely arithmetical proofs performing the same function as a trial balance to a particular ledger. Larger organisations would, however, incorporate them as part of the double entry records.

30.3 The format of control accounts

It is usual to find them in the same form as any ledger account, with the totals of the debit entries in the ledger on the left-hand side of the control account, and the totals of the various credit entries in the ledger on the right-hand side of the control account.

Exhibit 30.1 shows an example of a sales ledger control account for a sales ledger in which all the entries are arithmetically correct.

Exhibit 30.1 Sales ledger control account

	£
Debit balances at 1 January	1,894
Total credit sales for the month of January	10,290
Cheques received from customers in January	7,284
Cash received from customers in January	1,236
Returns inwards from customers during January	296
Debit balances on 31 January as extracted from the sales ledger	3,368

Sales Ledger Control

		£				£
Jan	1 Balance b/d	1,894	Jan	31	Bank	7,284
„	31 Sales	10,290			Cash	1,236
					Returns inwards	296
					Balance c/d	3,368
		12,184				12,184

We have proved the ledger to be arithmetically correct, because the totals of the control account equal each other. If the totals are not equal, then this proves there is an error somewhere.

Exhibit 30.2 shows an example where an error is found to exist in a purchases ledger. The ledger will have to be checked in detail, the error found, and the control account then corrected.

Exhibit 30.2 Purchases ledger control account

	£
Credit balances on 1 January	3,890
Cheques paid to suppliers during January	3,620
Returns outwards to suppliers in January	95
Bought from suppliers during January	4,936
Credit balances on 31 January as extracted from the purchases ledger	5,151

Purchases Ledger Control

		£				£
Jan	31 Bank	3,620	Jan	1	Balance b/d	3,890
„	31 Returns outwards	95	„	31	Purchases	4,936
„	31 Balance c/d	5,151				
		8,866*				8,826*

*The debit and credit totals differ by £40. Therefore, there is a £40 error in the purchases ledger. That ledger will have to be checked in detail to find the error.

30.4 Advantages of control accounts

Control accounts have merits other than that of locating errors. Normally the preparation of control accounts is the responsibility of a person other than the person who records individual sales, purchase and cash/bank transactions. This makes fraud concerning debtors or creditors more difficult than it would otherwise be as the control accounts and individual ledgers, prepared independently, are compared against each other.

For management purposes the balances on the control accounts can be entered as debtors and creditors in the balance sheet without waiting for an extraction of individual balances. Management control is thereby aided, for the speed at which information is obtained is one of the prerequisites of efficient control.

30.5 The sources of information for control accounts

In a large organisation there may well be more than one sales ledger or purchases ledger. The accounts in the sales ledgers may be divided up in ways such as:

- Alphabetically. Thus we may have for example three sales ledgers split A–F, G–O and P–Z.
- Geographically. This could be split: Europe, Far East, Asia, The Americas.

For each ledger we must therefore have a separate control account. An example of a sales book analysed in such a way as to facilitate three separate sales ledgers is shown below.

Exhibit 30.3

Sales Book

Date		Details	Total	Ledgers		
				A–F	G–O	P–Z
			£	£	£	£
Feb	1	J Archer	58	58		
"	3	G Gaunt	103		103	
"	4	T Brown	116	116		
"	8	C Dunn	205	205		
"	10	A Smith	16			16
"	12	P Smith	114			114
"	15	D Owen	88		88	
"	18	B Blake	17	17		
"	22	T Green	1,396		1,396	
"	27	C Males	48		48	
			2,161	396	1,635	130

The totals of the A–F column will be the total sales figure for the sales ledger A–F control account, the total of the G–O column for the G–O control account and so on.

A similar form of analysis can be used in the purchases book, returns inwards book, returns outwards book and the cash book. The *totals* necessary for each of the control accounts can be obtained from the appropriate columns in these books.

Other items, such as bad debts written off or transfers from one ledger to another, will be found in the journal where such items are recorded.

30.6 Transfers and other items in control accounts

Transfers to bad debt accounts will have to be recorded in the sales ledger control account as they involve entries in the sales ledgers.

Similarly, a contra entry, whereby the same firm is both a supplier and a customer, and debtor and creditor balances are offset, will also need to be entered in the control accounts. An example of this follows:

1 The firm has sold A Hughes goods valued at £600.
2 Hughes has supplied the firm with goods valued at £880.
3 The £600 owing by Hughes is set off against the £880 owing to him.
4 This leaves £280 owing to Hughes.

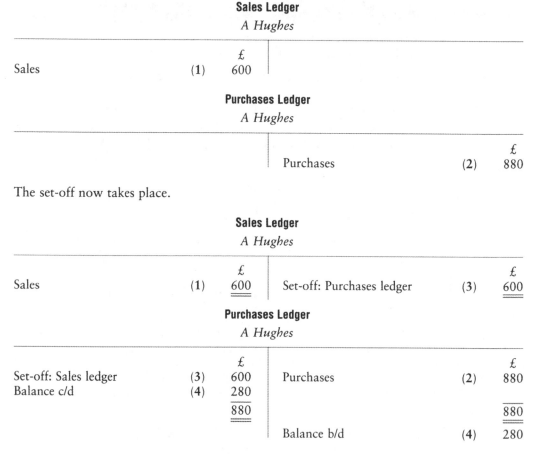

Sales Ledger

A Hughes

		£			
Sales	(1)	600			

Purchases Ledger

A Hughes

					£
			Purchases	(2)	880

The set-off now takes place.

Sales Ledger

A Hughes

		£			£
Sales	(1)	600	Set-off: Purchases ledger	(3)	600

Purchases Ledger

A Hughes

		£			£
Set-off: Sales ledger	(3)	600	Purchases	(2)	880
Balance c/d	(4)	280			
		880			880
			Balance b/d	(4)	280

The transfer of the £600 will therefore appear on the credit side of the sales ledger control account and on the debit side of the purchases ledger control account.

30.7 A detailed example of a control account

Exhibit 30.4 shows a worked example of a more detailed control account.

You will see that there are sometimes credit balances in the sales ledger as well as debit balances. Suppose for instance we sold £500 worth of goods to W Young, he then paid in full for them, and then afterwards he returned £40 worth to us. This would leave a credit

balance of £40 on the account, whereas usually the balances in the sales ledger are debit balances.

Exhibit 30.4

			£
Aug	1	Sales ledger – debit balances	3,816
,,	1	Sales ledger – credit balances	22
		Transactions for the month of August:	
		Cash received from debtors	104
		Cheques received from debtors	6,239
		Sales on credit	7,090
		Bad debts written off	306
		Discounts allowed	298
		Returns inwards	664
		Cash refunded to a customer who had overpaid his account	37
		Cheques received from debtors not honoured by their bank	29
		Interest charged by us on overdue debts	50
		At the end of the month:	
		Sales ledger – debit balances	3,429
		Sales ledger – credit balances	40

Sales Ledger Control

			£				£
Aug	1	Balance b/d	3,816	Aug	1	Balance b/d	22
,,	31	Sales on credit	7,090	,,	31	Cash	104
		Cash refunded	37			Bank	6,239
		Bank: dishonoured				Bad debts	306
		cheques	29			Discounts allowed	298
		Interest on debt	50			Returns inwards	664
		Balance c/d	40			Balance c/d	3,429
			11,062				11,062

30.8 Control accounts as part of the double entry system

In larger organisations it would be normal to find that control accounts are an integral part of the double entry system, the balances of the control accounts being taken for the purpose of extracting a trial balance. In this case the personal accounts are being used as **subsidiary records**, i.e. records where the detail of transactions is shown and which are compared to the control accounts.

Review questions

In addition to the questions which follow, you should attempt questions 197–218 in the accompanying book of multiple-choice questions (see back cover for details).

Suggested solutions to review questions with the letter 'A' after the question number are given in Appendix I (pages 628–30).

30.1A Prepare a sales ledger control account from the following for the month of May:

			£
May	1	Sales ledger balances	4,936
		Totals for May:	
		Sales journal	49,916
		Returns inwards journal	1,139
		Cheques and cash received from customers	46,490
		Discounts allowed	1,455
May	31	Sales ledger balances	5,768

30.2 Prepare a purchases ledger control account from the following for the month of June. The balance of the account is to be taken as the amount of creditors as at 30 June.

			£
June	1	Purchases ledger balances	3,676
		Totals for June:	
		Purchases journal	42,257
		Returns outwards journal	1,098
		Cheques paid to suppliers	38,765
		Discounts received from suppliers	887
June	30	Purchases ledger balances	?

30.3A The trial balance of Queen and Square Ltd revealed a difference in the books. In order that the error(s) could be located it was decided to prepare control accounts for both the purchases ledger and the sales ledger.

From the following prepare the control accounts and show where an error may have been made:

			£
Jan	1	Purchases ledger balances	11,874
		Sales ledger balances	19,744
		Totals for the year:	
		Purchases journal	154,562
		Sales journal	199,662
		Returns outwards journal	2,648
		Returns inwards journal	4,556
		Cheques paid to suppliers	146,100
		Petty cash paid to suppliers	78
		Cheques and cash received from customers	185,960
		Discounts allowed	5,830
		Discounts received	2,134
		Balances on the sales ledger set off against balances in the purchases ledger	1,036
Dec	31	The list of balances from the purchases ledger shows a total of £14,530 and that from the sales ledger a total of £22,024	

30.4 The following information relates to the purchases and sales of Ted Sweeney, a sole trader, for the year ended 31st December, 1997.

	£
Debtors at 1st January	170,000
Creditors at 1st January	130,000
Sales on Credit	450,000
Purchases on Credit	320,000
Sales Returns	18,000
Purchases Returns	22,000
Cash Receipts from Debtors	410,000
Payments to Creditors	290,000
Discount Allowed to Debtors	16,000
Discount Received from Creditors	25,000
Bad Debts Written Off	14,000

Additional information:
1 The total of the credit balances in the Debtors Ledger at 31st December was £7,000.
The total of the debit balances in the Creditors Ledger at 31st December was £11,000.
2 Sam Smith is both a debtor and creditor of Ted Sweeney and £2,500 due from him is to be offset against the balance due to him in the Creditors Ledger.

Required:
Prepare the Debtors and Creditors Control Accounts for Ted Sweeney for the year ended 31st December, 1997.

(IATI Foundation Examination)

30.5 The following information relates to the debtors and creditors of Beta Ltd for the year ended 31st December, 1997:

1 Balances as at 1st January:	£	
Debtors' Ledger Debit Balances	20,000	Dr
Debtors' Ledger Credit Balances	2,000	Cr
Creditors' Ledger Credit Balances	18,000	Cr
Creditors' Ledger Debit Balances	8,000	Dr

2 Transactions for the year:	£
Sales on Credit	140,000
Sales Returns	8,000
Purchases on Credit	90,000
Purchases Returns	4,000
Amount Received from Debtors	120,000
Discount Allowed to Debtors	2,000
Bad Debts Written Off	6,000
Payments to Creditors	75,000
Discounts Allowed by Creditors	3,000

3 At 31st December the total of the credit balances in the debtors' ledger was £3,000 and the total of the debit balances in the creditors' ledger was £1,200.

Required:
(a) Prepare the Debtors' and Creditors' Control Accounts for Beta Ltd for the year ended 31st December, 1997, and
(b) Explain briefly the advantages of preparing control accounts.

(IATI Foundation Examination)

30.6A The financial year of The Better Trading Company ended on 30 November 19X7. You have been asked to prepare a Total Debtors Account and a Total Creditors Account in order to produce end-of-year figures for Debtors and Creditors for the draft final accounts.

You are able to obtain the following information for the financial year from the books of original entry:

	£
Sales – cash	344,890
– credit	268,187
Purchases – cash	14,440
– credit	496,600
Total receipts from customers	600,570
Total payments to suppliers	503,970
Discounts allowed (all to credit customers)	5,520
Discounts received (all from credit suppliers)	3,510
Refunds given to cash customers	5,070
Balance in the sales ledger set off against balance in the purchases ledger	70
Bad debts written off	780
Increase in the provision for bad debts	90
Credit notes issued to credit customers	4,140
Credit notes received from credit suppliers	1,480

According to the audited financial statements for the previous year debtors and creditors as at 1 December 19X6 were £26,555 and £43,450 respectively.

Required:
Draw up the relevant Total Accounts entering end-of-year totals for debtors and creditors.

(*Association of Accounting Technicians*)

30.7A
(*a*) Why are many accounting systems designed with a purchase ledger (creditors ledger) control account, as well as with a purchase ledger (creditors ledger)?

(*b*) The following errors have been discovered:

(i)   An invoice for £654 has been entered in the purchase day book as £456;
(ii) A prompt payment discount of £100 from a creditor had been completely omitted from the accounting records;
(iii) Purchases of £250 had been entered on the wrong side of a supplier's account in the purchase ledger;
(iv) No entry had been made to record an agreement to contra an amount owed to X of £600 against an amount owed by X of £400;
(v) A credit note for £60 had been entered as if it was an invoice.

State the numerical effect on the purchase ledger control account balance of correcting each of these items (treating each item separately).

(*c*) Information technology and computerised systems are rapidly increasing in importance in data recording. Do you consider that this trend will eventually remove the need for control accounts to be incorporated in the design of accounting systems? Explain your answer briefly.

(*Association of Chartered Certified Accountants*)

30.8   The trial balance of Happy Bookkeeper Ltd, as produced by its bookkeeper includes the following items:

Sales ledger control account	£110,172
Purchase ledger control account	£78,266
Suspense account (debit balance)	£2,315

You have been given the following information:

(i)   The sales ledger debit balances total £111,111 and the credit balances total £1,234.

(ii) The purchase ledger credit balances total £77,777 and the debit balances total £1,111.

(iii) The sales ledger includes a debit balance of £700 for business X, and the purchase ledger includes a credit balance of £800 relating to the same business X. Only the net amount will eventually be paid.

(iv) Included in the credit balance on the sales ledger is a balance of £600 in the name of H Smith. This arose because a sales invoice for £600 had earlier been posted in error from the sales day book to the debit of the account of M Smith in the purchase ledger.

(v)   An allowance of £300 against some damaged goods had been omitted from the appropriate account in the sales ledger. This allowance had been included in the control account.

(vi) An invoice for £456 had been entered in the purchase day book as £654.

(vii) A cash receipt from a credit customer for £345 had been entered in the cash book as £245.

(viii)The purchase day book had been overcast by £1,000.

(ix) The bank balance of £1,200 had been included in the trial balance, in error, as an overdraft.

(x)   The bookkeeper had been instructed to write off £500 from customer Y's account as a bad debt, and to reduce the provision for doubtful debts by £700. By mistake, however, he had written off £700 from customer Y's account and *increased* the provision for doubtful debts by £500.

(xi) The debit balance on the insurance account in the nominal ledger of £3,456 had been included in the trial balance as £3,546.

Required:
Record corrections in the control and suspense accounts. Attempt to reconcile the sales ledger control account with the sales ledger balances, and the purchase ledger control account with the purchase ledger balances. What further action do you recommend?

(*Association of Chartered Certified Accountants*)

30.9A   The Debtors Control Account of M Twain as at 31st March, 1997 showed a balance of £257,200 while the Creditors Control Account showed £191,400. Neither of these balances agreed with the relevant List of Balances. The following errors were discovered and when these had been corrected the Books balanced:

(a)   The Purchases Book had been overcast by £10,000.

(b)   Goods worth £750 returned to a supplier had not been entered anywhere in the Books.

(c)   A credit balance of £250 on the debtors list had been shown as a debit balance.

(d)   A bad debt of £800 had been written off in the debtors ledger but no entry had been made in the Control Account.

(e)   It had been agreed with J Kelly to set the balance on his account in the Creditors Ledger of £1,500 against his account in the Debtors Ledger. This had been entered in the Debtors Ledger and in both Control Accounts but was not shown in the Creditors Ledger.

(f)   A balance of £1,300 had been omitted from the list of debtors balances.

(g)   A purchase of goods from C Temple of £3,500 had been posted to the wrong side of his ledger account.

(*h*) A refund of £500 to a customer, A Smith, had been posted to the credit side of B Smith's account in the Creditors Ledger.

(*i*) Discounts received of £320 had been entered in the Creditors Control Account but not in the Creditors Ledger Account.

(*j*) The Sales Returns Book had been overcast by £1,000.

You are required to prepare:

(*a*) Your computation of the corrected balances at 31st March, 1997 on the Debtors and Creditors Control Accounts, and

(*b*) A statement reconciling the original total balances extracted from the ledger with the corrected balance for each ledger.

(*ICPAI Formation I*)

30.10A The Debtors Control Account of D Swift as at 31st December, 1997 showed a balance of £78,214, while the Creditors Control Account showed a balance of £56,191. Neither of these balances agreed with the respective lists of balances.

Following investigation the following errors were found:

1 Sale of goods to T Evans of £2,300 had been posted to the wrong side of his ledger account.

2 A bad debt of £600 had been written off in the debtors' ledger account but no entry had been made in the Control Account.

3 A balance of £670 had been omitted from the list of creditors' balances.

4 Goods worth £635 returned by a customer had not been entered anywhere in the books.

5 A refund of £1,200 to a customer, P Moran, had been posted to the credit side of T Moran's account in the creditors ledger.

6 A £90 debit balance on the creditors list had been shown as a credit balance.

7 Discounts received of £215 had not been entered anywhere in the books.

8 The Sales Book had been undercast by £1,000.

9 It had been agreed with C Smith to set the balance on his account in the debtors ledger of £1,260 against his account in the creditors ledger. This had been entered in the creditors ledger and in both control accounts but was not shown in the debtors ledger.

10 The Purchases Book had been undercast by £900.

You are required to prepare:

(*a*) Your computation of the corrected balances at 31st December, 1997 of the Debtors Control Account and Creditors Control Account, and

(*b*) A statement reconciling the original total balances extracted from the ledger with the corrected balance for each ledger.

(*ICPAI Formation I*)

30.11 The balance on the Debtors Control Account of Trimleaf Ltd at 31st March, 1998 was £17,370, while the total of the list of the balances in the Debtors Ledger was £16,580.

On investigation of the difference, the following items were discovered:

1 A credit balance of £250 on Black's account had been listed as a debit balance.

2 No entry had been made in respect of a contra of £200 (which had been agreed) between Blue's accounts in the Debtors and Creditors ledgers.

3 In June 1997, sales returns of £350 were posted to the Control Account as £530.

4 In August 1997, cash received from debtors of £11,480 was posted to the debit side of the Creditors Control Account, while cheques issued to creditors of £10,170 were posted to the credit side of the Debtors Control Account.

5 A balance of £300 due from White was omitted from the List of Balances.

6 A balance of £470 due from Yellow Ltd was listed as £740.

7 In January 1998, the debtors column of the Cash Book was incorrectly totted as £11,780 and posted to the Control Account. The correct amount should have been £12,460.

8 In February 1998, a debt of £450 was written off as bad. The only entry made to record this was to credit the Debtors Control Account and debit the Bad Debts Account.

9 In March 1998, £100 was received in respect of a debt previously written off as bad. The only entry made to record this was to debit the Bank Account and credit the Debtors Control Account.

Required:

Prepare a reconciliation of the balance on the Debtors Control Account with the total of the List of Balances in the Debtors Ledger.

(*ICAI Professional Examination One*)

31

The correction of errors not affecting trial balance agreement

31.1 Types of errors which do not affect the agreement of the trial balance

In Chapter 7 it was seen that despite certain errors being made when recording transactions the trial balance would still 'balance'. These errors were

1 Errors of omission;
2 Errors of commission;
3 Errors of principle;
4 Compensating errors;
5 Errors of original entry, and
6 Complete reversal of entries.

If you do not remember each of the above types of error you should revise Chapter 7 before proceeding.

31.2 The correction of these errors

When an error is found it has to be corrected. The entries to effect the correction have to be made in the double entry accounts. In addition, an entry should be made in the journal, to explain the correction. An example of an error and its correction in this way is shown below for each type of error listed in section 31.1.

1 Error of omission

A £59 sale to E George has been completely omitted from the books. We must correct this by entering the sale in the books.

The Journal	Dr	Cr
E George Sales *Correction of omission of Sales Invoice No.......* *from the sales journal*	£59	£59

2 Error of commission

A £44 purchase from C Simons was entered in error in C Simpson's account. To correct this, it must be cancelled out of C Simpson's account, and then entered where it should be in C Simons' account. The double entry will be:

C Simpson

Sept 30 C Simons: Error corrected	£44	Sept 30 Purchases	£44

C Simons

	Sept 30 Purchases: Entered originally in C Simpson's a/c	£44

The Journal entry will be:

The Journal	Dr	Cr
C Simpson	£44	
C Simons		£44
Purchase Invoice No......entered in the wrong personal account, now corrected.		

3 Error of principle

The purchase of a machine for £200 is debited to the Purchases account instead of being debited to a Machinery account. We therefore cancel the item out of the Purchases account by crediting that account. It is then entered where it should be by debiting the Machinery account.

The Journal	Dr	Cr
Machinery	£200	
Purchases		£200
Correction of error: purchase of a fixed asset incorrectly debited to the purchases account.		

4 Compensating error

The sales account is overcast by £200, as is the wages account. The trial balance therefore still 'balances'. This assumes that these are the only two errors found in the books.

The Journal	Dr	Cr
Sales	£200	
Wages		£200
Correction of overcasts of £200 each in the sales account and the wages account which compensated for each other.		

5 Error of original entry

A sale of £98 to A Smailes was entered in the books as £89. Therefore, another £9 of sales needs to be entered now.

The Journal	Dr	Cr
A Smailes	£9	
Sales		£9
Correction of error whereby sales were understated by £9		

6 Complete reversal of entries

A payment of cash of £16 to M Dickson was entered on the receipts side of the cash book in error and credited to M Dickson's account. This is somewhat more difficult to adjust. First must come the amount needed to cancel the error, then comes the actual entry itself. Because of this, the correcting entry is double the actual amount first recorded. We can now look at why this is so:

What we should have had:

Cash

		M Dickson	£16

M Dickson

Cash	£16		

Was entered as:

Cash

M Dickson	£16		

M Dickson

		Cash	£16

We can now see that we have to enter double the original amount to correct the error.

Cash

M Dickson	£16	M Dickson (error corrected)	£32

M Dickson

Cash (error corrected)	£32	M Dickson	£16

Overall, when corrected, the cash account showing £16 debit and £32 credit means a net credit of £16. Similarly, Dickson's account shows £32 debit and £16 credit, a net debit of £16. As the final (net) answer is the same as what should have been entered originally, the error is now corrected.

The Journal entry appears:

The Journal	Dr	Cr
M Dickson	£32	
Cash		£32
Payment of cash £16 debited to cash and credited to		
M Dickson in error on .... Error now corrected.		

31.3 'Casting'

You will often notice the use of the expression 'to cast', which means 'to add up'. **Overcasting** means incorrectly adding up a column of figures to give an answer which is greater than it should be. **Undercasting** means incorrectly adding up a column of figures to give an answer which is less than it should be.

31.4 Errors of transposition

These are errors whereby the correct figures are recorded, but in the wrong order, e.g. £3,546 becomes £3,456.

Review questions

In addition to the questions which follow, you should attempt questions 219–221 in the accompanying book of multiple-choice questions (see back cover for details).

Suggested solutions to review questions with the letter 'A' after the question number are given in Appendix I (pages 630–1).

31.1A Show the journal entries necessary to correct the following errors:
(*a*) A sale of goods £678 to J Harris had been entered in J Hart's account.
(*b*) The purchase of a machine on credit from L Pyle for £4,390 had been completely omitted from our books.
(*c*) The purchase of a van for £3,800 had been entered in error in the Motor Expenses account.
(*d*) A sale of £221 to E Fitzwilliam had been entered in the books, both debit and credit, as £212.
(*e*) Commission received £257 had been entered in error in the Sales account.
(*f*) A receipt of cash from T Heath £77 had been entered on the credit side of the cash book and the debit side of T Heath's account.
(*g*) A purchase of goods £189 had been entered in error on the debit side of the Drawings account.
(*h*) Discounts Allowed £366 had been entered in error on the debit side of the Discounts Received account.

31.2 Show the journal entries needed to correct the following errors:

(a) Purchases £699 on credit from K Ward had been entered in H Wood's account.

(b) A cheque of £189 paid for advertisements had been entered in the cash column of the cash book instead of in the bank column.

(c) Sale of goods £443 on credit to B Gordon had been entered in error in B Gorton's account.

(d) Purchase of goods on credit from K Isaacs £89 entered in two places in error as £99.

(e) Cash paid to H Moore £89 entered on the debit side of the cash book and the credit side of H Moore's account.

(f) A sale of fittings £500 had been entered in the Sales account.

(g) Cash withdrawn from the bank £100, had been entered in the cash column on the credit side of the cash book, and in the bank column on the debit side.

(h) Purchase of goods £428 has been entered in error in the Fittings account.

31.3A After preparing its draft final accounts for the year ended 31 March 19X6 and its draft balance sheet as at 31 March 19X6 a business discovered that the stock lists used to compute the value of stock as at 31 March 19X6 contained the following entry:

Stock item	Number	Cost per unit	Total cost
Y 4003	100	£1.39	£1,390

Required:

(a) What is wrong with this particular entry?

(b) What would the effect of the error have been on
  (i) the value of stock as at 31 March 19X6?
  (ii) the cost of goods sold for the year ended 31 March 19X6?
  (iii) the net profit for the year ended 31 March 19X6?
  (iv) the total for Current Assets as at 31 March 19X6?
  (v) the Owner's Capital as at 31 March 19X6?

(*Association of Accounting Technicians*)

31.4A Show the journal entries needed to record the corrections of the following, narratives are not required.

(a) Extra capital of £10,000 paid into the bank has been credited to the Sales account.

(b) Goods taken for own use £700 had been debited to General Expenses.

(c) Private insurance £89 had been debited to the Insurance account.

(d) A purchase of goods from C Kelly £857 had been entered in the books as £587.

(e) Cash lodged £390 had been credited to the bank column and debited to the cash column in the cash book.

(f) Cash drawings of £400 had been credited to the bank column of the cash book.

(g) Returns inwards £168 from M McCarthy had been entered in error in J Charlton's account.

(h) A sale of an old delivery van for £1,000 has been credited to Motor Expenses.

31.5 Journal entries to correct the following are required, narratives may be omitted.

(a) Commissions Received of £880 have been credited to the Rent Received account.

(b) Bank charges of £77 have been debited to the Rent account.

(c) Completely omitted from the books is a payment of Sundry Expenses by cheque £23.

(d) A Purchase of fixtures £478 has been entered in the Purchases account.

(e) Returns inwards £833 have been entered on the debit side of the Returns outwards account.

(f) A loan from R Smiley £5,000 has been entered on the credit side of the Capital account.

(g) Loan interest of £500 has been debited to the Premises account.

(h) Goods taken for own use £250 have been debited to the Purchases account and credited to Drawings.

31.6 Thomas Smith, a retail trader, has very limited accounting knowledge. In the absence of his accounting technician, he extracted the following trial balance as at 31 March 19X8 from his business's accounting records:

	£	£
Stock in trade at 1 April 19X7		10,700
Stock in trade at 31 March 19X8	7,800	
Discounts allowed		310
Discounts received	450	
Provision for doubtful debts	960	
Purchases	94,000	
Purchases returns	1,400	
Sales		132,100
Sales returns	1,100	
Freehold property: at cost	70,000	
provision for depreciation	3,500	
Motor vehicles: at cost	15,000	
provision for depreciation	4,500	
Capital — Thomas Smith		84,600
Balance at bank	7,100	
Trade debtors		11,300
Trade creditors	7,600	
Establishment and administrative expenditure	16,600	
Drawings	9,000	
	£239,010	£239,010

Required:

(a) Prepare a corrected trial balance as at 31 March 19X8.

(b) After the preparation of the above trial balance, but before the completion of the final accounts for the year ended 31 March 19X8, the following discoveries were made:

(i) The correct valuation of the stock in trade at 1 April 19X7 is £12,000; apparently some stock lists had been mislaid.

(ii) A credit note for £210 has now been received from J Hardwell Limited; this relates to goods returned in December 19X7 by Thomas Smith. However, up to now J Hardwell Limited had not accepted that the goods were not of merchantable quality and Thomas Smith's accounting records did not record the return of the goods.

(iii) Trade sample goods were sent to John Grey in February 19X8. These were free samples, but were charged wrongly at £1,000 to John Grey. A credit note is now being prepared to rectify the error.

(iv) In March 19X8, Thomas Smith painted the inside walls of his stockroom using materials costing £150 which were included in the purchases figure in the above trial balance. Thomas Smith estimates that he saved £800 by doing all the painting himself.

Prepare the journal entries necessary to amend the accounts for the above discoveries.
Note: narratives are required.

(*Association of Accounting Technicians*)

31.7A In preparing the final accounts of Knight Ltd. for the year ended 31st December you have discovered the following items for which adjustments are required:

1 £1,700 received for the sale of fixtures and fittings, which had originally cost £3,400, was debited to the bank account and credited to the sales account. No entries were made in the books for the disposal of these fixtures and fittings. Accumulated depreciation on the items disposed of amounted to £1,530.

2   £2,800 of direct debits in respect of advertising, which had been included in the bank statement, were excluded from expenses and from the company's bank account.
3   £4,800 received from a debtor of the company was treated incorrectly as a cash sale.
4   Goods purchased for £3,800 had been returned to suppliers. No entries were made in the company's books to reflect this transaction.

Required:
(a) Draft the journal entries to post the above adjustments, and
(b) Assuming that a net profit of £7,800 had been calculated before the discovery of the above adjustments, calculate the revised profit figure.

(*IATI Foundation Examination*)

31.8   The bookkeeper of one of your clients has prepared draft final accounts for the year ended 31st December and has asked you to check them before they are finalised.

You discover the following:

1   A vehicle was sold for £5,000 and this amount was credited to the Vehicles account. This vehicle had originally cost £12,000 and depreciation of £5,856 had been provided on it. The only entry in the accounts was to credit the proceeds to the Vehicles account.
2   A machine which had cost £7,000 and on which depreciation of £4,200 had been provided was traded in for £4,000 against another machine. The only entry made in the accounts was to debit Machinery and credit Bank with the balance of £10,000 paid.
3   Insurances were effected on 1st March costing £3,600 and on 1st July costing £6,000, each providing cover for twelve months. The earlier insurance was cancelled on 31st August and credit was due in respect of unused premiums. A payment of £4,000 was made to the Insurance Broker on 1st November. The only entry made in the accounts was to debit bank and credit Insurances with the amount paid.
4   An entry appears in the Draft Accounts shown as 'Value Added Tax £17,400'. This represents the net tax due and paid to the Revenue Commissioners. The relevant accounts are all shown inclusive of Value Added Tax. A summary of the Value Added Tax Returns is as follows:

VAT on Sales		£80,000
Less		
VAT on Purchases	£48,000	
VAT on Advertising and Stationery	£6,100	
VAT on Repairs and Renewals	£8,500	£62,600
Payments		£17,400

Required:
Show the journal entries necessary to correctly treat these transactions.

(*ICPAI Formation I*)

32

The correction of errors which affect trial balance agreement

32.1 Errors which mean that the trial balance will not balance

In the previous chapter we looked at errors which still left equal totals in the trial balance. However, many errors will mean that trial balance totals will not be equal. Let us now look at some of these:

- Incorrect additions in any account.
- Making an entry on only one side of the accounts, e.g. a debit but no credit; a credit but no debit.
- Entering a different amount on the debit side from the amount on the credit side.

32.2 The suspense account as a means of balancing the trial balance

We should try very hard to find errors immediately when the trial balance totals are not equal. When they cannot be found, the trial balance totals should be made to agree with each other by inserting the amount of the difference between the two sides in a **suspense account**. This occurs in Exhibit 32.1 where there is a £40 difference.

Exhibit 32.1

Trial Balance as at 31 December 1997	Dr	Cr
	£	£
Totals after all the accounts have been listed	100,000	99,960
Suspense account		40
	100,000	100,000

To make the two totals the same, a figure of £40 for the suspense account has been shown on the credit side. A suspense account is opened and the £40 difference is also shown there on the credit side.

Suspense

	1997	£
	Dec 31 Difference per trial balance	40

32.3 The suspense account and the balance sheet

If the errors are not found before the final accounts are prepared, the suspense account balance will be included in the balance sheet. Where the balance is a credit balance, it should be included with capital and liabilities in the balance sheet. When the balance is a debit balance, it should be shown with the assets in the balance sheet.

32.4 The correction of errors affecting the suspense account

As with the errors described in the previous chapter, when errors affecting the suspense account are found they must be corrected, using double entry. Each correction must also have an entry in the journal describing it.

One error only causing the difference in the trial balance

We will look at two examples:

1. Assume that the error of £40 as shown in Exhibit 32.1 is found in the following year on 31 March 1998. The error was that the sales account was undercast by £40. The action taken to correct this is:

   Debit the suspense account to close it: £40.
   Credit the sales account to show item where it should have been: £40.

The accounts now appear as Exhibit 32.2:

Exhibit 32.2

Suspense

1997		£	1997		£
Dec 31 Balance c/d		40	Dec 31 Difference per trial balance		40
1998			1998		
Mar 31 Sales		40	Jan 1 Balance c/d		40

Sales

			1998		£
			Mar 31 Suspense		40

This can be shown in journal form as:

	The Journal	*Dr*	*Cr*
1998		£	£
Mar 31	Suspense	40	
	Sales		40
	Correction of undercasting of sales by £40 in last year's accounts.		

2. The trial balance on 31 December 1997 had a difference of £168. It was a shortage on the debit side.

A suspense account is opened, the difference of £168 is entered on the debit side. In May 1998 the error was found. We had made a payment of £168 to K Leek to close his account. It was correctly entered in the cash book, but it was not entered in K Leek's account.

First of all, (a) the account of K Leek is debited with £168, as it should have been in 1997. Second (b) the suspense account is credited with £168 so that the account can be closed.

K Leek

1998		£	1998		£
May 31 Bank	(a)	168	Jan 1 Balance b/d		168

The account of K Leek is now correct.

Suspense

1997	£	1997	£
Dec 31 Difference per trial balance	168	Dec 31 Balance c/d	168
1998		1998	
Jan 1 Balance b/d	168	May 31 K Leek (b)	168

The Journal entries are:

	The Journal	*Dr*	*Cr*
1998 Mar 31	K Leek Suspense *Correction of non-entry of payment last* *year in K Leek's account*	£ 168	£ 168

More than one error causing the difference in the trial balance

Exhibit 32.3 shows a situation where the suspense account difference was caused by more than one error.

Exhibit 32.3

The trial balance at 31 December 1997 showed a difference of £77, being a shortage on the debit side. A suspense account is opened, and the difference of £77 is entered on the debit side of the account.

On 28 February 1998 all the errors from the previous year were found.

1   A cheque of £150 paid to L Kent had been correctly entered in the cash book, but had not been entered in Kent's account.
2   The purchases account had been undercast by £20.
3   A cheque of £93 received from K Sand had been correctly entered in the cash book, but had not been entered in Sand's account.

These three errors resulted in a net error of £77, shown by a debit of £77 on the debit side of the suspense account. These are corrected as follows:

(*a*) Make correcting entries in accounts for **1**, **2** and **3**.
(*b*) Record double entry for these items in the suspense account.

L Kent

1998		£	
Feb 28 Suspense (1)		150	

Purchases

1998		£	
Feb 28 Suspense (2)		20	

K Sand

		1998		£
		Feb 28 Suspense (3)		93

Suspense

1998		£	1998		£
Jan 1 Balance b/d		77	Feb 28 L Kent (1)		150
Feb 28 K Sand (3)		93	Feb 28 Purchases (2)		20
		170			170

The Journal		Dr	Cr
1998		£	£
Feb 28	L Kent	150	
	Suspense		150
	Cheque paid omitted from Kent's account		
Feb 28	Purchases	20	
	Suspense		20
	Undercasting of purchases by £20 in last year's accounts		
Feb 28	Suspense	93	
	K Sand		93
	Cheque received omitted from Sand's account		
		263	263

NB Only those errors which make the trial balance totals different from each other have to be corrected via the suspense account. Errors which do not make the trial balance totals different are corrected as described in the previous chapter.

32.5 The effect of errors on profit

Some of the errors will have meant that original profits calculated will be wrong. Other errors will have no effect upon profits. Exhibit 32.4 which shows a set of accounts in which errors have been made, illustrates the different kinds of errors.

Exhibit 32.4

K Davis
Trading and Profit and Loss Account for the year ended 31 December 1997

	£	£
Sales		8,000
Opening stock	500	
Add Purchases	6,100	
	6,600	
Less Closing stock	700	5,900
Gross profit		2,100
Discounts received		250
		2,350
Expenses		
Rent	200	
Insurance	120	
Lighting	180	
Depreciation	250	750
Net profit		1,600

Balance Sheet as at 31 December 1997

	£	£
Fixed assets		
Fixtures at cost		2,200
Less Provision for depreciation		800
		1,400
Current assets		
Suspense account	60	
Stock	700	
Debtors	600	
Bank	340	
	1,700	
Creditors	600	1,100
		2,500
Capital		
Balance at 1 January		1,800
Add Net profit		1,600
		3,400
Less Drawings		900
		2,500

1 Errors which do not affect profit

If an error affects items only in the balance sheet, then the profit originally calculated will be correct. Exhibit 32.5 shows this:

Exhibit 32.5

Assume that in Exhibit 32.4 the £60 debit balance on the suspense account was because of the following error:

On 1 November 1997 we paid £60 to a creditor T Monk. It was correctly entered in the cash book. It was not entered anywhere else. The error was found on 1 June 1998.

The journal entry to correct it will be:

The Journal		Dr	Cr
1998		£	£
June 1	T Monk	60	
	Suspense		60
	Payment to T Monk on 1 November 1997 not		
	entered in his account. Correction now made.		

Both of these accounts appeared in the balance sheet only with T Monk as part of creditors. The net profit of £1,600 does not have to be changed.

2 Errors which do affect profit

If the error is in one of the figures shown in the trading and profit and loss account, then the profit shown before the error(s) are corrected will be incorrect. Exhibit 32.6 shows this:

Exhibit 32.6

Assume that in Exhibit 32.4 the £60 debit balance was because the rent account was added up incorrectly. It should be shown as £260 instead of £200. The error was found on 1 June 1998. The journal entries to correct it are:

The Journal		Dr	Cr
1998		£	£
June 1	Rent	60	
	Suspense		60
	Correction of rent undercast last year.		

Rent last year should have been increased by £60. This would have reduced net profit by £60. A statement of corrected profit for the year is now shown.

K Davis
Statement of corrected net profit for the year ended 31 December 1997

	£
Net profit per the accounts	1,600
Less Rent understated	60
	1,540

3 Where there have been several errors

If in Exhibit 32.4 there had been four errors in the accounts of K Davis, found on 31 March 1998, their correction can now be seen. Assume that the net difference had also been £60.

1 Sales overcast by	£70
2 Insurance undercast by	£40
3 Cash received from a debtor entered in the cash book only	£50
4 A purchase of £59 is entered in the books, both debit and credit as	£95

The entries in the suspense account, and the journal entries will be as follows:

Suspense

1998		£	1998		£
Jan 1	Balance b/d	60	Mar 31	Sales	70
Mar 31	Debtor	50	„ 31	Insurance	40
		110			110

	The Journal	Dr	Cr
1998		£	£
(1) Mar 31	Sales	70	
	Suspense		70
	Sales overcast of £70 in 1997		
(2) Mar 31	Insurance	40	
	Suspense		40
	Insurance expense undercast by £40 in 1997		
(3) Mar 31	Suspense	50	
	Debtor's account		50
	Cash received omitted from debtor's account in 1997		
(4) Mar 31	Creditor's account	36	
	Purchases		36
	Credit purchase of £59 entered both as debit and credit as £95 in 1997		
		196	196

Note: In (4), the correction of the understatement of purchases does not pass through the suspense account.

Now we can calculate the corrected net profit for 1997. Only items **1, 2** and **4** affect figures in the trading and profit and loss account. These are the only adjustments to be made to profit.

K Davis
Statement of corrected net profit for the year ended 31 December 1997

		£
Net profit per the accounts		1,600
Add Purchases overstated (4)		36
	£	1,636
Less Sales overcast (1)	70	
Rent undercast (2)	40	110
Corrected net profit for the year		1,526

Error 3, the cash not posted to a debtor's account, did not affect profit calculations.

Review questions

In addition to the questions which follow, you should attempt questions 222–226 in the accompanying book of multiple-choice questions (see back cover for details).

Suggested solutions to review questions with the letter 'A' after the question number are given in Appendix I (pages 631–3).

32.1A   Your bookkeeper extracted a trial balance on 31 December 1997 which failed to agree by £330, a shortage on the credit side of the trial balance. A suspense account was opened for the difference.

In January 1998 the following errors made in 1997 were found:

(i)   The Sales day book had been undercast by £100.
(ii)   Sales of £250 to J Cantrell had been debited in error to J Cochrane's account.
(iii)   The Rent account had been undercast by £70.
(iv)   The Discounts Received account had been undercast by £300.
(v)   The sale of a delivery van at book value had been credited in error to the Sales account £360.

You are required to:
(*a*)   Show the journal entries necessary to correct the errors.
(*b*)   Draw up the suspense account after the errors described have been corrected.
(*c*)   If the net profit had previously been calculated at £7,900 for the year ended 31 December 1997, show the calculations of the corrected net profit.

32.2   You have extracted a trial balance and drawn up accounts for the year ended 31 December 1997. There was a shortage of £292 on the credit side of the trial balance, a suspense account being opened for that amount.

During 1998 the following errors made in 1997 were located:

(i)   £55 received from sales of old office equipment has been entered in the sales account.
(ii)   The purchases day book had been overcast by £60.
(iii)   A private purchase of £115 had been included in the business purchases.
(iv)   Bank charges of £38 entered in the cash book have not been posted to the bank charges account.
(v)   A sale of goods to B Cross for £690 was correctly entered in the sales book but entered in the personal account as £960.

Required:

(a) Show the requisite journal entries to correct the errors.

(b) Write up the suspense account showing the correction of the errors.

(c) The net profit originally calculated for 1997 was £11,370. Show your calculation of the correct figure.

32.3A The trial balance as at 30 April 19X7 of Timber Products Limited was balanced by the inclusion of the following debit balance:

Difference on trial balance suspense account £2,513.

Subsequent investigations revealed the following errors:

(i) Discounts received of £324 in January 19X7 have been posted to the debit of the discounts allowed account.

(ii) Wages of £2,963 paid in February 19X7 have not been posted from the cash book.

(iii) A remittance of £940 received from K Mitcham in November 19X6 has been posted to the credit of B Mansell Limited.

(iv) In December 19X6, the company took advantage of an opportunity to purchase a large quantity of stationery at a bargain price of £2,000. No adjustments have been made in the accounts for the fact that three quarters, in value, of this stationery was in stock on 30 April 19X7.

(v) A payment of £341 to J Winters in January 19X7 has been posted in the personal account as £143.

(vi) A remittance of £3,000 received from D North, a credit customer, in April 19X7 has been credited to sales.

The draft accounts for the year ended 30 April 19X7 of Timber Products Limited show a net profit of £24,760.

Timber Products Limited has very few personal accounts and therefore does not maintain either a purchases ledger control account or a sales ledger control account.

Required:

(a) Prepare the difference on trial balance suspense account showing, where appropriate, the entries necessary to correct the accounting errors.

(b) Prepare a computation of the corrected net profit for the year ended 30 April 19X7 following corrections for the above accounting errors.

(c) Outline the principal uses of trial balances.

(Association of Accounting Technicians)

32.4 Chi Knitwear Ltd is an old-fashioned firm with a handwritten set of books. A trial balance is extracted at the end of each month, and a profit and loss account and balance sheet are computed. This month however the trial balance will not balance, the credits exceeding debits by £1,536.

You are asked to help and after inspection of the ledgers discover the following errors.

(i) A balance of £87 on a debtors account has been omitted from the schedule of debtors, the total of which was entered as debtors in the trial balance.

(ii) A small piece of machinery purchased for £1,200 had been written off to repairs.

(iii) The receipts side of the cash book had been undercast by £720.

(iv) The total of one page of the sales day book had been carried forward as £8,154, whereas the correct amount was £8,514.

(v) A credit note for £179 received from a supplier had been posted to the wrong side of his account.

(vi) An electricity bill in the sum of £152, not yet accrued for, is discovered in a filing tray.

(vii) Mr Smith whose past debts to the company had been the subject of a provision, at last paid £731 to clear his account. His personal account has been credited but the cheque has not yet passed through the cash book.

Required:
(a) Write up the suspense account to clear the difference, and
(b) State the effect on the accounts of correcting each error.

(*Association of Chartered Certified Accountants*)

32.5A The draft Financial Statements of Thomas Keynes for the year ended 31st January, 1997 showed a net loss of £2,800. During the audit of these accounts the following errors were discovered. A Suspense Account had been opened to record the net difference in the Trial Balance.

1 A fixed asset which had cost £2,500 was posted to Repairs. Depreciation is charged on this asset at 10% of cost.
2 An accrual for Bank Interest and Charges of £1,400, and a prepayment for Insurance of £600 at 31st January, 1996 had not been brought down as opening balances.
3 A Value Added Tax credit of £500 on Motor Expenses had been incorrectly claimed and must be repaid to the Revenue Commissioners.
4 Mr Keynes took stock costing £1,200 for his personal use. No entry had been made in the accounts for this.
5 Capital introduced by Mr Keynes of £5,000 had been entered correctly in the Cash Book but was debited to Sales.
6 A prepayment on Rent Payable of £850 at 31st January, 1997 had been omitted from the accounts.
7 A contra entry between the Sales Ledger and the Purchases Ledger of £2,500 had been correctly entered in the Purchases Ledger but was omitted from the Sales Ledger.
8 Trade debtors were shown as £57,800. However,

    (a) Bad Debts of £3,800 had not been written off;
    (b) The existing provision for doubtful debts of £3,400 should have been shown as 5% of debtors; and
    (c) A provision for discounts on debtors of 2% should have been raised.

Required:
(a) Prepare a statement correcting the net loss, and
(b) Complete the Suspense Account.

(*ICPAI Formation I*)

32.6 One of your friends, who is self employed, has prepared his draft accounts for the year ended 31st December, 1997 and has asked you to check them before he submits them to his auditor. You discover the following:

1 An entry appears in the accounts shown as 'Value Added Tax £4,950'. This represents the net tax due and paid to the Revenue Commissioners, based on the Value Added Tax returns. A summary of the returns is as follows:

VAT on Sales		£32,000
Less		
VAT on – Purchases	£21,000	
– Stationery	£1,200	
– Repairs	£2,450	
– Motor Expenses	£2,400	£27,050
		£4,950

The tax credit on Motor Expenses was non-allowable and was claimed in error.

2 Your friend changed his car during the year and paid £7,000. This has been included in Motor Expenses. The new car cost £15,000 and an allowance of £8,000 was given on the old car. The old car had cost £12,000 and depreciation of £4,800 had been charged up to 31st December, 1996, and a further £2,400 had been charged in 1997. Your friend's depreciation policy is to charge 20% per annum on the cost of vehicles held at the year-end.

3 An entry for Rent of £6,000 is shown in the draft accounts. This comprises £8,400 paid and £2,400 received. The payment refers to premises rented to your friend at £8,400 per annum, payable in advance and effective from 1st March, 1997. Your friend sublet part of the premises for £2,400 per annum, payable in advance, with effect from 1st July, 1997.

4 Your friend wrote off a bad debt of £5,000 at 31st December, 1997. Debtors before this write-off were £80,000. Provision for doubtful debts is carried at 2.5% of debtors, but is shown in the draft accounts at 2.5% of the 31st December, 1996 debtors of £60,000.

5 The draft accounts contain an entry for Suspense of £5,500. You attribute this to the following:
 (a) Discounts received of £2,000 shown as discounts allowed, and
 (b) The opening balance on the Stationery account of £1,500 was not included in the account.

Required:
Show the journal entries necessary to correctly treat these transactions.

(*ICPAI Formation I*)

32.7A The draft Financial Statements of Paul Benton for the year ended 31st March, 1998 showed a net profit of £13,360. During the audit of these accounts the following errors were discovered. A Suspense Account had been opened to record the net difference in the draft accounts.

(a) Capital introduced by Mr Benton of £12,000 had been entered correctly in the Cash Book but had been debited to drawings.

(b) A fixed asset which had cost £7,500 was posted to Purchases. Depreciation is 10% of cost.

(c) An insurance prepayment of £1,500 at 31st March, 1997 had not been brought down as an opening balance.

(d) No adjustment has been made to either the Creditors Ledger or discounts account for discounts of £650 which had been granted.

(e) Trade Debtors were shown as £36,600. However,
 (i) Bad Debts of £2,600 had not been written off.
 (ii) The existing provision for doubtful debts of £2,000 should have been adjusted to 5% of debtors.
 (iii) A provision of 2% for discounts on debtors should have been raised.

(f) A contra entry between the Sales Ledger and the Purchases Ledger of £1,000 had been correctly entered in the Sales Ledger but was omitted from the Purchases Ledger.

(g) Credit Sales of £2,500 had been correctly credited to the Sales Account but had been debited to the customer's account as £250.

(h) On 31st March, 1998 both an accrual of £1,300 for bank interest and a rent prepayment of £800 had been omitted from the accounts.

Required:
1 Prepare a statement correcting the net profit, and
2 Complete the Suspense Account.

(*ICPAI Formation I*)

Part IV Revision questions

Suggested solutions to questions with the letter 'A' after the question number are given in Appendix II (pages 683–7)

R4.1A The Trial Balance of J Charleton as at 31st March, 1998 was as follows:

	£ Debit	£ Credit
Premises	220,000	
Vehicles (cost £56,000)	44,800	
Equipment (cost £24,000)	16,800	
Stocks as at 1st April, 1997	74,000	
Debtors	85,000	
Bank		16,250
Creditors		43,500
Sales		750,000
Purchases	465,000	
Wages and Salaries	87,000	
Motor Expenses	26,500	
Telephone and Postage	8,600	
Light and Heat	17,410	
Rates	6,900	
Insurances	13,400	
Bank Interest and Charges	18,950	
Legal Fees	15,000	
Accountancy Charges	3,200	
Rent		12,000
Value Added Tax	2,200	
Miscellaneous Expenses	8,470	
Drawings	20,600	
Capital		162,080
Bank Loan		150,000
	1,133,830	1,133,830

Notes

1 Depreciation is to be charged on the cost of fixed assets as follows:

   Vehicles 20% per annum; Equipment 10% per annum

2 Stocks at 31st March, 1998 were £68,000.

3 'Value Added Tax' represents a refund due from the Revenue Commissioners at 31st March, 1998.

4 'Legal Fees' includes an amount of £12,500 which relates to the purchase of the premises. A further £5,000 is due in relation to this transaction.

5 Part of the premises was let on 1st January, 1998 at a rent of £12,000 per annum, payable in advance.

6 Insurances prepaid as at 31st March, 1998 were £2,200.

7 Amounts due but unpaid as at 31st March, 1998 were:

Bank Interest £5,600; Miscellaneous Expenses £4,200

8 Bad debts of £5,500 are to be written off. A provision of 2% of the remaining debtors is to be made.

You are required to prepare:

(a) a Trading and Profit and Loss Account for the year ended 31st March, 1998; and

(b) a Balance Sheet as at that date.

(*ICPAI Formation I*)

R4.2 Pat O'Neill is a sole trader. The following trial balance was extracted from his books at 31st December, 1998:

	£ Debit	£ Credit
Sales		550,000
Purchases	300,000	
Wages	80,000	
Rent and Rates	5,000	
Insurance	8,000	
Motor Travel	12,000	
Repairs and Renewals	11,000	
Bank Interest and Charges	3,000	
Bad Debts written off	9,000	
Plant and Equipment at cost	75,000	
Plant and Equipment – accumulated depreciation		27,000
Debtors	90,000	
Bank Balance	75,000	
Stock at cost at 1st January, 1998	50,000	
Creditors		40,000
Capital		116,000
Drawings	15,000	
	733,000	733,000

Additional information:

1 Stock at 31st December, 1998 was £65,000.

2 Depreciation is to be provided on plant and equipment at 20% per annum using the reducing balance method.

3 A bad debts provision equal to 15% of debtors is to be created.

4 No provision has been made for bank interest and charges amounting to £800, due to the bank at 31st December, 1998.

Required:

(a) Prepare the Trading and Profit and Loss Account of Pat O'Neill for the year ended 31st December, 1998 and

(b) Prepare the Balance Sheet as at that date.

(*IATI Foundation Examination*)

R4.3A The trial balance of B Harton as at 31st December, 1998 was as follows:

	£ Debit	£ Credit
Capital		165,000
Bank Loan		100,000
Plant and Equipment (cost £40,000)	36,000	
Vehicles (cost £60,000)	48,000	
Office Equipment (cost £8,000)	7,200	
Stocks as at 1st January, 1998	180,000	
Debtors	114,000	
Provision for doubtful debts		1,500
Creditors		76,000
Bank		34,500
Sales		746,000
Rent Received		7,400
Purchases	556,000	
Wages	68,000	
Rent and Rates	24,000	
Motor Expenses	16,000	
Insurances	7,600	
Telephone and Postage	8,400	
Light and Heat	6,200	
Bank Interest and Charges	12,800	
Accountancy Charges	3,500	
Income Tax paid	10,000	
Miscellaneous Expenses	12,400	
Value Added Tax	4,800	
PAYE/PRSI		6,300
Drawings	21,800	
	1,136,700	1,136,700

Notes

1 Depreciation is to be charged on the cost of fixed assets as follows:

Plant and Equipment, and Office Equipment	10% per annum
Vehicles	20% per annum

2 Stocks at 31st December, 1998 were £160,000.
3 Amounts due but unpaid at 31st December, 1998 were:

Accountancy Charges	£1,500
Miscellaneous Expenses	£2,300

4 Amounts prepaid at 31st December 1998 were:

Rent Payable	£6,000
Rent Receivable	£1,200

5 Amounts shown for PAYE/PRSI, and Value Added Tax represent balances due to, or from, the Revenue Commissioners.
6 Bad Debts of £6,000 are to be written off. A provision for doubtful debts of 2.5% is to be carried.

You are required to prepare:
(*a*) a Trading and Profit and Loss Account for the year ended 31st December, 1998, and
(*b*) a Balance Sheet as at that date.

(*ICPAI Formation I*)

R4.4   The following trial balance was extracted from the books of Michael Davis, a carpet retailer, at 30th June, 1998:

	Debit £'000	Credit £'000
Capital at 1st July, 1997		110
12% Loan repayable 2003		50
Drawings	30	
Sales		690
Purchases	478	
Stock at 1st July, 1997	45	
Wages and Salaries	70	
Rent, Rates and Insurance	24	
Light and Heat	12	
Sales Commissions	24	
Advertising	25	
Loan Interest	3	
Leasehold Premises (cost £60,000)	40	
Fittings and Furniture (cost £50,000)	30	
Vehicles (cost £70,000)	50	
Debtors	72	
Bad Debts provision		3
Bank Balance		20
Creditors		30
	903	903

The following additional information is available:

1 Purchases include £10,000 in respect of new furniture for the showroom.
2 Sales commissions are payable at the rate of 5% of sales.
3 In June 1998, goods which had cost £20,000 were sent to a customer on sale or return at an invoice price of £30,000. The goods were returned in July 1998. These goods are included in sales in the trial balance.
4 No record has been made of carpets which cost £5,000 and which were taken by Mr. Davis for his own use.
5 The annual rent of the premises is £24,000. Rent has been paid up to 30th April, 1998.
6 Stocks at 30th June, 1998, consisted of:

Goods for re-sale	£40,000
Advertising literature	£1,000

7 Depreciation is to be provided annually as follows:

Leasehold Premises	10% on cost
Fittings and Furniture	10% on cost
Vehicles	20% on cost

8 Bad debts of £2,000 are to be written off and the bad debts provision is to be maintained at 5% of debtors.

You are required to:
(a) prepare the Trading and Profit and Loss Account for Michael Davis for the year ended 30th June, 1998; and
(b) prepare the Balance Sheet as at that date.

(*ICAI Professional Examination One*)

R4.5A The following trial balance was extracted from the books of T Hardy on 31st December, 1998:

	£ Debit	£ Credit
Sales		610,000
Purchases	385,000	
Wages and Salaries	48,000	
Telephone and Postage	10,700	
Motor Expenses	18,400	
Rent and Rates	13,240	
Light and Heat	11,470	
Insurances	14,150	
Bank Interest and Charges	9,100	
Accountancy Fees	2,460	
General Expenses	8,190	
Value Added Tax	3,240	
PAYE/PRSI	34,700	
Stocks as at 1st January, 1998	37,200	
Debtors	27,400	
Creditors		49,280
Bank		13,740
Vehicles (Cost £48,000)	38,400	
Equipment (Cost £16,000)	11,200	
Drawings	18,750	
Capital		18,580
	691,600	691,600

Notes

1 Depreciation is to be charged on the cost of fixed assets as follows:

Vehicles	20% per annum
Equipment	10% per annum

2 Stocks as at 31st December, 1998 were £28,500.

3 Amounts due but unpaid at 31st December, 1998 were:

Telephone and Postage	£1,500
Bank Interest and Charges	£800

4 Rent Prepaid as at 31st December, 1998 was £2,400.

5 An amount of £2,400 is to be written off debtors in respect of bad debts. In addition, a provision for doubtful debts of 5% of debtors is to be made.

6 In relation to PAYE/PRSI:

 (a) The figure shown represents payments to the Revenue Commissioners and includes Mr. Hardy's personal income tax liability of £8,000.

 (b) An amount of £2,500 remains due and unpaid at 31st December, 1998.

 (c) The Profit and Loss charge is to be included in 'Wages and Salaries' which have been shown net in the Trial Balance.

7 'Value Added Tax' represents a refund due from the Revenue Commissioners at 31st December, 1998. Subsequent to the balancing date the Revenue Commissioners correctly disallowed £1,200 of this figure as relating to non-allowable motor expenses.

You are required to prepare:

(a) a Trading and Profit and Loss Account for the year ended 31st December, 1998, and

(b) a Balance Sheet as at that date.

(ICPAI Formation I)

R4.6A The following trial balance was extracted from the books of Tony Coakley as at 31st March, 1998:

	£ Debit	£ Credit
Capital		43,450
Vehicles (Cost £66,000)...	52,800	
Fixtures and Fittings (Cost £15,600)	14,040	
Office Equipment (Cost £6,700)..	6,030	
Sales		510,000
Purchases	310,800	
Stock as at 1st April, 1997	27,200	
Wages and Salaries	37,470	
Motor Expenses	15,470	
Rent and Rates	5,950	
Telephone and Postage	2,190	
Light and Heat..	4,010	
Repairs and Renewals..	1,750	
Insurances	2,460	
Bank Interest and Charges	2,140	
Stationery and Advertising...	3,430	
Accountancy Charges...	1,570	
Drawings...	18,400	
Taxation	48,950	
Trade Debtors..	51,400	
Trade Creditors		43,200
Bank..		9,410
	606,060	606,060

You are given the following additional information:

(a) Depreciation is to be charged on the cost of fixed assets at the following rates:

Vehicles	20% per annum
Fixtures and Fittings and Office Equipment	10% per annum

(b) Stock as at 31st March, 1998 was £29,500.

(c) Insurances prepaid at 31st March, 1998 were £660.

(d) 'Taxation' comprises the following:

Mr. Coakley's Personal Income Tax Paid	£9,600
Value Added Tax Paid	£22,650
PAYE/PRSI Paid	£16,700
	£48,950

(e) The amount shown for Value Added Tax paid is made up as follows:

VAT on Sales		£76,300
Less		
VAT on Purchases	£53,200	
VAT on Stationery and Advertising	£450	£53,650
		£22,650

(f) PAYE/PRSI is to be included in wages and salaries. An amount of £1,500 is due and unpaid at 31st March, 1998.

(g) Expenses due but unpaid at 31st March, 1998 were:

Bank Interest and Charges	£660
Accountancy Charges	£550

(*h*) Bad Debts totalling £4,400 are to be written off and a provision of 2.5% of debtors is to be made for doubtful debts.

You are required to prepare:
(*a*) a Trading and Profit and Loss Account for the year ended 31st March, 1998, and
(*b*) a Balance Sheet as at that date.

(*ICPAI Formation I*)

R4.7 Henry McCrea is a draper who maintains full accounting records. His accountant extracted the following trial balance from the accounts at 30th April, 1998:

	£ Debit	£ Credit
Land and Buildings, at cost	312,000	
Machinery, at cost	45,000	
Accumulated Depreciation		
– on buildings		36,000
– on machinery		22,500
Stocks at 1st May, 1997		
– Menswear	44,200	
– Childrenswear	4,600	
Purchases		
– Menswear	30,800	
– Childrenswear	8,800	
Sales		
– Menswear		48,300
– Childrenswear		39,100
Bank		16,000
Wages	22,000	
Electricity	2,100	
Fuel Oils	5,400	
Drawings	14,800	
Interest	3,200	
Capital		331,000
	492,900	492,900

The following information is also available:

1 Closing stocks consisted of:

   Menswear   £31,200
   Childrenswear   £400

2 During the year Henry and his family took clothing from stock which could otherwise have been sold for £3,800. It was estimated that the purchase cost of this clothing was £3,200.
3 Approximately one third of the cost of electricity and fuel oil is attributable to Henry's private use.
4 Depreciation is charged annually as follows:

   Machinery   10% on cost
   Buildings   1% on cost

5 Repairs to machinery were carried out in April 1998 at a cost of £800. They had not been paid for at the end of the month.

Required:
(*a*) Prepare the Trading Account and Profit and Loss Account of Henry McCrea for the year ended 30th April, 1998.
(*b*) Prepare a Balance Sheet as at that date.

(*ICAI Professional Examination Two*)

Part V

PARTNERSHIP ACCOUNTING

33

An introduction to partnerships and their accounts

33.1 The need for partnerships

So far we have mainly considered businesses owned by only one person. However, businesses can often have more than one owner. There are various reasons for multiple ownership. For example,

1 The capital required is more than one person can provide.
2 The experience or ability required to manage the business cannot be found in one person alone.
3 Many people want to share management instead of doing everything on their own.
4 Very often the partners will be members of the same family.

There are two types of multiple ownership: **partnerships** and companies. This part of the book deals only with partnerships. Part VI deals with companies.

33.2 The nature of partnerships

A partnership has the following characteristics.

1 It is formed to make profits.
2 It must obey the law as given in the Partnership Act 1890. If there is a limited partner, as described in section 33.3, there is also the Limited Partnership Act of 1907 to comply with as well.
3 Normally there can be a minimum of two partners and a maximum of 20 partners. There is no maximum limit in law for professional practices such as firms of accountants or solicitors. The Minister for Industry and Commerce also has the power to disapply the 20 partner limit in the case of certain other partnerships.
4 Each partner (except for limited partners described below) must pay his share of any debts that the partnership could not pay. If necessary, he could be forced to sell all his private possessions to pay his share of the debts.

33.3 Limited partners

A **limited partner**, unlike ordinary partners, is not liable for his/her share of the debts of the partnership. He has the following characteristics.

1 His liability for the debts of the partnership is limited to the capital he has put in. He can lose that capital, but he cannot be asked for any more money to pay the debts.

2 He is not allowed to take part in the management of the partnership business.
3 All of the partners cannot be limited partners.

33.4 Partnership agreements

Agreements in writing are not necessary. However, it is better if a proper written agreement is drawn up by a solicitor or accountant. Where there is a proper written agreement there will be fewer problems between partners. A written agreement means less confusion about what has been agreed.

33.5 Likely contents of partnership agreements

The written agreement can contain as much, or as little, as the partners want. The law does not say what it must contain. The usual contents with regard to accounting are:

1 The capital to be contributed by each partner.
2 The ratio in which profits (or losses) are to be shared.
3 The rate of interest, if any, to be paid on capital before the profits are shared.
4 The rate of interest, if any, to be charged on partners' drawings.
5 Salaries to be paid to partners.

Capital contributions

Partners need *not* contribute equal amounts of capital. What matters is how much capital each partner *agrees* to contribute.

Profit (or loss) sharing ratios

It is often thought by students that profits should be shared in the same ratio as that in which capital is contributed. For example, suppose the capitals were Allen £2,000 and Beet £1,000, many people would share the profits in the ratio of two-thirds to one-third, even though the work to be done by each partner is similar. A look at the division of the first few years' profits on such a basis would be:

Years	1	2	3	4	5	Total
	£	£	£	£	£	£
Net profit	1,800	2,400	3,000	3,000	3,600	13,800
Shared:						
Allen ⅔	1,200	1,600	2,000	2,000	2,400	9,200
Beet ⅓	600	800	1,000	1,000	1,200	4,600

It can now be seen that Allen would receive £9,200, or £4,600 more than Beet. Equitably the difference between the two shares of profit in this case, as the duties of the partners are the same, should be adequate to compensate Allen for putting extra capital into the firm. It is obvious that £4,600 extra profits is far more than adequate for this purpose.

Consider too the position of capital ratio sharing of profits if one partner put in £99,000 and the other put in £1,000 as capital.

To overcome the difficulty of compensating for the investment of extra capital, the concept of interest on capital was devised.

Interest on capital

If the work to be done by each partner is of equal value but the capital contributed is unequal, it is equitable to grant interest on the partners' capitals. This interest is treated as a deduction prior to the calculation of profits and their distribution according to the profit-sharing ratio.

The rate of interest is a matter of agreement between the partners, but it should theoretically equal the return which they would have received if they had invested the capital elsewhere.

Taking Allen and Beet's firm again, but sharing the profits equally after charging 5% per annum interest on capital, the division of profits would become:

Years	1	2	3	4	5	Total
	£	£	£	£	£	£
Net profit	1,800	2,400	3,000	3,000	3,600	13,800
Interest on capitals						
Allen	100	100	100	100	100	= 500
Beet	50	50	50	50	50	= 250
Remainder shared:						
Allen ½	825	1,125	1,425	1,425	1,725	= 6,525
Beet ½	825	1,125	1,425	1,425	1,725	= 6,525

Summary	Allen	Beet
	£	£
Interest on capital	500	250
Balance of profits	6,525	6,525
	7,025	6,775

Allen has thus received £250 more than Beet, this being adequate return (in the partners' estimation) for having invested an extra £1,000 in the firm for five years.

Interest on drawings

It is obviously in the best interests of the firm if cash is withdrawn from the firm by the partners in accordance with the two basic principles of: (*a*) as little as possible, and (*b*) as late as possible. The more cash that is left in the firm the more expansion that can be financed, the greater the economies of having ample cash to take advantage of bargains and of not missing cash discounts because cash is not available and so on.

To deter the partners from taking out cash unnecessarily the concept can be used of charging the partners interest on each withdrawal, calculated from the date of withdrawal to the end of the financial year. The amount charged to them helps to swell the profits divisible between the partners.

The rate of interest should be sufficient to achieve this end without being unduly penal.

Suppose that Allen and Beet have decided to charge interest on drawings at 5% per annum, and that their year end was 31 December. The following drawings are made:

Allen

Drawings		Interest on drawings	
			£
1 January	£100	£100 × 5% × 12 months =	5
1 March	£240	£240 × 5% × 10 months =	10
1 May	£120	£120 × 5% × 8 months =	4
1 July	£240	£240 × 5% × 6 months =	6
1 October	£80	£80 × 5% × 3 months =	1
		Interest charged to Allen =	26

Beet

Drawings		Interest on drawings	
			£
1 January	£60	£60 × 5% × 12 months =	3
1 August	£480	£480 × 5% × 5 months =	10
1 December	£240	£240 × 5% × 1 month =	1
		Interest charged to Beet =	14

Partners' salary entitlement

One partner may have more responsibility or tasks than the other(s). As a reward for this, rather than change the profit and loss sharing ratio, he may have a salary which is deducted before sharing the balance of profits.

33.6 An example of the distribution of profits amongst partners

Taylor and Clarke are in partnership sharing profits and losses in the ratio of Taylor ⅗ths, Clarke ⅖ths. They are entitled to 5% per annum interest on capitals, Taylor having £2,000 capital and Clarke £6,000. Clarke is to receive a salary of £500. They charge interest on drawings, Taylor being charged £50 and Clarke £100. The net profit, before any distributions to the partners, amounted to £5,000 for the year ended 31 December 1997.

	£	£	£
Net profit			5,000
Add Interest charged on drawings:			
Taylor		50	
Clarke		100	
			150
			5,150
Less Salary: Clarke		500	
Interest on capital:			
Taylor	100		
Clarke	300		
		400	
			900
Profit to be shared			4,250
Shared:			
Taylor ⅗ths			2,550
Clarke ⅖ths			1,700
			4,250

The £5,000 net profits have therefore been shared:

	Taylor £	Clarke £
Profit shares	2,550	1,700
Interest on capital	100	300
Salary	–	500
	2,650	2,500
Less Interest on drawings	50	100
	2,600	2,400
	£5,000	

33.7 The final accounts of partnerships

If the sales, stock and expenses of a partnership were exactly the same as those of a sole trader, then the trading and profit and loss account would be identical to that prepared for the sole trader. However, a partnership would have an extra section shown under the profit and loss account. This section is called the **profit and loss appropriation account**, and it is in this account that the distribution of profits is shown. The heading to the trading and profit and loss account does not include the words 'appropriation account'. It is purely an accounting custom not to include it in the heading.

The trading and profit and loss account of Taylor and Clarke from the details given would appear:

Taylor and Clarke
Trading and Profit and Loss Account for the year ended 31 December 1997

(Trading Account – same as for sole trader)

(Profit and Loss Account – same as for sole trader)

Profit and Loss Appropriation Account	£	£	£
Net profit			5,000
Interest on drawings:			
Taylor		50	
Clarke		100	150
			5,150
Less:			
Interest on capitals			
Taylor	100		
Clarke	300	400	
Salary: Clarke		500	900
			4,250
Balance of profits shared:			
Taylor ⅗ths			2,550
Clarke ⅖ths			1,700
			4,250

33.8 Fixed and fluctuating capital accounts

When accounting for capital, salaries and interest on either drawings or capital one can choose between maintaining a **fixed capital account combined with a current account** or maintaining a **fluctuating capital account** in place of both of these.

(i) Fixed capital accounts plus current accounts

Under this method the capital account for each partner remains year by year at the figure of capital put into the firm by that partner. The profits, interest on capital and the salaries to which the partner may be entitled are then credited to a separate current account for the partner, and the drawings and the interest on drawings are debited to it. The balance of the current account at the end of each financial year will then represent the amount of undrawn (or withdrawn) profits. A credit balance will be undrawn profits, while a debit balance will be drawings in excess of the profits to which the partner was entitled.

For Taylor and Clarke, capital and current accounts, assuming drawings of £2,000 each, will appear:

Taylor – Capital Account

				£
	1997			
	Jan	1	Balance b/d	2,000

Clarke – Capital Account

				£
	1997			
	Jan	1	Balance b/d	6,000

Taylor – Current Account

1997		£	1997		£
Dec 31	Cash: Drawings	2,000	Dec 31	Profit and loss appropriation account:	
„ 31	Profit and loss appropriation: Interest on drawings	50		Interest on capital	100
				Share of profits	2,550
„ 31	Balance c/d	600			
		2,650			2,650
			1998		
			Jan 1	Balance b/d	600

Clarke – Current Account

1997		£	1997		£
Dec 31	Cash: Drawings	2,000	Dec 31	Profit and loss appropriation account:	
„ 31	Profit and loss appropriation: Interest on drawings	100		Interest on capital	300
				Share of profits	1,700
„ 31	Balance c/d	400		Salary	500
		2,500			2,500
			1998		
			Jan 1	Balance b/d	400

Notice that the salary of Clarke was not paid to him, it was merely credited to his account. If in fact it was paid in addition to his drawings, the £500 cash paid would have been debited to the current account changing the £400 credit balance into a £100 debit balance.

Examiners often ask for the capital accounts and current accounts to be shown in *columnar form*. For the previous accounts of Taylor & Clarke these would appear as follows:

Capitals

	Taylor £	Clarke £	1997		Taylor £	Clarke £
			Jan 1	Balances b/d	2,000	6,000

Current Accounts

1997		Taylor £	Clarke £	1997		Taylor £	Clarke £
Dec 31	Cash: Drawings	2,000	2,000	Dec 31	Interest on capital	100	300
„ 31	Interest on drawings	50	100	„ 31	Share of profits	2,550	1,700
„ 31	Balances c/d	600	400	„ 31	Salary		500
		2,650	2,500			2,650	2,500
				1998			
				Jan 1	Balances b/d	600	400

(ii) Fluctuating capital accounts

Under this method the distribution of profits would be credited to the capital account, and the drawings and interest on drawings debited to it. Therefore, the balance on the capital account will change each year, i.e. it will fluctuate.

If fluctuating capital accounts had been kept for Taylor and Clarke they would have appeared:

Taylor – Capital Account

1997			£	1997			£
Dec	31	Cash: Drawings	2,000	Jan	1	Balance b/d	2,000
„	31	Profit and loss		Dec	31	Profit and loss	
		appropriation account:				appropriation account:	
		Interest on				Interest on capital	100
		drawings	50			Share of profits	2,550
„	31	Balance c/d	2,600				
			4,650				4,650
				1998			
				Jan	1	Balance b/d	2,600

Clarke – Capital Account

1997			£	1997			£
Dec	31	Cash: Drawings	2,000	Jan	1	Balance b/d	6,000
„	31	Profit and loss		Dec	31	Profit and loss	
		appropriation account:				appropriation account:	
		Interest on				Interest on capital	300
		drawings	100			Salary	500
„	31	Balance c/d	6,400			Share of profit	1,700
			8,500				8,500
				1998			
				Jan	1	Balance b/d	6,400

Fixed capital accounts are preferable

The keeping of fixed capital accounts plus current accounts is considered preferable to fluctuating capital accounts. When partners are taking out greater amounts than the share of the profits that they are entitled to, this is shown up by a debit balance on the current account and so acts as a warning.

33.9 Where a partnership agreement does not exist

Where no partnership agreement exists, express or implied, Section 24 of the Partnership Act 1890 governs the situation. This section, amongst other things, states that:

(a) Profits and losses are to be shared *equally* between the partners.
(b) Interest is *not* to be allowed on capital.
(c) Interest is *not* to be charged on drawings.
(d) Salaries are *not* allowed.

(e) If a partner puts a sum of money into a firm *in excess* of the capital he has agreed to subscribe, he is entitled to interest at the rate of 5% per annum on such an advance (but only on this excess – see (b) above).

This section applies where there is no agreement. There may be an agreement not by a partnership deed but in a letter, or it may be implied by conduct, for instance when a partner signs a balance sheet which shows profits shared in some ratio other than equally.

In some cases of dispute as to whether agreement existed or not only the courts would be competent to decide.

33.10 The balance sheet of a partnership

In a partnership the capital part of the balance sheet will appear:

Balance Sheet as at 31 December 1997

	Taylor £	Clarke £	Total £
Capitals:	2,000	6,000	8,000
Current accounts			
Interest on capital	100	300	
Share of profits	2,550	1,700	
Salary	–	500	
	2,650	2,500	
Less Drawings	2,000	2,000	
Interest on drawings	50	100	
	600	400	1,000
			9,000

If one of the current accounts had a debit balance, for instance if the current account of Clarke had finished up as £400 debit, the figure of £400 would appear in brackets and the balances would appear net in the totals column:

	Taylor £	Clarke £	Total £
Closing balance	600	(400)	200

If the net figure turned out to be a debit figure then this would be deducted from the total of the capital accounts.

Review questions

In addition to the questions which follow, you should attempt questions 227–234 in the accompanying book of multiple-choice questions (see back cover for details).

Suggested solutions to review questions with the letter 'A' after the question number are given in Appendix I (pages 633–7).

33.1A Rooster and Scarecrow are business partners sharing profits and losses equally. Their first financial year ended on 31st December, 1998 at which date the following balances were taken from their books.

	Rooster	Scarecrow
Capital	£50,000	£30,000
Salary	£20,000	£18,000
Drawings	£2,000	£3,000

The firm's net profit for the year was £60,000.
Interest on capital is to be allowed at 10% per annum.

Required:
Prepare the firm's Profit and Loss Appropriation Account and the partners' current accounts.

33.2 Pat and William are in partnership, sharing profits and losses in the ratio of 3:2, respectively. The following information relates to their business for the year ended 31st December, 1998, before the completion of their profit and loss appropriation account.

Net (trading) profit £46,000

	Pat £		William £	
Current accounts (1st January, 1998)	800	Dr	300	Cr
Drawings	3,000		2,000	
Interest on capital	500		700	
Salary entitlement	12,000		–	
Interest on drawings	200		150	

Required:
(a) Prepare, for the year ended 31st December, 1998:
  (i) the profit and loss appropriation account of the firm, and
  (ii) the partners' current accounts.
(b) Explain:
  (i) why partners' current accounts are often prepared as well as capital accounts;
  (ii) the significance of a debit balance on a partner's current account;
  (iii) the purpose of preparing a partnership profit and loss appropriation account;
  (iv) why interest is frequently allowed to partners on their capital; and
  (v) why interest is frequently charged on partners' drawings.

33.3A Bee, Cee and Dee have been holding preliminary discussions with a view to forming a partnership to buy and sell antiques.

The position has now been reached where the prospective partners have agreed the basic arrangements under which the partnership will operate.

Bee will contribute £40,000 as capital and up to £10,000 as a long-term loan to the partnership, if needed. He has extensive other business interests and will not therefore be taking an active part in the running of the business.

Cee is unable to bring in more than £2,000 as capital initially, but, because he has an expert knowledge of the antique trade, will act as the manager of the business on a full-time basis.

Dee is willing to contribute £10,000 as capital. He will also assist in running the business as the need arises. In particular, he is prepared to attend auctions anywhere within the United Kingdom in order to acquire trading stock which he will transport back to the firm's premises in his van. On occasions he may also help Cee to restore the articles prior to sale to the public.

At the meeting, the three prospective partners intend to decide upon the financial arrangements for sharing out the profits (or losses) made by the firm and have approached you for advice.

You are required to prepare a set of explanatory notes, under suitable headings, of the considerations which the prospective partners should take into account in arriving at their decisions at the next meeting.

(*Association of Chartered Certified Accountants*)

33.4 On 1st March 1997 Rob, Sam and Tom went into partnership without making an agreement about profit sharing. On that date the three partners introduced £25,000, £30,000 and £50,000 capital respectively. Half way through the year Rob introduced a further £5,000 in capital. During the business's first year of trading the partners withdrew cash as follows: Rob £2,000, Sam £6,000 and Tom £3,000. Tom also took stock which had cost the partnership £300 for his own use. Sam paid expenses of £500 incurred by the partnership out of his private funds and was not reimbursed by the firm. The partnership's net profit, after making any adjustments for the above, for the year ended 28th February, 1998 was £40,000.

Required:
Show the partners' capital and current accounts for the year ended 28th February, 1998 as they would appear in the books of the partnership.

33.5A Mendez and Marshall are in partnership sharing profits and losses equally. The following is their trial balance as at 30 June 1998.

	Dr £	Cr £
Buildings (cost £75,000)	50,000	
Fixtures at cost	11,000	
Provision for depreciation: Fixtures		3,300
Debtors	16,243	
Creditors		11,150
Cash at bank	677	
Stock at 30 June 1997	41,979	
Sales		123,650
Purchases	85,416	
Carriage outwards	1,288	
Discounts allowed	115	
Loan interest: King	4,000	
Office expenses	2,416	
Salaries and wages	18,917	
Bad debts	503	
Provision for bad debts		400
Loan from J King		40,000
Capitals: Mendez		35,000
Marshall		29,500
Current accounts: Mendez		1,306
Marshall		298
Drawings: Mendez	6,400	
Marshall	5,650	
	244,604	244,604

(a) Stock at 30 June 1998 £56,340.
(b) Expenses to be accrued: Office Expenses £96; Wages £200.
(c) Depreciate fixtures 10% on reducing balance basis, buildings £1,000.
(d) Reduce provision for bad debts to £320.
(e) Partnership salary: £800 to Mendez. Not yet entered.
(f) Interest on drawings: Mendez £180; Marshall £120.
(g) Interest on capital account balances at 10% per annum.

Required:
Prepare a trading and profit and loss appropriation account for the year ended 30 June 1998, and a balance sheet as at that date.

33.6 Oscar and Felix are in partnership. They share profits in the ratio: Oscar 60%; Felix 40%. The following trial balance was extracted as at 31 March 1998.

	Dr £	Cr £
Office equipment at cost	6,500	
Vehicle at cost	9,200	
Provision for depreciation at 31 March 1997:		
Vehicle		3,680
Office equipment		1,950
Stock at 31 March 1997	24,970	
Debtors and creditors	20,960	16,275
Cash at bank	615	
Cash in hand	140	
Sales		90,370
Purchases	71,630	
Salaries	8,417	
Office expenses	1,370	
Discounts allowed	563	
Current accounts at 31 March 1997		
Oscar		1,379
Felix		1,211
Capital accounts: Oscar		27,000
Felix		12,000
Drawings: Oscar	5,500	
Felix	4,000	
	153,865	153,865

Notes
(a) Stock was £27,340.
(b) Office expenses owing £110.
(c) Provide for depreciation: vehicle 20% of cost, office equipment 10% of cost.
(d) Charge interest on capitals at 10% per annum.
(e) Charge interest on drawings: Oscar £180; Felix £210.

Required:
Draw up a set of final accounts for the year ended 31 March 1998 for the partnership.

33.7A Henson and Pierce are in partnership and share profits and losses equally. The following trial balance was extracted from their books on 31st March, 1998.

	Dr £	Cr £
Premises (cost £120,000)	120,000	
Vehicles (cost £34,000)	27,200	
Equipment (cost £12,000)	9,600	
Stocks as at 1st April, 1997	65,000	
Debtors	42,700	
Creditors		69,400
Sales		680,000
Purchases	482,000	
Wages	86,000	
Motor expenses	15,600	
Light and heat	9,100	
Telephone and postage	6,100	
Rent and rates	4,750	
Discount		8,460
Insurance	9,350	
General expenses	7,400	
Bank		12,900
Drawings: Henson	19,500	
Pierce	15,000	
Capital: Henson		95,000
Pierce		50,000
Current accounts as at 31st March, 1997		
Henson		5,720
Pierce	2,180	
	921,480	921,480

Notes

1 Stocks as at 31st March, 1998 were £72,000.
2 Depreciation for the year ended 31st March, 1998 is to be charged on the cost of fixed assets as follows:

Vehicles	20% per annum
Equipment	10% per annum

3 Expenses due but unpaid at 31st March, 1998 were:

Insurance	£1,500
General expenses	£1,200

4 £4,700 is to be written off debtors in respect of bad debts. In addition, a provision for doubtful debts of 5% of debtors is to be made.
5 Interest is to be charged at 10% of Capital Account balances which remain fixed.
6 Henson is to be credited with a salary of £8,000.
7 Included in 'Purchases' is £5,000 relating to goods purchased for Henson's personal use.

You are required to prepare:
(*a*) A Trading and Profit and Loss Account for the year ended 31st March, 1998, and
(*b*) a Balance Sheet as at that date.

(*ICPAI Formation I*)

33.8A The following list of balances as at 30 September 19X0 has been extracted from the books of Brick and Stone, trading in partnership, sharing the balance of profits and losses in the proportions 3:2 respectively.

	£
Printing, stationery and postages	3,500
Sales	322,100
Stock at 1 October 19X9	23,000
Purchases	208,200
Rent and rates	10,300
Heat and light	8,700
Staff salaries	36,100
Telephone charges	2,900
Vehicle running costs	5,620
Discounts allowable	950
Discounts receivable	370
Sales returns	2,100
Purchases returns	6,100
Carriage inwards	1,700
Carriage outwards	2,400
Fixtures and fittings: at cost	26,000
provision for depreciation	11,200
Vehicles: at cost	46,000
provision for depreciation	25,000
Provision for doubtful debts	300
Cash drawings: Brick	24,000
Stone	11,000
Current account balances at 1 October 19X9:	
Brick	3,600 credit
Stone	2,400 credit
Capital account balances at 1 October 19X9:	
Brick	33,000
Stone	17,000
Debtors	9,300
Creditors	8,400
Balance at bank	7,700

Additional information

1 £10,000 is to be transferred from Brick's capital account to a newly opened Brick Loan Account on 1 July 19X0.
   Interest at 10% per annum on the loan is to be credited to Brick.
2 Stone is to be credited with a salary at the rate of £12,000 per annum from 1 April 19X0.
3 Stock in hand at 30 September 19X0 has been valued at cost at £32,000.
4 Telephone charges accrued due at 30 September 19X0 amounted to £400 and rent of £600 prepaid at that date.
5 During the year ended 30 September 19X0 Stone has taken goods costing £1,000 for his own use.
6 Depreciation is to be provided at the following annual rates on the straight line basis:

Fixtures and fittings	10%
Vehicles	20%

Required:
(a) Prepare a trading and profit and loss account for the year ended 30 September 19X0.
(b) Prepare a balance sheet as at 30 September 19X0 which should include summaries of the partners' capital and current accounts for the year ended on that date.

(Association of Accounting Technicians)

33.9 Coyne and Malone are in partnership sharing profits and losses equally. The following trial balance was taken from their books on 30th June, 1998.

	Dr £	Cr £
Sales		275,000
Purchases	168,000	
Wages and salaries	27,400	
Light and heat	6,700	
Telephone and postage	4,100	
Motor expenses	12,150	
Repairs and renewals..	3,190	
Insurances	4,200	
Advertising and stationery	3,470	
Bank interest and charges	6,100	
Accountancy fees	1,300	
Rent and rates	9,100	
General expenses	4,500	
Stocks as at 1st July, 1997...	21,600	
Debtors	23,500	
Creditors		19,480
PAYE/PRSI..		3,400
Value Added Tax	2,100	
Bank		13,400
Drawings – Coyne..	10,700	
– Malone	11,400	
Capital – Coyne		18,000
– Malone		15,000
Current account – Coyne	4,700	
– Malone		3,250
Vehicles (cost £17,000)...	13,600	
Equipment (cost £12,000)	9,720	
	347,530	347,530

Notes

1 Depreciation is to be charged on the cost of fixed assets as follows:

Vehicles	20% per annum
Equipment	10% per annum

2 Stocks as at 30th June, 1998 were £28,500.

3 Expenses due but unpaid as at 30th June, 1998 were:

Telephone and postage	£750
Bank interest	£870

4 Malone is to be credited with a salary of £7,500.

5 'PAYE/PRSI' and 'Value Added Tax' represent amounts due to, or from, the Revenue Commissioners.

6 Interest is to be charged at 10% of Capital Balances which remain fixed.

7 Included in purchases is an amount of £3,000 relating to goods purchased for Coyne's personal use.

8 £3,500 is to be written off debtors in respect of bad debts. In addition, a provision for doubtful debts of 5% of debtors is to be made.

You are required to prepare:
(*a*) a Trading and Profit and Loss Account for the year ended 30th June, 1998, and
(*b*) a Balance Sheet as at that date.

(*ICPAI Formation I*)

33.10 Owen and Steel are in partnership, sharing profits equally after Owen has been allowed a salary of £5,000 per year. No interest is charged on drawings or allowed on current accounts, but interest of 10% p.a. is allowed on the opening capital account balances for each year. Their bookkeeper has been having trouble balancing the books and has eventually produced the following list of balances as at 31 December.

	£
Capital account: Owen	9,000
Capital account: Steel	10,000
10% loan account: Steel	5,000
10% loan account: Williams	6,000
Current account balance 1 January: Owen	1,000
Current account balance 1 January: Steel	2,000
Drawings: Owen	6,500
Drawings: Steel	5,500
Sales	113,100
Sales returns	3,000
Closing stock	17,000
Cost of goods sold	70,000
Sales ledger control account	30,000
Purchase ledger control account	25,000
Operating expenses	26,100
Fixed assets at cost	37,000
Provision for depreciation	18,000
Bank overdraft	3,000
Suspense account	?

You ascertain the following information:
(i)   The sales ledger control account does not agree with the list of balances from the ledger. The following errors when corrected will remove the difference:
   (a) the sales returns day book has been undercast by £100;
   (b) a contra entry with the creditors ledger for £200 has been omitted from the control accounts;
   (c) an invoice for £2,000 was incorrectly entered in the sales day book as £200.
(ii) A fully depreciated fixed asset, original cost £5,000, was sold during the year. The proceeds of £1,000 were entered in the bank account only, and no other entries in connection with the disposal were made.
(iii) It is agreed that hotel bills for £500 paid by Steel from his personal bank account are proper business expenses. Owen has taken goods out of the business for his own use, costing £1,000. No entry has been made for either of these items.
(iv) No interest of any kind has yet been paid or recorded.
(v)   Any remaining balance on the suspense account cannot be traced, and is to be treated in the most suitable manner.

Required:
(a) Prepare a trial balance and establish the balance on the suspense account.
(b) Incorporate the necessary adjustments, showing your workings clearly in any way you feel appropriate.
(c) Prepare final accounts for presentation to the partners.

(Association of Chartered Certified Accountants)

34

Goodwill in partnership accounts

34.1 The nature of goodwill

Suppose that you have owned a business for some years and now want to sell it. How much would you ask as the total sale price of the business? In order to arrive at a value for the business you decide to separately value all of the individual assets and liabilities and treat the excess of the value of the assets over the liabilities as being the value of the business. If your business did not have any liabilities your list of asset values might be as follows:

	£
Buildings	225,000
Machinery	75,000
Debtors	60,000
Stock	40,000
	400,000

Instead of selling the assets individually you may be able to sell the business as a going concern for, say, £450,000, £50,000 more than the total for all the assets. This extra amount of £50,000 is called **goodwill**. The purchaser has paid this because he wanted to take over the business as a going concern. Thus:

Purchased Goodwill = Purchase Price *less* the value of identifiable net assets.

34.2 Reasons for the payment of goodwill

In buying an existing business which has been established for some time there may be quite a few possible advantages. Some of them are listed here:

- A large number of regular customers who will continue to deal with the new owner.
- The business has a good reputation.
- It has experienced, efficient and reliable employees.
- The business is situated in a good location.
- It has good contacts with suppliers.

None of these advantages is available to completely new businesses. For this reason, many people would decide to buy an existing business and pay an amount for goodwill.

34.3 The existence of goodwill in a business

Goodwill does not necessarily exist in a business. If the business had a bad reputation, an inefficient labour force or other negative factors, the owner is unlikely to be paid for goodwill on selling the business.

34.4 Methods of calculating goodwill

There is no single way of calculating goodwill to which everyone can agree. The seller will probably want more for the goodwill than the buyer will want to pay. All that is certain is that when an agreement is reached between buyer and seller, that determines the amount of goodwill. Various methods are used to help buyer and seller come to an agreed figure. The calculations give buyer and seller a figure with which to begin discussions of the value.

Very often each industry or occupation has its own customary way of calculating goodwill. For example,

(a) In some types of retail business it has been the custom to value goodwill at the average weekly sales for the past year multiplied by a given figure. The given figure will, of course, differ between different types of businesses, and often changes gradually in the same types of business in the long term.

(b) With many professional firms, such as accountants in public practice, it is the custom to value goodwill as being the gross annual fees times a given number. For instance, what is termed a two years' purchase of a firm with gross fees of £100,000 means goodwill = 2 × £100,000 = £200,000.

(c) The average net annual profit for a specified past number of years multiplied by an agreed number. This is often said to be x years' purchase of the net profits.

(d) The super-profits method (see below).

It may be argued, as in the case of a sole trader for example, that the net profits are not 'true profits'. This is because the sole trader has not charged for the following expenses:

(a) Services of the proprietor. He has worked in the business, but he has not charged for such services. Any drawings he makes are charged to a capital account, not to the profit and loss account.

(b) The use of the money he has invested in the business. If he had invested his money elsewhere he would have earned interest or dividends on such investments.

Super profits are what is left of the net profits after allowances have been made for (a) services of the proprietor and (b) the use of the capital.

It is usually calculated as, for example,

	£	£
Annual net profits		80,000
Less (i) Remuneration that the proprietor would have earned for similar work elsewhere	20,000	
(ii) Interest that would have been earned if capital had been invested elsewhere	10,000	30,000
Annual super profits		50,000

The annual super profits are then multiplied by a number agreed by the seller and the purchaser of the business.

34.5 Existence of goodwill in a sole trader's books

Goodwill is not entered in a sole trader's accounts unless he has actually bought it. This will show that he did not start the business himself, but bought an existing business.

34.6 Existence of goodwill in partnership books

Although goodwill is not normally entered in the accounts unless it has been purchased, sometimes it is necessary in partnerships.

Unless it has been agreed differently, a partner will own a share in the goodwill in the same ratio in which he shares profits. For instance, if A takes one-quarter of the profits he will be the owner of one-quarter of the goodwill. This is true even if there is no goodwill account.

This means that when something happens such as:

(a) existing partners decide to change profit and loss sharing ratios, or
(b) a new partner is introduced, or
(c) a partner retires or dies,

then the ownership of goodwill by partners changes in some way.

The change may involve cash passing from one partner to another, or an adjustment in the books, so that the changes in ownership do not lead to a partner (or partners) giving away his share of ownership for nothing.

34.7 Change in the profit sharing ratios of existing partners

Sometimes the profit and loss sharing ratios have to be changed. Typical reasons are:

- A partner may not work as much as he used to, possibly because of old age or ill-health.
- His skills and ability may have changed.
- He may be doing much more for the business than he used to.

If the partners decide to change their profit sharing ratios, an adjustment for goodwill passing from one partner to another will be needed. If this was not done then some partners would lose a share of the goodwill without being rewarded for it. Other partners would also gain shares of the goodwill without paying anything or being charged for them in any way. This would never be agreed to by partners losing a share of goodwill, so we have to make adjustments to reward them for their loss of goodwill.

Exhibit 34.1

E, F and G have been in business for ten years. They have always shared profits equally. No goodwill account has ever existed in the books. On 31 December 1997 they agreed that G will take only a one-fifth share of the profits as from 1 January 1998, because he will be devoting less of his time to the business in the future. E and F will each take two-fifths of the profits. The summarised balance sheet of the business on 31 December 1997 appeared as follows:

Balance Sheet as at 31 December 1997

		£
Net assets		7,000
Capital:	E	3,000
	F	1,800
	G	2,200
		7,000

The partners agree that the goodwill should be valued at £3,000. Answer (1) shows the solution when a goodwill account is opened. Answer (2) is the solution when a goodwill account is not opened.

1 Goodwill account opened. Open a goodwill account. Then make the following entries:
Debit the goodwill account with the total value of goodwill.
Credit the individual partners' capital accounts: each one with his share of goodwill in the old profit sharing ratio.

The goodwill account will appear as:

Goodwill

Capitals: valuation shared (old)	£		£
E	1,000		
F	1,000		
G	1,000	Balance c/d	3,000
	3,000		3,000

The capital accounts may be shown in columnar fashion as:

Capitals

	E £	F £	G £		E £	F £	G £
Balances c/d	4,000	2,800	3,200	Balances b/d	3,000	1,800	2,200
				Goodwill: old ratios	1,000	1,000	1,000
	4,000	2,800	3,200		4,000	2,800	3,200

The balance sheet items before and after the adjustments will appear as:

		Before £	After £
Goodwill		–	3,000
Other assets		7,000	7,000
		7,000	10,000
Capitals:	E	3,000	4,000
	F	1,800	2,800
	G	2,200	3,200
		7,000	10,000

2 Goodwill account not opened. The effect of the change of ownership of goodwill may be shown in the following form:

Before		After		Loss or Gain	Action Required
	£		£		
E One-third	1,000	Two-fifths	1,200	Gain £200	Debit E's capital account £200
F One-third	1,000	Two-fifths	1,200	Gain £200	Debit F's capital account £200
G One-third	1,000	One-fifth	600	Loss £400	Credit G's capital account £400
	3,000		3,000		

The column headed 'Action Required' shows that a partner who has gained goodwill because of the change must be charged for it by having his capital account debited with

the value of the gain. A partner who has lost goodwill must be compensated for it by having his capital account credited.

The capital accounts will appear as:

Capitals

	E £	F £	G £		E £	F £	G £
Goodwill	200	200	–	Balances b/d	3,000	1,800	2,200
Balances c/d	2,800	1,600	2,600	Goodwill	–	–	400
	3,000	1,800	2,600		3,000	1,800	2,600

As there is no goodwill account the balance sheet items before and after the adjustments will therefore appear as:

		Before £	After £
Net assets		7,000	7,000
Capitals:	E	3,000	2,800
	F	1,800	1,600
	G	2,200	2,600
		7,000	7,000

Comparison of methods 1 and 2

Let us see how the methods compare. Assume that shortly afterwards the assets in 1 and 2 are sold for £7,000 and the goodwill for £3,000. The total of £10,000 would be distributed as follows, using each of the methods:

Method 1 The £10,000 is exactly the amount needed to pay the partners according to the balances on their capital accounts. The payments are therefore made of

Capitals paid to E	4,000
F	2,800
G	3,200
Total cash paid	£10,000

Method 2 First of all the balances on capital accounts, totalling £7,000, are to be paid. Then the £3,000 received for goodwill will be split between the partners in their profit and loss ratios. This will result in payments as follows:

	Capitals	Goodwill Shared		Total Paid
E	2,800	(2/5ths)	1,200	4,000
F	1,600	(2/5ths)	1,200	2,800
G	2,600	(1/5th)	600	3,200
	£7,000		£3,000	£10,000

You can see that the final amounts paid to the partners are the same whether a goodwill account is opened or not.

34.8 Admission of new partners into the firm

New partners may be admitted, usually for one of two reasons:

1 As an extra partner, either because the firm has grown or someone is needed with different skills.
2 To replace partners who are leaving the firm. This might be because of retirement or death of the partner.

34.9 The effect of the admission of new partners on goodwill

The new partner will be entitled to a share in the profits. Normally, he will also be entitled to the same share of the value of goodwill. It is correct to charge him for his taking over that share of the goodwill.

34.10 Goodwill adjustments required when a new partner is admitted

This calculation is done in three stages:

1 Show the value of goodwill divided between the existing partners in their profit and loss sharing ratio.
2 Then show the value of goodwill divided between all of the partners (including the new partner) in the new profit and loss sharing ratio.
3 Goodwill gain shown: charge these partners for the gain.
   Goodwill loss shown: give these partners an allowance for their losses.

This is illustrated in Exhibits 34.2 and 34.3.

Exhibit 34.2

A and B are in partnership, sharing profits and losses equally. C is admitted as a new partner. The three partners will share profits and losses one-third each.
   Goodwill is valued at £60,000.

Stage 1			Stage 2		Stage 3	
Partners	Old profit shares	Share of goodwill £	New profit shares	Share of goodwill £	Gain or loss £	Adjustment needed
A	1/2	30,000	1/3	20,000	10,000 Loss	Cr A Capital
B	1/2	30,000	1/3	20,000	10,000 Loss	Cr B Capital
C		–	1/3	20,000	20,000 Gain	Dr C Capital
		60,000		60,000	Nil	

This means that A and B need to have their capitals increased by £10,000 each. C's capital needs to be reduced by £20,000.

   Note that A and B have kept their profits in the same ratio to each other. While they used to have one-half each, now they have one-third each.

We will now see in Exhibit 34.3 that the method shown is the same even when old partners take a different share of the profit to each other than before the change.

Exhibit 34.3

D and E are in partnership sharing profits equally. A new partner F is admitted. Profits will now be shared D one-fifth, and E and F two-fifths each. D and E have therefore not kept their shares the same relative to each other. Goodwill is valued at £60,000.

Stage 1			Stage 2		Stage 3	
Partners	Old profit shares	Share of goodwill £	New profit shares	Share of goodwill £	Gain or loss £	Adjustment needed
D	1/2	30,000	1/5	12,000	18,000 Loss	Cr D Capital
E	1/2	30,000	2/5	24,000	6,000 Loss	Cr E Capital
F		–	2/5	24,000	24,000 Gain	Dr F Capital
		60,000		60,000		

D's capital is to be increased by £18,000. E's capital is to be increased by £6,000. F's capital is to be reduced by £24,000.

34.11 Accounting entries for goodwill adjustments

These depend on how the partners wish to arrange the adjustment. Three methods are usually used:

1 Cash is paid by the new partner privately to the old partners for his share of the goodwill. No goodwill account is to be opened.
   In Exhibit 34.3, F would therefore give £24,000 in cash, being £18,000 to D and £6,000 to E. They could lodge these amounts in their *private* bank accounts. No entry is made for this in the *accounts of the partnership*.
2 Cash is paid by the new partner into the *business* bank account for his share of the goodwill. No goodwill account is to be opened. Assume that the capital balances before F was admitted were: D £50,000, E £50,000, and F was to pay in £50,000 as capital plus £24,000 for goodwill.

In Exhibit 34.3 the entries would be shown in the capital accounts as:

Capital

	D £	E £	F £		D £	E £	F £
Adjustments for gain in goodwill				Balances b/d	50,000	50,000	–
				Cash (for capital)	–	–	50,000
	–	–	24,000	Adjustments for loss of goodwill	18,000	6,000	–
Balances c/d	68,000	56,000	50,000	Cash (for goodwill)	–	–	24,000
	68,000	56,000	74,000		68,000	56,000	74,000

3 Goodwill account to be opened. No extra cash to be paid in by the new partner for goodwill.
The opening capitals were D £50,000, E £50,000. F paid in £50,000 as capital.

Here the action required is:

(a) Debit the goodwill account with the value of goodwill.
Credit the capitals of the old partners with their shares of goodwill in their old profit sharing ratios.
(b) Debit adjustment gains to partners' capitals.
Credit adjustment losses to partners' capitals.

For Exhibit 34.3 the entries would appear as:

Goodwill

	£		£
Value divided:			
D Capital	30,000		
E Capital	30,000	Balance c/d	60,000
	60,000		60,000

Capital

	D £	E £	F £		D £	E £	F £
Adjustments for gain of goodwill	–	–	24,000	Balances b/d	50,000	50,000	–
				Cash for capital	–	–	50,000
Balances c/d	98,000	86,000	26,000	Goodwill	30,000	30,000	–
				Adjustments for loss of goodwill	18,000	6,000	–
	98,000	86,000	50,000		98,000	86,000	50,000

34.12 The valuation of goodwill where new partners pay for their share

Unless otherwise agreed, the assumption is that the total value of goodwill is directly proportionate to the amount paid by the new partner for the share taken by him. For example, if a new partner pays £1,200 for a one-fifth share of the profits, then goodwill is taken to be £6,000. A sum of £800 for a one-quarter share of the profits would therefore be taken to imply a total value of £3,200 for goodwill.

34.13 Goodwill on the retirement withdrawal or death of partners

This depends on whether or not a goodwill account exists.

If there was no goodwill account

If no goodwill account already existed the partnership goodwill should be valued because the outgoing partner is entitled to his share of its value. This value is entered in the double entry accounts:

Debit the goodwill account with the valuation.
Credit each old partner's capital account in their profit sharing ratios.

Example

H, I and J have been in partnership for many years sharing profit and losses equally. No goodwill account has ever existed.

J is leaving the partnership. The other two partners are to take over his share of profits equally. Capitals entered before goodwill were £50,000 each. The goodwill is valued at £45,000.

Goodwill

	£		£
Valuation: Capital H	15,000		
Capital I	15,000		
Capital J	15,000	Balance c/d	45,000
	45,000		45,000
Balance b/d	45,000		

Capital

	H £	I £	J £		H £	I £	J £
Balances c/d	65,000	65,000	65,000	Balances b/d	50,000	50,000	50,000
				Goodwill	15,000	15,000	15,000
	65,000	65,000	65,000		65,000	65,000	65,000
				Balances b/d	65,000	65,000	65,000

When J leaves the partnership, his capital balance of £65,000 will be paid to him.

If a goodwill account exists

1 If a goodwill account exists with the correct valuation of goodwill entered in it, no further action is required.
2 If the valuation in the goodwill account needs to be changed, the following will apply:

Goodwill undervalued: Debit the increase needed to the goodwill account.
Credit the increase to the old partners' capital accounts in their old profit sharing ratios.

Goodwill overvalued: Debit the reduction to the old partners' capital accounts in their old profit sharing ratios.
Credit the reduction needed to the goodwill account.

Review questions

In addition to the questions which follow, you should attempt questions 235–237 in the accompanying book of multiple-choice questions (see back cover for further details).

Suggested solutions to review questions with the letter 'A' after the question number are given in Appendix I (pages 637–9).

34.1A X, Y and Z have been in partnership for many years. They have always shared their profits in the ratios of X4: Y3: Z1. They are to alter their profit ratios to X3: Y5: Z2. The last balance sheet before the change was:

Balance Sheet as at 31 December 1998

	£
Net Assets (not including goodwill)	14,000
Capitals:	
X	6,000
Y	4,800
Z	3,200
	14,000

The partners agree to bring in goodwill, being valued at £12,000 on the change.

Required:
Show the balance sheets on 1 January 1999 after goodwill has been taken into account if:
(*a*) A goodwill account was opened.
(*b*) A goodwill account was not opened.

34.2 X and Y are in partnership, sharing profits and losses equally. They decide to admit Z. By agreement, goodwill, valued at £6,000, is to be introduced into the business books. Z is required to provide capital equal to that of Y after he (Y) has been credited with his share of goodwill. The new profit sharing ratios are to be 4:3:3 respectively for X, Y and Z.

The Balance Sheet before the admission of Z showed:

		£
Fixed and current assets (excl. cash)		15,000
Cash		2,000
		17,000
Current liabilities		5,000
		12,000
Capital	X	8,000
Capital	Y	4,000
		12,000

Show:
(*a*) Journal entries to record the admission of Z.
(*b*) The balance sheet of the partnership after admitting Z.
(*c*) Journal entries for writing off the goodwill which the new partners decided to do soon after the start of the new business.

34.3A A new partner has joined the business during the year and has paid in £10,000 for 'goodwill'. This £10,000 has been credited by the bookkeeper to the account of the new partner. The senior partner had objected to this, but the bookkeeper had replied: 'Why not credit the £10,000 to the account of the new partner? It is his money after all.'

Required:

Give your advice as to the proper treatment of this £10,000. Explain your reasons fully.

(*Association of Chartered Certified Accountants*)

34.4 Al and Bert are in partnership, sharing profits equally. At 30 June they have balances on their capital accounts of £12,000 (Al) and £15,000 (Bert). On that day they agree to bring in their friend Hall as a third partner. All three partners are to share profits equally from now on. Hall is to introduce £20,000 as capital into the business. Goodwill on 30 June is agreed at £18,000.

Required:

(*a*) Show the partners' capital accounts for 30 June and 1 July on the assumption that the goodwill, previously unrecorded, is to be included in the accounts.

(*b*) Show the additional entries necessary to eliminate goodwill again from the accounts.

(*c*) Explain briefly what goodwill is. Why are adjustments necessary when a new partner joins a partnership?

(*Association of Chartered Certified Accountants*)

34.5A Owing to staff illnesses, the draft final accounts for the year ended 31 March 19X0 of Messrs Stone, Pebble and Brick, trading in partnership as the Bigtime Building Supply Company, have been prepared by an inexperienced, but keen, clerk. The draft summarised balance sheet as at 31 March 19X0 is as follows:

	£	£
Tangible fixed assets: At cost less depreciation to date		45,400
Current assets	32,290	
Less: Trade creditors	6,390	25,900
		£71,300

Represented by:	Stone	Pebble	Brick	Total
	£	£	£	£
Capital accounts: at 1 April 19X9	26,000	18,000	16,000	60,000
Current accounts:				
Share of net profit for the year ended 31 March 19X0	12,100	12,100	12,100	
Drawings year ended 31 March 19X0	(8,200)	(9,600)	(7,200)	
At 31 March 19X0	3,900	2,500	4,900	11,300
				£71,300

The partnership commenced on 1 April 19X9 when each of the partners introduced, as their partnership capital, the net tangible fixed and current assets of their previously separate businesses. However, it has now been discovered that, contrary to what was agreed, no adjustments were made in the partnership books for the goodwill of the partners' former businesses now incorporated in the partnership. The agreed valuations of goodwill at 1 April 19X9 are as follows:

	£
Stone's business	30,000
Pebble's business	20,000
Brick's business	16,000

It is agreed that a goodwill account should not be opened in the partnership's books.

It has now been discovered that effect has not been given in the accounts to the following provisions in the partnership agreement effective from 1 January 19X0:

1 Stone's capital to be reduced to £20,000 the balance being transferred to a loan account upon which interest at the rate of 11% per annum will be paid on 31 December each year.
2 Partners to be credited with interest on their capital account balances at the rate of 5% per annum.
3 Brick to be credited with a partner's salary at the rate of £8,500 per annum.
4 The balance of the net profit or loss to be shared between Stone, Pebble and Brick in the ratio 5:3:2 respectively.

Notes
1 It can be assumed that the net profit indicated in the draft accounts accrued uniformly throughout the year.
2 It has been agreed between the partners that no adjustments should be made for any partnership goodwill as at 1 January 19X0.

Required:
(*a*) Prepare the profit and loss appropriation account for the year ended 31 March 19X0.
(*b*) Prepare a corrected statement of the partners' capital and current accounts for inclusion in the partnership balance sheet as at 31 March 19X0.

(*Association of Accounting Technicians*)

34.6A   Apple, Pear and Orange are in partnership sharing profits and losses in the ratio of 3:2:1. Partners receive no salary but are entitled to interest on capital at 10% of the balance on their capital accounts for the year. The following is the draft balance sheet of the partnership as at 31st March, 1998.

Balance Sheet as at 31st March, 1998

	Cost	Accumulated Depreciation	Net Book Value
	£	£	£
Fixed assets			
Premises	20,000	2,000	18,000
Vehicles	11,000	4,600	6,400
	31,000	6,600	24,400
Current assets			
Stocks		12,000	
Debtors		10,600	
Bank		1,200	
		23,800	
Current liabilities			
Creditors		12,400	11,400
			35,800
Represented by:			
Capital Accounts			
Apple		4,000	
Pear		10,000	
Orange		2,000	16,000
Current Accounts			
Apple		2,050	
Pear		–600	
Orange		800	2,250
			18,250
Profit for the Year (not yet divided between the partners)			10,000
Long-term Loan			7,550
			35,800

On investigation you ascertain that adjustment is required in respect of the following items:

1 Stocks valued at £1,200 in the draft accounts have a net realisable value of £300.
2 Apple has not been charged for goods to the value of £300 supplied to him out of goods purchased by the partnership.

On 31st March, 1998 it was agreed that Pear would retire from the partnership. Apart from the adjustments required in respect of items (1) and (2) mentioned above, all assets and liabilities are correctly valued in the books. Pear is to receive an immediate cash payment of £4,000, with any balance due to him to be repaid within one year. Also on 31st March, 1998 Lemon is to be admitted to the partnership on the introduction of capital of £10,000.

You are required to prepare:

(a) a statement setting out the adjustments required to the profit for the year arising because of the items mentioned at (1) and (2) above;
(b) a statement setting out the division of the adjusted profit between the partners;
(c) the current accounts of the partners; and
(d) the revised Balance Sheet of the partnership after the retirement of Pear and the introduction of Lemon as a partner.

(IATI Admission Examination)

34.7 Tom, Dick and Harry have been in partnership sharing profits and losses in the ratio of 5:2:3 respectively. Their agreed annual salaries are £12,000, £25,000 and £20,000 respectively. Interest accruing to the partners from the balances on their capital accounts has been agreed at 8% per annum.

On 1st February, 1998 Joan was admitted as another partner and the profits and losses are now to be shared in the ratio of 4:3:2:2 to Tom, Dick, Harry and Joan respectively. Revised annual salaries are £15,000, £21,000, £18,000 and £18,000 respectively. Interest on the capital accounts is charged at 9% per annum. Joan is to introduce cash of £40,000.

Due to ill health, Dick retired from the partnership on 1st May, 1998 taking with him £34,000 in cash and computer equipment at an agreed value of £5,400. The capital account balance then due to him is to be treated as a loan to the partnership, accruing interest at 1% per month, after a repayment to Dick of £1,500 in principal each month. This repayment is to be processed on the 10th of each month. The interest and current account balances then due to Dick will be re-paid to him in full on 31st March, 1999.

The partners Tom, Harry and Joan now share profits and losses in the ratio of 7:4:3 respectively. Their annual salaries are now agreed to be £18,000, £21,000 and £21,000 respectively, and interest on capital accounts is to be charged at 11% per annum.

On 1st September, 1997 the then partners' accounts were as follows:

	Tom	Dick	Harry
Capital Accounts	£70,000	£28,000	£42,000
Current Accounts	£15,800	£6,700	–£1,200

The partnership goodwill was valued at £100,000 on 1st September, 1997, at £150,000 on 1st February, 1998 and at £110,000 on 1st May, 1998.

In the year to 31st August, 1998 the net profit of the partnership was £86,400 before adjusting for any loan interest payable to Dick from 1st May, 1998 and before any salary or interest apportionment to any partner.

There were no drawings by any partner during the year ended 31st August, 1998. Profits accrued evenly throughout the year. No figure for goodwill is to be maintained in the partnership books of account. Interest on capital is to be charged on the opening balance for any period.

Required:

Set out the interest, current, and capital accounts for each partner for the year ended 31st August 1998.

N.B. Figures should be rounded to the nearest pound, where appropriate.

(ICAI Professional Examination Two)

35

The revaluation of partnership assets

35.1 Why the revaluation of assets is necessary

When a partnership business is sold, if the sale price of the net assets exceeds their book values, there will be a profit on the sale. This profit will be shared between the partners in their profit and loss sharing ratios. Any loss on sale would be shared in the same way. This means that whenever one of the following happens:

- A new partner is admitted;
- A partner leaves the firm; or
- The partners change their profit and loss sharing ratios;

the assets will have to be revalued.

If this was not done any new partner admitted would benefit from increases in value before he joined the firm, without having to pay anything for it.

Similarly, if the value of assets had fallen before he had joined the firm, and no revaluation took place, he would share that loss of value without any adjustment being made for it.

Partners who leave or whose profit and loss sharing ratio is changed would also either gain or lose, without payments or allowances for such gains or losses.

35.2 Profit or loss arising on the revaluation of assets

We have already seen that there should be a revaluation of assets when there is a change of partners or a change in profit sharing ratios.

If the revaluation shows no difference in asset values, no further action is necessary. This will not happen very often, especially if assets include buildings. These are normally shown at cost, but this is very rarely the actual value after the buildings have been owned for a few years. If there is a difference on revaluation then a profit or loss will be calculated as follows:

		£
If:	The new valuation of net assets (say)	90,000
Is more than:	The old valuation of net assets (say)	60,000
The result is:	A profit on revaluation (of)	30,000

		£
If:	The old valuation of net assets (say)	50,000
Is more than:	The new valuation of net assets (say)	40,000
The result is:	A loss on revaluation (of)	10,000

35.3 Accounting for the revaluation of assets

A revaluation account is opened

1 For each asset showing a gain on revaluation:
   Debit the asset account and
   Credit the revaluation account with the amount of the gain.
2 For each asset showing a loss on revaluation:
   Debit the revaluation account and
   Credit the asset account with the amount of the loss.
3 If there is an increase in the total valuation of assets:
   Debit the profit to the revaluation account.
   Credit the old partners' capital accounts in their old profit and loss sharing ratios.
4 If there is a fall in the total valuation of assets:
   Debit the old partners' capital accounts in their old profit and loss sharing ratios.
   Credit the loss to the revaluation account.

Exhibit 35.1

The following is the balance sheet as at 31 December 1998 of W and Y, who shared profit and losses in the ratios W two-thirds; Y one-third. From 1 January 1999 the profit and loss sharing ratios are to be altered to W one-half; Y one-half.

Balance Sheet as at 31 December 1998

	£
Premises at cost	6,500
Fixtures (at cost less depreciation)	1,500
Stock	2,000
Debtors	1,200
Bank	800
	12,000
Capitals: W	7,000
Y	5,000
	12,000

The assets were revalued on 1 January 1999 to be: Premises £9,000, Fixtures £1,100. Other assets remained at the same values.

Accounts to show the assets at revalued amounts follow:

Revaluation

	£	£		£
Assets reduced in value:			*Assets increased in value:*	
Fixtures		400	Premises	2,500
Profit on revaluation transferred to Capital accounts: (old ratios)				
W two-thirds	1,400			
Y one-third	700	2,100		
		2,500		2,500

Premises

	£		£
Balance b/d	6,500	Balance c/d	9,000
Revaluation: Increase	2,500		
	9,000		9,000
Balance b/d	9,000		

Fixtures

	£		£
Balance b/d	1,500	Revaluation: Reduction	400
		Balance c/d	1,100
	1,500		1,500
Balance b/d	1,100		

Capital: W

	£		£
Balance c/d	8,400	Balance b/d	7,000
		Revaluation: Share of profit	1,400
	8,400		8,400
		Balance b/d	8,400

Capital: Y

	£		£
Balance c/d	5,700	Balance b/d	5,000
		Revaluation: Share of profit	700
	5,700		5,700
		Balance b/d	5,700

35.4 The revaluation of goodwill

This chapter dealt with the revaluation of assets other than goodwill. The revaluation of goodwill has already been dealt with in Chapter 34.

Review questions

In addition to the questions which follow, you should attempt questions 238 and 239 in the accompanying book of multiple-choice questions (see back cover for details).

Suggested solutions to review questions with the letter 'A' after the question number are given in Appendix I (pages 639–41).

35.1A   **Hughes, Allen and Elliott**
Balance Sheet as at 31 December 1998

	£
Buildings at cost	8,000
Vehicles (at cost *less* depreciation)	3,550
Office fittings (at cost *less* depreciation)	1,310
Stock	2,040
Debtors	4,530
Bank	1,390
	20,820

Capital:	£
Hughes	9,560
Allen	6,420
Elliott	4,840
	20,820

The above partners have always shared profits and losses in the ratio: Hughes 5: Allen 3: Elliott 2.

From 1 January 1999 the assets were to be revalued prior to the profit sharing ratios being altered. The following assets are to be revalued to the figures shown: Buildings £17,500, Vehicles £2,600, Stock £1,890, Office fittings £1,090.

Required:
(*a*) Show all the ledger accounts necessary to record the revaluation.
(*b*) Draw up a balance sheet as at 1 January 1999.

35.2 Avon and Brown have been in partnership for many years sharing profits and losses in the ratio 3:2 respectively. The following was their balance sheet as at 31 December 1998.

	£
Goodwill	2,000
Plant and machinery	1,800
Stock	1,960
Debtors	2,130
Bank	90
	7,980
Sundry Creditors	980
	7,000

Capital: Avon	4,000
Brown	3,000
	7,000

On 1 January 1999, they decided to admit Charles as a partner on the condition that he contributed £2,000 as his capital but that the plant and machinery and stock should be revalued at £2,000 and £1,900 respectively, the other assets, except for goodwill, remaining at their present book values. The goodwill was agreed to be valueless.

You are required to show:

(a) The ledger entries dealing with the above in the following accounts:
   (i)   Goodwill account,
   (ii) Revaluation account,
   (iii) Capital accounts;
(b) The balance sheet of the partnership immediately after the admission of Charles.

35.3A Alan, Bob and Charles are in partnership sharing profits and losses in the ratio 3:2:1 respectively.

The balance sheet for the partnership as at 30 June 19X2 is as follows:

Fixed assets	£	£
Premises		90,000
Plant		37,000
Vehicles		15,000
Fixtures		2,000
		144,000
Current assets		
Stock	62,379	
Debtors	34,980	
Cash	760	98,119
		£242,119

Capital	£	£
Alan		85,000
Bob		65,000
Charles		35,000
		185,000
Current account		
Alan	3,714	
Bob	(2,509)	
Charles	4,678	5,883
Loan – Charles		28,000
Current liabilities		
Creditors		19,036
Bank overdraft		4,200
		£242,119

Charles decides to retire from the business on 30 June 19X2, and Don is admitted as a partner on that date. The following matters are agreed:

(a) Certain assets were revalued   – Premises   £120,000
                                     – Plant   £35,000
                                     – Stock   £54,179
(b) Provision is to be made for doubtful debts in the sum of £3,000.
(c) Goodwill is to be recorded in the books on the day Charles retires in the sum of £42,000. The partners in the new firm do not wish to maintain a goodwill account so that amount is to be written back against the new partners' capital accounts.

(d) Alan and Bob are to share profits in the same ratio as before, and Don is to have the same share of profits as Bob.

(e) Charles is to take his car at its book value of £3,900 in part payment, and the balance of all he is owed by the firm in cash except £20,000 which he is willing to leave as a loan account.

(f) The partners in the new firm are to start on an equal footing so far as capital and current accounts are concerned. Don is to contribute cash to bring his capital and current accounts to the same amount as the original partner from the old firm who has the lower investment in the business.

The original partner in the old firm who has the higher investment will draw out cash so that his capital and current account balances equal those of his new partners.

Required:

(a) Account for the above transactions, including goodwill and retiring partners' accounts.

(b) Draft a balance sheet for the partnership of Alan, Bob and Don as at 30 June 19X2.

(*Association of Accounting Technicians*)

35.4A Tom, Gerry and Mary are in partnership sharing profits and losses in the ratio of 2:1:1. Each partner receives a salary of £2,000 per annum and interest on capital at 15% per annum, based on their capital balances at the beginning of the year. The following is the draft Balance Sheet of the partnership as at 31st March, 1998 (before the profit for the year has been divided between the partners).

Draft Balance Sheet as at 31st March, 1998

	Cost £'000	Accumulated Depreciation £'000	Net Book Value £'000
Fixed Assets			
Furniture and Fittings	25	15	10
Vehicles	12	6	6
	37	21	16
Current Assets			
Stocks		14	
Debtors		8	
Bank		12	
		34	
Current Liabilities			
Creditors		10	24
			40
Represented by:			
Capital Accounts			
Tom		4	
Gerry		8	
Mary		4	16
Current Accounts			
Tom		2	
Gerry		–1	
Mary		3	4
			20
Profit for the year (not yet divided between the partners)			16
			36
Long-term Loan			4
			40

It is agreed that Ann is to join the partnership on 31st March, 1998 introducing capital of £10,000. The partners are to share profits from 1st April, 1998 in the ratio – Tom 4: Gerry 3: Mary 2: Ann 1.

Goodwill at 31st March, 1998 is valued at £30,000 and is to be brought into the books. In addition, it is agreed that stocks are to be re-valued at £18,000 and debtors at £7,000.

All other assets and liabilities are to remain at their Balance Sheet values as per the draft Balance Sheet at 31st March, 1998.

You are required to prepare:
(a) the Profit and Loss Appropriation Account for the year ended 31st March, 1998;
(b) a revaluation account to account for the changes in the values of stocks and debtors;
(c) the partners' capital and current accounts to deal with the introduction of goodwill, the distribution of profits and any profit or loss on revaluation; and
(d) a revised Balance Sheet at 31st March, 1998, after the introduction of Ann as a partner.

(*IATI Admission Examination*)

35.5 Lemon, Plum and Orange are in partnership sharing profits and losses in the ratio 5:3:1. The Balance Sheet of the partnership as at 30th June, 1998, was as follows.

Balance Sheet as at 30th June, 1998

	Cost £	Accumulated Depreciation £	Net Book Value £
Fixed Assets			
Premises	125,000	15,000	110,000
Vehicles	80,000	40,000	40,000
	205,000	55,000	150,000
Current Assets			
Stock		28,000	
Debtors		46,000	
		74,000	
Current liabilities			
Bank Overdraft	18,000		
Creditors	22,000	40,000	
Net Current Assets			34,000
			184,000
Represented by:			
Capital Accounts			
Lemon			50,000
Plum			60,000
Orange			40,000
			150,000
Current Accounts			
Lemon		20,000	
Plum		–1,000	
Orange		15,000	34,000
			184,000

On 1st July, 1998, Plum retired from the partnership. At that date the assets and liabilities were valued as follows:

1 Goodwill was valued at £18,000 and is to be brought into the books.
2 Premises were valued at £94,000.
3 Vehicles were valued at their book value.

4 Stocks and debtors were valued at £30,000 and £42,000 respectively.
5 Creditors were valued at their book value.

It was agreed that, in part payment of the amount due to him on retirement, Plum should take:

(*i*) a vehicle at its book value of £15,000; and
(*ii*) cash of £20,000.

The remaining balance due to Plum is to be repaid six months after his retirement.

You are required to prepare:
(*a*) the revaluation account;
(*b*) the partners' capital accounts; and
(*c*) a Balance Sheet as at 1st July, 1998, after the retirement of Plum.

(*IATI Admission Examination*)

35.6 Sam, Reg and Bob are in partnership sharing profits and losses in the ratio 5:3:2. The following is the Balance Sheet of the partnership as at 31st December, 1997:

Balance Sheet as at 31st December, 1997

Fixed Assets	£	£	£
Freehold Premises			60,000
Furniture and Equipment			32,000
Vehicles			18,000
			110,000
Investments			8,000
			118,000
Current Assets			
Stock	12,000		
Debtors	23,000		
Bank	6,000	41,000	
Current Liabilities			
Creditors	13,000		
Loan from Tom	5,000	18,000	
Net Current Assets			23,000
			141,000

Represented by:	Capital Accounts	Current Accounts	
Sam	40,000	11,000	
Reg	40,000	6,000	
Bob	40,000	4,000	
	120,000	21,000	141,000

Additional information

1 On 1st January, 1998, Reg retired from the partnership and Tom was admitted on the introduction of £12,000 capital. It was agreed that, in addition to the capital introduced in cash by Tom, Tom's loan to the partnership was also to be considered as part of his capital on admission.
2 It was also agreed that, at the date of the change of partnership, the investments were to be taken over by Reg at their book value.
3 At the date of the change of partnership, the other assets were re-valued as follows:

Freehold premises	£70,000	Furniture and equipment	£28,000
Vehicles	£22,000	Stock	£14,000
Debtors	£24,000	Goodwill	£16,000

These assets are to be included in the new partnership at the revalued amounts, with the exception of goodwill, which is to be excluded from the books of the new partnership.

4 The new partnership agreement between Sam, Bob and Tom provides for a profit sharing ratio of 3:3:2 respectively.

5 One half of the balance due to Reg at the date of his retirement is to be paid to him immediately and the other half is to be left in the partnership as a loan to be repaid in two years' time.

You are required to prepare:

(*a*) a revaluation account to reflect the revaluation of the partnership assets;

(*b*) the partners' capital accounts to reflect the effect of the partnership changes; and

(*c*) a Balance Sheet of the new partnership immediately after the effects of the change in the partnership have been recorded.

(*IATI Admission Examination*)

36

The dissolution of partnerships

The **dissolution** of a partnership simply means that the partnership ceases to exist. Reasons for dissolution include the following:

(*i*) The partnership is no longer profitable, and there is no longer any reason to carry on trading.

(*ii*) The partners cannot agree between themselves how to operate the partnership. They therefore decide to finish the partnership.

(*iii*) Factors such as ill-health or old age may bring about the close of the partnership.

36.2 The sequence of events upon dissolution

Upon dissolution the partnership firm stops trading or operating. Then, in accordance with the Partnership Act 1890:

(*i*) The assets of the partnership are disposed of;

(*ii*) The liabilities of the firm are paid to everyone other than the partners;

(*iii*) The partners are repaid their advances and current account balances. Advances are the amounts they have put in above and beyond the capital; and

(*iv*) The partners are paid the final amounts due to them on their capital accounts.

Any profit or loss on dissolution would be shared by all the partners in their profit and loss sharing ratios. Profits would increase capitals repayable to partners. Losses would reduce the capitals repayable.

If a partner's final balance on his capital and current accounts is in deficit, he will have to pay that amount into the partnership bank account.

36.3 The disposal of assets

The assets do not have to be sold to external parties. Quite often one or more existing partners will take assets at values agreed by all of the partners. In such a case the partner may not pay in cash for such assets; instead they will be charged to his capital account.

36.4 Accounting for partnership dissolution: introduction

The main account in which the dissolution entries are made is known as the **realisation account**. Whether assets disposed of realised a profit or a loss is calculated in this account.

Exhibit 36.1 A simple partnership dissolution

The last balance sheet of A and B, who share profits A two-thirds: B one-third is shown below. On this date they are to dissolve the partnership.

Balance Sheet at 31 December

	£	£
Fixed assets		
Buildings		10,000
Vehicle		2,000
		12,000
Current assets		
Stock	3,000	
Debtors	4,000	
Bank	1,000	
	8,000	
Current liabilities		
Creditors	2,000	6,000
		18,000
Capital: A		12,000
B		6,000
		18,000

The buildings were sold for £10,500 and the stock for £2,600. £3,500 was collected from debtors. The vehicle was taken over by A at an agreed value of £1,700, but he did not pay any cash for it. £2,000 was paid to creditors. The costs of the dissolution, £200, were paid.

The accounting entries needed to record the above are:

(A) Transfer the book values of all the assets to the realisation account:
　　　Debit the realisation account with the book values of the assets and
　　　Credit the individual asset accounts
(B) Amounts received from the disposal of assets:
　　　Debit the bank account with the amounts received and
　　　Credit the realisation account
(C) Values of assets taken over by any partner without payment:
　　　Debit that partner's capital account with the agreed value and
　　　Credit the realisation account
(D) Creditors paid:
　　　Debit the creditors' accounts with the amounts paid and
　　　Credit the bank account
(E) Costs of dissolution:
　　　Debit the realisation account with the amount of costs paid and
　　　Credit the bank account
(F) Profit or loss on realisation to be shared between the partners in their profit and loss sharing ratios:
　　　If a profit: Debit the realisation account with the amount of the profit and
　　　　　　　　　Credit the partners' capital accounts
　　　If a loss:　 Debit the partners' capital accounts with the amount of the loss and
　　　　　　　　　Credit the realisation account
(G) Pay to the partners their final balances on their capital accounts:
　　　Debit the capital accounts with the payment to each partner and
　　　Credit the bank account

The entries are now shown. The letters (A) to (G) as above are shown against each entry following:

Buildings

		£			£
Balance b/d		10,000	Realisation	(A)	10,000

Vehicle

		£			£
Balance b/d		2,000	Realisation	(A)	2,000

Stock

		£			£
Balance b/d		3,000	Realisation	(A)	3,000

Debtors

		£			£
Balance b/d		4,000	Realisation	(A)	4,000

Realisation

		£				£	£
Assets to be realised:			Bank: Assets sold				
Buildings	(A)	10,000	Buildings	(B)			10,500
Vehicle	(A)	2,000	Stock	(B)			2,600
Stock	(A)	3,000	Debtors	(B)			3,500
Debtors	(A)	4,000	Taken over by partner A:				
Bank:			Vehicle	(C)			1,700
Dissolution costs	(E)	200	Loss on realisation				
			A 2/3	(F)		600	
			B 1/3	(F)		300	900
		19,200					19,200

Bank

		£			£
Balance b/d		1,000	Creditors	(D)	2,000
Realisation: Assets sold			Realisation: Costs	(E)	200
Buildings	(B)	10,500	Capitals: to clear		
Stock	(B)	2,600	A	(G)	9,700
Debtors	(B)	3,500	B	(G)	5,700
		17,600			17,600

Creditors

		£		£
Bank	(D)	2,000	Balance b/d	2,000

A: Capital

		£		£
Realisation: Vehicle	(C)	1,700	Balance b/d	12,000
Realisation: Share of loss	(F)	600		
Bank: to close	(G)	9,700		
		12,000		12,000

B: Capital

		£		£
Realisation: Share of loss	(F)	300	Balance b/d	6,000
Bank: to close	(G)	5,700		
		6,000		6,000

The final balances on the partners' capital accounts should always equal the amount in the bank account from which they are to be paid. For instance, in the above exhibit there was £15,400 in the bank from which to pay A £9,700 and B £5,700. If the final bank balance does not equal the balances on the partners' capital accounts, a mistake has been made somewhere.

36.5 Accounting for partnership dissolution: further aspects

Exhibit 36.1 did not show the more difficult accounting entries. A more difficult example appears in Exhibit 36.2.

The extra information is:

(*i*)   Any provision such as a bad debt provision or depreciation is to be transferred to the credit of the related asset account. See entries (A) in Exhibit 36.2.

(*ii*) Discounts on creditors. To balance the creditors' account, transfer the discounts on creditors to the credit of the realisation account. See entries (F) in the exhibit.

(*iii*) Transfer the balances on the partners' current accounts to their capital accounts. See entries (I) of the exhibit.

(*iv*) A partner who owes the firm money because his capital account is in deficit must now pay the money owing. See entries (J) of the exhibit.

Exhibit 36.2 A more detailed partnership dissolution

On 31 December, P, Q and R decided to dissolve their partnership. They had always shared profits in the ratio of P 3:Q 2:R 1.

Their goodwill was sold for £3,000, the machinery for £1,800 and the stock for £1,900. There were three cars, all taken over by the partners at agreed values, P taking one for £800, Q one for £1,000 and R one for £500. The premises were taken over by R at an agreed value of £5,500. The amounts collected from debtors amounted to £2,700 after bad debts and discounts had been deducted. The creditors were discharged for £1,600, the difference being due to discounts received. The costs of dissolution amounted to £1,000.

Their last balance sheet is summarised as:

Balance Sheet as at 31 December

	£	£	£
Fixed assets			
Premises			5,000
Machinery			3,000
Vehicles			2,500
			10,500
Current assets			
Stock		1,800	
Debtors	3,000		
Less Provision for bad debts	200	2,800	
Bank		1,400	
		6,000	
Current liabilities			
Creditors		1,700	4,300
			14,800

	P	Q	R	Total
Capital	6,000	5,000	3,000	14,000
Current account	200	100	500	800
				14,800

The accounts recording the dissolution are shown below. A description of each entry follows the accounts. The letters (A) to (K) opposite each entry indicate the relevant descriptions.

Premises

	£			£
Balance b/d	5,000	Realisation	(B)	5,000

Machinery

	£			£
Balance b/d	3,000	Realisation	(B)	3,000

Vehicles

	£			£
Balance b/d	2,500	Realisation	(B)	2,500

Stock

	£			£
Balance b/d	1,800	Realisation	(B)	1,800

Debtors

		£			£
Balance b/d		3,000	Provision for bad debts	(A)	200
			Realisation	(B)	2,800
		3,000			3,000

Realisation

		£	£			£
Assets to be realised:				Bank: Assets sold		
Premises	(B)		5,000	Goodwill	(C)	3,000
Machinery	(B)		3,000	Machinery	(C)	1,800
Vehicles	(B)		2,500	Stock	(C)	1,900
Stock	(B)		1,800	Debtors	(C)	2,700
Debtors	(B)		2,800	Taken over by partners:		
Bank: Costs	(G)		1,000	P: Car	(D)	800
Profit on realisation:	(H)			Q: Car	(D)	1,000
P		600		R: Car	(D)	500
Q		400		R: Premises	(D)	5,500
R		200	1,200	Creditors: Discounts	(F)	100
			17,300			17,300

Creditors

		£		£
Bank	(E)	1,600	Balance b/d	1,700
Realisation (Discounts)	(F)	100		
		1,700		1,700

Bank

		£			£
Balance b/d		1,400	Creditors	(E)	1,600
Realisation: Assets sold			Realisation: Costs	(G)	1,000
Goodwill	(C)	3,000	P: Capital	(K)	6,000
Machinery	(C)	1,800	Q: Capital	(K)	4,500
Stock	(C)	1,900			
Debtors	(C)	2,700			
R: Capital	(J)	2,300			
		13,100			13,100

P Capital

		£			£
Realisation: Car	(D)	800	Balance b/d		6,000
Bank	(K)	6,000	Current account		
			transferred	(I)	200
			Realisation: Share of		
			profit	(H)	600
		6,800			6,800

Provision for Bad Debts

		£			£
Debtors	(A)	200	Balance b/d		200

P Current Account

		£			£
P: Capital	(I)	200	Balance b/d		200

Q Current Account

		£			£
Q: Capital	(I)	100	Balance b/d		100

Q Capital

		£			£
Realisation: Car	(D)	1,000	Balance b/d		5,000
Bank	(K)	4,500	Current account transferred	(I)	100
			Realisation: Share of profit	(H)	400
		5,500			5,500

R Capital

		£			£
Realisation: Car	(D)	500	Balance b/d		3,000
Realisation: Premises	(D)	5,500	Current account transferred	(I)	500
			Realisation: Share of profit	(H)	200
			Bank	(J)	2,300
		6,000			6,000

R Current Account

		£			£
R: Capital	(I)	500	Balance b/d		500

Description of transactions:

(A) The provision accounts are transferred to the relevant asset accounts so that the net balance on the asset accounts may be transferred to the realisation account. Debit provision accounts. Credit asset accounts.

(B) The net book values of the assets are transferred to the realisation account. Debit realisation account. Credit asset accounts.

(C) Assets sold. Debit bank account. Credit realisation account.

(D) Assets taken over by partners. Debit partners' capital accounts. Credit realisation account.

(E) Liabilities discharged. Credit bank account. Debit liability accounts.

(F) Discounts on creditors. Debit creditors' account. Credit realisation account.

(G) Costs of dissolution. Credit bank account. Debit realisation account.

(H) Profit or loss split in profit/loss sharing ratio. Profit – debit realisation account. Credit partners' capital accounts. The opposite if a loss.

(I) Transfer the balances on the partners' current accounts to their capital accounts.

(J) Any partner with a capital account in deficit, i.e. debits exceeding credits, must now pay in the amount needed to cancel his indebtedness to the firm. Debit bank account. Credit capital account.

(K) The credit balances on the partners' capital accounts can now be paid to them. Credit bank account. Debit partners' capital accounts.

The payments made under (K) should complete the payment of all the balances in the partnership books.

36.6 The rule in the case of *Garner* v. *Murray*

It sometimes happens that a partner's capital account finishes up with a debit balance. Normally the partner will pay in an amount to clear his indebtedness to the firm. However, sometimes he will be unable to pay all, or part, of such a balance. In the legal case of *Garner* v. *Murray* the court ruled that, subject to any agreement to the contrary, such a deficiency was to be shared by the other partners *not* in their profit and loss sharing ratios but in the ratio of their 'last agreed capitals'. By 'their last agreed capitals' is meant the credit balances on their capital accounts in the normal balance sheet drawn up at the end of their last accounting period.

It must be borne in mind that the balances on their capital accounts after the assets have been realised may be far different from those on the last balance sheet. Where a partnership deed is drawn up it is commonly found that agreement is made to use normal profit and loss sharing ratios instead, thus rendering the *Garner* v. *Murray* rule inoperative.

Exhibit 36.3

After completing the realisation of all the assets, in respect of which a loss of £4,200 was incurred, but before making the final payments to the partners, the Balance Sheet appears:

Balance Sheet

	£	£
Bank		6,400
		6,400
Capitals: R	5,800	
S	1,400	
T	400	
	7,600	
Less Q (debit balance)	1,200	6,400
		6,400

According to the last balance sheet drawn up before the dissolution, the partners' capital account credit balances were: Q £600; R £7,000; S £2,000; T £1,000; while the profits and losses were shared Q 3:R 2:S 1:T 1.

Q is unable to meet any part of his deficiency. Each of the other partners therefore suffers the deficiency as follows:

$$\frac{\text{Own capital per balance sheet before dissolution}}{\text{Total of all solvent partners' capitals per same balance sheet}} \times \text{Deficiency}$$

This can now be calculated.

$$R \quad \frac{£7,000}{£7,000 + £2,000 + £1,000} \times £1,200 = \quad £840$$

$$S \quad \frac{£2,000}{£7,000 + £2,000 + £1,000} \times £1,200 = \quad £240$$

$$T \quad \frac{£1,000}{£7,000 + £2,000 + £1,000} \times £1,200 = \quad £120$$

$$\overline{£1,200}$$

When these amounts have been charged to the capital accounts, then the balances remaining on them will equal the amount of the bank balance. Payments may therefore be made to clear their capital accounts.

	Credit balance B/fwd		Share of deficiency now debited		Final credit balances
	£		£		£
R	5,800	–	840	=	4,960
S	1,400	–	240	=	1,160
T	400	–	120	=	280
Equals the bank balance					6,400

36.7 Piecemeal realisation of assets

Frequently the assets may take a long time to realise. The partners will naturally want payments made to them on account as cash is received. They will not want to wait for payments until the dissolution is completed just for the convenience of the accountant. There is, however, a danger that if too much is paid to a partner, and he is unable to repay it, then the person handling the dissolution could be placed in a very awkward position.

To counteract this, the concept of prudence is brought into play. This is done by:

(*i*) Treating each receipt of money as being the final receipt, even though more could be received.

(*ii*) Any loss then calculated so far to be shared between the partners in their profit and loss sharing ratios.

(*iii*) Should any partner's capital account after each receipt show a debit balance, then he is assumed to be unable to pay in the deficiency. This deficit will be shared (failing any other agreement) between the partners using the *Garner* v. *Murray* rule.

(*iv*) After payments of liabilities and the costs of dissolution the remainder of the cash is then paid to the partners.

(*v*) In this manner, even if no further money were received, or should a partner become insolvent, the division of the available cash would be strictly in accordance with the legal requirements. Exhibit 36.4 shows such a series of calculations.

Exhibit 36.4

The following is the summarised balance sheet of H, I, J and K as at 31 December 1997. The partners had shared profits in the ratios H 6:I 4:J 1:K 1.

Balance Sheet as at 31 December 1997

	£
Assets	8,400
Creditors	1,800
	6,600
Capitals:	
H	600
I	3,000
J	2,000
K	1,000
	6,600

On 1 March 1998 some of the assets were sold for cash £5,000. Out of this the creditors £1,800 and the cost of dissolution £200 are paid, leaving £3,000 distributable to the partners.

On 1 July 1998 some more assets are sold for £2,100. As all of the liabilities and the costs of dissolution have already been paid, then the whole of the £2,100 is available for distribution between the partners.

On 1 October 1998 the final sale of the assets realised £1,200.

First Distribution 1 March 1998	H £		I £		J £		K £	
Capital balances before dissolution	600		3,000		2,000		1,000	
Loss if no further assets realised:								
Assets £8,400 – Sales £5,000								
= £3,400 + Costs £200 = £3,600 loss								
Loss shared in profit/loss ratios	1,800		1,200		300		300	
	1,200	Dr	1,800	Cr	1,700	Cr	700	Cr
H's deficiency shared in *Garner* v. *Murray* ratios		³⁄₆	600	²⁄₆	400	¹⁄₆	200	
Cash paid to partners (£3,000)			1,200		1,300		500	

Second Distribution: 1 July 1998	H £		I £		J £		K £	
Capital balances before dissolution	600		3,000		2,000		1,000	
Loss if no further assets realised:								
Assets £8,400 – Sales (£5,000 + £2,100)								
= £1,300 + Costs £200 = £1,500 loss								
Loss shared in profit/loss ratios	750		500		125		125	
	150	Dr	2,500	Cr	1,875	Cr	875	Cr
H's deficiency shared in *Garner* v. *Murray* ratios			75		50		25	
			2,425		1,825		850	
Less first distribution already paid			1,200		1,300		500	
Cash now paid to partners (£2,100)			1,225		525		350	

Third and Final Distribution: 1 October 1998	H		I		J		K	
	£		£		£		£	
Capital balances before dissolution	600		3,000		2,000		1,000	
Loss finally ascertained –								
Assets £8,400 – Sales (£5,000 + £2,100 + £1,200) = £100 + Costs £200 = £300 loss								
Loss shared in profit/loss ratios	$\frac{150}{450}$	Cr	$\frac{100}{2,900}$	Cr	$\frac{25}{1,975}$	Cr	$\frac{25}{975}$	Cr
(No deficiency now exists on any Capital Account)								
Less first and second distributions	–		2,425		1,825		850	
Cash now paid to partners (£1,200)	$\overline{450}$		$\overline{475}$		$\overline{150}$		$\overline{125}$	

In any subsequent distribution following that in which all the partners have shared, i.e. no partner could then have had a deficiency left on his capital account, all receipts of cash are divided between the partners in their profit and loss sharing ratios. Following the above method would give the same answer for these subsequent distributions but obviously an immediate division in the profit and loss sharing ratios would be quicker. You should undertake the calculations necessary to prove to yourself that this is the case.

Review questions

In addition to the questions which follow, you should attempt questions 240–243 in the accompanying book of multiple-choice questions (see back cover for details).

Suggested solutions to review questions with the letter 'A' after the question number are given in Appendix I (pages 641–4).

36.1A S, W and M are partners. They share profits and losses in the ratios of ⅖, ⅖ and ⅕ respectively.

For the year ended 31 December 1998 their capital accounts remained fixed at the following amounts:

S	£6,000
W	£4,000
M	£2,000

They have agreed to give each other 10% interest per annum on their capital accounts.

In addition to the above, partnership salaries of £3,000 for W and £1,000 for M are to be charged.

The net profit of the partnership before taking any of the above into account was £25,200.

Required:

Draw up the appropriation account of the partnership for the year ended 31 December 1998.

36.2 Draw up a profit and loss appropriation account for Winn, Pool and Howe for the year ended 31 December, and balance sheet extracts at that date, from the following:

(*i*) Net profits £30,350.
(*ii*) Interest to be charged on capitals: Winn £2,000; Pool £1,500; Howe £900.
(*iii*) Interest to be charged on drawings: Winn £240; Pool £180; Howe £130.
(*iv*) Salaries to be credited: Pool £2,000; Howe £3,500.
(*v*) Profits to be shared: Winn 50%; Pool 30%; Howe 20%.
(*vi*) Current accounts: Winn £1,860; Pool £946; Howe £717.
(*vii*) Capital accounts: Winn £40,000; Pool £30,000; Howe £18,000.
(*viii*) Drawings: Winn £9,200; Pool £7,100; Howe £6,900.

36.3A Moore and Stephens, who share profits and losses equally, decide to dissolve their partnership as at 31 December. Their balance sheet on that date was as follows:

Balance Sheet as at 31 December

Fixed assets	£	£
Buildings		800
Tools and fixtures		850
		1,650
Current assets		
Debtors	2,800	
Cash	1,800	
	4,600	
Current liabilities		
Sundry creditors	2,750	1,850
		3,500
Capital: Moore		2,000
Stephens		1,500
		3,500

The debtors realised £2,700, the buildings £400 and the tools and fixtures £950. The expenses of dissolution were £100 and discounts totalling £200 were received from creditors.

Required:
Prepare the accounts necessary to show the results of the realisation and of the disposal of the cash.

36.4A Ann, Mary and Joan are in partnership sharing profits and losses in the ratio 5:3:2. The partners decided to dissolve the partnership on 31st December, 1997. The balance sheet of the partnership at that date was as follows:

Balance Sheet as at 31st December, 1997

Fixed Assets	£	£	£
Premises			50,000
Furniture and Fittings			12,500
Vehicle			6,800
			69,300
Current Assets			
Stock		5,400	
Debtors		5,300	
Bank		2,100	
		12,800	
Current Liabilities			
Creditors	4,800		
Loan from Bank	2,000	6,800	
Net Current Assets			6,000
			75,300

Financed by:	Ann	Mary	Joan	Total
Capital	40,000	30,000	11,600	81,600
Current Accounts	12,000	12,000	–30,300	–6,300
				75,300

Additional information
1 The premises were sold for £45,000.
2 The furniture and fittings were taken over by Mary at their book value.
3 The vehicle was taken over by Ann at an agreed valuation of £5,000.
4 The costs of dissolution, amounting to £1,500, were paid.
5 The stock and debtors realised £4,600 and £5,000 respectively.
6 The bank loan and the creditors were paid in full.
7 Joan is insolvent at 31st December, 1997, and unable to pay in cash in respect of any debit balance remaining on her combined Capital and Current Accounts.

Requirements:
Prepare the following accounts to record the dissolution of the partnership:
(*a*) The Realisation Account;
(*b*) The Bank Account; and
(*c*) The combined Capital and Current Accounts.

(IATI Admission Examination)

36.5 Thomas and Carol have carried on a business in partnership selling ladies' and gents' fashions for a number of years sharing profits and losses in the ratio 3:2, respectively. Under the partnership agreement, interest is allowed at 8% per annum on the capital account balances at the beginning of the year, before the division of the profits or losses. No interest is charged on drawings.

The partners have decided to dissolve the partnership on 31st May, 1998. Thomas is to take over the gents' outfitters and Carol is to take over the ladies' outfitters.

Carol will conduct her business from new premises of which she has become a tenant.

Trial Balance as at 31st May, 1998

	Debit £	Credit £
Capital accounts at 1st June, 1997		
Thomas		25,500
Carol		17,125
Drawings 1997/98		
Thomas	8,130	
Carol	6,150	
Thomas – loan at 12% interest per annum		25,000
Goodwill	6,000	
Freehold premises (cost)	41,000	
Fixtures and fittings (book value)		
Gents' outfitters	5,475	
Ladies' outfitters	4,910	
Investments (cost)	1,100	
Stock at 31st May, 1998		
Gents' outfitters	9,955	
Ladies' outfitters	7,120	
Debtors	950	
Cash at bank	1,215	
Creditors		2,395
Sales		89,995
Cost of goods sold	52,145	
General expenses	5,685	
Wages	10,180	
	160,015	160,015

The terms of the dissolution were agreed as follows:

1 Goodwill is to be written off.
2 Thomas' loan is to be repaid.
3 Thomas is to take over the freehold premises at a valuation of £48,500, the gents' department fixtures and fittings at £5,000 and the gents' department stock at £9,900.
4 Carol is to take over the ladies' department fixtures and fittings at £4,800 and the ladies' department stock at £7,000.
5 Any loss on debtors is to be shared equally.
6 Thomas is to pay the creditors in full and retain the proceeds from the debtors. (These eventually realised £850.)
7 The investments were sold and realised £1,250.
8 Dissolution expenses amounted to £800.

You are required to prepare:
(*a*) the realisation account;
(*b*) the cash account; and
(*c*) the partners' capital and current accounts in columnar form to reflect the foregoing.

(*ICAI Professional Examination Two*)

36.6 The following trial balance has been extracted from the books of Gain and Main as at 31 March 19X2; Gain and Main are in partnership sharing profits and losses in the ratio 3 to 2:

	£	£
Capital accounts:		
Gain		10,000
Main		5,000
Cash at bank	1,550	
Creditors		500
Current accounts:		
Gain		1,000
Main	2,000	
Debtors	2,000	
Depreciation: Fixtures and fittings		1,000
Motor vehicles		1,300
Fixtures and fittings	2,000	
Land and buildings	30,000	
Motor vehicles	4,500	
Net profit (for the year to 31 March 19X2)		26,250
Stock, at cost	3,000	
	£45,050	£45,050

In appropriating the net profit for the year, it has been agreed that Main should be entitled to a salary of £9,750. Each partner is also entitled to interest on his opening capital account balance at the rate of 10 per cent per annum.

Gain and Main have decided to convert the parnership into a limited company, Plain Limited, as from 1 April 19X2. The company is to take over all the assets and liabilities of the partnership, except that Gain is to retain for his personal use one of the motor vehicles at an agreed transfer price of £1,000.

The purchase consideration will consist of 40,000 ordinary shares of £1 each in Plain Limited, to be divided between the partners in profit sharing ratio. Any balance on the partners' current accounts is to be settled in cash.

You are required to:
Prepare the main ledger accounts of the partnership in order to close off the books as at 31 March 19X2.

(*Association of Accounting Technicians*)

36.7 A, B & C are partners sharing profits and losses in the ratio 2:2:1. The balance sheet of the partnership as at 30 September 19X7 was as follows:

	£	£
Freehold premises		18,000
Equipment and machinery		12,000
Cars		3,000
Stock		11,000
Debtors		14,000
Bank		9,000
		67,000
Creditors	10,000	
Loan – A	7,000	17,000
		50,000
Capital: A		22,000
B		18,000
C		10,000
		50,000

The partners agreed to dispose of the business to CNO Limited with effect from 1 October 19X7 under the following conditions and terms:

(*i*)   CNO Limited will acquire the goodwill, all fixed assets and the inventory for the purchase consideration of £58,000. This consideration will include a payment of £10,000 in cash and the issue of 12,000 10 per cent preference shares of £1 each at par, and the balance by the issue of £1 ordinary shares at £1.25 per share.

(*ii*) The partnership business will settle amounts owing to creditors.

(*iii*) CNO Limited will collect the debts on behalf of the vendors.

Purchase consideration payments and allotments of shares were made on 1 October 19X7.

The partnership creditors were paid off by 31 October 19X7 after taking cash discounts of £190.

CNO Limited collected and paid over all partnership debts by 30 November 19X7 except for bad debts amounting to £800. Discounts allowed to debtors amounted to £400.

Required:

(*a*) Journal entries (including those relating to cash) necessary to close the books of the partnership, and

(*b*) Set out the basis on which the shares in CNO Limited are allotted to partners. Ignore interest.

(*Institute of Chartered Secretaries and Administrators*)

36.8A Amis, Lodge and Pym were in partnership sharing profits and losses in the ratio 5:3:2. The following trial balance has been extracted from their books of account as at 31 March 19X8:

	£	£
Bank interest received		750
Capital accounts (as at 1 April 19X7):		
Amis		80,000
Lodge		15,000
Pym		5,000
Carriage inwards	4,000	
Carriage outwards	12,000	
Cash at bank	4,900	
Current accounts:		
Amis	1,000	
Lodge	500	
Pym	400	
Discounts allowed	10,000	
Discounts received		4,530
Drawings:		
Amis	25,000	
Lodge	22,000	
Pym	15,000	
Vehicles:		
at cost	80,000	
accumulated depreciation (at 1 April 19X7)		20,000
Office expenses	30,400	
Plant and machinery:		
at cost	100,000	
accumulated depreciation (at 1 April 19X7)		36,600
Provision for bad and doubtful debts		
(at 1 April 19X7)		420
Purchases	225,000	
Rent, rates, heat and light	8,800	
Sales		404,500
Stock (at 1 April 19X7)	30,000	
Trade creditors		16,500
Trade debtors	14,300	
	£583,300	£583,300

Additional information
(a) Stock at 31 March 19X8 was valued at £35,000.
(b) Depreciation on the fixed assets is to be charged as follows:
    Vehicles – 25% on the reduced balance.
    Plant and machinery – 20% on the original cost.
    There were no purchases or sales of fixed assets during the year to 31 March 19X8.
(c) The provision for bad and doubtful debts is to be maintained at a level equivalent to 5% of the total trade debtors as at 31 March 19X8.
(d) An office expense of £405 was owing at 31 March 19X8, and some rent amounting to £1,500 had been paid in advance as at that date. These items had not been included in the list of balances shown in the trial balance.

(e) Interest on drawings and on the debit balance on each partner's current account is to be charged as follows:

	£
Amis	1,000
Lodge	900
Pym	720

(f) According to the partnership agreement, Pym is allowed a salary of £13,000 per annum. This amount was owing to Pym for the year to 31 March 19X8, and needs to be accounted for.

(g) The partnership agreement also allows each partner interest on his capital account at a rate of 10% per annum. There were no movements on the respective partners' capital accounts during the year to 31 March 19X8, and the interest had not been credited to them as at that date.

Note: The information given above is sufficient to answer part (a) (i) and (ii) of the question, and notes (h) and (i) below are pertinent to requirements (b) (i), (ii) and (iii) of the question.

(h) On 1 April 19X8, Fowles Limited agreed to purchase the business on the following terms:
- (i) Amis to purchase one of the partnership's motor vehicles at an agreed value of £5,000, the remaining vehicles being taken over by the company at an agreed value of £30,000;
- (ii) the company agreed to purchase the plant and machinery at a value of £35,000 and the stock at a value of £38,500;
- (iii) the partners to settle the trade creditors: the total amount agreed with the creditors being £16,000;
- (iv) the trade debtors were not to be taken over by the company, the partners receiving cheques on 1 April 19X8 amounting to £12,985 in total from the trade debtors in settlement of the outstanding debts;
- (v) the partners paid the outstanding office expense on 1 April 19X8, and the landlord returned the rent paid in advance by cheque on the same day;
- (vi) as consideration for the sale of the partnership, the partners were to be paid £63,500 in cash by Fowles Limited, and to receive £75,000 in £1 ordinary shares in the company, the shares to be apportioned equally amongst the partners.

(i) Assume that all the matters relating to the dissolution of the partnership and its sales to the company took place on 1 April 19X8.

Required:

(a) Prepare:
- (i) Amis', Lodge's and Pym's trading, profit and loss and profit and loss appropriation account for the year to 31 March 19X8;
- (ii) Amis', Lodge's and Pym's current accounts (in columnar format) for the year to 31 March 19X8 (the final balance on each account is to be then transferred to each partner's respective capital account);

and

(b) Compile the following accounts:
- (i) the partnership realisation account for the period up to and including 1 April 19X8;
- (ii) the partners' bank account for the period up to and including 1 April 19X8; and
- (iii) the partners' capital accounts (in columnar format) for the period up to and including 1 April 19X8.

Note: Detailed workings should be submitted with your answer.

(Association of Accounting Technicians)

36.9   Proudie, Slope and Thorne were in partnership sharing profits and losses in the ratio 3:1:1. The draft balance sheet of the partnership as at 31 May 19X6 is shown below:

	£000 Cost	£000 Depreciation	£000 Net Book Value
Fixed assets			
Land and buildings	200	40	160
Furniture	30	18	12
Vehicles	60	40	20
	£290	£98	£192
Current assets			
Stocks		23	
Trade debtors	42		
Less Provision for doubtful debts	1		
		41	
Prepayments		2	
Cash		10	
		76	
Less Current liabilities			
Trade creditors	15		
Accruals	3		
		18	
			58
			£250
Financed by:			
Capital accounts			
Proudie		100	
Slope		60	
Thorne		40	
			200
Current accounts			
Proudie		24	
Slope		10	
Thorne		8	
			42
			242
Loan			
Proudie			8
			£250

Additional information

1 Proudie decided to retire on 31 May 19X6. However, Slope and Thorne agreed to form a new partnership out of the old one, as from 1 June 19X6. They agreed to share profits and losses in the same ratio as in the old partnership.

2 Upon the dissolution of the old partnership, it was agreed that the following adjustments were to be made to the partnership balance sheet as at 31 May 19X6.

   (*a*) Land and buildings were to be revalued at £200,000;

   (*b*) Furniture was to be revalued at £5,000;

   (*c*) Proudie agreed to take over one of the vehicles at a value of £4,000, the remaining vehicles being revalued at £10,000;

   (*d*) Stocks were to be written down by £5,000;

   (*e*) A bad debt of £2,000 was to be written off, and the provision for doubtful debts was then to be adjusted so that it represented 5 per cent of the then outstanding trade debtors as at 31 May 19X6.

(*f*) A further accrual of £3,000 for office expenses was to be made;

(*g*) Professional charges relating to the dissolution were estimated to be £1,000.

3 It has not been the practice of the partners to carry goodwill in the books of the partnership, but on the retirement of a partner it had been agreed that goodwill should be taken into account. Goodwill was to be valued at an amount equal to the average annual profits of the three years expiring on the retirement. For the purpose of including goodwill in the dissolution arrangement when Proudie retired, the net profits for the last three years were as follows:

	£000
Year to 31 May 19X4	130
Year to 31 May 19X5	150
Year to 31 May 19X6	181

The net profit for the year to 31 May 19X6 had been calculated before any of the items listed in 2 above were taken into account. The net profit was only to be adjusted for items listed in 2(*d*), 2(*e*) and 2(*f*) above.

4 Goodwill is not to be carried in the books of the new partnership.

5 It was agreed that Proudie's old loan of £8,000 should be repaid to him on 31 May 19X6, but any further amount owing to him as a result of the dissolution of the partnership should be left as a long-term loan in the books of the new partnership.

6 The partners' current accounts were to be closed and any balances on them as at 31 May 19X6 were to be transferred to their respective capital accounts.

Required:

(*a*) Prepare the revaluation account as at 31 May 19X6.

(*b*) Prepare the partners' capital accounts as at the date of dissolution of the partnership, and bring down any balances on them in the books of the new partnership.

(*c*) Prepare Slope and Thorne's balance sheet as at 1 June 19X6.

(*Association of Accounting Technicians*)

36.10 John, Kevin and Leonard have been in partnership for many years, sharing profits and losses in the ratio 3:1:1. The partnership agreement stipulates that the rule established in the case of *Garner* v. *Murray* shall apply to this partnership. The balance sheet of the partnership at 31st December, 1997, was as follows:

Balance Sheet as at 31st December, 1997

	£	£	£	£
Fixed assets				103,000
Stock				21,000
Debtors				17,000
Cash				5,000
				146,000
Bank			15,000	
Trade creditors			16,000	31,000
				115,000

	John	Kevin	Leonard	Total
Capital	36,000	32,000	30,000	98,000
Current Accounts	8,500	1,000	7,500	17,000
				115,000

The following events occurred during 1998:

1 On 1st January it was agreed that the goodwill of the partnership had a value of £24,000, and that the profit-sharing ratio of the partnership should henceforth be 2:1:1. Goodwill is not to be recorded permanently in the accounts.
2 Trading profit for the year amounted to £18,000. Drawings of £5,800 were taken by each partner.
3 Because of disagreements among the partners, it was decided that, with effect from 31st December, 1998, the partnership should cease trading and should be dissolved. A summary of the balance sheet at that date (prior to the dissolution) was as follows:

Balance Sheet as at 31st December, 1998

	£	£
Fixed assets		100,000
Stocks and debtors		43,000
Cash		4,600
		147,600
Bank	17,000	
Trade creditors	15,000	32,000
		115,600
Partners' capital accounts		98,000
Partners' current accounts		17,600
		115,600

The dissolution took some time because there was a delay in disposing of some of the assets. The stock and debtors were realised in full on 1st January, 1999, for £38,000, but the fixed assets were not sold until 25th January, when they realised £104,000. The expenses of the realisation and dissolution amounted to £2,000.

Required:
Prepare the following ledger accounts to record the above events and transactions:
(a) Capital account of each partner;
(b) Current account of each partner; and
(c) Realisation account.

It should be assumed that, in the dissolution, cash was distributed to the partners as quickly as was legally possible.

(ICAI Professional Examination Two)

36.11 Helen, Jane and Irene have been in partnership sharing profits and losses in the ratio 5:3:2, respectively. The partnership was dissolved as at 31st August, 1998. The Balance Sheet as at that date is shown below:

Balance Sheet as at 31 August 1998

	£	£	£	£
Bank				5,475
Debtors				23,207
Stocks				14,751
Fixtures and fittings				8,450
Creditors				−13,008
				38,875

	Helen	*Jane*	*Irene*	*Total*
Capital Accounts	16,000	13,475	9,400	38,875

You note that the following transactions took place during September 1998:

1 4th September   The fixtures and fittings realised £8,000.
   7th September   Some of the stock realised £7,250.
   11th September   Creditors were paid £12,500 in full settlement of the amounts due to them.
   14th September   More stock realised £3,600.
   26th September   Debtors paid in £23,060 to close off all balances due to the partnership.
   29th September   The remaining stock realised £3,700.
   30th September   Realisation expenses of £590 were paid.

2 Interim distributions were made on 13th September and 19th September and a final distribution on 30th September.

You also note that, under the partnership agreement, any profit or loss arising on dissolution which would accrue to Irene is to be divided between Helen and Jane in the ratio 2:3, respectively.

Required:
Prepare, in columnar form, the accounts necessary to record the above transactions for September 1998, ensuring that at no stage of the realisation is there any over-distribution to a partner.

(ICAI Professional Examination Two)

36.12A Lock, Stock and Barrel have been in partnership as builders and contractors for many years. Owing to adverse trading conditions it has been decided to dissolve the partnership. Profits are shared Lock 40%, Stock 30% and Barrel 30%. The partnership deed also provides that in the event of a partner being unable to pay off a debit balance the remaining partners will treat this as a trading loss.

The latest partnership balance sheet was as follows:

	Cost £	Depreciation £	Net £
Fixed tangible assets			
Freehold yard and buildings	20,000	3,000	17,000
Plant and equipment	150,000	82,000	68,000
Vehicles	36,000	23,000	13,000
	206,000	108,000	98,000
Current assets			
Stock of land for building		75,000	
Houses in the course of construction		115,000	
Stocks of materials		23,000	
Debtors for completed houses		62,000	
		275,000	
Current liabilities			
Trade creditors	77,000		
Deposits and progress payments	82,000		
Bank overdraft	132,500		
	291,500		
Excess of current liabilities over current assets			(16,500)
			81,500
Partners' capital accounts			
Lock		52,000	
Stock		26,000	
Barrel		3,500	
			81,500

During the six months from the date of the latest balance sheet to the date of dissolution the following transactions have taken place:

	£
Purchase of materials	20,250
Materials used for houses in course of construction	35,750
Payments for wages and subcontractors on building sites	78,000
Payments to trade creditors for materials	45,000
Sales of completed houses	280,000
Cash received from customers for houses	225,000
Payments for various general expenses	12,500
Payments for administration salaries	17,250
Cash withdrawn by partners: Lock	6,000
Stock	5,000
Barrel	4,000

All deposits and progress payments have been used for completed transactions.

Depreciation is normally provided each year at £600 on the freehold yard and buildings, at 10 per cent on cost for plant and equipment and 25 per cent on cost for vehicles.

The partners decide to dissolve the partnership on 1 February 19X7 and wish to take out the maximum cash possible, as items are sold. At this date there are no houses in course of construction and one third of the stock of land had been used for building.

It is agreed that Barrel is insolvent and cannot bring any money into the partnership. The partners take over the partnership cars at an agreed figure of £2,000 each. All other vehicles were sold on 28 February 19X7 for £6,200. At the same date stocks of materials were sold for £7,000, and the stock of the land realised £72,500. On 30 April 19X7 the debtors paid in full and all the plant and equipment was sold for £50,000.

The freehold yard and buildings realised £100,000 on 1 June 19X7, on which date all remaining cash was distributed.

There are no costs of realisation or distribution.

Required:

(a) Prepare a partnership profit and loss account for the six months to 1 February 19X7, partners' capital accounts for the same period and a balance sheet at 1 February 19X7.

(b) Show calculations of the amounts distributable to the partners.

(c) Prepare a realisation account and the capital accounts of the partners to the final distribution.

(*Association of Chartered Certified Accountants*)

Part V Revision questions

Suggested solutions to questions with the letter 'A' after the question number are given in Appendix II.

R5.1 Simon and Ann were in partnership sharing profits in the ratio 3:1. The Balance Sheet of the partnership as at 31st December, 1998 was as follows:

Balance Sheet as at 31st December, 1998

	£	£	£
Fixed Assets			
Premises			60,000
Furniture and fittings			18,000
Vehicle			9,000
			87,000
Current Assets			
Stocks		30,000	
Debtors		22,000	
		52,000	
Current Liabilities			
Creditors	18,000		
Loan from Ann	5,000		
Bank overdraft	12,000	35,000	
			17,000
			104,000
Capital Accounts			
Simon			55,000
Ann			49,000
			104,000

Additional information

1 On 1st January, 1999, John was admitted as a partner on payment of £30,000. From that date the partners are to share profits in the ratio Simon 3: Ann 2: John 1.

2 The assets were valued on 1st January, 1999, and the values at that date are as shown below. The new values are to be incorporated into the books.

Premises	£65,000
Furniture and Fittings	£19,000
Vehicle	£11,000
Stock	£26,000
Debtors	£22,000

3 Goodwill was valued at £12,000 on 1st January, 1999, and is not to be brought into the books.

4 It is agreed that the loan from Ann is to be repaid immediately out of the partnership bank account.

5 It is agreed that, in addition to the £30,000 cash introduced by John, he is to introduce into the partnership the following:
  (*i*) A premises at a valuation of £25,000.
  (*ii*) Stock valued at £5,000.
  (*iii*) A vehicle valued at £6,000.

You are required to prepare:
(*a*) the revaluation account;
(*b*) the capital accounts of the partners to give effect to the admission of John into the partnership; and
(*c*) the revised Balance Sheet of the partnership after giving effect to the admission of John into the partnership.

(*IATI Admission Examination*)

R5.2 Albert, Brian and Colin were in partnership sharing profits and losses in the ratio 4:3:2 respectively except that Brian (but not Albert) had guaranteed that Colin's share of the profit (excluding interest on capital) in any year should be not less than £6,800.

Interest was allowed on capital account balances at the beginning of the year at 10% per annum before the division of profits or losses. No interest was charged on drawings.

The Trial Balance as at 31st May, 1998 was as follows:

Trial Balance as at 31 May 1998

	Debit £	Credit £
Capital accounts at 1st June, 1997		
Albert		45,000
Brian		31,500
Colin		24,750
Drawings – 1997/98		
Albert	6,050	
Brian	5,175	
Colin	6,320	
Goodwill	31,500	
Plant and fittings (net book value)	18,435	
Vehicles (net book value)	19,970	
Stocks	17,072	
Debtors	14,315	
Cash at bank	39,565	
Creditors		18,155
Net profit for the year ended 31st May, 1998		
(before interest on capital)		38,997
	158,402	158,402

Albert retired from the partnership on 31st May, 1998 and took over a vehicle at book value of £4,000. In computing the amount to be paid to him on retirement, goodwill of the firm was revalued at £36,000.

On 1st June, 1998 David was admitted to the partnership on payment of £16,000, including a premium for his share of the goodwill of the firm, which was then to be eliminated from the books. From 1st June, 1998, profits and losses in the new firm were to be shared between Brian, Colin and David in the ratio 3:2:1, respectively.

You are required to prepare:
(*a*) the capital and current accounts of Albert, Brian, Colin and David in columnar form to reflect the foregoing; and
(*b*) the Balance Sheet as at 1st June, 1998.

(*ICAI Professional Examination Two*)

R5.3   Alice and Betty were in partnership for many years sharing profits and losses in the ratio 7:3, respectively. The balance sheet of the firm at 31st December, 1996, was as follows:

Balance Sheet as at 31 December, 1996

	£	£	£
Fixed assets (net)			32,400
Stocks			8,400
Trade debtors			3,700
Bank			1,500
			46,000
Trade creditors			1,900
			44,100

	Alice	Betty	Total
Capital	24,900	16,600	41,500
Current accounts:	1,500	1,100	2,600
			44,100

On 1st January, 1997, Carla was admitted as a partner on payment of £12,000 into the firm, including a premium of £6,000 in respect of goodwill. A goodwill account was not maintained permanently in the accounts. The new partnership agreement specified that profits were to be shared between Alice, Betty and Carla in a ratio of 5:2:3 respectively, after crediting an annual salary of £6,000 to Alice.

Details of profits (before deduction of Alice's salary) and of drawings by each partner in the years ended 31st December, 1997, and 1998, are as follows:

	Years Ended 31st December	
	1997	1998
Profits	£28,400	£24,500
Drawings by Alice	£10,000	£8,900
Drawings by Betty	£3,800	£3,100
Drawings by Carla	£6,700	£6,100

Alice withdrew her salary each year in addition to the above drawings.

On 1st January, 1999, Carla became insolvent and the partnership was dissolved. The firm paid its creditors in full (£11,600) and paid realisation expenses of £2,300. The assets of the firm realised £41,800.

Required:
Prepare, in columnar form, the capital and current accounts of the partners to reflect the above events and transactions. The rule in *Garner* v. *Murray* should be applied.

(*ICAI Professional Examination Two*)

R5.4 Martin and Nicholas are in partnership sharing profits in the ratio of 5:4. The following is the Balance Sheet of the partnership as at 31st December, 1996:

Balance Sheet as at 31 December 1996

Fixed assets			£50,000
Stocks			£20,000
Debtors			£15,000
Bank			£5,000
Creditors			–£13,000
			£77,000

	Martin	*Nicholas*	*Total*
Capital	£40,000	£31,400	£71,400
Current accounts	£3,000	£2,600	£5,600
			£77,000

1 Profits for the year to 31st December, 1997, were £18,000. No drawings were taken during that year.
2 On 31st December, 1997, Martin retired and Oliver and Peter were admitted to the partnership. Goodwill, which is not to be included in the accounts, was valued at 3 times the 1997 profits. The balances on Martin's capital and current accounts were transferred to a loan account. Oliver and Peter each introduced capital of £20,000. The new profit sharing ratio between Nicholas, Oliver and Peter was 3:1:1 respectively. Oliver is to get an annual salary of £5,000.
3 Profits for the year to 31st December, 1998, were £15,000 and drawings during the year were as follows:

Nicholas	£7,000
Oliver	£8,000
Peter	£10,000

4 Owing to the insolvency of Peter at 31st December, 1998, the partnership was dissolved. After the firm paid its creditors and Martin's loan account in full, the assets realised £27,250.

Required:
Prepare the capital and current accounts of the partners in columnar form to reflect the above transactions and events using the rule in *Garner* v. *Murray*.

(ICAI Professional Examination Two)

R5.5 Nora, Olga and Patricia have been in partnership for several years, sharing profits and losses in the ratio 1:1:3 respectively. They agreed to dissolve the partnership at 31st May, 1998. The following is the Balance Sheet of the partnership at that date:

Balance Sheet as at 31 May 1998

Fixed assets	£13,200
Stocks	£8,500
Trade debtors	£7,200
Bank	£1,300
	£30,200
Trade creditors	£6,200
	£24,000
Capital accounts	
Nora	£12,000
Olga	£8,000
Patricia	£4,000
	£24,000

The fixed assets were sold for £12,000 on 2nd June, and the stock was sold for £7,900 on 6th June. Payment of £7,000 was received from trade debtors (in full settlement) on 21st June.

Trade creditors were paid £6,100 (in full settlement) on 9th June, An interim distribution was made to the partners on 19th June and a final distribution on 23rd June.

Required:

Calculate the amounts of cash which may be paid to each partner on each of the two distribution dates, assuming that the rule in *Garner* v. *Murray* applies to this partnership.

(*ICAI Professional Examination Two*)

Part VI

COMPANY ACCOUNTING

37

Introduction to companies

37.1 The general nature of companies

This chapter introduces students to companies, a common form of business organisation. As it is only an introduction some generalisations will be made. Exceptions to these generalisations will be covered at a later stage in your studies.

A **company** is a form of business organisation which is owned by all those who invest in it. These investors are known as **shareholders** as they own or 'hold' a share of the company. The size of their share of the company will depend upon the amount of money they have invested in it.

The total investment by all of the shareholders is known as the **share capital** of the company. Thus, unlike a sole trader, where one person owns the business, or a partnership, where a small number of people own a business, a company may be owned by several hundred or even several thousand shareholders.

Obviously, all of these people cannot be involved in running the company. Instead, the shareholders appoint **directors** to run the company on their behalf. If the directors run the company efficiently and make a profit the shareholders will receive a **dividend** each year as a return on their investment.

37.2 Characteristics of companies

The characteristics of companies differ in several respects from both sole traders and partnerships. The following are among the more important differences.

Separate legal entity

A unique feature of a company is that, no matter how many individuals have bought shares in it, it is treated in its dealings with the outside world as if it was a person in its own right. It is said to be a **separate legal entity**. Just as the law can create this separate legal person, so also can it eliminate it, but its existence can only be terminated by using the proper legal procedures.

Thus, the identity of the shareholders in a large concern may be changing daily as shares are bought and sold by different people. On the other hand, a small private company may have the same shareholders from the date it is incorporated (the day it legally came into being), until the date when liquidation is completed (the cessation of the company, often known also as 'winding up' or being 'wound up'). A prime example of its identity as a separate legal entity is that it may sue its own shareholders, or in turn be sued by them.

The legal formalities by which a company comes into existence can be found in any textbook on company law. It is not the purpose of this book to discuss company law in detail. As companies must, however, comply with the law, the essential company law concerning accounting matters will be dealt with in this book insofar as it is considered

necessary. It is important to note that this book provides only an introduction to companies and their accounts. This is a complex area, which, for those undertaking further study of accounting, will be covered in much greater detail at a later stage.

Limited liability

Most companies are 'limited' companies. This means that any shareholder who has paid for the share(s) which he has bought cannot be forced to pay more money into the company if, for example, it is making losses or has gone into liquidation. Thus, the maximum amount of money any shareholder can lose by investing in a company is the amount he has invested. Unlike in sole traders or partnerships a shareholder in a limited company cannot be forced to sell his house, car etc. to pay the debts of the business.

If a shareholder has not paid in full for the shares he has agreed to buy, he can be forced to pay the balance owing on the shares. Once he has paid that amount he cannot be forced to pay any further amount. Thus, his liability is limited to the amount he has agreed to pay but has not yet paid.

This is known as **limited liability** and the company is known as a limited company. It is important to note that it is the liability of the shareholders that is limited not the liability of the company. Companies can incur debts well beyond what they are able to pay and therefore their liabilities can exceed their assets.

There are, as will be seen later, some companies, known as unlimited companies, in which the liability of the shareholders is not limited.

Limited liability and the ability to raise large amounts of finance are the principal reasons why limited companies are the most common form of business organisation.

37.3 The law governing companies

In the same way that partnerships are governed by the Partnership Act, 1890 companies are regulated by the Companies Acts. All of the Companies Acts do not apply to all companies. For example, banks and insurance companies are often excluded from some company law provisions. The principal Companies Acts and Companies (Amendment) Acts are:

The Companies Act, 1963;
The Companies (Amendment) Act, 1983;
The Companies (Amendment) Act, 1986;
The Companies Act, 1990; and
The Companies (Amendment) Act, 1990.

Because of the impact of EC Directives which have attempted to harmonise company law throughout the EC (now EU) Irish company law is similar to, though not exactly the same as, company law in the UK and other EU member states.

The format and content of company accounts are governed by the Companies Acts as well as by Accounting Standards, Financial Reporting Standards, other professional pronouncements and, in the case of public companies, Stock Exchange regulations. Company accounts are discussed in greater detail in Chapters 38 and 39.

37.4 Public companies and private companies

Broadly speaking, there are two classes of company, the **public company** and the **private company**. In Ireland private companies far outnumber public companies. Public companies are also known as PLCs, that is, public limited companies.

A private company may not have less than two, or more than fifty, shareholders (excluding employees and ex-employees) and may not offer its shares to the general public. Once someone has purchased shares in a private company the right to transfer those shares to someone else is severely restricted.

A PLC is a company which fulfils the following conditions:

It must be able to issue share capital of at least £30,000;

It must have at least seven shareholders. There is no maximum.

Its name must end with the words 'public limited company', the abbreviation 'plc' or the Irish equivalent 'cpt'.

A private company is usually, but not always, smaller than a public company.

The shares that are dealt in on the Stock Exchange are all of public limited companies. This does not mean that all public companies' shares are traded on the Stock Exchange, as, for various reasons, some public companies have either chosen not to, or not been allowed to, have their shares traded there. The ones that are traded in are known as **quoted companies** or **listed companies** meaning that the price of shares in them is quoted (or listed) by the Stock Exchange. Quoted companies have to comply with Stock Exchange rules and regulations.

37.5 Company directors

The day-to-day business of a company is not carried out by the shareholders. Shareholders can normally attend, and vote at, general meetings of their company. At one of these meetings the shareholders will vote for **directors**, the people to whom the running of the business is entrusted. At each **Annual General Meeting** (AGM) the directors have to report to the shareholders. They write a directors' report and this is accompanied by a set of final accounts for the year. If there is a change in the directors of a company, for example, a new director being appointed or an existing director resigning, this change must be notified to the Companies Office within fourteen days of the change. The **board of directors** (usually known simply as 'the board') is the term used to mean all of the directors.

37.6 The company secretary

The **Company Secretary** must, among other things, attend all board meetings, consult with the chief executive on the agenda and keep a record of the minutes of board meetings and general meetings of the shareholders. It is normally the company secretary who makes returns to the Companies Office including notifying the Registrar of changes in the company's board, auditors, registered office etc. The company secretary is usually an individual although many companies pay firms of accountants to undertake this role.

37.7 Share capital and dividends

A shareholder in a limited company obtains his reward for investing in the form of a share of the profits, known as a dividend. The directors decide how much of the profits is to be retained in the company and used for expansion. Out of the profits remaining they propose the payment of a certain amount of dividend. The shareholders cannot propose a dividend for themselves higher than that already proposed by the directors. They can, however, propose that a lesser dividend should be paid, although this action is very rare. If the directors propose that no dividend be paid, then the shareholders are powerless to alter the decision.

The decision by the directors as to the amount proposed as dividends is a very complex one and cannot be fully discussed here. Such matters as the effect of taxation, the availability of bank balances to pay the dividends, the possibility of take-over bids and so on will all be taken into account.

Dividends are usually expressed as a percentage of the share capital. A dividend of 10% in Company A on 500,000 Ordinary Shares of £1 each will amount to £50,000, or a dividend of 6% in Company B on 200,000 Ordinary Shares of £2 each will amount to £24,000. A shareholder having 100 shares in each firm would receive £10 from Company A and £12 from Company B.

There are two main types of shares:

Preference shares

These get an agreed percentage rate of dividend before the ordinary shareholders receive anything.

Ordinary shares

These receive the remainder of the total profits available for dividends. The amount of profit available is the only upper limit to the amount of dividends they can receive.

Example 37.1

If a company had 10,000 5% preference shares of £1 each and 20,000 ordinary shares of £1 each, then the dividends would be payable as follows:

	Year 1	Year 2	Year 3	Year 4	Year 5
Profits appropriated for dividends	£900	£1,300	£1,600	£3,100	£2,000
Preference dividends (5%)	£500	£500	£500	£500	£500
Ordinary dividends	£400	£800	£1,100	£2,600	£1,500
Rate of Ordinary Dividend	2%	4%	5.5%	13%	7.5%

The two main types of preference shares are non-cumulative preference shares and cumulative preference shares.

Non-cumulative preference shares

These can receive a dividend up to an agreed percentage each year. If the amount paid is less than the maximum agreed amount, the shortage is lost by the shareholder. He cannot carry forward that shortage and get it in a future year.

Cumulative preference shares

These also have an agreed maximum percentage dividend. However, any shortage of dividend paid in a year can be carried forward. All arrears of preference dividends will have to be paid in a subsequent year before the ordinary shareholders receive anything in that year.

Example 37.2

A company has 5,000 £1 ordinary shares and 2,000 5% non-cumulative preference shares of £1 each. The profits available for dividends are: Year 1 £150, Year 2 £80, Year 3 £250, Year 4 £60, Year 5 £500.

	Year 1	Year 2	Year 3	Year 4	Year 5
Profits	£150	£80	£250	£60	£500
Preference dividend (limited in years 2 and 4)	£100	£80	£100	£60	£100
Dividends on ordinary shares	£50	–	£150	–	£400

Example 37.3

Assuming that the preference shares in Example 37.2 had been cumulative, the dividends would have been:

	Year 1	Year 2	Year 3	Year 4	Year 5
Profits	£150	£80	£250	£60	£500
Preference dividend	£100	£80	*£120	£60	*£140
Dividends on ordinary shares	£50	–	£130	–	£360

including arrears.

37.8 Different meanings of 'share capital'

The term 'share capital' can have any of the following meanings:

Authorised share capital (or nominal share capital)

This is the maximum amount of share capital which a company can issue to shareholders. The maximum can be increased at a general meeting of the company. When nominal capital is increased the Companies Office must be notified of the increase within fifteen days of the meeting at which the decision was made to increase it.

Issued share capital

This is the share capital actually issued to shareholders.

If all of the authorised share capital has been issued, then authorised share capital and issued share capital would be the same amount.

Called-up share capital

Where only part of the amounts payable on each share has been asked for, the total amount asked for on all the shares is known as the called-up capital. The issued shares in a PLC must be paid in full when the company is incorporated.

Uncalled share capital

This is the total amount which is to be received in future, but which has not yet been asked for.

Calls in arrear

The amount of payment which has been asked for (i.e. called for), but has not yet been paid by shareholders.

Paid-up share capital

This is the amount of share capital which has been paid for by shareholders.

Example 37.4

1 Better Enterprises Ltd was formed with the legal right to issue 100,000 shares of £1 each.
2 The company has actually issued 75,000 of these shares.
3 None of the shares has yet been fully paid up. So far, the company has made calls of £0.80 per share.
4 All the calls have been paid by shareholders except for £200 owing from one shareholder
   (a) Authorised or nominal share capital is £100,000.
   (b) Issued share capital is £75,000.
   (c) Called-up capital is 75,000 × £0.80 = £60,000.
   (d) Calls in arrear amounted to £200.
   (e) Paid-up capital is (c) £60,000 less (d) £200 = £59,800.

37.9 Debentures

The term **debenture** is used when a limited company receives money on loan, and certificates called debenture certificates are issued to the lender. Interest will be paid to the holder at the rate shown on the certificate. Instead of always being called debentures they are often known as loan stock or as loan capital.

Debenture interest has to be paid whether or not profits are earned. They are therefore different from ordinary shares, where dividends depend upon profits. A debenture may be either:

Redeemable, i.e. repayable at or by a particular date, or
Irredeemable, normally repayable only when the company is officially terminated, known as liquidation.

If a date is shown after a debenture, e.g. '7% Debenture 2001/2008', it means that the company can redeem it in any of the years 2001 to 2008 inclusive.

People lending money to companies in the form of debentures will obviously be interested in how safe their investment will be. Some debentures are given the legal right that, on certain happenings, the debenture holders will be able to take control of specific assets, or of the whole of the assets. They can then sell the assets and recoup the amount due under their debentures, or deal with the assets in ways specified in the deed under which the debentures were issued. Such debentures are known as being 'secured against the assets', the term **mortgage debenture** often being used. Other debentures have no prior right to control the assets under any circumstances. These are known as **simple** or **naked** debentures.

37.10 The Companies Registration Office

The Companies Registration Office (CRO or Companies Office), keeps a file on every Irish company. Its main functions are registering (or incorporating) companies when they are first set up, registering business names, registering documents which companies must send to it regularly and providing information on companies to anyone who wants it.

Since 1994 the Companies Office has facilitated companies or professional company secretaries to file information electronically using electronic data interchange (EDI). Documents sent in by companies are scanned and held on optical disk.

Information in the Companies Office may be accessed in person, by post, by telex or electronically using a PC and modem. A printout of information held on the company 'searched' will be issued.

37.11 Books of account

Companies are required to keep detailed and accurate accounting records, usually known as **proper books of account**. These books must correctly record and explain a company's transactions, enable the company's financial position to be determined with reasonable accuracy, enable the directors to ensure that the company's annual accounts give the information required by the Companies Acts and enable those accounts to be audited.

37.12 Records and registers to be kept by companies

Apart from the normal accounting records already described in this text, there are other records and registers which, by law, must be kept by companies. These are known as **statutory books**. A list of them, what they should contain, and the need for them is given below.

Book	Contains	Purpose
Register of Members	Details of shareholders, giving names, addresses and amounts of shareholdings.	To enable anyone to establish the identities of shareholders
Register of Debenture-Holders	Details of debenture-holders, giving names, addresses and amounts of debentures held	To enable anyone to establish the identities of debenture-holders
Register of Charges	Full details of each charge	To enable anyone to establish amounts of charges, what they have been secured on and the parties involved
Register of Directors and Secretaries	Particulars of each person concerned	To enable anyone to establish their identities
Register of Directors' Interests in Shares and Debentures	Full details of shares and debentures held by directors or their close relatives	To enable anyone to ascertain exact involvement of director with the company
Minute Book: general meetings	Proper account of items discussed, resolutions and voting	To enable anyone to discover details of business concerned
Minute Book: directors' meetings	Proper account of items discussed and decisions taken	Not generally open to examination. Serves as a record of business undertaken
Record of Declarations by Directors of Interests in Company Contracts	Details of declarations by directors of personal interests in company contracts	To avoid ethical problems and conflict of interest claims arising from directors having a personal interest in company business

37.13 Memorandum of Association and Articles of Association

Every company is governed by two documents, known as the **Memorandum of Association** and the **Articles of Association**, generally referred to as the memorandum and the articles. The memorandum of a private limited company must contain the following four clauses:

1 The name of the company;
2 The objects of the company (what it has powers to do in terms of trading);
3 A statement that the liability of its members is limited, and
4 Details of the share capital which the company is authorised to issue.

The memorandum of a PLC must, in addition to the above, state that the company is a public limited company.

The memorandum is said to be the document which discloses the conditions which govern the company's relationship with the outside world.

Table A Articles of Association

Every company must also have Articles of Association. Just as the memorandum governs the company's dealings with the outside world, the articles govern the relationships which exist between the members of a company (the shareholders) and the company itself, between one member and the other members, and other necessary regulations. The Companies Act, 1963 contains a 'model' set of articles known as **Table A**. A company may, if it so wishes, have its articles exactly the same as Table A, commonly known as 'adopting Table A', or else adopt part of it and have some sections altered. The adoption of the major part of Table A is normal for most private companies. In this book, unless stated to the contrary, the examples shown are on the basis that Table A has been adopted.

Table A lays down regulations concerning the powers of the directors of the company. On the other hand, the company may draft its own regulations for the powers of directors. Any such regulations are of the utmost importance because the legal owners of the business, the shareholders, have entrusted the running of the company to the directors. The shareholders' own rights are largely limited to attending, and voting at, Annual General Meetings, although some shares do not carry voting rights. The Companies Acts make the keeping of proper sets of accounting records and the preparation of final accounts compulsory for every company. In addition, the accounts must be audited. This is different from a partnership or a sole trader's business where an audit is not compulsory.

37.14 Publication of company accounts

Limited companies, whether private or public, have to send a copy of their final accounts, drawn up in a prescribed manner, to the Registrar of Companies. Further details regarding the publication of accounts are given in Chapter 39.

37.15 Meetings of company shareholders

Every company must hold an Annual General Meeting (AGM) once in every calendar year and there must not be more than fifteen months between successive AGMs. An AGM must be held within nine months of the end of each accounting period.

A profit and loss account and balance sheet covering the period since the previous set of accounts must be presented at each AGM.

37.16 Annual returns

Under the Companies Acts, every company must make an **Annual Return,** accompanied by the relevant financial statements, dated fourteen days after the AGM and file it within sixty days of the meeting, for example, dated 14 October if the meeting was held on 30 September.

Under a recent Ministerial Order the Annual Return must be filed in Dublin Castle within Seventy-seven days of the date of the return, for example, before 30 December when the return is dated 14 October. The Companies Office charges a late filing fee on all returns filed later than seventy-seven days after the date of the return. The fee is currently £150. If, however, a company is summonsed to appear in court for not filing an annual return the provisions of the Companies Acts apply and fines of up to £1,000 per return may be payable.

37.17 Public companies and the stock exchange

The shares of most of the public companies are traded on the Stock Exchange. The shares of private companies cannot be bought and sold on the Stock Exchange, as this would contravene the requirements for the company being recognised as a 'private' company. The sale and purchase of shares on the Stock Exchange have no effect on the accounting entries made in the company's books. The only entry made in the company's 'books' when a shareholder sells all, or some, of his shares to someone else, is to record the change of identity of the shareholders in the register of shareholders. The price at which shares are sold on the Stock Exchange does not enter into the company's books.

The price of the shares on the Stock Exchange has repercussions on the financial policy of the company. If some new shares are to be issued, the price at which they are to be issued will be largely dependent on the Stock Exchange valuation. If another firm is to be taken over by the company, part of the purchase price being by the means of shares in the company, then the Stock Exchange value will also affect the value placed upon the shares being given. A take-over bid from another firm may well be caused because the Stock Exchange value of the shares has made a take-over seem worthwhile.

The Stock Exchange is the 'second-hand market' for a company's shares. The company does not actually sell (normally called issue) its shares by using the Stock Exchange as a selling place. The company issues new shares directly to the people who make application to it for the shares at the time when the company has shares available for issue. The company does not sell to, or buy from, the Stock Exchange. This means that the shares in a public company sold and bought on the Stock Exchange are passing from a shareholder to another person who will then become a shareholder. The double entry accounts of the company are not affected.

Review questions

Questions 244–260 in the accompanying book of multiple-choice questions examine the material covered in this chapter (see back cover of this book for further details).

38

An introduction to the final accounts of companies

38.1 Trading and profit and loss accounts of companies

The trading and profit and loss account of a limited company, whether private or public, prepared for use by the management of the company (not for publication) is drawn up using the same principles as for a sole trader or a partnership. Profit and loss accounts (and balance sheets) for publication must adhere to very strict layouts specified in the Companies Acts.

Although the principles are the same, there are, however, some differences which may be found in the profit and loss account of a company when compared with that of a sole trader or partnership. The two main expenses which are found only in company accounts are:

1 **Directors' remuneration**

Only companies have directors, so the expense of paying them is found only in company accounts.

Directors are legally employees of the company, appointed by the shareholders. Their remuneration is charged in the main profit and loss account. Emoluments paid to directors must be shown in the profit and loss account in accordance with the Companies Acts – they cannot be omitted or mixed in with another figure.

2 **Debenture interest**

The interest payable for the use of the money borrowed is an expense to the company whether or not a profit is earned. This means that debenture interest is charged as an expense in the profit and loss account itself. Contrast this with dividends, which are dependent upon profits being earned.

38.2 Profit and loss appropriation accounts of companies

As for partnerships a profit and loss appropriation account is prepared to show how the net profit is to be appropriated, i.e. how it is to be distributed or reinvested.

We may find any of the following in the appropriation account:

Credit

1 **Net profit for the year**

This is the net profit brought down from the main profit and loss account.

2 **Balance brought forward from last year**

As you will see, all the profits may not be appropriated during a period. This then will be the balance on the appropriation account, as brought forward from the previous year (usually called retained profits). Under the Companies Acts this must be shown.

Debit

3 Transfers to reserves

The directors may decide that some of the profits should not be included in the calculation of how much should be paid out as dividends. These profits are transferred to reserve accounts. There may, or may not, be a specific reason for the transfer, such as a need to replace fixed assets. In this case an amount would be transferred to a fixed assets replacement reserve. Where there is not a specific reason an amount would be transferred to a general reserve account. Under the Companies Acts any transfers to reserves must be shown.

4 Amounts written off goodwill

Any amounts written off goodwill should be shown in the appropriation account and not in the main profit and loss account.

5 Taxation payable on profits (Corporation Tax)

At this point in your studies you do not need to know very much about taxation. However, it does affect the preparation of accounts, and so we will tell you here as much as you need to know now. Sole traders and partnerships pay income tax based on their profits. Such income tax, when paid, is simply charged as drawings – it is not an expense.

Companies, on the other hand, pay corporation tax. It is also based on the amount of profits earned. For the moment you do not need to know how to calculate the amount of tax payable. Therefore, in questions and examples at this point you will be told how much it is, or be given a simple arithmetical way of ascertaining the amount.

Corporation tax is not an expense, it is an appropriation of profits. However, for the sake of presentation and to make the accounts more understandable to the general reader, it is not shown with the other appropriations. Instead, as in Example 1 it is shown as a deduction from profit for the year before taxation (i.e. the net profit figure) to show the net result, i.e. profit for the year after taxation.

6 Dividends

Out of the remainder of the profits the directors propose what dividends should be paid. Under the Companies Acts both dividends paid and proposed must be shown.

7 Balance carried forward to next year

After the dividends have been proposed there will probably be some profits that have not been appropriated. These retained profits, which must be shown under the Companies Acts, will be carried forward to the following year.

Example 38.1 shows the profit and loss appropriation account of a new business for its first three years of trading.

Example 38.1

C O'Byrne Ltd has an ordinary share capital of 40,000 ordinary shares of £1 each and 20,000 5% preference shares of £1 each. The company prepares its accounts for the year ended on 31st December each year. Details for its first three years in business are as follows:

	1996	1997	1998
Net Profit	£10,967	£14,864	£15,822
Transfer to general reserve	nil	£1,000	nil
Transfer to fixed assets replacement reserve	nil	nil	£2,250
Dividends on ordinary shares	10%	12.5%	15%
Corporation tax	£4,100	£5,250	£6,300

Dividends were proposed for each year on the preference shares at 5%.

C O'Byrne Ltd
Profit and Loss Appropriation Account for the year ended 31st December 1996

	£	£
Profit for the year before taxation		10,967
Less Corporation tax		4,100
Profit for the year after taxation		6,867
Less Proposed dividends:		
Preference dividend of 5%	1,000	
Ordinary dividend of 10%	4,000	5,000
Retained profits carried forward to next year		1,867

C O'Byrne Ltd
Profit and Loss Appropriation Account for the year ended 31st December 1997

	£	£
Profit for the year before taxation		14,864
Less Corporation tax		5,250
Profit for the year after taxation		9,614
Add Retained profits from last year		1,867
		11,481
Less Transfer to general reserve	1,000	
Proposed dividends:		
Preference dividend of 5%	1,000	
Ordinary dividend of 12.5%	5,000	7,000
Retained profits carried forward to next year		4,481

C O'Byrne Ltd
Profit and Loss Appropriation Account for the year ended 31st December 1998

	£	£
Profit for the year before taxation		15,822
Less Corporation tax		6,300
Profit for the year after taxation		9,522
Add Retained profits from last year		4,481
		14,003
Less Transfer to fixed assets replacement reserve	2,250	
Proposed dividends:		
Preference dividend of 5%	1,000	
Ordinary dividend of 15%	6,000	9,250
Retained profits carried forward to next year		4,753

In a balance sheet, corporation tax owing will be shown as a current liability.

38.3 Presentation of balance sheets of companies

Although this book does not cover the presentation requirements of the Companies Acts, the balance sheet shown in Example 38.2 is presented in a way similar to that required by the Acts. This is done because it is always advisable in exams that you present final accounts in a professional manner. Example 38.2 is intended to assist you in this regard. You should adopt a similar professional approach to profit and loss accounts and there is no good reason why the balance sheet format shown on page 366 could not be used in the case of a sole trader or partnership (apart from the 'Capital and Reserves' section).

Fixed assets

Generally fixed assets are shown under two separate headings, **tangible fixed assets** and **intangible fixed assets** with only one total figure for each. Whilst the Companies Acts require only one figure for each in published accounts it is better to show more detail when accounts are not being published. This is done in Example 38.2. Tangible fixed assets are assets that have 'physical substance', meaning that they can be seen and touched. Examples include buildings and machinery. They are normally shown net of depreciation. In a note accompanying the accounts the cost and depreciation for each category of tangible fixed asset, for example, land, buildings and vehicles, would be given. Intangible fixed assets are those not having a 'physical' existence, such as goodwill. The net book value of tangible fixed assets may be calculated as either cost less aggregate depreciation or some valuation less aggregate depreciation (or simply cost or valuation in the case of land, which is not depreciated). Whether assets are valued at cost or valuation will also be stated in the notes to the accounts.

Creditors

Creditors are also generally shown under two separate headings: **Creditors – amounts falling due within one year** and **Creditors – amounts falling due after more than one year**. Again, whilst it is normal to only show one figure for each heading in published accounts more detail is shown in the example. The only difference between the two categories is that the former includes only those creditors which are payable within a year of the balance sheet date, for example, trade creditors, and the latter includes only creditors payable after that time, for example, long-term loans.

Working capital

'Working capital' is normally referred to as **net current assets**.

Share capital

The main types of share capital and reserves will each be given a heading in the balance sheet. Shares are valued in a balance sheet at whatever their **par** or **nominal** value is according to the memorandum of association, not what they can be sold for. More detailed information, including the authorised share capital and the nominal value of each share, will be found in supplementary notes to the balance sheet. The total of capital plus reserves is often referred to as **shareholders' funds**. Where shares are only partly called-up, then it is the amount actually called-up that appears in the balance sheet and not the full amount.

Reserves

Reserves consist either of those unused profits remaining in the appropriation account, or transferred to an appropriately titled reserve account, for example, General Reserve or Fixed Assets Replacement Reserve. At this juncture all that needs to be said is that any account labelled as a reserve has originated by being charged as a debit in the appropriation account and credited to a reserve account.

One reserve that is in fact not labelled with the word 'reserve' in its title is the Share Premium account. For various reasons (discussed in Chapter 41) shares can be issued for more than their face or nominal value. The excess of the price at which they are issued over the nominal value of the shares is credited to a share premium account.

There are two types of reserves namely 'Revenue Reserves' and 'Capital Reserves'. The main importance of the distinction is in deciding how much can be treated as being available for payment to shareholders in the form of dividends. 'Revenue Reserves', which include the Appropriation Account balance and the General Reserve, can be treated as being available for such dividends. 'Capital Reserves' which include revaluation reserves on property and land, also some reserves (which you have not yet met) which, legally, have to be created cannot be treated as being available for payment as dividends.

The closing balance on the profit and loss appropriation account is shown under the heading 'Reserves'. These are profits not already appropriated, and therefore 'reserved' for future use.

Example 38.2

C O'Byrne Ltd
Balance Sheet as at 31 December 1998

	£	£	£
Tangible Fixed Assets			
Buildings	9,000		
Machinery	5,600		
Vehicles	2,400	17,000	
Intangible Fixed Assets			
Goodwill		10,000	27,000
Current Assets			
Stock	6,000		
Debtors	3,000		
Bank	4,000	13,000	
Current liabilities			
Proposed dividend	1,000		
Creditors	3,000		
Corporation tax payable	2,000	6,000	
Net current assets			7,000
Total assets less current liabilities			34,000
Long-term liabilities			
Debenture loans			8,000
			26,000
Capital and Reserves			
Called-up share capital			20,000
Share premium account			1,200
General reserve			3,800
Profit and loss account			1,000
			26,000

38.4 An example of the preparation of company final accounts

The following trial balance was extracted from the books of Barker Pharmaceutical Components Ltd as at 31 December 1998.

Trial Balance as at 31 December 1998

	£ Debit	£ Credit
10% preference share capital		20,000
Ordinary share capital		70,000
10% debentures (repayable 2002)		30,000
Goodwill at cost	15,500	
Buildings at cost	95,000	
Equipment at cost	8,000	
Vehicles at cost	17,200	
Provision for depreciation of equipment at 1 January, 1998		2,400
Provision for depreciation of vehicles at 1 January, 1998		5,160
Stock at 1 January, 1998	22,690	
Sales		98,200
Purchases	53,910	
Carriage inwards	1,620	
Salaries and Wages	9,240	
Directors' remuneration	6,300	
Motor expenses	8,120	
Rates and insurances	2,930	
General expenses	560	
Debenture interest	1,500	
Debtors	18,610	
Creditors		11,370
Bank	8,390	
General reserve		5,000
Share premium account		14,000
Interim ordinary dividend paid	3,500	
Profit and loss account at 31 December, 1997		16,940
	273,070	273,070

Additional information:

(i) Stock at 31 December, 1998 was £27,220.
(ii) Vehicles are to be depreciated by £3,000 and equipment by £1,200.
(iii) Debenture interest of £1,500 is to be accrued.
(iv) A preference dividend of £2,000 and a final ordinary dividend of 10% are to be provided for.
(v) £2,000 is to be transferred to the general reserve.
(vi) £3,000 is to be written off goodwill.
(vii) Authorised share capital is £20,000 in preference shares and £100,000 in £1 ordinary shares.
(viii) Corporation tax of £5,000 is to be provided for.

The final accounts, prepared in a form suitable for presentation to the company's management, follow.

Barker Pharmaceutical Components Ltd
Trading and Profit and Loss Account for the year ended 31 December 1998

	£	£	£
Sales			98,200
Less Cost of sales:			
Opening Stock		22,690	
Add Purchases	53,910		
Add Carriage inwards	1,620	55,530	
		78,220	
Less Closing stock		27,220	51,000
Gross profit			47,200
Less Expenses:			
Salaries and wages		9,240	
Motor expenses		8,120	
Rates and insurances		2,930	
General expenses		560	
Directors' remuneration		6,300	
Debenture interest		3,000	
Depreciation of vehicles	3,000		
Depreciation of equipment	1,200	4,200	34,350
Profit for the year before taxation			12,850
Less Corporation tax			5,000
Profit for the year after taxation			7,850
Add Retained profits from last year			16,940
			24,790
Less Appropriations:			
Transfer to general reserve		2,000	
Goodwill written off		3,000	
Preference share dividend		2,000	
Ordinary share dividends			
Interim	3,500		
Final*	7,000	10,500	17,500
Retained profits carried forward to next year			7,290

* Note: Dividends on ordinary share capital, when expressed as a percentage, are always based on issued ordinary share capital, not authorised ordinary share capital.

Barker Pharmaceutical Components Ltd
Balance Sheet as at 31 December 1998

	£	£	£
Tangible fixed assets*			
Buildings	95,000		
Equipment	4,400		
Vehicles	9,040	108,440	
Intangible fixed assets			
Goodwill		12,500	120,940
Current assets			
Stock	27,220		
Debtors	18,610		
Bank	8,390	54,220	
Current liabilities			
Trade Creditors	11,370		
Proposed dividend	9,000		
Debenture interest accrued	1,500		
Corporation Tax	5,000	26,870	
Net current assets			27,350
Total assets less current liabilities			148,290
Long-term liabilities			
Debentures			30,000
			118,290
Capital and reserves			
Called-up share capital**			90,000
Share premium account			14,000
General reserve			7,000
Profit and loss account			7,290
			118,290

* Details of cost, acquisitions and disposals in the year and depreciation would be shown as a note to the balance sheet.

** The authorised share capital, where it is different from the issued share capital, is shown as a note. Notice that the total figure of £120,000 for authorised capital is not included when calculating the balance sheet totals. Only the issued capital figures are included in balance sheet totals.

38.5 Requirement for company accounts to give a true and fair view

The Companies Act, 1963 requires every company to prepare a profit and loss account which gives a **true and fair view** of the company's results for the period covered by it.

A profit and loss account and balance sheet covering the period since the previous set of accounts must be presented at each AGM. These accounts must give a true and fair view of the state of affairs of the company at the date of the balance sheet and of the profit or loss of the company for the period. In order to give a true and fair view published accounts must normally comply with the formats given in the Companies (Amendment) Act, 1986. Compliance with Accounting Standards and Financial Reporting Standards is also normally required and the four fundamental accounting concepts (going concern, consistency, prudence and accruals) must be adhered to.

38.6 Accounting Standards and Financial Reporting Standards

Accounting Standards and Financial Reporting Standards are documents which prescribe 'rules' which accountants must follow when preparing accounts which are intended to give a true and fair view. Although the accounts of many businesses other than companies are intended to give a true and fair view, it is a legal requirement for companies. Therefore, Accounting Standards and Financial Reporting Standards are discussed here rather than elsewhere in the text.

Statements of Standard Accounting Practice (SSAPs or Accounting Standards) and Financial Reporting Standards (FRSs) provide guidance to accountants by either prescribing fixed rules or stating a number of options from which accountants may choose when preparing accounts. For example, you have already seen that SSAP 12 gives guidance in relation to how depreciation should be calculated but does not actually specify the method of calculation (for example, straight line or reducing balance) that should be used. It can be seen from this that the objective of such standards is to limit the number of different acceptable ways of accounting for certain items rather than to set inflexible rules.

Statements of Standard Accounting Practice were developed between 1970 and 1990 by the Accounting Standards Committee (ASC), a subcommittee of the Consultative Committee of Accountancy Bodies (CCAB), which is the representative body of the six main professional accounting bodies, namely, the Institute of Chartered Accountants in Ireland (ICAI), the Chartered Association of Certified Accountants (ACCA), the Chartered Institute of Management Accountants (CIMA), the Chartered Institute of Public Finance and Accountancy (CIPFA), the Institute of Chartered Accountants in England and Wales (ICAEW) and the Institute of Chartered Accountants of Scotland (ICAS). During these years twenty-five SSAPs were issued, of which three were subsequently withdrawn, leaving twenty-two in force when the ASC ceased issuing standards in 1990. The SSAPs developed by the ASC were then issued separately by each of the member bodies of the CCAB.

In 1990, following much criticism of the way in which SSAPs were issued, essentially by the accounting profession itself, as the CCAB is the representative body of the professional accounting bodies, a new system for issuing standards was put in place. Under this system Financial Reporting Standards, applicable in the UK and Northern Ireland, are now issued by the Accounting Standards Board (ASB), a body independent of the accounting profession. In the Republic of Ireland the ICAI, at the request of the government, issues standards for the Republic by adopting FRSs issued by the ASB and making any amendments necessary to comply with Irish legislation.

The ASB took on board the twenty-two SSAPs in force when it was set up. Therefore, all of these, except for those subsequently replaced by a Financial Reporting Standard, are still in force, even though SSAPs are no longer issued.

SSAPs and FRSs, in themselves, are not legally binding in the Republic of Ireland. However, as company accounts must, by law, give a true and fair view, which, almost invariably requires SSAPs and FRSs to be followed, they are indirectly legally binding.

38.7 Stock Exchange regulations

PLCs whose shares are traded on the Stock Exchange must, in addition to complying with the Companies Acts, SSAPs and FRSs, also comply with regulations issued by the Stock Exchange. These regulations are not applicable to other companies.

Review questions

In addition to the questions which follow, you should attempt questions 261–290 in the accompanying book of multiple-choice questions (see back cover for details).

Suggested solutions to review questions with the letter 'A' after the question number are given in Appendix I (pages 644–8).

38.1A   The trial balance extracted from the books of Chang Ltd at 31 December 1998 was as follows:

	£	£
Ordinary share capital		100,000
Profit and loss account at 31 December 1997		34,280
Freehold premises at cost	65,000	
Machinery at cost	55,000	
Provision for depreciation on machinery account as at 31 December 1997		15,800
Purchases	201,698	
Sales		316,810
General expenses	32,168	
Wages and salaries	54,207	
Rent	4,300	
Lighting expenses	1,549	
Bad debts	748	
Provision for doubtful debts at 31 December 1997		861
Debtors	21,784	
Creditors		17,493
Stock as at 31 December 1997	25,689	
Bank	23,101	
	485,244	485,244

You are given the following additional information:
(i)   The authorised and issued share capital is divided into 100,000 ordinary shares of £1 each.
(ii)   Stock as at 31 December 1998 was £29,142.
(iii)   Wages and salaries due at 31 December 1998 amounted to £581.
(iv)   Rent paid in advance at 31 December 1998 amounted to £300.
(v)   A dividend of £10,000 is proposed for 1998.
(vi)   The provision for doubtful debts is to be increased to £938.
(vii)   A depreciation charge is to be made on machinery at the rate of 10% per annum on cost.

Required:
A trading and profit and loss account for 1998 and a balance sheet as at 31 December 1998.

38.2 The following is the trial balance of ABC Ltd as at 31 December 1998:

	Dr £	Cr £
Share capital issued: ordinary shares £1		75,000
Debtors and creditors	28,560	22,472
Stock as at 31 December 1997	41,415	
Bank	16,255	
Machinery at cost	45,000	
Vehicles at cost	28,000	
Depreciation provisions at 31 December 1997		
Machinery		18,000
Vehicles		12,600
Sales		97,500
Purchases	51,380	
Motor expenses	8,144	
Repairs to machinery	2,308	
Sundry expenses	1,076	
Wages and salaries	11,372	
Directors' remuneration	6,200	
Profit and loss account as at 31 December 1997		6,138
General reserve		8,000
	239,710	239,710

You are given the following information:

(i) Authorised share capital: £100,000 in ordinary shares of £1.
(ii) Stock at 31 December 1998 was £54,300.
(iii) Motor expenses owing £445.
(iv) Ordinary dividend proposed of 20%.
(v) Transfer £2,000 to general reserve.
(vi) Provide for depreciation of all fixed assets at 20% using the reducing balance method.

Required:
A trading and profit and loss account for 1998 and a balance sheet as at 31 December 1998.

38.3A You are to draw up a trading and profit and loss account for the year ended 31 December 1998, and a balance sheet as at that date from the following trial balance and other information concerning T Howe Ltd:

	Dr £	Cr £
Bank	6,723	
Debtors	18,910	
Creditors		12,304
Stock as at 31 December 1997	40,360	
Buildings at cost	100,000	
Equipment at cost	45,000	
Profit and loss account as at 31 December 1997		15,286
General reserve		12,200
Authorised and issued ordinary share capital		100,000
Purchases	72,360	
Sales		135,486
Carriage inwards	1,570	
Carriage outwards	1,390	
Salaries	18,310	
Rates and occupancy expenses	4,235	
Office expenses	3,022	
Sundry expenses	1,896	
Provisions for depreciation at 31 December 1997:		
Buildings		32,000
Equipment		16,000
Directors' remuneration	9,500	
	323,276	323,276

Notes at 31 December 1998:
(i) Stock at 31 December 1998 was £52,360.
(ii) Rates owing £280; Office expenses owing £190.
(iii) A dividend of 10% is proposed.
(iv) Transfer to General reserves: £1,800.
(v) Depreciation on cost: Buildings 5%; Equipment 20%.

38.4 The accountant of Fiddles plc has begun preparing final accounts but the work is not yet complete. At this stage, the items included in the trial balance are as follows:

	£000
Land	100
Buildings	120
Plant and machinery	170
Depreciation provision	120
Share capital	100
Profit and loss balance brought forward	200
Debtors	200
Creditors	110
Stock	190
Operating profit	80
Debentures (16%)	180
Provision for doubtful debts	3
Bank balance (asset)	12
Suspense	1

The following points are to be taken into account:

(i) The debtors control account figure, which is used in the trial balance, does not agree with the total of the debtors ledger. A contra of £5,000 has been entered correctly in the individual ledger accounts but has been entered on the wrong side of both control accounts.

A batch total of sales of £12,345 had been entered in the double entry system as £13,345, although individual ledger account entries for these sales were correct. The balance of £4,000 on sales returns account has inadvertently been omitted from the trial balance, though correctly entered in the ledger records.

(ii) A standing order of receipt from a regular customer for £2,000, and bank charges of £1,000, have been completely omitted from the records.

(iii) A debtor for £1,000 is to be written off. The provision for doubtful debts balance is to be adjusted to 1% of debtors.

(iv) The opening stock figure had been overstated by £1,000 and the closing stock figure had been understated by £2,000.

(v) Any remaining balance on suspense account should be treated as purchases if a debit balance and as sales if a credit balance.

(vi) The debentures were issued three months before the year end. No entries have been made as regards interest.

(vii) A dividend of 10% of share capital is to be proposed.

Required:

(a) Prepare journal entries to cover items in notes (i) to (v) above. You are NOT to open any new accounts and may use only those accounts included in the trial balance as given.

(b) Prepare final accounts for internal use in good order within the limits of the available information. For presentation purposes all the items arising from notes (i) to (vii) above should be regarded as material.

(*Association of Chartered Certified Accountants*)

38.5A On 31 December the accounting records of Rulers plc contained the following balances. All figures are in £000s.

£1 ordinary shares	500
£1 10% preference shares	100
Share premium	200
Profit and loss balance 1 January	400
Land	200
Plant and machinery – cost	550
– depreciation 1 January	250
Sales	3,500
Cost of sales	2,100
Stocks	600
Debtors	550
Bank (debit balance)	200
Operating expenses	900
10% debentures	100
Value added tax (debit balance)	150
Creditors	200
Bad debts	5
Bad debt provision	6
Discounts received	7
Discounts allowed	8

The following notes need additionally to be taken into account:

(i)   The firm's products are zero-rated for VAT purposes.
(ii) Bank charges of £2,000 and a standing order receipt of £50,000 from a customer have been omitted.
(iii) On 31 December the preference shares are redeemed at par.†
(iv) The bad debt provision is required to be 1% of debtors.
(v)   Debenture interest and preference dividend both need to be provided for.
(vi) Depreciation on plant and machinery is to be provided at 20% on the reducing balance method.
(vii) The land is to be revalued by £30,000.

Required:
(a) Prepare profit and loss account and balance sheet for internal use, in good order.
(b) Briefly explain and justify your treatment of the value added tax balance.

(*Association of Chartered Certified Accountants*)

Notes
†   Debit appropriation account £100,000.
     Credit capital redemption reserve £100,000.
     Debit preference share capital £100,000.
     Credit bank £100,000.

38.6A 'The historical cost convention looks backwards but the going concern convention looks forwards.'

Required:
(a) Explain clearly what is meant by:
     (i)   the historical cost convention;
     (ii) the going concern convention.
(b) Does traditional financial accounting, using the historical cost convention, make the going concern convention unnecessary? Explain your answer fully.
(c) Which do you think a shareholder is likely to find more useful – a report on the past or an estimate of the future? Why?

(*Association of Chartered Certified Accountants*)

38.7A The chairman of a public limited company has written his annual report to the shareholders, extracts of which are quoted below.

Extract 1
'In May 19X6, in order to provide a basis for more efficient operations, we acquired PAG Warehousing and Transport Ltd. The agreed valuation of the net tangible assets acquired was £1.4 million. The purchase consideration, £1.7 million, was satisfied by an issue of 6.4 million equity shares, of £0.25 per share, to PAG's shareholders. These shares do not rank for dividend until 19X7.'

Extract 2
'As a measure of confidence in our ability to expand operations in 19X7 and 19X8, and to provide the necessary financial base, we issued £0.5 million 8% Redeemable Debenture Stock, 2000/2007, 20 million 6% £1 Redeemable Preference Shares and 4 million £1 equity shares. The opportunity was also taken to redeem the whole of the 5 million 11% £1 Redeemable Preference Shares.'

Required:
Answer the following questions on the above extracts.

Extract 1
(a) What does the difference of £0.3 million between the purchase consideration (£1.7m) and the net tangible assets value (£1.4m) represent?
(b) What does the difference of £0.1 million between the purchase consideration (£1.7m) and the nominal value of the equity shares (£1.6m) represent?
(c) What is the meaning of the term 'equity shares'?
(d) What is the meaning of the phrase 'do not rank for dividend'?

Extract 2
(e) In the description of the debenture stock issue, what is the significance of
   (i) 8%?
   (ii) 2000/2007?
(f) In the description of the preference share issue, what is the significance of
   (i) 6%?
   (ii) Redeemable?
(g) What is the most likely explanation for the company to have redeemed existing preference shares but at the same time to have issued others?
(h) What effect will these structural changes have had on the gearing of the company?
(j) Contrast the accounting treatment, in the company's profit and loss accounts, of the interest due on the debentures with dividends proposed on the equity shares.
(k) Explain the reasons for the different treatments you have outlined in your answer to (j) above.

(Association of Chartered Certified Accountants)

38.8A The directors of the company by which you are employed as an accountant have received the forecast profit and loss account for 19X3 which disclosed a net profit for the year of £36,000.

This is considered to be an unacceptably low figure and a working party has been set up to investigate ways and means of improving the forecast profit.

The following suggestions have been put forward by various members of the working party:

(a) 'Every six months we deduct income tax of £10,000 from the debenture interest and pay it over to the Inland Revenue. If we withhold these payments, the company's profit will be increased considerably.'
(b) 'I see that in the three months August to October 19X3 we have forecast a total amount of £40,000 for repainting the exterior of the company's premises. If, instead, we charge this amount as capital expenditure, the company's profit will be increased by £40,000.'
(c) 'In November 19X3, the replacement of a machine is forecast. The proceeds from the sale of the old machinery should be credited to profit and loss account.'
(d) 'There is a credit balance of £86,000 on general reserve account. We can transfer some of this to profit and loss account to increase the 19X3 profit.'
(e) 'The company's £1 ordinary shares, which were originally issued at £1 per share, currently have a market value of £1.60 per share and this price is likely to be maintained. We can credit the surplus £0.60 per share to the 19X3 profit and loss account.'
(f) 'The company's premises were bought many years ago for £68,000, but following the rise in property values, they are now worth at least £300,000. This enhancement in value can be utilised to increase the 19X3 profit.'

You are required as the accounting member of the working party, to comment on the feasibility of each of the above suggestions for increasing the 19X3 forecast profit.

(Association of Chartered Certified Accountants)

38.9 The trial balance of Hall Ltd, a clothing manufacturer, on 31st May, 1998 was presented as follows:

	Debit £	Credit £
Sales		610,000
Cost of sales	420,000	
Stock (31st May, 1998)	220,000	
Wages and salaries	84,000	
Rent, rates and insurance	1,200	
Directors' remuneration	4,000	
Administration expenses	7,100	
Debenture interest	1,600	
Light and heat	2,400	
Audit fees	1,500	
Preference dividend	1,000	
Interim ordinary dividend	2,000	
Ordinary shares of 50p each		200,000
10% preference shares of £1 each		20,000
Profit and loss account – 1st June, 1997		9,400
Bank overdraft		6,400
10% debentures		50,000
Machinery (cost £200,000)	127,000	
Vehicles (cost £25,000)	15,000	
Debtors and creditors	53,000	42,000
Bad debt provision		2,000
	939,800	939,800

You are provided with the following additional information:
1 Audit fees of £2,000 have not been paid at the end of the year.
2 During the year rates of £600 for the year ended 30th November, 1998 were paid.
3 Depreciation is to be provided on fixed assets at the following rates, with a full year's depreciation being provided in the year of acquisition and none in the year of sale.

    Machinery   20% per annum on cost
    Vehicles   20% per annum on book-value

4 Provision is to be made for the preference dividend and a dividend of 3p per share on the ordinary shares.
5 Machinery costing £4,000 with a book-value of £1,700 was sold during the year for £2,800. This amount has not yet been received and no record has been made of this transaction.
6 Bad debts of £1,800 are to be written off and the bad debt provision is to be maintained at 5% of trading debtors.
7 Administration expenses include £1,000 paid to a director by way of an interest free loan.
8 The authorised share capital consisted of £600,000 divided into 800,000 ordinary shares of 50p each and 200,000 10% cumulative preference shares of £1 each.

You are required to prepare:
(a) the Trading, Profit and Loss and Profit and Loss Appropriation Accounts for the year ended 31st May, 1998; and
(b) a Balance Sheet as at that date.

(*ICAI Professional Examination One*)

38.10   The following trial balance was extracted from the books of Candles Ltd as at 31st May, 1998.

	Debit £000	Credit £000
Ordinary shares of £1 each		500
Profit and loss account 1st June, 1997		290
Land and buildings (cost £600,000)	450	
Plant and machinery (cost £500,000)	260	
Vehicles (cost £299,000)	119	
Stock as at 31st May, 1998	260	
Debtors	250	
Creditors		210
Sales		1,700
Cost of sales	960	
Rent and rates	60	
Insurance	80	
Wages and salaries	150	
Distribution costs	40	
Administration expenses	60	
Heat and light	10	
Printing, postage and stationery	16	
Bad debts provision		10
Interim dividend paid	25	
Bank overdraft		30
	2,740	2,740

The following additional information is available.

1   Due to an error on the stock sheets, the stock at 31st May, 1998 was overstated by £30,000.

2   No record was made of goods purchased on credit for £40,000 on 30th May, 1998 as the goods were not delivered until 2nd June, 1998.

3   Bad debts of £10,000 are to be written off and the bad debts provision is to be adjusted to 5% of debtors.

4   The rent of the company's showrooms has been paid up to 31st July, 1998. The rent of the showrooms is £6,000 per annum.

5   In April 1998 the company paid rates of £12,000 for the half year to 30th September, 1998.

6   In June 1997 the company sold an old vehicle for £1,000. This vehicle had originally cost £20,000 and had a book value at the date of sale of £4,000. The only entry made in the books in respect of this transaction was to debit the bank account and credit the vehicles account.

7   Depreciation is to be provided on fixed assets on hand at 31st May, 1998 at the following rates.

Land and buildings	2% on cost
Plant and machinery	10% on cost
Vehicles	20% on cost

8   Provision is to be made for a final dividend of 10%.

You are required to prepare:

(a)   the Trading and Profit and Loss Account and the Profit and Loss Appropriation Account of Candles Ltd for the year ended 31st May, 1998; and

(b)   the Balance Sheet as at that date.

(*ICAI Professional Examination One*)

38.11 The following trial balance was extracted from the books of Brackets Ltd as at 30th June, 1998.

	Debit £000	Credit £000
Ordinary shares of £1 each		750
Profit and loss account 1st July, 1997		338
10% debentures		100
Land and buildings (cost £900,000)	700	
Plant and machinery (cost £800,000)	400	
Vehicles (cost £500,000)	180	
Stock at 30th June, 1998	400	
Debtors	380	
Creditors		340
Sales		2,570
Cost of sales	1,440	
Rent and rates	90	
Insurance	120	
Wages and salaries	320	
Advertising and promotion	65	
Heat and light	15	
Printing, postage and stationery	20	
Debenture interest		5
Bad debts provision		12
Interim dividend paid	40	
Bank overdraft		55
	4,170	4,170

The following additional information is available.
1 Sales include £65,000 in respect of goods invoiced to a customer on 26th June, 1998, on a sale or return basis. These goods were returned by the customer in July 1998. The cost of these goods was £50,000.
2 Bad debts of £15,000 are to be written off and the bad debts provision is to be adjusted to 5% of debtors.
3 The rent on the company's showrooms has been paid up to 31st July, 1998. The rent of the showrooms is £12,000 per annum.
4 In April 1998, the company paid rates of £24,000 for the half year to 30th September, 1998.
5 In July 1997, the company sold an old vehicle for £5,000. This vehicle had originally cost £20,000 and had a book value of £8,000 at the date of sale. The only entry made in the books in respect of this transaction was to debit the bank account and credit the sales account.
6 Sales staff are entitled to a commission of 10% on sales in excess of £2 million.
7 No debenture interest was paid during the year.
8 Depreciation is to be provided on fixed assets on hand at 30th June, 1998, at the following rates:

Land and buildings	2% on cost
Plant and machinery	10% on cost
Vehicles	20% on cost

9 Provision is to be made for a final dividend of 10%.

You are required to prepare:
(a) the Trading and Profit and Loss Account for the year ended 30th June, 1998; and
(b) the Balance Sheet as at that date.

(*ICAI Professional Examination One*)

38.12 Chestnutt Limited has an Authorised Share Capital of £500,000 divided into 400,000 Ordinary Shares of £1 each and 10,000 8% Redeemable Preference Shares of £10 each. The following trial balance was extracted from the books of the company as at 31st December, 1998:

	£	£
Ordinary Shares		400,000
8% Redeemable preference shares		100,000
Communication costs	35,000	
Purchases/Sales	927,000	1,498,000
Stock at 1 January 1998	148,000	
Leasehold Factory (cost £300,000)	256,000	
Accommodation costs	26,000	
Goodwill	70,000	
Bank		53,000
Capital reserve		48,000
Interim dividend on preference shares	4,000	
Carriage Inwards	105,000	
10% Debentures 2003		150,000
Salaries and wages	158,000	
Investments at cost	100,000	
Advertising	75,000	
Interim dividend on ordinary shares	20,000	
Trade debtors	220,000	
Trade creditors		125,000
Bad debt reserve		8,000
Transport costs	50,500	
Debenture interest	7,500	
Plant and equipment (cost £387,000)	287,000	
Finance and insurance costs	13,000	
Appropriation account at 1 January 1998		125,000
Bad debts	5,000	
	2,507,000	2,507,000

You are given the following information:
(a) Stock on hand at 31 December 1998 was £145,000.
(b) An invoice for goods ordered, but still in transit, was received on 31 December 1998. The amount shown on the invoice was £25,000 being the recommended selling price which is cost price plus 25%. No entry was made in the books.
(c) An item of plant was purchased during the year, the delivery costs of £5,000 are included with Carriage Inwards. The costs of installation amounting to £8,000 are included with Salaries and Wages.
(d) Investments were sold on 31 December 1998 for £80,000, these investments cost £50,000 and had a market value on 31 December 1997 of £60,000. No entry was made in the books. The market value of the remaining investments on 31 December 1998 is £70,000.
(e) Debtors include an amount of £10,000 since found to be bad. No entries have been passed in the books. Bad Debts reserve is to be maintained at 5% of Trade Debtors.
(f) The benefit of advertising expenditure is expected to accrue evenly over the years 1998, 1999 and 2000.
(g) Sales income includes £18,000 in error, being proceeds of sale of plant which had been wholly written-off in the accounts in previous years.
(h) Directors fees of £25,000 should be provided for.
(i) Provide depreciation on Leasehold Factory at 2% p.a. of cost price and on Plant and Equipment at 20% p.a. of net book value.
(j) The Directors are proposing that the preference dividend due be provided for, a final dividend of 10% be provided for and that a sum of £10,000 be written off Goodwill.

Required:
Prepare a Trading and Profit and Loss Account for the year ended 31st December, 1998 and a Balance Sheet as at that date.

(*The Institute of Bankers in Ireland*)

39

Published company reports and accounts

The Companies (Amendment) Act 1986

The principal Act governing the publication of accounts in Ireland is the Companies (Amendment) Act 1986 (CAA86). All companies covered by this Act are required to publish annual accounts, in a specified format, by filing them in the Companies Registration Office in Dublin Castle. Thus, most Irish limited companies, both public and private, are required to do so. The accounts to be published must be prepared in accordance with generally accepted accounting practices and presented in specified formats providing much more detailed information than was previously necessary. Other information is also required to be disclosed.

Companies excluded or partly excluded from the provisions of the Act

Some companies, for example, certain charities and unlimited companies, are fully excluded from the provisions of CAA86.

Others such as most banks, financial institutions and insurance and assurance companies, are partly excluded. However, these companies are governed by other Irish and/or European legislation or other forms of regulation. For example, insurance companies are required to make financial returns to the Department of Industry and Commerce. Non-Life insurance companies are obliged to file their accounts in the Companies Registration Office under the European Communities (Non-Life Insurance Accounts) Regulations, 1977. Banks are regulated by the Central Bank.

Private companies which are deemed under the Act to be either 'small' or 'medium-sized' may file audited modified accounts with the Registrar of Companies. A full set of accounts, including a directors' report and an auditors' report, must be provided to shareholders.

Small companies are required to file an abridged balance sheet together with certain notes. They are not required to file a profit and loss account or directors' report. The documentation to be filed must be accompanied by a special report by the auditors.

'Medium-sized' companies may combine certain items under the heading 'Gross Profit or Loss' in their profit and loss account to be filed with their annual return.

'Medium-sized' companies may also file an abridged balance sheet provided certain other additional items and amounts are disclosed separately or in the notes to the accounts.

In both cases the accounts filed will have to comply with accounting, and financial reporting, standards and give a true and fair view.

Criteria for qualifying as small and medium-sized companies

Since 1st January, 1994 private companies qualify as small or medium-sized if, in the current year and in the immediately preceding year, they satisfy at least TWO of the following conditions:

Category	Balance Sheet totals not exceeding	Annual Turnover not exceeding	Average no. of employees not exceeding
Small company	£1.5m	£3m	50
Medium-sized company	£6m	£12m	250

39.3 Directors' reports

The directors of a company must write a report, commonly known as a Directors' Report, which must include, amongst other things:

- a review of the business during the year and an indication of likely future developments in the business
- important events affecting the company which have happened since the balance sheet date
- an indication of activities, if any, in the field of research and development.

The company's auditors are under a duty to consider, and give an opinion as to, whether the information in the directors' report is consistent with the accounts.

The Safety, Health and Welfare at Work Act 1989 requires companies to have a safety statement. The directors are required to evaluate the extent to which the policy(ies) set out in that statement has (have) been fulfilled during the period and state it in their report.

39.4 Audit reports

These are discussed in Chapter 40.

39.5 Financial highlights

Some companies produce selected figures from their current and previous profit and loss accounts, as two columns or as graphs, showing improvements over the previous year. Companies are not required to do this and it is normally done as a public relations exercise rather than an accounting one.

39.6 Historical summaries

Some companies produce historical summaries which give the same type of information as the financial highlights referred to above except that it is usually given for the past five years and in more detail. For example, more detailed information from the profit and loss

account may be given as well as some information from the balance sheet and the **cash flow statement** (see Chapter 42).

Historical Summaries are a convenient way of identifying trends over a period of years as a lot of information is given in a single statement. However, the information given is that selected by the company rather than that which is required as there is no requirement to produce a historical summary. Clearly a more detailed picture of trends will be possible by looking at the accounts for each of the last five years. This is clearly more time consuming than simply reading the historical summary.

39.7 Chairman's Statement etc.

The **annual reports** of most listed PLCs include reports such as a 'Chairman's Statement' and/or 'Chief Executive's Review'. These are not required either by law or by the Stock Exchange.

Review questions

Questions 291–295 in the accompanying book of multiple-choice questions examine the material covered in this chapter (see back cover of this book for details).

40

Introduction to auditing

40.1 What is an audit?

An **audit** is an examination of the financial statements of a business by persons who are independent from that business (auditors) with a view to forming a judgement as to whether those financial statements give a true and fair view of the state of affairs and performance of the business.

The judgement formed by the auditor is known as the **audit opinion** and is formally expressed in an **audit report** which is usually included with financial statements which are published, sent to the Registrar of Companies or given to banks. It is important that you realise that an audit opinion is just that, an opinion, as to whether the financial statements examined give a true and fair view – it is not a guarantee that they do.

Auditors must be independent and be seen to be such, as the opinion of someone who is not independent may well be biased and therefore not of much use to persons relying on it.

It can be seen from the first paragraph that auditors *examine* financial statements with a view to forming, and expressing an opinion on them – it is not their responsibility to *prepare* those financial statements. The preparation of the financial statements and the maintenance of the accounting records of a company are the responsibility of its directors.

40.2 Reasons for audits

Companies are required by law to have their accounts audited. The reason for this requirement is to add credibility to the financial statements prepared by the directors and presented to shareholders, banks and others.

40.3 Objectives of an audit

Primary objective

The primary objective of an audit is to enable the auditor to form an opinion as to, and to report upon, the truth and fairness of the financial position shown by the balance sheet, the profit or loss shown by the profit and loss account and of any other information disclosed in the financial statements and covered by the audit report.

Auditors are *required* to state in their reports whether, in their *opinion*, the financial statements examined give a true and fair view of the state of the company's affairs at the balance sheet date and of its profit or loss for the period then ended and whether the information required by the Companies Acts 1963 to 1990 is given in the required manner.

In cases where the auditor's opinion is that the financial statements do not give a true and fair view of the above he must 'qualify' his audit report in such a way as to state

clearly why he considers that a true and fair view is not presented and in what respects and to what extent he considers the accounts to be mis-stated.

Secondary objectives

Other objectives of audits include the detection of fraud and other irregularities and the provision of advice to the management of the company.

40.4 Auditors' relationship with the directors and members of a company

The shareholders in a company appoint the directors who are responsible for ensuring that the company maintains proper accounting records, the preparation of financial statements for presentation to the members, safeguarding the company's assets and preventing errors and fraud. These are not part of auditors' duties. It is the responsibility of auditors to report, to the members, on the accounts prepared by the directors.

Strictly, auditors are appointed by the members of a company although they usually empower the directors to do so on their behalf.

The duties of auditors are specified in the Companies Acts and cannot be limited by the directors or the members.

Review questions

Questions 296–303 in the accompanying book of multiple-choice questions examine the material covered in this chapter (see back cover of this book for details).

41

Accounting for the issue of shares and debentures

41.1 The issue of shares

In the case of public companies a new issue of shares can be very costly indeed, and the number of shares issued must be sufficient to make the cost worthwhile. However, for simplicity, so that the principles are not obscured by the difficulties of grappling with large amounts, the numbers of shares shown as issued in the illustrations that follow will be quite small.

Shares can be issued being payable (a) immediately on application, or (b) by instalments. The first instances will be of shares being paid for immediately. Issues of shares may take place on the following terms connected with the price of the shares:

(a) **Shares issued at par.** This would mean that shares of £1 nominal value would be issued for £1 each.
(b) **Shares issued at a premium.** In this case shares of £1 nominal value would be issued for more than £1 each, say for £3 each.

Shares cannot be issued at a discount, that is, they cannot be issued for less than their 'nominal' or 'par' value.

When companies issue new shares they must pay companies capital duty within thirty days of the issue. If this is paid late the company is liable to pay interest at the rate of 1.25% per month.

41.2 Share premium account

This will all seem rather strange at first. How can a £1 share, which states that value on the face of it, be issued for £3 each, and who would be foolish enough to buy it? The reasons for this apparently strange state of affairs stem from the Companies Act requirement that the Share Capital Accounts always show shares at their nominal value, irrespective of how much the shares are worth or how much they are issued for. To illustrate this, the progress of two companies can be looked at, Company A and Company B. Both companies started in business on 1 January 1994 and issued 1,000 ordinary shares each of £4 nominal value at par. Ignoring any issue expenses, the balance sheets of both companies on that date would appear:

Balance Sheet as at 1 January 1994

	£
Bank	4,000
Capital	4,000

Five years later, on 31 December 1998, the companies have fared quite differently. It is to be assumed here, for purposes of illustration, that the balance sheet values and any other interpretation of values happen to be identical.

£4,000 capital is needed by A Ltd, and this is to be met by issuing more ordinary shares. Suppose that another 1,000 ordinary shares of £4 nominal value each are issued at par. Column (a) shows the balance sheet before the issue, and column (b) shows the balance sheet after the issue has taken place.

A Ltd Balance Sheets (Solution 1) as at 31 December 1998

	(a) £	(b) £
Fixed and current assets (other than bank)	9,000	9,000
Bank	1,000	5,000
	10,000	14,000
Financed by:		
Ordinary share capital	4,000	8,000
Profit and loss account	6,000	6,000
	10,000	14,000

Now the effect of what has happened can be appreciated. Before the new issue there were 1,000 shares. As there were £10,000 of assets and no liabilities, then each share was worth £10. After the issue there are 2,000 shares and £14,000 of assets, so that now each share is worth £7. This would be extremely disconcerting to the original shareholders who see the value of each of their shares fall immediately by £3.

On the other hand, the new shareholder who has just bought shares for £4 each sees them rise immediately to be worth £7 each. Only in one specific case would this be just, and that is where each original shareholder buys an equivalent number of new shares. Otherwise this obviously cannot be the correct solution. What is required is a price which is equitable as far as the interests of the old shareholders are concerned, and yet will attract sufficient applications to provide the capital required. As in this case the balance sheet value and the real value are the same, the answer is that each old share was worth £10 and therefore each new share should be issued for £10 each. The balance sheets will now appear:

A Ltd Balance Sheets (Solution 2) as at 31 December 1998

	(a) £	(b) £
Fixed and current assets (other than bank)	9,000	9,000
Bank	1,000	11,000
	10,000	20,000
Financed by:		
Ordinary share capital (at nominal value)	4,000	8,000
Share premium account (*see* note below)	–	6,000
Profit and loss account	6,000	6,000
	10,000	20,000

Thus in (a) above 1,000 shares own between them £10,000 of assets = £10 each, while in (b) 2,000 shares are shown as owning £20,000 of assets = £10 each. Both the old and new shareholders are therefore satisfied with the bargain that has been made.

Note: The **share premium** account shown in the balance sheet is needed, ignoring for a moment the legal requirements to be complied with in company balance sheets, simply because the balance sheet would not balance without it. If shares are stated at nominal value, but issued at another price, the actual amount received increases the bank balance, but the share capital shown is increased by a different figure. The share premium therefore represents the excess of the cash received over the nominal value of the shares issued.

B Ltd has not fared so well. It has, in fact, lost £1,000. The accumulated losses are reflected in a debit balance on the profit and loss appropriation account. There are £3,000 of assets to represent the shareholders' stake in the firm of 1,000 shares, i.e. each share is worth £3 each. If more capital was needed 1,000 more shares could be issued. From the previous case it will now be obvious that each new share of £4 nominal value is really only worth £3. As shares cannot be issued at a discount, no new shares are likely to be issued as nobody would be willing to pay more than £3.

For the purpose of making the foregoing explanations easier it was assumed that balance sheet values and other values were the same. This is very rarely true for all the assets, and in fact there is more than one other 'value'. A balance sheet is a historical view of the past based on records made according to the firm's interpretation and use of accounting concepts and conventions. When shares are being issued it is not the historical view of the past that is important, but the view of the future. Therefore the actual premium on shares being issued is not merely a matter of balance sheet values, but on the issuing company's view of the future and its estimate of how the investing public will react to the price at which the shares are being offered.

The actual double entry accounts can now be seen.

41.3 Accounting for shares issued which are payable in full on application

The issue of shares in illustrations (1), (2) and (3) which follow are based on the balance sheets that have just been considered.

1 Shares issued at par

1,000 ordinary shares with a nominal value of £4 each are to be issued. Applications, together with the necessary money, are received for exactly 1,000 shares. The shares are then allotted to the applicants.

Bank

		£			
Ordinary share applicants	A	4,000			

Ordinary Share Applicants

		£			£
Ordinary share capital	B	4,000	Bank	A	4,000

Ordinary Share Capital

					£
			Ordinary share applicants	B	4,000

It may appear that the ordinary share applicants account is unnecessary, and that the only entries needed are a debit in the bank account and a credit in the ordinary share capital account. However, applicants do not always become shareholders; this is shown later. The applicant must make an offer for the shares being issued, accompanied by the necessary money, this is the application. After the applications have been vetted the allotments of shares are made by the company. This represents the acceptance of the offer by the company and it is at this point that the applicant becomes a shareholder. Therefore 'A' represents the offer by the applicant, while 'B' is the acceptance by the company. No entry must therefore be made in the share capital account until B happens, for it is not until that point that the share capital is in fact in existence. The share applicants account is therefore an intermediary account pending allotments being made.

2 Shares issued at a premium

1,000 ordinary shares with a nominal value of £4 each are to be issued for £10 each (*see* A Ltd previously). Thus a premium of £6 per share has been charged. Applications and the money are received for exactly 1,000 shares.

Bank

	£		
Balance b/d	1,000		
Ordinary share applicants	10,000		

Ordinary Share Applicants

		£			£
Ordinary share capital	A	4,000	Bank		10,000
Share premium	B	6,000			
		10,000			10,000

Share Premium

		£
Ordinary share applicants	B	6,000

Ordinary Share Capital

		£
Balance b/d		4,000
Ordinary share applicants	A	4,000

Note: 'A' is shown as £4,000 because the share capital is shown at nominal value and not as total issued value. 'B', the £6,000 share premium in total must therefore be credited to a share premium account to preserve double entry balancing.

3 Oversubscription and undersubscription for shares

When a public company invites investors to apply for its shares it is unlikely that applications for shares exactly equal the number of shares to be issued. Where more shares are applied for than are available for issue, then the issue is said to be **oversubscribed**. Where fewer shares are applied for than are available for issue, then the issue has been **undersubscribed**.

With a brand-new company a minimum amount is fixed as being necessary to carry on any further with the running of the company. If the applications are less than the minimum stated, then the application monies must be returned to the senders. This does not apply to an established company. If therefore 1,000 shares of £1 each are available for issue, but only 875 shares are applied for, then only 875 will be issued, assuming that this is above the fixed minimum figure. The accounting entries will be in respect of 875 shares, no entries being needed for the 125 shares not applied for, as this part does not represent a transaction.

The opposite of this is where the shares are oversubscribed. In this case some sort of rationing is applied so that the issue is restricted to the shares available for issue. The process of selecting who will get how many shares depends on the policy of the firm. Some firms favour few large shareholders because this leads to lower administrative costs. Why the costs will be lower will be obvious if the cost of two companies each with 20,000 shares calling a meeting is considered. For example, H Ltd has 20 shareholders with an average holding of 1,000 shares each. J Ltd has 1,000 shareholders with an average holding of 20 shares each. They all have to be notified by post and given various documents including a set of the final accounts. The cost of printing and sending these is less for H Ltd with 20 shareholders than for J Ltd with 1,000 shareholders. This is only one example of the costs involved, but it will also apply with equal force to many items connected with the shares. Conversely, the directors may prefer to have more shareholders with smaller holdings, one reason being that it decreases the amount of voting power in any one individual's hands. The actual process of rationing the shares is then a simple matter once a policy has been agreed. It may consist of scaling down applications, of drawing lots or some other chance selection, but it will eventually bring the number of shares to be issued down to the number of shares available. Excess application monies will then be refunded by the company.

An issue of shares where 1,000 ordinary shares of £1 nominal value each are to be issued at par payable in full, but 1,550 shares are applied for, will appear as follows:

Bank

	£		£
Ordinary share applicants	1,550	Ordinary share applicants (refunds)	550

Ordinary Share Applicants

	£		£
Bank	550	Bank	1,550
Ordinary share capital	1,000		
	1,550		1,550

Ordinary Share Capital

			£
		Ordinary share applicants	1,000

41.4 Accounting for shares issued and payable by instalments

The shares considered so far have all been issued as paid in full on application. However, many issues are made which require payment by instalments. These are probably more common with public companies than with private companies. It should be noted that a

public company is now not allowed to allot shares unless it has received a certain minimum amount of money. This minimum is decided upon by the directors of the company.

The various stages, after the initial invitation has been made to the public to buy shares by means of advertisements (if it is a public company), etc., are as follows:

A   Applications are received together with the application monies.

B   The applications are vetted and the shares allotted, letters of allotment being sent out.

C   The excess application monies from wholly unsuccessful, or where the application monies received exceed both the application and allotment monies required, and partly unsuccessful applicants, are returned to them. Usually, if a person has been partly unsuccessful, his excess application monies are held by the company and will reduce the amount needed to be paid by him on allotment.

D   Allotment monies are received.

E   The next instalment, known as the first call, is requested.

F   The monies are received from the first call.

G   The next instalment, known as the second call, is requested.

H   The monies are received from the second call.

This carries on until the full number of calls has been made, although there is not usually a large number of calls to be made in an issue.

The reasons for the payments by instalments become obvious if it is realised that a company will not necessarily require the immediate use of all the money to be raised by the issue. Suppose a new company is to be formed, it is to buy land, build a factory, equip it with machinery and then go into production. This might take two years altogether. If the total sum needed was £1,000,000, the allocation of this money could be:

Ordinary Share Capital

	£
Cost of land, payable within 1 month	300,000
Cost of buildings, payable in 1 year's time	200,000
Cost of machinery, payable in 18 months' time	200,000
Working capital required in 2 years' time	300,000
	1,000,000

The issue may therefore be on the following terms:

	%
Application money per share, payable immediately	10
Allotment money per share, payable within 1 month	20
First call, money payable in 12 months' time	20
Second call, money payable in 18 months' time	20
Third call, money payable in 24 months' time	30
	100

The entries made in the share capital account should equal the amount of money requested to that point in time. However, instead of one share applicants account, this is usually split into several accounts to represent the different instalments. For this purpose application and allotment are usually joined together in one account, the application and allotment account, as this cuts out the need for transfers where excess application monies are held over and set off against allotment monies needed. When allotment is made, and not until then, an entry of £300,000 (10% + 20%) would be made in the share capital account. On the first call an entry of £200,000 would be made in the share capital account, likewise £200,000 on the second call and £300,000 on the third call. The share capital account will therefore contain not the monies received, but the amount of money requested. An example of a share issue by instalment follows.

Example 41.1

A company is issuing 1,000 7% preference shares of £1 each, payable 10% on application, 20% on allotment, 40% on the first call and 30% on the second call. Applications are received for 1,550 shares. A refund of the money is made in respect of 50 shares, while for the remaining 1,500 applied for, an allotment is to be made on the basis of 2 shares for every 3 applied for (assume that this will not involve any fractions of shares). The excess application monies are set off against the allotment monies asked for. The remaining requested instalments are all paid in full. The letters beside each entry refer to the various stages outlined earlier.

Bank

		£			£
Application and allotment:			Application and allotment:		
Application monies	A	155	refund	C	5
Allotment monies					
(£1,000 × 20% *less* excess					
application monies £50)	B	150			
First call	F	400			
Second call	H	300			

Application and Allotment

		£			£
Bank – refund of			Bank	A	155
Application monies	C	5	Bank	B	150
Preference share capital	B	300			
		305			305

First Call

		£			£
Preference share capital	E	400	Bank	F	400

Second Call

		£			£
Preference share capital	G	300	Bank	H	300

7% Preference Share Capital

		£			£
			Application and allotment	B	300
			First call	E	400
Balance c/d		1,000	Second call	G	300
		1,000			1,000
			Balance b/d		1,000

If more than one type of share is being issued at the same time, e.g. preference shares and ordinary shares, then separate share capital accounts and separate application and allotment accounts and call accounts should be opened.

41.5 Forfeited shares

Sometimes a shareholder fails to pay the calls requested from him. The Articles of Association of the company will probably state that the shareholder will have his shares forfeited, provided that certain safeguards for his protection are fully observed. In this case the shares will be cancelled, and the instalments already paid by the shareholder will be lost by him.

After the forfeiture, the company may reissue the shares, on such terms and in such manner as the directors think fit unless there is a provision in its Articles of Association to prevent it. Credit will be given for any sums paid by the previous shareholder.

Example 41.2

Take the same information as in Example 41.1, but instead of all the calls being paid, Allen, the holder of 100 shares, fails to pay the first and second calls. He had already paid the application and allotment monies on the required dates. The directors conform to the provisions of the Articles of Association and (A) Allen is forced to suffer the forfeiture of his shares. (B) The amount still outstanding from Allen will be written off. (C) The directors then reissue the shares at 75% of nominal value to J Dougan. (D) Dougan pays for the shares.

First Call

	£			£
7% Preference share capital	400	Bank		360
		Forfeited shares	(B)	40
	400			400

Second Call

	£			£
7% Preference share capital	300	Bank		270
		Forfeited shares	(B)	30
	300			300

7% Preference Share Capital

		£			£
Forfeited shares	(A)	100	Application and allotment		300
Balance c/d		900	First call		400
			Second call		300
		1,000			1,000
			Balance b/d		900
Balance c/d		1,000	J Dougan	(C)	100
		1,000			1,000
			Balance b/d		1,000

Forfeited Shares

		£			£
First call	(B)	40	7% Preference share capital	(A)	100
Second call	(B)	30			
Balance c/d		30			
		100			100
J Dougan (*see* following note)		25	Balance c/d		30
Balance c/d		5			
		30			30

Bank

		£			
First call (£900 × 40%)		360			
Second call					
(£900 × 30%)		270			
J Dougan	(D)	75			

J Dougan

	£			£
Preference share capital	100	Bank	(D)	75
		Forfeited shares (discount on		
		reissue) *see* following note		25
	100			100

Note The transfer of £25 from the forfeited shares account to J Dougan's account is needed because the reissue was entered in the preference share capital account and Dougan's account at nominal value, i.e. following standard practice of a share capital account being concerned with nominal values, but Dougan was not to pay the full nominal price. Therefore, the transfer of £25 is needed to close his account.

The balance of £5 on the forfeited shares account can be seen to be: Cash received from the original shareholder on application and allotment £30 + cash from Dougan £75 = £105. This is £5 over the nominal value so that the £5 appears as a credit balance. This is usually stated to be either transferred to a profit on reissue of forfeited shares account, but it really cannot be thought that this is followed in practice for small amounts. Normally it would be transferred to the credit of a share premium account.

41.6 Calls in advance and in arrear and the balance sheet

At the balance sheet date some shareholders will not have paid all the calls made, these are collectively known as **calls in arrear**. On the other hand, some shareholders may have paid amounts in respect of calls not made by the balance sheet date. These are **calls in advance.**

Both calls in arrear and calls in advance should be shown in the 'Capital and Reserves' section of the balance sheet.

41.7 Rights issues

The costs of making a new issue of shares can be quite high. A way to reduce the costs of raising new long-term capital in the form of issuing shares may be by way of a **rights issue**, an issue of new shares to existing shareholders at a price lower than the current market price. To do this the company circularises its existing shareholders, and informs them of the new issue to be made and the number of shares which each one of them is entitled to buy of the new issue. In most cases the shareholder is allowed to renounce his rights to the new shares in favour of someone else. The issue is usually pitched at a price which will make the rights capable of being sold, i.e. if the existing shareholder does not want the shares he can renounce them to someone else who will pay him for the right to apply for the shares in his place, a right which that person could not otherwise obtain. If any shareholder does not either buy the shares or transfer his rights, then the directors will usually have the power to dispose of such shares not taken up by issuing them in some other way.

The price at which the shares of a very profitable company are quoted in the Stock Exchange is usually higher than the nominal value of the shares. For instance, the market price of the shares of a company might be quoted at £2.50 while the nominal value per share is only £1.00. If the company has 8,000 shares of £1 each and declares a rights issue of one for every eight held at a price of £1.50 per share, it is obvious that it will be cheaper for the existing shareholders to buy the rights issue at this price instead of buying the same shares in the open market for £2.50 per share. Assuming that all the rights issued were taken up, then the number of shares taken up will be 1,000 (i.e. 8,000 ÷ 8). The amount paid for them will be £1,500. The journal entries will be:

The Journal	Dr	Cr
	£	£
Bank	1,500	
Share capital		1,000
Share premium		500
Being the rights issue of 1 new share for every 8 shares held at a price of £1.50 (nominal value being £1.00).		

Note that because the nominal value of each share is £1.00 while £1.50 was paid, the extra 50p constitutes a share premium to the company.

Notice also that the market value of the shares will be reduced or 'diluted' by the rights issue. Before the rights issue there were 8,000 shares at a price of £2.50, giving a market capitalisation of £20,000. After the issue there are 9,000 shares and the assets have increased by £1,500. The market value may therefore reduce to £2.39 [(20,000 + 1,500)/9,000], although the precise market price at the end of the issue will have been influenced by the information given surrounding the sale about the future prospects of the company and may not be exactly the amount calculated.

41.8 Bonus issues

A **bonus issue** is an issue of new ordinary shares to existing ordinary shareholders free of charge. An alternative name is a **scrip issue**.

If a company's articles of association give the power, and if the requisite legal formalities are observed, the following reserves may be capitalised when issuing bonus shares:

1 The balance on the profit and loss account (as shown in the balance sheet).
2 Any other revenue reserve.
3 Any capital reserve, e.g. share premium account.

This thus comprises all of the reserves.

The reason why this should ever be needed can be illustrated by taking a somewhat exaggerated example, shown below.

Example 41.3

A company, Better Price Ltd, started business 50 years ago with 1,000 ordinary shares of £1 each and £1,000 in the bank. The company has constantly had to retain a proportion of its profits to finance its operations, thus diverting them from being used for cash dividend purposes. Such a policy has conserved working capital.

The firm's balance sheet as at 31 December 1998 is shown as:

Better Price Ltd
Balance Sheet as at 31 December 1998
(before bonus shares are issued)

	£
Fixed assets	5,000
Current assets *less* current liabilities	5,000
	10,000
Share capital	1,000
Reserves (including profit and loss account balance)	9,000
	10,000

If an annual profit of £1,500 is now being earned, this being 15% of capital employed, and £1,000 could be paid annually as cash dividends, then the dividend declared each year would be 100%, i.e. a dividend of £1,000 on shares of £1,000 nominal value. It is obvious that the dividends and the share capital have got out of step with one another. Employees and trade unions may well become quite belligerent, as, owing to the lack of accounting knowledge, or even misuse of it, it might be believed that the firm was making unduly excessive profits. Customers, especially if they are members of the general public, may also be deluded into thinking that they are being charged excessive prices, or, even though this could be demonstrated not to be true because of the prices charged by competitors, they may well still have the feeling that they are somehow being duped.

However, an efficient firm in this particular industry or trade may well be only reasonably rewarded for the risks it has taken by making a profit of 15% on capital employed. The figure of 100% for the dividend is due to the very misleading convention in accounting of calculating dividends in relationship to the nominal amount of the share capital.

If it is considered that £7,000 of the reserves could not be used for dividend purposes, due to the fact that the net assets should remain at £8,000, made up of fixed assets £5,000 and working capital £3,000, then besides the £1,000 share capital which cannot be returned to the shareholders there are also £7,000 reserves which cannot be rationally returned to them. Instead of this £7,000 being called reserves, it might as well be called capital, as it is needed by the business on a permanent basis.

To remedy this position, as well as some other needs less obvious, bonus shares were envisaged. The reserves are made non-returnable to the shareholders by being converted into share capital. Each holder of one ordinary share of £1 each will receive seven bonus shares (in the shape of seven ordinary shares) of £1 each. The balance sheet, if the bonus shares had been issued immediately, would then appear:

Better Price Ltd
Balance sheet as at 31 December 1998
(after bonus shares are issued)

	£
Fixed assets	5,000
Current assets *less* current liabilities	5,000
	10,000
Share capital (£1,000 + £7,000)	8,000
Reserves (£9,000 – £7,000)	2,000
	10,000

When the dividends of £1,000 per annum are declared in the future, they will amount to:

$$\frac{£1,000}{£8,000} \times \frac{100}{1} = 12.5\%.$$

This will cause less disturbance in the minds of employees, trade unions, and customers.

Of course the issue of bonus shares may be seen by any of the interested parties to be some form of diabolical liberty. To give seven shares of £1 each free for one previously owned may be seen as a travesty of social justice. In point of fact the shareholders have not gained at all. Before the bonus issue there were 1,000 shares that owned between them £10,000 of net assets. Therefore, assuming just for this purpose that the book 'value' is the same as any other 'value', each share was worth £10. After the bonus issue each previous holder now has eight shares for every one share he held before. If he had owned one share only, he now owns eight shares. He is therefore the owner of $^8/_{8,000}$ part of the firm, i.e. a one thousandth part. The 'value' of the net assets are £10,000, so that he owns £10 of them, so his shares are worth £10. This is exactly the same 'value' as that applying before the bonus issue was made.

It would be useful in addition, to refer to other matters for comparison. Anyone who had owned a £1 share 50 years ago, then worth £1, would now have (if he was still living) eight shares worth £8. A new house of a certain type 50 years ago might have cost £x, it may now cost £$8x$, the cost of a bottle of beer may now be y times greater than it was 50 years ago, a packet of cigarettes may be z times more and so on. Of course, the firm has brought a lot of trouble on itself by waiting so many years to capitalise reserves. It should have been done by several stages over the years.

This is a very simplified, and in many ways an exaggerated version. There is, however, no doubt that misunderstanding of accounting and financial matters has caused a great deal of unnecessary friction in the past and will probably still do so in the future. Yet another very common misunderstanding is that the assumption the reader was asked to accept, namely that the balance sheet values equalled 'real values', is often one taken by the reader of a balance sheet. Thus a profit of £10,000 when the net assets book values are £20,000 may appear to be excessive, yet in fact a more realistic value of the assets may be saleable value, in this case the value may be £100,000.

The accounting entries necessary are to debit the reserve accounts utilised, and to credit a bonus account. The shares are then issued and the entry required to record this is to credit the share capital account and to debit the bonus account. The journal entries would be:

The Journal	Dr	Cr
	£	£
Reserve account(s) (show each account separately)	7,000	
Bonus account		7,000
Transfer of an amount equal to the bonus payable in fully-paid *shares*		
Bonus account	7,000	
Share capital		7,000
Allotment and issue of 7,000 shares of £1 each, in satisfaction *of the bonus declared*		
	14,000	14,000

41.9 The issue of debentures

The entries for the issue of debentures are similar to those for shares. It would, however, not be normal practice to issue debentures at a premium.

Review questions

In addition to the questions which follow, you should attempt questions 304–313 in the accompanying book of multiple-choice questions (see back cover for details).

Suggested solutions to review questions with the letter 'A' after the question number are given in Appendix I (pages 648–50).

41.1A A company has a nominal capital of £120,000 divided into 120,000 ordinary shares of £1 each. The whole of the capital was issued at par on the following terms:

	Per share
Payable on application	£0.125
Payable on allotment	£0.25
First call	£0.25
Second call	£0.375

Applications were received for 160,000 shares and it was decided to allot the shares on the basis of three for every four for which applications had been made. The balance of application monies were applied to the allotment, no cash being refunded. The balance of allotment monies were paid by the members.

The calls were made and paid in full by the members, with the exception of a member who failed to pay the first and second calls on the 800 shares allotted to him. A resolution was passed by the directors to forfeit the shares. The forfeited shares were later issued to D Reagan at £0.90 each.

Required:
Show the ledger accounts recording all the above transactions, and the relevant extracts from the balance sheet after all the above transactions had been completed.

41.2A Badger Ltd has an authorised capital of £100,000 divided into 20,000 ordinary shares of £5 each. The whole of the shares were issued at par, payments being made as follows:

	£
Payable on application	0.50
Payable on allotment	1.50
First call	2.00
Second call	1.00

Applications were received for 32,600 shares. It was decided to refund application monies on 2,600 shares and to allot the shares on the basis of two for every three applied for. The excess application monies sent by the successful applicants is not to be refunded but is to be held and so reduce the amount payable on allotment.

The calls were made and paid in full with the exception of one member holding 100 shares who paid neither the first nor the second call and another member who did not pay the second call on 20 shares. After requisite action by the directors the shares were forfeited. They were later reissued to B Mills at a price of £4 per share.

Required:
Draft the ledger accounts to record the above transactions.

41.3A The authorised and issued share capital of Cosy Fires Ltd was £75,000 divided into 75,000 ordinary shares of £1 each, fully paid. On 2 January 19X7, the authorised capital was increased by a further 85,000 ordinary shares of £1 each to £160,000. On the same date 40,000 ordinary shares of £1 each were offered to the public at £1.25 per share payable as to £0.60 on application (including the premium), £0.35 on allotment and £0.30 on 6 April 19X7.

The lists were closed on 10 January 19X7, and by that date applications for 65,000 shares had been received. Applications for 5,000 shares received no allotment and the cash paid in respect of such shares was returned. All shares were then allocated to the remaining applicants pro rata to their original applications, the balance of the monies received on applications being applied to the amounts due on allotment.

The balances due on allotment were received on 31 January 19X7, with the exception of one allottee of 500 shares and these were declared forfeited on 4 April 19X7. These shares were reissued as fully paid on 2 May 19X7, at £1.10 per share. The call due on 6 April 19X7 was duly paid by the other shareholders.

You are required
(a) To record the above-mentioned transactions in the appropriate ledger accounts; and
(b) To show how the balances on such accounts should appear in the company's balance sheet as on 31 May 19X7.

(*Association of Chartered Certified Accountants*)

41.4 During the year to 30 September 19X7, Kammer plc made a new offer of shares. The details of the offer were as follows:

1 100,000 ordinary shares of £1 each were issued payable in instalments as follows:

	Per Share
On application at 1 November 19X6	£0.65
On allotment (including the share premium of £0.50 per share) on 1/12/19X6	£0.55
On first and final call on 1 June 19X7	£0.30
	£1.50

2 Applications for 200,000 shares were received, and it was decided to deal with them as follows:
  (*a*) to return cheques for 75,000 shares;
  (*b*) to accept in full applications for 25,000 shares; and
  (*c*) to allot the remaining shares on the basis of three shares for every four shares applied for.
3 On the first and final call, one applicant who had been allotted 5,000 shares, failed to pay the due amount, and his shares were duly declared forfeited. They were then re-issued to Amber Ltd on 1 September 19X7 at a price of £0.80 per share fully paid.

Note: Kammer's issued share capital on 1 October 19X6 consisted of 500,000 ordinary shares of £1 each.

Required:
Record the above transactions in the following ledger accounts:

(*a*) ordinary share capital;
(*b*) share premium;
(*c*) application and allotment;
(*d*) first and final call;
(*e*) forfeited shares; and
(*f*) Amber Ltd's account.

(*Association of Accounting Technicians*)

41.5A M Limited has an authorised share capital of £1,500,000 divided into 1,500,000 ordinary shares of £1 each. The issued share capital at 31 March 19X7 was £500,000 which was fully paid, and had been issued at par. On 1 April 19X7, the directors, in accordance with the company's Articles, decided to increase the share capital of the company by offering a further 500,000 ordinary shares of £1 each at a price of £1.60 per share, payable as follows:

on application, including the premium	£0.85 per share
on allotment	£0.25 per share
on first and final call on 3 August 19X7	£0.50 per share

On 13 April 19X7, applications had been received for 750,000 shares and it was decided to allot the shares to applicants for 625,000 shares, on the basis of four shares for every five shares for which applications had been received. The balance of the money received on application was to be applied to the amounts due on allotment. The shares were allotted on 1 May 19X7, the unsuccessful applicants being repaid their cash on this date. The balance of the allotment money was received in full by 15 May 19X7.

With the exception of one member who failed to pay the call on the 5,000 shares allotted to him, the remainder of the call was paid in full within two weeks of the call being made.

The directors resolved to forfeit these shares on 1 September 19X7, after giving the required notice. The forfeited shares were re-issued on 30 September 19X7 to another member at £0.90 per share.

You are required to write up the ledger accounts necessary to record these transactions in the books of M Limited.

(*Chartered Institute of Management Accountants*)

41.6 Simplex Ltd has an authorised share capital of 300,000 ordinary shares of £1 each, of which 100,000 shares had already been issued by 31st December, 1997. At that date, all application and allotment money had been received in respect of the shares which were issued. The final call of 30p per share was made on 28th December, 1997, in respect of which no money had been received by 31st December, 1997.

During January 1998, all call money was received with the exception of the amount due in respect of 1,500 shares. The shares were forfeited by the company on 31st January, 1998 and were not re-issued.

On 1st March, 1998, the company issued a further 50,000 shares at a premium of 20p per share payable as follows:

Payable on application on 25th April	60p
Payable on allotment on 25th May (including premium)	40p
Payable on first and final call on 1st June	20p

Applications were received for exactly the number of shares on offer. All money in respect of the issue of these shares was received on the due dates.

Requirement:
Prepare all the relevant ledger accounts for the period from 1st January, 1998 to 30th June, 1998 to record the above transactions in the books of Simplex Ltd.

(*IATI Admission Examination*)

41.7 Bell Ltd has an authorised share capital of 500,000 ordinary shares of £1 each and 150,000 6% preference shares of £2 each.

At 31st December, 1997 the company had already issued 200,000 of the ordinary shares and all of the preference shares at par.

On 1st January, 1998 the company decided to offer the remaining 300,000 ordinary shares to the public on the following terms:

Payable on application on 20th January, 1998	25p
Payable on allotment on 10th February, 1998	60p (including premium)
Payable on first and final call on 31st March, 1998	35p

Applications were received for 480,000 shares. Of these, applications in respect of 30,000 shares were not accepted by the company and the application money was refunded. In respect of the remaining applications, the shares were issued on a pro-rata basis, the remaining excess application money being retained in lieu of allotment money. All allotment money due was received on the appropriate date.

The first and final call was paid in full on the due date with the exception of the money due from one shareholder who had been allotted 2,000 shares. These shares were forfeited on 30th April, 1998 and were re-issued on 1st May as fully paid shares, on payment by the new shareholder of 50p per share.

Requirement:
Prepare all the relevant ledger accounts to record the above information.

(*IATI Admission Examination*)

41.8 Applications were invited by the directors of Grobigg Ltd for 150,000 of its £1 ordinary shares at £1.15 per share payable as follows:

	Per Share
On application on 1 April 19X8	£0.75
On allotment on 30 April 19X8 (including the premium of £0.15 per share)	£0.20
On first and final call on 31 May 19X8	£0.20

Applications were received for 180,000 shares and it was decided to deal with these as follows:

1 To refuse allotment to applicants for 8,000 shares.
2 To give full allotment to applicants for 22,000 shares.
3 To allot the remainder of the available shares pro rata among the other applicants.
4 To utilise the surplus received on applications in part payment of amounts due on allotment.

An applicant, to whom 400 shares had been allotted, failed to pay the amount due on the first and final call and his shares were declared forfeit on 31 July 19X8. These shares were re-issued on 3 September 19X8 as fully paid at £0.90 per share.

Show how the transactions would be recorded in the company's books.

(*Association of Chartered Certified Accountants*)

42

Cash flow statements

Profit and loss accounts for each period are published by each company, as well as a balance sheet as at the period's closing date. These disclose the profit, or loss, made by the company for that period, and how the resources were being used at the end of the period.

However, when we want to try to assess whether or not the company has used its resources to good effect during the period, these two statements do not give us enough information. What we could also do with is something that shows the cash coming into the company or firm during the period, and what it has done with this. The financial statement which gives us this information is usually called **a cash flow statement.** Cash flow statements are concerned with examining the reasons underlying the rise or fall in cash held during a period.

The Accounting Standards Board in September 1991 issued Financial Reporting Standard No. 1 'Cash Flow Statements' (FRS 1). This standard requires businesses, whose accounts are intended to give a true and fair view, to prepare a cash flow statement, in addition to a profit and loss account and balance sheet.

Before we start to construct cash flow statements, let us look at where the cash can come from, and where it can go to. Remember, we are looking at the following:

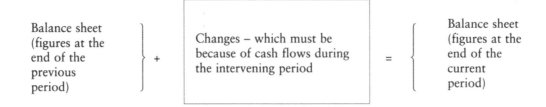

Balance sheet (figures at the end of the previous period)

+

Changes – which must be because of cash flows during the intervening period

=

Balance sheet (figures at the end of the current period)

We will show cash flows in the form of a diagram, Exhibit 42.1, and then look at them in greater detail.

Exhibit 42.1

Where cash comes from	Cash flow		Where cash goes to
	In	Out	

1 Profits ————————————→ ————→ 1 Losses
2 Sales of Fixed Assets ————→ ————→ 2 Purchase of Fixed Assets
3 Decrease in Stock ————————→ ————→ 3 Increase in Stock
4 Decrease in Debtors ————→ ————→ 4 Increase in Debtors
5 Capital Introduced ————→ ————→ 5 Drawings/Dividends
6 Loans Received ————————→ ————→ 6 Loans Repaid
7 Increase in Creditors ————→ ————→ 7 Decrease in Creditors

These can be explained as:

1 Profits bring a flow of cash into the firm. Losses take cash out of it.
2 The cash received from sales of fixed assets comes into the firm. A purchase of fixed assets takes it out.
3 Reducing stock in the normal course of business means turning it into cash. An increase in stock ties up cash.
4 A reduction in debtors means that the extra amount paid comes into the firm as cash. Letting debtors increase stops that extra amount of cash coming in.
5 An increase in a sole proprietor's capital, or issues of shares in a company, bring cash in. Drawings or dividends take it out.
6 Loans received bring in cash, while their repayment reduces cash.
7 An increase in creditors keeps the extra cash in the firm. A decrease in creditors means that the extra payments take cash out.

42.3 Illustration of cash flows

Exhibit 42.2

The following are the balance sheets of T Holmes as at 31 December 1997 and 31 December 1998:

	31 December 1997		31 December 1998	
Fixed assets	£	£	£	£
Premises at cost		25,000		28,800
Current assets				
Stock	12,500		12,850	
Debtors	21,650		23,140	
Cash and bank balances	4,300		5,620	
	38,450		41,610	
Less Current liabilities				
Creditors	11,350		11,120	
Working capital		27,100		30,490
		52,100		59,290
Financed by:				
Capital				
Opening balance		52,660		52,100
Add Net profit for the year		16,550		25,440
		69,210		77,540
Less Drawings		17,110		18,250
		52,100		59,290

Note: No depreciation has been charged in the accounts.

A summary of cash flows based on the above can be prepared as follows:

T Holmes
Summary of Cash Flows for the year ended 31 December 1998

	£	£
Cash inflows		
Net profit		25,440
Cash outflows		
Drawings	18,250	
Extra premises bought	3,800	
Increase in stock	350	
Increase in debtors	1,490	
Decrease in creditors	230	24,120
Increase in cash		1,320

Proof:

Cash and bank balances at 31 December 1997	4,300
Cash and bank balances at 31 December 1998	5,620
Increase in cash and bank balances	1,320

You will see that the summary of cash flows matches up with the previous descriptions. At the bottom of the summary you will see a reconciliation which shows the increase in cash explained in terms of the change between opening and closing cash and bank balances.

42.4 Note on the use of brackets

In accounting, it is customary to show a figure in brackets if it is a minus figure. This would be deducted from the other figures to arrive at the total of the column. These are seen very frequently in cash flow statements.

For instance suppose that the increase in cash in Exhibit 42.3 had been £1,760 instead of £1,320 and that there had been a decrease in stock of £90 instead of an increase of £350. In this case the latter part of the summary of cash flows would have been shown as:

	£	£
Cash inflows		
Net profit		25,440
Drawings	18,250	
Extra premises bought	3,800	
Decrease in stock	(90)	
Increase in debtors	1,490	
Decrease in creditors	230	23,680
Increase in cash		1,760

42.5 Adjustments needed to net profit to find cash flow

When net profit is included as a source of cash, we usually have to adjust the net profit figure to take account of items included which do not involve cash flow *in the period covered by the cash flow statement*.

Depreciation

For instance, suppose we bought equipment costing £3,000 during the year ended 31 December 1997. It is depreciated by £1,000 per annum for 3 years and then scrapped, disposal value being nil. This would result in the following:

		Years to 31 December		
		1997	1998	1999
		£	£	£
(i)	Item involving cash flow:			
	Cost of equipment	3,000	Nil	Nil
(ii)	Item not involving cash flow:			
	Depreciation	(1,000)	(1,000)	(1,000)
(iii)	Net profit before depreciation	12,000	13,000	15,000
(iv)	Net profit after depreciation	11,000	12,000	14,000

Now the question arises as to which of figures (i) to (iv) are the ones to be used when showing cash flows. Let us examine items (i) to (iv) accordingly.

(i) A payment of £3,000 is made to buy equipment. This *does* involve cash flow and should therefore be included when showing cash flows for 1997.

(ii) Depreciation is represented by a bookkeeping entry: Debit profit and loss: Credit provision for depreciation. This does *not* involve cash flow and cannot be shown as an inflow or outflow.

(iii) Net profit before depreciation. This brings cash flowing into the firm and therefore should be shown in a summary of cash flows.

(iv) Net profit after depreciation. Depreciation does not involve cash flow, and therefore (iii) is the net profit we need.

In most examination questions (iii) will not be shown. Therefore, you will have to do some calculations to arrive at it.

Provisions for bad or doubtful debts

If a debt is written off as bad, then that involves a cash flow. A debt would have become cash when paid. Now you are saying that this will not happen and have written it off to the profit and loss account.

On the other hand a provision for bad debts is similar in this respect to a provision for depreciation. The cash flow occurs when a bad debt is written off, *not* when a provision is made in case there may be bad debts in the future.

If an examination question gives you the net profit *after* the bad debt provision, then the provision has to be added back to exclude it from the profit calculations.

Book profits or losses on sales of fixed assets

If a fixed asset with a book value (after depreciation) of £5,000 is sold for £6,400 cash, then the cash flow is £6,400. The fact that there has been a book profit of £1,400 does not provide any more cash above the figure of £6,400. Similarly, the sale of an asset with a book value of £3,000 for £2,200 cash produces a cash flow of £2,200. The £800 book loss does mean that there has been an outflow.

Example of adjustments for depreciation, bad debt provisions and profits or losses on the sale of fixed assets

As the net profit figure in accounts is:

(i) *after* adjustments for depreciation;
(ii) *after* any provision for bad debts, and
(iii) *after* book profits or losses on sales of fixed assets

the profit figure will need to be adjusted to find the actual cash flow. Note that the adjustments needed are only for depreciation in *that period*, fixed asset book profits/losses for *that period* and *changes* in the provision for bad debts. No adjustments are needed in respect of previous periods.

Examples of such adjustments for three firms follow.

Exhibit 42.1

	Firm A £	Firm B £	Firm C £
Net profit (after taking account of the items below)	16,270	21,390	32,410

The following items were shown in the Profit and Loss Account:

	£	£	£
Depreciation for the year	2,690	4,120	6,640
Increase in bad debt provision	540	360	–
Decrease in bad debt provision	–	–	200
Book loss on sale of fixed assets	1,200	–	490
Book profit on sale of fixed assets	–	750	–

Cash inflow	£	£	£
Net profit	16,270	21,390	32,410
Adjustment for items not involving cash flow			
Depreciation	2,690	4,120	6,640
Book profit on sale of fixed assets	–	(750)	–
Book loss on sale of fixed assets	1,200	–	490
Increase in bad debt provision	540	360	–
Decrease in bad debt provision	–	–	(200)
Cash inflow	20,700	25,120	39,340

You will notice that the items in brackets, i.e. (750) and (200), had been credits in the profit and loss accounts and need to be deducted, while the other items were debits and need to be added back.

Adjustments to profit for changes in working capital

In addition to the adjustments to profit for items which do not involve cash flow the overall effect, on cash, of running a business will include changes in stock, debtors and creditors. These changes in working capital should, therefore, be shown alongside the profit to show the net cash flow from operating activities, for example:

	£'000
Profit before adjustments	5,000
Depreciation charges	100
Loss on sale of fixed assets	50
Increase in stocks	(180)
Increase in debtors	(90)
Increase in creditors	200
Net cash flow from operating activities	5,080

42.6 A further example of cash flows

The balance sheets of R Lester are as follows:

	31 December 1997			31 December 1998		
	£	£	£	£	£	£
Fixed assets						
Equipment at cost		28,500			26,100	
Less Depreciation to date		11,450	17,050		13,010	13,090
Current assets						
Stock		18,570			16,250	
Debtors	8,470			14,190		
Less Bad debts provision	420	8,050		800	13,390	
Cash and bank balances		4,060			3,700	
		30,680			33,340	
Less Current liabilities						
Creditors		4,140			5,730	
Working capital			26,540			27,610
			43,590			40,700
Financed by:						
Capital						
Opening balance			35,760			33,590
Add Net profit			10,240			11,070
Add Cash introduced			–			600
			46,000			45,260
Less Drawings			12,410			8,560
			33,590			36,700
Loan from J Gorsey			10,000			4,000
			43,590			40,700

Notes: Equipment with a book value of £1,350 was sold for £900. Depreciation written off equipment during the year was £2,610.

From the foregoing balance sheets a summary of cash flows could be drawn up as follows:

R Lester
Summary of Cash Flows for the year ended 31 December 1998

	£	£
Cash inflows		
Net profit		11,070
Depreciation	2,610	
Loss on sale of fixed assets	450	
Increase in bad debt provision	380	
Decrease in stock	2,320	
Increase in creditors	1,590	
Increase in debtors	(5,720)	1,630
Cash inflow from operating activities		12,700
Sale of fixed assets	900	
Capital introduced	600	
Loan repaid to J Gorsey	(6,000)	
Drawings	(8,560)	
Cash outflow from non-operating activities		(13,060)
Decrease in cash		(360)
Proof:		
Cash and bank balances at 31 December 1997		4,060
Cash and bank balances at 31 December 1998		3,700
Decrease in cash and bank balances		(360)

42.7 Financial Reporting Standard No. 1 (FRS 1)

We have already stated that FRS 1 requires most companies to prepare a cash flow statement for each accounting period. FRS 1 also proposes a standard layout for such a statement. This layout is shown in Exhibit 42.2.

Exhibit 42.2

X Ltd
Cash flow statement for the year ended 31 December 1998

	£000	£000
Operating Activities		
Net cash inflow/(outflow) from operating activities (*see* note 1)		XXX
Returns on investments and servicing of finance		
Interest received	XXX	
Interest paid	(XXX)	
Dividends paid	(XXX)	
Net cash inflow/(outflow) from returns on investments and servicing of finance		XXX
Taxation		
Corporation tax paid	(XXX)	(XXX)
Capital expenditure and financial investment		
Payments to acquire intangible fixed assets	(XXX)	
Payments to acquire tangible fixed assets	(XXX)	
Receipts from sales of tangible fixed assets	XXX	
Net cash inflow/(outflow) from capital expenditure and financial investment		(XXX)
Acquisitions and disposals		
Purchase of subsidiary undertaking	(XXX)	
Sale of business	XXX	
Net cash inflow/(outflow) from acquisitions and disposals		XXX
Equity dividends paid		(XXX)
Management of liquid resources		
Cash withdrawn from 7-day deposit	XXX	
Purchase of government securities	(XXX)	
Sale of corporate bonds	XXX	
Net cash inflow/(outflow) from management of liquid resources		XXX
Financing		
Issue of ordinary share capital	XXX	
Repayment of loan	(XXX)	
Net cash inflow/(outflow) from financing (*see* note 2)		XXX
Increase/(decrease) in cash		XXX

Notes to the cash flow statement

1 *Reconciliation of operating profit to net cash inflow from operating activities*

	£000
Operating profit	XXX
Depreciation charges	XXX
Loss on sale of tangible fixed assets	XXX
Increase in stocks	(XXX)
Increase in debtors	(XXX)
Increase in creditors	XXX
Net cash inflow from operating activities	XXX

2 *Analysis of changes in cash and cash equivalents during the year*

	£000
Balance at 1 January 1998	XXX
Net cash inflow	XXX
Balance at 31 December 1998	XXX

Standard headings included in FRS 1

As can be seen from Exhibit 42.2 there are standardised headings in cash flow statements prepared in accordance with FRS 1. These are:

	£
Operating activities	xxx
Returns on investments and servicing of finance	xxx
Taxation	xxx
Capital expenditure and financial investment	xxx
Acquisitions and disposals	xxx
Equity dividends paid	xxx
Management of liquid reserves	xxx
Financing	xxx
Increase/decrease in cash	xxx

Section 1 – Operating activities

Cash flows from operating activities are, in general, the cash effects of transactions and other events relating to operating or trading activities.

There are two methods of showing operating cash flow which are allowed:

1 **The direct method.** This shows operating cash receipts and payments in a 'gross' form such as:

Operating activities	£
Cash received from customers	xxx
Cash payments to suppliers	(xxx)
Cash paid to, and on behalf of, employees	(xxx)
Other cash payments	(xxx)
Net cash in/(out) flow from operating activities	xxx

2 **The indirect method.** This starts with the operating profit and adjusts it for non-cash charges and credits to reconcile it to the net cash flow from operating activities in the following form:

Operating activities	£
Operating profit	xxx
Depreciation charges	xxx
Loss (profit) on sale of tangible fixed assets	xxx
Increase in stocks	(xxx)
Decrease in debtors	xxx
Increase in creditors	(xxx)
Net cash in/(out) flow from operating activities	xxx

The Standard requires that a reconciliation must be shown between the operating profit reported in the profit and loss account and the net cash flow from operating activities in the cash flow statement. This reconciliation gives the same information as the 'Indirect Method' gives. The FRS recommends organisations to use the Direct Method – but does not insist on it.

For an organisation to use the Direct Method it will have to undertake a special analysis of its cash book in order to obtain the necessary breakdown of cash flow information, whereas the Indirect Method can be prepared from the existing profit and loss and balance sheet data. In an examination question, if you are given the breakdown of cash flows, you should follow the recommended method and give the Direct Method layout.

Section 2 – Returns on investments and servicing of finance

Cash flows shown under this heading are receipts resulting from ownership of investments and payments to providers of finance. However, this heading does not include items which may be classed either as 'operating', 'investing' or 'financing' activities, which will be shown separately. The Cash Inflow will include interest received and dividends received. The Cash Outflow will include interest paid and dividends paid.

Section 3 – Taxation

Under this heading are shown cash flows to or from taxation authorities in respect of the entity's taxes based on revenue profits (i.e. income) and capital profits.

In the case of value added tax, the net cash payable to, or receivable from, the Collector-General will *not* be shown under this heading but under the heading of operating activities. This will apply to any taxes such as sales taxes or property taxes which are not based on profits.

Section 4 – Capital expenditure and financial investment

This heading covers cash flows from the purchase or sale of any fixed assets.
Cash inflows under this heading will include cash from sales of fixed assets.
Cash outflows will include purchases of fixed assets.
It is worth pointing out under this heading that the Standard requires a note to be included in respect of material transactions not resulting in any cash flow, if this is necessary for the understanding of the underlying transactions. This type of note is likely to be required where assets are acquired under operating leases. In this situation the cash flow to acquire an asset is paid by the leasing company and the only cash flow in the company accounts would be rental payments.

Section 5 – Acquisitions and disposals

Included in this section are those cash flows relating to the acquisition or disposal of any trade or business, or of an investment in an entity that is or, as a result of the transaction, becomes or ceases to be either an associate, a joint venture, or a subsidiary undertaking.

Section 6 – Equity dividends paid

This section includes the dividends paid on the reporting entity's equity shares.

Section 7 – Management of liquid resources

Cash flows in respect of liquid resources are included in this section. The FRS defines liquid resources as 'current asset investments held as readily disposable stores of value'. A 'readily disposable investment' is one that is disposable without curtailing or disrupting the entity's business and is either readily convertible into known amounts of cash or traded in an active market.

Each entity must explain what it includes in liquid resources and declare any change in its policy.

Cash inflows in this section include withdrawals from short-term deposits not qualifying as cash and inflows from the disposal or redemption of any other investments held as liquid resources.

Cash outflows in this section include payments into short-term deposits not qualifying as cash and outflows to acquire any other investment held as a liquid resource.

Section 8 – Financing

Cash flows under this heading will include receipts from, or repayments to, external providers of finance in respect of principal amounts (i.e. not interest payments which are shown under the heading returns on investment and servicing of finance).

Inflows will include cash received from share issues and from issues of debentures and other loans both long- and short-term.

Outflows will include repayments of loans as well as the payments of expenses or commissions paid when shares are issued.

A reconciliation must be shown between the above figures and the relevant items shown in the balance sheet.

42.8 Examples of cash flow statements

Two examples will now be worked through. The following are important points to consider.

(i)   It is taxation *paid*, not taxation charged that is needed.
(ii) It is dividends *paid* not dividends proposed that is needed.
(iii) Do *not* include any profit on sales of fixed assets; such profit is already automatically included in any figure of sales of fixed assets.
(iv) Look for other adjustments to the starting figure of profit before tax which do not involve cash flow, e.g. provision for bad debts.

Example 42.2

PQ Ltd
Balance Sheets as at

	31 December 1997			31 December 1998		
	£	£	£	£	£	£
Fixed assets at cost		3,200			4,000	
Less Depreciation		1,200	2,000		1,600	2,400
Current assets						
Stock		4,218			5,654	
Debtors		1,560			1,842	
Bank		840			695	
		6,618			8,191	
Less Current liabilities						
Creditors	922			988		
Taxation	306			410		
Proposed dividend	500	1,728	4,890	750	2,148	6,043
			6,890			8,443
Financed by:						
Issue share capital			5,000			6,000
Profit and loss account			1,890			2,443
			6,890			8,443

PQ Ltd
Profit and Loss Account for the year ended 31 December 1998

	£
Profit on ordinary activities before taxation (after charging depreciation £400)	1,713
Tax on profit on ordinary activities	410
	1,303
Undistributed profits from last year	1,890
	3,193
Proposed dividend	750
Undistributed profits carried on to next year	2,443

Outline solution (not strictly in the format required by FRS1)

PQ Ltd
Cash Flow Statement for year ended 31 December 1998

	£	£
Operating activities		
Net profit before tax	1,713	
Add Depreciation	400	
Increase in creditors	66	
Less Increase in stock	(1,436)	
Increase in debtors	(282)	
Net cash inflow from operating activities		461
Returns on investments and servicing of finance		
Dividends paid (A)		(500)
Taxation:		
Tax paid (B)		(306)
Capital expenditure and financial investment		
Payments to acquire fixed assets		(800)
Financing		
Issue of shares		1,000
Decrease in cash		(145)

Notes:

1 Analysis of balances of cash and cash equivalents shown in the balance sheet.

Cash at bank at 31 December 1997	840
Reduction in balance	(145)
Cash at bank at 31 December 1998	695

2 Analysis of changes in financing during the year

Balance of share capital 31 December 1997	5,000
Issue of new shares	1,000
Balance of share capital 31 December 1998	6,000

Notes

(A) Dividends *paid*. The dividend in the profit and loss account of £750 is owing and shown in the balance sheet as a proposed dividend. The amount owing in the 1997 balance sheet of £500 has been paid in 1998.

(B) Tax *paid*. The tax in the profit and loss account of £410 based on this year's profit will be paid next year. The amount owing last year was £306 and has been paid in 1998.

A more detailed example is now given.

Example 42.3

No Money Ltd
Balance Sheets as at

	31 December 1997			31 December 1998		
	£	£	£	£	£	£
Fixed assets at cost		5,600			8,300	
Less Depreciation		2,300	3,300		3,150	5,150
Investments			–			1,000
Current assets						
Stock		7,204			4,516	
Debtors	3,120			3,994		
Less Provision for bad debts	210	2,910		180	3,814	
Cash		60			90	
		10,174			8,420	
Less Current liabilities						
Creditors	1,520			1,416		
Taxation	580			735		
Proposed dividend	800			1,200		
Bank overdraft	105	3,005	7,169	629	3,980	4,440
			10,469			10,590
Financed by:						
Issued share capital			4,000			5,000
Share premium account			–			1,000
Profit and loss account			3,469			4,090
Loan capital			3,000			500
			10,469			10,590

No Money Ltd
Profit and Loss Account for the year ended 31 December 1998

	£
Operating profit*	2,536
Interest on loans received	120
	2,656
Interest paid	(100)
Profit on ordinary activities before taxation*	2,556
Tax on profit on ordinary activities	(735)
	1,821
Undistributed profits from last year	3,469
	5,290
Proposed dividend	(1,200)
Undistributed profits carried to next year	4,090

*Includes profit of £85 on fixed assets sold. The items sold had cost £1,120, had been depreciated by £740 and were sold for £465.

The change in provision for bad debts had also been taken into account before arriving at a profit of £2,556.

One thousand ordinary shares of £1 had been issued at a price of £2 per share. In the balance sheet the issued share capital increases by £1,000 and the share premium account increases by £1,000. In the cash flow statement the overall impact of issuing the shares, £2,000 will be shown.

In getting the figures together for the cash flow statement, some figures need to be deduced so that the profit figure can be adjusted. These are (a) the cost of fixed assets bought and (b) depreciation charged. To find these it is necessary to reconstruct (a) the fixed asset account and (b) the depreciation account. The figures needed will be those necessary to balance the accounts. (In a real company these figures would be readily available, but examiners are fond of making students deduce the figures instead.)

Workings

Fixed Assets

1998		£	1998		£
Jan 1	Balance b/d	5,600	Dec 31	Assets disposal	1,120
Dec 31	Bank (missing figure)	3,820	„ 31	Balance c/d	8,300
		9,420			9,420

Provision for Depreciation

1998		£	1998		£
Dec 31	Assets disposal	740	Jan 1	Balance b/d	2,300
„ 31	Balance c/d	3,150	Dec 31	Profit & loss (missing figure)	1,590
		3,890			3,890

The missing figures calculated will form part of the cash flow statement. In addition you are given the following analysis of the cash book:

	£
Cash received from customers	91,900
Cash payments to suppliers	(62,080)
Cash paid to, and on behalf of, employees	(22,600)
Other cash payments	(1,499)
Net cash inflow	5,721

The cash flow statement can now be prepared.

No Money Ltd
Cash Flow Statement for the year ended 31 December 1998

	£	£
Operating activities		
Cash received from customers	91,900	
Cash payments to suppliers	(62,080)	
Cash paid to and on behalf of employees	(22,600)	
Other cash payments	(1,499)	
Net cash inflow from operating activities (note 1)		5,721
Returns on investments and servicing of finance		
Interest received	120	
Interest paid	(100)	
Dividends paid	(800)	
Net cash outflow from returns on investments and servicing of finance		(780)
Taxation		
Corporation tax on profit on ordinary activities		(580)
	£	
Capital expenditure and financial investment		
Purchase of tangible fixed assets	(3,820)	
Sale of tangible fixed assets	465	
Purchase of investments	(1,000)	
Net cash outflow from capital expenditure and financial investments		(4,355)
Financing		
Issue of share capital	2,000	
Repayment of loan capital	(2,500)	(500)
Decrease in cash (note 2)		(494)

Notes to the cash flow statement

1 *Reconciliation of operating profit to net cash inflow from operating activities*:

	£
Operating profit	2,536
Depreciation charges	1,590
Profit on sale of fixed assets	(85)
Reduction in provision for bad debts	(30)
Reduction in stocks	2,688
Increase in debtors	(874)
Reduction in creditors	(104)
Net cash inflow from operating activities	5,721

2 *Analysis of changes in cash*:

Balance at 31 December 1997		
Cash	60	
Overdraft	(105)	(45)
Decrease in cash and cash equivalents		(494)
Balance at 31 December 1998		
Cash	90	
Overdraft	(629)	(539)

In addition to the questions which follow, you should attempt questions 314–334 in the accompanying book of multiple-choice questions (see back cover for details).

Suggested solutions to review questions with the letter 'A' after the question number are given in Appendix I (pages 650–5).

42.1A Draw up a cash flow statement, in accordance with FRS 1 for 1998 from the following information:

JJ Ltd
Balance Sheets as at

	31 December 1997			31 December 1998		
	£	£	£	£	£	£
Fixed assets at cost		8,650			11,170	
Less Depreciation		2,890	5,760		3,905	7,265
Current assets						
Stock		3,720			3,604	
Debtors		4,896			5,001	
Bank		544			–	
		9,160			8,605	
Less Current liabilities						
Creditors	2,072			1,854		
Bank overdraft	–			116		
Taxation	856			620		
Proposed dividend	500	3,428	5,732	600	3,190	5,415
			11,492			12,680
Financed by						
Issued share capital			10,000			10,000
Profit and loss account			1,492			2,680
			11,492			12,680

Profit and Loss Account for the year ended 31 December 1998

	£
Profit on ordinary activities before taxation (after charging depreciation £1,015)	2,408
Tax on profit on ordinary activities	620
	1,788
Undistributed profits from last year	1,492
	3,280
Proposed dividend	600
Undistributed profits carried to next year	2,680

42.2   Draw up a cash flow statement, in accordance with FRS 1 for 1998 from the following:

TX Ltd
Balance Sheets as at

	31 December 1997			31 December 1998		
	£	£	£	£	£	£
Fixed assets at cost		6,723			7,418	
Less Depreciation		2,946	3,777		3,572	3,846
Current assets						
Stock		6,012			8,219	
Debtors	4,192			4,381		
Less Provision for bad debts	200	3,992		240	4,141	
Cash		100			35	
		10,104			12,395	
Less Current liabilities						
Creditors	2,189			2,924		
Taxation	622			504		
Proposed dividend	1,200			750		
Bank overdraft	416	4,427	5,677	294	4,472	7,923
			9,454			11,769
Debentures			3,000			2,000
			6,454			9,769
Financed by						
Issued share capital			6,000			7,500
Profit and loss account			454			2,269
			6,454			9,769

Profit and Loss Account for the year ended 31 December 1998

	£
Profit on ordinary activities before taxation*	3,069
Tax on profit on ordinary activities	504
	2,565
Undistributed profits from last year	454
	3,019
Proposed dividend	750
Undistributed profits carried to next year	2,269

*Includes loss on fixed assets sold of £114. The items sold had cost £2,070, had been depreciated by £1,290 and were sold for £666.

42.3A   The summarised balance sheets as at 31 March 1997 and 1998 of NITE Limited are as follows:

	1998 £000	1998 £000	1997 £000	1997 £000	Additional Information
Fixed assets; at net book value		175		150	(1)
Current assets	90		80		(2)
Trade creditors	(70)		(50)		
		20		30	
		195		180	
Long-term creditors		(30)		(30)	
		165		150	
Capital and reserves					
Ordinary shares of £1 each		90		80	(3)
Share premium account		40		20	(3)
Profit and loss account		35		20	
		165		120	
8% Debentures		–		30	(3)
		165		150	

Additional information

1   Fixed assets

	Cost £000	Depreciation £000	Net Book Value £000
Balance at 31 March 1997	200	50	150
Additions	60	–	60
Disposals	(40)	(25)	(15)
Depreciation for the year to 31 March 1998	–	20	(20)
Balance at 31 March 1998	220	45	175

Fixed assets disposed of during the year were sold for £22,000.

2   Current assets at 31 March for each of the two years comprise the following:

	1998 £000	1997 £000
Stocks	35	27
Debtors	22	28
Bank	24	22
Cash	9	3
	90	80

3   The 8% debentures were repaid during the year ended 31 March 1998. This repayment was funded by a new issue of ordinary shares at a premium.

Required:
Prepare a cash flow statement for NITE Limited for the year ended 31 March 1998.

42.4A The following information has been extracted from the books of Nimmo Limited for the year to 31 December 19X9:

Profit and Loss Accounts for the Years to 31 December

	19X8	19X9
	£000	£000
Profit before taxation	9,500	20,400
Taxation	(3,200)	(5,200)
Profit after taxation	6,300	15,200
Dividends:		
Preference (paid)	(100)	(100)
Ordinary: interim (paid)	(1,000)	(2,000)
final (proposed)	(3,000)	(6,000)
Retained profit for the year	£2,200	£7,100

Balance Sheets as at 31 December

	19X8	19X9
	£000	£000
Fixed assets		
Plant, machinery and equipment, at cost	17,600	23,900
Less: Accumulated depreciation	9,500	10,750
	8,100	13,150
Current assets		
Stocks	5,000	15,000
Trade debtors	8,600	26,700
Prepayments	300	400
Cash at bank and in hand	600	–
	14,500	42,100
Current liabilities		
Bank overdraft	–	(16,200)
Trade creditors	(6,000)	(10,000)
Accruals	(800)	(1,000)
Taxation	(3,200)	(5,200)
Dividends	(3,000)	(6,000)
	(13,000)	(38,400)
	£9,600	£16,850
Share capital		
Ordinary shares of £1 each	5,000	5,000
10% preference shares of £1 each	1,000	1,000
Profit and loss account	3,000	10,100
	9,000	16,100
Loans		
15% debenture stock	600	750
	£9,600	£16,850

Additional information

1 The directors are extremely concerned about the large bank overdraft as at 31 December 19X9 and they attribute this mainly to the increase in trade debtors as a result of alleged poor credit control.
2 During the year to 31 December 19X9, fixed assets originally costing £5,500,000 were sold for £1,000,000. The accumulated depreciation on these assets as at 31 December 19X8 was £3,800,000.

Required:
Prepare a cash flow statement for the year to 31 December 19X9.

(*Association of Accounting Technicians*)

42.5A   Based on the following information you are required to prepare a Cash Flow Statement for A Trader for the year ended 30th June, 1998 in accordance with the requirements of Financial Reporting Standard No. 1.

A Trader
Draft Balance Sheets as at

	30th June 1997		30th June 1998	
	£	£	£	£
Tangible fixed assets				
Premises		20,000		50,000
Machinery at cost	120,000		160,000	
Less provision for depreciation	−58,000	62,000	−72,500	87,500
		82,000		137,500
Financial fixed assets				
Investments		1,000		Nil
		83,000		137,500
Current assets				
Stock	32,500		60,000	
Trade debtors	16,000		25,250	
Prepayments (no interest)	1,000		1,250	
Cash	6,000		Nil	
	55,500		86,500	
Current liabilities				
Trade creditors	20,000		45,000	
Bank overdraft	Nil		17,500	
	−20,000		−62,500	
Net current assets		35,500		24,000
Net assets		118,500		161,500
Financed by:				
Capital		118,500		131,500
Premises revaluation reserve		Nil		30,000
		118,500		161,500

The following information may be relevant:
(i) Investments were sold during the year for £900.
(ii) Machinery which originally cost £12,000 and which had a net book value at the time of sale of £5,000 was sold during the year for £6,400.
(iii) Cash drawings by A Trader during the year amounted to £14,000.
(iv) No new capital was introduced into the business during the year.

42.6A   Based on the Draft Balance Sheets, Profit and Loss Account and note which follow, prepare a Cash Flow Statement, including relevant notes thereto, for 'Short of Cash Ltd' for the year ended 30th June, 1998 in a form consistent with Financial Reporting Standard No. 1.

Short of Cash Ltd
Draft Balance Sheets as at

	30th June 1997		30th June 1998	
Tangible fixed assets	£	£	£	£
Land		200,000		250,000
Buildings at cost	270,000		275,000	
less Aggregate depreciation	–80,000	190,000	–100,000	175,000
Plant and equipment at cost	100,000		150,000	
less Aggregate depreciation	–60,000	40,000	–90,000	60,000
		430,000		485,000
Financial fixed assets				
Quoted investments (at cost)		40,000		120,000
Current assets				
Stock	30,000		70,000	
Trade debtors	180,000		190,000	
Bank	20,000		Nil	
	230,000		260,000	
Current liabilities				
Trade creditors	130,000		135,000	
Taxation payable	15,000		2,000	
Bank overdraft	Nil		140,000	
	–145,000		–277,000	
Net current assets/liabilities		85,000		–17,000
Long-term loans		175,000		178,000
Net assets		380,000		410,000
Financed by:				
Ordinary share capital		200,000		250,000
Retained profits		180,000		160,000
Shareholders' funds		380,000		410,000

Short of Cash Ltd
Draft Profit and Loss Account for the Year Ended 30th June, 1998

	£	£
Gross profit		106,000
Expenses:		
Depreciation of buildings	–20,000	
Depreciation of plant and equipment	–60,000	
Interest paid and payable	–11,000	
Other expenses	–45,000	–136,000
		–30,000
Income:		
Interest received and receivable	2,000	
Dividends received and receivable	6,000	
Profit on sale of plant and equipment	4,000	12,000
Loss before taxation		–18,000
Taxation		–2,000
Loss retained for the year		–20,000

Note

Plant and Equipment which originally cost £30,000 and had been fully depreciated was sold during the year.

42.7 Based on the following information you are required to prepare a Cash Flow Statement, including relevant notes thereto, for Cash Rich Ltd, a computer equipment retailer, for the year ended 31st December, 1998 in accordance with the requirements of FRS 1.

Cash Rich Ltd
Draft Balance Sheets as at

	31st December 1997		31st December 1998	
	£	£	£	£
Tangible fixed assets				
Land		95,000		70,000
Furniture and fittings at cost	55,000		65,000	
less Provision for depreciation	−18,000	37,000	−20,000	45,000
Vehicles at cost	60,000		70,000	
less Provision for depreciation	−25,000	35,000	−36,000	34,000
		167,000		149,000
Financial fixed assets				
Investments		125,000		400,000
		292,000		549,000
Current assets				
Stock	100,000		130,000	
Investments	30,000		40,000	
Trade debtors	40,000		50,000	
Cash at bank and in hand	8,000		20,000	
	178,000		240,000	
Current liabilities				
Trade creditors	40,000		40,000	
Proposed dividend	50,000		58,000	
Taxation payable	80,000		91,000	
	−170,000		−189,000	
Net current assets		8,000		51,000
Net assets		300,000		600,000
Financed by:				
Ordinary share capital		160,000		160,000
Revenue reserves		140,000		440,000
		300,000		600,000

Cash Rich Ltd
Extracts from the Draft Profit and Loss Account for the Year Ended 31st December 1998

	£	£
Turnover		2,000,000
Profit before interest, dividends and capital profits/losses		400,000
Interest paid and payable		−4,000
Interest received and receivable		25,000
Dividends received and receivable		85,000
Profit on sale of land		14,000
Loss on sale of furniture and fittings		−1,000
Net profit before tax		519,000
Taxation		−91,000
		428,000
Dividends:		
Interim Ordinary Dividend	70,000	
Proposed Final Dividend	58,000	−128,000
Profit Retained for the Year		300,000

The following information may be relevant:

(i) Land which originally cost £30,000 was sold during the year.

(ii) Furniture and Fittings, which originally cost £5,000 and which had a net book value at the time of sale of £2,000, were sold on 1st January. Further purchases of furniture and fittings were made during the year.

(iii) No disposal of vehicles took place during the year.

(iv) The short-term investments were within three months of maturity when acquired.

42.8 Based on the following information you are required to prepare a Cash Flow Statement for A Counting Ltd for the year ended 31st December, 1998 in a form consistent with Financial Reporting Standard No. 1.

A Counting Ltd
Draft Balance Sheets as at

	31st December 1997		31st December 1998	
Tangible fixed assets	£	£	£	£
Land		100,000		120,000
Buildings at cost	120,000		145,000	
less Provision for depreciation	–12,000	108,000	–24,000	121,000
Vehicles at cost	15,000		18,000	
less Provision for depreciation	–5,000	10,000	–9,000	9,000
		218,000		250,000
Financial fixed assets				
Investments		13,000		Nil
		231,000		250,000
Current assets				
Stock	50,000		80,000	
Trade debtors	25,000		45,000	
Cash	1,000		2,000	
	76,000		127,000	
Current liabilities				
Trade creditors	30,000		45,000	
Dividends payable	4,000		8,000	
Taxation payable	6,000		12,000	
Bank overdraft	12,000		24,000	
	–52,000		–89,000	
Net current assets		24,000		38,000
Net assets		255,000		288,000
Financed by:				
Ordinary Share Capital		187,000		200,000
Profit and Loss Account		68,000		88,000
		255,000		288,000

A Counting Ltd
Draft Profit and Loss Account for the Year Ended 31st December 1998

	£	£
Profit before interest, dividends and profits/losses on fixed assets		37,000
Interest paid and payable		–2,400
Interest received and receivable		400
Dividends received and receivable		2,000
Profit on sale of land		10,000
Loss on disposal of building		–2,000
Loss on sale of investments		–5,000
Net profit before tax		40,000
Taxation		–12,000
		28,000
Dividends		
Interim ordinary dividend	3,000	
Proposed final dividend	5,000	–8,000
Profit retained for the year		20,000

The following information may be relevant:

(i)   Land which originally cost £30,000 was sold during the year.

(ii) A pre-fabricated building which originally cost £5,000 and which had a net book value at the time of sale of £2,000 was disposed of on 1st January, 1998.

(iii) No vehicles were disposed of during the year.

42.9A Based on the following information you are required to prepare a Cash Flow Statement for Revalue Ltd for the year ended 30th June, 1998 in accordance with the requirements of Financial Reporting Standard No. 1.

Revalue Ltd
Draft Balance Sheets as at

	30th June 1997		30th June 1998	
Tangible fixed assets	£	£	£	£
Freehold land (at valuation)		100,000		134,500
Buildings (at cost or valuation)	170,000		175,000	
less Provision for depreciation	−6,800	163,200	−13,800	161,200
Plant and equipment at cost	210,560		264,380	
less Provision for depreciation	−56,620	153,940	−85,600	178,780
		417,140		474,480
Financial fixed assets				
Quoted investments (at cost)		58,340		Nil
Current assets				
Stock	132,900		174,240	
Trade debtors	83,020		93,180	
Bank	21,460		Nil	
	237,380		267,420	
Current liabilities				
Trade creditors	34,220		37,440	
Taxation payable	14,500		18,000	
Bank overdraft	Nil		36,360	
	−48,720		−91,800	
Net current assets		188,660		175,620
Long-term loans		252,000		52,000
Net assets		412,140		598,100
Financed by:				
Share capital		200,000		260,000
Share premium account		25,000		70,500
Retained profits		117,140		163,100
Capital reserve		70,000		104,500
		412,140		598,100

Revalue Ltd
Draft Profit and Loss Account for the Year Ended 30th June 1998

	£
Sales	552,200
Cost of sales	−372,600
Gross profit	179,600
Depreciation of buildings	−7,000
Depreciation of plant and equipment	−39,600
Interest paid and payable	−6,000
Other expenses	−97,400
Interest received and receivable	1,000
Dividends received and receivable	5,000
Profit on sale of quoted investments	22,860
Profit on sale of plant and equipment	3,500
Net profit before taxation	61,960
Taxation	−16,000
Profit retained for the year	45,960

Notes

(i) Freehold land is revalued annually and the increase in value is credited to the Capital Reserve account. Buildings were last revalued on 30th June, 1996; subsequent additions are included at cost.

(ii) Plant and Equipment which originally cost £10,620 and had been fully depreciated was sold during the year.

42.10 Based on the following information you are required to prepare a Cash Flow Statement for Small Company Ltd for the year ended 30th June, 1998 in a form consistent with Financial Reporting Standard No. 1.

Small Company Ltd
Draft Balance Sheets as at

	30th June 1997		30th June 1998	
Tangible fixed assets	£	£	£	£
Freehold land (at valuation)		100,000		150,000
Buildings (at cost or valuation)	170,000		175,000	
less Provision for depreciation	−20,000	150,000	−30,000	145,000
Plant and equipment at cost	200,000		250,000	
less Provision for depreciation	−60,000	140,000	−90,000	160,000
		390,000		455,000
Financial fixed assets				
Quoted investments (at cost)		60,000		Nil
Current assets				
Stock	130,000		170,000	
Trade debtors	80,000		90,000	
Bank	20,000		Nil	
	230,000		260,000	
Current liabilities				
Trade creditors	30,000		35,000	
Taxation payable	15,000		20,000	
Bank overdraft	Nil		40,000	
	−45,000		−95,000	
Net current assets		185,000		165,000
Long-term loans		250,000		60,000
Net assets		385,000		560,000
Financed by:				
Share capital		200,000		250,000
Share premium account		25,000		50,000
Retained profits		110,000		160,000
Capital reserve		50,000		100,000
Shareholders' funds		385,000		560,000

Small Company Ltd
Draft Profit and Loss Account for the Year Ended 30th June 1998

	£
Sales	500,000
Cost of goods sold	−375,000
Gross profit	125,000
Depreciation of buildings	−10,000
Depreciation of plant and equipment	−40,000
Interest paid and payable	−6,000
Other expenses	−37,000
Interest received and receivable	1,000
Dividends received and receivable	5,000
Profit on sale of quoted investments	45,000
Profit on sale of plant and equipment	3,000
Net profit before taxation	86,000
Taxation	−36,000
Profit retained for the year	50,000

Notes
(i) 'Freehold Land' is revalued annually and the increase in value is credited to the Capital Reserve account. Buildings were last revalued on 30th June, 1994. Subsequent additions are included at cost.
(ii) Plant and Equipment which originally cost £10,000 and had been fully depreciated was sold during the year.

42.11 The following are the Balance Sheets of Premium Issue Limited as at 31st December, 1997 and 1998 together with the Profit and Loss account for the year ended 31st December, 1998.

Premium Issue Limited
Balance Sheets as at

	31st December, 1997		31st December, 1998	
Tangible fixed assets	£000	£000	£000	£000
Freehold land and buildings	500		300	
Less Provision for depreciation	−140	360	−60	240
Plant and equipment	600		2,400	
Less Provision for depreciation	−500	100	−640	1,760
		460		2,000
Financial fixed assets				
Investments		120		–
Current assets				
Stock	300		400	
Debtors	180		200	
Cash	140		–	
	620		600	
Current liabilities				
Creditors	−80		−140	
Taxation payable	−120		−70	
Dividends payable	–		−12	
Bank overdraft	–		−260	
	200		−482	
Net current assets		420		118
10% Debentures		60		400
Net assets		940		1,718
Financed by:				
Share capital				
£1 8% Preference shares	–		100	
£1 Ordinary shares	480	480	640	740
Reserves				
Revaluation reserve	–		100	
Share premium	40		80	
Revenue reserves	420	460	798	978
Shareholders' funds		940		1,718

Premium Issue Limited
Profit and Loss Account for the Year Ended 31st December 1998

	£000
Operating Profit	482
Interest Paid	−10
Profit Before Tax	472
Taxation	−70
Profit After Tax	402
Dividends	−24
Profit Retained for the Year	378

The following information is also available:

1 There were no disposals of plant and equipment during the year.
2 There were no additions to buildings during the year. Buildings disposed of for £340,000 had cost £300,000. Aggregate depreciation on these buildings amounted to £100,000.
3 Investments were disposed of for £140,000 on 1st January, 1998.

Requirement:
Prepare a Cash Flow Statement, including notes thereto, for Premium Issue Limited for the year ended 31st December, 1998 in a form consistent with FRS 1.

42.12 The following summarised balance sheets relate to Track Limited:

Balance Sheets at 30 June

	19X0	19X1
	£000	£000
Fixed assets at cost	500	650
Less Accumulated depreciation	200	300
	300	350
Investments at cost	200	50
Current assets		
Stocks	400	700
Debtors	1,350	1,550
Cash and bank	100	–
	1,850	2,250
Current liabilities		
Bank overdraft	–	(60)
Creditors	(650)	(790)
Taxation	(230)	(190)
Proposed dividend	(150)	(130)
	(1,030)	(1,170)
	£1,320	£1,480
Capital and reserves		
Called-up share capital (£1 ordinary shares)	500	750
Share premium account	150	200
Profit and loss account	670	530
	£1,320	£1,480

Additional information
1 During the year to 30 June 19X1, some fixed assets originally costing £25,000 had been sold for £20,000 in cash. The accumulated depreciation on these fixed assets at 30 June 19X0 amounted to £10,000. Similarly, some of the investments originally costing £150,000 had been sold for cash at their book value.
2 The taxation balances disclosed in the above balance sheets represent the actual amounts agreed with the Inland Revenue. All taxes were paid on their due dates. Advance corporation tax may be ignored.
3 No interim dividend was paid during the year to 30 June 19X1.
4 During the year to 30 June 19X1, the company made a 1-for-2 rights issue of 250 ordinary £1 shares at 120p per share.

Required:
Prepare Track Ltd's cash flow statement for the year to 30 June 19X1 in accordance with the requirements of FRS 1.

(*Association of Accounting Technicians*)

Part VI Revision questions

Suggested solutions to questions with the letter 'A' after the question number are given in Appendix II (pages 687–9).

R6.1A The following trial balance was extracted from the books of Robin Ltd, after a draft Profit and Loss Account had been prepared, for the year ended 31st December, 1998.

	£ Debit	£ Credit
Premises at cost and accumulated depreciation	200,000	40,000
Vehicles at cost and accumulated depreciation	35,000	7,000
Debtors and prepayments	130,000	
Stock at 31st December, 1998	90,000	
Bank overdraft		33,000
Creditors and accruals		80,000
Debentures (2010)		30,000
Issued share capital		
62,500 ordinary shares at 40p each		25,000
100,000 preference shares at 50p each		50,000
General reserve		24,000
Net profit for the year ended 31st December, 1998, before adjustments		79,000
Profit retained at 1st January, 1998		87,000
	455,000	455,000

Additional information

1 The following items, which require adjustments to the net profit, have been discovered in a review of the Trial Balance.
   (i) Stock amounting to £25,000 at cost has been found to have a net realisable value of £18,000.
   (ii) A vehicle costing £5,000 has been incorrectly charged to repairs and renewals. This vehicle is to be depreciated at the rate of 20% per annum straight line.
   (iii) An additional PAYE provision of £6,000 is required for salaries paid to directors.
2 Debenture interest at the rate of 20% per annum is to be provided.
3 The following dividends are proposed.

Ordinary shares	5p per share
Preference shares	10%

4 £15,000 is to be transferred to the general reserve.

You are required to prepare for Robin Ltd:
(a) a statement showing the revised net profit for the year ended 31st December, 1998;
(b) the Profit and Loss Appropriation Account for the year ended 31st December, 1998; and
(c) the Balance Sheet as at that date.

(IATI Foundation Examination)

R6.2 The following trial balance was extracted from the books of Keogh Ltd at 31st December, 1998:

	Debit £000	Credit £000
150,000 ordinary shares of 50p each fully paid		75
80,000 12% preference shares of 25p each fully paid		20
Profit and loss account – 1st January, 1998		105
Premises at cost	220	
Accumulated depreciation on premises at 1st January, 1998		44
Debtors and prepayments	80	
Bank current account	25	
Stock at 1st January, 1998	60	
Creditors and accruals		95
Sales		286
Purchases	160	
Wages	30	
Rent and rates	5	
Administration expenses	15	
Selling and distribution expenses	18	
Bank interest and charges	4	
Bad debts written off	8	
	625	625

Additional information
1 Stock at 31st December, 1998, amounted to £85,000.
2 Rates amounting to £6,000 were due at 31st December, 1998, and were not provided for.
3 Depreciation is to be provided on premises at the rate of 2% on cost.
4 A dividend of 10p per ordinary share is to be provided for.
5 The preference share dividend due for the year is to be provided for.

You are required to prepare:
(*a*) the Trading and Profit and Loss Account of Keogh Ltd for the year ended 31st December, 1998;
(*b*) the Profit and Loss Appropriation Account for the year ended 31st December, 1998; and
(*c*) the Balance Sheet as at 31st December, 1998.

(IATI Foundation Examination)

R6.3 The following trial balance was extracted from the books of Timber Ltd, as at 31st March, 1998:

	Debit £000	Credit £000
Ordinary shares of £1 each		1,500
Profit and loss account 1st April, 1997		870
Buildings (cost £1,800,000)	1,350	
Plant and machinery (cost £1,500,000)	780	
Vehicles (cost £900,000)	360	
Stock 31st March, 1998	780	
Debtors	750	
Creditors		630
Bank balance		90
Sales		5,120
Cost of sales	2,880	
Wages and salaries	450	
Distribution costs	120	
Administration expenses	180	
Rent and rates	180	
Heat and light	30	
Insurance	240	
Advertising	50	
Bad debts provision 1st April, 1997		30
Interim dividend paid	90	
	8,240	8,240

Additional information
1 Due to an error on the stock sheets, the stock at 31st March, 1998, was understated by £80,000.
2 No record was made of goods purchased on credit for £120,000 on 30th March, 1998, as the goods were not delivered until 2nd April, 1998.
3 Bad debts of £30,000 are to be written off and the bad debts provision is to be adjusted to 5% of debtors.
4 The rent on the company's showrooms has been paid up to 31st January, 1998. The rent of the showrooms is £18,000 per annum.
5 In March 1998, the company paid rates of £25,000 for the half year to 30th September, 1998.
6 In April 1997, the company sold an old vehicle for £20,000. This vehicle had originally cost £30,000 and it had a book value at the date of sale of £15,000. The only entry made in the books in respect of this transaction was to debit the bank account and credit the sales account.
7 Depreciation is to be provided on fixed assets on hand at 31st March, 1998, at the following rates:

Buildings	2% on cost
Plant and machinery	10% on cost
Vehicles	20% on cost

8 Provision is to be made for a final dividend of 10%.

Requirements:
(a) Prepare the Trading and Profit and Loss Account and the Profit and Loss Appropriation Account for Timber Ltd for the year ended 31st March, 1998, and
(b) Prepare the Balance Sheet as at that date.

(ICAI Professional Examination One)

R6.4 The following trial balance was extracted from the books of Caruth Ltd at 31st December, 1998:

	Debit £000	Credit £000
Land..	200	
Buildings (cost £200,000)	180	
Plant and machinery (cost £120,000)	95	
Vehicles (cost £80,000)...	65	
Stock at 1st January, 1998	60	
Trade debtors and creditors...	120	135
Bank...	15	
Ordinary shares (£1 each, fully paid)		200
10% preference shares £1 each...		100
10% debentures		60
Profit and loss account at 1st January, 1998...............................		178
Sales...		890
Purchases	620	
Wages and salaries..	95	
Rent	12	
Advertising costs	40	
Printing and stationery...	14	
Professional fees..	28	
Telephone and fax	22	
Bad debts provision		8
Preference dividend paid...	5	
	1,571	1,571

Additional information
1 Stock at 31st December, 1998, amounted to £80,000.
2 During the year a van was bought for £20,000; this amount was posted to the purchases account. Also included in purchases was £1,500 which related to alterations to provide more space for storage in the interior of the van.
3 Depreciation is to be provided on fixed assets on hand at 31st December, 1998, as follows:

Buildings	2% on cost
Plant and machinery	10% on written down value
Vehicles	20% on written down value

It is company policy to charge a full year's depreciation on assets in the year of purchase, regardless of the date of purchase, and none in the year of sale.
4 During 1997 a debt of £4,000 owing by Dawson Ltd was written off. On 30th December, 1998, Dawson Ltd indicated that, following an upturn in the company's fortunes, it would be in a position to repay the full amount of the debt on 2nd January, 1999. The recovery of this bad debt has not been reflected in the trial balance.
5 No debenture interest was paid during the year.
6 Provision is to be made for the final dividend on preference shares and an ordinary dividend of 5p per share.
7 Directors' fees of £30,000 have not yet been provided for.
8 Annual rent amounts to £8,000. Rent has been paid up to 30th June, 1999.

Requirements:
(*a*) Prepare the Trading and Profit and Loss Account and the Profit and Loss Appropriation Account for Caruth Ltd for the year ended 31st December, 1998, and
(*b*) Prepare the Balance Sheet as at that date.

(*ICAI Professional Examination One*)

R6.5 Explain what is meant by the 'independence' of an auditor and discuss the extent to which the current legal framework helps to ensure independence.

(ICAI Professional Examination Two)

R6.6A The balance sheet of Hall Ltd at 1st April, 1998 was as follows:

Fixed assets		£150,000
Current assets		
Bank	£25,000	
Other	£33,000	
	£58,000	
Creditors	£21,000	£37,000
		£187,000
Represented by:		
Capital and reserves		
Ordinary share capital		£150,000
Reserves		£37,000
		£187,000

Hall Ltd has an authorised share capital of 300,000 ordinary shares of £1 each of which 150,000 have already been issued as at 1st April, 1998.

On 1st April, 1998 the company decided to issue a further 100,000 shares on the following terms.

Payable on application on 1st May, 1998 (including premium)	40p
Payable on allotment on 1st June, 1998	25p
Payable on first and final call on 1st July, 1998	50p

Applications were received for 165,000 shares. Applications for 15,000 shares were refused and the application money was refunded. The remaining excess application money was retained in lieu of allotment money. All allotment money was received on the due date.

The first and final call was paid in full by all shareholders with the exception of one, who had originally *applied for* 1,500 shares, and who failed to pay the first and final call on the shares allotted to him.

On 15th July, those shares were forfeited for non-payment and were not re-issued.

Requirement:
Prepare all the relevant ledger accounts in the books of Hall Ltd to record the above transactions.

(IATI Admission Examination)

R6.7 Crossword Ltd has an authorised share capital of 500,000 ordinary shares of 50p each, of which 200,000 shares had already been issued by 31st December, 1997. During January 1998 the company issued a further 200,000 shares of 50p each at a premium or 10p per share payable as follows:

Payable on application on 31st January	20p
Payable on allotment on 28th February (including premium)	25p
Payable on first and final call on 30th April	15p

Applications were received for 280,000 shares. Of these, applications in respect of 30,000 shares were refused by the company and the application money was refunded. In respect of the other applications, shares were issued on a pro-rata basis, with the remaining excess application money being retained in lieu of allotment money. All allotment money was paid on the appropriate date.

The first and final call was made on the due date and was paid in full, with the exception of the money due from one shareholder who had originally applied for 2,500 shares. These shares were forfeited on 30th June and were re-issued to a new shareholder on 1st July as fully paid shares on payment of 15p per share by the new shareholder.

Requirement:
Prepare all the relevant ledger accounts to record the above information.

(*IATI Admission Examination*)

R6.8 Set out below are the Profit and Loss Account, Balance Sheet and appropriate notes to the accounts of Court Ltd for the year ended 31st December, 1998 (with comparative figures for the year ended 31st December, 1997, where required).

Profit and Loss Account for the Year Ended 31st December 1998

	£000
Profit before interest	210
Debenture interest paid	–10
Profit before taxation [Note (1)]	200
Taxation	–100
Profit after taxation	100
Dividends – proposed ordinary dividend	–40
Retained profit for the year	60
Retained profit brought forward from previous year	180
Retained profit carried forward to next year	240

Balance Sheets as at

	31st December 1998		31st December 1997	
	£000	£000	£000	£000
Fixed assets				
Tangible assets [note 2]		470		370
Current assets				
Stock	40		76	
Debtors	168		120	
Bank balance	154		130	
	362		326	
Current liabilities				
Creditors	52		76	
Taxation payable	100		120	
Proposed dividends	40		20	
	192		216	
Net current assets		170		110
Debenture loan		100		50
		540		430
Financed by:				
Share capital – ordinary shares of £1 each		300		250
Retained profits		240		180
		540		430

Notes

1 The profit before taxation is arrived at after charging:

Depreciation	£70,000
Auditors' remuneration	£4,000
Directors' remuneration	£6,000

2 Tangible Assets:	£ Cost	Agg. Deprec.	£ NBV
At 1st January, 1998	700,000	330,000	370,000
Additions during the year/charge for the year	170,000	70,000	
At 31st December, 1998	870,000	400,000	470,000

Requirements:

(a) Prepare a Cash Flow Statement, to include relevant notes, for the year ended 31st December, 1998, and

(b) Set out in your own words the benefits of including a Cash Flow Statement as part of a set of accounts.

(*IATI Admission Examination*)

R6.9 The following are the summarised balance sheets of Glenside Ltd at 31st July, 1998 and 1997.

	31st July 1998 £000		31st July 1997 £000	
Fixed assets at cost		390		380
Provision for depreciation		−138		−104
		252		276
Current assets				
Stocks	84		90	
Debtors	73		69	
Bank	12		–	
	169		159	
Current liabilities				
Creditors	−32		−35	
Dividends	−12		−5	
	−44		−40	
Net current assets		125		119
12% Debentures		100		150
		277		245
Share capital		250		230
Share premium		10		5
Profit and loss account		17		10
		277		245

The following additional information is also provided:

1 Fixed assets, which had cost £20,000 and had a book value of £8,000, were sold for £9,000 cash on 1st August, 1997.

2 Dividends of £9,000 for the year ended 31st July, 1998, were declared shortly before the end of that year.

3 Some of the debentures were repaid on 31st July, 1998.

4 On 31st July, 1998, interest in respect of the financial year ended on that date was paid on the full amount of the debentures which were outstanding at the beginning of the year. No other interest was paid or received by the company during the year.

Requirement:

Prepare a Cash Flow Statement for Glenside Ltd for the financial year ended 31st July, 1998, in compliance with FRS 1.

(*ICAI Professional Examination Two*)

R6.10 Based on the following information you are required to prepare a Cash Flow Statement for Capital Ltd for the year ended 31st August, 1998 in accordance with the requirements of Financial Reporting Standard No. 1.

Capital Ltd
Draft Balance Sheets as at

	31st August 1998		31st August 1997	
Tangible fixed assets	£000s	£000s	£000s	£000s
Freehold land		100		50
Buildings at cost	50		200	
less Provision for depreciation	−30	20	−70	130
Plant and equipment at cost	1,200		300	
less Provision for depreciation	−320	880	−250	50
		1,000		230
Financial fixed assets				
Investments (at cost)		Nil		60
Current assets				
Stock	200		200	
Trade debtors	100		100	
Cash on hand	Nil		10	
	300		310	
Current liabilities				
Trade creditors	70		40	
Taxation payable	65		60	
Bank overdraft	94		Nil	
	−229		−100	
Net current assets		71		210
Debentures		200		30
Net assets		871		470
Financed by:				
Share capital				
£1 Ordinary shares fully paid	320		200	
£1 Preference shares fully paid	50	370	Nil	200
Reserves				
Capital redemption reserve	Nil		40	
Revaluation reserve	50		Nil	
Share premium account	40		20	
Retained profits	411	501	210	270
		871		470

Capital Ltd
Extract from the Draft Profit and Loss Account
for the Year Ended 31st August 1998

	£000
Trading profit (after charging depreciation)	96
Interest paid and payable	−5
Dividends received and receivable	5
Profit on sale of buildings	120
Profit on sale of investments	20
Profit before taxation	236
Taxation	−35
Profit retained for the year	201

The following information may be relevant:

(i)   There were no sales of plant and equipment during the year.

(ii) The freehold land was revalued at the start of the year.

(iii) There were no additions to buildings during the year. Some of the buildings were sold during the year. The company agreed to rent back some of these buildings from the purchaser. The depreciation on the buildings sold was £50,000.

(iv) The preference shares were issued for cash at par.

(v)   A bonus issue of ordinary shares on the basis of one new share for every five held was made. The capital redemption reserve fund was used for this purpose.

(vi) An issue of £1 ordinary shares was made at a price of £1.25 per share.

Part VII

THE ANALYSIS AND INTERPRETATION OF FINANCIAL INFORMATION

43

Analysis of financial information I: Introduction to ratio analysis

43.1 Ratio analysis as a tool for comparison

Let us examine the performance of four companies, all dealing in the same type of goods.

	Gross profit £	Sales £
Company A	10,000	84,800
Company B	15,000	125,200
Company C	25,000	192,750
Company D	17,500	146,840

Suppose you want to know which company achieves the best profit margins. Using only the above figures it is difficult to gauge which performance was the best, and which was the worst. In order for the figures to be comparable some form of common measure is needed. The common measure used would be a ratio – in this case the amount of gross profit as a percentage of sales. The comparison now becomes:

Gross profit as a percentage of sales

Company A	11.79%
Company B	11.98%
Company C	12.97%
Company D	11.91%

Company C, with 12.97% (or £12.97 gross profit per £100 sales) has performed better than the other companies in terms of the amount of gross profit it earns on its sales.

43.2 Ratio analysis can be misleading

You can only sensibly compare like with like. There is not much point in comparing the gross profit percentage of a wholesale chemist with that of a restaurant, for example.

Similarly, figures are only comparable if they have been built up on a similar basis. The sales figures of Company X which treat items as sales only when cash is received cannot be properly compared with Company Z which treats items as sales as soon as they are invoiced.

Ratios therefore need very careful handling. They are extremely useful if used properly, and very misleading otherwise.

43.3 Liquidity ratios

Profit as a percentage of capital employed, as you will see, gives an overall picture of profitability. It cannot always be assumed, however, that profitability is everything that is desirable. It must be stressed that accounting is needed, not just to calculate profitability, but also to know whether or not the business will be able to meet its financial commitments as they fall due.

The two main measures of liquidity are the **current ratio** and the **acid test ratio**.

1 Current ratio (also known as the *working capital ratio*)

$$\text{Current ratio} = \frac{\text{Current assets}}{\text{Current liabilities}}$$

This compares assets which will become liquid in approximately 12 months with liabilities which will be due for payment in the same period.

2 Acid test ratio (also known as the *quick ratio* or the *liquid ratio*)

$$\text{Acid test ratio} = \frac{\text{Current assets} - \text{Stock}}{\text{Current liabilities}}$$

This shows that provided creditors and debtors are paid at approximately the same time, a view might be made as to whether the business has sufficient liquid resources to meet its current liabilities.

Example 43.1 shows how two businesses may have similar profitability, yet their liquidity positions may be quite different.

Example 43.1

	Business E		Business F	
	£	£	£	£
Fixed assets		40,000		70,000
Current assets				
Stock	30,000		50,000	
Debtors	45,000		9,000	
Bank	15,000		1,000	
	90,000		60,000	
Less Current liabilities: creditors	30,000	60,000	30,000	30,000
		100,000		100,000
Capital				
Opening capital		80,000		80,000
Add Net profit		36,000		36,000
		116,000		116,000
Less Drawings		16,000		16,000
		100,000		100,000

Notes: sales for both E and F amounted to £144,000. Gross profits for E and F were identical at £48,000.

Profitability: this is the same for both businesses. However, there is a vast difference in the liquidity of the two businesses. The current ratios for both businesses are as follows:

$$E = \frac{90,000}{30,000} = 3: \quad F = \frac{60,000}{30,000} = 2$$

This looks adequate on the face of it, but the acid test ratio reveals that F is in distress, as it will probably find it difficult to pay its current liabilities on time. The acid test ratios are calculated as follows:

$$E = \frac{60,000}{30,000} = 2: \quad F = \frac{10,000}{30,000} = 0.33$$

Therefore, for a business to be profitable is not enough, it should also be adequately liquid as well.

3 Stockturn (or rate of stock turnover)

If we always kept just £100 of stock at cost, which when we sold it would sell for £125, then if we sold this amount eight times in a year we would make 8 × £25 = £200 gross profit. The quicker we sell our stock (we could say the quicker we turn over our stock) the more profit we will make, if our gross profit as a percentage of sales remains the same.

To check on how quickly we are turning over our stock we can use the formula:

$$\frac{\text{Cost of goods sold}}{\text{Average stock}} = \text{Number of times stock is turned over within a period}$$

It would be best if the average stock held could be calculated by valuing the stock several times each year, then dividing the totals of the figures obtained by the number of valuations. For instance, monthly stock figures are added up then divided by twelve.

However, it is quite common, especially in examinations or in cases where no other information is available, to calculate the average stock as the opening stock plus the closing stock and the answer divided by two.

Instead of saying that the stockturn is so many times per annum, we could instead say, on average, how long we keep stock before we sell it. We do this by the formula:

To express it in months: $12 \div \text{Stockturn} = x$ months
To express it in days: $365 \div \text{Stockturn} = x$ days

The ratio does not prove anything by itself, it merely prompts inquiries as to why it should be changing. A reduction in stockturn can mean that the business is slowing down. Stocks may be piling up and not being sold. This could lead to a liquidity crisis, as money may be being taken out of the bank simply to increase stocks which are not then sold quickly enough.

The cost of sales for each company was £144,000 – £48,000 = £96,000. If opening stocks had been E £34,000 and F £46,000, then stockturns would have been:

	E	F
$\dfrac{\text{Cost of sales}}{\text{Average stock}}$	$\dfrac{96,000}{(34,000 + 30,000) \div 2}$	$\dfrac{96,000}{(46,000 + 50,000) \div 2}$
	$= \dfrac{96,000}{32,000} = 3$ times	$= \dfrac{96,000}{48,000} = 2$ times

It appears that F's stock is starting to pile up. Business F is having more difficulty selling its stock than business E.

4   Average period of credit given to debtors

The resources tied up in debtors is an important ratio subject. Money tied up unnecessarily in debtors is unproductive money. This can be calculated for the two companies as:

	E	F
$\dfrac{\text{Debtors}}{\text{Sales}} \times 365$	$\dfrac{45,000}{144,000} \times 365$	$\dfrac{9,000}{144,000} \times 365$
	$= 114$ days	$= 22.8$ days

Why business E should have allowed so much time for its debtors to pay is a matter for investigation. Possibly the business was finding it harder to sell goods, and to sell at all, was eventually forced to sell to customers on long credit terms. It could well be that E has no proper credit control system, whereas F has an extremely efficient one.

5 Average period of credit taken from creditors

Assuming that purchases for E amounted to £92,000 and for F £100,000 then the figures are:

	E	F
$\dfrac{\text{Creditors}}{\text{Purchases}} \times 365$	$\dfrac{30,000}{92,000} \times 365$	$\dfrac{30,000}{100,000} \times 365$
	$= 119$ days	$= 109.5$ days

43.4 Profitability ratios

1 Return on capital employed (ROCE)

This is the most important of all profitability ratios, as it encompasses all the other ratios, and the earning of an adequate return on capital employed is why the person(s) invested their money in the first place.

(a) Sole traders

In an earlier chapter it was stated that the term 'capital employed' had not been standardised. In this chapter the average of the capital account will be used, i.e. (opening balance + closing balance) ÷ 2.

In businesses C and D in Example 43.2 the same net profits have been earned, but capitals employed are different.

Example 43.2

Balance Sheets

	C $£$	D $£$
Fixed + Current assets − Current liabilities	10,000	16,000
Capital accounts		
Opening balance	8,000	14,000
Add Net profits	3,600	3,600
	11,600	17,600
Less Drawings	1,600	1,600
	10,000	16,000

Return on capital employed is:

$$\boxed{\frac{\text{Net profit}}{\text{Capital employed}} \times 100}$$

$$C \; \frac{3,600}{(8,000 + 10,000) \div 2} \times \frac{100}{1} = 40\%$$

$$D \; \frac{3,600}{(14,000 + 16,000) \div 2} \times \frac{100}{1} = 24\%$$

The ratio illustrates that what is important is not simply how much profit has been made but how well capital has been employed. Business C has made far better use of its capital, achieving a return of £40 net profit for every £100 invested, whereas D has received only a net profit of £24 per £100.

(b) Limited companies

Again, different meanings are attached to return on capital employed. The main ones are:

(i)   return on capital employed by ordinary shareholders;
(ii) return on capital employed by all long-term suppliers of capital.

To distinguish between these two meanings, in a limited company (i) is usually known as 'Return on Owners' Equity' (ROOE). The word 'Return' in this case is the net profit for the period. The words 'Owners' Equity' means the book value of all things owned by the

owners of the ordinary share capital. This is calculated as: Ordinary Share Capital + all Reserves including Profit and Loss Account.

In the case of (ii) this is often known simply as 'Return on Capital Employed' (ROCE). The word 'Return' in this case means net profit + any preference share dividends + debenture and long-term loan interest. The word 'Capital' means Ordinary Share Capital + Reserves including Profit and Loss Account + Preference Shares + Debentures and Long-term Loans.

Given the following balance sheets of two companies, P Ltd and Q Ltd, the calculations of (i) and (ii) will be shown:

Balance sheets as at 31 December

	P Ltd		Q Ltd	
	£	£	£	£
	1997	1998	1997	1998
Fixed assets	5,200	5,600	8,400	9,300
Net current assets	2,800	3,400	1,600	2,700
10% debentures			1,200	1,200
	8,000	9,000	8,800	10,800
Share capital (ordinary)	3,000	3,000	5,000	5,000
Reserves	5,000	6,000	3,800	5,800
	8,000	9,000	8,800	10,800

Profit and Loss Accounts for the year ended 31 December 1998

	P Ltd	Q Ltd
	£	£
Net profit	2,200	3,800
Dividends	1,200	1,800
	1,000	2,000

Return on Owners' Equity (ROOE)

$$P\ Ltd \qquad\qquad Q\ Ltd$$

$$\frac{2,200}{(8,000 + 9,000) \div 2} \times \frac{100}{1} = 25.9\% \qquad \frac{3,800}{(8,800 + 10,800) \div 2} \times \frac{100}{1} = 38.8\%$$

The return on capital employed by all long-term suppliers of capital is not relevant in the case of P Ltd, as there are only ordinary shareholders in P Ltd.

$$\text{ROCE: } Q\ Ltd = \frac{3,800 + 120*}{(10,000 + 12,000) \div 2} \times \frac{100}{1} = 35.6\%$$

*The debenture interest 10% of £1,200 = £120 must be added back here, as it was an expense in calculating the £3,800 net profit.

2 Gross profit as a percentage of sales

The basic formula is:

$$\frac{\text{Gross Profit}}{\text{Sales}} \times \frac{100}{1} = \text{Gross Profit as a percentage of sales.}$$

Put another way, this represents the amount of gross profit for every £100 of sales. If the answer turned out to be 15%, this would mean that for every £100 of sales £15 gross profit was made before any expenses were paid.

This ratio is used as a test of the profitability of the sales. Just because the sales are increased does not of itself mean that the gross profit will increase. The trading accounts in the following example illustrate this.

Example 43.3

Trading Accounts for the year ended 31 December

	£	1997 £	£	1998 £
Sales		7,000		8,000
Opening stock	500		900	
Purchases	6,000		7,200	
	6,500		8,100	
Closing stock	900	5,600	1,100	7,000
Gross profit		1,400		1,000

In 1997 the gross profit as a percentage of sales was:

$$\frac{1,400}{7,000} \times \frac{100}{1} = 20\%$$

In 1998 it became:

$$\frac{1,000}{8,000} \times \frac{100}{1} = 12\frac{1}{2}\%$$

Sales increased, but as the gross profit percentage has fallen by a relatively greater amount the gross profit has fallen. There could be many reasons for such a fall in the gross profit percentage, such as:

1 Perhaps the goods being sold have cost more, but the selling price of the goods has not risen to the same extent.
2 Perhaps in order to increase sales, reductions have been made in the selling price of goods.
3 There could be a difference in how much has been sold of each sort of goods, called the sales-mix, between this year and last, with different kinds of goods carrying different rates of gross profit per £100 of sales.
4 There may have been a greater wastage or theft of goods.

These are only some of the possible reasons for the decrease. The idea of calculating the ratio is to show whether the profitability per £100 of sales has changed. The firm would then try to find out why and how such a change has taken place.

As the figure of sales less returns inwards is also known as **turnover**, the ratio is also known as the **gross profit percentage on turnover**.

3 Net profit as a percentage of sales

The formula is:

$$\frac{\text{Net profit}}{\text{Sales}} \times \frac{100}{1} = \text{Net Profit as a percentage of sales.}$$

43.5 Other ratios

There is a large number of other ratios which could be used to analyse accounting information; far more than can be mentioned in a textbook such as this. The ratios which should be calculated in any particular case will depend on the type of business being analysed and the purpose for which the analysis is being undertaken.

Different users of accounts will want to calculate the ratios which are of vital concern to them. If we can take a bank as an example, which lends money to a company, it will want to ensure two things:

(*a*) that the company will be able to pay interest on the loan as it falls due; *and*
(*b*) that it will be able to repay the loan on the agreed date.

The bank is therefore interested in:

(*a*) short-term liquidity, concerning payment of loan interest; and
(*b*) long-term solvency for eventual repayment of the loan.

Ratios which a bank could calculate to measure the above would include:

1 Short-term liquidity

Short-term liquidity is generally measured using the *acid test ratio* and the *current ratio*, already described.

2 Long-term solvency

Ratios to measure this might include:

(a) **Operating profit/loan interest.** This indicates how much of the profits is taken up by paying loan interest. Too great a proportion would mean that the company was borrowing more than was sensible, as a small fall in profits could mean the company operating at a loss with the consequent effect upon long-term solvency.

(b) **Total external liabilities/shareholders' funds.** This ratio measures how much financing is done via share capital and retained profits, and how much is from external sources. Too high a proportion of external liabilities could bring about long-term solvency problems if the company's profit making capacity falls by a relatively small amount, as outside liabilities still have to be met.

(c) **Shareholders' funds/total assets (excluding intangible assets).** This highlights the proportion of assets financed by the company's own funds. Large falls in this ratio will tend to show a difficulty with long-term solvency. Similarly, investors will want to see ratios suitable for their purposes, which are not the same as those for the bank. These will not only be used on a single company comparison, but probably with the average of the same type of ratios for other companies in the same industry.

These will include the following ratios.

(i) Earnings per share (EPS)
The formula is:

$$\text{Earnings per share} = \frac{\text{Net profit after both tax and preference dividends}}{\text{Number of ordinary shares issued}}$$

This gives the shareholder (or prospective shareholder) a chance to compare one year's earnings with another in terms easily understood.

(ii) Price/earnings ratio (P/E Ratio)
The formula is:

$$\text{Price/earnings ratio} = \frac{\text{Market price per share on the Stock Exchange}}{\text{Earnings per share}}$$

This puts the price into context as a multiple of the earnings. The greater the P/E ratio, the greater the demand for the shares. A low P/E means there is little demand for shares.

(iii) Dividend cover
This is found by the formula:

$$\text{Dividend cover} = \frac{\text{Net profit after both tax and preference dividends}}{\text{Ordinary dividends paid and proposed}}$$

This gives the shareholder some idea as to the proportion that the ordinary dividends bear to the amount available for distribution to ordinary shareholders. Usually, the dividend is described as being so many times covered by profits made. If therefore the dividend is said to be *three times covered*, it means that one-third of the available profits are being distributed as dividends.

3 Capital gearing ratio

There is more than one way of calculating this ratio. The most common method is:

$$\text{Capital gearing ratio} = \frac{\text{Preference shares + long-term loans}}{\text{All shareholders' funds + long-term loans}} \times 100$$

Let us look at the calculations for three companies:

	R Ltd £	S Ltd £	T Ltd £
Ordinary shares of £1	6,000	4,000	2,000
Profit and loss account	1,000	1,000	1,000
8% preference shares of £1	1,000	2,000	3,000
10% debentures	2,000	3,000	4,000
	10,000	10,000	10,000

R Ltd	S Ltd	T Ltd
$\dfrac{1,000 + 2,000}{10,000} \times 100 = 30\%$	$\dfrac{2,000 + 3,000}{10,000} \times 100 = 50\%$	$\dfrac{3,000 + 4,000}{10,000} \times 100 = 70\%$

A company financed by a high level of borrowing (whether long-term loans or preference shares) is called a **highly-geared company**. A company is **lowly-geared** when it has a low level of borrowing.

With a highly-geared company a change in profits has a much greater proportionate effect upon profits available for ordinary shareholders than in a lowly-geared company. Example 43.3 illustrates this.

Example 43.3

For each of the three companies, R Ltd, S Ltd and T Ltd, the amounts payable in debenture interest and preference dividends are:

	R Ltd £	S Ltd £	T Ltd £
8% preference dividend	80	160	240
10% debenture interest	200	300	400
Total prior charges	280	460	640

The profit, before debenture interest and preference dividends, was identical for each of the companies for the first three years of their existence. The profits were: *Year 1* £640; *Year 2* £1,000; *Year 3* £2,000. The profits available to ordinary shareholders were as follows:

	Gearing		
	Low	*Medium*	*High*
Year 1	R Ltd	S Ltd	T Ltd
Profits	640	640	640
Less prior charges	280	460	640
Available to ordinary shareholders	360	180	–
Year 2			
Profits	1,000	1,000	1,000
Less prior charges	280	460	640
Available to ordinary shareholders	720	540	360
Year 3			
Profits	2,000	2,000	2,000
Less prior charges	280	460	640
Available to ordinary shareholders	1,720	1,540	1,360

Profit available per ordinary share, is found by dividing the available profit by the number of ordinary shares:

	R Ltd	S Ltd	T Ltd
Year 1	6.0p	4.5p	–
Year 2	12.0p	13.5p	18.0p
Year 3	28.7p	38.5p	68.0p

Lowly-geared companies see a lesser change in ordinary dividends than highly-geared companies.

43.6 Fixed costs and variable costs

Some costs will remain constant whether the level of business activity increases or falls, at least within a given range of change of activity. These costs are called **fixed costs**. An example of this would be the rent of a shop which would remain at the same figure, whether sales increased 10% or fell 10%. The same would remain true of such things as rates, fire insurance and so on.

Wages of shop assistants could also remain constant in such a case. If, for instance, the shop employed two assistants, then it would probably keep the same two assistants, on the same wages, whether sales increased or fell by 10%.

Of course, such 'fixed costs' can only be viewed as fixed in the short term. If sales doubled, then the business might well need a larger shop or more assistants. A larger shop would also certainly mean higher rates, higher fire insurance and so on, and with more assistants the total wage bill would be larger.

Variable costs on the other hand will change with swings in activity. Suppose that wrapping materials are used in the shop, then it could well be that an increase in sales of 10% may see 10% more wrapping materials used. Similarly an increase of 10% of sales, if all sales are despatched by parcel post, could well see delivery charges increase by 10%.

Some costs could be partly fixed and partly variable. Suppose that because of an increase in sales of 10%, telephone calls made increased by 10%. With telephone bills the cost falls into two parts, one for the rent of the phone and the second part corresponding to the actual number of calls made. The rent would not change in such a case, and therefore this part of the telephone expense would be 'fixed' whereas the calls part of the expense could increase by 10%.

This means that the effect of a percentage change in the level of business activity could result in a different percentage change in net profit, because the fixed costs (within that range of activity) may not alter.

Example 43.4 shows the change in net profit in Business A which has a low proportion of its costs as 'fixed' costs, whereas in Business B the 'fixed' costs are a relatively higher proportion of its expenses.

Example 43.4

Business A	Actual £	Actual £	If sales fell 10% £	If sales fell 10% £	If sales rose 10% £	If sales rose 10% £
Sales		50,000		45,000		55,000
Less Cost of goods sold		30,000		27,000		33,000
		20,000		18,000		22,000
Gross profit						
Less Expenses:						
Fixed	3,000		3,000		3,000	
Variable	13,000	16,000	11,700	14,700	14,300	17,300
Net profit		4,000		3,300		4,700

Business B	Actual £	£	If sales fell 10% £	£	If sales rose 10% £	£
Sales		50,000		45,000		55,000
Less Cost of goods sold		30,000		27,000		33,000
		20,000		18,000		22,000
Gross profit						
Less Expenses:						
Fixed	12,000		12,000		12,000	
Variable	4,000	16,000	3,600	15,600	4,400	16,400
Net profit		4,000		2,400		5,600

The comparison of percentage changes in net profit therefore works out as follows:

Business A | **Business B**

10% decrease in sales

$$\frac{\text{Reduction in profit}}{\text{Original profit}} \times \frac{100}{1} \quad \frac{700}{4,000} \times \frac{100}{1} = 17.5\% \qquad \frac{1,600}{4,000} \times \frac{100}{1} = 40\%$$

10% increase in sales

$$\frac{\text{Increase in profit}}{\text{Original profit}} \times \frac{100}{1} \quad \frac{700}{4,000} \times \frac{100}{1} = 17.5\% \qquad \frac{1,600}{4,000} \times \frac{100}{1} = 40\%$$

It can be seen that a change in the level of business activity in Business B which has a higher proportion of fixed costs relative to its total costs, will result in greater percentage changes in profit, 40% in B compared with 17.5% in A.

43.7 Trend figures

It is not advisable to base decisions on just one year's accounts, if more information is available. What is important for a business is not just what accounting ratios are for one year, but what the trend has been.

Given two similar types of businesses G and H, both having existed for 5 years, if both of them had exactly the same ratios in year 5, are they both exactly desirable as investments? Given one year's accounts it may appear so, but if one had all the 5 years' figures it may not give the same picture, as Example 43.5 illustrates.

Example 43.5

		1	2	3	4	5 (current)
		Years				
Gross profit as % of sales	G	40%	38%	36%	35%	34%
	H	30%	32%	33%	33%	34%
Net profit as % of sales	G	15%	13%	12%	12%	11%
	H	10%	10%	10%	11%	11%
Net profit as % of capital employed	G	13%	12%	11%	11%	10%
	H	8%	8%	9%	9%	10%
Current ratio	G	3	2.8	2.6	2.3	2.0
	H	1.5	1.7	1.9	2.0	2.0

From these figures G appears to be the worst investment for the future, as the trend appears to be downwards. If the trend for G is continued it could be in a very dangerous financial situation in a year or two. Business H, on the other hand, is strengthening its position all the time.

Of course, it would be ridiculous to assert that H will continue on an upward trend. One would have to know more about the business to be able to judge whether or not that could be true.

However, given all other desirable information, trend figures would be an extra important indicator.

43.8 Some limitations of accounting statements

Final accounts are only partial information. They show the reader of them, in financial terms, what has happened *in the past*. This is better than having no information at all, but one needs to know much more.

First, it is impossible to sensibly compare two businesses which are completely unlike one another. To compare a supermarket's figures with those of a chemical factory would be rather pointless.

Second, there are a whole lot of factors that the past accounts do not disclose. The desire to keep to the money measurement concept, and the desire to be objective, both dealt with in Chapter 11, exclude a great deal of potentially useful information. Some such information can be listed, but beware, the list is indicative rather than exhaustive.

(*a*) What are the future plans of the business? Without this an investment in a business would be sheer guesswork.

(*b*) Has the firm got good quality staff?

(*c*) Is the business situated in a location desirable for such a business? A ship-building business situated a long way up a river which was becoming unnavigable, to use an extreme example, could soon be in trouble.

(*d*) What is its position as compared with its competitors? A business manufacturing a single product, which has a foreign competitor which has just invented a much improved product which will capture the whole market, is obviously in for a bad time.

(*e*) Will future government regulations affect it? Suppose that a business which is an importer of goods from Country X, which is outside the EU, finds that the EU is to ban all imports from Country X?

(*f*) Is its plant and machinery obsolete? If so, the business may not have sufficient funds to be able to replace it.

(*g*) Is the business of a high-risk type or in a relatively stable industry?

(*h*) Has the business got good customers? A business selling largely to Country Y, which is getting into trouble because of shortage of foreign exchange, could soon lose most of its trade. Also if one customer was responsible for, say, 60% of sales, then the loss of that one customer would be calamitous.

(*i*) Has the business got good suppliers? A business in wholesaling could, for example, be forced to close down if manufacturers decided to sell directly to the general public.

(*j*) Problems concerned with the effects of distortion of accounting figures caused by inflation (or deflation).

The reader can now see that the list would have to be an extremely long one if it was intended to cover all possibilities.

43.9 Further aspects of accounting concepts and conventions

In Chapter 11 you were introduced to the concepts and conventions used in accounting. Since then further chapters have consolidated your knowledge on specific points.

In recent years there has been a considerable change in the style of examinations in accounting at all levels. At one time practically every examination question was simply of a computational nature, requiring you to prepare final accounts, draft journal entries, extract a trial balance and so on. Now, *in addition* to all that (which is still important) there are quite a lot of questions asking such things as:

- Why do we do it?
- What does it mean?
- How does it relate to the concepts and conventions?

Such questions depend very much on the interests and ingenuity of examiners. They like to set questions worded to find out those who can understand and interpret financial information, and eliminate those who cannot and simply try to repeat information learned by rote.

The examiners will often draw on knowledge from any part of a syllabus. It is therefore impossible for a student (or an author) to guess exactly how an examiner will select a question and how he will word it.

An example of this is where the examiner could ask you to show how different concepts contradict one another. Someone who has read about the concepts, and memorised them, could not answer this unless they had thought further about it. Think about whether or not you could have answered that question before you read further.

One example is the use of the concept of consistency. Basically that concept states that one should be consistent in accounting for similar items from year to year. Yet if the net realisable value of stock is less than cost, then the normal method of showing it at cost should be abandoned and the net realisable value used instead. Thus, at the end of one period, stock may be shown at cost and at the end of the next period it will be shown at net realisable value. In this case the concept of prudence has overridden the concept of consistency.

Another example is that of calculating profit based on sales whether they have been paid for or not. If the prudence concept was taken to an extreme, then profit would only be calculated on a sale when the sale had been paid for. Instead the realisation concept has overridden the prudence concept.

Review questions 43.11 to 43.18 are typical examination questions which relate to concepts and conventions, and to a general understanding of the subject.

Review questions

In addition to the questions which follow, you should attempt questions 335–349 in the accompanying book of multiple-choice questions (see back cover for details).

Suggested solutions to review questions with the letter 'A' after the question number are given in Appendix I (pages 655–61).

43.1A   You are to study the following financial statements for two similar types of retail store and then answer the questions which follow.

Summary of Profit & Loss Accounts	Retail Store A		Retail Store B	
	£	£	£	£
Sales		80,000		120,000
Less Cost of goods sold				
Opening stock	25,000		22,500	
Add Purchases	50,000		91,000	
	75,000		113,500	
Less Closing stock	15,000	60,000	17,500	96,000
Gross profit		20,000		24,000
Less Depreciation	1,000		3,000	
Other expenses	9,000	10,000	6,000	9,000
Net profit		10,000		15,000

Summary of Balance Sheets	Retail Store A		Retail Store B	
Fixed assets				
Equipment at cost	10,000		20,000	
Less Depreciation to date	8,000	2,000	6,000	14,000
Current assets				
Stock	15,000		17,500	
Debtors	25,000		20,000	
Bank	5,000		2,500	
	45,000		40,000	
Less Current liabilities				
Creditors	5,000	40,000	10,000	30,000
		42,000		44,000
Financed by:				
Capital				
Balance at the start of the year		38,000		36,000
Add Net profit for the year		10,000		15,000
		48,000		51,000
Less Drawings		6,000		7,000
		42,000		44,000

Required:

(a) Calculate the following ratios:

(i) gross profit as percentage of sales;
(ii) net profit as percentage of sales;
(iii) expenses as percentage of sales;
(iv) stockturn;
(v) rate of return of net profit on capital employed (use the average of the capital account for this purpose);

(vi) current ratio;
(vii) acid test ratio;
(viii) average period of credit given to debtors;
(ix) average period of credit taken from creditors.

(b) Drawing upon all your knowledge of accounting, comment upon the differences, and similarities of the accounting ratios for A and B. Which business seems to be more efficient? Give possible reasons.

43.2 Study the following accounts of two companies and then answer the questions which follow. Both companies are stores selling textile goods.

Trading and Profit and Loss Accounts

	R Ltd		T Ltd	
	£	£	£	£
Sales		250,000		160,000
Less Cost of goods sold				
Opening stock	90,000		30,000	
Add Purchases	210,000		120,000	
	300,000		150,000	
Less Closing stock	110,000	190,000	50,000	100,000
Gross profit		60,000		60,000
Less Expenses:				
Wages and salaries	14,000		10,000	
Directors' remuneration	10,000		10,000	
Other expenses	11,000	35,000	8,000	28,000
Net profit		25,000		32,000
Add Balance from last year		15,000		8,000
		40,000		40,000
Less Appropriations				
General reserve	2,000		2,000	
Dividend	25,000	27,000	20,000	22,000
Balance carried to next year		13,000		18,000

Balance sheets

	R Ltd		T Ltd	
	£	£	£	£
Fixed assets				
Equipment at cost	20,000		5,000	
Less Depreciation to date	8,000	12,000	2,000	3,000
Lorries	30,000		20,000	
Less Depreciation to date	12,000	18,000	7,000	13,000
		30,000		16,000
Current assets				
Stock	110,000		50,000	
Debtors	62,500		20,000	
Bank	7,500		10,000	
	180,000		80,000	
Less Current liabilities				
Creditors	90,000		16,000	
		90,000		64,000
		120,000		80,000
Financed by:				
Issued share capital		100,000		50,000
Reserves				
General reserve	7,000		12,000	
Profit and loss	13,000	20,000	18,000	30,000
		120,000		80,000

Required:

(a) Calculate the following ratios for each of *R Ltd* and *T Ltd*:

(i) gross profit as percentage of sales;	(vi) current ratio;
(ii) net profit as percentage of sales;	(vii) acid test ratio;
(iii) expenses as percentage of sales;	(viii) average period of credit given to debtors;
(iv) stockturn;	
(v) return on capital employed (for the purpose of this question only, take capital as being total of share capitals + reserves at the balance sheet date);	(ix) average period of credit taken from creditors.

(b) Comment briefly on the comparison of each ratio as between the two companies. State which company appears to be the more efficient, giving what you consider to be possible reasons.

43.3 The following information has been extracted from the books of Jones Ltd for the year ended 31st December:

Extract from the Profit and Loss Account

Sales	£150,000
Purchases	£100,000
Opening stock 1st January	£30,000
Closing stock 31st December	£50,000

Extract from the Balance Sheet

Fixed assets	£170,000
Cash in bank	£6,000
Debtors	£25,000
Stock	£50,000
Creditors	£30,000
Accruals	£10,000
Short-term bank loan	£14,000

Requirements:

(a) Calculate the following ratios for Jones Ltd:
   (i) Stock turnover;
   (ii) Current ratio;
   (iii) Liquid (or acid-test) ratio; and
(b) Explain briefly the significance of any one of the above ratios.

(*IATI Foundation Examination*)

43.4A Balance Sheets of J Giles are as follows:

	Year 1		Year 2	
	£	£	£	£
Fixed assets		260,000		205,000
Current assets				
Stocks	86,000		84,000	
Debtors	94,000		58,000	
	180,000		142,000	
Current liabilities	(174,000)	6,000	(59,000)	83,000
		266,000		288,000
Capital				
Opening balance		262,900		266,000
Add net profit		15,600		36,000
Less drawings		(12,500)		(14,000)
Closing balance		266,000		288,000

The following information was extracted from the Trading Accounts for the two years:

	Year 1	Year 2
Sales	£505,000	£385,000
Gross profit	£152,900	£172,750
Opening stock	£82,000	£86,000

Required:
Calculate the following ratios for each year and comment on the position shown for the second year as compared to the first:

1 Gross Profit Ratio;
2 Stock Turnover;
3 Working Capital Ratio;
4 Acid-Test Ratio; and
5 Period of Credit Given.

(*ICPAI Formation I*)

43.5 Ted Sharp has completed his first year of business. The following figures have been extracted from his trading and profit and loss account and balance sheet.

Trading and Profit and Loss Account for the year ended 31st December

	£	£
Sales		400,000
Opening stock	80,000	
Purchases	310,000	
	390,000	
Closing stock	(120,000)	270,000
Gross profit		130,000
Selling expenses	32,000	
Entertainment expenses	41,000	
Administration expenses	23,000	
Financial expenses	9,000	
Depreciation	4,000	(109,000)
Net profit		21,000

Ted Sharp
Balance Sheet as at 31st December

	£	£
Fixed assets		
Cost	80,000	
Provision for depreciation	(15,000)	65,000
Current assets		
Stock	120,000	
Debtors	55,000	
Bank	38,000	
	213,000	
Current liabilities		
Creditors	(48,000)	
Net current assets		165,000
Net assets		230,000

All sales are on credit.

You are required to:
(a) Calculate each of the following ratios:
   (i)   Current ratio;
   (ii) Acid-test ratio;
   (iii) Stock turnover;
   (iv) Average period of credit given to debtors; and
(b) Comment briefly on any one of the above ratios.

(*IATI Foundation Examination*)

43.6A The following are the management accounts of Appliances Ltd, a retail electrical business, for the year ended 31st December:

Trading and Profit and Loss Account
for the Year Ended 31st December

	Small Electrical Goods		Large Electrical Goods		Total	
	£	£	£	£	£	£
Sales		30,000		70,000		100,000
Cost of goods sold						
Opening stock	4,000		10,000		14,000	
Purchases	24,000		60,000		84,000	
	28,000		70,000		98,000	
Less closing stock	(6,000)	22,000	(8,000)	62,000	(14,000)	84,000
Gross profit		8,000		8,000		16,000
Less expenses						(12,000)
Net profit						4,000

Appliances Ltd
Balance Sheet as at 31st December

Tangible fixed assets	Cost	Depreciation	Net book value
Leasehold property	80,000	16,000	64,000
Vehicles	24,000	12,000	12,000
Furniture and fittings	8,000	2,000	6,000
	112,000	30,000	82,000
Current assets			
Stocks	14,000		
Debtors	18,000	32,000	
Current liabilities			
Trade creditors	12,000		
VAT payable	12,000		
Bank overdraft	16,000	(40,000)	
Net current liabilities			−8,000
			74,000
Long-term liabilities			
Long-term loan			−39,000
			35,000
Capital and reserves			
Ordinary share capital			25,000
Revenue reserves			10,000
			35,000

Requirements:
(a) Calculate the following ratios for the year ended 31st December:
   (i) Gross profit percentage (for both small and large electrical goods);
   (ii) Stock turnover (for both small and large electrical goods);
   (iii) Current ratio;
   (iv) Liquid (acid-test) ratio;
   (v) Debtors days outstanding; and
   (vi) Creditors days outstanding.
(b) Comment on the financial position of Appliances Ltd in terms of both immediate liquidity and long-term liquidity; and
(c) Make suggestions as to how Appliances Ltd might improve its present financial position.

(IATI Admission Examination)

43.7A The trading stock of Joan Street, retailer, has been reduced during the year ended 31 March 19X8 by £6,000 from its commencing figure of £21,000.

A number of financial ratios and related statistics have been compiled relating to the business of Joan Street for the year ended 31 March 19X8; these are shown below alongside comparative figures for a number of retailers who are members of the trade association to which Joan Street belongs:

		Joan Street %	Trade association %
Net profit as % Net capital employed*		15	16
Net profit/sales		9	8
Sales/net capital employed		166⅔	200
Fixed assets/sales		45	35
Working capital ratio:	$\dfrac{\text{Current assets}}{\text{Current liabilities}}$	400	287½
Acid-test ratio:	$\dfrac{\text{Bank} + \text{Debtors}}{\text{Current liabilities}}$	275	187½
Gross profit/sales		25	26
Debtors collection period:	$\dfrac{\text{Debtors} \times 365}{\text{Sales}}$	36½ days	2¹⁷⁄₂₀ days
Stock turnover (based on average stock for the year)		10 times	8 times

Joan Street has supplied all the capital for her business and has had no drawings from the business during the year ended 31 March 19X8.

Required:

(a) Prepare the trading and profit and loss account for the year ended 31 March 19X8 and balance sheet as at that date of Joan Street in as much detail as possible.

(b) Identify two aspects of Joan Street's results for the year ended 31 March 19X8 which compare favourably with the trade association's figures and identify two aspects which compare unfavourably.

(c) Outline two drawbacks of the type of comparison used in this question.

(*Association of Accounting Technicians*)

Note from authors: Take closing figure at 31 March 19X8.

43.8 Harold Smart, a small manufacturer trading as Space Age Projects is very pleased with his recently completed financial results which show that a planned 20% increase in turnover has been achieved in the last accounting year.

The summarised results relating to the last three financial years are as follows:

Year ended 30 September	19X9 £	19X0 £	19X1 £
Sales	90,000	100,000	120,000
Cost of sales	74,000	75,000	92,000
Gross profit	16,000	25,000	28,000
Administrative overheads	3,000	5,000	6,000
Net profit	13,000	20,000	22,000

As at 30 September	19X8 £	19X9 £	19X0 £	19X1 £
Fixed assets:				
At cost	155,000	165,000	190,000	206,000
Provision for depreciation	42,000	45,000	49,000	53,000
	113,000	120,000	141,000	153,000
Current assets:				
Stock	3,000	4,000	7,000	30,000
Debtors	14,000	19,000	15,000	10,000
Balance at bank	2,000	1,000	3,000	–
	19,000	24,000	25,000	40,000
Current liabilities:				
Creditors	5,000	4,000	6,000	9,000
Bank overdraft	–	–	–	2,000
	5,000	4,000	6,000	11,000

Since 30 September 19X8, Harold Smart has not taken any drawings from the business.

Harold Smart has been invited recently to invest £150,000 for a 5-year fixed term government loan stock earning interest at 12½% per annum.

Note: Taxation is to be ignored.

Notwithstanding his response to these financial results. Harold Smart is a very cautious person and therefore has asked a financial consultant for a report.

Required:
(a) A schedule of six accounting ratios or measures of resource utilisation covering each of the three years ended 30 September 19X1 of Space Age Projects.
(b) As financial consultant prepare a report to Harold Smart on the financial results of Space Age Projects given above including comments on the alternative future actions that he might take.

Note: Reports should utilise the information given in answers to part (a) of this question.

(Association of Accounting Technicians)

43.9A   Business A and Business B are both engaged in retailing, but seem to take a different approach to this trade according to the information available. This information consists of a table of ratios, shown below:

Ratio	Business A	Business B
Current ratio	2:1	1.5:1
Quick (acid-test) ratio	1.7:1	0.7:1
Return on capital employed (ROCE)	20%	17%
Return on owners' equity (ROOE)	30%	18%
Period of credit given to debtors	63 days	21 days
Period of credit taken from creditors	50 days	45 days
Gross profit percentage	40%	15%
Net profit percentage	10%	10%
Stock turnover	52 days	25 days

Required:

(a) Explain briefly how each ratio is calculated.

(b) Describe what this information indicates about the differences in approach between the two businesses. If one of them prides itself on personal service and one of them on competitive prices, which do you think is which and why?

(*Association of Chartered Certified Accountants*)

43.10   You are given summarised information about two firms in the same line of business; A and B, as follows.

Balance Sheets as at 30 June	A			B		
	£000	*£000*	*£000*	*£000*	*£000*	*£000*
Land			80			260
Buildings		120			200	
Less: Depreciation		40	80		–	200
Plant		90			150	
Less: Depreciation		70	20		40	110
			180			570
Stocks		80			100	
Debtors		100			90	
Bank		–			10	
		180			200	
Creditors	110			120		
Bank	50			–		
		160			120	
Net current assets			20			80
			200			650
Capital at start of year			100			300
Profit for year			30			100
			130			400
Less: Drawings			30			40
			100			360
Land revaluation			–			160
Loan (10% p.a.)			100			130
			200			650

Profit and Loss information						
Sales			1,000			3,000
Cost of sales			400			2,000

Required:
(a) Produce a table of eight ratios calculated for both businesses.
(b) Write a report briefly outlining the strengths and weaknesses of the two businesses. Include comment on any major areas where the simple use of the figures could be misleading.

(Association of Chartered Certified Accountants)

43.11A The following letter has been received from a client. 'I gave my bank manager those audited accounts you prepared for last year. But he says he needs more information before he will agree to increase my overdraft. What could he possibly want to know that he can't get from those accounts? If they are not good enough why bother to prepare them?

Required:
Outline the major points which should be included in a reply to this letter.

(Association of Chartered Certified Accountants)

43.12A An acquaintance of yours, H Gee, has recently set up in business for the first time as a general dealer.

The majority of his sales will be on credit to trade buyers but he will sell some goods to the public for cash.

He is not sure at which point of the business cycle he can regard his cash and credit sales to have taken place.

After seeking guidance on this matter from his friends, he is thoroughly confused by the conflicting advice he has received. Samples of the advice he has been given include:

The sale takes place when:
(a) 'you have bought goods which you know you should be able to sell easily';
(b) 'the customer places the order';
(c) 'you deliver the goods to the customer';
(d) 'you invoice the goods to the customer';
(e) 'the customer pays for the goods';
(f) 'the customer's cheque has been cleared by the bank'.

He now asks you to clarify the position for him.

Required:
(a) Write notes for Gee, setting out, in as easily understood a manner as possible, the accounting conventions and principles which should generally be followed when recognising sales revenue.
(b) Examine each of the statements (a) to (f) above and advise Gee (stating your reasons) whether the method advocated is appropriate to the particular circumstances of his business.

(Association of Chartered Certified Accountants)

43.13A The annual final accounts of businesses are normally prepared on the assumption that the business is a going concern.

Required:
Explain and give a simple illustration of

(a) the effect of this convention on the figures which appear in those final accounts.
(b) the implications for the final accounts figures if this convention were deemed to be inoperative.

(Association of Chartered Certified Accountants)

43.14A One of the well-known accounting concepts is that of materiality.

Required:
(*a*) Explain what is meant by this concept.
(*b*) State and explain three types of situation to which this concept might be applicable.
(*c*) State and explain two specific difficulties in applying this concept.

(*Association of Chartered Certified Accountants*)

43.15A State three classes of people, other than managers and owners, who are likely to need to use financial accounting information. Discuss whether you think their requirements are compatible.

(*Association of Chartered Certified Accountants*)

43.16A A firm produces a standard manufactured product. The stages of the production and sale of the product may be summarised as follows:

Stage Activity	A Raw material	B WIP-I	C WIP-II	D Finished product
	£	£	£	£
Costs to date	100	120	150	170
Net realisable value	80	130	190	300

Stage Activity	E For sale	F Sale agreed	G Delivered	H Paid for
	£	£	£	£
Costs to date	170	170	180	180
Net realisable value	300	300	300	300

Required:
(*a*) What general rule do accountants apply when deciding when to recognise revenue on any particular transaction?
(*b*) Apply this rule to the above situation. State and explain the stage at which you think revenue will be recognised by accountants.
(*c*) How much would the gross profit on a unit of this product be? Why?
(*d*) Suggest arguments in favour of delaying the recognition of revenue until stage H.
(*e*) Suggest arguments in favour of recognising revenue in appropriate successive amounts at stages B, C and D.

(*Association of Chartered Certified Accountants*)

43.17A
(*a*) In accounting practice a distinction is drawn between the terms 'reserves' and 'provisions' and between 'accrued expenses' and 'creditors'.

Required:
Briefly define each of the four terms quoted and explain the effect of each on the preparation of accounts.

(*b*) While preparing the final accounts for year ended 30 September 19X3, the accountant of Lanep Lighting Ltd had to deal with the following matters:
(i) the exterior of the company's premises were being repaired. The contractors had started work in August but were unlikely to finish before the end of November 19X3. The total cost would not be known until after completion. Cost of work carried out to 30 September 19X3 was estimated at £21,000:
(ii) the company rented a sales showroom from Commercial Properties plc at a rental of £6,000 per annum payable half yearly in arrear on 1 August and 1 February;

(iii) on 3 October 19X3 an invoice was received for £2,500, less a trade discount of 30 per cent, from Lucifer Ltd for goods for resale supplied during September 19X3;

(iv) the directors of Lanep Lighting Ltd have decided that an annual amount of £5,000 should be set aside, starting with year ended 30 Sept 19X3, for the purpose of plant replacement.

Required:

State the accounting treatment which should be accorded to each of the above matters in the Lanep Lighting Ltd profit and loss account for year ended 30 September 19X3 and balance sheet at that date.

(Association of Chartered Certified Accountants)

43.18A Bradwich plc is a medium-sized engineering company whose shares are listed on a major Stock Exchange.

It has recently applied to its bankers for a 7-year loan of £500,000 to finance a modernisation and expansion programme.

Mr Whitehall, a recently retired civil servant, is contemplating investing £10,000 of his lump sum pension in the company's ordinary shares in order to provide both an income during his retirement and a legacy to his grandchildren after his death.

The bank and Mr Whitehall have each acquired copies of the company's most recent annual report and accounts.

Required:

(a) State, separately for each of the two parties, those aspects of the company's performance and financial position which would be of particular interest and relevance to their respective interests.

(b) State, separately for each of the two parties, the formula of four ratios which would assist in measuring or assessing the matters raised in your answer to (a).

(Association of Chartered Certified Accountants)

44

Analysis of financial information II: Ratio analysis continued

44.1 Introduction

In Chapter 43 accounting ratios and the interpretation of final accounts were introduced. The present chapter takes the reader one stage further. On occasion the reader will be required to look again at factors already dealt with in the previous chapter, but it may be in greater depth or with a different slant.

Accounting information summarises the economic performance and situation of a business. In order to make use of this information the user needs to analyse and interpret its meaning. When confronted with information it is useful to have a framework of analysis available to make an attempt to distil what is important from the mass of less important data.

A mechanic confronted with a car that is refusing to start has a set of routine checks which will by elimination help to identify the problem. Someone without the appropriate knowledge can feel helpless faced with the complex array of electrical and mechanical parts under the bonnet of a car.

A business is in many ways more complex than a car. In a car cause and effect can be traced through a mechanical sequence. A thorough check will show the fault and a repair can be made. If a business's sales decline, however, the cause may be clearly identifiable; on the other hand the problem may be due to a variety of causes, some of which are human problems and may not be so easily diagnosed. A business consists of people interacting amongst themselves as well as with the mechanical means of production at their disposal. The human behaviour element may not always lend itself to logical and systematic analysis.

Having said this, however, the first stage in analysis is the development of a systematic review of the accounting data. In this respect accounting ratios are relationships which bring together the results of activity which experience shows identify the key areas for success of the business.

The choice of ratios will be determined by the needs of the user of the information. In this chapter the ratios which are illustrated are divided into main groups which may be identified with the requirements of particular users. However, this division, whilst it is useful as an aid to our memory and in developing a logical approach, should not be taken as a set of rigid rules. A supplier of goods on credit to a firm will mainly be interested in his customer's immediate ability to repay him, which will be measured by liquidity ratios, but he will also be interested in the overall future and prospects of the customer measured by the profitability and other ratios.

The main parties interested in accounts include shareholders and potential shareholders, creditors, lenders, the Government for taxation and statistical purposes, potential take-over bidders, employees particularly through their trade unions, as well as management.

The interests of the various parties have been summarised in Exhibit 44.1 which divides the types of ratio into five main categories. In this book it is not possible to show all possibly useful ratios since these can run to many hundreds, rather generally useful common ratios are illustrated. In practice it is sensible to calculate as many ratios as appear useful for the required objective.

Exhibit 44.1

Examples of parties with an immediate interest	Type of ratio
Potential suppliers of goods on credit; lenders, e.g. bank managers and debenture holders; management.	*Liquidity (credit risk)*: Ratios indicating how well equipped the business is to pay its way.
Shareholders (actual and potential); potential take-over bidders; lenders; management; competitive firms; tax authorities; employees.	*Profitability*: How successfully is the business trading?
Shareholders (actual and potential); potential take-over bidders; management; competitive firms; employees.	*Use of assets*: How effectively are the assets of the firm utilised?
Shareholders (actual and potential); potential take-over bidders; management lenders; and creditors in assessing risk.	*Capital structure*: How does the capital structure of the firm affect the cost of capital and the return to shareholders?
Shareholders (actual and potential); potential take-over bidders; management.	*Investment*: Show how the market prices for a share reflect a company's performance.

Exhibit 44.2 shows a set of accounts prepared for The Rational Company Ltd. The various types of ratio mentioned in Exhibit 44.1 will be illustrated using the data for The Rational Company Ltd.

Exhibit 44.2

The Rational Co. Ltd
Profit and Loss Account for the year ended 31 December

	£	£
Turnover		900,000
Cost of sales		780,000
Gross profit		120,000
Distribution costs	27,000	
Administrative expenses	30,000	57,000
		63,000
Other operating income (Royalties)		4,700
		67,700
Interest payable		15,700
Profit on ordinary activities before taxation		52,000
Tax on profit on ordinary activities		22,000
Profit for the year on ordinary activities after taxation		30,000
Undistributed profits from last year		107,400
		137,400
Preference dividend paid	2,400	
Proposed ordinary dividend	15,000	17,400
Undistributed profits carried to next year		120,000

The Rational Co. Ltd
Abridged Balance Sheet as at 31 December

	Cost £	Depreciation £	Net £
Fixed Assets			
Land and buildings	500,000	140,000	360,000
Plant	40,000	10,000	30,000
	540,000	150,000	390,000
Current Assets			
Stock		90,000	
Debtors		105,000	
Bank		15,000	
		210,000	
Less Current liabilities			
Trade creditors	21,000		
Bank overdraft	32,000		
Current taxation	22,000		
Proposed ordinary dividend	15,000	90,000	
Net current assets			120,000
			510,000
Debentures 7%			210,000
			300,000
Capital and reserves			
Called-up share capital			
Ordinary shares		150,000	
8% preference shares		30,000	180,000
Profit and loss account			120,000
			300,000

NB The market price of an ordinary share at 31 December was £3.

44.2 Liquidity ratios in more detail

The analysis of credit risk was the historic starting point for formal ratio analysis. With widely scattered markets a firm is frequently asked to trade with companies of which it has little or no knowledge. The risks of supplying goods on credit to a strange company are fairly obvious and in practice can be very hazardous. Many small businesses have themselves been forced to wind up because a large customer has failed to pay its debt. It is hardly surprising that firms specialising in giving advice on credit risks should have come into existence. These firms started the consistent use of ratios to analyse company balance sheets. Usually they are operating as outsiders and therefore have to rely on published information, in contrast to the management of a business who can obtain much more detailed information about that business. The following ratios are useful in the measurement of liquidity.

The current ratio

The **current ratio** measures current assets : current liabilities. In general terms we are comparing assets which will become liquid in approximately twelve months with liabilities which will be due for payment in the same period.

In interpreting the ratio a creditor will want to see a sufficiently large amount of current assets to cover liabilities and the eventuality of losses. It is hard, however, to say exactly what is satisfactory, since factors of type of industry and overall size and reputation of the firm will play a part. A commonly used rule of thumb would be 2:1, in other words £2 of current assets for £1 of current liability, but many very good firms show a lower ratio, whilst some bad ones, by over-valuing assets, show a much higher ratio. Referring to Exhibit 44.2 the current ratio is 210,000 : 90,000 = 2.3:1. This may also be conveniently expressed by $\frac{210,000}{90,000}$ = 2.3 times.

The acid test ratio

In order to refine the analysis of the current ratio another ratio is used which takes only those current assets which are cash or will convert very quickly into cash. This will normally mean cash and debtors or current assets *less* stock. The **acid test ratio** may, therefore, be stated as:

Current assets *less* stock : Current liabilities
The ratio calculated from Exhibit 44.2 is:

$$\frac{120,000}{90,000} = 1.3 \text{ times.}$$

This shows that provided creditors and debtors are paid at approximately the same time, the company has sufficient liquid resources to meet its current liabilities. If a large proportion of the current assets had been in the form of stock the liquid position might have been dangerously low.

The ratios shown under credit risk have been concerned with liquidity. A useful supplement to this type of analysis is provided by **cash flow statements.** From the point of view of management, the forecast cash flow statement is the most useful statement for control of credit. For those outside the firm, however, this information is not usually available and they must rely on the ratios.

44.3 Profitability ratios in more detail

Profitability is the end-product of the policies and decisions taken by a firm, and is its single most important measure of success.

Gross profit/sales

From Exhibit 44.2 the ratio for the Rational Company Ltd is $\dfrac{120,000}{900,000} = 0.133$ or as a percentage on sales = 13.3%.

It is impossible to state a rule of thumb for this figure which will vary considerably from firm to firm and industry to industry.

Net profit (after tax)/sales

The same comments apply to Net profit/Sales as to Gross profit/Sales. The difference between the two ratios will be explained by measuring the ratios of sales to the expenses in the profit and loss account. The ratio from Exhibit 44.2 is $\dfrac{30,000}{900,000} = 0.033 = 3.3\%$.

This percentage of 3.3 indicates by how much the profit margin can decline before the firm makes losses.

Return on capital employed

Great care must be exercised in measuring ratios of profit to capital employed. There are no standard definitions and thus for comparability it is necessary to ensure that the same method is used over time for the same firm or between different firms. Another problem is inherent in comparing profit which arises over a period of time, with capital employed which is taken from the balance sheet and is thus measured at one point of time. For a proper evaluation the capital employed needs to be an average figure for the accounting period in which the profit was calculated. As an external analyst the only data available is at the beginning and end of the accounting period. Since the year end is by no means likely to be representative of the average for a period any calculated figure must be taken with caution. If, for example, an analyst knows that a major investment in fixed assets took place mid-way through the year, he would tend to average the opening and closing figures. If little change has taken place, then the year end figure may be used.

Net profit (after tax)/total assets

In this calculation of return on capital employed the total assets are defined as all fixed and other non-current assets plus working capital. Working capital is simply the figure reached by deducting current liabilities from current assets (assuming that current assets exceed current liabilities). Using the data from Exhibit 44.2 the working capital is Current assets £210,000 *less* Current liabilities £90,000 = £120,000. The total assets are therefore fixed assets £390,000 + Working capital £120,000 = £510,000 and the return is:

$$\frac{\text{Net profit (after tax)}}{\text{Total assets}} = \frac{30,000}{510,000} = 5.88\%$$

One of the problems with using this approach to return on capital is that net profit after tax will already have had interest on debentures, loans and overdrafts charged against it and thus if this interest is significant the return on assets will be understated.

Similarly if the assets of the business include items of an intangible nature such as goodwill it is often felt that the return on assets is better related to tangible assets alone, since the accounting valuation of intangibles varies so much.

To answer these problems the following ratio is often used:

> **Net operating profit/Operating assets**

The aim here is to take the operating profit which is the outcome of operations before interest charges are made or any investment income is included. This profit will then be taken over operating assets which are the tangible assets used in the generation of the operating income. Operating assets will not include intangibles nor investments in shares or other securities outside the firm, whether shown under a separate heading or as current assets.

As with the previous calculation of total assets it is appropriate to take working capital as part of operating assets but in this definition it is frequently appropriate to exclude bank overdraft from current liabilities. Although from a legal point of view and from the bank's intention it is a current liability, since repayment can be demanded at short notice: in practice for a well-run business the bank is usually happy to maintain an overdraft over extended periods of time. Unlike most of the other current liabilities interest is chargeable on overdrafts.

Thus this definition of return on capital employed is Net operating profit: Tangible operating fixed assets + (Working capital + Overdraft). Referring to Exhibit 44.2 this is equal to £390,000 + £120,000 + £32,000 = £542,000. This is equivalent to:

> Share capital £180,000 + Reserves £120,000 + Debentures £210,000 +
> Bank overdraft £32,000 = £542,000.

The net operating profit which in Exhibit 44.2 = £67,700 is the profit obtained from the capital employed before paying interest or dividends to any of these sources of capital. This return on capital employed in the Rational Company Ltd is therefore

$$\frac{67,700}{542,000} = 12.49\%.$$

Net profit (after taxes)/owners' equity

In this case the net profit after tax (*less* preference dividends) is compared with the ordinary shareholders' stake in the business, i.e. ordinary share capital plus reserves. From Exhibit 44.2 the ratio is $\frac{£27,600}{£270,000} = 10.2\%$.

In contrast to the previous ratio this one is not an overall measure of profitability but is specially concerned with the return an ordinary shareholder might expect.

44.4 Asset utilisation ratios

Although the way assets are utilised will affect profitability, these particular ratios deserve to be evaluated separately as they are of great importance. In effect they show how effectively management has been using the assets at their disposal.

A straightforward ratio between assets and sales can be used by the external analyst. For the Rational Co Ltd we should show:

Land and buildings	: Sales	360,000:900,000	= 1: 2.5
Plant	: Sales	30,000:900,000	= 1: 30.0
Total fixed assets	: Sales	390,000:900,000	= 1: 2.3
Stock-in-trade	: Sales	90,000:900,000	= 1: 10.0
Debtors	: Sales	105,000:900,000	= 1: 8.6
Cash at bank	: Sales	15,000:900,000	= 1: 60.0
Total current assets	: Sales	210,000:900,000	= 1: 4.3

It is often convenient to express these ratios in terms of 'per £1,000 of sales' to avoid too much 'rounding off'. For example, land and buildings per £1,000 of sales would be £400, i.e. (360,000 ÷ 900).

A number of these activity ratios are sufficiently important to merit special mention and in some cases detailed development.

Sales/fixed assets

The ratio of sales to fixed assets measures the utilisation a firm is obtaining from its investment in fixed plant. If the ratio is low, it indicates that management may not be utilising its plant very effectively. In the illustration from Exhibit 44.2 the ratio is 2.3 times, or £433.3 per £1,000 of sales.

Stock turnover

This important ratio, which may also be considered as a liquidity ratio, was introduced in Section 43.3, is measured in the first instance by dividing sales by stock. Since sales are at selling prices, the stock should also be measured at selling price. Usually an easier way is to divide sales at cost price (which is the cost of goods sold total) by stock at cost value. The stock figure used should be an average figure for the year. While the true average will be known to management it will often not be available to outsiders. In this situation a very rough approximation is used by taking the average of the opening and closing stocks. If in the example in Exhibit 44.2, the stock at 1 January had been £50,000 and the stock at 31 December is £90,000 the average would be taken as:

$$\frac{50,000 + 90,000}{2} = £70,000.$$

The stock turnover therefore is

$$\frac{\text{Cost of goods sold}}{\text{Stock}} = \frac{780,000}{70,000} = 11.1 \text{ times.}$$

If the cost of goods sold is not known, it may be necessary to use the sales figure instead. Although this is not a satisfactory basis, it may be better than nothing if like is compared with like. Notice that in this example stock turnover = 12.86 times if the sales figure is used (900,000 ÷ 70,000).

Collection period for debtors

We have already calculated the relationship of debtors to sales in Section 43.3 where this was considered under the heading of liquidity, which in the example is 1:8.6. This means that for every £8.6 sold there is £1 of debtors outstanding.

This relationship is often translated into the length of time a debtor takes to pay. If we assume that the sales for the Rational Company Ltd are made over the whole of one year, i.e. 365 days, this means that on average a debt is outstanding for

$365 \times \dfrac{1}{8.6} = 42.4$ days. Notice that it is assumed that sales take place evenly over the year, and we have ignored holidays. However it is useful to know that our customers take about 6 weeks to pay!

In recent years the interest in productivity measurement has focused interest on many ratios which combine information which is not essentially part of the accounts with accounting data. Published accounts for example are now required to show as supplementary information the average number of people employed by a limited company. This information may be related to sales to give an index of sales per employee. For example, if the average number employed by the Rational Company was 215, then sales per employee would be $\dfrac{£900,000}{215} = £4,186$. This example is given as an illustration of the development of this type of measurement which may be a useful guide to assessment of a company's performance.

44.5 Capital structure ratios

The capital structure of a business is important because it has a significant influence on the risk to lenders, and on the return to shareholders.

In the first instance it is worthwhile to express the balance sheet in percentage terms. For the Rational Company using the main sub-totals it would be as follows:

Balance Sheet as at 31 December

		% of Balance Sheet Totals
Fixed assets		130
Current assets	70	
Less Current liabilities	30	40
		170
Less Debentures		(70)
		100
Ordinary shares		50
Preference shares		10
Profit and loss account		40
		100

Net worth/total assets

From this it can be seen that ordinary shares and preference shares together with reserves, the total of which is often called net worth, is providing 50% of the financing of fixed and current assets. Thus the ratio Net worth : Fixed assets + Current assets is an important measure of the shareholder stake in a business (300,000 : 390,000 + 210,000 = 1:2).

Fixed assets/net worth

From the balance sheet it is also easy to see that a high proportion of the assets (65%) are fixed assets. A comparison of the fixed assets with net worth shows whether the longer term investment usually involved in fixed assets is provided by shareholders. In our example the ratio is £390,000 : £300,000 (or 65% : 50%) = 1 : 0.77. This ratio shows that shareholders are not providing all the investment required to finance the fixed assets

quite apart from current assets. The remainder of the funding of assets is provided by borrowing. The important thing here is to ensure that the borrowing is sufficiently long-term to match the investment in fixed assets. If the company has to repay borrowing whilst all its resources are locked into assets which cannot easily be converted into cash, it can only make repayment by fresh borrowing or new capital issues which may cause problems.

Fixed assets/net worth and long-term loans

Provided the mortgage debenture has a reasonably long life the Rational Company provides reasonable cover of its fixed assets since Fixed assets : Net worth + Long-term loan are in the ratio 1:1.31 (390 : 510).

Coverage of fixed charges

This relationship is obtained by dividing net profit by any fixed interest charges or rentals. Since these charges are allowable expenses for tax purposes, the profit before tax will be used. From Exhibit 44.2 the interest charges are £15,700 with no rental expense. The available profit before tax is £52,000 + £15,700 = £67,700. The fixed charges are, therefore, covered:

$$\frac{\text{Profit before tax} + \text{Fixed charges}}{\text{Fixed charges}} = \frac{67,700}{15,700} = 4.3 \text{ times.}$$

This is low enough to indicate a company which is high geared.

By 'high geared' is meant a company which has a high proportion of borrowing to net worth. A company with no gearing has all its funds provided by the ordinary shareholder. Gearing has also been measured indirectly in the ratio of Net worth : Total assets. The lower the proportion of funds provided from net worth, the higher the borrowing and hence gearing.

The coverage of fixed charges gives a very important measure of the extent to which the profit may decline before the company is not able to earn enough to cover the interest etc. it is legally obliged to pay. If charges are not paid, legal steps will be taken against the company which usually end in its being taken over or wound up.

Borrowings/net worth

This ratio is the most direct measure of gearing since it indicates the proportions in which all funds are provided for the business. Borrowing is taken as all the long-term and current liabilities of the business and net worth as share capital and reserves. In this definition preference shares are included in net worth. Although the return to preference shareholders is a fixed rate interest there is no legal obligation for the company to pay it, hence the inclusion with net worth. If you are, however, looking at the effect of gearing on the return to ordinary shareholders, it may then be appropriate to treat preference share dividends as a fixed charge.

The ratio for the Rational Co Ltd is thus £210,000 + £90,000 : 300,000 = 1:1.

44.6 Investment ratios

These ratios are important for the investor and financial manager who is interested in the market prices of the shares of a company on the Stock Exchange.

Dividend yield

This measures the real rate of return on an investment in shares, as distinct from the declared dividend rate which is based on the nominal value of a share. The yield is calculated as follows, illustrated from Exhibit 44.2:

$$\frac{\text{The dividend per share}}{\text{Market price per share}} = \frac{£1 \times 10\%}{£3} = 3.3\%.$$

Dividend cover for ordinary shares

This indicates the amount of profit for an ordinary dividend and indicates the amount of profit retained in the business. The cover is:

$$\frac{\text{Net profit for the year after tax} - \text{Preference dividend}}{\text{Dividend on ordinary shares}}$$

$$= \frac{£30,000 - 2,400}{15,000} = 1.8 \text{ times.}$$

EPS: Earnings per (ordinary) share

As is implied by the name this ratio is:

$$\frac{\text{Net profit for the year after tax} - \text{Preference dividend}}{\text{Number of ordinary shares}}$$

$$= \frac{£30,000 - 2,400}{150,000} = £0.18 \text{ per share.}$$

The calculation of this important ratio is governed by Statement of Standard Accounting Practice 3, as amended by Financial Reporting Standard 3.

PE ratio: the price earnings ratio

Finally the price earnings ratio relates the earnings per share to the price the shares sell at in the market. From Exhibit 44.2 the ratio is:

$$\frac{\text{Market price}}{\text{Earnings per share}} = \frac{£3}{£0.18} = 16.7$$

This relationship is an important indicator both to investor and financial manager of the market's evaluation of a share, and is very important when a new issue of shares is due since it shows the earnings the market expects in relation to the current share prices.

44.7 Summary of principal ratios

Type of ratio	Method of calculation
● *Liquidity**	
Current ratio	$\dfrac{\text{Current assets}}{\text{Current liabilities}}$
Acid test ratio	$\dfrac{\text{Current assets } less \text{ Stock}}{\text{Current liabilities}}$
● *Profitability*	
Gross profit/Sales	$\dfrac{\text{Gross profit}}{\text{Sales}}$
Net profit after tax/Sales	$\dfrac{\text{Net profit after tax}}{\text{Sales}}$
● *Return on capital employed*	
Net profit after tax/Total assets	$\dfrac{\text{Net profit after tax}}{\text{Fixed and other assets + Working capital}}$
Net operating profit/Operating assets	$\dfrac{\text{Net operating income}}{\text{Tangible operating fixed assets + Working capital and overdraft}}$
Net profit (after tax)/Owners' equity	$\dfrac{\text{Net profit after tax } less \text{ Preference dividend}}{\text{Ordinary share capital + reserves}}$
● *Asset Utilisation*	
Asset/Sales	$\dfrac{\text{Individual asset totals}}{\text{Sales}}$
Sales/Fixed assets	$\dfrac{\text{Sales}}{\text{Fixed assets}}$
Stock turnover**	$\dfrac{\text{Cost of goods sold}}{\text{Average stock}}$
Collection period for debtors**	$365 \times \dfrac{\text{Debtors}}{\text{Sales}}$
● *Capital structure*	
Net worth/Total assets	$\dfrac{\text{Ordinary share capital + Preference S C + Reserves}}{\text{Fixed assets + Current assets}}$
Fixed assets/Net worth	$\dfrac{\text{Fixed assets}}{\text{Net worth}}$
Fixed assets/Net worth and Long-term loans	$\dfrac{\text{Fixed assets}}{\text{Net worth + Long-term loan}}$
Coverage of fixed charges	$\dfrac{\text{Net profit before tax and fixed charges}}{\text{Fixed charges}}$
Borrowings/Net worth	$\dfrac{\text{Long term + Current liabilities}}{\text{Net worth}}$
Capital gearing ratio	$\dfrac{\text{Preference shares + long-term loans}}{\text{All shareholders' fund + long-term loans}} \times 100$

Type of ratio	Method of calculation
● *Investment*	
Dividend yield	$\dfrac{\text{Dividend per share}}{\text{Market price per share}}$
Dividend cover for ordinary shares	$\dfrac{\text{Net profit after tax} - \text{Pref div}}{\text{Ordinary share dividends}}$
Earnings per ordinary share	$\dfrac{\text{Net profit after tax} - \text{Pref div}}{\text{Number of ordinary shares issued}}$
Price earnings ratio	$\dfrac{\text{Market price per share}}{\text{Earnings per share}}$

   * See also Asset Utilisation section.
 ** Could also be shown as liquidity ratios.

Review questions

In addition to the questions which follow, you should attempt questions 350–354 in the accompanying book of multiple-choice questions (see back cover for details).

    Suggested solutions to review questions with the letter 'A' after the question number are given in Appendix I (pages 661–2).

44.1 Describe five main groups of ratios and indicate who may be interested in each type.

44.2 Explain what you think the following ratios indicate about a firm:
(*a*) Acid test ratio.
(*b*) Net operating profit/Capital employed.
(*c*) Collection period for debtors.
(*d*) Net worth/Total assets.
(*e*) Dividend cover for ordinary shares.

44.3 Stock turnover is sometimes calculated by dividing sales by the average of the opening and closing stock in trade figures. What is wrong with this method of computation?

44.4A For each of the following items select the lettered item(s) which indicate(s) its effect(s) on the company accounts. More than one item may be affected.
1 Declaration and payment of a dividend on preference share capital.
2 Declaration of a proposed dividend on ordinary shares due for payment in one month.
3 Purchase of stock for cash.
4 Payment of creditors.
5 Bad debt written off against an existing provision for bad and doubtful debts.

Effect
A Reduces working capital.
B Increases working capital.
C Reduces current ratio.
D Increases current ratio.
E Reduces acid test ratio.
F Increases acid test ratio.

44.5 Describe four ratios which might help you to assess the profitability of a company and explain their significance.

44.6A A limited company with 100,000 £1 ordinary shares as its capital earns a profit after tax of £15,000. It pays a dividend of 10%. The market price of the shares is £1.50. What is the:

(a) Yield on ordinary shares?
(b) Earnings per share?
(c) Price/earnings ratio?

44.7 What ratios might be of particular interest to a potential holder of debentures in a limited company?

44.8A The following is a trading and profit and loss account of a small limited company engaged in manufacturing for the year ending 31 December.

	£000	£000
Sales (Credit)		150
Opening stock	20	
Purchases (credit)	120	
	140	
Less Closing stock	40	
	100	
Direct manufacturing expenses	20	
Overhead expenditure	10	130
Net profit		20

Balance Sheet as at 31 December

	£000	£000	£000
Fixed assets:	*Cost*	*Depreciation*	*Net*
Freehold property	100	–	100
Plant and machinery	40	20	20
	140	20	120
Current assets:			
Stocks at cost		40	
Debtors		50	
Quoted investments at cost		60	
Bank		20	
		170	
Less Current liabilities:			
Corporation tax	10		
Bills payable	20		
Trade creditors	60	90	80
			200
5% Debentures			60
			140
Authorised and issued share capital			100
Reserves			40
			140

Required:
Select five major ratios, apply them to the above accounts and comment upon their relevance.

44.9

Ironsides Limited
Balance Sheet as at 31 December

	£	£	£
Fixed assets at cost			7,200,000
Depreciation			2,000,000
			5,200,000
Current assets			
Stock		1,200,000	
Debtors		800,000	
Investments		600,000	
Cash		200,000	
		2,800,000	
Less Current liabilities			
Creditors	280,000		
Taxation	520,000	800,000	
Net current assets			2,000,000
			7,200,000
6% Debenture		800,000	
5% Mortgage		2,000,000	
Bank loan 8%		400,000	3,200,000
			4,000,000
Capital and reserves			
Share capital: Ordinary £1 shares			
Authorised		2,500,000	
Issued			2,400,000
General reserve			1,600,000
			4,000,000

Condensed Profit and Loss Account for the year ended 31 December

	£
Sales	12,000,000
Cost of production	10,320,000
Gross Profit	1,680,000

	£	£
Other Expenses:		
Administration	120,000	
Selling	68,000	
Rent	112,000	
Depreciation	400,000	700,000
		980,000
Less Interest		
Bank	32,000	
Mortgage	100,000	
Debenture	48,000	180,000
		800,000
Less Corporation tax at 45%		360,000
		440,000
Less Dividend		400,000
Transfer to general reserve		£40,000

Required:
Calculate ten significant ratios for Ironsides Ltd and comment on the meaning of each.

44.10A The annual accounts of the Wholesale Textile Company Limited have been summarised for two years as follows:

	Year 1		Year 2	
Sales	£	£	£	£
Cash		60,000		64,000
Credit		540,000		684,000
		600,000		748,000
Cost of sales		472,000		596,000
Gross profit		128,000		152,000
Expenses				
Warehousing	26,000		28,000	
Transport	12,000		20,000	
Administration	38,000		38,000	
Selling	22,000		28,000	
Debenture interest	–		4,000	
		98,000		118,000
Net profit		30,000		34,000

	On 31 Dec. Year 1		On 31 Dec. Year 2	
	£	£	£	£
Fixed assets				
(*Less* depreciation)		60,000		80,000
Current assets				
Stock	120,000		188,000	
Debtors	100,000		164,000	
Cash	20,000		14,000	
	240,000		366,000	
Less Current liabilities				
Trade creditors	100,000		152,000	
Net current assets		140,000		214,000
		200,000		294,000
Share capital		150,000		150,000
Reserves and undistributed profit		50,000		84,000
Debenture loan		–		60,000
		200,000		294,000

You are informed that:
1 All sales were from stocks in the company's warehouse.
2 The range of merchandise was not changed and buying prices remained steady throughout the two years.
3 Budgeted total sales for Year 2 were £780,000.
4 The debenture loan was received on 1 January, Year 2, and additional fixed assets were purchased on that date.

Required:
State the internal accounting ratios that you would use in this type of business to assist the management of the company in measuring the efficiency of its operation, including its use of capital.

Your answer should name the ratios and give the figures (calculated to one decimal place) for Year 1 and Year 2, together with possible reasons for changes in the ratios for the two years. Ratios relating to capital employed should be based on the capital at the year end. Ignore taxation.

45

Interpretation of financial information

45.1 Introduction

The interpretation of final accounts through the use of ratios can conveniently be divided into two parts. Firstly there is analysis by those outside the firm who are seeking to understand more from the published accounting data. On the other side there is management wishing to interpret a much fuller range of internal information in a meaningful way. In both situations current information will be assessed in relation to past trends of the same business and with comparative information for similar firms.

45.2 Comparisons over time

One of the most helpful ways in which accounting ratios can be used is to compare them with previous periods' ratios for the same organisation. Taking as an example Net profit after tax/Sales the results for the Rational Co Ltd are as follows:

	1993	1994	1995	1996	1997	1998
Net profit after tax/Sales	3.5%	3.4%	3.4%	3.1%	3.8%	3.3%

This year's result (1998) acquires much more significance when compared to the previous five years. The appreciation of the trends is usually assisted by graphing the results as in Exhibit 45.1.

Exhibit 45.1

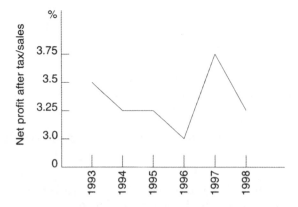

This graph very clearly illustrates how the net profit margin has fluctuated. In this type of case the ratio which is a comparative number is not expected to 'grow' in the way that an expanding firm expects its sales to grow. Thus for ratios an ordinary graph would normally be appropriate.

However, when the ratio points have been plotted it can be helpful to insert a line of best fit to these points. Thus on the graph we drew of Net profit after tax/Sales a line of best fit gives a useful idea of the past trends of the ratio as in Exhibit 45.2.

Exhibit 45.2

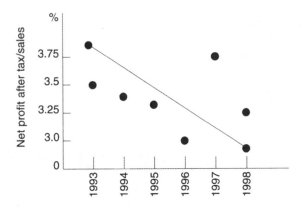

This can be drawn either by eye or by using a statistical technique such as least squares.

It is very tempting to extend these trend lines into the future as a form of forecast. Past trends should not be used mechanically to predict the future. Only if you are sure that all conditions influencing a ratio are likely to remain constant next year should you extend the trend. Notice that in the graph we have just plotted the linear trend is not significantly influenced by the upturn in the current year. This improvement may in fact represent the start of an upward movement if we had sufficient information to explain it. Thus great care must be taken with predictions.

As with the interpretation of all ratios the best approach is to structure the analysis in an orderly fashion. The pyramid type of structuring explained later in the chapter is a useful model since it links together a set of ratios, in a way that helps to develop understanding – one ratio being explained by other more detailed ratios.

It is also often helpful to combine with the comparison of ratios over time, some information about the trends in the real accounting data. In the example we have just examined of the Net profit after tax/Sales ratio it is likely to be helpful for someone interpreting the accounts to have alongside his graphical analysis of the ratio other graphs showing the sales in £ and net profit after tax in £. The ratio analysis must always be kept in the perspective of the real accounting results. The graphs of key figures from the profit and loss account for example can usefully be developed on logarithmic scales to emphasise trends.

45.3 Comparisons of ratios of one firm with those of other firms

Comparisons over time are useful since they give a perspective on trends developing within a firm. However, since firms operate in a competitive environment it is always necessary to have some basis of comparison with other organisations, particularly those in the same type of business.

While in principle inter-firm comparisons are very worthwhile there are considerable practical differences. First, in many cases organisations are not directly comparable with others in size or in the exact nature of business carried on. A large multinational company

can be involved in a wide range of industries and countries of operation, as a whole therefore it is probably unique. Size can in itself have an important bearing on ratios. For example the capital structure ratios of a large public company are not comparable with one which is small and privately owned. Second, inter-company comparisons are frequently made misleading by differences in accounting methods and factors such as the age structure and location of assets.

Most of the difficulties mentioned can be overcome by a properly structured scheme of inter-firm comparison. Here firms agree to pool data and employ experts to ensure comparability of the data. However, this type of scheme is only available internally for the management. For the external analyst relying on published data the development of accounting standards is helping to ensure a better basic source of information. The external analyst must by necessity look at the overall ratios for more general guidelines to a firm's performance.

45.4 External analysis of ratios

The outsider is at a disadvantage in undertaking ratio analysis since he will have relatively little information about the underlying bases of accounting. He will, however, be able to obtain information which is now published, showing ratios by industry. These are calculated from the published accounts of public companies, and more limited information on accounts of private companies. This information would tend to be in a form similar to that shown in Exhibit 45.3, which is an abbreviated form of a broad schedule of ratios.

Using some information from Exhibit 44.2 (in the previous chapter), let us set up the information we have available to assess the Rational Co Ltd, which is a Building and Civil Engineering Firm.

Exhibit 45.3

Illustration of Published Ratios by Industry Quoted Companies Years 1 and 2							
Industry Classification	*Year*	*Financial Performance*				*Credit Control*	
		P/CE %	NP/S %	S/FA times	S/ST times	CA/CL times	LA/CL times
Building and Civil Engineering	1	14.5	3.9	7.7	10.1	1.32	0.96
	2	14.8	4.6	7.0	7.3	1.36	0.93
Specialist Construction Contractors	1	14.5	5.3	6.0	9.8	1.55	1.15
	2	17.8	6.0	6.3	12.1	1.66	1.08

Notes:

P	=	Net operating profit	ST =	Stock
NP	=	Net profit after tax	CA =	Current assets
CE	=	Capital employed	CL =	Current liabilities
S	=	Sales	LA =	Liquid assets or current assets
FA	=	Fixed assets		*less* stock

The ratios shown are the median figures for the companies in the sample. In practice it would be common to show the two quartile figures as well.

Ratio	Rational Co Ltd		Industry Median for Building and Civil Engineering	
	Year 1	*Year 2*	*Year 1*	*Year 2*
Operating profit/Capital employed	13.2	11.7	14.5	14.8
Net profit after tax/Sales	3.8	3.3	3.9	4.6
Sales/Fixed assets	3.1	2.3	7.7	7.0
Sales/Stock	13.5	12.9	10.1	7.3
Current assets/Current liabilities	2.2	2.3	1.32	1.36
Liquid assets/Current liabilities	1.1	1.3	0.96	0.93

Whilst it must be appreciated that we are working with only a few ratios when ideally we would look at least at five years' information we might draw some tentative conclusions:

Operating profit/Capital employed is lower than the median figure for the industry. Looking further we see that Sales/Fixed assets ratio is considerably below average. The two ratios are closely linked since Sales is an important contributor to profit and Fixed assets are part of Capital employed. Net profit after tax to Sales is also below average but the company is utilising its stock above the average level. Both the liquidity ratios are above average, which may mean from the company's point of view that excessive resources are tied up in non-productive cash or debtor balances, which would also contribute to a low return on capital employed.

In practice we could also look at the quartile figures in addition to the median. Our conclusions from the analysis can only be tentative, but there is an impression which develops even from the limited information we have looked at that all is not right with the Rational Co Ltd. Profitability is below average and the explanation seems to lie in a low net profit margin, and low utilisation of fixed assets plus too many liquid assets. The trend of profitability figures cannot be assessed from two years, and it would have been useful to see information covering as many years back such as will give a reasonable guide. In preparing the graphs of trends over time for the ratios it is often very useful to show the Industry Data on the same graph as that from the firm. Using the example previously illustrated the graph for the Rational Co Ltd, Profit after tax/Sales would be improved by adding the Industry Median figures as in Exhibit 45.4.

Exhibit 45.4

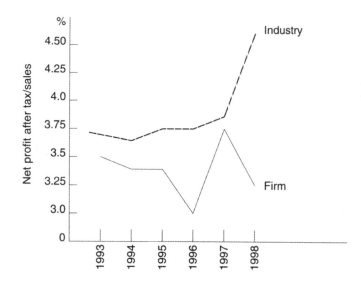

45.5 Internal analysis of ratios

From a management point of view very useful information can be drawn from a detailed ratio analysis between companies using a full range of information not normally published. The UK Centre for Inter-firm Comparisons is a specialist organisation undertaking this work, maintaining secrecy as to the identity of participating firms, but ensuring that all firms taking part prepare their information on a comparable basis. Several trade associations and professional bodies run similar schemes for their members. The Centre for Inter-firm Comparison have developed what is known as the 'pyramid' approach to ratios. This simply means that a key ratio at the top of the pyramid is explained by more detailed ratios which branch out below.

One example is shown in Exhibit 45.5 developed from the key ratio Operating profit/Operating assets. Note that $\dfrac{\text{Operating profit}}{\text{Operating assets}}$ is the same as:

$$\frac{\text{Sales}}{\text{Operating assets}} \times \frac{\text{Operating profit}}{\text{Sales}} \text{ (cancelling out Sales in the multiplication).}$$

Exhibit 45.5

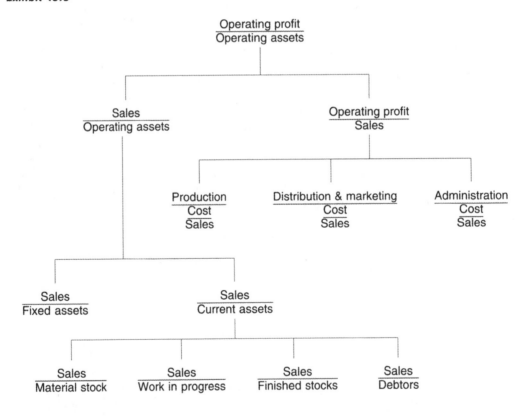

In a working scheme very many detailed ratios would be developed from the framework illustrated in this chapter. The main benefit usually arises by the more general comparison, but the detail allows backup research if things are going wrong.

The ratios are as follows:

Ratio	Last Year	This Year
Return on assets		
1 Operating profit/Operating assets (%)	8.2	11.1
Profit margin on sales and turnover of assets		
2 Operating profit/sales (%)	6.7	5.8
3 Sales/Operating assets (times per year)	2.5	1.7
Departmental costs (as a percentage of sales)		
4 Production	71.0	70.9
5 Distribution and marketing	16.3	18.2
6 Administration	6.0	5.1
Asset utilisation (£'s per £1,000 of sales)		
3a Operating assets	703	653
10 Current assets	593	480
11 Fixed assets	102	101
Current asset utilisation (£'s per £1,000 of sales)		
12 Material stocks	142	141
13 Work in progress	156	152
14 Finished stocks	152	94
15 Debtors	143	103

The results of our firm can now be appraised alongside the other companies in the sample. Our firm is identified by 'C'.

The Inter-firm Comparison

Ratio	A	B	C	D	E
Return on assets					
1 Operating profit/Operating assets (%)	17.2	14.5	11.1	8.6	3.9
Profit margin on sales and turnover of assets					
2 Operating profit/Sales (%)	14.0	14.3	5.8	7.9	2.0
3 Sales/Operating assets (times per year)	1.3	1.1	1.7	1.0	2.4
Departmental costs (as a percentage of sales)					
4 Production	74.0	70.5	70.9	71.7	77.0
5 Distribution and marketing	8.5	12.2	18.2	14.2	16.0
6 Administration	3.5	3.0	5.1	6.2	5.0
Asset utilisation (£'s per £1,000 of sales)					
3a Operating assets	842	908	653	1,030	500
10 Current assets	616	609	480	800	370
11 Fixed assets	250	320	101	241	160
Current asset utilisation (£'s per £1,000 of sales)					
12 Material stocks	131	120	141	172	84
13 Work in progress	148	120	132	175	140
14 Finished stocks	203	164	94	259	68
15 Debtors	134	205	123	194	78

Interpreting the Inter-firm Comparison we are able to see that our firm is below two other firms in terms of return on operating assets. This can be traced to Operating profit/Sales. Note that total departmental costs + operating profit as per cent sales = 100%. The main factor in the profit being below firms A and B is high distribution and marketing costs. Action can be taken on these costs if appropriate.

Since firm C will have details of the general size and description of all the firms in the sample (although the names of firms are confidential) and knows that the Centre for Inter-firm Comparison makes sure that the figures used are comparable, very valuable information can be drawn for management.

When several periods' data is available this type of information is much more readily appreciated in graphical form.

45.6 Further aspects of gearing

In the previous chapter, ratios to measure gearing were discussed. The most important aspect of gearing is its relation to risk.

The break-even chart shows clearly how risk emanates from variations in sales in relation to costs. Risk is usually defined in terms of the variability in profits and of course ultimately in the likelihood of failure, implied in bankruptcy or liquidations. A business with a high proportion of fixed cost will show a much higher rate of increase in profit as sales rise above break-even compared to one with a high proportion of variable cost. Correspondingly the high fixed cost company will show a much more dramatic decline into loss as sales reduce.

Exhibit 45.6

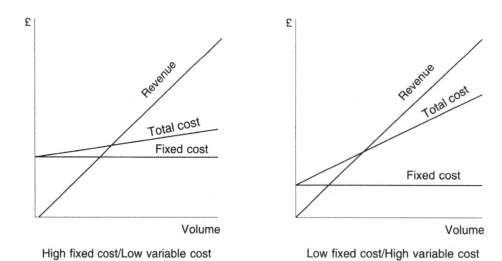

High fixed cost/Low variable cost   Low fixed cost/High variable cost

In numerical terms this can be illustrated as follows:

Fixed costs are £200 and variable costs are 60% of Sales. The break-even point is therefore at Sales of £500. The break-even is worked out from the fact that we know fixed cost is £200 and that the contribution is: Sales – 60% Sales = 40% Sales. Thus every £1 sold will make a contribution of 40p. The point of break-even is where contribution equals fixed costs, i.e. $\frac{200}{0.4}$ = £500 sales.

	£	£	£	£	£	£
Sales	400	500	600	700	800	900
Variable cost	240	300	360	420	480	540
Contribution	160	200	240	280	320	360
Fixed cost	200	200	200	200	200	200
Profit/Loss before interest and tax	−40	0	40	80	120	160

Exhibit 45.7

The impact of changes in sales level can be seen to have a more than proportional impact on profit:

Sales increase	from	£600 to £700	= +	16.7%
Profit increases	from	£40 to £80	= +	100.0%

Sales increase	from	£600 to £800	= +	33.3%
Profit increases	from	£40 to £120	= +	200.0%

The effect of the level of fixed cost on the returns of a business is the cause of what has been called gearing. A highly geared company is one with a high proportion of fixed cost.

A business often has to think carefully about investing in new plant because of its impact on gearing. Using the data in Exhibit 45.7 as a starting point, we can see the effect on its profitability if the business invests in some new plant. The impact will be to increase fixed cost from £200 to £300 and reduce variable cost to 50% of sales. The break-even point will move this up to sales of £600.

	£	£	£	£	£	£
Sales	400	500	600	700	800	900
Variable cost	200	250	300	350	400	450
Contribution	200	250	300	350	400	450
Fixed cost	300	300	300	300	300	300
Profit/Loss before interest or tax	−100	−50	0	50	100	150

The impact of the new investment has been to increase the break-even sales from £500 to £600 in exchange for which the rate of profitability has increased. This can best be seen on the graph, Exhibit 45.6, where a higher geared situation shows the widest angle between the Revenue and Total cost line.

In numerical terms increasing sales from £700 to £800, i.e. 14.3% increases profits from £50 to £100, i.e. 100%.

The analysis we have examined which relates to the change in gearing from operating factors does not in itself indicate whether the investment is a good one or not. It does, however, show that new investment can have a significant impact on the operational risk of the business. The decision will have to be taken as to whether the increased profitability justifies the increase in break-even position. If sales are hard to come by, this may not be justified.

45.7 Financial gearing

The impact of a firm borrowing money and paying interest on it, rather than funding itself entirely from its equity capital is very similar in effect to operational gearing. The interest on borrowing is the same in its impact as a fixed cost.

To illustrate this the data from Exhibit 45.7 will be taken.

	£	£	£	£	£	£
Sales	400	500	600	700	800	900
Profit/Loss before interest and tax	− 40	0	40	80	120	160

If the business is funded entirely from ordinary share capital amounting to £1,000, then if we ignore tax, the rates of return would be:

	£	£	£	£	£	£
Sales	400	500	600	700	800	900
Return = $\dfrac{\text{Profit/Loss}}{\text{Share capital of £1,000}}$	− 4%	0	4%	8%	12%	16%

If, instead of funding entirely from ordinary shares, the business raised its £1,000 funds – £600 from ordinary shares and £400 from a 10% loan, the amended returns would be as follows:

	£	£	£	£	£	£
Sales	400	500	600	700	800	900
Profit/Loss before Interest and tax	− 40	0	40	80	120	160
Interest	− 40	− 40	− 40	− 40	− 40	− 40
Net Profit before tax	− 80	− 40	0	40	80	120
Return = $\dfrac{\text{Profit/Loss}}{\text{Share capital of £600}}$	−13.3%	−6.7%	0	6.7%	13.3%	20%

The impact of borrowing money on the return to the ordinary shareholders is to increase the return to him beyond the point where operating profits exceed a return of 10% on the capital, i.e. sales of £750. After this point the returns to the ordinary shareholder accelerate. Notice, however, the significant increase in break-even point from £500 to £600 and that sales must in fact exceed £750 before the shareholder is better off.

Apart from the increased risk from gearing, the introduction of borrowing brings a legal risk that the lender may, if for example interest is not paid on time, take a legal charge over the company's assets.

The net cost of borrowing is reduced if tax is taken into account, since the interest charge is deductible from profit subject to tax. If we assumed a 50% tax rate the figures would be as follows:

100% Share Capital

Sales	£400	£500	£600	£700	£800	£900
Net of tax profit (Loss)	£(−20)	£0	£20	£40	£60	£80
Return	(−2%)	0	2%	4%	6%	8%

60% Share Capital

Net of tax profit	−£40	−£20	£0	£20	£40	£60
Return	−6.7%	−3.3%	0%	3.3%	6.7%	10%

45.8 Some problems with return on capital employed

Considerable difficulty is caused by the wide use of return on capital employed (ROCE) as a measure of the performance of a business. Perhaps the main issue is the valuation of the fixed assets which are subject to depreciation. The problem can be illustrated from the following facts: A business acquires an asset costing £9,000 which will have a life of three years with a nil residual value. Profits generated before depreciation will be £5,000 per annum and the profit after depreciation (straight line) will be £5,000 – £3,000 = £2,000 per annum.

	Period			
	0	*1*	*2*	*3*
Cost of asset	£9,000	£9,000	£9,000	£9,000
Less Aggregate depreciation	0	3,000	6,000	9,000
	9,000	6,000	3,000	0

In year 1 if the average value of assets is used the return will be 26.7%

$$\left(2,000 \Big/ \frac{9,000 + 6,000}{2}\right) = 26.7\%$$

and in year 3 it will have increased to 133.3%

$$\left(2,000 \Big/ \frac{3,000 + 0}{2}\right) = 133.3\%$$

If the profits happened to be earned by using the fully depreciated assets in Year 4 – the return would be infinite – in relation to a zero capital value.

The fact which emerges from this example is that if performance is to be judged by ROCE there is an incentive for the manager not to invest in new fixed assets which will increase the capital base. With depreciating assets the performance will appear to improve automatically.

Although much has been written about this problem of measurement, this is no practical alternative that has been adopted. The interpreter of the accounts must be vigilant.

45.9 Some limitations of ratio analysis

The advantages of ratio analyses which have been brought out in this text are that they provide a consistent and disciplined approach to the analysis of accounts. In addition they are a convenient method of comparing the performance of a particular firm with others and of seeing trends over time. Nonetheless there are dangers in accepting answers which appear to be put forward by ratios in too rigid a manner. The following points are relevant:

1 Accounting statements present a limited picture only of the business. The information included in accounts does not cover all aspects of the business.
2 The problem associated with differing bases of accounting are nowhere more important than in ratio analysis. In particular differences in valuing fixed assets, depreciation methods and in valuation of stock-in-trade can be mentioned. As you will appreciate from your study of accounting there is usually a variety of accounting methods which may be appropriate to a particular firm.
3 The accounts of large organisations frequently aggregate operations in different industries and an external analyst will not be able to split up the results of one sector from another.
4 Comparison of a firm which finances its fixed plant through rental, thus not showing it as an asset, with a firm which purchases its own assets will be difficult.
5 External analysis of balances can be misleading because the picture at that particular moment of time may not be representative of the year as a whole. For example firms frequently take stock when their stock levels are lowest. Average figures should be used but are not available externally.
6 Interpretation of a change in a ratio needs careful examination of changes in both numerator and denominator. Without a very full and detailed investigation some wrong conclusions can be drawn.
7 There is room for considerable difference between individual companies. It is wrong to lay down too rigid guidelines since what may be good for one successful firm may be wrong for another.

8 In general it is incorrect to compare small firms with very large firms. Many of the general industrial analyses of ratios are overall averages, and are, therefore, not strictly comparable to any particular firm.

The lesson is that while ratios are useful in indicating areas for investigation they cannot be relied upon to answer all the questions raised. Many of the limitations may, however, be reduced if a properly supervised scheme of inter-firm comparison is introduced.

45.10 Interpretation of accounts for employees

The interpretation which has been reviewed so far in this chapter has been for people with a good knowledge of the basis of accounting. Many firms have realised in recent years that it can be of great interest to their employees, if they attempt to make important features of the accounts generally available. Experience has tended to show that the average employee is very easily put off if too much detail is presented to him. Most firms attempt therefore to give a much more limited amount of information and to present it as imaginatively as possible in a special employee report. It is always far better to get over a limited amount of important information than to include so much detail that the message is obscured. Those who are interested can look for more detail in the main published accounts.

Firms have developed many different approaches in preparing their reports to employees. Many succeed by capturing interest through good graphics and design. Care must be taken, however, not to make these reports appear too trivial or condescending. There is a very wide range of approach between different firms many of which include cartoons and 'comic-strip' types of presentation to capture interest. Space is not available here to do justice to this type of presentation. Try to find examples of company reports in libraries.

In addition to the questions which follow, you should attempt questions 355–361 in the accompanying book of multiple-choice questions (see back cover for details).

Suggested solutions to review questions with the letter 'A' after the question number are given in Appendix I (pages 662–6).

45.1 Comparative financial data from three companies in the same industrial sector is as follows:

	A Ltd £	B Ltd £	C Ltd £
Fixed assets (net)	52,000	76,000	54,000
Current assets:			
Stock	48,000	40,000	64,000
Debtors	30,000	56,000	80,000
Cash	42,000	24,000	16,000
	172,000	196,000	214,000
Less Current liabilities			
Creditors	(24,400)	(44,600)	(64,000)
Proposed dividends	(7,600)	(11,400)	(30,000)
	140,000	140,000	120,000
Issued capital:			
6% £1 preference shares	10,000	40,000	–
£1 ordinary shares	70,000	60,000	120,000
Revenue reserves	60,000	40,000	–
	140,000	140,000	120,000
Average stock	50,000	72,000	60,000
Sales	250,000	240,000	800,000
Gross profit	50,000	60,000	80,000
Net profit	30,000	30,000	30,000

Required:
(*a*) write a report analysing and comparing the performance of the three companies;
(*b*) advise a client with £5,000 to invest in shares of one of the three companies, which company to choose and which type of share to select.

45.2 Identify and discuss some of the more important limitations of ratio analysis as a financial analysis technique.

45.3 Morgan & Lee Limited are manufacturers. The following are the summarised revenue accounts of the company for 1996, 1997 and 1998, with balance sheets as at 31st December, each year.

Revenue Accounts	1996	1997	1998
	£000	£000	£000
Cost of sales	600	900	1,210
Expenses	200	250	320
Net profit	200	250	270
Sales (credit)	1,000	1,400	1,800

Balance Sheets	1996	1997	1998
	£000	£000	£000
Share capital	500	700	700
Retained profits	300	500	550
Creditors	80	140	210
Bank	–	50	160
	880	1,390	1,620
Plant (net)	650	1,000	1,000
Stock	100	200	350
Debtors	120	190	270
Bank	10	–	–
	880	1,390	1,620

Note: Ignore Taxation

Required:
Your commentary, supported by appropriate ratios, on the profitability and liquidity trends of Morgan & Lee Limited.

(*The Institute of Bankers in Ireland*)

45.4 The following are the summarised final accounts of two manufacturing companies, Soda Ltd and Tonic Ltd, for the year ended 31st December, 1998:

Summarised Profit and Loss Accounts
for the year ended 31st December 1998

	Soda Ltd		Tonic Ltd	
	£000	£000	£000	£000
Sales		700		540
Cost of goods sold		310		230
Gross profit		390		310
Debenture interest	40		20	
Other expenses	190	230	140	160
Net profit		160		150

Balance Sheets as at 31st December 1998

	£000	£000	£000	£000
Fixed Assets at cost		820		370
Accumulated depreciation		360		80
		460		290
Current Assets				
Trade debtors	115		60	
Stocks	80		40	
Bank	10		–	
	205		100	
Current liabilities				
Trade creditors	80		55	
Net current assets		125		45
		585		335
Financed by:				
Shareholders' funds		345		220
Debentures		240		115
		585		335

The following information is also available:
1 Approximately 90% of each company's sales are made on credit.
2 Each company's stock level remains approximately constant throughout the year.

Requirement:
Write a report to the Managing Director of Soda Ltd, comparing the performance of his company with that of Tonic Ltd.

Your report should include reference to appropriate ratios and any other information which you consider relevant.

(ICAI Professional Examination Two)

45.5 The following are the summarised accounts of Charlie Ltd, for the two years ended on 31st March, 1997 and 1998:

Profit and Loss Accounts for the Years Ended

	31st March, 1998 £	31st March, 1998 £	31st March, 1997 £	31st March, 1997 £
Sales		92,000		89,000
Cost of goods sold		48,000		46,000
Gross profit		44,000		43,000
Administration costs	11,000		9,500	
Distribution costs	15,900		12,800	
Interest	3,000	29,900	1,000	23,300
Net profit		14,100		19,700

Balance Sheets as at

	31st March, 1998 £	31st March, 1998 £	31st March, 1997 £	31st March, 1997 £
Fixed assets (net of depreciation)		68,000		51,000
Current assets				
Debtors	32,000		35,000	
Stocks	35,000		18,000	
Cash	–		2,700	
	67,000		55,700	
Current liabilities				
Creditors	24,500		27,300	
Bank overdraft	12,000		–	
	36,500		27,300	
Net current assets		30,500		28,400
		98,500		79,400
Ordinary share capital (in £5 shares)		55,000		55,000
Share premium account		5,000		5,000
Profit and loss account		33,500		19,400
		93,500		79,400
Debentures		5,000		–
		98,500		79,400

Requirements:
(a) Calculate and comment upon the earnings per share for 1997 and 1998 of Charlie Ltd, and
(b) Write a report to a shareholder in Charlie Ltd, commenting on the trends in each of the following:
  (i) Liquidity;
  (ii) Use of assets;
  (iii) Profitability and return on capital employed; and
  (iv) Solvency and capital structure.

NB *Your report should include reference to appropriate ratios and any other information which you consider relevant.*

(*ICAI Professional Examination Two*)

45.6 Set out below are the profit and loss accounts of Cone Ltd for the years ended 31st March, 1997 and 1998:

Profit and Loss Accounts for the Years Ended

	31st March, 1998		31st March, 1997	
	£000	£000	£000	£000
Sales		400		200
Trading Profit		50		20
Investment Income		6		3
		56		23
Debenture Interest		6		3
Profit before Taxation		50		20
Taxation		15		6
Profit after Taxation		35		14
Dividends Paid and Proposed				
Preference	4		6	
Ordinary	21	25	2	8
Profit Retained for the Year		10		6
Retained Profit at the Start of the Year		86		80
Retained Profit at the End of the Year		96		86

Set out below are the balance sheets of Cone Ltd as at 31st March, 1997 and 1998:

Balance Sheets as at

	31st March, 1998		31st March, 1997	
	£000	£000	£000	£000
Fixed Assets (at net book value)		355		180
Quoted Investments		20		20
Unquoted Investments		30		20
Current Assets				
Stocks	50		25	
Debtors	54		29	
Cash	40		2	
	144		56	
Current Liabilities				
Creditors	93		25	
Bank Overdraft	–		20	
	93		45	
Net Current Assets		51		11
		456		231
Ordinary Share Capital		140		20
8% Preference Shares		50		75
Share Premium		70		–
Revenue Reserves		96		86
6% Debentures		100		50
		456		231

You are required to:

(a) calculate the return on capital employed for 1997 and 1998 and comment on the reasons for the change;

(b) calculate appropriate liquidity ratios and comment on their significance; and

(c) compute the borrowing and gearing ratios and comment on the change in the capital structure of the company.

(ICAI Professional Examination Two)

45.7 The following information has been extracted from the accounts of Witton Way Ltd:

Profit and Loss Account for the Year to 30 April 19X6

	19X5 £000	19X6 £000
Turnover (all credit sales)	7,650	11,500
Less Cost of sales	(5,800)	(9,430)
Gross profit	1,850	2,070
Other expenses	(150)	(170)
Loan interest	(50)	(350)
Profit before taxation	1,650	1,550
Taxation	(600)	(550)
Profit after taxation	1,050	1,000
Dividends (all ordinary shares)	(300)	(300)
Retained profits	£750	£700

Balance Sheet as at 30 April 19X6

	19X5 £000	19X6 £000
Fixed assets		
Tangible assets	10,050	11,350
Current assets		
Stocks	1,500	2,450
Trade debtors	1,200	3,800
Cash	900	50
	3,600	6,300
Creditors: Amounts falling due within one year	2,400	2,700
Net current assets	1,200	3,600
Total assets less current liabilities	11,250	14,950
Creditors:		
Amounts falling due after more than one year		
Loans and other borrowings	350	3,350
	£10,900	£11,600
Capital and reserves		
Called-up share capital	5,900	5,900
Profit and loss account	5,000	5,700
	£10,900	£11,600

Additional information:
During the year to 30 April 19X6, the company tried to stimulate sales by reducing the selling price of its products and by offering more generous credit terms to its customers.

Required:
(a) Calculate six accounting ratios specifying the basis of your calculations for each of the two years to 30 April 19X5 and 19X6 respectively which will enable you to examine the company's progress during 19X6.
(b) From the information available to you, including the ratios calculated in part (a) of the question, comment upon the company's results for the year to 30 April 19X6 under the heads of 'profitability', 'liquidity', 'efficiency' and 'shareholders' interests'.
(c) State what additional information you would require in order to assess the company's attempts to stimulate sales during the year to 30 April 19X6.

(Association of Accounting Technicians)

45.8A You are presented with the following information for three quite separate and independent companies:

Summarised Balance Sheets at 31 March 19X7

	Chan plc £000	Ling plc £000	Wong plc £000
Total assets *less* current liabilities	600	600	700
Long-term liabilities			
10% Debenture stock	–	–	(100)
	£600	£600	£600
Capital and reserves:			
Called-up share capital			
Ordinary shares of £1 each	500	300	200
10% Cumulative preference shares of £1 each	–	200	300
Profit and loss account	100	100	100
	£600	£600	£600

Additional information:

1 The operating profit before interest and tax for the year to 31 March 19X8 earned by each of the three companies was £300,000.
2 The effective rate of corporation tax for all three companies for the year to 31 March 19X8 is 30%. This rate is to be used in calculating each company's tax payable on ordinary profit.
3 An ordinary dividend of 20p for the year to 31 March 19X8 is proposed by all three companies, and any preference dividends are to be provided for.
4 The market prices per ordinary share at 31 March 19X8 were as follows:

	£
Chan plc	8.40
Ling plc	9.50
Wong plc	10.38

5 There were no changes in the share capital structure or in long-term loans of any of the companies during the year to 31 March 19X8.

Required:

(a) Insofar as the information permits, prepare the profit and loss account for each of the three companies (in columnar format) for the year to 31 March 19X8 (formal notes to the accounts are not required):
(b) calculate the following accounting ratios for each company:
  (i) earnings per share;
  (ii) price earnings;
  (iii) gearing [taken as total borrowings (preference share capital and long-term loans) to ordinary shareholders' funds]; and
(c) using the gearing ratios calculated in answering part (b) of the question, briefly examine the importance of gearing if you were thinking of investing in some ordinary shares in one of the three companies assuming that the profits of the three companies were fluctuating.

(*Association of Accounting Technicians*)

45.9A The following information is provided for Bessemer Ltd which operates in an industry subject to marked variations in consumer demand.

(*i*) Shareholders' equity at 30 September 19X5.

	£000
Issued ordinary shares of £1 each fully paid	5,000
Retained profits	1,650
	6,650

There were no loans outstanding at the balance sheet date.

(*ii*) Profit and loss account extracts: year to 30 September 19X5.

	£000
Net profit before tax	900
Less Corporation tax	270
	630
Less Dividends	600
Retained profit for the year	30
Retained profit at 1 October 19X4	1,620
Retained profit at 30 September 19X5	1,650

(*iii*) The directors are planning to expand output. This will require an additional investment of £2,000,000 which may be financed either by issuing 1,000,000 ordinary shares each with a nominal value of £1, or by raising a 12 per cent debenture.

(*iv*) Forecast profits before interest charges, if any, for the year to 30 September:

	£000
19X6	1,800
19X7	500
19X8	2,200

A corporation tax rate of 30 per cent on reported profit before tax may be assumed; the directors plan to pay out the entire post-tax profit as dividends.

Required:
(*a*) The forecast profit and loss appropriation accounts for each of the next three years and year-end balance sheet extracts, so far as the information permits, assuming that the expansion is financed by:
   (*i*) issuing additional shares, or
   (*ii*) raising a debenture.
(*b*) Calculate the forecast return on shareholders' equity, for each of the next three years, under the alternative methods for financing the planned expansion.
(*c*) An assessment of the merits and demerits of the alternative methods of finance based on the calculations made under (*a*) and (*b*) and any other relevant methods of comparison.

(*Institute of Chartered Secretaries and Administrators*)

45.10 An investor is considering the purchase of shares in either AA plc or BB plc whose latest accounts are summarised below. Both companies carry on similar manufacturing activities with similar selling prices and costs of materials, labour and services.

Balance Sheets at 30 September 19X7

	AA plc		BB plc	
	£000	£000	£000	£000
Freehold property at revaluation 19X5		2,400		–
Plant, machinery and equipment:				
at cost	1,800		1,800	
depreciation	1,200		400	
		600		1,400
Goodwill		–		800
Stocks: finished goods		400		200
work in progress		300		100
Debtors		800		500
Bank deposit		–		400
		4,500		3,400
Less Liabilities due within one year				
Creditors	600		900	
Overdraft	200		–	
	800		900	
Liabilities due after one year	1,400		1,000	
		2,200		1,900
		2,300		1,500
Ordinary £1 shares		1,000		500
Reserves		1,300		1,000
		2,300		1,500

Profit and Loss Accounts – Year to 30 September 19X7

	AA plc		BB plc	
	£000	£000	£000	£000
Sales		2,500		2,500
Operating profit		400		600
Depreciation – plant, machinery and equipment	180		180	
Loan interest	150		160	
		330		340
		70		260
Bank interest		–		100
		70		360
Taxation		20		90
Available to ordinary shareholders		50		270
Dividend		40		130
Retained		£10		£140
Price/earnings ratio	30		5	
Market value of share	£1.50		£2.70	

Required:

(a) Write a report to the investor, giving an appraisal of the results and state of each business, and

(b) advise the investor whether, in your opinion, the price earnings ratios and market price of the shares can be justified in the light of the figures in the accounts, giving your reasons.

(*Institute of Chartered Secretaries and Administrators*)

45.11A The following are the summarised accounts for B Limited, a company with an accounting year ending on 30 September.

Summarised Balance Sheets	19X5/6		19X6/7	
	£000	£000	£000	£000
Tangible fixed assets – at cost				
Less Depreciation		4,995		12,700
Curent assets:				
Stocks	40,145		50,455	
Debtors	40,210		43,370	
Cash at bank	12,092		5,790	
	92,447		99,615	
Creditors: amounts falling due within one year:				
Trade creditors	32,604		37,230	
Taxation	2,473		3,260	
Proposed dividend	1,785		1,985	
	36,862		42,475	
Net current assets		55,585		57,140
Total assets less current liabilities		60,580		69,840
Creditors: amounts falling due after more than one year:				
10% Debentures 2006/2010		19,840		19,840
		40,740		50,000
Capital and reserves:				
Called-up share capital of £0.25 per share		9,920		9,920
Profit and loss account		30,820		40,080
Shareholders' funds		40,740		50,000

Summarised Profit and Loss Accounts	19X5/6	19X6/7
	£000	£000
Turnover	486,300	583,900
Operating profit	17,238	20,670
Interest payable	1,984	1,984
Profit on ordinary activities before taxation	15,254	18,686
Tax on profit on ordinary activities	5,734	7,026
Profit for the financial year	9,520	11,660
Dividends	2,240	2,400
	7,280	9,260
Retained profit brought forward	23,540	30,820
Retained profit carried forward	30,820	40,080

You are required to:
(a) calculate, for each year, two ratios for each of the following user groups, which are of particular significance to them:
   (i) shareholders,
   (ii) trade creditors,
   (iii) internal management;
(b) make brief comments upon the changes, between the two years, in the ratios calculated in (a) above.

(*Chartered Institute of Management Accountants*)

45.12 The following are the financial statements of D Limited, a wholesaling company, for the year ended 31 December:

Profit and Loss Accounts	*19X4*	*19X4*	*19X5*	*19X5*
	£000	£000	£000	£000
Turnover – credit sales	2,200		2,640	
– cash sales	200		160	
		2,400		2,800
Cost of sales		(1,872)		(2,212)
Gross profit		528		588
Distribution costs		(278)		(300)
Administration expenses		(112)		(114)
Operating profit		138		174
Interest payable		–		(32)
Profit on ordinary activities before tax		138		142

Balance Sheets as at 31 December	*19X4*	*19X4*	*19X5*	*19X5*
	£000	£000	£000	£000
Tangible fixed assets		220		286
Current assets: Stocks	544		660	
Debtors	384		644	
Cash at bank	8		110	
	936		1,414	
Creditors: amounts falling due within one year:				
Trade creditors	(256)		(338)	
Net current assets		680		1,076
Total assets *less* current liabilities		900		1,362
Creditors: Amounts falling due after more than one year:				
Debenture loans				(320)
Shareholders' funds		900		1,042

The following information should be taken into consideration.

1 You may assume that:
   (*i*) The range of products sold by D Limited remained unchanged over the two years;
   (*ii*) the company managed to acquire its products in 19X5 at the same prices as it acquired them for in 19X4;
   (*iii*) the effects of any inflationary aspects have been taken into account in the figures.
2 Ignore taxation.
3 All calculations must be shown to one decimal place.

You are required, using the information above, to assess and comment briefly on the company, from the point-of-view of:
(*a*) profitability;
(*b*) liquidity.

(*Chartered Institute of Management Accountants*)

45.13A G plc is a holding company with subsidiaries that have diversified interests. G plc's board of directors is interested in the group acquiring a subsidiary in the machine tool manufacturing sector. Two companies have been identified as potential acquisitions, A Ltd and B Ltd. Summaries of both these companies' accounts are shown below:

Profit and Loss Accounts for the Year ended 30 April 19X8

	A Ltd	B Ltd
	£000	£000
Turnover	985	560
Cost of goods sold		
Opening stock	150	145
Materials	255	136
Labour	160	125
Factory overheads	205	111
Depreciation	35	20
Closing stock	(155)	(140)
	650	397
Gross profit	335	163
Selling and administration expenses	(124)	(75)
Interest	(35)	(10)
Profit before taxation	176	78
Taxation	65	25
Profit after taxation	111	53

Balance Sheets at 30 April 19X8

	A Ltd		B Ltd	
	£000	£000	£000	£000
Fixed assets		765		410
Current assets				
Stock	155		140	
Debtors	170		395	
Bank	50		45	
	375		580	
Current liabilities				
Trade creditors	235		300	
Other	130		125	
	365		425	
Net current assets		10		155
Debentures		(220)		(70)
		555		495
Share capital		450		440
Profit and loss account		105		55
		555		495

You are required to prepare a report for the board of G plc assessing the financial performance and position of A Ltd and B Ltd. Your report should be prepared in the context of G plc's interests in these two companies and should be illustrated with financial ratios where appropriate. You should state any assumptions you make as well as any limitations of your analysis.

(*Chartered Institute of Management Accountants*)

Part VII   Revision questions

Suggested solutions to questions with the letter 'A' after the question number are given in Appendix II (pages 689–91).

R7.1 Financial ratios have been compared to a thermometer for taking the temperature of a business. Like a thermometer they give only a limited part of the diagnosis and must be interpreted.

Required:

Comment on the above statement. Suggest five significant ratios explaining the use of each.

(*The Institute of Bankers in Ireland*)

R7.2 The term 'accounting ratios' is used to describe significant relationships which exist between figures shown in the Profit and Loss Account and Balance Sheet. By examining certain key ratios over a period of time it is possible to build up a clear picture of the profitability and solvency of a company.

Requirement:

You are required to explain the purpose, and to indicate the method of calculation, of each of the following ratios:

(*a*) Return on capital employed;

(*b*) Net profit to sales;

(*c*) Stock turnover;

(*d*) Current ratio;

(*e*) Acid test ratio (liquidity ratio); and

(*f*) Average collection period for debtors.

(*ICAI Professional Examination Two*)

R7.3A Balance Sheets of James Parker are as follows:

	Year 1 £	Year 1 £	Year 2 £	Year 2 £
Fixed assets		85,300		131,300
Current assets				
Stocks	54,500		79,500	
Debtors	55,200	109,700	80,700	160,200
		195,000		291,500
Current liabilities		55,000		160,000
		140,000		131,500
Capital				
Opening balance		126,000		140,000
Add net profit		24,000		4,000
Less drawings		10,000		12,500
		140,000		131,500

The following information was extracted from the Trading Accounts for the two years.

	Year 1	Year 2
Sales	£350,000	£460,000
Gross profit	£122,500	£92,000
Opening stock	£52,500	£54,500

Required:

Calculate the following ratios for each year and comment on the position shown for the second year as compared to the first:

(a) Gross profit percentage;

(b) Stock turnover;

(c) Working capital ratio;

(d) Acid test ratio; and

(e) Period of credit given.

(*ICPAI Formation I*)

R7.4A One of your clients has provided you with the following extracts from his final accounts:

	1999	1998
Sales	£960,000	£720,000
Cost of Sales	£576,000	£360,000
Gross Profit	£384,000	£360,000

The Gross Profit Rate achieved in 1998 is the norm for the type of goods sold and your client is concerned about the decrease in 1999 relative to 1998.

The following occurred in 1999:

1 Sales of a new line of goods amounted to £100,000. The Gross Profit Rate on these sales is 35%. These goods were not affected by items (2) to (6) below.

2 Stock which had cost £20,000 became obsolete and was sold for £5,000.

3 Goods purchased for half price at a supplier's closing down sale cost £40,000. Half of these were sold prior to the year end.

4 Sales revenue from seasonal promotions totalled £60,000. All items sold during these promotions were sold at 75% of normal price.

5 Goods costing £30,000 had to be destroyed when they became damp.

6 In order to meet a large order it was necessary to buy some stock from a new supplier. These goods cost 20% more than normal and were sold for £50,000.

Required:

Determine whether the above factors account for the fall in the Gross Profit Rate or whether further investigations are necessary.

(*ICPAI Formation I*)

R7.5A Puzzles Ltd has been trading for several years. Its authorised share capital is comprised of 400,000 ordinary shares of £1 each. The information set out below relates to the year ended 31st March, 1998.

1 Capital employed at the year end, 31st March, 1998, consisted of 'Fixed Assets' and 'Net Current Assets'. Net Current Assets consist of Current Assets less Current Liabilities (Creditors: amounts falling due within one year).

2 The cost of Fixed Assets at 31st March, 1998, was £600,000. The accumulated depreciation, after charging depreciation for the year ended 31st March, 1998, amounted to 40% of the cost of fixed assets.

3 The ratio of the net book value of Fixed Assets to Net Current Assets was 1.5 : 1.

4 Current Assets (stocks, debtors and cash) were twice the value of Current Liabilities.

5 The ratio of annual sales to year-end Capital Employed was 2 : 1.

6 Mark up on cost was 33⅓%.

7 Annual net profit (gross profit less business expenses and depreciation) amounted to 10% of sales.

8 The depreciation charge for the year was 10% of the cost of Fixed Assets held.

9 The issued ordinary share capital was £280,000.

10 Stock turnover for the year was 3 times. (The value of stock at the beginning and end of the year was the same.)

11 Debtors days outstanding at 31st March, 1998, were 30 (assume 360 days in a year).

12 The balancing figure between net profit for the year and retained profits at the end of the year is the retained profit brought forward from last year.

Requirement:

You are required to construct from the above information the Profit and Loss Account and the Balance Sheet for Puzzles Ltd for the year ended 31st March, 1998, in as much detail as the information supplied permits.

(*IATI Admission Examination*)

R7.6 Your employer's finance department has recently developed a computer model to assist in the prediction of the profit and loss account and balance sheet for the first year of trading. By entering the sales forecast and the values of the various parameters the model will print a summary profit and loss account and an outline balance sheet. The model parameters are as follows:

Gross profit as a percentage of sales	40%
Selling expenses as a percentage of sales	14%
Administration costs, excluding interest	£12,000
Interest rate on long-term debt	10%
Return on capital employed – being:	
(Profit before interest divided by closing capital employed)	20%
Ratio of long-term debt to equity	1 : 1
Ratio of fixed to net current assets	3 : 1
Current ratio	2 : 1

The first trial of the model has a sales value of £100,000. The only expense items to be considered are selling, administration and interest.

You are required to prepare a forecast:

(*a*) Profit Statement based on the above information using an initial sales value of £100,000, and

(*b*) Balance Sheet in as much detail as possible.

(*ICAI Professional Examination One*)

R7.7 The following information relates to Jigsaw Ltd for the year ended 31st March:

1 Balance Sheet at 31st March:

	%
Stock	45
Debtors	35
Cash	15
	95
Creditors	40
	55
Fixed assets	55
Debentures	10
	100
Share capital	30
Share premium	10
Revenue reserves	60
	100

2 Number of Shares in Issue	2 million
3 Earnings per Share	12 pence
4 Tax Rate	40%
5 Profit before Tax: Shareholders Funds	25%
6 Profit before Interest and Tax: Sales	15%
7 Credit Sales: Total Sales	80%
8 Debtors Turnover	4 times
9 Stock Turnover	3 times

You are required to:

(a) explain briefly what are meant by solvency and liquidity ratios and profitability ratios, and

(b) reconstruct the Balance Sheet of Jigsaw Ltd as at 31st March and the Trading and Profit and Loss Account for the year ended on that date.

NB *A balancing figure for expenses, other than cost of sales and also for interest, should be inserted.*

(*ICAI Professional Examination Two*)

R7.8

(a) 'The choice of ratios will be determined by the needs of the user of the information.'

Conflux plc, a public company manufacturing farm machinery, is your client. The Managing Director has written to you requesting information on the uses of ratios.

Required:

Write a brief letter to the Managing Director outlining:

(i) the types of ratios which may be extracted from the accounts of a company and indicating those which are most useful to management; and

(ii) the limitations on using ratios as a means of analysing company results.

(b) The following statistics relate to Conflux plc for the year ended 30th June:

(1) *Fixed assets*			
Tangible assets	£x		
Financial assets	£x		£x
Current assets			
Stock	£x		
Debtors	£x	£x	
Creditors (amounts falling due within 1 year)		£x	
Net current assets			£x
Total assets less current liabilities			£x
Creditors (amounts falling due after more than 1 year)			10%
Capital and reserves			
Called up share capital in shares of £1 each	36%		
Share premium	15%		
Profit and loss account	39%	90%	
			£x

(2) Stock turnover	4 times
Debtors days	50 days
Current ratio	2 : 1
Return on capital employed – being:	
Profit before interest and taxation/shareholders' funds	8%
Dividend cover	4 times
Dividend paid	£40,000
Margin on goods sold	20%
Tax rate	45%
Net Profit to Sales	15%

'Financial Assets' represents an investment in an unlisted company of 3.8 million shares at 10p each.

Requirement:

Reconstruct the Balance Sheet and Profit and Loss Account for the year ended 30th June, noting any assumptions made.

(ICAI Professional Examination Two)

Part VIII

THE FINAL ACCOUNTS OF OTHER TYPES OF ORGANISATIONS

46

Final accounts of firms which do not maintain complete accounting records

46.1 Gross profit mark-up and gross profit margin

The purchase and sale of goods may be shown as:

Cost Price + Profit = Selling Price

Profit when shown as a fraction, or percentage, of cost price is known as the **mark-up**.
   Profit when shown as a fraction, or percentage, of selling price is known as the **margin**.
   Both mark-up and margin are calculated in the following example.

Example of the calculation of mark-up and margin

Cost Price + Profit = Selling Price
   £4   +   £1 = £5.

Mark-up = $\dfrac{\text{Profit}}{\text{Cost Price}}$ as a fraction, or if required as a percentage, multiply by 100:

$$£\tfrac{1}{4} = \tfrac{1}{4}, \text{ or } \tfrac{1}{4} \times 100 = 25\%.$$

Margin = $\dfrac{\text{Profit}}{\text{Selling Price}}$ as a fraction, or if required as a percentage, multiply by 100:

$$£\tfrac{1}{5} = \tfrac{1}{5}, \text{ or } \tfrac{1}{5} \times 100 = 20\%.$$

46.2 Calculating missing figures using mark-up or margin

We can use these ratios to complete trading accounts where some of the figures are missing. All examples in this chapter:

- assume that all the goods in a firm have the same rate of mark-ups, and
- ignore wastages and theft of goods.

Example of the calculation of gross profit and sales using mark-up

Given the following figures find gross profit and sales.

	£
Opening stock	400
Closing stock	600
Purchases	5,200

A uniform rate of mark-up of 20% is applied.

Trading Account

	£	£
Sales		?
Cost of sales		
Opening stock	400	
Add Purchases	5,200	
	5,600	
Closing stock	600	5,000
Gross profit		?

Answer:

It is known that:	Cost of goods sold + Gross profit = Sales
and also that:	Cost of goods sold + Percentage Mark-up = Sales

The following figures
are also known: £5,000 + 20% = Sales
After doing the arithmetic: £5,000 + £1,000 = £6,000

The trading account can be completed by inserting the gross profit of £1,000 and £6,000 for Sales.

Example of the calculation of gross profit and purchases using margin

Another firm has the following figures.

	£
Opening stock	500
Closing stock	800
Sales	6,400

The firm earns a gross profit margin of 25% on all sales.

Find the gross profit and the purchases figure.

Trading Account

	£	£
Sales		6,400
Cost of sales		
Opening stock	500	
Purchases	?	
Closing stock	800	?
Gross profit		?

Answer:

	Cost of goods sold	+ Gross profit	= Sales
Therefore	Sales	– Gross profit	= Cost of goods sold
	Sales	– 25% margin	= Cost of goods sold
	£6,400	– £1,600	= £4,800

Now the following figures are known:

		£
Opening stock		500
Add Purchases	(1)	?
	(2)	?
Less Closing stock		800
Cost of goods sold		4,800

The two missing figures are found by normal arithmetical deduction:

No. (2) less £800	= £4,800
Therefore No. (2)	= £5,600
So that: £500 opening stock + No. (1)	= £5,600
Therefore No. (1)	= £5,100

The completed trading account can now be shown:

Trading Account

	£	£
Sales		6,400
Cost of sales		
Opening stock	500	
Purchases	5,100	
	5,600	
Closing stock	800	4,800
Gross profit		1,600

This technique is often used by retail stores when estimating the amount to be bought if a certain sales target is to be achieved. Alternatively, stock levels or sales figures can be estimated given information as to purchases and opening stock figures.

46.3 The relationship between mark-up and margin

As both of these figures refer to the same profit, but expressed as a fraction or a percentage of different figures, there is bound to be a relationship. If one is known as a fraction, the other can soon be found.

If the mark-up is known, to find the margin take the same numerator to be numerator of the margin, then for the denominator of the margin take the total of the mark-up's denominator plus the numerator. An example can now be shown:

Mark-up	*Margin*
$\dfrac{1}{4}$	$\dfrac{1}{4+1} = \dfrac{1}{5}$
$\dfrac{2}{11}$	$\dfrac{2}{11+2} = \dfrac{2}{13}$

If the margin is known, to find the mark-up take the same numerator to be the numerator of the mark-up, then for the denominator of the mark-up take the figure of the margin's denominator less the numerator:

Margin	Mark-up
$\dfrac{1}{6}$	$\dfrac{1}{6-1} = \dfrac{1}{5}$
$\dfrac{3}{13}$	$\dfrac{3}{13-3} = \dfrac{3}{10}$

46.4 Manager's commission

Managers of businesses are very often remunerated by a basic salary plus a percentage of profits. It is quite common to find the percentage expressed not as a percentage of profits before such commission has been deducted, but as a percentage of the amount remaining after deduction of the commission.

For example, assume that profits before the manager's commission was deducted amounted to £8,400, and that the manager was entitled to 5% of the profits remaining after such commission was deducted. If 5% of £8,400 was taken, this amounts to £420, and the profits remaining would amount to £7,980. However, 5% of £7,980 amounts to £399 so that the answer of £420 is wrong.

The formula to be used to arrive at the correct answer is:

$$\frac{\text{Percentage commission}}{100 + \text{Percentage commission}} \times \text{Profit before commission}$$

In the above problem this would be used as follows:

$$\frac{5}{100 + 5} \times £8,400 = £400 \text{ manager's commission.}$$

The profits remaining are £8,000 and as £400 represents 5% of it the answer is verified.

46.5 Not all firms keep full double entry accounting records

Every small shop, market stall or other small business does not keep its books using a full double entry system. A large number of the owners of such firms would not know how to write up double entry records, even if they wanted to.

It is more likely that they would enter details of a transaction once only, using a single entry system. Also many of them would fail to record every transaction, resulting in incomplete records.

It is perhaps only fair to remember that accounting is after all supposed to be an aid to management; it is not something to be done as an end in itself. Therefore, many small firms, especially retail shops, can have all the information they want by merely keeping a cash book and having some form of record, not necessarily in double entry form, of their debtors and creditors.

Somehow, however, the profits will have to be calculated. This could be for the purpose of calculating income tax payable. How can profits be calculated if the bookkeeping records are inadequate or incomplete?

46.6 Profit viewed as an increase in capital

Probably the way to start is to recall that, unless there has been an introduction of extra cash or resources into the firm, the only way that capital can be increased is by making profits. Therefore, profits can be found by comparing capital at the end of last period with that at the end of this period.

Let us look at a firm where capital at the end of last year was £2,000. During this year there have been no drawings, and no extra capital has been brought in by the owner. At the end of this year the capital was £3,000.

$$\text{Net profit} = \underset{\text{capital}}{\underset{\text{This year's}}{£3,000}} - \underset{\text{capital}}{\underset{\text{Last year's}}{£2,000}} = £1,000$$

If, on the other hand, the drawings had been £700, the profits must have been £1,700, calculated thus:

$$\text{Last year's Capital} + \text{Profits} - \text{Drawings} = \text{This year's Capital}$$
$$£2,000 \quad + \quad ? \quad - \quad £700 \quad = \quad £3,000$$

We can see that £1,700 profits was the figure needed to complete the formula, filling in the missing figure by normal arithmetical deduction:

$$£2,000 + £1,700 - £700 = £3,000$$

The following example shows the calculation of profit where insufficient information is available to draft a trading and profit and loss account, only information of assets and liabilities being known.

Example of the calculation of profit using asset and liability information

H Taylor provides information as to his assets and liabilities at certain dates.

At 31 December 1997. *Assets*: Van £1,000; Fixtures £700; Stock £850; Debtors £950; Bank £1,100; Cash £100. *Liabilities*: Creditors £200; Loan from J Ogden £600.

At 31 December 1998. *Assets*: Van (after depreciation) £800; Fixtures (after depreciation) £630; Stock £990; Debtors £1,240; Bank £1,700; Cash £200. *Liabilities*: Creditors £300; Loan from J Ogden £400; Drawings were £900.

First of all a **Statement of Affairs** is drawn up as at 31 December 1997. This is the name given to what would have been called a balance sheet if it had been drawn up from a complete set of records. The capital is the difference between the assets and liabilities.

Statement of Affairs as at 31 December 1997

	£	£
Fixed assets		
Van		1,000
Fixtures		700
		1,700
Current assets		
Stock	850	
Debtors	950	
Bank	1,100	
Cash	100	
	3,000	
Less Current liabilities		
Creditors	200	
		2,800
		4,500
Financed by		
Capital (difference)		3,900
Long-term liability		
Loan from J Ogden		600
		4,500

A statement of affairs is now drawn up at the end of 1998. The formula of Opening Capital + Profit – Drawings = Closing Capital is then used to deduce the profit figure.

Statement of Affairs as at 31 December 1998

		£	£
Fixed assets			
Van			800
Fixtures			630
			1,430
Current assets			
Stock		990	
Debtors		1,240	
Bank		1,700	
Cash		200	
		4,130	
Less Current liabilities			
Creditors		300	3,830
			5,260
Financed by:			
Capital			
Balance at 1 January 1998		3,900	
Add Net Profit	(c)	?	
	(b)	?	
Less Drawings		900	(a) ?
Long-term loan			
Loan from J Ogden			400
			5,260

Deduction of net profit:

Opening Capital + Net Profit − Drawings = Closing Capital. Finding the missing figures (a)
(b) and (c) by deduction,

(a) is the figure needed to make the balance sheet totals equal, i.e. £4,860.

(b) is therefore £4,860 + £900 = £5,760

(c) is therefore £5,760 − £3,900 = £1,860.

To check:

Capital		3,900
Add Net profit	(c)	1,860
	(b)	5,760
Less Drawings		900
	(a)	4,860

Obviously, this method of calculating profit is very unsatisfactory as it is much more informative when a trading and profit and loss account can be drawn up. Therefore, whenever possible the 'comparisons of capital' method of ascertaining profit should be avoided and a full set of final accounts drawn up from the available records.

It is important to realise that a business would have exactly the same trading and profit and loss account and balance sheet whether they kept their books by single entry or double entry. However, as you will see, whereas the double entry system uses the trial balance in preparing the final accounts, the single entry system will have to arrive at the same answer by different means.

46.7 Preparing final accounts from an incomplete set of records

The following example shows the various stages of drawing up final accounts from a single entry set of records.

The accountant discerns the following details of transactions for J Frank's retail store for the year ended 31 December 1998.

(a) The sales are mostly on a credit basis. No record of sales has been made, but £10,000 has been received, £9,500 by cheque and £500 by cash, from persons to whom goods have been sold.

(b) Amount paid by cheque to suppliers during the year = £7,200.

(c) Expenses paid during the year: by cheque, Rent £200, General Expenses £180; by cash, Rent £50.

(d) J Frank took £10 cash per week (for 52 weeks) as drawings.

(e) Other information is available:

	At 31.12.1997 £	At 31.12.1998 £
Debtors	1,100	1,320
Creditors for goods	400	650
Rent owing	–	50
Bank balance	1,130	3,050
Cash balance	80	10
Stock	1,590	1,700

(f) The only fixed asset consists of fixtures which were valued at 31 December 1997 at £800. These are to be depreciated at 10% per annum.

Stage 1: Draw up a Statement of Affairs on the closing day of the last accounting period. This is now shown:

Statement of Affairs as at 31 December 1997

	£	£
Fixed assets		
Fixtures		800
Current assets		
Stock	1,590	
Debtors	1,100	
Bank	1,130	
Cash	80	
	3,900	
Less Current liabilities		
Creditors	400	
		3,500
		4,300
Financed by:		
Capital (difference)		4,300

All of these opening figures are then taken into account when drawing up the final accounts for 1998.

Stage 2: Next a cash and bank summary, showing the totals of each separate item, plus opening and closing balances, is drawn up.

	Cash	Bank		Cash	Bank
	£	£		£	£
Balances at 31.12.1997	80	1,130	Suppliers		7,200
Receipts from debtors	500	9,500	Rent	50	200
			General Expenses		180
			Drawings	520	
			Balances 31.12.1998	10	3,050
	580	10,630		580	10,630

Stage 3: Calculate the figures for purchases and sales to be shown in the trading account. Remember that the figures needed are the same as those which would have been found if double entry records had been kept.

Purchases: In double entry, purchases means the goods that have been bought in the period irrespective of whether they have been paid for or not during the period. The figure of payments to suppliers must therefore be adjusted to find the figures of purchases.

	£
Paid during the year	7,200
Less payments made, but which were for goods which were purchased in a previous year (creditors 31 December 1997)	400
	6,800
Add purchases made in this year, but for which payment has not yet been made (creditors at 31 December 1998)	650
Goods bought in this year, i.e. purchases	7,450

The same answer could have been obtained if the information had been shown in the form of a total creditors account, the figure of purchases being the amount required to make the account totals agree.

Creditors

	£		£
Bank (cash paid to suppliers)	7,200	Balance b/d	400
Balance c/d	650	Purchases (missing figure)	7,450
	7,850		7,850

Sales: The sales figure will only equal receipts where all the sales are for cash. Therefore, the receipts figures need to be adjusted to find sales. This can only be done by constructing a total debtors account, the sales figure being the one needed to make the totals agree.

Debtors

	£		£
Balance b/d	1,100	Receipts: Cash	500
		Cheque	9,500
Sales (missing figure)	10,220	Balance c/d	1,320
	11,320		11,320

Stage 4: Expenses. Where there are no accruals or prepayments either at the beginning or end of the accounting period, then expenses paid will equal expenses used up during the period. These figures will be charged to the trading and profit and loss account.

On the other hand, where such prepayments or accruals exist, then an expense account should be drawn up for that particular item. When all known items are entered, the missing figure will be the expenses to be charged for the accounting period. In this case only the rent account needs to be drawn up.

Rent

	£		£
Cheques	200	Profit and loss (missing figure)	300
Cash	50		
Balance c/d (accrual)	50		
	300		300

Stage 5: Draw up the final accounts.

J Frank
Trading and Profit and Loss Account for the year ended 31 December 1998

	£	£
Sales (stage 3)		10,220
Less Cost of goods sold:		
Opening stock	1,590	
Add Purchases (stage 3)	7,450	
	9,040	
Less Closing stock	1,700	7,340
Gross profit		2,880
Less Expenses:		
Rent (stage 4)	300	
General expenses	180	
Depreciation: Fixtures	80	560
Net profit		2,320

Balance Sheet as at 31 December 1998

	£	£	£
Fixed assets			
Fixtures at 1 January 1998		800	
Less Depreciation		80	720
Current assets			
Stock		1,700	
Debtors		1,320	
Bank		3,050	
Cash		10	
		6,080	
Less Current liabilities			
Creditors	650		
Rent owing	50	700	
Working capital			5,380
			6,100
Financed by:			
Capital			
Balance 1 January 1998 (per Opening Statement of Affairs)			4,300
Add Net profit			2,320
			6,620
Less Drawings			520
			6,100

46.8 Incomplete records and missing figures

In practice, part of the information relating to cash receipts or payments is often missing. If the missing information is in respect of one type of payment, then it is normal to assume that the missing figure is the amount required to make both totals agree in the cash column of the cash and bank summary. This does not happen with bank items owing to the fact that another copy of the bank account can always be obtained from the bank. Exhibit 46.2 shows an example when the drawings figure is unknown; Exhibit 46.3 is an example where the receipts from debtors had not been recorded.

Exhibit 46.2

The following information regarding cash and bank receipts and payments is available:

	Cash	Bank
	£	£
Cash paid into the bank during the year	5,500	
Receipts from debtors	7,250	800
Paid to suppliers	320	4,930
Drawings during the year	?	–
Expenses paid	150	900
Balances at 1 January	35	1,200
Balances at 31 December	50	1,670

	Cash	Bank		Cash	Bank
	£	£		£	£
Balances at 1 January	35	1,200	Lodgements (C)	5,500	
Received from debtors	7,250	800	Suppliers	320	4,930
Lodgements (C)		5,500	Expenses	150	900
			Drawings	?	
			Balances at 31 December	50	1,670
	7,285	7,500		7,285	7,500

The amount needed to make the two sides of the cash columns agree is £1,265. Therefore, this is taken as the figure of drawings.

Exhibit 46.3

Information regarding cash and bank transactions is available as follows:

	Cash	Bank
	£	£
Receipts from debtors	?	6,080
Cash withdrawn from the bank for business use (this is the amount which is used besides cash receipts from debtors to pay drawings and expenses)		920
Paid to suppliers		5,800
Expenses paid	640	230
Drawings	1,180	315
Balances at 1 January	40	1,560
Balances at 31 December	70	375

	Cash	Bank		Cash	Bank
	£	£		£	£
Balances at 1 January	40	1,560	Suppliers		5,800
Received from debtors	?	6,080	Expenses	640	230
Withdrawn from Bank (C)	920		Withdrawn from Bank (C)		920
			Drawings	1,180	315
			Balances at 31 December	70	375
	1,890	7,640		1,890	7,640

Receipts from debtors is, therefore, the amount needed to make each side of the cash column agree, £930.

It must be emphasised that balancing figures are acceptable only when all the other figures have been verified. Should, for instance, a cash expense be omitted when cash received from debtors is being calculated, then this would result in an understatement not only of expenses but also ultimately of sales.

46.9 Finding figures where there are two missing pieces of information

If both cash drawings and cash receipts from debtors were not known it would not be possible to deduce both of these figures. The only course open would be to estimate whichever figure was more capable of being accurately assessed, use this as a known figure, then deduce the other figure. However, this is a most unsatisfactory position as both of the figures are no more than pure estimates, the accuracy of each one relying entirely upon the accuracy of the other.

46.10 Goods stolen, destroyed by fire or lost in some other way

When goods are stolen, destroyed by fire, or lost in some other way, then the value of those goods will have to be calculated. This could be needed to substantiate an insurance claim or to settle problems concerning taxation etc.

If the stock had been properly valued immediately before the fire, burglary, etc., then the stock loss would obviously be known. Also if a full and detailed system of stock records were kept, then the value would also be known. However, as the occurrence of fires or burglaries cannot be foreseen, and not many businesses keep full and proper stock records, the stock loss will have to be calculated in some other way.

The methods described in this chapter for determining missing figures are used instead. The only difference is that instead of computing closing stock at a year end, for example, the closing stock will be that as at immediately before the fire consumed it or it was stolen.

Two examples will now be looked at. The first is a very simple case, where figures of purchases and sales are known and all goods are sold at a uniform profit ratio. The second is rather more complicated.

Example 1

J Collins lost the whole of his stock by fire on 17 March 1999. The last time that a stocktake had been done was on 31 December 1998, the last balance sheet date, when it was £1,950 at cost. Purchases from then to 17 March 1999 amounted to £6,870 and sales for the period were £9,600. All sales were made at a uniform profit margin of 20%.

First, the Trading Account can be drawn up with the known figures included. Then the missing figures can be deduced afterwards.

J Collins
Trading Account for the period 1 January to 17 March 1999

	£	£
Sales		9,600
Cost of sales		
Opening stock	1,950	
Purchases	6,870	
	8,820	
Closing stock	(c) ?	(b) ?
Gross profit		(a) ?

Now the missing figures can be deduced.

It is known that the gross profit margin is 20%, therefore gross profit (a) is 20% of £9,600 = £1,920.

Now (b) ? + (a) £1,920 = £9,600, so that (b) is difference, i.e. £7,680.

Now that (b) is known (c) can be deduced, £8,820 – (c) ? = £7,680, so (c) is difference, i.e. £1,140.

The figure for goods destroyed by fire, at cost, is therefore £1,140.

Example 2

T Scott had the whole of his stock stolen from his warehouse on the night of 20 August. Also destroyed were his sales and purchases journals, but the sales and purchases ledgers were salvaged. The following facts are known:

(*a*) Stock was known at the last balance sheet date, the previous 31 March, to be £12,480 at cost.

(*b*) Receipts from debtors during the period 1 April to 20 August amounted to £31,745. Debtors were: at 31 March £14,278, at 20 August £12,333.

(*c*) Payments to creditors during the period 1 April to 20 August amounted to £17,270. Creditors were: at 31 March £7,633, at 20 August £6,289.

(*d*) The margin on sales has been constant at 25%. Before we can start to construct a trading account for the period, we need to find out the figures of sales and of purchases. These can be found by drawing up total debtors' and total creditors' accounts, sales and purchases figures being the difference on the accounts.

Creditors

	£		£
Cash and bank	17,270	Balance b/d	7,633
Balance c/d	6,289	Purchases (difference)	15,926
	23,559		23,559

Debtors

	£		£
Balance b/d	14,278	Cash and bank	31,745
Sales (difference)	29,800	Balance c/d	12,333
	44,078		44,078

The trading account can now show the figures already known.

Trading Account for the period 1 April to 20 August

		£		£
Sales				29,800
Cost of sales				
Opening stock		12,480		
Purchases		15,926		
		28,406		
Less Closing stock	(c)	?	(b)	?
Gross profit			(a)	?

Gross profit can be found, as the margin on sales is known to be 25%, therefore (a) = 25% of £29,800 = £7,450.
Cost of goods sold (b) ? + Gross profit £7,450 = £29,800 therefore (b) is £22,350.
£28,406 – (c) ? = (b) £22,350, therefore (c) is £6,056.
The figure for cost of goods stolen is therefore £6,056.

Review questions

In addition to the questions which follow, you should attempt questions 362–374 in the accompanying book of multiple-choice questions (see back cover for details).

Suggested solutions to review questions with the letter 'A' after the question number are given in Appendix I (pages 666–71).

46.1A   R Stubbs is a trader who sells all of his goods at 25% above cost.
His books give the following information at 31 December:

	£
Stock at 1 January	9,872
Stock at 31 December	12,620
Sales for the year	60,000

You are required to:
(*a*) Ascertain the cost of goods sold.
(*b*) Show the value of purchases during the year.
(*c*) Calculate the gross profit earned by Stubbs.

Show your answer in the form of a trading account.

46.2   C White gives you the following information as at 30 June 1998:

	£
Stock at 1 July 1997	6,000
Purchases during the year	54,000

White's mark-up is 50% on 'cost of goods sold'. His average stock during the year was £12,000. Draw up a trading and profit and loss account for the year ended 30 June 1998 showing clearly:

(*a*) the closing stock as at 30 June 1998.
(*b*) the total amount of profit and loss expenditure White must not exceed if he is to maintain a *net* profit on sales of 10%.

46.3A J Green's business has a rate of stock turnover of 7 times. Average stock is £12,600. Trade discount (i.e. margin allowed) is 33⅓% off all selling prices. Expenses are 66⅔% of gross profit.

You are to calculate:
(a) Cost of goods sold;
(b) Gross profit;
(c) Turnover;
(d) Total expenses; and
(e) Net profit.

46.4 The following figures relate to the retail business of J Clarke for the month of May. Goods which are on sale fall into two categories, A and B.

	Category A	Category B
Sales to the public at manufacturer's recommended list price	£6,000	£14,000
Trade discount allowed to retailers	20%	25%
Total expenses as a percentage of sales	10%	10%
Rate of stock turnover	12 times	20 times

Calculate for each category:
(a) Cost of goods sold;
(b) Gross profit;
(c) Total expenses;
(d) Net profit; and
(e) Average stock at cost, assuming that sales are distributed evenly over the year, and that there are twelve equal months in the year.

46.5A B Arkwright started in business on 1 January with £10,000 in a business bank account. Unfortunately he did not keep proper books of account.

He is forced to submit a calculation of profit for the year to 31 December to the Revenue Commissioners. He ascertains that at 31 December he had stock valued at cost £3,950, a van which had cost £2,800 during the year and which had depreciated by £550, debtors of £4,970, expenses prepaid of £170, bank balance £2,564, cash balance £55, trade creditors £1,030, and expenses owing £470.

His drawings were: cash £100 per week for 50 weeks, cheque payments £673.

Required:
Draw up a statement to show the profit or loss for the year.

46.6 J Kirkwood is a dealer who has not kept proper books of account. At 31 August 1997 he had the following assets and liabilities:

	£
Cash	115
Bank balance	2,209
Fixtures	4,000
Stock	16,740
Debtors	11,890
Creditors	9,052
Van (at valuation)	3,000

During the year to 31 August 1998 his drawings amounted to £7,560. Winnings from a competition £2,800 were put into the business. Extra fixtures were bought for £2,000.

At 31 August 1998 his assets and liabilities were: Cash £84, Bank overdraft £165, Stock £21,491, Creditors for goods £6,002, Creditors for expenses £236, Fixtures to be depreciated £600, Van to be valued at £2,500, Debtors £15,821, Prepaid expenses £72.

Required:
Draw up a statement showing the profit or loss made by Kirkwood for the year ended 31 August 1998.

46.7A William Brook is a sole trader. He has asked you to prepare accounts for his first year of business which ended on 31st December, 1998, and has supplied you with the following information:

1 Summarised bank account for the year ended 31st December, 1998:

	£000		£000
Lodgements	164	Purchases	65
		Administration costs	45
		Selling expenses	15
		Financial expenses	8
		Drawings	10
		Balance at 31st December, 1998	21
	164		164

2 All cash received from debtors was lodged to the bank.
3 Lodgements included £27,000 capital introduced on 1st January, 1998.
4 Other assets and liabilities at 31st December, 1998, comprised the following:

Stock	£8,000
Debtors	£24,000
Amount due in respect of purchases	£15,000

You are required to prepare:
(a) the Trading and Profit and Loss Account of William Brook for the year ended 31st December, 1998, and
(b) the Balance Sheet as at that date.

(*IATI Foundation Examination*)

46.8 Mary Lambe owns a boutique. She does not maintain full accounting records but has supplied you with the following information in respect of 1998:

1 Summarised bank account:

Lodgements	£283,000	Balance at 1st January, 1998	£2,000
Balance at 31st December, 1998	£24,000	Payments to creditors	£209,000
		Wages	£40,000
		Business expenses	£36,000
		Purchase of fixed assets	£20,000
	£307,000		£307,000

2 Mary lodges all cash receipts to the bank account, except for £1,000 per month which she takes for her own use.
3 Wages include £8,000 which Mary paid to her mother who does not work in the business.
4 Assets and liabilities at 1st January and 31st December, 1998 included the following:

	1st January 1998	31st December 1998
Fixed assets	£100,000	£108,000
Stock	£60,000	£40,000
Debtors	£50,000	£55,000
Creditors	£15,000	£14,000
Accrued expenses	£1,000	£2,000
Prepaid expenses	£2,000	£1,000

You are required to prepare:
(a) a Trading and Profit and Loss Account for Mary Lambe for the year ended 31st December, 1998, and
(b) a Balance Sheet as at that date.
(*ICAI Professional Examination One*)

46.9A   Following is a summary of Kelly's bank account for the year ended 31 December.

	£		£
Balance at 1 January	405	Payments to creditors	
Receipts from debtors	37,936	for goods	29,487
Balance at 31 December	602	Rent	1,650
		Rates	890
		Sundry expenses	375
		Drawings	6,541
	38,943		38,943

All of the business takings have been lodged with the exception of £9,630. Out of this, Kelly has paid wages of £5,472, drawings of £1,164 and purchase of goods £2,994.
   The following additional information is available:

	1 January	31 December
Stock	13,862	15,144
Creditors for goods	5,624	7,389
Debtors for goods	9,031	8,624
Rates prepaid	210	225
Rent owing	150	–
Fixtures at valuation	2,500	2,250

Required:
Draw up a set of final accounts for the year ended 31 December. Show all of your workings.

46.10   Terry White, a sole trader, has provided you with the following information from his records for the year ended 31st December, 1998:

	1st January 1998	31st December 1998
Stock	£22,000	£28,000
Debtors	£18,000	£26,000
Creditors	£20,000	£16,000
Cash at bank	£2,000	Unknown

He had the following transactions during the year to 31st December, 1998:

Amounts received from debtors	£120,000
Amounts paid to creditors	80,000
Wages paid	12,000
Expenses paid	10,000
Drawings	13,000

Requirements:
(a) Prepare the Trading and Profit and Loss Account for Terry White for the year ended 31st December, 1998; and
(b) Prepare the Balance Sheet as at that date.

(*IATI Foundation Examination*)

46.11A On 14th July a fire destroyed a large portion of the stock of Morgan Limited. The following information was extracted from the books of the company:

	1 January £	14 July £
Trade creditors	48,000	39,000
Trade debtors	55,000	60,000
Stock	46,000	3,500

Relevant cash receipts and payments during the period 1st January to 14th July were as follows:

Cash paid to suppliers	£263,500
Cash received from debtors	225,000
Cash Sales	90,000

Goods sold during the period were sold at a gross profit margin of 20% on sales.

Required:
A calculation of the cost of goods destroyed.

(*The Institute of Bankers in Ireland*)

46.12 John Blank owns a confectionery shop. Turnover is comprised solely of cash sales. In January 1998, the manager of the shop suddenly disappeared and John, alarmed by this and by a serious disimprovement in the business bank balance, asked you to conduct an investigation.

You obtained the following information:

1 For the first six months of 1997 goods were sold to yield a rate of gross profit of 33⅓%. The rate of VAT during this period was 15%.
2 From 1st July, 1997 the rate of gross profit was reduced to 25% and the rate of VAT was reduced to 10%.
3 The quantity of goods sold in the second six months of 1993 was 50% higher than in the first six months of the year.
4 Purchases for the year (excluding VAT) amounted to £520,000.
5 Stocks, valued at cost, were as follows:

1st January, 1997	£60,000
31st December, 1997	£80,000

6 Cash lodgements in respect of sales amounted to £635,000.

Requirement:
Calculate the amount of any cash deficiency.

(*ICAI Professional Examination One*)

46.13A John McCarthy is a Supermarket Proprietor. The following is his summarised bank account for 1998:

	£		£
Balance at 1 January	5,300	Cash purchases	90,000
Cash sales	175,000	Payments to creditors	82,000
Cash received from debtors	41,700	Wages	10,900
		Delivery expenses	3,200
		Purchase of van	6,000
		Fuel, light and heat	1,600
		Cash withdrawals	12,000
		Deposit account	10,000
		Rates	860
		Balance at 31 December	5,440
	222,000		222,000

You are given the following additional information:

(a) Balances outstanding as at 31 December:

	1997	1998
	£	£
Freehold premises at cost	109,680	109,680
Stock	26,500	30,100
Trade creditors	48,800	62,000
Debtors for: – Goods	8,000	11,300
– Rates	120	180

(b) He purchased a van in 1996 for £12,000. Depreciation amounting to £4,800 i.e. 20% on cost price, had been provided in each of the years 1996 and 1997. Fittings costing £8,000 have a net value in the books as at 31 December 1997 of £6,500. Depreciation is provided at 10% on cost price.

(c) McCarthy took goods from stock during 1998 valued at £7,600 at cost price. No entries were made in the books.

(d) The figure for 'Cash Withdrawals' includes £7,300 for personal use; the balance is sundry expenses connected with the business.

(e) McCarthy lives on the premises and 25% of Rates and Fuel, Light and Heat is attributable to private use.

Required:
(a) McCarthy's Capital Account as at 31st December, 1997; and
(b) His Profit and Loss Account for the year ended 31st December, 1998 and a Balance Sheet as at that date.

(*The Institute of Bankers in Ireland*)

46.14   Alan Strong, a sole trader, has asked you to prepare the accounts for his business for the year ended 31st December, 1998, and has provided you with the following information:

Summarised Bank Account for the Year Ended 31st December, 1998

	Note	£		Note	£
Lodgements	(5)	84,000	Balance at 1st January		2,016
			Payments to creditors		42,900
			Wages and salaries		8,100
			Rent and rates		1,250
			Light and heat		3,200
			Printing and stationery		2,300
			Telephone		1,100
			Transfer to deposit a/c	(3)	5,000
			Purchase of van	(4)	6,500
			Miscellaneous expenses		4,300
			Balance at 31st December		7,334
		84,000			84,000
Balance b/d		7,334			

Additional information

1   Details of other assets and liabilities are as follows:

	At 1st January, 1998 £	At 31st December, 1998 £
Stock (at Cost)	6,300	8,400
Debtors	4,100	4,600
Creditors	3,900	4,200
Wages and Salaries Due	500	750
Rates Due	200	300
Light and Heat Prepaid	400	300

2   The business owns a premises which was valued at £25,000 on 1st January, 1998, and is to be valued at £22,500 on 31st December, 1998.
3   The sum of £5,000 deposited in a bank deposit account during the year had earned interest of £400 by 31st December, 1998. This interest is outstanding at 31st December, 1998.
4   The new van is to be depreciated by 10% in respect of the year ended 31st December, 1998.
5   The following cash payments were made out of sales proceeds before the lodgements were made to the bank:

£800	paid in general expenses
£1,000	paid to creditors
£3,600	withdrawn by the owner to cover personal expenses.

Requirements:

(*a*) Prepare a Statement of Affairs (opening Balance Sheet) for Alan Strong as at 1st January, 1998;
(*b*) Prepare a Trading and Profit and Loss Account for the year ended 31st December, 1998; and
(*c*) Prepare a Balance Sheet as at 31st December, 1998.

(*IATI Admission Examination*)

46.15A Although Janet Lambert has run a small business for many years, she has never kept adequate accounting records. However, a need to obtain a bank loan for the expansion of the business has necessitated the preparation of 'final' accounts for the year ended 31 August 19X1. As a result, the following information has been obtained after much careful research:

1 Janet Lambert's business assets and liabilities are as follows:

As at	1 September 19X0	31 August 19X1
	£	£
Stock	8,600	16,800
Debtors for sales	3,900	4,300
Creditors for purchases	7,400	8,900
Rent prepaid	300	420
Electricity accrued due	210	160
Balance at bank	2,300	1,650
Cash in hand	360	330

2 All takings have been banked after deducting the following payments:

Cash drawings – Janet Lambert has not kept a record of cash drawings, but suggests these will be in the region of	£8,000
Casual labour	£1,200
Purchase of goods for resale	£1,800

Note: Takings have been the source of all amounts banked.

3 Bank payments during the year ended 31 August 19X1 have been summarised as follows:

	£
Purchases	101,500
Rent	5,040
Electricity	1,390
Delivery costs (to customers)	3,000
Casual labour	6,620

4 It has been established that a gross profit of 33⅓% on cost has been obtained on all goods sold.

5 Despite her apparent lack of precise accounting records, Janet Lambert is able to confirm that she has taken out of the business during the year under review goods for her own use costing £600.

Required:

(a) Prepare a computation of total purchases for the year ended 31 August 19X1.

(b) Prepare a trading and profit and loss account for the year ended 31 August 19X1 and a balance sheet as at that date, both in as much detail as possible.

(c) Explain why it is necessary to introduce accruals and prepayments into accounting.

(*Association of Accounting Technicians*)

46.16 Jean Smith, who retails wooden ornaments, has been so busy since she commenced business on 1 April 19X5 that she has neglected to keep adequate accounting records. Jean's opening capital consisted of her life savings of £15,000 which she used to open a business bank account. The transactions in this bank account during the year ended 31 March 19X6 have been summarised from the bank account as follows:

	£
Receipts:	
Loan from John Peacock, uncle	10,000
Takings	42,000
Payments:	
Purchases of goods for resale	26,400
Electricity for period to 31 December 19X5	760
Rent of premises for 15 months to 30 June 19X6	3,500
Rates of premises for the year ended 31 March 19X6	1,200
Wages of assistants	14,700
Purchase of van, 1 October 19X5	7,600
Purchase of holiday caravan for Jean Smith's private use	8,500
Van licence and insurance, payments covering a year	250

According to the bank account, the balance in hand on 31 March 19X6 was £4,090 in Jean Smith's favour.

While the intention was to bank all takings intact, it now transpires that, in addition to cash drawings, the following payments were made out of takings before bankings:

	£
Van running expenses	890
Postages, stationery and other sundry expenses	355

On 31 March 19X6, takings of £640 awaited banking; this was done on 1 April 19X6. It has been discovered that amounts paid into the bank of £340 on 29 March 19X6 were not credited to Jean's bank account until 2 April 19X6 and a cheque of £120, drawn on 28 March 19X6 for purchases was not paid until 10 April 19X6. The normal rate of gross profit on the goods sold by Jean Smith is 50% on sales. However, during the year a purchase of ornamental goldfish costing £600 proved to be unpopular with customers and therefore the entire stock bought had to be sold at cost price.

Interest at the rate of 5% per annum is payable on each anniversary of the loan from John Peacock on 1 January 19X6.

Depreciation is to be provided on the van on the straight line basis; it is estimated that the van will be disposed of after five years' use for £100.

The stock of goods for resale at 31 March 19X6 has been valued at cost at £1,900.

Creditors for purchases at 31 March 19X6 amounted to £880 and electricity charges accrued due at that date were £180.

Trade debtors at 31 March 19X6 totalled £2,300.

Required:
Prepare a trading and profit and loss account for the year ended 31 March 19X6 and a balance sheet as at that date.

(Association of Accounting Technicians)

46.17A David Denton set up in business as a plumber a year ago, and he has asked you to act as his accountant. His instructions to you are in the form of the following letter.

Dear Henry,

I was pleased when you agreed to act as my accountant and look forward to your first visit to check my records. The proposed fee of £250 p.a. is acceptable. I regret that the paperwork for the work done during the year is incomplete. I started my business on 1 January last, and put £6,500 into a business bank account on that date. I brought my van into the firm at that time, and reckon that it was worth £3,600 then. I think it will last another three years after the end of the first year of business use.

I have drawn £90 per week from the business bank account during the year. In my trade it is difficult to take a holiday, but my wife managed to get away for a while. The travel agent's bill for £280 was paid out of the business account. I bought the lease of the yard and office for £6,500. The lease has ten years to run, and the rent is only £300 a year payable in advance on the anniversary of the date of purchase, which was 1 April. I borrowed £4,000 on that day from Aunt Jane to help pay for the lease. I have agreed to pay her 10% interest per annum, but have been too busy to do anything about this yet.

I was lucky enough to meet Miss Prism shortly before I set up on my own, and she has worked for me as an office organiser right from the start. She is paid a salary of £3,000 p.a. All the bills for the year have been carefully preserved in a tool box, and we analysed them last week. The materials I have bought cost me £9,600, but I reckon there was £580 worth left in the yard on 31 December. I have not yet paid for them all yet, I think we owed £714 to the suppliers on 31 December. I was surprised to see that I had spent £4,800 on plumbing equipment, but it should last me five years or so. Electricity bills received up to 30 September came to £1,122; but motor expenses were £912, and general expenses £1,349 for the year. The insurance premium for the year to 31 March next was £800. All these have been paid by cheque but Miss Prism has lost the rate demand. I expect the Local Authority will send a reminder soon since I have not yet paid. I seem to remember that rates came to £180 for the year to 31 March next.

Miss Prism sent out bills to my customers for work done, but some of them are very slow to pay. Altogether the charges made were £29,863, but only £25,613 had been received by 31 December. Miss Prism thinks that 10% of the remaining bills are not likely to be paid. Other customers for jobs too small to bill have paid £3,418 in cash for work done, but I only managed to bank £2,600 of this money. I used £400 of the difference to pay the family's grocery bills, and Miss Prism used the rest for general expenses, except for £123 which was left over in a drawer in the office on 31 December.

Kind regards,

Yours sincerely,

David.

You are required to draw up a profit and loss account for the year ended 31 December, and a balance sheet as at that date.

(*Association of Chartered Certified Accountants*)

46.18 Since commencing business several years ago as a cloth dealer, Tom Smith has relied on annual receipts and payments accounts for assessing progress. These accounts have been prepared from his business bank account through which all business receipts and payments are passed.

Tom Smith's receipts and payments account for the year ended 31 March 19X0 is as follows:

	£		£
Opening balance	1,680	Drawings	6,300
Sales receipts	42,310	Payments for purchases	37,700
Proceeds of sale of		Van expenses	2,900
grandfather clock	870	Workshop: rent	700
Loan from John Scott	5,000	rates	570
Closing balance	1,510	Wages – John Jones	3,200
	51,370		51,370

Additional information

(a) The grandfather clock sold during the year ended 31 March 19X0 was a legacy received by Tom Smith from the estate of his late father.

(b) The loan from John Scott was received on 1 January 19X0; interest is payable on the loan at the rate of 10% per annum.

(c) In May 19X0 Tom Smith received from his suppliers a special commission of 5% of the cost of purchases during the year ended 31 March 19X0.

(d) On 1 October 19X9, Tom Smith engaged John Jones as a salesman. In addition to his wages, Jones receives a bonus of 2% of the business's sales during the period of his employment; the bonus is payable on 1 April and 1 October in respect of the immediately preceding six months' period.

Note: It can be assumed that sales have been at a uniform level throughout the year ended 31 March 19X0.

(e) In addition to the items mentioned above, the assets and liabilities of Tom Smith were as follows:

At 31 March	19X9	19X0
	£	£
Van, at cost	4,000	4,000
Stock at cost	5,000	8,000
Trade debtors	4,600	12,290
Vehicle expenses prepaid	–	100
Workshop rent accrued due	–	200
Trade creditors	2,900	2,200

(f) It can be assumed that the opening and closing balances in the above receipts and payments account require no adjustment for the purpose of Tom Smith's accounts.

(g) As from 1 April 19X9, it has been decided to provide for depreciation on the van annually at the rate of 20% of the cost.

Required:

The trading and profit and loss account for the year ended 31 March 19X0, and a balance sheet at that date of Tom Smith.

(*Association of Chartered Certified Accountants*)

46.19 On 1st September, 1997 John Wells commenced trading as a wholesaler of ladies and gents' fashion garments. On 28th March, 1998 his premises were engulfed in a fire in which all accounting records, cash, stocks and office equipment therein were destroyed.

From duplicate records and other information supplied to you, you have been able to assemble the information set out in Schedules 1 to 4 inclusive.

Schedule 1 – Analysis of Bank Statements

Payments	£	Receipts	£
Drawings	7,420	Government training grants	1,800
Trade creditors	95,600	Cash introduced	12,000
Wages	21,425	Receipts from trade debtors	125,500
PAYE taxation	3,750	Cash sales	17,481
Expense creditors	1,800	Long-term loan finance	30,000
Cash expenses (see schedule 2)	4,080		186,781
Office equipment	7,500		
Transit van	22,000		
Loan repayments	5,000		
Rent	2,400		
	170,975		

Schedule 2 – Analysis of cash expenses

Drawings	£980
Wages	£350
Expenses	£450
Purchases	£2,300
	£4,080

Schedule 3 – Balances as at 28 March 1998

Trade creditors	£10,090
Expense creditors	£120
Wages due	£2,250
PAYE taxation due	£625
Trade debtors	£11,500

Schedule 4 – Other Information

1 A customer's balance of £2,760 had been set off against a balance due to him for goods supplied.
2 Bad debts written off amounted to £804 in the period.
3 Discounts of £2,405 had been allowed to customers for early settlement of their accounts.
4 The insurance company has agreed to pay the following claims submitted in respect of the fire.

Stocks	£7,800
Office equipment	£6,800
Cash	£160

5 The transit van and the stocks loaded in the van were not damaged in the fire. These stocks were valued at £4,500.
6 Depreciation on the transit van is to be charged at the rate of 20% per annum, or part thereof.
7 The rent charged to the business is £4,800 per annum.
8 The government grants were received in respect of staff training.

Requirement:
Prepare for John Wells a Profit and Loss Account for the period 1st September, 1997, to 28th March, 1998, and a Balance Sheet as at 28th March, 1998.

NB   *Ignore any interest chargeable on the loan.*
     Ignore any VAT implications in the details supplied.

(*ICAI Professional Examination Two*)

47

The final accounts of non-profit organisations

Clubs, associations and other non-profit organisations do not have trading and profit and loss accounts drawn up for them, as their main purpose is not trading or profit making. They are run so that their members can do things such as play football or chess. The final accounts prepared by these organisations are **receipts and payments accounts, income and expenditure accounts** and balance sheets.

47.2 Receipts and payments accounts

A receipts and payments account for an organisation is a summary of its cash book for the period for which the account is prepared.

Example of a Receipts and Payments Account

The Homers Running Club
Receipts and Payments Account for the year ended 31 December 1998

Receipts	£	Payments	£
Bank balance as at 1 January	236	Groundsman's wages	728
Subscriptions received during the year	1,148	Sports stadium expenses	296
Rent received	116	Committee expenses	58
		Printing and stationery	33
		Bank balance at 31 December	385
	1,500		1,500

47.3 Income and expenditure accounts

When assets are owned, and there are liabilities, the receipts and payments account is not a good way of drawing up final accounts. Other than the cash received and paid out, it shows only the cash balances. The other assets and liabilities are not shown at all. What is required is:

1 a balance sheet, and
2 an account showing whether the association's capital has increased.

In a business, **2** would be a trading and profit and loss account. In a non-profit organisation **2** would be an income and expenditure account.

An income and expenditure account follows the same rules as trading and profit and loss accounts. The only differences are the terms used. A comparison now follows:

Terms used

Business	Non-profit Organisation
1 Trading and Profit and Loss Account	1 Income and Expenditure Account
2 Net Profit	2 Surplus of Income over Expenditure
3 Net Loss	3 Excess of Expenditure over Income

47.4 Profit or loss on a trading operation

Sometimes there are reasons why a non-profit making organisation would prepare a profit and loss account.

This is where something is done to make a profit. The profit is not to be kept, but used to pay for the main purpose of the organisation.

For instance, a football club may have discos or dances which people pay to go to. Any profit from these helps to pay club expenses. For these discos and dances a trading and profit and loss account would be drawn up. Any profit (or loss) would be transferred to the income and expenditure account.

47.5 Accumulated fund

A sole trader or a partnership would have capital accounts. A non-profit making organisation would instead have an **accumulated fund**. It is in effect the same as a capital account, as it is the difference between assets and liabilities.

In the case of a sole trader or partnership:

$$\textbf{Capital} \ = \textbf{Assets} - \textbf{Liabilities}$$

In a non-profit making organisation:

$$\textbf{Accumulated Fund} = \textbf{Assets} - \textbf{Liabilities}$$

47.6 Preparing income and expenditure accounts

We will now look at the preparation of an income and expenditure account and a balance sheet of a club in the example overleaf. A separate trading account is to be prepared for a bar, where beverages are sold to make a profit.

The majority of clubs and associations keep their accounts using single entry methods. This example will therefore be from single entry records, using the principles already described.

Example of the Preparation of an Income and Expenditure Account

Long Lane Football Club

Receipts and Payments Account for the year ended 31 December 1998

Receipts	£	Payments	£
Bank balance at 1 January	524	Payment for bar supplies	3,962
Subscriptions received for		Wages:	
1997 (arrears)	55	Groundsman and assistant	939
1998	1,236	Barman	624
1999 (in advance)	40	Bar expenses	234
Bar sales	5,628	Repairs to stands	119
Donations received	120	Ground upkeep	229
		Secretary's expenses	138
		Transport costs	305
		Bank balance at 31 December	1,053
	7,603		7,603

The treasurer of the Long Lane Football Club has prepared a receipts and payments account, but members have complained about the inadequacy of such an account. He therefore asks an accountant to prepare a trading account for the bar, an income and expenditure account and a balance sheet. The treasurer gives the accountant a copy of the receipts and payments account together with the following information regarding assets and liabilities at the beginning and end of the year:

1		31.12.1997	31.12.1998
		£	£
Stocks in the bar – at cost		496	558
Owing for bar supplies		294	340
Bar expenses owing		25	36
Transport costs		–	65

2 The land and football stands were valued at 31 December 1997 at: land £4,000; football stands £2,000; the stands are to be depreciated by 10% per annum.

3 The equipment at 31 December 1997 was valued at £550, and is to be depreciated at 20% per annum.

4 Subscriptions owing by members amounted to £55 on 31 December 1997, and £66 on 31 December 1998.

From this information, the accountant drew up the accounts that follow using the stage by stage approach that is shown.

Stage 1: Draw up a Statement of Affairs as at the beginning of the period.

Statement of Affairs as at 31 December 1997

	£	£	£
Fixed assets			
Land			4,000
Stands			2,000
Equipment			550
			6,550
Current assets			
Stock in bar		496	
Debtors for subscriptions		55	
Cash at bank		524	
		1,075	
Less Current liabilities			
Creditors	294		
Bar expenses owing	25	319	
Working capital			756
			7,306
Financed by:			
Accumulated fund (difference)			7,306

Stage 2: Draw up a Trading Account for any trading activities.

Long Lane Football Club
Bar Trading and Profit and Loss Account for the year ended 31 December 1998

	£	£
Sales		5,628
Less Cost of goods sold:		
Opening stock	496	
Add Purchases*	4,008	
	4,504	
Less Closing stock	558	3,946
Gross profit		1,682
Less Bar expenses*	245	
Barman's wages	624	869
Net profit (transfer to income and expenditure account)		813

*Working of purchases and bar expenses figures:

Purchases Control

	£		£
Cash	3,962	Balance b/d (creditors)	294
Balance c/d	340	Trading account (difference)	4,008
	4,302		4,302

Bar Expenses

	£		£
Cash	234	Balance b/d	25
Balance c/d	36	Trading account (difference)	245
	270		270

Stage 3: Draw up the Final Accounts.

Long Lane Football Club
Income and Expenditure Account for the year ended 31 December 1998

	£	£	£
Income			
Subscriptions for 1998*			1,302
Profit from the bar			813
Donations received			120
			2,235
Less Expenditure			
Wages – Groundsman and assistant		939	
Repairs to stands		119	
Ground upkeep		229	
Secretary's expenses		138	
Transport costs*		370	
Depreciation			
Stands	200		
Equipment	110	310	2,105
Surplus of income over expenditure			130

*Workings on transport costs and subscriptions figures:

Transport Costs

	£			£
Cash	305	Income and expenditure		370
Balance c/d (accrual)	65			
	370			370

Subscriptions

	£			£
Balance b/d (debtors)	55	Cash 1997		55
Income and expenditure		1998		1,236
account (difference)	1,302	1999		40
Balance c/d (in advance)	40	Balance c/d (owing)		66
	1,397			1,397

Note that subscriptions received in advance are carried down as a credit balance to the following period.

The Long Lane Football Club
Balance Sheet as at 31 December 1998

	£	£	£
Fixed assets			
Land at valuation			4,000
Pavilion at valuation		2,000	
Less Depreciation		200	1,800
Equipment at valuation		550	
Less Depreciation		110	440
			6,240
Current assets			
Stock of bar supplies		558	
Debtors for subscriptions		66	
Cash at bank		1,053	
		1,677	
Less Current liabilities			
Creditors for bar supplies	340		
Bar expenses owing	36		
Transport costs owing	65		
Subscriptions received in advance	40	481	
Working capital			1,196
			7,436
Financed by:			
Accumulated fund			
Balance as at 1 January 1998			7,306
Add Surplus of income over expenditure			130
			7,436

47.7 Outstanding subscriptions and the prudence concept

So far we have treated subscriptions owing as being an asset. However, as any treasurer of a club would tell you, most subscriptions that have been owing for a long time are never paid. A lot of clubs do not therefore show unpaid subscriptions as an asset in the balance sheet. This is obviously consistent with the prudence concept which states that assets should not be over-valued. They are therefore ignored by these clubs for final accounts purposes.

However, in an examination a student should assume that subscriptions are to be brought into the final accounts unless instructions to the contrary are given.

The following example includes subscriptions in arrears and in advance at the beginning and end of a period.

Example

An amateur theatre organisation charges an annual subscription of £20 per member. It accrues for subscriptions owing at the end of each year and also adjusts for subscriptions received in advance.

(i) On 1 January 1998, 18 members owed £360 for 1997.
(ii) In December 1997, 4 members paid £80 for 1998.

(iii) During 1998 the organisation received cash for subscriptions £7,420.

For 1997	£360
For 1998	£6,920
For 1999	£140
	£7,420

(iv) At 31 December 1998, 11 members had not paid their 1998 subscriptions.

Subscriptions

1998		£	1998		£
Jan 1	Balance (owing) b/d (i)	360	Jan 1	Balance (prepaid) b/d (ii)	80
Dec 31	Income and expenditure	*7,220	Dec 31	Bank (iii)	7,420
Dec 31	Balance (prepaid) c/d (iii)	140	Dec 31	Balance (owing) c/d (iv)	220
		7,720			7,720
1999			1999		
Jan 1	Balance owing b/d (iv)	220	Jan 1	Balance prepaid b/d (iii)	140

* Difference between two sides of the account.

47.8 Life membership

In some clubs and societies members can make a payment for life membership. This means that by paying a fairly substantial amount now the member can enjoy the facilities of the club for the rest of his life.

Such a receipt should not be treated as income in the Income and Expenditure Account solely in the year in which the member paid the money. It should be credited to a Life Membership Account, and transfers should be made from that account to the credit of the Income and Expenditure Account of an appropriate amount annually.

Exactly what is meant by an appropriate amount is decided by the committee of the club or society. The usual basis is to establish, on average, how long members will continue to use the benefits of the club. To take an extreme case, if a club was in existence which could not be joined until one achieved the age of 70, then the expected number of years' use of the club on average per member would be relatively few. Another club, such as a golf club, where a fair proportion of the members joined when reasonably young, and where the game is capable of being played by members until and during old age, would expect a much higher average of years of use per member. The club should decide for itself the average number of years of usage.

The credit balance remaining on the account, after the transfer of the agreed amount has been made to the credit of the Income and Expenditure Account, should be shown on the Balance Sheet as a liability. It is, after all, the liability of the club to provide amenities for the member without any further payment by him.

47.9 Donations received

Any donations received are usually shown as income in the year that they are received.

47.10 Entrance fees

New members often have to pay an entrance fee in the year that they join, in addition to the membership fee for that year. Entrance fees are normally included as income in the year that they are received. The club could, however, decide to treat them differently. It all depends on the circumstances.

Review questions

In addition to the questions which follow, you should attempt questions 375–382 in the accompanying book of multiple-choice questions (see back cover for details).

Suggested solutions to review questions with the letter 'A' after the question number are given in Appendix I (pages 672–7).

47.1A A summary of the Uppertown Football Club's cash book is shown below. From it, and the additional information provided you are to construct an income and expenditure account for the year ended 31 December 1998, and a balance sheet as at that date.

Cash Book Summary

	£		£
Balance at 1 January 1998	180	Purchase of equipment	125
Collections at matches	1,650	Rent for football pitch	300
Profit on sale of refreshments	315	Printing and stationery	65
		Secretary's expenses	144
		Repairs to equipment	46
		Groundsman's wages	520
		Miscellaneous expenses	66
		Balance at 31 December 1998	879
	2,145		2,145

Additional information
(i)   At 1 January 1998 equipment was valued at £500.
(ii) Depreciate all equipment 20% for 1998.
(iii) At 31 December 1998 rent paid in advance was £60.
(iv) At 31 December 1998 there was £33 owing for printing.

47.2 The Slice Golf Club has two classes of membership – full members who pay an annual subscription of £300, and associate members who pay an annual subscription of £100.

On 1st January, 1997, there were 200 full members, of whom 7 had paid their subscriptions for 1997 in advance, and 2 had still to pay their subscriptions for 1996. At the same date, there were 100 associate members, of whom 3 had paid their subscriptions for 1997 in advance.

During 1997, the 2 full members who had not paid their subscriptions for 1996 were expelled from the Club, while 12 new full members and 10 new associate members were admitted to the Club.

During 1997, the total cash received in respect of subscriptions amounted to £75,100. At 31st December, 1997, there were no arrears of subscriptions outstanding in respect of 1997.

Requirement:
Write up the Subscriptions Account for 1997.

(ICAI Professional Examination One)

47.3A The Balance Sheet of the Barwell Bowling Club as at 31st December, 1997 was as follows:

Fixed assets	£	£	£
Land and clubhouse, at cost			75,000
Equipment and furniture (cost £20,000)			11,500
			86,500
Current assets			
Bar stocks		4,600	
Subscriptions owing		1,250	
Bank current account		1,120	
Bank deposit account		3,000	
		9,970	
Current liabilities			
Creditors for bar supplies	4,200		
Subscriptions	400		
Wages due	1,150	5,750	4,220
			90,720
Long-term loan			24,000
			66,720
Accumulated fund			66,720

The club's summarised Bank Current Account for 1998 was as follows:

	£		£
Balance at 1st January	1,120	Bar purchases	50,150
Subscriptions	48,530	Bar expenses	16,600
Bar sales	85,000	Wages	23,400
Competition entries	6,700	Rates	1,500
		Loan repayment	7,200
		Competition expenses	5,200
		Equipment	5,000
		General expenses	25,500
		Transfer to deposit a/c	2,000
		Balance at 31 December	4,800
	141,350		141,350

The following information is also provided:

(a) Balances as at 31st December, 1998:

		£
Bar Stocks		5,600
Subscriptions Owing		2,500
Creditors for: Bar Supplies		6,450
Subscriptions		780
Wages		1,750

(b) The Long-term loan is to be repaid in six annual instalments of £4,000, plus interest. The interest applicable to 1998 is £3,200.

(c) Interest accrued on the Deposit Account for 1998 is £300.

(d) Depreciation is provided on Equipment and Furniture at 10% p.a. of cost price.

(e) All cash transactions were passed through the Current Account.

Required:
Prepare a Bar Trading Account and an Income and Expenditure Account for the year ended 31st December, 1998 and a Balance Sheet as at that date.

(*The Institute of Bankers in Ireland*)

47.4 The following summarised bank account was prepared for the Bunker Golf Club.

Receipts	£	Payments	£
Balance at 1st January, 1998	1,200	Bar supplies	36,000
Subscriptions	14,900	Wages and salaries	22,700
Bar receipts	51,000	Course repairs	3,000
Green fees	3,000	Rates	2,600
Dance receipts	700	Light and heat	1,400
Competition fees	2,500	Dance expenses	500
		Competition expenses	3,700
		Purchase of mower	2,700
		Sundry expenses	600
		Balance at 31st December, 1998	100
	73,300		73,300

The following additional information is available.

1

	1st January 1998	31st December 1998
	£	£
Bar creditors	5,000	4,000
Bar stock	7,000	8,000
Subscriptions in arrears	400	700
Subscriptions in advance	300	500
Light and heat due	100	200
Rates prepaid	300	500

2 At 1st January, 1998, the clubhouse and course were valued at £25,000, the fittings and furniture at £10,000 and the mowers and equipment at £5,500.
3 During 1998, an old mower with a book value of £500 at 1st January, 1998, was traded in against a new mower, the list price of which was £3,000. £2,700 was paid to the supplier of the new mower.
4 Depreciation of fixed assets is to be provided on a straight line basis as follows: Clubhouse and Course 2%, Fittings and Furniture 10%, Mowers and Equipment 20%.

You are required to prepare:
(*a*) the Income and Expenditure Account of the Bunker Golf Club for the year ended 31st December, 1998, and
(*b*) the Balance Sheet of the club as at that date.

(*ICAI Professional Examination One*)

47.5A   The following is a summary of the South Yard Football Club's Bank Account for the year ended 31st December, 1998.

Receipts	£	Payments	£
Bar receipts	56,000	Balance at 1st January	650
Members' subscriptions	7,400	Bar supplies	40,100
Members' tour contributions	7,100	Bar wages	2,200
Fund raising for tour	8,400	Light and heat	2,400
		Telephone	650
		Insurances	6,400
		Tour cost	17,500
		Buildings	7,500
Balance at 31 December	3,900	Miscellaneous expenses	5,400
	82,800		82,800

You are given the following additional information:

1 The assets of the club as at 1st January, 1998 were:
   Premises £30,000; Furniture and Equipment £8,500; Bar Stock £7,500 and Bar Suppliers were owed £3,100.
2 On 31st December, 1998 Bar Stocks were £5,600 and suppliers were owed £2,900.
3 Furniture and Equipment is to be depreciated at 10% per annum.
4 Insurances prepaid were as follows:

31st December, 1997	£1,400
31st December, 1998	£1,200

5 Subscriptions were received in advance as follows:

31st December, 1997	£750
31st December, 1998	£850

6 Light and Heat, Telephone, Insurances, Miscellaneous Expenses and Depreciation are to be apportioned equally between the bar and general activities.

You are required to prepare:
(a) a Bar Trading and Profit and Loss Account for the year ended 31st December, 1998, and
(b) the Club's Income and Expenditure Account for the year ended 31st December, 1998 and a Balance Sheet as at that date.

(*ICPAI Formation I*)

47.6A   The following receipts and payments account for the year ended 31 March 19X1 of the High Towers Rural Pursuits Society has been prepared by the society's treasurer John Higham.

	£	£
1 April 19X0 balance brought forward		1,347
Receipts:		
Membership subscriptions:		
For the year ended 31 March 19X0	252	
For the year ended 31 March 19X1	6,810	
For the year ended 31 March 19X2	330	
	7,392	
Sale of photographic equipment	28,100	
Sale of small transit coach	2,560	38,052
		39,399
Payments:		
Purchase of photographic equipment	22,734	
Lecturer for rural hobbies course	460	
Purchase of land for proposed new meeting room and office	10,000	
Bank investment deposit account	3,000	
Stationery and postages	600	
Printing year book	810	
Advertising for new members	230	
National Society affiliation fee	180	
Meeting room hire	340	
Secretary's honorarium	300	38,654
31 March 19X1 balance carried forward		£745

Additional information:

1 The Society has a policy of not accounting for subscriptions until received.
2 In addition to the items mentioned previously, the Society's assets and liabilities as at 1 April 19X0 were as follows:

	£
Stock of photographic equipment for resale, at cost	3,420
Subscriptions for the year ended 31 March 19X1	
received prior to 31 March 19X0	420
Small transit coach at cost bought 1 April 19X6	18,000
Video equipment bought 31 March 19X0	1,200

Notes:

(i)   When bought by the Society, the small transit coach was expected to be in use by the Society for five years and have a nil residual value.
(ii) The video equipment is expected to be in use by the Society until 31 March 19X4 when its residual value is expected to be £200.
(iii) The Society uses the straight line basis when providing for depreciation.

3 All receipts and payments are passed through the Society's bank current account.
4 The Society buys photographic equipment for sale to members on a cash basis at favourable prices; the photographic equipment in stock at 31 March 19X1 has been valued, at cost, at £1,800.

Members have requested that the Society's annual accounts should show the profit or loss arising from the sale of photographic equipment.

5 The Society's bank investment deposit account was credited with interest of £82 on 31 March 19X1.
6 The Society has now decided that an income and expenditure account for the year ended 31 March 19X1 and a balance sheet as at that date should be prepared.

Required:

The Society's income and expenditure account for the year ended 31 March 19X1 and a balance sheet as at that date.

(*Association of Accounting Technicians*)

47.7 The following is a summary of the receipts and payments of the Miniville Rotary Club during the year ended 31 July 19X6.

Miniville Rotary Club

Receipts and Payments Account for the year ended 31 July 19X6

	£		£
Cash and bank balances b/d	210	Secretarial expenses	163
Sales of competition tickets	437	Rent	1,402
Members' subscriptions	1,987	Visiting speakers' expenses	1,275
Donations	177	Donations to charities	35
Refund of rent	500	Prizes for competitions	270
Balance c/d	13	Stationery and printing	179
	£3,324		£3,324

The following valuations are also available:

as at 31 July	19X5	19X6
	£	£
Equipment	975	780
(original cost £1,420)		
Subscriptions in arrears	65	85
Subscriptions in advance	10	37
Owing to suppliers of competition prizes	58	68
Stocks of competition prizes	38	46

Required:

(*a*) Calculate the value of the accumulated fund of the Miniville Rotary Club as at the 1 August 19X5.

(*b*) Reconstruct the following accounts for the year ended 31 July 19X6.
  (i) the subscriptions account,
  (ii) the competition prizes account.

(*c*) Prepare an income and expenditure account for the Miniville Rotary Club for the year ended 31 July 19X6 and a balance sheet as at that date.

(*Association of Accounting Technicians*)

47.8A The accounting records of the Happy Tickers Sports and Social Club are in a mess. You manage to find the following information to help you prepare the accounts for the year to 31 December 19X0.

Summarised Balance Sheet as at 31 December 19X9

Assets	£	£
Half-share in motorised roller		600
New sports equipment unsold		1,000
Used sports equipment at valuation		700
Rent (2 months)		200
Subscriptions 19X9		60
Café stocks		800
Cash and bank		1,210
		4,570
Liabilities		
Insurance	150	
Subscriptions	120	
Life subscriptions	1,400	1,670
		2,900
Accumulated fund		2,900

Receipts during 19X0:		£
Subscriptions	– 19X9	40
	– 19X0	1,100
	– 19X1	80
	– life	200
From sales of new sports equipment		900
From sales of used sports equipment		14
Café takings		4,660
		6,994

Payments during 19X0:	£
Rent (for 12 months)	1,200
Insurance (for 18 months)	900
To suppliers of sports equipment	1,000
To café suppliers	1,900
Wages of café manager	2,000
Total cost of repairing motorised roller	450
	7,450

Notes:

(i) Ownership and all expenses of the motorised roller are agreed to be shared equally with the Carefree Conveyancers Sports and Social Club which occupies a nearby site. The roller cost a total of £2,000 on 1 January 19X6 and had an estimated life of 10 years.

(ii) Life subscriptions are brought into income equally over 10 years, in a scheme begun 5 years ago in 19X5. Since the scheme began the cost of £200 per person has been constant. Prior to 31 December 19X9 10 life subscriptions had been received.

(iii) Four more annual subscriptions of £20 each had been promised relating to 19X0, but not yet received. Annual subscriptions promised but unpaid are carried forward for a maximum of 12 months.

(iv) New sports equipment is sold to members at cost plus 50%. Used equipment is sold off to members at book valuation. Half the sports equipment bought in the year (all from a cash and carry supplier) has been used within the club, and half made available for sale, new,

to members. The 'used equipment at valuation' figure in the 31 December 19X0 balance sheet is to remain at £700.

(v) Closing café stocks are £850, and £80 is owed to suppliers at 31 December 19X0.

Required:

(*a*) Calculate profit on café operations and profit on sale of sports equipment.

(*b*) Prepare statement of subscription income for 19X0.

(*c*) Prepare income and expenditure statement for the year to 31 December 19X0, and balance sheet as at 31 December 19X0.

(*d*) Why do life subscriptions appear as a liability?

(*Association of Chartered Certified Accountants*)

47.9 The following receipts and payments account for the year ended 31 March 19X1 for the Green Bank Sports Club has been prepared by the treasurer, Andrew Swann:

Receipts	£	Payments	£
Balances brought forward		Painting of clubhouse	580
1 April 19X0		Maintenance of grounds	1,310
Cash in hand	196	Bar steward's salary	5,800
Bank current account	5,250	Insurances	240
Members subscriptions:		General expenses	1,100
Ordinary	1,575	Building society investment	
Life	800	account	1,500
Annual dinner – ticket sales	560	Secretary's honorarium	200
Bar takings	21,790	Annual dinner – expenses	610
		New furniture and fittings	1,870
		Bar purchases	13,100
		Rent of clubhouse	520
		Balances carried forward	
		31 March 19X1:	
		Bank current account	3,102
		Cash in hand	239
	£30,171		£30,171

The following additional information has been given:

(i) Ordinary membership subscriptions. £
    Received in advance at 31 March 19X0 200
    The subscriptions received during the year ended 31 March 19X1 included £150 in advance for the following year.

(ii) A life membership scheme was introduced on 1 April 19X9; under the scheme life membership subscriptions are £100 and are appointed to revenue over a ten-year period.
    Life membership subscriptions totalling £1,100 were received during the first year of the scheme.

(iii) The club's building society investment account balance at 31 March 19X0 was £2,676; during the year ended 31 March 19X1 interest of £278 was credited to the account.

(iv) All the furniture and fittings in the club's accounts at 31 March 19X0 were bought in January 19X8 at a total cost of £8,000; it is the club's policy to provide depreciation annually on fixed assets at 10% of the cost of such assets held at the relevant year end.

(v) Other assets and liabilities of the club were:

At 31 March	19X0	19X1
	£	£
Bar stocks	1,860	2,110
Insurance prepaid	70	40
Rent accrued due	130	140
Bar purchases creditors	370	460

Required:

(*a*) The bar trading and profit and loss account for the year ended 31 March 19X1.

(*b*) The club's income and expenditure account for the year ended 31 March 19X1 and a balance sheet at that date.

(*c*) Outline the advantages and disadvantages of receipts and payments accounts for organisations such as the Green Bank Sports Club.

(*Association of Chartered Certified Accountants*)

48

The final accounts of manufacturing firms

48.1 Introduction

When preparing the final accounts of manufacturing firms a **manufacturing account** is prepared in addition to the normal trading and profit and loss account and balance sheet.

48.2 The divisions of costs

In a manufacturing firm costs are divided into different types. These may be summarised in chart form as follows:

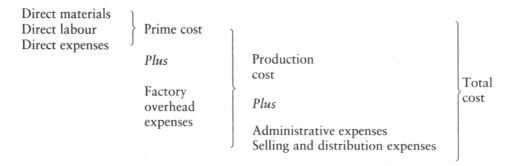

48.3 Direct and indirect costs

When you see the words **direct costs** you know that the costs of making an item have been able to be traced to the item being manufactured. If it cannot easily be traced to the item being manufactured, then it is an indirect expense and will be included under factory overhead expenses.

For example, the wages of a machine operator making a particular item will be **direct** labour. The wages of a foreman in charge of many men on different jobs will be **indirect** labour, and will be part of factory overhead expenses. Other instances of costs being direct costs include carriage inwards on raw materials (included in 'direct materials') and hire of special machinery for a job (included in 'direct expenses').

48.4 Factory overhead expenses

Factory overhead costs are all those costs which arise in the factory where production takes place, but which cannot easily be traced to the items being manufactured. Examples are:

- Wages of cleaners.
- Wages of crane drivers.
- Rent and rates of the factory.
- Depreciation of plant and machinery.
- Costs of operating fork-lift trucks.
- Factory power.
- Factory lighting.

48.5 Administration expenses

Administration expenses consist of such items as managers' salaries, legal and accountancy charges, the depreciation of accounting machinery and secretarial salaries. Administration expenses are shown in the profit and loss account **not** the manufacturing account.

48.6 Selling and distribution expenses

Selling and distribution expenses are items such as sales staff's salaries and commission, carriage outwards, depreciation of delivery vans, advertising and display expenses. Selling and distribution expenses are also shown in the profit and loss account.

48.7 Format of the final accounts of manufacturing firms

Manufacturing account

This is debited with the production cost of goods completed during the accounting period for which the account is prepared. The production cost of goods completed is made up of:

- Direct materials.
- Direct labour.
- Direct expenses.
- Factory overhead expenses.

When completed this account will show the total of production cost. This figure will then be transferred to the trading account.

Trading account

This account includes:

- Production cost transferred from the manufacturing account.
- Opening and closing stocks of finished goods.
- Sales.

When completed this account will disclose the gross profit. This will then be carried down to the profit and loss account.

Thus, the manufacturing account and the trading account and the relationship between them can be shown as follows:

Manufacturing Account

	£
Cost of direct materials	xxx
Cost of direct labour	xxx
Direct expenses	xxx
Factory overhead expenses	xxx
Production cost of goods completed	xxx

Trading Account

	£	£
Sales		xxx
Cost of sales		
Opening stock of finished goods (a)	xxx	
Production cost of goods completed	xxx	
Less closing stock of finished goods (b)	xxx	xxx
Gross profit		xxx

(a) is the production cost of goods unsold in the previous period

(b) is the production cost of goods unsold at the end of this period

Note: The above assumes that all finished goods are manufactured rather than being bought in for re-sale.

Profit and loss account

This account includes:

- Gross profit transferred from the trading account.
- All administration expenses.
- All selling and distribution expenses.

When completed, this account will show the net profit.

48.8 Example of the preparation of a simple manufacturing account

Details necessary to prepare a simple manufacturing account are given below. It has been assumed that there were no partly completed units (known as **work in progress**) either at the beginning or end of the period.

Details of production costs for the year ended 31 December 1998:

	£
1 January 1998, stock of raw materials	500
31 December 1998, stock of raw materials	700
Raw materials purchased during the year	8,000
Manufacturing (direct) wages	21,000
Royalties	150
Indirect wages	9,000
Rent of Factory – excluding administration and selling and distribution blocks	440
Depreciation of plant and machinery in factory	400
General indirect expenses	310

Manufacturing Account for the year ended 31 December 1998

	£	£
Stock of raw materials at 1 January 1998		500
Add Purchases		8,000
		8,500
Less Stock of raw materials at 31 December 1998		700
Cost of raw materials consumed		7,800
Manufacturing wages		21,000
Royalties		150
Prime cost		28,950
Factory overhead expenses		
Rent	440	
Indirect wages	9,000	
General expenses	310	
Depreciation of plant and machinery	400	10,150
Production cost of goods completed		39,100

Sometimes, if a firm has produced less than the customers have demanded, then the firm may well have bought an outside supply of finished goods. In this case, the trading account will have both a figure for purchases and for production cost of goods completed. This will also happen where a manufacturing firm does not manufacture all of the finished goods which it sells.

48.9 Work in progress

The production cost to be transferred to the trading account is the production cost of the goods *completed* during the period. If items have not been completed, they cannot be sold. Therefore, they should not appear in the trading account.

For instance, if we have the following information, we can calculate the transfer to the trading account:

	£
Total production costs incurred during the year	5,000
Production costs last year on goods not completed last year, but completed in this year (work in progress)	300
Production costs this year on goods which were not completed by the year end (work in progress)	440

The calculation of the production cost of goods completed this year is:

	£
Total production costs incurred this year	5,000
Add Costs from last year, in respect of goods completed in this year (work in progress)	300
	5,300
Less Costs in this year, for goods to be completed next year (work in progress)	440
Production cost of goods completed this year	4,860

48.10 A further example of the preparation of a manufacturing account

Given the following information, prepare a manufacturing account and trading account for the year ended 31 December 1998:

	£
1 January 1998, Stock of raw materials	800
31 December 1998, Stock of raw materials	1,050
1 January 1998, Work in progress	350
31 December 1998, Work in progress	420
Year to 31 December 1998:	
Wages: Direct	3,960
Indirect	2,550
Purchase of raw materials	8,700
Fuel and power	990
Direct expenses	140
Lubricants	300
Carriage inwards on raw materials	200
Rent of factory	720
Depreciation of factory plant and machinery	420
Internal transport expenses	180
Insurance of factory buildings and plant	150
General factory expenses	330

Manufacturing Account for the year ended 31 December 1998

	£	£
Stock of raw materials at 1 January 1998		800
Add Purchases		8,700
" Carriage inwards		200
		9,700
Less Stock of raw materials at 31 December 1998		1,050
Cost of raw materials consumed		8,650
Direct wages		3,960
Direct expenses		140
PRIME COST		12,750
Factory overhead expenses:		
Fuel and power	990	
Indirect wages	2,550	
Lubricants	300	
Rent	720	
Depreciation of plant	420	
Internal transport expenses	180	
Insurance	150	
General factory expenses	330	5,640
		18,390
Add Work in progress at 1 January 1998		350
		18,740
Less Work in progress at 31 December 1998		420
PRODUCTION COST OF GOODS COMPLETED		18,320

The trading account is concerned with finished goods. If in the foregoing example there had been £3,500 stock of finished goods at 1 January 1998 and £4,400 at 31 December 1998, and the sales of finished goods amounted to £25,000, then the trading account would appear:

Trading Account for the year ended 31 December 1998

	£	£
Sales		25,000
Less Cost of goods sold:		
Stock of finished goods at 1 January 1998	3,500	
Add Production cost of goods completed	18,320	
	21,820	
Less Stock of finished goods at 31 December 1998	4,400	17,420
Gross profit		7,580

The profit and loss account is then prepared in the normal way.

48.11 Apportionment of expenses

Quite often expenses will have to be split between

- Factory overhead expenses: to be charged in the manufacturing account
- Administration expenses: } to be charged in the profit and
- Selling and distribution expenses: loss account

An example of this could be the rent expense. If the rent is paid separately for each part of the organisation, then it is easy to charge the rent to each sort of expense. However, only one amount of rent may be paid, without any indication as to how much is for the factory part, how much is for the selling and distribution part and how much for the administration buildings.

How the rent expense will be apportioned in the latter case will depend on circumstances. The objective is to apportion costs in the most equitable way possible. This may be achieved, for example, by apportioning costs on the basis of the floor area used by the factory, the sales department and the administration department. Costs could, however, be apportioned in numerous other ways.

48.12 A comprehensive example of the final accounts of a manufacturing firm

A complete worked example is now given. Note that in the profit and loss account the expenses have been separated so as to show whether they are administration expenses, selling and distribution expenses, or financial charges.

The trial balance extracted from the books of J Jarvis, a Toy Manufacturer, as at 31 December 1998 was as follows:

J Jarvis

Trial Balance as at 31 December 1998	Dr	Cr
	£	£
Stock of raw materials at 1 January 1998	2,100	
Stock of finished goods at 1 January 1998	3,890	
Work in progress at 1 January 1998	1,350	
Wages (direct £18,000; Factory indirect £14,500)	32,500	
Royalties	700	
Carriage inwards (on raw materials)	350	
Purchases of raw materials	37,000	
Productive machinery (cost £28,000)	23,000	
Office equipment (cost £2,000)	1,200	
General factory expenses	3,100	
Lighting	750	
Factory power	1,370	
Administrative salaries	4,400	
Salesmen's salaries	3,000	
Commission on sales	1,150	
Rent	1,200	
Insurance	420	
General administration expenses	1,340	
Bank charges	230	
Discounts allowed	480	
Carriage outwards	590	
Sales		100,000
Debtors and creditors	14,230	12,500
Bank	5,680	
Cash	150	
Drawings	2,000	
Capital as at 1 January 1998		29,680
	142,180	142,180

Notes at 31 December 1998:

1 Stock of raw materials £2,400, stock of finished goods £4,000, work in progress £1,500.

2 Lighting, and rent and insurance are to be apportioned: factory ⅚ths, administration ⅙th.

3 Depreciate productive machinery and office equipment at 10% per annum on cost.

J Jarvis

Manufacturing, Trading and Profit and Loss Account for the year ended 31 December 1998

	£	£	£
Stock of raw materials at 1 January 1998			2,100
Add Purchases			37,000
„ Carriage inwards			350
			39,450
Less Stock raw materials at 31 December 1998			2,400
Cost of raw materials consumed			37,050
Direct labour			18,000
Royalties			700
PRIME COST			55,750
Factory overhead expenses:			
General factory expenses		3,100	
Lighting ⅚ths		625	
Power		1,370	
Rent ⅚ths		1,000	
Insurance ⅚ths		350	
Depreciation of productive machinery		2,800	
Indirect labour		14,500	23,745
			79,495
Add Work in progress at 1 January 1998			1,350
			80,845
Less Work in progress at 31 December 1998			1,500
Production cost of goods completed			79,345
Sales			100,000
Less Cost of goods sold:			
Stock of finished goods at 1 January 1998		3,890	
Add Production cost of goods completed		79,345	
		83,235	
Less Stock of finished goods at 31 December 1998		4,000	79,235
Gross profit			20,765
Administration expenses			
Administrative salaries	4,400		
Rent ⅙th	200		
Insurance ⅙th	70		
General expenses	1,340		
Lighting ⅙th	125		
Depreciation of office equipment	200	6,335	
Selling and distribution expenses			
Salesmen's salaries	3,000		
Commission on sales	1,150		
Carriage outwards	590	4,740	
Financial charges			
Bank charges	230		
Discounts allowed	480	710	11,785
Net profit			8,980

J Jarvis
Balance Sheet as at 31 December 1998

	£	£
Fixed assets		
Productive machinery at cost	28,000	
Less Depreciation to date	7,800	20,200
Office equipment at cost	2,000	
Less Depreciation to date	1,000	1,000
		21,200
Current assets		
Stock		
Raw materials	2,400	
Finished goods	4,000	
Work in progress	1,500	
Debtors	14,230	
Bank	5,680	
Cash	150	
	27,960	
Less Current liabilities		
Creditors	12,500	
Working capital		15,460
		36,660
Financed by:		
Capital		
Balance as at 1 January 1998		29,680
Add Net profit		8,980
		38,660
Less Drawings		2,000
		36,660

48.13 Market value of goods manufactured

The accounts of J Jarvis, just illustrated, are subject to the limitation that the respective amounts of the gross profit which are attributable to the manufacturing side or to the selling side of the firm are not known. A technique is sometimes used to bring out this additional information. Using this method the cost which would have been incurred if the goods had been bought in their finished state instead of being manufactured by the firm is brought into account. This is credited to the manufacturing account and debited to the trading account so as to produce two gross profit figures instead of one. The net profit will remain unaffected. All that will have happened will be that the figure of £20,765 gross profit will be shown as two figures instead of one.

The accounts in summarised form will appear:

Manufacturing, Trading and Profit and Loss Account for the year ended 31 December 1998

	£	£
Market value of goods completed		95,000
Less Production cost of goods completed (as before)		79,345
Gross profit on manufacture		15,655
Sales		100,000
Stock of finished goods at 1 January 1998	3,890	
Add Market value of goods completed	95,000	
	98,890	
Less Stock of finished goods 31 December 1998	4,000	94,890
Gross profit on trading		5,110
Gross profit:		
On manufacturing	15,655	
On trading	5,110	20,765

48.14 Depreciation in the context of manufacturing firms

In Chapter 24 the straight line and reducing balance methods of depreciation were examined. We can now look at some further methods.

There is no information easily available to show how many organisations are using each method. It is possible to devise one's own special method. If it brings about an equitable charge for depreciation for that organisation, then the method will be suitable.

The revaluation method of calculating depreciation

When there are a few expensive fixed assets, it is not difficult to draw up the necessary accounts for depreciation. For each item we:

(i)   Find its cost;
(ii) Estimate its years of use to the firm;
(iii) Calculate and provide depreciation;
(iv) Make the adjustments when the asset is disposed of; and
(v)   Calculate the profit or loss on disposal.

This is worth doing for expensive items. There are, however, many examples of fixed assets for which the calculation would not be worth doing, and in fact may be impossible.

Some firms will have many low cost fixed assets. Garages or engineering works will have a lot of spanners, screwdrivers and other small tools; brewers will have crates; laboratories will have many small, low cost glass instruments. All of these items are fixed assets because they have an expected useful life greater than one year and therefore, must be depreciated.

It would be impossible to follow procedures (i) to (v) above for every screwdriver or crate. Instead the revaluation method is used.

The method is not difficult to use. An example of this method follows.

Example of the Revaluation Method of Calculating Depreciation

A firm has a lot of small loose tools which are not sold but are used by the firm for repairs, etc.

	£
On 1 January 1998 the tools were valued at	3,500
During the year to 31 December tools were purchased costing	1,300
On 31 December 1998 the tools were valued at	3,800

The depreciation is calculated as follows:

	£
Value at the start of the period	3,500
Add Cost of items bought during the period	1,300
	4,800
Less Value at the end of the period	3,800
Depreciation for the period	1,000

The depreciation figure of £1,000 will be charged as an expense. Using this idea, we can see in the following example, where depreciation is entered in the books for the first three years of a firm starting trading. This example could apply equally to packing crates, containers, etc.

Double entry records for depreciation calculated using the revaluation method

The firm started in business on 1 January 1996.

	£
In its first year it buys tools costing	800
Their estimated value at 31 December 1996	540
Tools bought in the year ended 31 December 1997	320
Estimated value of all tools in hand on 31 December 1997	530
Tools bought in the year ended 31 December 1998	590
Estimated value of all tools in hand on 31 December 1998	700

Tools

1996		£	1996		£
Dec 31 Cash (during the year)		800	Dec 31 Profit and loss		260
			„ 31 Balance c/d (valuation)		540
		800			800
1997			1997		
Jan 1 Balance b/d (valuation)		540	Dec 31 Profit and loss		330
Dec 31 Cash (during the year)		320	„ 31 Balance c/d (valuation)		530
		860			860
1998			1998		
Jan 1 Balance b/d (valuation)		530	Dec 31 Profit and loss		420
Dec 31 Cash (during the year)		590	„ 31 Balance c/d (valuation)		700
		1,120			1,120
1999					
Jan 1 Balance b/d (valuation)		700			

Profit and Loss Account charges for the years ended 31 December

		£
1996	Use of tools	260
1997	Use of tools	330
1998	Use of tools	420

The balance of the tools account at the end of each year is shown as a fixed asset in the balance sheet.

Sometimes the firm may make its own items such as tools or crates. In these instances the tools account or crates account should be debited with labour costs and material costs.

Revaluation is also used, for instance, by a farmer for his cattle. Like other fixed assets depreciation should be provided for, but during the early life of an animal it will be appreciating in value only to depreciate later. The task of calculating the cost of an animal becomes virtually impossible if it has been born on the farm, reared on the farm by grazing on the pasture land and from other foodstuffs, some grown by the farmer and others bought by him.

To get over this problem the revaluation method is used. Because of the difficulty of calculating the cost of the animals, they are valued at the price which they would fetch if sold at market. This is an exception to the general rule of assets being shown at cost price.

The depletion unit method of calculating depreciation

With fixed assets such as a quarry from which raw materials are extracted to be sold to the building industry, a different method is needed.

If a quarry was bought for £5,000 and it was expected to contain 1,000 tons of saleable materials, then for each ton taken out we would depreciate it by £5, i.e. £5,000 ÷ 1,000 = £5.

This can be shown as:

$$\frac{\text{Cost of fixed asset}}{\text{Expected total contents in units}} \times \text{Number of units taken in period}$$

= Depreciation for that period.

The machine hour method of calculating depreciation

With a machine the depreciation provision may be based on the number of hours that the machine was operated during the period compared with the total expected running hours during the machine's life with the firm. A firm which bought a machine costing £2,000 having an expected running life of 1,000 hours, and no scrap value, could provide for depreciation of the machine at the rate of £2 for every hour it was operated during a particular accounting period.

The sum of the years' digits method of calculating depreciation

This method is popular in the USA but not common in Ireland. It provides for higher depreciation to be charged early in the life of an asset with lower depreciation in later years.

Given an asset costing £3,000 which will be in use for 5 years, the calculations will be:

From the date of purchase the asset will last for	5 years
From the second year the asset will last for	4 years
From the third year the asset will last for	3 years
From the fourth year the asset will last for	2 years
From the fifth year the asset will last for	1 year
Sum of these digits	15

	£
1st Year of 5/15ths of £3,000 is charged =	1,000
2nd Year of 4/15ths of £3,000 is charged =	800
3rd Year of 3/15ths of £3,000 is charged =	600
4th Year of 2/15ths of £3,000 is charged =	400
5th Year of 1/15th of £3,000 is charged =	200
	3,000

The units of output method of calculating depreciation

This method establishes the total expected units of output expected from the asset. Depreciation, based on cost less salvage value, is then calculated for the period by taking that period's units of output as a proportion of the total expected output over the life of the asset.

An example of this could be a machine which is expected to be able to produce 10,000 units of a particular product over its useful life. It has cost £6,000 and has an expected salvage value of £1,000. In year one 1,500 units are produced, and in year two the production is 2,500 units.

The depreciation per period is calculated :

$$\text{Cost} - \text{salvage value} \times \frac{\text{period's production}}{\text{total expected production}}$$

$$\text{Year 1: } £5,000 \times \frac{1,500}{10,000} = £750 \text{ depreciation}$$

$$\text{Year 2: } £5,000 \times \frac{2,500}{10,000} = £1,250 \text{ depreciation}$$

Review questions

In addition to the questions which follow, you should attempt questions 383–398 in the accompanying book of multiple-choice questions (see back cover for details).

Suggested solutions to review questions with the letter 'A' after the question number are given in Appendix I (pages 677–82).

48.1A A firm both buys loose tools and also makes some loose tools itself. The following data is available concerning the years ended 31 December 1996, 1997, and 1998.

1996		£
Jan 1	Value of loose tools	1,250
	During the year:	
	Bought loose tools from suppliers	2,000
	Made own loose tools: the cost of wages of employees being	
	£275 and the materials cost £169	
Dec 31	Loose tools valued at	2,700
1997		
	During the year:	
	Loose tools bought from suppliers	1,450
	Made own loose tools: the cost of wages of employees being	
	£495 and the materials cost £390	
Dec 31	Loose tools valued at	3,340
1998		
	During the year:	
	Loose tools bought from suppliers	1,890
	Made own loose tools: the cost of wages of employees being	
	£145 and the materials cost £290. Received refund from a	
	supplier for faulty tools returned to him	88
Dec 31	Loose tools valued at	3,680

Required:
You are to draw up the Loose Tools Account for the three years, showing the amount transferred as an expense in each year to the Manufacturing Account.

48.2A On 1 April 19X6 a business purchased a machine costing £112,000. The machine can be used for a total of 20,000 hours over an estimated life of 48 months. At the end of that time the machine is expected to have a trade-in value of £12,000.

The financial year of the business ends on the 31 December each year. It is expected that the machine will be used for:

4,000 hours during the financial year ending 31 December 19X6
5,000 hours during the financial year ending 31 December 19X7
5,000 hours during the financial year ending 31 December 19X8
5,000 hours during the financial year ending 31 December 19X9
1,000 hours during the financial year ending 31 December 19X0

Required:
(a) Calculate the annual depreciation charges on the machine on each of the following bases for each of the financial years ending on the 31 December 19X6, 19X7, 19X8, 19X9 and 19X0:
   (i) the straight line method applied on a month for month basis,
   (ii) the diminishing balance method at 40% per annum applied on a full year basis, and
   (iii) the units of output method.
(b) Suppose that during the financial year ended 31 December 19X7 the machine was used for only 1,500 hours before being sold for £80,000 on the 30 June.

   Assuming that the business has chosen to apply the straight line method on a month for month basis show the following accounts for 19X7 only:
   (i) the Machine Account,
   (ii) the Provision for Depreciation — Machine Account, and
   (iii) the Assets Disposals Account.

(Association of Accounting Technicians)

48.3 On 1 January 19X1 a business purchased a laser printer costing £1,800. The printer has an estimated life of 4 years after which it will have no residual value.

It is expected that the output from the printer will be:

Year	Sheets printed
19X1	35,000
19X2	45,000
19X3	45,000
19X4	55,000
	180,000

Required:

(a) Calculate the annual depreciation charges for 19X1, 19X2, 19X3 and 19X4 on the laser printer on the following bases:
(i) the straight line basis,
(ii) the diminishing balance method at 60% per annum, and
(iii) the units of output method.
   Note: Your workings should be to the nearest £.
(b) Suppose that in 19X4 the laser printer were to be sold on 1 July for £200 and that the business had chosen to depreciate it at 60% per annum using the diminishing balance method applied on a month for month basis.
   Reconstruct the following accounts for 19X4 only:
(i) the Laser Printer account,
(ii) the Provision for Depreciation – Laser Printer account, and
(iii) the Assets Disposals account.

(*Association of Accounting Technicians*)

48.4A Prepare manufacturing, trading and profit and loss accounts from the following balances of T Jackson for the year ended 31 December 1998.

	£
Stocks at 1 January 1998:	
Raw materials	18,450
Work in progress	23,600
Finished goods	17,470
Purchases: Raw materials	64,300
Carriage on raw materials	1,605
Direct labour	65,810
Office salaries	16,920
Rent	2,700
Office lighting and heating	5,760
Depreciation: Factory machinery	8,300
Depreciation: Office equipment	1,950
Sales	200,600
Factory fuel and power	5,920

Rent is to be apportioned: Factory ⅔rds; Office ⅓. Stocks at 31 December 1994 were: Raw materials £20,210, Work in progress £17,390, Finished goods £21,485.

48.5A Manufacturers Ltd is a small Irish company which produces automotive components for both the domestic and export markets. The following balances as at the year-end date have been extracted from the books of the company.

Manufacturers Ltd
Draft List of Selected Balances as at 31st December, 1997

	£
Purchases of raw materials during 1997	45,000
Carriage in on purchases of raw materials	2,000
Direct labour	26,000
Variable factory overheads	11,000
Fixed factory overheads	8,000
Rent and rates	16,000
Light and heat	4,000
Import duty charged on 1997 raw material purchases	4,500
Loose tools purchased	2,000
Plant and machinery (cost £30,000)	18,000
Royalties on manufacturing processes	5,000
Hire of special equipment to manufacture complex components	3,000
Quality control supervisor's wages	12,000
Stocks on hand on January 1st, 1997	
• Raw materials	8,000
• Work in progress	6,000
• Loose tools	1,000

The following information may be relevant:

1 Depreciation is to be provided for 1997 on Plant and Machinery at 10% of original cost.
2 An additional amount of £3,000, representing the direct factory wages for December 1997 as yet unpaid, should be accrued. Rent and Rates prepaid amount to £2,000.
3 Stocks on Hand on December 31st, 1997 were as follows:

Raw materials	£9,000
Loose tools	£750
Work in progress	£8,000

4 The 'Rent and Rates' and 'Light and Heat' expenses are to be apportioned 50:50 between Factory costs and Administrative expenses respectively.

Required:
Prepare a Manufacturing Account for the company for the year ended 31st December 1997.

48.6A   Mr Murphy has been in business for some years as a manufacturer and the following list of balances were extracted from his books on 31st December, 1997.

	£ Debit	£ Credit
Purchases of raw materials	60,000	
Sales		150,000
Carriage inwards	1,000	
Stock of raw materials at 1st January, 1997	6,000	
Direct manufacturing wages	55,000	
Stock of work-in-progress at 1st January, 1997	7,000	
Debtors	22,000	
Creditors		17,000
Provision for bad debts		600
Bad debts	400	
Machinery at cost	40,000	
Provision for depreciation of machinery		10,000
Rent of premises	12,000	
Capital		28,000
Drawings	1,500	
Stock of finished goods at 1st January, 1997	3,300	
Manufacturing overheads	16,000	
Selling and distribution overheads	11,000	
Balance at bank (overdrawn)		39,600
Administration overheads (non-manufacturing)	10,000	
	245,200	245,200

Additional information
1   Stocks at 31st December, 1997, were as follows.

Raw materials	£8,000
Work-in-progress	£5,000
Finished goods	£4,400

2   Depreciation is to be provided on machinery at 25% of cost.
3   The provision for bad debts is to be made equal to 10% of debtors.
4   £500 is due for rent and was not included in the books at the year end. Rent of premises is to be apportioned 50% to manufacturing and 50% to selling and distribution overheads.

You are required to prepare for Mr Murphy:
(*a*)   the Manufacturing, Trading and Profit and Loss Account, for the year ended 31st December, 1997; and
(*b*)   the Balance Sheet at that date.

(*IATI Foundation Examination*)

48.7 A client of your firm, Denis O'Connor, operates a manufacturing business. The following list of balances was extracted from his books at 31st December, 1997:

	£ Debit	£ Credit
Sales		375,000
Purchases of raw materials	135,000	
Carriage inwards	3,000	
Direct wages	40,000	
Factory overheads	50,000	
Administrative overheads	35,000	
Selling and distribution overheads	45,000	
Rent and rates	14,000	
Bank interest and charges	2,000	
Bad debts	7,000	
Premises at cost	95,000	
Accumulated depreciation on premises		19,000
Plant and equipment at cost	50,000	
Accumulated depreciation on plant and equipment		18,000
Stock of raw materials at 1st January, 1997	37,000	
Stock of work-in-progress at 1st January, 1997	28,000	
Stock of finished goods at 1st January, 1997	8,000	
Debtors	76,000	
Provision for bad debts as at 31st December, 1997		12,000
Prepayments	15,000	
Balance at bank	38,000	
Creditors		56,000
Accruals		29,000
Capital: 1st January, 1997		188,000
Drawings	19,000	
	697,000	697,000

Additional information
1 The entire premises measures 10,000 square feet. The administration area amounts to 3,900 square feet. The sales and distribution area amounts to 1,500 square feet. The balance of 4,600 square feet is devoted exclusively to manufacturing. Rent and rates is to be apportioned in proportion to the area occupied.
2 Depreciation is to be provided for premises at 2% on the straight line basis. Depreciation is to be provided for plant and equipment at 20% on the reducing balance basis. All depreciation is to be included in 'Factory overheads'.
3 Stocks and work-in-progress at 31st December, 1997, were as follows:

Raw materials	£34,000
Finished goods	£6,000
Work-in-progress	£32,000

You are required to prepare:
(a) the Manufacturing Account and Trading and Profit and Loss Account for Denis O'Connor for the year ended 31st December, 1997.
(b) the Balance Sheet as at that date.

(*IATI Foundation Examination*)

48.8 The following Trial Balance was extracted from the books of Selkirk Ltd for the year ended 31st December, 1998:

	Debit £000	Credit £000
Stocks of raw materials, 1st January, 1998	20	
Work-in-progress, 1st January, 1998	7	
Finished goods, 1st January, 1998	31	
Raw material purchases	250	
Carriage on purchases of raw material	1	
Raw material returns outwards		2
Wages	63	
Indirect production materials	2	
Royalties	3	
Salesmen's salaries and commission	9	
Heat and light	10	
Postage and telephone	2	
Rental of office space	12	
Office salaries	8	
General expenses	14	
Insurance	9	
Production plant and machinery (cost £120,000)	84	
Office equipment (cost £50,000)	30	
Delivery vans (cost £30,000)	24	
Sales		450
Sales returns	3	
Debtors and creditors	68	52
Ordinary share capital (Ordinary shares of £1 each fully paid)		100
Bank	12	
Provision for bad debts		2
Retained profit at 1st January, 1998		56
	662	662

Additional information

1 A stock-take was carried out at 31st December, 1998, which produced the following results:

Raw materials	£15,000
Work-in-progress	£9,000
Finished goods	£32,000

Included in the finished goods stock is stock at an original cost of £4,000 which was damaged in a fire. This stock would only realise £2,000, if sold on the open market.

2 Wages included in the Trial Balance are to be split as follows:

Direct wages	£40,000
Indirect factory wages	£23,000
	£63,000

3 Depreciation is to be provided as follows:

Production plant and machinery	10% on cost
Office equipment	20% on cost
Delivery vans	20% on net book value

4 Professional fees of £4,000 have not been provided for.

5 Rental of office space amounts to £8,000 per annum. Rent has been paid up to 30th June, 1999.

6 Bad debts amounting to £1,200 should be written off. The bad debts provision is to be adjusted to 5% of debtors.

7 Expenses are to be apportioned as follows:

	Production	Administration
Insurance	2/3	1/3
Heat and light	3/4	1/4
General expenses	1/2	1/2

You are required to prepare:

(a) the Manufacturing, Trading and Profit and Loss Account for the year ended 31st December, 1998.

(b) the Balance Sheet as at that date.

(ICAI Professional Examination One)

48.9A The following Trial Balance was extracted from the books of B. Sharpe on 31st July, 1998.

	£ Debit	£ Credit
Vehicles (cost £48,000)	28,800	
Factory machinery (cost £80,000)	64,000	
Office equipment (cost £7,800)	6,240	
Stocks as at 1st August, 1997		
Raw materials	64,000	
Work-in-progress	13,200	
Finished goods	125,000	
Trade debtors	116,000	
Trade creditors		68,000
Bank		13,140
Sales		971,000
Purchases of raw materials	546,000	
Purchases of finished goods	59,800	
Carriage on raw materials	18,600	
Factory wages	121,000	
Machine maintenance and repairs	21,500	
Rent and rates	12,600	
Insurance	17,400	
Light, heat and power	25,200	
Motor and travelling expenses	36,000	
Telephone and postage	8,900	
General office expenses	14,600	
Office wages	16,400	
Bank interest and charges	9,100	
Drawings	26,100	
Capital		298,300
	1,350,440	1,350,440

Notes

1 Stocks as at 31st July, 1998 were:

Raw materials	£56,000
Work-in-progress	£9,100
Finished goods	£137,000

2 Expenses due but unpaid at 31st July, 1998 were:

General office expenses	£3,200
Insurance	£1,200
Accountancy charges	£2,500

3 Provide for depreciation on the cost of fixed assets at the following rates:

Vehicles	20% per annum
Factory machinery	20% per annum
Office equipment	10% per annum

4 Expenses are to be apportioned as follows:

	Factory	*Office*
Rent and rates	5/6	1/6
Insurances	5/6	1/6
Light, heat and power	5/6	1/6

5 Bad Debts totalling £8,000 are to be written off and a provision of 2.5% of debtors is to be made for doubtful debts.

6 Discounts received during the year amounted to £4,500. No entries were made in the Creditors Ledger in respect of these.

You are required to prepare:
(*a*) a Trading and Profit and Loss Account for the year ended 31st July, 1998, and
(*b*) a Balance Sheet as at that date.

(*ICPAI Formation I*)

48.10A The following list of balances as at 31 July 19X6 has been extracted from the books of Jane Seymour who commenced business on 1 August 19X5 as a designer and manufacturer of kitchen furniture:

	£
Plant and machinery, at cost on 1 August 19X5	60,000
Vehicles, at cost on 1 August 19X5	30,000
Loose tools, at cost	9,000
Sales	170,000
Raw materials purchased	43,000
Direct factory wages	39,000
Light and power	5,000
Indirect factory wages	8,000
Machinery repairs	1,600
Vehicle running expenses	12,000
Rent and insurances	11,600
Administrative staff salaries	31,000
Administrative expenses	9,000
Sales and distribution staff salaries	13,000
Capital at 1 August 19X5	122,000
Sundry debtors	16,500
Sundry creditors	11,200
Balance at bank	8,500
Drawings	6,000

Additional information for the year ended 31 July 19X6:

(i) It is estimated that the plant and machinery will be used in the business for 10 years and the vehicles used for 4 years: in both cases it is estimated that the residual value will be nil. The straight line method of providing for depreciation is to be used.

(ii) Light and power charges accrued due at 31 July 19X6 amounted to £1,000 and insurances prepaid at 31 July 19X6 totalled £800.

(iii) Stocks were valued at cost at 31 July 19X6 as follows:

| Raw materials | £7,000 |
| Finished goods | £10,000 |

(iv) The valuation of work in progress at 31 July 19X6 included variable and fixed factory overheads and amounted to £12,300.

(v) Two-thirds of the light and power and rent and insurances costs are to be allocated to the factory costs and one-third to general administration costs.

(vi) Vehicle costs are to be allocated equally to factory costs and general administration costs.

(vii) Goods manufactured during the year are to be transferred to the trading account at £95,000.

(viii) Loose tools in hand on 31 July 19X6 were valued at £5,000.

Required:

(a) Prepare a manufacturing, trading and profit and loss account for the year ended 31 July 19X6 of Jane Seymour.

(b) An explanation of how each of the following accounting concepts have affected the preparation of the above accounts:

- conservatism,
- matching,
- going concern.

(*Association of Accounting Technicians*)

48.11 The following balances as at 31 December 19X5 have been extracted from the books of William Speed, a small manufacturer:

		£
Stocks at 1 January 19X5:	Raw materials...	7,000
	Work in progress......................................	5,000
	Finished goods...	6,900
Purchases of raw materials	....	38,000
Direct labour	....	28,000
Factory overheads:	Variable...	16,000
	Fixed	9,000
Administrative expenses:	Rent and rates	19,000
	Heat and light	6,000
	Stationery and postage	2,000
	Staff salaries	19,380
Sales	....	192,000
Plant and machinery:	At cost..	30,000
	Provision for depreciation	12,000
Vehicles (for sales deliveries):		
At cost	....	16,000
Provision for depreciation	....	4,000
Creditors	....	5,500
Debtors	....	28,000
Drawings	....	11,500
Balance at bank	....	16,600
Capital at 1 January 19X5	....	48,000
Provision for unrealised profit at 1 January 19X5....................		1,380
Vehicle running costs	....	4,500

Additional information

(i)   Stocks at 31 December 19X5 were as follows:

	£
Raw materials	9,000
Work in progress	8,000
Finished goods	10,350

(ii)   The factory output is transferred to the trading account at factory cost plus 25% for factory profit. The finished goods stock is valued on the basis of amounts transferred to the debit of the trading account.

(iii) Depreciation is provided annually at the following percentages of the original cost of fixed assets held at the end of each financial year:

Plant and machinery	10%
Vehicles	25%

(iv) Amounts accrued due at 31 December 19X5 for direct labour amounted to £3,000 and rent and rates prepaid at 31 December 19X5 amounted to £2,000.

Required:

Prepare a manufacturing, trading and profit and loss account for the year ended 31 December 19X5 and a balance sheet as at that date.

Note: The prime cost and total factory cost should be clearly shown.

(*Association of Accounting Technicians*)

49

Departmental accounts

49.1 Usefulness of departmental accounts

Some accounting information is more useful than others. For a retail store with five departments, it is better to know that the store has made £10,000 gross profit than not to know what the gross profit was. Obviously it would be better if we know how much gross profit was made in each department.

Assume that the gross profits and losses of the departments were as follows:

Department	Gross profit	Gross loss
	£	£
A	4,000	
B	3,000	
C	5,000	
D		8,000
E	6,000	
	18,000	8,000

Gross profit of the firm, £10,000.

If we knew the above, we could see how well, or how badly, each part of the business was doing. If we closed down department D we could make a greater total gross profit of £18,000. Perhaps we could replace department D with a department which would make a gross profit instead of a loss.

You would have to know more about the business before you could be certain what the figures mean. Some stores deliberately allow parts of their business to lose money, so that customers come to the store to buy the cheap goods and then spend money in the other departments.

Accounting information therefore seldom tells the full story. It serves as one measure, but there are other non-accounting factors to be considered before a relevant decision for action can be made.

The various pros and cons of the actions to be taken to increase the overall profitability of the business cannot therefore be properly considered until the departmental gross profits or losses are known. It must not be thought that departmental accounts refer only to departmental stores. They refer to the various facets of a business.

The reputations of many successful businesspeople have been built up on their ability to utilise the departmental account principle to guide their actions to increase the profitability of a firm. The lesson still has to be learned by many medium-sized and small firms. It is one of accounting's greatest, and simplest, aids to business efficiency.

To find out how profitable each part of the business is, we will have to prepare departmental accounts to give us the facts for each department.

49.2 The apportionment of expenses between departments

The expenses of a firm are often split between its various departments, and the net profit for each department then calculated. Each expense is divided between the departments on what is considered to be the most logical basis. This will differ considerably between businesses. An example of a trading and profit and loss account drawn up in such a manner is shown below.

Example of a departmental trading, profit and loss account

Northern Stores have three departments in their store:

	(a) Jewellery	(b) Ladies hairdressing	(c) Clothing
	£	£	£
Stock of goods or materials, 1 January 1998	2,000	1,500	3,000
Purchases	11,000	3,000	15,000
Stock of goods or materials, 31 December 1998	3,000	2,500	4,000
Sales and work done	18,000	9,000	27,000
Wages of assistants in each department	2,800	5,000	6,000

The following expenses cannot be traced to any particular department:

	£
Rent	3,500
Administration expenses	4,800
Air conditioning and lighting	2,000
General expenses	1,200

It is decided to apportion rent together with air conditioning and lighting in accordance with the floor space occupied by each department. These were taken up in the ratios of (a) one-fifth, (b) half, (c) three-tenths. Administration expenses and general expenses are to be split in the ratio of sales and work done.

The Northern Stores
Trading and Profit and Loss Account for the year ended 31 December 1998

	(a) Jewellery		(b) Hairdressing		(c) Clothing	
	£	£	£	£	£	£
Sales and work done		18,000		9,000		27,000
Cost of goods or materials:						
Stock at 1 January	2,000		1,500		3,000	
Add Purchases	11,000		3,000		15,000	
	13,000		4,500		18,000	
Less Stock at 31 December	3,000	10,000	2,500	2,000	4,000	14,000
Gross profit		8,000		7,000		13,000
Less Expenses:						
Wages	2,800		5,000		6,000	
Rent	700		1,750		1,050	
Administration expenses	1,600		800		2,400	
Air conditioning and lighting	400		1,000		600	
General expenses	400	5,900	200	8,750	600	10,650
Net Profit/loss		2,100		(1,750)		2,350

This way of calculating net profits and losses seems to imply a precision that is lacking in fact, and would often lead to an interpretation that the hairdressing department has lost £1,750 this year, and that this amount would be saved if the department was closed down. It has already been stated that different departments are very often dependent on one another, therefore it will be realised that this would not necessarily be the case.

The calculation of net profits and losses are also dependent on the arbitrary division of overhead expenses. It is by no means obvious that the overheads of department (b) would be avoided if it was closed down. Assuming that the sales staff of the department could be discharged without compensation, then £5,000 would be saved in wages. The other overhead expenses shown under department (b) would not, however, necessarily disappear. The rent may still be payable in full even though the department was closed down. The administration expenses may turn out to be only slightly down, say from £4,800 to £4,600, a saving of £200; air conditioning and lighting down to £1,500, a saving of £500; general expenses down to £1,100, a saving of £100. Therefore the department, when open, costs an additional £5,800 compared with when the department is closed. This is made up as follows:

	£
Administration expenses	200
Air conditioning and lighting	500
General expenses	100
Wages	5,000
	5,800

But when open, assuming this year is typical, the department makes £7,000 gross profit. The firm is therefore £1,200 a year better off when the department is open than when it is closed, subject to certain assumptions. These include:

(a) That the remaining departments would not be profitably expanded into the space vacated to give greater proportionate benefits than the hairdressing department.

(b) That a new type of department which would be more profitable than hairdressing could not be set up.

(c) That the department could not be leased to another firm at a more profitable figure than that shown by hairdressing.

There are also other factors which, though not easily seen in an accounting context, are still extremely pertinent. They are concerned with the possible loss of confidence in the firm by customers generally; what appears to be an ailing business does not usually attract good customers. Also the effect on the remaining staff should not be ignored. The dismissal of the hairdressing staff may instil fear in the other staff, some of whom may leave, especially the most competent members who could easily find work elsewhere, and so the general quality of the staff may decline with serious consequences for the firm.

49.3 A better method of apportioning expenses

It is less misleading to show costs split as follows:

First section of trading and profit and loss account	Direct costs allocated entirely to the department and which would *not* be paid if department closed down
Second section of trading and profit and loss account	Costs not directly traceable to the department or which would still be payable even if the department closed down

The *surpluses* brought down from the first section represent the *contribution* that each department has made to cover the expenses, the remainder being the net profit for the whole of the firm.

From the figures given in the previous example the accounts using the above method to apportion expenses would appear as follows.

The Northern Stores
Trading and Profit and Loss Account for the year ended 31 December 1998

	(a) Jewellery £	£	(b) Hairdressing £	£	(c) Clothing £	£	Total £
Sales and work done		18,000		9,000		27,000	
Less cost of goods or materials:							
Stock at 1 January	2,000		1,500		3,000		
Add Purchases	11,000		3,000		15,000		
	13,000		4,500		18,000		
Less Stock 31 December	3,000		2,500		4,000		
	10,000		2,000		14,000		
Wages	2,800	12,800	5,000	7,000	6,000	20,000	
Surpluses (contribution)		5,200		2,000		7,000	14,200

All Departments

Less		
Rent	3,500	
Administration expenses	4,800	
Air conditioning and lighting	2,000	
General expenses	1,200	11,500
Net profit		2,700

The contribution of a department is the result of activities which are under the control of a departmental manager. The efficiency of their control will affect the amount of the contribution.

The costs in the second section, such as rent, insurance or lighting cannot be affected by the departmental manager. It is therefore only fair if the departmental manager is judged by the *contribution* of his department rather than the net profit of his department.

49.4 The balance sheet of departmental organisations

The balance sheet does not usually show assets and liabilities split between different departments.

49.5 Inter-departmental transfers

Purchases made for one department may be subsequently sold in another department. In such a case the items should be deducted from the figure for Purchases of the original purchasing department, and added to the figure for Purchases for the subsequent selling department.

Review questions

In addition to the questions which follow, you should attempt questions 399 and 400 in the accompanying book of multiple-choice questions (see back cover for details).

Suggested solutions to review questions with the letter 'A' after the question number are given in Appendix I (page 682).

49.1A From the following you are to draw up the trading account for Charnley's Department Store for the year ended 31 December 1998.

	1.1.1998		31.12.1998
	£		£
Stocks:			
Electrical Department	6,080		7,920
Furniture Department	17,298		16,150
Leisure Goods Department	14,370		22,395
Sales for the year:		£	
Electrical Department		29,840	
Furniture Department		73,060	
Leisure Goods Department		39,581	
Purchases for the year:			
Electrical Department		18,195	
Furniture Department		54,632	
Leisure Goods Department		27,388	

49.2A   J Spratt is the proprietor of a shop selling books, periodicals, newspapers and children's games and toys. For the purposes of his accounts he wishes the business to be divided into two departments:

Department A   Books, periodicals and newspapers.
Department B   Games, toys and fancy goods.

The following balances have been extracted from his nominal ledger at 31 March 1999:

	Dr	Cr
	£	£
Sales Department A		15,000
Sales Department B		10,000
Stocks Department A, 1 April 1998	250	
Stocks Department B, 1 April 1998	200	
Purchases Department A	11,800	
Purchases Department B	8,200	
Wages of sales assistants Department A	1,000	
Wages of sales assistants Department B	750	
Newspaper delivery wages	150	
General office salaries	750	
Rates	130	
Fire insurance – buildings	50	
Lighting and air conditioning	120	
Repairs to premises	25	
Internal telephone	25	
Cleaning	30	
Accountancy and audit charges	120	
General office expenses	60	

Stocks at 31 March 1999 were valued at:
Department A £300
Department B £150

The proportion of the total floor area occupied by each department was:
Department A One-fifth
Department B Four-fifths

Prepare J Spratt's trading and profit and loss account for the year ended 31 March 1999, apportioning the overhead expenses, where necessary, to show the Departmental profit or loss. The apportionment should be made by using the methods as shown:

Area – Rates, Fire insurance, Lighting and air conditioning, Repairs, Telephone, Cleaning;
Turnover – General office salaries, Accountancy, General office expenses.

49.3   From the following list of balances you are required to prepare a departmental trading and profit and loss account in columnar form for the year ended 31 March 1999, in respect of the business carried on under the name of Ivor's Superstores:

			£	£
Rent and rates				4,200
Delivery expenses				2,400
Commission				3,840
Insurance				900
Purchases:	Dept. A		52,800	
	B		43,600	
	C		34,800	131,200
Discounts received				1,968
Salaries and wages				31,500
Advertising				1,944
Sales:	Dept. A		80,000	
	B		64,000	
	C		48,000	192,000
Depreciation				2,940
Opening stock:	Dept. A		14,600	
	B		11,240	
	C		9,120	34,960
Administration and general expenses				7,890
Closing stock:	Dept. A		12,400	
	B		8,654	
	C		9,746	30,800

Except as follows, expenses are to be apportioned equally between the departments.

Delivery expenses – proportionate to sales.
Commission – 2% of sales.
Salaries and wages – in the proportion of 6:5:4.
Discounts received – 1.5% of purchases.

49.4 Ned Ryan has been in business for many years as a hardware merchant. The business is comprised of two retail departments, one selling building materials and one selling electrical goods. The following trial balance was extracted from his books at 31st December, 1997.

	£ Debit	£ Credit
Sales of Building Materials		300,000
Sales of Electrical Goods		200,000
Purchases of Building Materials	170,000	
Purchases of Electrical Goods	95,000	
Wages	160,000	
Administration Costs	12,300	
Selling and Distribution Expenses	7,100	
Bank Charges	600	
Premises at Cost	80,000	
Plant and Equipment at Cost	30,000	
Accumulated Depreciation – Premises		6,000
Accumulated Depreciation – Plant and Equipment		10,000
Stock of Building Materials at 1st January, 1997	15,000	
Stock of Electrical Goods at 1st January, 1997	20,000	
Debtors	20,000	
Prepayments	5,000	
Bad Debts Provision		5,000
Creditors and Accruals		18,000
Bank Overdraft		15,000
Capital Account		61,000
	615,000	615,000

Additional information

1 Stock at 31st December, 1997, was as follows:

Building Materials	£35,000
Electrical Equipment	£20,000

2 The bad debts provision is to be made equal to 40% of debtors.
3 Depreciation is to be provided as follows:

Premises	2% on the straight line basis
Plant and Equipment	20% on the reducing balance basis

4 Expenses are to be allocated to each department in accordance with its ratio of sales to total sales.

You are required to prepare:
(*a*) a Departmental Trading and Profit and Loss Account for the year ended 31st December, 1997, using in each case separate columns for the building materials department, the electrical goods department and the total business, and
(*b*) the Balance Sheet for the total business as at 31st December, 1997.
    (A Departmental Balance Sheet is not required.)

(*IATI Foundation Examination*)

Additional question
Question R4.7 (page 282) may also be answered as a Departmental Accounts question.

Part VIII Revision questions

Suggested solutions to questions with the letter 'A' after the question number are given in Appendix II (pages 691–8).

R8.1A William Greene, a butcher, commenced in business on the 1st January, 1997, and completed his first year's trading on 31st December, 1997. He has presented you with the following summaries:

Cheque payment summary	£	Bank lodgement summary	£
Purchases	130,000	Sales (net of cash withdrawn)	200,000
Light and heat	8,950	Capital introduced	30,000
Print, packaging and stationery	17,860	Refunds from creditors	3,000
Motor expenses	18,940		
Wages, PAYE and PRSI	15,400		
Rent	15,000		
Insurance	9,000		
	215,150		233,000

He has also explained that each month he withdrew £4,500 cash from the business which he spent as follows:

Wages	£2,800
Drawings	£400
Cash purchases	£1,100
Motor expenses	£200
	£4,500

Additional information
1 Closing stock was £12,000.
2 Direct debits for bank charges not shown in the Cheque Payment Summary amount to £2,800.
3 Light and heat includes a refundable deposit of £2,500 which will be repaid if he remains in business for two years.
4 Motor expenses includes his personal motor and travel expenses which are calculated at 20% of the total motor expenses.
5 Closing stock of stationery and packaging materials was £1,920.
6 The wages paid comprises the net wages for the year and PAYE and PRSI for the 11 months to 30th November, 1997. The PAYE and PRSI due for the month ended 31st December, 1997, amounts to £1,400.
7 Rent has been paid for three months in advance.
8 Insurance is paid three months in arrears.

You are required to prepare:
(a) the Trading and Profit and Loss Account for William Greene for the year ended 31st December, 1997; and
(b) the Balance Sheet as at that date.

(IATI Foundation Examination)

R8.2 George Martin is a sole trader whose financial year end is 31st December. The following balances were extracted from his books:

	31st December, 1996	31st December, 1995
Stocks	£30,000	£26,000
Debtors	£36,000	£42,000
Prepayments (light and heat)	£15,000	£10,000
Trade creditors	£50,000	£48,000
Accruals (office expenses)	£19,000	£20,000

Additional information
1 Gross profit is at a mark-up of 25% on cost.
2 Fixed assets at 31st December, 1995 were £60,000.
3 Capital at 31st December, 1995 was £80,000.
4 Receipts from customers for the year ended 31st December, 1996 were £350,000. All sales are made on credit.
5 Payments for the year ended 31st December, 1996 were as follows:

Light and Heat	£25,000
Office Expenses	£27,000

6 The proprietor's personal expenses amounted to £13,500, for the year ended 31st December, 1996.
7 Bad debts of £4,000 were written off during the year ended 31st December, 1996.
8 During 1996, discounts received amounted to £6,000 while discounts allowed amounted to £5,000.
9 Depreciation for the year ended 31st December, 1996, amounted to £4,000.
10 The bank balance at 31st December, 1995, was £10,000.

You are required to prepare:
(a) the Trading and Profit and Loss Account of George Martin for the year ended 31st December, 1996, and
(b) the Balance Sheet as at that date.

(ICAI Professional Examination One)

R8.3 Ms Ryan was made redundant in April 1997 and she started up a small retail business on 1st May, 1997. She opened a business bank account with her accumulated savings of £5,000 and arranged, with her bank, a short-term loan of £2,000 and overdraft facilities of £3,000. Simultaneously, she purchased a three year lease on suitable business premises for £3,000 with responsibility for rates of £600 per annum.

At the end of the first accounting year you have been requested by Ms Ryan to prepare final accounting reports. However, you find that the accounting records are incomplete. After some investigation you obtain the following information:

1 Personal drawings of £40 per week for the 52 week period were made from the business bank account.
2 Shop equipment was purchased for £3,000. The equipment has an estimated useful life of five years with an estimated re-sale value of £500 and is to be depreciated using the Straight Line method.
3 Total payments to the bank during the year in respect of the term loan amounted to £1,100 which includes £120 interest. At the end of the year £150 interest was accrued on the loan. The agreed overdraft limit remained at £3,000.
4 A payment of £900 was made for rates on 5th May, 1997 for the period up to 31st October, 1998. Payments in respect of miscellaneous expenses during the accounting year to 30th April, 1998 amounted to £4,000.

5 The Bank Statement for the Current Account on 30th April, 1998 showed a debit balance of £414, but you learn from the Cash Book that a recent deposit in the bank's night safe of £800 has not been credited by the bank and cheques amounting to £269 have not been presented. In addition, the Bank Statement reveals bank interest and charges of £55, and a dishonoured cheque for £68, which have not been recorded in the Cash Book.

6 The total amount owed per suppliers' statements at 30th April, 1998 amounted to £1,750. On checking you discover that:
   (i) a suppliers' invoice charged at £93 should have been charged at £39; and
   (ii) a cheque payment for £243 has not been credited by a supplier.

7 Closing stock, valued at selling price, amounted to £2,100. The average mark up on cost was 25%.

8 Sales invoices unpaid at the end of the year amounted to £1,900.

You are required to:
(a) prepare a Bank Reconciliation Statement as at 30th April, 1998;
(b) prepare a Balance Sheet of the business as at 30th April, 1998 and indicate clearly the profit or loss made during the year ended on that date; and
(c) explain briefly the disadvantages associated with this method of profit determination.

(*ICAI Professional Examination One*)

R8.4 The following is a letter which you received from a friend of yours, Mr B. Ward, who has not kept proper accounting records for his business.

Dear John,

Thank you for your kind offer to help me in organising my accounts. As you know, I won £10,000 in the Prize Bonds, which I received in December, 1996, and decided to commence my own business as a contractor. On 2nd January, 1997, I purchased a JCB digger, which I hope will last for 5 years, for £6,500.

    Business was slow at first but picked up eventually. I kept a note of all work done and, on 31st December, 1997 I had received cheques totalling £4,714 from various customers which had been lodged. This sum did not include work done just before Christmas which I did not get a chance to invoice and which amounted to £360.

    I incurred very few expenses during the year except for repair bills. I added these up the other day and the cheque payments amounted to £572. Some other cheques which I wrote were in respect of insurance of £245, which coincided with the calendar year, and £416 in respect of petrol and diesel oil. The bank charged me £95 interest as I had a small overdraft during the year.

    The debit balance per my bank statement on 31st December, 1997 was £2,498 but I noticed that a cheque for £200 had not yet been presented.

    I wrote a few other non-business cheques during the year. I do not know for how much exactly as I did not fill in the cheque stubs properly. Best to say that if there is any money missing then it should be charged by way of drawings.

    I hope from what I have said that you can prepare some sort of accounts for me. Don't forget to provide for your own accountancy fee of £100.

Yours sincerely,

Brian Ward

You are required to:
(a) prepare a Profit and Loss Account for the year ended 31st December, 1997;
(b) prepare a Balance Sheet as at that date; and
(c) comment briefly on whether Mr. Ward should be registered for VAT.

(*ICAI Professional Examination One*)

R8.5A Set out below is a letter you received recently from a friend, Joe Singleton.

31st January, 1998

Dear Pat,

I would appreciate your help with my accounts. On 1st January, 1997, I started a business as a retail stationer. To open a business bank account, I lodged the £12,000 redundancy payment cheque which I had received. The following were all my transactions for the year.

(1)	Total purchases on credit	£30,000
(2)	Total payments to creditors for purchases	£27,000
(3)	Total sales on credit	£50,000
(4)	Total receipts from debtors	£48,000
(5)	Payments for expenses and rent	£20,000
(6)	Drawings for my own use	£6,000

Stock at 31st December, 1997, amounted to £4,000. All receipts and payments were put through the bank account.

I look forward to receiving your reply at your earliest convenience.

Yours sincerely,

Joe Singleton

You are required to:
(*a*) prepare for Joe Singleton for the year ended 31st December, 1997
    (i) the bank account;
    (ii) the Trading and Profit and Loss account;
    (iii) the Balance Sheet at that date; and
(*b*) list the reasons why the balance per the bank account in Joe Singleton's books might be different from the bank balance according to the Bank Statement at the same date.

(*IATI Foundation Examination*)

R8.6 The entire stock of Folders Ltd, whose financial year ends on 31st December, was destroyed by fire on 25th April, 1998. The company requires an estimate of the cost of the stock destroyed in order to make a claim against its insurance company. It supplies you with the following information.

1 Purchases of goods for re-sale amounted to £296,750 in the year ended 31st December, 1997, and to £102,250 in the period 1st January to 25th April, 1998.
2 Sales, as shown in the Sales Journal, amounted to £376,000 in the year ended 31st December, 1997, and to £127,300 in the period 1st January to 25th April, 1998.
3 The rate of gross profit is approximately the same in each year.
4 Stock, at cost, amounted to £94,500 on 31st December, 1996, and to £106,600 on 31st December, 1997.
5 Goods costing £2,650 were misappropriated by an employee in February 1997. The same employee admitted to misappropriating £500 from cash sales in January 1998.

Requirement:
Estimate the cost of the stock destroyed in the fire.

(*ICAI Professional Examination One*)

R8.7 Mr. Patterson is trading as a retail merchant selling two categories of goods as follows:

	Category A	*Category B*
Percentage Mark-up on Cost	25%	33⅓%

On 11th August, 1998 a fire destroyed his entire stock. The following information has been extracted from the books:

1	*1st January, 1998*	*11th August, 1998*
Trade debtors (gross)	£8,027	£11,000
Bad debts provision	£1,000	£2,000
Trade creditors	£6,492	£4,925
Stock on hand		
– Category A	£16,843	Unknown
– Category B	£8,106	Unknown
Cash on hand	£900	£1,200

2 Cash movements during the period from 1st January, 1998 to 11th August, 1998 were as follows:

Cheque payments for purchases for re-sale	£59,126
Cash till lodgements arising from credit sales	£83,555
Cash till payments to trade creditors for goods for re-sale	£1,800

3 Bad debts amounting to £760 were written off and bad debts recovered amounting to £48 were received and immediately lodged during the period. In addition, discounts allowed amounted to £612 and discounts received amounted to £641.

The mix of purchases and sales consists of:

Category A	70%
Category B	30%

You are required to:

(a) reconstruct the cash account and debtors and creditors control accounts for the above period, and

(b) compute the cost of goods destroyed by fire on 11th August, 1998.

(*ICAI Professional Examination One*)

R8.8A Ben Lewis is a sole trader, who carries on a cabinet manufacturing business. He has no accountant and he himself has no experience in maintaining proper books and records. Accordingly, he has sought your assistance as he wishes to extract accounts for the year ended 31st March, 1998. From information supplied by Mr. Lewis and from your own investigations, you ascertain the following.

1 The Trial Balance at 1st April, 1997, was as follows.

	£ Debit	*£ Credit*
Premises	40,000	
Accumulated depreciation on premises		2,000
Plant	18,000	
Accumulated depreciation on plant		4,500
Stock	16,000	
Debtors	14,000	
Bank	3,000	
Cash	500	
Creditors		18,000
Provision for legal claim		5,000
Owner's capital		62,000
	91,500	91,500

2 An analysis of the bank lodgement dockets for the year revealed the following receipts.

Disposal of old machine as scrap	£2,000
Receipts from debtors	£64,000
Cash lodgements	£27,000
Insurance proceeds [see 6 below]	£5,000
Inheritance from uncle	£12,000
	£110,000

3 An analysis of the cheque stubs for the year revealed the following payments.

Payments to suppliers	£58,000
New machine	£14,000
Wages and expenses	£11,100
Legal claim [see 7 below]	£6,400
Cash	£5,700
Drawings	£13,400
	£108,600

4 The cash balance at 31st March, 1998, was £400. During the year, £9,400 in wages and expenses were paid out of cash.

5 All purchases were made on credit and all receipts from credit sales were lodged intact to the bank. Receipts from cash sales were occasionally used to pay cash expenses [see 4 above].

6 At 1st April, 1997, Mr Lewis had two machines. These had been bought for £9,000 each 12 months previously when he commenced business. During the year, one of the machines was damaged by fire and had to be replaced. The insurance proceeds relate to the damaged machine which was ultimately disposed of.

7 At 31st March, 1997, there was a legal claim pending against the business arising from the supply of defective cabinets. The amount paid out during the year was the final settlement of this claim (including legal fees).

8 When you reconciled the bank account, you noted that the bank had dishonoured a cheque for £3,000 from a customer. This had not been noted anywhere in Mr Lewis' books. According to Mr Lewis, this balance should be written off as a bad debt. There were no other bad debts during the year.

9 Discounts of £1,200 and £2,100 were allowed and received respectively. At 31st March, 1998, debtors owed £15,700, creditors were owed £16,100 and stocks on hand were £18,400.

10 Depreciation is to be provided using the straight line method on premises at 5% per annum and on plant at 25% per annum. A full year's depreciation is charged in the year of acquisition and none is charged in the year of disposal.

Requirement:
Prepare for Mr Lewis a Profit and Loss Account for the year ended 31st March, 1998, and a Balance Sheet as at that date.

(*ICAI Professional Examination Two*)

R8.9A You are the Treasurer of Crookstown Golf Club and have prepared the following receipts and payments account for the year ended 31st December, 1995:

Receipts	£	£	Payments	£	£
Balance forward: cash on hand		75	Balance forward: bank account		1,200
Membership subscriptions:			Wages and salaries		
Ordinary members	11,000		Restaurant staff	3,800	
Associate members	1,600		Other staff	8,300	12,100
Life members	800	13,400	Restaurant purchases		8,600
Restaurant receipts		13,800	Rent and rates		1,600
Donations received		950	Light and heat		1,800
Deposit account		1,220	New computer		1,600
			Restaurant expenses		750
			Bank interest		240
			Deposit account		1,200
			Balance forward:		
			Bank account	315	
			Cash on hand	40	355
		29,445			29,445
Balance forward:					
Bank account	315				
Cash on hand	40	355			

As Treasurer, you have been asked by the club's Management Committee to prepare additional financial statements (as set out in the requirement below) and you have been supplied with the following information:

Notes
1 The clubhouse should be valued at £18,000 at 31st December, 1994, and at 31st December, 1995.
2 All club equipment was valued at £10,400 at 31st December, 1994. Depreciation should be charged at 20% on the book value of all equipment held at the club's year-end.
3 Other assets and liabilities of the club are as follows:

	31st December, 1995	31st December, 1994
Subscriptions due	£400	Nil
Rates prepaid	£320	£200
Light and heat unpaid (accrued)	£310	£250
Restaurant creditors	£1,400	£1,600
Restaurant stocks	£930	£850

4 Life subscriptions received are credited to a life subscriptions fund and written off to income over a ten year period commencing in the year of receipt. The life subscriptions fund account balance on 1st January, 1995, was £900, being in respect of £1,000 of life subscriptions received in the year ended 31st December, 1994.
5 All subscriptions received from ordinary and associate members during 1995 were for the year ended 31st December, 1995.
6 One half of the charges for rent and rates and light and heat are in respect of the restaurant.
7 £1,200 was placed on deposit during the year and withdrawn, with interest earned, before the year end.

You are required to prepare:
(*a*) a Statement of Affairs (opening Balance Sheet) as at 31st December, 1994;
(*b*) a Restaurant Trading Account for the year ended 31st December, 1995;
(*c*) an Income and Expenditure Account for the year ended 31st December, 1995; and
(*d*) a Balance Sheet as at that date.

(IATI Admission Examination)

R8.10 The following is the Receipts and Payments Account of the Greenogue Rugby Club for the year ended 30th June, 1998.

Receipts	£	£	Payments	£	£
Balance at start of year:			Light and heat		1,400
Bank account	1,100		Wages and Salaries:		
Cash on hand	150	1,250	Bar staff	4,200	
			Other staff	8,090	12,290
Membership Subscriptions			Rent and Rates		2,000
Ordinary members	10,600		Insurances		780
Associate members	1,200		Bar Purchases		8,400
Life members	600	12,400	Repairs to Clubhouse		630
			New Equipment		1,500
Annual Dinner Dance			New Computer		2,000
Sale of tickets	1,500		Bank Interest and Charges		320
Raffle	230	1,730	Bar Expenses		620
			Dance Expenses		400
Bar Receipts		14,200			
Balance at end of year – bank		820	Balance at end of year – cash		60
		30,400			30,400
Balance at start of year – cash		60	Balance at start of year – bank		820

Additional information

1 At 30th June, 1997, and 30th June, 1998, the clubhouse was valued at £15,000.
2 Club equipment had a net book value of £9,300 at 30th June, 1997. Depreciation, on the reducing balance method, should be charged at 10% per annum on club equipment, including new equipment. The new computer is to be depreciated at 20% per annum on the straight line basis. A full year's depreciation is charged in the year of purchase on club equipment and the computer.
3 The figure for ordinary members' subscriptions received is comprised of:

Subscriptions for the year ended 30th June, 1998	£9,800
Subscriptions for the year ended 30th June, 1999	£800
	£10,600

The associate members' subscriptions received are all in respect of the year ended 30th June, 1998.
4 The club introduced a life subscription membership scheme for the first time in the year ended 30th June, 1998. The life subscriptions received are to be credited to a life subscriptions fund and written off to income over a ten year period, commencing in the year of receipt.
5 Other assets and liabilities of the club at 30th June were as follows:

	1997	1998
Rates prepaid	£300	£350
Insurances prepaid	£400	£350
Electricity bills unpaid (accrued)	£250	£320
Bar creditors	£1,800	£1,900
Bar stocks	£2,300	£2,600

You are required to prepare:
(a) a Statement of Affairs at 30th June, 1997;
(b) a Bar Trading Account for the year ended 30th June, 1998;
(c) an Income and Expenditure Account for the year ended 30th June, 1998; and
(d) a Balance Sheet as at that date.

(IATI Admission Examination)

R8.11A Make-it Ltd is a manufacturing company. The following balances appeared in its books on September 30th, 1996.

Make-it Ltd
Trial Balance as at 30th September, 1996

	£	£
Advertising	39,960	
Audit fee	7,875	
Bank	1,753,942	
Creditors		398,009
Debtors	167,400	
Direct factory wages	795,157	
Discounts given for prompt settlement	25,702	
Doubtful debt provision		16,065
Factory general expenses	11,925	
Factory power	213,157	
Finished goods packaging and delivery expense	30,720	
Insurance	5,344	
Issued ordinary share capital		1,500,000
Light and heat	20,880	
Office furniture at cost	120,750	
Office general expenses	53,047	
Plant and machinery at cost	384,487	
Production manager's salary	23,437	
Profit and loss account as at 30th September, 1995		259,815
Provisions for depreciation to 30th September, 1995:		
• Office furniture		63,060
• Plant and machinery		173,220
Office salaries	69,457	
Purchases of raw materials	1,618,252	
Rent and rates	28,080	
Repairs to Plant	11,827	
Sales		3,688,042
Sales director's salary	26,250	
Stocks on hand as at 30th September, 1995:		
• Finished goods	450,697	
• Raw materials	92,565	
• Work in progress	147,300	
	6,098,211	6,098,211

The following information may be relevant:
(i)   Stocks as at 30th September, 1996:

	£
• Finished Goods	541,365
• Raw Materials	63,187
• Work in Progress	137,220

(ii) Seven eighths of Rent and Rates, Light and Heat and Insurance are to be allocated to the factory. The figure for Insurance arises principally due to the cost of insuring property.
(iii) The doubtful debt provision is to be adjusted to 5% of relevant debtors.
(iv) Depreciation is to be provided using the straight line method on plant and machinery at the rate of 25% per annum and on office furniture at the rate of 20% per annum.

Required:

Based on the foregoing information separately prepare a Manufacturing Account and a Trading and Profit and Loss Account for the year ended 30th September, 1996 for presentation to the directors of Make-it Ltd in as much detail as the information given permits.

(Show clearly all relevant workings. All calculations should be rounded to the nearest pound.)

R8.12 Tony Limited is a company which specialises in the manufacture of packing cases used for the despatch of goods in bulk.

At 31st December, 1995 the following balances appeared in the company's books:

	£ Debit	£ Credit
Fixed assets at cost:		
Premises..	370,000	
Plant and machinery..	387,600	
Vehicles	79,700	
Aggregate depreciation:		
Premises..		21,400
Plant and Machinery		201,800
Vehicles		25,200
Purchases (less returns):		
Raw Materials..	265,040	
Packing cases (see note 4)...	7,430	
Wages and salaries:		
Factory operatives	121,732	
Factory manager...	28,019	
Administrative...	87,932	
Power heat and light..	92,238	
Rates and Insurance	69,800	
Directors' fees...	15,000	
Sales		876,863
Revenue reserves...		10,030
Ordinary share capital (£1 shares)		100,000
8% Preference share capital (£1 shares).........................		50,000
7% Debentures..		500,000
Preference dividend paid..	4,000	
Debenture Interest paid	35,000	
Stocks at 1st January 1995:		
Raw materials..	49,562	
Work-in-Progress..	27,930	
Finished goods..	61,070	
Packing cases (see Note 4)..	987	
Trade debtors..	62,731	
Discount allowed...	1,462	
Trade creditors..		28,540
Discount received		639
Bank..	34,165	
Cash	13,074	
	1,814,472	1,814,472

Notes:

1 Depreciation is to be provided using the method and annual rate below:

Premises	Straight line	2%
Plant and machinery	Reducing balance	20%
Vehicles	Straight line	20%

2 Adjustment has not yet been made for:

Power heat and light accrued	£3,462
Accrued wages and salaries – factory operatives	£1,569
Rates and Insurance Prepaid	£10,600

3 Expenses should be apportioned as follows:

	Factory	*Office*
Rates and insurance	60%	40%
Power heat and light	80%	20%
Depreciation – premises	60%	40%
Depreciation – plant and machinery	70%	30%

4 Occasionally, when production facilities are fully committed, Tony Limited has to buy in packing cases from another manufacturer to fulfil an urgent order.

5 Stocks at 31st December, 1995:

Raw materials	£53,667
Work-in-progress	£16,420
Finished goods	£43,407
Packing cases	Nil

6 Corporation tax of £8,200 is to be provided.

7 The directors have proposed an ordinary dividend of 20p per share.

Requirement:

Prepare, for presentation to the directors of the company, a Manufacturing, Trading, Profit and Loss account of Tony Limited for the year ended 31st December, 1995 and a Balance Sheet as at that date.

R8.13 Manufacturing Company Ltd is engaged in the manufacture and wholesale of automotive components. The following balances, as at 31st December, 1997, have been extracted from the books of the company.

Manufacturing Company Ltd
Extract from the List of Balances as at 31st December, 1997

	£
Stocks on hand as at January 1st, 1997:	
Raw materials	17,000
Work in progress	5,000
Finished goods	6,000
Loose tools	1,000
Finished goods packing materials	500
Purchases of raw materials	48,000
Carriage in on raw materials	1,500
Direct labour	38,000
Variable factory overheads	12,500
Fixed factory overheads	19,000
Rent and rates	10,000
Light and heat	14,000
Purchase of finished goods packing materials	2,500
10% Import duty on raw materials	4,800
Loose tools	3,000
Office stationery	800
Salaries of administrative staff	19,000
Sales	226,400
Plant and machinery (cost £40,000)	22,000
Manager's company car (cost £18,000)	10,000
Car running expenses	3,500
Royalties on manufacturing processes	7,000
Hire of special equipment to manufacture complex components	500
Factory supervisor's wages	12,000

The following information may be relevant:
(i) Factory Output is transferred to the trading account at a figure calculated so as to show a profit of 25% of Production Cost in the Manufacturing Account.
(ii) Depreciation is to be provided for 1997 at the following annual rates:

Plant and machinery	10% of original cost
Manager's company car	20% using the reducing balance method

(iii) An additional amount of £4,000, representing the direct factory wages for December 1997, as yet unpaid, should be accrued. Rent and Rates prepaid as at the year end amount to £2,000.
(iv) Stocks on Hand on December 31st, 1997 were as follows:

	£
Raw materials	10,000
Finished goods	11,000
Finished goods packing materials	1,200
Loose tools	800
Work in progress	8,000

(v) The 'Rent and Rates' and 'Light and Heat' expenses are to be apportioned as follows:
Factory 75% Administration 25%

Required:
Prepare a Manufacturing Account for the company for the year ended 31st December, 1997.

Appendix I
Suggested solutions to selected review questions

2.1

(a) 10,700	(b) 23,100	(c) 4,300
(d) 3,150	(e) 25,500	(f) 51,400

2.3

(a) Asset	(b) Liability	(c) Asset
(d) Asset	(e) Liability	(f) Asset

2.5

Wrong: Assets: Loan from C Smith; Creditors; Liabilities: Stock of goods; Debtors.

2.7

Assets: Vehicle 2,000; Premises 5,000; Stock 1,000; Bank 700; Cash 100 = total 8,800:
Liabilities: Loan from Bevan 3,000; Creditors 400 = total 3,400.
Capital 8,800 – 3,400 = 5,400.

2.9

A Foster
Balance Sheet as at 31 December 1997

Assets		
Fixtures		5,500
Vehicles		5,700
Stock of Goods		8,800
Debtors		4,950
Cash at Bank		1,250
		26,200
Creditors		2,450
		23,750
Capital		23,750

2.11

	Assets	Liabilities	Capital
(a)	– Cash	– Creditors	
(b)	– Bank		+ Capital
	+ Fixtures		
(c)	+ Stock	+ Creditors	
(d)	+ Cash		
(e)	+ Cash	+ Loan from J Walker	
(f)	+ Bank		
	– Debtors		
(g)	– Stock	– Creditors	
(h)	+ Premises		
	+ Bank		

2.13

C Sangster
Balance Sheet as at 7 May 1998

Assets		
Fixtures		4,500
Vehicle		4,200
Stock		5,720
Debtors		3,000
Bank		5,450
Cash		400
		23,270
Liabilities		
Loan from T Sharples	2,000	
Creditors	2,370	
		4,370
		18,900
Capital		18,900

3.1

Debited	Credited		Debited	Credited
(a) Office Machinery	D Isaacs Ltd	(b) C Jones	Capital
(c) Cash	N Fox	(d) Loan: P Exeter	Bank
(e) D Isaacs Ltd	Office Machinery	(f) Bank	N Lyn
(g) Van	Cash		

Dates are shown in brackets in double entry accounts

3.3

Bank

(1) Capital	2,500	(2) Office F.	150
		(15) Planers Ltd	750
		(31) Machinery	280

Capital

		(1) Bank	2,500

Office Furniture

(2) Bank	150	(8) J Walker	60

Machinery

(3) Planers Ltd	750
(31) Bank	280

Cash

(23) J Walker	60		
(15) Bank	750	(3) Machinery	750

Planers Ltd

J Walker & Sons

(8) Office Furn	60	(23) Cash	60

3.4

Cash

(1) Capital	2,000	(2) Bank	1,800
(25) W Machinery	75		
(28) Bank	100		

Capital

		(1) Cash	2,000

Office Furniture

(5) Betta-Built	120	B Built	

Works Machinery

(12) Evans & Sons	560	(25) Cash	75

Bank

(2) Cash	1,800	(26) Betta-Built	58
(30) J Smith	500	(28) Cash	100

Betta-Built Ltd

(18) Office Furn	62	(5) Office F	120
(26) Bank	58		

Evans & Sons

		(12) W Machy	560

J Smith (Loan)

		(30) Bank	500

4.1

Debited	Credited		Debited	Credited
(a) Purchases	J Reid	(b) B Perkins	Sales
(c) Van	H Thomas	(d) Bank	Sales
(e) Cash	Sales	(f) H Hardy	Returns Outwards
(g) Cash	Machinery	(h) Returns Inwards	J Nelson
(i) Purchases	D Simpson	(j) H Forbes	Returns Outwards

4.3

Cash

(1) Capital	500	(3) Purchases	85
(10) Sales	42	(25) E Morgan	88
(31) A Knight	55		

Purchases

(3) Cash	85
(7) E Morgan	116
(18) A Moses	98

Sales

		(10) Cash	42
		(24) A Knight	55

Returns Outwards

		(14) E Morgan	28
		(21) A Moses	19

A Knight

(24) Sales	55	(31) Cash	55

E Morgan

(14) Returns	28	(7) Purchases	116
(25) Cash	88		

A Moses

(21) Returns	19	(18) Purchases	98

Capital

		(1) Cash	500

4.4

Cash

(1) Capital	1,000	(2) Bank	900
(19) Sales	28	(7) Purchases	55

Purchases

(4) S Holmes	78
(7) Cash	55

Returns Outwards

		(12) S Holmes	18

S Holmes

(12) Returns	18	(4) Purchases	78
(29) Bank	60		

D Moore

(10) Sales	98

Bank

(2) Cash	900	(29) S Holmes	60
(24) D Watson (Loan)	100	(31) Kingston Eqt	150

Sales

		(10) D Moore	98
		(19) Cash	28

Fixtures

(22) Kingston Eqt	150

D Watson (Loan)

		(24) Bank	100

Kingston Equipment

(31) Bank	150	(22) Fixtures	150

Capital

		(1) Cash	1,000

4.5

Bank

Dr		Cr	
(1) Capital	10,000	(25) F Jones	1,070
(6) Cash	250	(29) Mid West Motors	2,600

Sales

Dr		Cr	
		(4) Cash	200
		(8) C Moody	180
		(10) J Newman	220
		(14) H Morgan	190
		(14) J Peat	320
		(24) Cash	70

Returns Inwards

Dr		Cr	
(12) C Moody	40		
(26) H Morgan	30		

Van

Dr		Cr	
(17) Mid West Motors	2,600		

Office Furniture

Dr		Cr	
(18) Faster S	600	(27) Faster S	160
(31) Cash	100		

Capital

Dr		Cr	
		(1) Bank	10,000
		(28) Cash	500

J Newman

Dr		Cr	
(10) Sales	220		

H Morgan

Dr		Cr	
(14) Sales	190	(26) Returns	30

C Moody

Dr		Cr	
(8) Sales	180	(12) Returns	40

J Peat

Dr		Cr	
(14) Sales	320		

Cash

Dr		Cr	
(2) T Cooper (Loan)	400	(6) Bank	250
(4) Sales	200	(20) Purchases	220
(24) Sales	70	(31) Office Furn	100
(28) Capital	500		

Purchases

Dr		Cr	
(3) F Jones	840		
(3) S Charles	3,600		
(11) F Jones	370		
(20) Cash	220		

Returns Outwards

Dr		Cr	
		(15) F Jones	140
		(19) S Charles	110

Mid West Motors

Dr		Cr	
(29) Bank	2,600	(17) Van	2,600

Faster Supplies Ltd

Dr		Cr	
(27) Office Furn	160	(18) Office Furn	600

F Jones

Dr		Cr	
(15) Returns	140	(3) Purchases	840
(25) Bank	1,070	(11) Purchases	370

S Charles

Dr		Cr	
(19) Returns	110	(3) Purchases	3,600

T Cooper (Loan)

Dr		Cr	
		(2) Cash	400

5.1

Account to be debited	Account to be credited
(a) Insurance	Bank
(c) Cash	Rent received
(e) Bank	Rates
(g) Wages	Cash
(i) Bank	Sales commission

Account to be debited	Account to be credited
(b) Motor expenses	Cash
(d) Rates	Bank
(f) Stationery	Cash
(h) Bank	Stationery
(j) Van	Bank

5.2

Bank

Dr		Cr	
(1) Capital	20,000	(3) Fixtures	150
(21) Rent rec.	50	(24) Van	3,000

Cash

Dr		Cr	
(5) Sales	275	(10) Rent	150
		(12) Stationery	27
		(30) Wages	117
		(31) Drawings	44

Purchases

Dr		Cr	
(2) D Miller	175		
(6) S Waites	114		

Sales

Dr		Cr	
		(5) Cash	275
		(23) U Henry	77

Fixtures

Dr		Cr	
(3) Bank	150		

Rent

Dr		Cr	
(10) Cash	150		

Capital

Dr		Cr	
		(1) Bank	20,000

M Mills

Dr		Cr	
(18) Returns out	23	(2) Purchases	175

S Waites

Dr		Cr	
		(6) Purchases	114

U Henry

Dr		Cr	
		(23) Sales	77

Rent Received

Dr		Cr	
		(21) Bank	50

Stationery

Dr		Cr	
(12) Cash	27		

Returns Outwards

Dr		Cr	
		(18) M Mills	23

Van

Dr		Cr	
(24) Bank	3,000		

Wages

Dr		Cr	
(30) Cash	117		

Drawings

Dr		Cr	
(31) Cash	44		

5.3

Cash

Dr		Cr	
(1) Capital	1,500	(3) Rent	280
(11) Sales	49	(4) Bank	1,000
		(20) B Repairs	18
		(28) Purchases	125
		(30) Cleaning exps	15

Bank

Dr		Cr	
(4) Cash	1,000	(7) Stationery	15
		(27) A Hanson	279

Purchases

Dr		Cr	
(2) A Hanson	296		
(28) Cash	125		

Sales

Dr		Cr	
		(5) E Linton	54
		(11) Cash	49
		(17) S Morgan	29

Stationery

Dr		Cr	
(7) Bank	15		

Returns Outwards

Dr		Cr	
		(14) A Hanson	17

Fixtures

Dr		Cr	
(31) A Webster	120		

Capital

Dr		Cr	
		(1) Cash	1,500

Rent

Dr		Cr	
(3) Cash	280		

Building Repairs

Dr		Cr	
(20) Cash	18		

Cleaning Expenses

Dr		Cr	
(30) Cash	15		

A Hanson

Dr		Cr	
(14) Returns out	17	(2) Purchases	296
(27) Bank	279		

E Linton

Dr		Cr	
(5) Sales	54	(22) Returns in	14

S Morgan

Dr		Cr	
(17) Sales	29		

Returns Inwards

Dr		Cr	
(22) E Linton	14		

A Webster

Dr		Cr	
		(31) Fixtures	120

5.6

(A) Bought a vehicle £5,000, paying by cheque.
(B) Paid off £4,000 creditors in cash.
(C) Lee lent us £150,000, this being paid into the bank.
(D) Bought land and buildings £125,000, paying by bank.
(E) Debtors paid cheques £80,000, being paid into bank.
(F) Land and buildings sold for £300,000, the proceeds being paid into the bank.
(G) Loan from Lee repaid out of the bank.
(H) Creditors £8,000 paid in cash.
(I) Stock costing £17,000 sold for £12,000 on credit. Loss of £5,000 shown deducted from Capital.

6.1

H Harvey

(1) Sales	690	(10) Returns	40
(4) Sales	66	(24) Cash	300
		(31) Balance c/d	416
	756		756
(1) Balance b/d	416		

L Masters

(4) Sales	418	(31) Balance c/d	621
(31) Sales	203		
	621		621
(1) Balance b/d	621		

N Morgan

(1) Sales	153	(18) Bank	153

J Lindo

(1) Sales	420	(10) Returns	20
		(20) Bank	400
	420		420

6.2

J Young

(10) Returns	55	(1) Purchases	458
(28) Cash	250	(15) Purchases	80
(30) Balance c/d	233		
	538		538
		(1) Balance b/d	233

L Williams

(30) Returns	17	(1) Purchases	120
(30) Balance c/d	180	(3) Purchases	77
	197		197
		(1) Balance b/d	180

G Norman

(10) Returns	22	(1) Purchases	708
(30) Balance c/d	686		
	708		708
		(1) Balance b/d	686

T Harris

(19) Bank	880	(3) Purchases	880

6.3

H Harvey

	Dr	Cr	Balance	
May 1	Sales	690		690	Dr
May 4	Sales	66		756	Dr
May 10	Returns		40	716	Dr
May 24	Cash		300	416	Dr

N Morgan

	Dr	Cr	Balance	
May 1	Sales	153		153	Dr
May 18	Bank		153	0	

J Lindo

	Dr	Cr	Balance	
May 1	Sales	420		420	Dr
May 10	Returns		20	400	Dr
May 20	Bank		400	0	

L Masters

	Dr	Cr	Balance	
May 4	Sales	418		418	Dr
May 31	Sales	203		621	Dr

6.4

J Young

	Dr	Cr	Balance	
Jun 1	Purchases		458	458	Cr
Jun 10	Returns	55		403	Cr
Jun 15	Purchases		80	483	Cr
Jun 28	Cash	250		233	Cr

L Williams

	Dr	Cr	Balance	
Jun 1	Purchases		120	120	Cr
Jun 3	Purchases		77	197	Cr
Jun 30	Returns	17		180	Cr

G Norman

	Dr	Cr	Balance	
Jun 1	Purchases		708	708	Cr
Jun 10	Returns	22		686	Cr

T Harris

	Dr	Cr	Balance	
Jun 3	Purchases		880	880	Cr
Jun 19	Bank	880		0	

6.5

D Williams
(1) Sales	458	(24) Bank	300
		(28) Cash	100
		(30) Balance c/d	58
	458		458
(1) Balance b/d	58		

A White
		(2) Purchases	77
	77		77

H Samuels
(17) Returns	24	(2) Purchases	231
(30) Balance c/d	219	(10) Purchases	12
	243		243
		(1) Balance b/d	219

J Moore
(1) Sales	235	(12) Returns	26
(8) Sales	444	(20) Balance c/d	653
	679		679
(1) Balance b/d	653		

P Owen
		(2) Purchases	65

G Grant
(1) Sales	98	(12) Returns	9
		(30) Balance c/d	89
	98		98
(1) Balance b/d	89		

O Oliver
(17) Returns	12	(10) Purchases	222
(26) Cash	210		
	222		222

F Franklin
(8) Sales	249	(30) Bank	249

7.1

Cash
(1) Capital	250	(6) Rent	12
		(15) Carriage	23
		(31) Balance c/d	215
	250		250

Bank
(9) C Bailey	43	(12) K Gibson	25
(10) H Spencer	150	(12) D Ellis	54
		(31) Rent	18
		(31) Balance c/d	96
	193		193

Capital
		(1) Cash	250

Rent
(6) Cash	12		
(31) Bank	18		

Carriage
(15) Cash	23		

D Ellis
(12) Bank	54	(2) Purchases	54

C Murphy
		(2) Purchases	87
		(18) Purchases	43

K Gibson
(12) Bank	25	(2) Purchases	25

D Booth
		(2) Purchases	76
		(18) Purchases	110

L Lowe
		(2) Purchases	64

C Bailey
(4) Sales	64	(9) Bank	43

B Hughes
		(4) Sales	62
		(21) Sales	67

H Spencer
(4) Sales	176	(10) Bank	150

Purchases
(2) D Ellis	54		
(2) C Murphy	87		
(2) K Gibson	25		
(2) D Booth	76		
(2) L Lowe	64		
(18) C Murphy	43		
(18) D Booth	110		

Sales
		(4) C Bailey	43
		(4) B Hughes	62
		(4) H Spencer	176
		(21) B Hughes	67

Trial Balance as at 31 May 1998

	Dr	Cr
Cash	215	
Bank	96	
Capital		250
Rent	30	
Carriage	23	
C Mendez		130
D Booth		186
L Lowe		64
B Hughes	129	
H Spencer	26	
Purchases	459	
Sales		348
	978	978

8.1

B Webb
Trading and Profit and Loss Account for the year ended 31 December 1997

Sales		18,462
Purchases	14,629	
Closing stock	3,548	
		12,081
Gross profit		6,381
Expenses		
Salaries	2,150	
Motor expenses	520	
Rent and rates	670	
Insurance	111	
General expenses	105	
		3,556
Net profit		2,825

8.2

C Worth
Trading and Profit and Loss Account for the year ended 30 June 1998

Sales		28,794
Purchases	23,803	
Closing stock	4,166	
		19,637
Gross profit		9,157
Expenses		
Salaries	3,164	
Rent	854	
Lighting	422	
Insurance	105	
Motor expenses	1,133	
Trade expenses	506	
		6,184
Net profit		2,973

7.2

Bank

(1) Capital	800	(17) M Hyatt	84
(24) J Carlton	95	(21) Betta Ltd	50
		(31) Balance c/d	761
	895		895

Cash

(5) Sales	87	(6) Wages	14
(30) J King (Loan)	60	(9) Purchases	46
		(12) Wages	14
		(31) Balance c/d	73
	147		147

Capital

| | | (1) Bank | 800 |

Wages

| (6) Cash | 14 |
| (12) Cash | 14 |

Shop Fixtures

| (15) Betta Ltd | 50 |

J King (Loan)

| | | (30) Cash | 60 |

H Elliott

| (7) Sales | 35 |

L Lane

| (7) Sales | 42 |
| (13) Sales | 32 |

J Carlton

| (7) Sales | 72 | (24) Bank | 95 |
| (13) Sales | 23 | | |

K Henry

| (27) Returns out | 24 | (2) Purchases | 76 |

M Hyatt

| (17) Bank | 84 | (2) Purchases | 27 |
| | | (10) Purchases | 57 |

T Braham

| (18) Returns out | 20 | (2) Purchases | 56 |
| | | (10) Purchases | 98 |

Betta Ltd

| (21) Bank | 50 | (15) Shop fixtures | 50 |

Sales

		(5) Cash	87
		(7) H Elliott	35
		(7) L Lane	42
		(7) J Carlton	72
		(13) L Lane	32
		(13) J Carlton	23

Purchases

(2) K Henry	76
(2) M Hyatt	27
(2) T Braham	56
(9) Cash	46
(10) M Hyatt	57
(10) T Braham	98

Returns Outwards

| | | (18) T Braham | 20 |
| | | (27) K Henry | 24 |

Trial Balance as at 31 March 1998

Bank	761	
Cash	73	
Capital		800
Wages	28	
Shop fixtures	50	
J King (Loan)		60
H Elliott	35	
L Lindo	74	
K Henry		52
T Braham		134
Sales		291
Purchases	360	
Returns outwards		44
	1,381	1,381

9.1

B Webb
Balance Sheet as at 31 December 1997

Fixed assets		
Premises		1,500
Vehicles		1,200
		2,700
Current assets		
Stock	2,548	
Debtors	1,950	
Bank	1,654	
Cash	40	
	6,192	
Current liabilities		
Creditors	1,538	
		4,654
		7,354
Capital		
Balance at the start of the year		5,424
Net profit for the year		2,825
		8,249
Drawings		895
		7,354

9.2

C Worth
Balance Sheet as at 30 June 1998

Fixed assets		
Buildings		50,000
Fixtures		1,000
Vans		5,500
		56,500
Current assets		
Stock	4,166	
Debtors	3,166	
Bank	3,847	
	11,179	
Current liabilities		
Creditors	1,206	
		9,973
		66,473
Capital		
Balance at the start of the year		65,900
Net profit for the year		2,973
		68,873
Drawings		2,400
		66,473

10.1

T Clarke
Trading Account for the year ended 31 December 1997

Sales		38,742
Less Returns inwards		890
		37,852
Purchases	33,333	
Less Returns outwards	495	
	32,838	
Carriage inwards	670	
	33,508	
Less Closing stock	7,489	
		26,019
Gross profit		11,833

10.3

R Graham
Trading and Profit and Loss Account for the year ended 30 September 1998

Sales		18,600
Less Returns inwards		205
		18,395
Opening stock		2,368
Purchases	11,874	
Less Returns outwards	322	
	11,552	
Carriage inwards		310
		14,230
Less Closing stock		2,946
		11,284
Gross profit		7,111
Expenses		
Salaries and wages	3,862	
Rent and rates	304	
Carriage outwards	200	
Insurance	78	
Motor expenses	664	
Office expenses	216	
Lighting and heating	166	
General expenses	314	
		5,804
Net profit		1,307

10.4

B Jackson

Balance Sheet as at 30 September 1998

Fixed assets		
Premises		5,000
Fixtures		350
Vehicles		1,800
		7,150
Current assets		
Stock	2,946	
Debtors	3,896	
Bank	482	
	7,324	
Current liabilities		
Creditors	1,731	
		5,593
		12,743
Capital		
Balance at the start of the year		12,636
Net profit for the year		1,307
		13,943
Drawings		1,200
		12,743

Trading and Profit and Loss Account for the year ended 30 April 1998

Sales			18,600
Less Returns inwards			440
			18,160
Opening stock		3,776	
Purchases	11,556		
Less Returns outwards	355		
		11,201	
Carriage inwards		234	
		15,211	
Less Closing stock		4,998	
			10,213
Gross profit			7,947
Expenses			
Salaries and wages		2,447	
Motor expenses		664	
Rent		576	
Carriage outwards		326	
Sundry expenses		1,202	
			5,215
Net profit			2,732

Balance Sheet as at 30 April 1998

Fixed assets		
Fixtures		600
Vehicles		2,400
		3,000
Current assets		
Stock	4,998	
Debtors	4,577	
Bank	3,876	
Cash	120	
	13,571	
Current liabilities		
Creditors	3,045	
		10,526
		13,526
Capital		
Balance at the start of the year		12,844
Net profit for the year		2,732
		15,576
Drawings		2,050
		13,526

13.1

Cash Book

	Cash	Bank		Cash	Bank
(1) Capital	100		(2) Rent	10	
(3) F Lake (Loan)		500	(4) B McKenzie		65
(5) Sales	98		(9) B Burton	22	
(7) N Miller		62	(16) Bank (Contra)	50	
(11) Sales		53	(19) F Lake (Loan)		100
(15) G Moores	65		(26) Motor Expenses		12
(16) Cash (Contra)		50	(30) Cash (Contra)		100
(22) Sales		66	(31) Wages	97	
(30) Bank (Contra)	100		(31) Balances c/d	184	454
	363	731		363	731

13.2

Cash Book

Dr	Cash	Bank	Cr	Cash	Bank
(1) Balances b/d	56	2,356	(2) Rates		156
(5) Sales	74		(3) Postages	5	
(7) Cash (Contra)		60	(7) Bank (Contra)	60	
(12) J Moores	50	100	(8) T Lee		75
(20) P Jones		79	(10) C Brooks	2	
(22) Bank (Contra)	200		(17) Drawings	20	
(31) Sales		105	(22) Cash (Contra)		200
			(24) Van		1,950
			(28) Rent		40
			(31) Balance c/d	293	279
	380	2,700		380	2,700

14.1

Cash Book

Dr	Disct	Cash	Bank	Cr	Disct	Cash	Bank
(1) Capital			6,000	(1) Fixtures			950
(3) Sales		407		(2) Purchases			1,240
(5) N Morgan	10		210	(4) Rent		200	
(9) S Cooper	20		380	(7) S Thompson & Co	4		76
(14) L Curtis			115	(12) Rates			410
(20) P Exeter	2		78	(16) M Monroe	6	114	
(31) Sales			88	(31) Balance c/d		93	4,195
	32	407	6,871		10	407	6,871

In General Ledger:
Debit Discounts Allowed £32: Credit Discounts Received £10.

14.2

Cash Book

Dr	Disct	Cash	Bank	Cr	Disct	Cash	Bank
(1) Balance b/d		230	4,756	(4) Rent			120
(2) R Burton	7		133	(8) N Black	9		351
(2) E Taylor	11		209	(8) P Towers	12		468
(2) R Harris	15		285	(8) C Rowse	20		780
(6) J Cotton: loan			1,000	(10) Motor expenses		44	
(12) H Hankins	3	74		(15) Wages		160	
(18) C Winston	13		247	(21) Cash			350
(18) R Wilson & Son	17		323	(24) Drawings		120	
(18) H Winter	23		437	(25) T Briers		133	
(21) Bank		350		(29) Fixtures	7		650
(31) Commission			88	(31) Balances c/d		123	4,833
	89	580	7,552		48	580	7,552

	Discounts Received	
(31) Total for the month		48

	Discounts Allowed	
(31) Total for month		89

15.1

Sales Journal

(1) J Gordon	187
(3) G Abrahams	166
(6) V White	12
(10) J Gordon	55
(17) F Williams	289
(19) U Richards	66
(27) V Wood	28
(31) L Simes	78
	881

Sales Ledger

J Gordon
(1) Sales 187
(10) Sales 55

G Abrahams
(3) Sales 166

V White
(6) Sales 12

F Williams
(17) Sales 289

U Richards
(19) Sales 66

V Wood
(27) Sales 28

L Simes
(31) Sales 78

General Ledger

Sales
(31) Total 881 for month

15.3

Workings of invoices:

(1) F Gray:
3 rolls white tape × 10 =	30	
5 sheets blue cotton × 6 =	30	
1 dress length × 20 =	20	80
Less trade discount 25%		20
		60

(4) A Gray:
6 rolls white tape × 10 =	60	
30 metres green baize × 4 =	120	180
Less trade discount 33⅓%		60
		120

(8) E Hines:
1 dress length black silk × 20 =		20

(20) M Allen:
10 rolls white tape × 10 =	100	
6 sheets blue cotton × 6 =	36	
3 dress lengths black silk × 20 =	60	
11 metres green baize × 4 =	44	240
Less trade discount 25%		60
		180

(31) B Cooper:
12 rolls white tape × 10 =	120	
14 sheets blue cotton × 6 =	84	
9 metres green baize × 4 =	36	240
Less trade discount 33⅓%		80
		160

16.1

Sales Journal

(1) F Gray	60
(4) A Gray	120
(8) E Hines	20
(20) M Allen	180
(31) B Cooper	160
	540

Sales Ledger

F Gray
(1) Sales	60

A Gray
(4) Sales	120

E Hines
(8) Sales	20

M Allen
(20) Sales	180

B Cooper
(31) Sales	160

General Ledger

Sales
(31) Total for month	540

Purchases Ledger

K King
	(1) Purchases 450

A Bell
	(3) Purchases 800

J Kelly
	(15) Purchases 600

B Powell
	(20) Purchases 280

B Lewis
	(30) Purchases 640

Purchases Journal

(1) K King	450
(3) A Bell	800
(15) J Kelly	600
(20) B Powell	280
(30) B Lewis	640
	2,770

General Ledger

Purchases
(31) Total for month	2,770

Workings of purchases invoices

(1) K King	4 radios × 30 =	120	
	3 music centres × 160 =	480	600
	Less trade discount 25%		150
			450
(3) A Bell	2 washing machines × 200 =	400	
	5 vacuum cleaners × 60 =	300	
	2 dish dryers × 150 =	300	1,000
	Less trade discount 20%		200
			800
(15) J Kelly	1 music centre × 300 =	300	
	2 washing machines × 250 =	500	800
	Less trade discount 25%		200
			600
(20) B Powell	6 radios × 70	420	
	Less trade discount 33⅓%	140	280
(30) B Lewis	4 dish dryers × 200	800	
	Less trade discount 20%	160	640

16.3

Purchases Journal

(1) Smith Stores	90
(23) C Kelly	105
(31) J Hamilton	180
	375

Purchases Ledger

Smith Stores
	(1) Purchases 90

C Kelly
	(23) Purchases 105

J Hamilton
	(31) Purchases 180

General Ledger

Purchases
(31) Total for month	375

Sales Journal

(8) A Grantley	72
(15) A Henry	240
(24) D Sangster	81
	393

Sales Ledger

A Grantley
(8) Sales	72

A Henry
(15) Sales	240

D Sangster
(24) Sales	81

General Ledger

Sales
(31) Total for month	393

17.1

Purchases Journal

(1) H Lloyd	119
(7) D Scott	98
(4) A Simpson	114
(4) A Williams	25
(4) S Wood	56
(10) A Simpson	59
(18) M White	89
(18) J Wong	67
(18) H Miller	196
(18) H Lewis	119
(31) A Williams	56
(31) C Cooper	98
	1,096

Returns Outwards Journal

(7) H Lloyd	16
(7) D Scott	14
(25) J Wong	5
(25) A Simpson	11
	46

General Ledger

Purchases

(31) Total for month 1,096

Returns Outwards

(31) Total for month 46

Purchases Ledger

H Lloyd

(7) Returns	16	(1) Purchases	119

D Scott

(7) Returns	14	(4) Purchases	98

A Simpson

(25) Returns	11	(4) Purchases	114
		(10) Purchases	59

A Williams

		(4) Purchases	25
		(31) Purchases	56

S Wood

		(4) Purchases	56

M White

		(18) Purchases	89

J Wong

(25) Returns	5	(18) Purchases	67

H Miller

		(18) Purchases	196

H Lewis

		(18) Purchases	119

C Cooper

		(31) Purchases	98

17.3

Sales Journal

(1) T Thompson	56
(1) L Rogers	148
(1) K Barton	145
(7) K Kelly	89
(7) N Mendes	78
(7) N Lee	257
(24) K Molloy	57
(24) K Kelly	65
(24) O Green	112
(31) N Lee	55
	1,062

Purchases Journal

(3) P Potter	144
(3) H Harris	25
(3) B Spencer	76
(9) B Perkins	24
(9) H Harris	58
(9) H Miles	123
(17) H Harris	54
(17) B Perkins	65
(17) L Nixon	75
	644

Returns Inwards Journal

(14) T Thompson	5
(14) K Barton	11
(14) K Kelly	14
(28) N Mendes	24
	54

Returns Outwards Journal

(11) P Potter	12
(11) B Spencer	22
(20) B Spencer	14
	48

Sales Ledger

T Thompson

(1) Sales	56	(14) Returns	5

L Rogers

(1) Sales	148		

K Barton

(1) Sales	145	(14) Returns	11

K Kelly

(7) Sales	89	(14) Returns	14
(24) Sales	65		

N Mendes

(7) Sales	78	(28) Returns	24

N Lee

(7) Sales	257		
(31) Sales	55		

K Molloy

(24) Sales	57		

O Green

(24) Sales	112		

Purchases Ledger

P Potter

(11) Returns	12	(3) Purchases	144

H Harris

		(3) Purchases	25
		(9) Purchases	58
		(17) Purchases	54

B Spencer

(11) Returns	22	(3) Purchases	76
(20) Returns	14		

B Perkins

		(9) Purchases	24
		(17) Purchases	65

H Miles

		(9) Purchases	123

L Nixon

		(17) Purchases	75

General Ledger

Sales

		(31) Total for month	1,062

Returns Outwards

		(31) Total for month	48

Purchases

(31) Total for month 644

Returns Inwards

(31) Total for month 54

18.1

The Journal

(1) Premises	2,000	
Van	450	
Fixtures	600	
Stock	1,289	
Debtors: N Hardy	40	
M Nelson	180	
Bank	1,254	
Cash	45	
Creditors: B Blake		60
V Reagan		200
Capital		5,598
	5,858	5,858
(14) Van	300	
Better Motors Ltd		300

Returns Inwards Journal

(11) K O'Connor	16
(11) L Staines	18
	34

Returns Outwards Journal

(19) N Lee	9

Purchases Journal

(2) B Blake	20
(2) C Harris	56
(2) H Gordon	38
(2) N Lee	69
(22) J Johnson	89
(22) T Best	72
	344

Sales Journal

(3) K O'Connor	56
(3) M Benjamin	78
(3) L Staines	98
(3) N Duffy	48
(3) B Green	118
(3) M Nelson	40
(9) M Benjamin	22
(9) L Pearson	67
	527

Ledger Accounts

T Best

Dr		Cr	
		(22) Purchases	72

N Hardy

Dr		Cr	
(1) Balance	40	(16) Bank & disct	40

M Nelson

Dr		Cr	
(1) Balance	180	(16) Bank & disct	220
(3) Sales	40		
	220		220

K O'Connor

Dr		Cr	
(3) Sales	56	(11) Returns	16
		(16) Bank & disct	40
			56

J Johnson

Dr		Cr	
		(22) Purchases	89

Trial Balance as at 31 May

	Dr	Cr
C Harris		56
H Gordon		38
J Johnson		89
T Best		72
M Benjamin	100	
N Duffy	48	
B Green	118	
L Pearson	67	
Capital		5,598
Rent	15	
Motor expenses	13	
Drawings	20	
Wages	56	
Rates	66	
Sales		527
Purchases	344	
Returns inwards	34	
Returns outwards		9
Premises	2,000	
Vans	750	
Fixtures	600	
Stock	1,289	
Discounts allowed	19	
Discounts received		17
Bank	855	
Cash	12	
	6,406	6,406

Cash Book

	Disct	Cash	Bank		Disct	Cash	Bank
(1) Balances		45	1,254	(1) Rent			15
(16) N Hardy	2		38	(4) Motor expenses		13	
(16) M Nelson	11		209	(7) Drawings		20	
(16) K O'Connor	2		38	(24) B Blake	4		76
(16) L Staines	4		76	(24) V Reagan	10		190
				(24) N Lee	3		57
				(27) Wages			56
				(30) Rates			66
				(31) Better Motors			300
				(31) Balance c/d		12	855
	19	45	1,615		17	45	1,615

General Ledger

Capital

	(1) Balance 5,598

Rent

(1) Bank 15	

Motor Expenses

(4) Cash 13	

Drawings

(7) Cash 20	

Wages

(27) Bank 56	

Rates

(30) Bank 38	

Sales

	(31) Total for month 527

Purchases

(31) Total for month 344	

Returns Inwards

(31) Total for month 34	

Returns Outwards

	(31) Total for month 9

Premises

(1) Balance 2,000	

Vans

(1) Balance 450	
(14) Better Motors 300	

Fixtures

(1) Balance 600	

Stock

(1) Balance 1,289	

Discounts Allowed

(31) Total for month 19	

Discounts Received

	(31) Total for month 17

B Blake

(24) Bank 76	(1) Balance 60
(24) Discount 4	(2) Purchases 20
80	80

V Reagan

(24) Bank & disct. 200	(1) Balance b/d 200

C Harris

	(2) Purchases 56

H Gordon

	(2) Purchases 38

N Lee

(19) Returns 9	(2) Purchases 69
(24) Bank & disct 60	
69	69

M Benjamin

(3) Sales 78	
(9) Sales 22	

L Staines

(3) Sales 98	(16) Returns 18
	(16) Bank & disct 80
98	98

N Duffy

(3) Sales 48	

B Green

(3) Sales 118	

L Pearson

(9) Sales 67	

Better Motors Ltd

(31) Bank 300	(14) Van 300

18.2

	Dr.			Cr.
(a) Vehicles	6,790	:	Kingston's Garage	6,790
(b) Bad debts	34	:	H Newman	34
(c) Unique Offices	490	:	Office furniture	490
(d) Bank	39	:	W Charles	150
Bad debts	111			
(e) Drawings	45	:	Purchases	45
(f) Drawings	76	:	Insurance	76
(g) Machinery	980	:	Systems Accelerated	980

19.1

Petty Cash Book

Receipts			Total	Cleaning	Motor Expenses	Postage	Stationery	Travelling
300								
	(1)	Postage	18			18		
	(2)	Travelling	12					12
	(3)	Cleaning	15	15				
	(4)	Petrol	22		22			
	(7)	Travelling	25					25
	(8)	Stationery	17				17	
	(9)	Cleaning	18	18				
	(11)	Postage	5			5		
	(14)	Travelling	8					8
	(15)	Stationery	9				9	
	(18)	Cleaning	23	23				
	(18)	Postage	13			13		
	(20)	Motor service	43		43			
	(26)	Petrol	18		18			
	(27)	Cleaning	21	21				
	(29)	Postage	5			5		
	(30)	Petrol	14		14			
			286	77	97	41	26	45
286	(31)	Cash						
	(31)	Balance c/d	300					
586			586					

20.1

(a) Style of invoice will vary

Calculations:

		£
3 sets of Boy Michael Golf Clubs × £270		810
150 Watson golf balls at £8 per 10 balls		120
4 Faldo golf bags at £30		120
		1,050
Less trade discount 33⅓%		350
		700
Add VAT 10%		70
		770

(b)

D Wilson Ltd Ledger
G Christie & Son

May 1 Sales	770	

G Christie & Son Ledger
D Wilson Ltd

	May 1 Purchases	770

20.3

Sales Book

	Net	VAT
(1) B Davies & Co	150	15
(4) C Grant Ltd	220	22
(16) C Grant Ltd	140	14
(31) B Kelly	80	8
	590	59

Purchases Book

	Net	VAT
(10) G Cooper & Son	400	40
(10) J Wayne Ltd	190	19
(14) B Lemon	50	5
(23) S Hayward	60	6
	700	70

Sales Ledger
B Davies & Co

(1) Sales	165	

C Grant Ltd

(4) Sales	242	
(16) Sales	154	

B Kelly

(31) Sales	88	

Purchases Ledger
G Cooper & Son

	(10) Purchases	440

J Wayne Ltd

	(10) Purchases	209

B Lemon

	(14) Purchases	55

S Hayward

	(23) Purchases	66

General Ledger
Sales

	(31) Credit Sales for month	590

Purchases

(31) Credit Purchases for month	700	

Value Added Tax

(31) VAT Content in purchases book	70	(31) VAT Content in sales book	59
		(31) Balance c/d	11
	70		70

21.1

		£
Gross pay (5 × 40)		200
Less Income tax	27	
National insurance	16	43
Net pay		157

21.2

Gross pay 40 × 4		160.00
[(45 − 40) = 5] × 6		30.00
		190.00
Less Income tax	27.50	
PRSI	17.00	44.50
Net pay		145.50

21.3

Salary		200.00
Commission (30,000 × 2%)		600.00
Gross pay		800.00
Less Income tax	87.50	
PRSI	66.00	153.50
Net pay		646.50

21.4

Salary		2,000.00
Bonus		400.00
		2,400.00
Less		
Superannuation	120.00	
Income tax	830.50	
PRSI	190.00	1,140.50
Net pay		1,259.50

22.1

Sales Analysis Book

		Inv No	Total	VAT	Hi Fi Dept	TV Dept	Sundries Dept
Feb 1	P Small	586	2,860	260		2,600	
" 2	L Goode	587	1,980	180	1,800		
" 3	R Daye	588	1,760	160		1,600	
" 5	B May	589	320	–			320
" 7	L Goode	590	990	90		900	
" 7	P Small	591	3,740	340	3,400		
			11,650	1,030	5,200	5,100	320

General Ledger

Sales

	Hi Fi	TV	Sundries
Feb 28 Total for month	5,200	5,100	320

Value Added Tax

Feb 28 Total for month	1,030

Sales Ledger

P Small

Feb 1	Sales	2,860
" 7	"	3,740

L Goode

Feb 2	Sales	1,980
" 7	"	990

R Daye

Feb 3	Sales	1,760

B May

Feb 5	Sales	320

22.2

M Barber
Purchases Analysis Book

		Total	Purchases	Light & Heat	Motor Exps	Stationery	Carriage Inwards
Jul 1	L Ogden	220	220				
" 3	E Evans	390	390				
" 4	ESB	88		88			
" 5	H Noone	110	110				
" 6	Kirk Motors	136			136		
" 8	Avon Enterprises	77				77	
" 10	Kirk Motors	55			55		
" 12	Bord Gais	134		134			
" 15	A Dodds	200	200				
" 17	O Smith	24		24			
" 18	J Kelly	310	310				
" 19	D Adams	85					85
" 21	J Moore	60				60	
" 23	H Noone	116	116				
" 27	D Flynn	62					62
" 31	Kirk Motors	185			185		
		2,252	1,346	246	376	137	147

22.3

General ledger : Purchases Dr 1,346: Lighting and heating Dr 246:
Motor expenses Dr 376: Stationery Dr 137:
Carriage inwards Dr 147.

Purchases ledger : Credits in Personal accounts should be obvious

23.1
Capital: (i) (ii) Machine part of (v) (vi)
Revenue: (iii) (iv) Drinks part of (v)

23.3
Capital (a) (c) (d) (f) (j) (l): Revenue (b) (e) (g) (h) (i) (k)

23.5
(a) Per text (sections 23.1–23.3)
(b) Microcomputer – acquisition cost

Basic cost	4,000	
Installation and testing	340	
	4,340	
Less 5% discount	217	
	4,123	
Special wiring	110	
Modifications	199	
Staff training	990	
Total cost	5,422	

(c) 1. Revenue. 2. Capital. 3. Capital. 4. Revenue. 5. Revenue.
6. Revenue. 7. Capital. 8. Revenue. 9. Capital. 10. Capital.

24.1

Straight Line

Cost	4,000
Yr 1 Depreciation	700
	3,300
Yr 2 Depreciation	700
	2,600
Yr 3 Depreciation	700
	1,900
Yr 4 Depreciation	700
	1,200
Yr 5 Depreciation	700
	500

Reducing Balance

Cost	4,000
Yr 1 Depn 40% of 4,000	1,600
	2,400
Yr 2 Depn 40% of 2,400	960
	1,440
Yr 3 Depn 40% of 1,440	576
	864
Yr 4 Depn 40% of 864	346
	518
Yr 5 Depn 40% of 518	207
	311

4,000 – 500 = 3,500 ÷ 5 = 700. The rate for reducing balance should clearly be slightly less than 40%.

24.2

(a) *Straight Line*

Cost	12,500
Yr 1 Depreciation	1,845
	10,655
Yr 2 Depreciation	1,845
	8,810
Yr 3 Depreciation	1,845
	6,965
Yr 4 Depreciation	1,845
	5,120

$$\frac{12,500 - 5,120}{4} = 1,845$$

(b) *Reducing Balance*

Cost	12,500
Yr 1 Depn 20% of 12,500	2,500
	10,000
Yr 2 Depn 20% of 10,000	2,000
	8,000
Yr 3 Depn 20% of 8,000	1,600
	6,400
Yr 4 Depn 20% of 6,400	1,280
	5,120

24.3

(a) *Reducing Balance*

Cost	6,400
Yr 1 Depn 50% of 6,400	3,200
	3,200
Yr 2 Depn 50% of 3,200	1,600
	1,600
Yr 3 Depn 50% of 1,600	800
	800
Yr 4 Depn 50% of 800	400
	400
Yr 5 Depn 50% of 400	200
	200

(b) *Straight Line*

Cost	6,400
Yr 1 Depreciation	1,240
	5,160
Yr 2 Depreciation	1,240
	3,920
Yr 3 Depreciation	1,240
	2,680
Yr 4 Depreciation	1,240
	1,440
Yr 5 Depreciation	1,240
	200

$$\frac{6,400 - 200}{5} = 1,240$$

24.7

		Machines		
		A	B	C
1995	Bought 1.1.1995	3,000		
	Depreciation 10% for 12 months	300		
		2,700		
1996	Bought 1.4.1996		2,000	
	Depreciation 10% × 2,700	270		
	" 10% for 9 months		150	
		2,430	1,850	
1997	Bought 1.7.1997			1,000
	Depreciation 10% × 2,430	243		
	" 10% × 1,850		185	
	" 10% for 6 months			50
		2,187	1,665	950

1997 Total Depreciation 243 + 185 + 50 = 478

25.1

Computers

Jan 1 Bank	2,400	Dec 31 Balance c/d	3,800
Jul 1 Bank	1,400		
	3,800		3,800

Provision for Depreciation: Computers

Dec 31 Balance c/d	620	Dec 31 Profit and loss	620

25.2

Machinery

1994			
Jan 1 Bank	800	Dec 31 Balance c/d	800
1995			
Jan 1 Balance b/d	800	Dec 31 Balance c/d	2,400
Jul 1 Bank	1,000		
Oct 1 Bank	600		
	2,400		2,400
1996			
Jan 1 Balance b/d	2,400		
1997			
Apl 1 Bank	200	Dec 31 Balance c/d	2,600
	2,600		2,600

Provision for Depreciation: Machinery

1994			
Dec 31 Balance c/d	80	Dec 31 Profit and loss	80
1995			
Dec 31 Balance c/d	225	Jan 1 Balance b/d	80
		Dec 31 Profit and loss	145
	225		225
1996			
Dec 31 Balance c/d	465	Jan 1 Balance b/d	225
		Dec 31 Profit and loss	240
	465		465
1997			
Dec 31 Balance c/d	720	Jan 1 Balance b/d	465
		Dec 31 Profit and loss	255
	720		720

Balance Sheet Extracts

	31 December 1994			*31 December 1996*	
Machinery at cost		800	Machinery at cost		2,400
Less Depreciation	80	720	*Less* Depreciation to date	465	1,935
	31 December 1995			*31 December 1997*	
Machinery at cost		2,400	Machinery at cost		2,600
Less Depreciation to date	225	2,175	*Less* Depreciation to date	720	1,880

25.5

Machinery

Jan 1 Balance b/d	52,590	Dec 31 Machinery disposals	2,800
Dec 31 Bank	2,480	,, 31 Balance c/d	52,270
	55,070		55,070

Office Furniture

Jan 1 Balance b/d	2,860	Dec 31 Balance c/d	3,180
Dec 31 Bank	320		
	3,180		3,180

Provision for Depreciation: Machinery

Dec 31 Machinery disposals	1,120	Jan 1 Balance b/d	25,670
,, 31 Balance c/d	29,777	Dec 31 Profit and loss	5,227
	30,897		30,897

Provison for Depreciation: Office Furniture

Dec 31 Balance c/d	1,649	Jan 1 Balance b/d	1,490
		Dec 31 Profit and loss	159
	1,649		1,649

Machinery Disposals

Dec 31 Machinery	2,800	Dec 31 Provision for depreciation	1,120
		,, 31 Bank	800
		,, 31 Profit and loss:	
		Loss on sale	880
	2,800		2,800

Balance Sheet as at 31 December

Machinery at cost	52,270	
Less Depreciation to date	29,777	22,493
Office furniture at cost	3,180	
Less Depreciation to date	1,649	1,531

25.6

(a) (i) Time factor (ii) Economic factors (iii) Deterioration physically (iv) Depletion.

(b) (i) Depletion (ii) Physical deterioration (iii) Time (iv) Not usually subject to depletion, but depends on circumstances (v) Economic factors, obsolescence for example (vi) Time factor.

(c)

Equipment

Balance b/d	135,620	Asset disposals	36,000
Bank	47,800	Balance c/d	147,420
	183,420		183,420
Balance b/d	147,420		

Provision for Depreciation – Equipment

Asset disposals	28,224	Balance b/d	81,374
Balance c/d	90,858	Profit and loss	37,708
	119,082		119,082
		Balance b/d	90,858

Asset Disposals

Equipment	36,000	Provision for depreciation	28,224
		Bank	5,700
		Profit and loss	2,076
	36,000		36,000

25.8

(a) (i) Straight line method of calculating depreciation

Fixed Asset

Year 1 Bank	10,000	Year 3 Asset disposals	10,000

Provision for Depreciation

		Year 1 Profit and loss	2,000
Year 2 Balance c/d	4,000	Year 2 Profit and loss	2,000
	4,000		4,000
		Year 3 Balance b/d	4,000

Asset Disposals

Year 3 Fixed asset	10,000	Year 3 Bank	5,000
		,, 3 Provision for depreciation	4,000
		,, 3 Profit and loss	1,000
	10,000		10,000

(ii) Reducing balance method of calculating depreciation

Fixed Asset

Year 1 Bank	10,000	Year 3 Asset disposals	10,000

Provision for Depreciation

		Year 1 Profit and loss	4,000
		,, 1 Profit and loss	2,400
			6,400
Year 2 Balance c/d	6,400		
	6,400		
Year 3 Asset disposals	6,400	Year 3 Balance b/d	6,400

Asset Disposals

Year 3 Fixed asset	10,000	Year 3 Bank	5,000
,, 3 Profit and loss	1,400	,, 3 Provn for depreciation	6,400
	11,400		11,400

(b) (i) The purpose of depreciation provisions is to apportion the cost of a fixed asset over the useful years of its life to the organisation.

The matching concept concerns the matching of costs against the revenues which those costs generate. If the benefit to be gained is equal in each year then the straight line method is to be preferred. If the benefits are greatest in year 1 and then falling year by year, then the reducing balance method would be preferred. The impact of maintenance costs of the fixed asset, if heavier in later years, may also give credence to the reducing balance method.

(ii) The net figure at the end of year 2 is the amount of original cost not yet expensed against revenue.

(c) The charge in year 1 should be nil in this case. The matching concept concerns matching costs against revenues. There have been no revenues in year 1, therefore there should be no costs.

25.10

(a)

Plant (at cost)

1996	£	1996	£
June 1 Balance b/d	84,000	Dec 31 Disposal of plant (W1)	25,000
1997		1997	
Jan 1 Bank (W2)	34,000	May 31 Balance c/d	93,000
	118,000		118,000

(b)

Provision for depreciation of plant

1996	£	1996	£
Dec 31 Disposal of plant (W3)	12,808	June 1 Balance b/d	32,000
1997		1997	
May 31 Balance c/d	33,954	May 31 Profit and loss (W4)	14,762
	46,762		46,762

W4 *Depreciation charge for the year ended 31st May, 1997*

	£	£
Cost balance at 31st May, 1997 (per plant account)		93,000
Accumulated depreciation at 31st May, 1997:		
Opening balance	32,000	
Depreciation on plant disposed of	12,808	
		−19,192
		73,808
Depreciation @ 20%		14,762

25.11

(a)

Machinery (at cost)

1996		£	1996		£
Jan 1	Balance b/d	150,000	Mar 31	Disposal of machinery (W1)	36,000
			Dec 31	Balance c/d	114,000
		150,000			150,000
1997			1997		
Jan 1	Balance b/d	114,000	Sept 30	Disposal of machinery (W1)	13,000
Dec 31	Purchases	13,000	Dec 31	Balance c/d	114,000
		127,000			127,000

(b)

Provision for depreciation of machinery

1996		£	1996		£
Mar 31	Disposal of machinery (W2)	11,457	Jan 1	Balance b/d	30,000
Dec 31	Balance c/d	28,089	Dec 31	Profit and loss (W3)	9,546
		39,546			39,546
1997			1997		
			Jan 1	Balance b/d	28,089
Dec 31	Balance c/d	36,680	Dec 31	Profit and loss (W3)	8,591
		36,680			36,680

(c)

Disposal of machinery

1996		£	1996		£
Dec 31	Machinery (W1)	36,000	Dec 31	Prov. for dep. of mach. (W2)	11,457
	Profit & loss – profit on sale	4,457		Cash	29,000
		40,457			40,457

(c)

(Profit and loss on) disposal of plant

1996		£	1996		£
Dec 31	Plant (W1)	25,000	Dec 31	Prov. for dep. of plant (W3)	12,808
			Dec 31	Cash	10,000
			1997		
			May 31	Profit and loss – loss on sale	2,192
		25,000			25,000

Workings

W1 *Cost of plant disposed of*

	£	£
Initial cost		16,000
Other capitalised costs		
Installation costs	1,000	
Transport costs	3,000	
Additional part	5,000	9,000
		25,000

The cost of repairs in August 1995 is revenue expenditure and is therefore not included above.

W2 *Cost of new machine*

	£	£
Initial cost		24,000
Other capitalised costs		
Installation costs	4,000	
Repairs to put the machine into working order	6,000	10,000
		34,000

The cost of repairs has been capitalised as they 'added value' to the machine by putting it into working order.

W3 *Depreciation on machine disposed of on 31/12/96*

	Value	*Depreciation*
Year ended 31/5/93		
Original cost	16,000	
Installation charges	1,000	
Transport costs	3,000	
	20,000	
Depreciation @ 20%	−4,000	4,000
	16,000	
Year ended 31/5/94 Depreciation @ 20%	−3,200	3,200
	12,800	
Year ended 31/5/95 Depreciation @ 20%	−2,560	2,560
	10,240	
Year ended 31/5/96 New part	5,000	
	15,240	
Depreciation @ 20%	−3,048	3,048
	12,192	12,808

1997

		1997	
Dec 31 Machinery (W1)	13,000	Dec 31	Cash (£8,000 – £2,000)	6,000
	13,000		Profit & loss – loss on sale	7,000
				13,000
				13,000

Workings

W1 *Cost of machines disposed of*

	1996	1997
Original cost	24,000	10,000
Installation charges	4,000	2,000
Transport costs	2,000	1,000
Additional part	6,000	–
	36,000	13,000

The cost of repairs in April 1994 is revenue expenditure and therefore is not included above.

W2 *Depreciation on machine disposed of in 1996*

		Value	Depreciation
1992	Original cost	24,000	
	Installation charges	4,000	
	Transport costs	2,000	
		30,000	
	Depreciation @ 10%	–3,000	3,000
		27,000	
1993	Depreciation @ 10%	–2,700	2,700
		24,300	
1994	New part	6,000	
		30,300	
	Depreciation @ 10%	–3,030	3,030
		27,270	
1995	Depreciation @ 10%	–2,727	2,727
		24,543	11,457

W3 *Depreciation charge for 1996 and 1997*

	Cost	Provision for deprec	Net	Charge
Balance at 1st January, 1996	150,000	30,000	120,000	
Machine sold in 1996 (W1 & 2)	36,000	11,457	–24,543	
			95,457	
1996 depreciation @ 10%			9,546	9,546
Net book value at 31st December, 1996			85,911	
1997 depreciation @ 10%			8,591	8,591
			77,320	

Note Depreciation was not charged in the above workings on the machine disposed of in 1997 as it was not held at any year end

25.14

1 The factors which should be considered in the assessment of depreciation and its allocation to accounting periods are:

(a) The amount at which the asset being depreciated is carried in the accounts;

(b) the length of assets' expected useful economic lives to the business of the enterprise, having due regard to the incidence of obsolescence; and

(c) the estimated residual value of assets at the end of their expected useful economic lives in the business of the enterprise.

2 A change from one method of providing for depreciation to another is permissible only on the grounds that the new method will give a fairer presentation of the results and of the financial position of the business.

3 If at any time there is a permanent diminution in the value of an asset and the net book value is considered not to be recoverable in full (perhaps as a result of obsolescence or a fall in demand for a product), the net book amount should be written down immediately to the estimated recoverable amount, which should then be written off over the remaining useful economic life of the asset. If at any time the reasons for making such a provision cease to apply, the provision should be written back to the extent that it is no longer necessary.

4 The charge for depreciation of re-valued fixed assets should be based on the re-valued amounts and the remaining useful economic lives. Depreciation charged prior to revaluation should not be written back to the Profit and Loss Account except to the extent that it relates to a provision for permanent diminution in value which is subsequently found to be unnecessary.

5 The disclosure requirements of SSAP 12 are:

(a) The following should be disclosed in the financial statements for each major class of depreciable asset:

(i) the depreciation method used;

(ii) the useful economic lives or the depreciation rates used;

(iii) total depreciation charged for the period; and

(iv) the gross amount of depreciable assets and the related accumulated depreciation;

(b) Where there has been a change in the depreciation method used, the effect, if material, should be disclosed in the year of change. The reason for the change should also be disclosed; and

(c) Where assets have been re-valued the effect of the revaluation on the depreciation charge should, if material, be disclosed in the year of revaluation.

26.1

Bad Debts

Apl 30	H Gordon	110	Dec 31 Profit and loss	186
Aug 31	D Bellamy	64		
Oct 31	J Alderton	12		
		186		186

Provision for Bad Debts

	Dec 31 Profit and loss	220

Charge to the Profit and Loss Account

Bad debts	186
Provision for bad debts	220

(Extracts from) Balance Sheet as at 31 December

Debtors	6,850
Less Provision for bad debts	220
	6,630

26.2

(i)

Bad Debts

1996			1996		
Aug 31	W Beet	85	Dec 31 Profit and loss		225
Sep 30	S Avon	140			
		225			225
1997			1997		
Feb 28	L J Friend	180	Dec 31 Profit and loss		490
Aug 31	N Kelly	60			
Nov 30	A Oliver	250			
		490			490

Provision for Bad Debts

			1996	
			Dec 31 Profit and loss	550
1997			1997	
Dec 31	Balance c/d	600	Dec 31 Profit and loss	50
		600		600

(ii)

Charges to the Profit and Loss Account

	1996	1997
Bad debts	225	490
Provision for bad debts	550	50
	775	540

(iii)

Balance Sheet (extracts) as at 31 December

	1996	1997
Debtors	40,500	47,300
Less Provision for bad debts	550	600
	39,950	46,700

26.5

(a)

Provision for Doubtful Debts

19X8			19X7	
May 31	Profit and loss (see W1)	1,390	Jun 1 Balance b/d	2,300
		910		
,, 31	Balance c/d	2,300	19X8	
		2,300	Jun 1 Balance b/d	910

(b)

Provision for Discounts Allowed on Debtors

		19X8	
		May 31 Profit and loss (W2)	594

Workings (W1) Provision 1.6.19X7 ... 2,300
Less Provision 31.5.19X8

1% × 24,000	240	
2% × 10,000	200	
4% × 8,000	320	
5% × 3,000	150	910

Reduction in Provision ... 1,390

(W2) Debtors liable for discounts ... 24,000
Less Provision for doubtful debts ... 240
... 23,760
Provision for discounts allowed 2½% × 23,760 = 594

26.7

(days and months omitted)

(a)

Bad Debts

1995 Debtors	1,200	1995 Profit and loss	1,200
1996 Debtors	1,600	1996 Profit and loss	1,600
1997 Debtors	2,350	1997 Profit and loss	2,350

(b)

Bad Debts Recovered

1996 Profit and loss	350	1996 Mrs P Iles	350
1997 Profit and loss	150	1997 Debtor	150

(c)

Provision for Bad Debts

1996 Balance c/d	2,800	1995 Profit and loss	2,000
	2,800	1996 Profit and loss	800
			2,800
1997 Profit and loss	700	1997 Balance b/d	2,800
1997 Balance c/d	2,100		
	2,800		2,800

(d)

Profit and Loss Account (extracts)

	Charge	Credit
1995 Bad debts	1,200	
Provision for bad debts	2,000	
1996 Bad debts	1,600	
Provision for bad debts	800	
Bad debt recovered		350
1997 Bad debts	2,350	
Reduction in provision for bad debts		700
Bad debt recovered		150

26.8

(a)

Bad debts

	£		£
1995		**1995**	
Dec 31 Debtors	12,500	Dec 31 Profit and loss	12,500
1996		**1996**	
Dec 31 Debtors	8,200	Dec 31 Profit and loss	8,200
1997		**1997**	
Dec 31 Debtors	8,000	Dec 31 Profit and loss	8,000

(b)

Provision for doubtful debts

	£		£
1995		**1995**	
Dec 31 Profit and loss	3,350	Jan 1 Balance b/d	8,750
Dec 31 Balance c/d	5,400		
	8,750		8,750
1996		**1996**	
Dec 31 Balance c/d	9,320	Jan 1 Balance b/d	5,400
(2,000 + *7,320)		Dec 31 Profit and loss	3,920
	9,320		9,320
(* see part 5)			
1997		**1997**	
Dec 31 Profit and loss	580	Jan 1 Balance b/d	9,320
Dec 31 Balance c/d	8,740		
	9,320		9,320

(c)

Provision for discount on debtors

	£		£
1995		**1995**	
Dec 31 Balance c/d (see part 5)	2,592	Dec 31 Profit and loss	2,592
1996		**1996**	
Dec 31 Balance c/d	3,514	Jan 1 Balance b/d	2,592
		Dec 31 Profit and loss	922
	3,514		3,514

1997		**1997**	
Dec 31 Balance c/d	4,195	Jan 1 Balance b/d	3,514
		Dec 31 Profit and loss	681
	4,195		4,195

(d) *Profit and loss account extracts for the years ended 31st December*

	1995	1996	1997
	£	£	£
Bad debts	12,500 Dr.	8,200 Dr.	8,000 Dr.
Increase in provision for discounts on debtors	2,592 Dr.	922 Dr.	681 Dr.
In/decrease in provision for doubtful debts	3,350 Cr.	3,920 Dr.	580 Cr.

(e) *Balance sheet extracts as at 31st December*

	1995	1996	1997
	£	£	£
Gross debtors	135,000	190,000	220,000
less Bad debts written off	–	5,000	1,500
less Specific provision for doubtful debts	–	2,000	–
Debtors for purposes of calculating debt provision	135,000	183,000	218,500
less 4% provision for doubtful debts	5,400	7,320	8,740
Debtors for purpose of calculating discount prov.	129,600	175,680	209,760
less 2% provision for discounts on debtors	2,592	3,514	4,195
	127,008	172,166	205,565

26.10

(i)

BDP = Bad Debt Provision

Bad Debt Provision

	£		£
Dec 31 P & L – Reduction in	3,455	Jan 1 Balance b/d	4,900
BDP		Dec 31 P & L – increase in	5,000
Dec 31 Balance c/d (W1)	6,445	BDP	
	9,900		9,900

(ii)

Profit and Loss Account entries

	Charge	Credit
Bad debts (4,500 + 5,900)	10,400	
Increase in BDP during the year	5,000	
Reduction in BDP at year end		3,455

W1 Calculation of provision for bad debts as at 31st December

	Amount	Rate	Bad Debt Provision
	£		£
Debtors 4 months old and older (excl. bad debt)	7,000	30%	2,100
Debtors over 3 months and less than 4 months old	8,000	25%	2,000
All other debtors	46,900	5%	2,345
[£12,000 + £21,000 + £13,900]			6,445

(iii) **Balance Sheet (Extract) as at 31 December**

Debtors (£67,800 – £5,900)	£61,900
Less: Bad Debt Provision	£6,445
	£55,455

(b) The Prudence concept means that revenue and profits are not anticipated. They are included in the Profit and Loss Account only when realised either in the form of cash, or of other assets the ultimate cash realisation of which can be assessed with reasonable certainty.

Provision is made for all known liabilities, both expenses and losses, as soon as they are known of, unless the expenses relate to a future period and it is reasonably certain that they will give rise to future revenue greater than or equal to, the amount of the expenses. If the amount of an expense to be provided for is not known with certainty an estimate should be made in the light of available information.

Where the prudence concept and the accruals concept conflict, the prudence concept takes precedence.

27.1

Motor Expenses

Dec 31 Cash and bank	744	Dec 31 Profit and loss	772
,, 31 Bal c/d (expenses owing)	28		
	772		772

Insurance

Dec 31 Cash and bank	420	Dec 31 Bal c/d (Insurance prepaid)	35
		,, 31 Profit and loss	385
	420		420

Stationery

Dec 31 Cash and bank	1,800	Jan 1 Bal b/d (owing)	250
,, 31 Bal c/d (owing)	490	Dec 31 Profit and loss	2,040
	2,290		2,290

Rates

Jan 1 Bal b/d (prepaid)	220	Dec 31 Bal c/d (prepaid)	290
Dec 31 Cash and bank	950	,, 31 Profit and loss	880
	1,170		1,170

Rent Receivable

Jan 1 Bal b/d (owing)	180	Dec 31 Cash and bank	550
Dec 31 Profit and loss	580	,, 31 Bal c/d (owing)	210
	760		760

27.3 Rent and Rates

1997	£	1997	£
Jan 1 Balance b/d – rent prepaid	6,000	Jan 1 Balance b/d – rates accrued	6,000
Feb 1 Bank – Rent	18,000	Dec 31 Profit and Loss	*102,500
Mar 31 ,, – Rates	12,000		
May 1 ,, – Rent	18,000		
Aug 1 ,, – Rates	21,000		
Sep 30 ,, – Rates	12,000		
Nov 1 ,, – Rent	21,000		
Dec 31 Balance c/d – rates accrued	7,500	Dec 31 Balance c/d – rent prepaid	7,000
	115,500		115,500
1998		**1998**	
Jan 1 Balance b/d – rent prepaid	7,000	Jan 1 Balance b/d – rates accrued	7,500

Proof of profit and loss account charge

		£
Rent:	1 Jan to 31 July = 7 Months × £72,000 per annum	42,000
	1 Aug to 31 Dec = 5 Months × £84,000 per annum	35,000
		77,000
Rates:	1 Jan to 30 Sep = 9 Months × £24,000 per annum	18,000
	1 Oct to 31 Dec = 3 Months × £30,000 per annum	7,500
		25,500
		102,500

27.5

Rent Receivable

	£			£
Dec 31 Profit and Loss (W1)	8,411	Dec 31 Cash / Bank (W1)		8,681
Dec 31 Balance c/d (693 + 336)	1,029	Dec 31 Balance c/d		759
	9,440			9,440

W1 *Income for the year and balances at the end of the year*

				Income	Received	Balance
Flat 1:	Jan – Mar	3 Mths × £210	630			
	Apr – Dec	9 Mths × (£210 × 110%)	2,079	2,709	3,402	693
Flat 2:	Jan – Apr	4 Mths × £220	880			
	Jul – Dec	6 Mths × (£220 × 115%)	1,518	2,398	1,639	-759
Flat 3:	Jan	1 Mth × £280	280			
	Mar – Aug	6 Mths × £280	1,680			
	Sept – Dec	4 Mths × (£280 × 120%)	1,344	3,304	3,640	336
				8,411	8,681	270

27.9

A Scholes
Trading and Profit and Loss Account for the year ended 28 February 1998

Sales			19,740
Less Cost of goods sold:			
Opening stock		2,970	
Add Purchases		11,280	
		14,250	
Less Closing stock		3,510	10,740
Gross profit			9,000
Add Discounts received			360
			9,360
Less Expenses:			
Wages and salaries (2,580 + 90)		2,670	
Rent (1,020 – 140)		880	
Discounts allowed		690	
Van running costs (450 + 60)		510	
Bad debts (810 + 60)		870	
Depreciation:			
Office furniture	180		
Delivery van	480	660	6,280
Net profit			3,080

A Scholes
Balance Sheet as at 28 February 1998

Fixed assets			
Office furniture		1,440	
Less Depreciation		180	1,260
Delivery van		2,400	
Less Depreciation		480	1,920
			3,180
Current assets			
Stock		3,510	
Debtors	4,920		
Less Provision for bad debts	330	4,590	
Prepaid expenses		140	
Cash at bank		1,140	
Cash in hand		210	
		9,590	
Less Current liabilities			
Creditors	2,490		
Expenses owing	150	2,640	
Working capital			6,950
			10,130
Financed by:			
Capital			
Balance at start of year			9,900
Add Net profit for the year			3,080
			12,980
Less Drawings			2,850
			10,130

27.11

John Brown

Trading and Profit and Loss Account for the year ended 31 December 1997

Sales			400,000
Less Returns inwards			5,000
			395,000
Less Cost of goods sold			
Opening stock		100,000	
Add Purchases	350,000		
Less Returns out	6,200	343,800	
		443,800	
Less Closing stock		120,000	323,800
Gross profit			71,200
Less Wages		35,000	
Rates		5,500	
Telephone		1,220	
Bad debts		200	
Provision for bad debts		180	
Depreciation: Shop fittings		4,000	
Van		6,000	52,100
Net profit			19,100

Balance Sheet as at 31 December 1997

Fixed Assets			
Shop fittings at cost		40,000	
Less Depreciation		4,000	36,000
Van at cost		30,000	
Less Depreciation		6,000	24,000
			60,000
Current assets			
Stock		120,000	
Debtors	9,800		
Less Provision	980	8,820	
Prepayments		500	
Bank		3,000	
		132,320	
Less Current liabilities			
Creditors	7,000		
Expenses accrued	5,220	12,220	
Working capital			120,100
			180,100
Financed by:			
Capital			
Balance at start of year			179,000
Add Net profit			19,100
			198,100
Less Drawings			18,000
			180,100

27.13

Mr Chai

Trading and Profit and Loss Account for the year ended 30 April 19X7

Sales (259,870 − 5,624)			254,246
Less Cost of goods sold			
Stock 1.5.19X6		15,654	
Purchases (135,680 − 13,407)		122,273	
Carriage inwards		11,830	
		149,757	
Less Stock 30.4.19X7		17,750	132,007
Gross profit			122,239
Discounts received			1,750
			123,989
Less Expenses			
Salaries and wages		38,521	
Rent, rates and insurances (25,973 − 1,120 − 5,435)		19,418	
Heating and lighting (11,010 + 1,360)		12,370	
Carriage out		4,562	
Advertising		5,980	
Postage, stationery and telephone		2,410	
Bad debts		2,008	
Provision for bad debts		223	
Discounts allowed		2,306	
Depreciation		12,074	99,872
Net profit			24,117

Balance Sheet as at 30.4.19X7

Fixed assets			
Fixtures and fittings at cost		120,740	
Less Depreciation to date		63,020	57,720
Current assets			
Stock		17,750	
Debtors	24,500		
Less Provision for bad debts	735	23,765	
Prepaid expenses		6,555	
Bank		4,440	
Cash		534	
		53,044	
Less Current liabilities			
Creditors	19,840		
Expenses accrued	1,360	21,200	
Working capital			31,844
			89,564
Financed by:			
Capital: Balance as at 1.5.19X6			83,887
Add Net profit			24,117
			108,004
Less Drawings			18,440
			89,564

28.1

(i) FIFO Closing Stock 20 × £40 = £800

(ii)

LIFO	Bought	Sold	Stock after each transaction	
Jan	10 × £30		10 × £30	300
Mar	10 × £34		10 × £30	300
			10 × £34	340 640
April		8 × £34	10 × £30	300
			2 × £34	68 368
Sept	20 × £40		10 × £30	300
			2 × £34	68
			20 × £40	800 1,168
Dec		12 × £40	10 × £30	300
			2 × £34	68
			8 × £40	320 688

(iii)

AVCO	Bought	Sold	Average cost per unit stock held	No. of units in stock	Total value of stock
Jan	10 × £30		£30	10	£300
Mar	10 × £34		£32	20	£640
Apl		8	£32	12	£384
Sept	20 × £40		£37	32	£1,184
Dec		12	£37	20	£740

28.2

Trading Account for the year ended December 31

	FIFO	LIFO	AVCO
Sales 8 × £46	368	368	368
12 × £56	672	672	672
	1,040	1,040	1,040
Purchases	1,440	1,440	1,440
Less closing stock	800	688	740
	640	752	700
Gross profit	400	288	340

28.7

(This is a brief answer showing the main points to be covered. In an examination the answer should be in report form and elaborated.)

1 For Charles Gray:
(i) The prudence concept says that stock should be valued at lower of cost or net realisable value. As 50% of the retail price £375 is lower than cost £560, then £375 will be taken as net realisable value and used for stock valuation.
(ii) The sale has not taken place by 30 April 19X1. The prudence concept does not anticipate profits and therefore the sale will not be assumed. The gun should therefore be included in stock, at cost price £560.

2 For Jean Kim:
It appears that it is doubtful if the business can still be treated as a going concern.
If the final decision is that the business cannot continue, then the stock valuation should be £510 each, as this is less than cost, with a further overall deduction of auction fees and expenses £300.

3 For Peter Fox:
Stock must be valued at the lower of cost or net realisable value in this case.
The cost to be used is the cost for Peter Fox. It is quite irrelevant what the cost may be for other distributors.
It would also be against the convention of consistency to adopt a different method. The consistency applies to Peter Fox, it is not a case of consistency with other businesses. Using selling prices as a basis is not acceptable for the vast majority of businesses.

28.9

(a) In one respect the consistency convention is not applied, as at one year end the stock may be shown at cost whereas the next year end may see stock valued at net realisable value.
On the other hand, as it is prudent to take the lower of cost or net realisable value, it can be said to be consistently prudent to consistently take the lower figure.

(b) Being prudent can be said to be an advantage. For instance, a shareholder can know that stocks are not overvalued and give him a false picture of his investment.
Someone to whom money is owed, such as a creditor, will know that the stocks in the balance sheet are realisable at least at that figure.
It is this knowledge that profits are not recorded because of excessive values placed on stocks that give outside parties confidence to rely on reported profits.

29.1   *Bank Reconciliation Statement as at 31 December*

Cash at bank as per cash book		678
Add Unpresented cheques	256	
Credit transfers	56	
		312
		990
Less Bank lodgements not yet credited		115
Cash at bank as per bank statement		875

> **Note to students**
>
> Both in theory and in practice you can start with the cash book balance working to the bank statement balance, or you can reverse this method. Many lecturers/teachers have their own preference, but this is a personal matter only. Examiners sometimes ask for them using one way, sometimes the other. You should therefore be able to tackle them both ways.

29.4

Bank

		£				£
Dec 18	Lodgement understated	110	Dec 1	Balance b/d		288
Dec 16	Cheque No. 8214 overstated	81	Dec 2	Life assurance direct debit		45
Dec 20	Cheque No. 8215 overstated	9	Dec 5	Motor lease direct debit		287
			Dec 5	Cheque No. 8209 understated		2
			Dec 12	Cheque dishonoured		450
			Dec 16	Interest		315
			Dec 16	Bank charges		204
			Dec 31	Bank charges		3
Dec 31	Balance c/d	1,394				1,594
		1,594				
			Jan 1	Balance b/d		1,394

Gerard Knight

Bank Reconciliation Statement as at 31st December

	£	£	
Adjusted balance per bank account (overdrawn)		1,394	Cr.
Add: Unpresented Cheques:			
No. 8208	350		
No. 8210	285		
No. 8211	487		
No. 8212	384		
No. 8216	33		
		1,539	
Balance per the bank statement		145	Cr.

Note 1

The bank account for the month could have been re-written instead of being adjusted. If this was done the rewritten account would appear as follows:

Bank

		£			£
Dec 2	Lodgement	900	Dec 1	Balance b/d	1,810
Dec 9	Lodgement	1,500	Dec 2	Life assurance direct debit	45
Dec 18	Lodgement	2,000	Dec 2	Cheque No. 8206	138
			Dec 4	Cheque No. 8207	200
			Dec 5	Motor lease direct debit	287
			Dec 5	Cheque No. 8208	350
			Dec 5	Cheque No. 8209	142
			Dec 6	Cheque No. 8210	285
			Dec 6	Cheque No. 8211	487
			Dec 7	Cheque No. 8212	384
			Dec 12	Cheque dishonoured	450
			Dec 16	Bank interest	315
			Dec 16	Bank charges	204
			Dec 16	Cheque No. 8213	140
			Dec 16	Cheque No. 8214	309
			Dec 20	Cheque No. 8215	212
			Dec 21	Cheque No. 8216	33
			Dec 31	Bank Charges	3
Dec 31	Balance c/d	1,394			5,794
		5,794			
			Jan 1	Balance b/d	1,394

Note 2

The difference between the opening balance per the bank account of £1,810 overdrawn and that per the Bank Statement of £1,500 overdrawn is as follows:

	£	£	
Balance per the bank statement (overdrawn)		1,500	Dr.
Add: November cheques presented in December:			
No. 8204	125		
No. 8205	185	310	
Balance per the bank account (overdrawn)		1,810	Cr.

29.5

(a)

Cash Book (bank columns)

19X1		£	19X1		£
May 31	Total per question	8,342		Total per question	13,130
May 29	Dividend	90	May 31	Traders Mutual	36
May 31	Balance c/d	4,863	,, 31	T Binder (dishonoured cheque)	19
			,, 31	Charges	110
		13,295			13,295
			Jun 1	Balance b/d	4,863

(b)

Bank Reconciliation Statement as at 31 May 19X1

	£	£
Overdraft per cash book		4,863 O/D
Less unpresented cheques:		
989	364	
992	39	
994	359	
995	133	
996	9,360	
998	337	
999	649	
		11,241
		6,378 Dr
Less lodgements not yet credited: (288 + 420)		708
Balance per bank statement		5,670 Dr

(c) Report to cover following points:

(i) Balance sheet shows company's relationship with others, not others relationship with company.

(ii) Suggestion would mean that cheques sent to (and possibly received by) creditors would be ignored. Creditors would therefore be overstated.

(iii) Also ignored would be cheques received from debtors which had not been banked. Debtors would accordingly be overstated.

(iv) Any fixed asset bought by cheque, as yet unpresented would be excluded from the balance sheet.

(v) All of the above points mean that the balance sheet would not show a correct view of assets and liabilities.

29.7

Cash Book

	(Totals so far)	737		(Totals so far)	6,017
Mar 31	M Turnbull	57	Mar 31	BKS	49
,, 31	Balance c/d	5,300	,, 31	Bank charges	28
		6,094			6,094

Bank Reconciliation Statement as at 31 March

Overdraft per Cash Book		5,300
Add Lodgement not yet in bank statement		160
		5,460
Less Unpresented cheque – No. 823 to J Shaw		490
Overdraft per bank statement		4,970

29.8

Reconciliation of Account of Nala Merchandising Company with J Cross
Supplier's Statement as on 31 May 19X4

Balance per our accounts		472.13
Add Adjustments:		
Goods not received by us:	134.07	
	251.12	
	204.80	
	91.36	
		681.35
Payments not credited by supplier		1,222.16
Discounts not credited		24.94
Adjustment not credited		5.80
Returns not credited		18.15
Balance per supplier's statement		2,424.53

30.1

Sales Ledger Control

Balance b/d	4,936	Returns inwards	1,139
Sales	49,916	Bank/cash	46,490
		Discounts allowed	1,455
		Balance c/d	5,768
	54,852		54,852

30.3

Purchases Ledger Control

	£		£
Returns outwards	2,648	Balance b/d	11,874
Bank	146,100	Purchases	154,562
Petty cash	78		
Discounts received	2,134		
Set-offs against sales ledger	1,036		
Balance c/d	14,530		
	*166,526		*166,436

*Difference between the two sides 90

Sales Ledger Control

	£		£
Balance b/d	19,744	Returns inwards	4,556
Sales	199,662	Bank/cash	185,960
		Discounts allowed	5,830
		Set-offs against purchase ledger	1,036
		Balance c/d	22,024
	219,406		219,406

30.6

Total Debtors Account

	£		£
Balance b/d	26,555	Cash (600,570 – 344,890)	255,680
Sales	268,187	Discounts allowed	5,520
		Set-offs (total debtors)	70
		Bad debts	780
		Returns inwards	4,140
		Balance c/d	28,552
	294,742		294,742
Balance b/d	28,552		

Total Creditors Account

	£		£
Cash (503,970 – 14,440)	489,530	Balance b/d	43,450
Discounts received	3,510	Purchases	496,600
Set-offs (total creditors)	70		
Returns outwards	1,480		
Balance c/d	45,460		
	540,050		540,050
		Balance b/d	45,460

30.7

(a) To ensure an arithmetical check on the accounting records. The agreement of the total of the individual creditors balances with that of the balance on the control account provides that check.

If the control account and ledger are kept by separate personnel, then a check on their work and honesty is provided.

(b) (i) Increase £198 (ii) Decrease £100 (iii) No effect (iv) Decrease £400 (v) Decrease £120

(c) A computer will automatically enter two figures in different directions and will then confirm it in total fashion. As such there may seem at first sight for there to be no need for control accounts.

However, there is still the need to check on the accuracy of data input. It is important that both the skill and the honesty of the programmer is checked.

Accordingly there will still be a need for control accounts.

30.9

(a) *Computation of Correct Balance on the Debtors Control Account*

		£
Original balance per control account		257,200
Add sales returns book overcast	(i)	1,000
		258,200
Deduct bad debt	(d)	800
Correct balance		257,400

Computation of Correct Balance on the Creditors Control Account

		£	£
Original balance per control account			191,400
Deduct:			
Purchases book overcast	(a)	10,000	
Goods returned	(b)	750	10,750
Correct Balance			180,650

(b) Reconciliation of Total per Original List of Debtors Balances with Corrected Balance

	£	£
Total per original list (balancing figure)		256,100
Add:		
Balance omitted (f)	1,300	
Refund to A. Smith (h)	500	1,800
		257,900
Deduct:		
Credit balance shown as a debit balance (c)		500
		257,400

Reconciliation of Total per Original List of Creditors Balances with Corrected Balance

	£	£
Total per original list (balancing figure)		176,720
Add purchase from C Temple (g)		7,000
		183,720
Deduct:		
Goods returned (b)	750	
Contra J Kelly (e)	1,500	
Refund to A Smith (h)	500	
Discounts Received (i)	320	3,070
		180,650

30.10

(a) Computation of Correct Balance per Debtors Control Account

	£	£
Original balance per control account		78,214
Add: sales book undercast (8)		1,000
		79,214
Less:		
Bad debt (2)	600	
Goods returned (4)	635	1,235
		77,979

Computation of Correct Balance per Creditors Control Account

	£
Original balance per control account	56,191
Add purchases book undercast (10)	900
Less discounts received (7)	215
	56,876

(b) Reconciliation of Original List of Debtors Balances with Correct Control Account Balance

	£	£
Total per original list (balancing figure)		74,074
Add:		
Sale to T Evans (1)	4,600	
Refund to P Moran (5)	1,200	5,800
		79,874
Less:		
Goods returned (4)	635	
Contra C Smith (9)	1,260	1,895
		77,979

Reconciliation of Original List of Creditors Balances with Correct Control Account Balance

	£	£
Total per original list (balancing figure)		57,801
Add balance omitted (3)		670
		58,471
Less:		
Refund to P Moran (5)	1,200	
Debit balance shown as credit balance (6)	180	
Discount received (7)	215	1,595
		56,876

31.1

To economise on space, all narratives for journal entries are omitted.

	Debit	Credit
(a) J Harris : L Hart	678	678
(b) Machinery : L Pyle	4,390	4,390
(c) Van : Motor expenses	3,800	3,800
(d) E Fitzwilliam : Sales	9	9
(e) Sales : Commissions rec'd	257	257
(f) Cash needs double the amount.		
(g) Purchases : T Heath	154	154
: Drawings	189	189
(h) Discounts allowed : Discounts received	366	366

31.3

(a) 100 units × £1.39 = £139 *not* £1,390.

(b)
- (i) Stock overstated by £1,251 (i.e. 1,390 − 139).
- (ii) Cost of goods sold understated by £1,251.
- (iii) Net profit overstated by £1,251.
- (iv) Current assets overstated by £1,251.
- (v) Owner's capital overstated by £1,251.

31.4

		Debit	Credit
(a) Sales	: Capital	10,000	10,000
(b) Drawings	: General expenses	700	700
(c) Drawings	: Insurance	89	89
(d) Purchases	: C Kelly	270	270
(e) Bank	: Cash	780	780
(f) Bank	: Cash	400	400
(g) J Charlton	: M McCarthy	168	168
(h) Motor expenses	: Motor disposals	1,000	1,000

31.7

(a)

		Debit	Credit
1	Sales	1,700	
	Fixtures and fittings disposal A/c		1,700
	Being proceeds on disposal of fixtures and fittings incorrectly posted to sales A/c		
	Fixtures and fittings disposal A/c	3,400	
	Fixtures and fittings A/c		3,400
	Being cost of assets disposed of transferred to disposal A/c		
	Accumulated depreciation A/c	1,530	
	Fixtures and fittings disposal A/c		1,530
	Being accumulated depreciation on assets disposed of transferred to disposal A/c		
	Profit and loss A/c	170	
	Fixtures and fittings disposal A/c		170
	Being loss on disposal transferred to profit and loss A/c		
2	Advertising – (profit and loss A/c)	2,800	
	Bank		2,800
	Being advertising expense recorded in Profit and Loss A/c and bank A/c		
3	Cash sales	4,800	
	Debtors		4,800
	Being amount received from debtors incorrectly posted to cash sales – transferred to debtors		
4	Creditors	3,800	
	Purchases returns		3,800
	Being goods purchased returned to suppliers		

(b)

Net profit	7,800
Add: Purchases returns	3,800
	11,600
Less	
Sales	1,700
Loss on disposal of fixtures and fittings	170
Advertising	2,800
Cash sales	4,800
	9,470
Revised net profit	2,130

32.1 (a)

The Journal (narratives omitted)

		Dr	Cr
(i)	Suspense	100	
	Sales		100
(ii)	J Cantrell	250	
	J Cochrane		250
(iii)	Rent	70	
	Suspense		70
(iv)	Suspense	300	
	Discounts received		300
(v)	Sales	360	
	Motor disposals		360

(b)

Suspense

Sales	100	Balance b/d	330
Discounts received	300	Rent	70
	400		400

(c)

Net profit per accounts		7,900
Add (i) Sales undercast	100	
(iv) Discounts undercast	300	400
		8,300
Less (iii) Rent undercast	70	
(v) Reduction in sales	360	430
Corrected net profit		7,870

32.3

(a)

Difference on Trial Balance Suspense

	£		£
Per trial balance	2,513	J Winters	198
Discounts received	324	Wages	2,963
Discounts allowed	324		
	3,161		3,161

(b) *Computation of Corrected Net Profit for year to 30 April 19X7*

		+	−
Net profit per draft accounts	24,760		
(i) Discounts			648
(ii) Wages		2,963	
(iv) Stationery stock		1,500	
(vi) Remittance:		3,000	
		5,963	2,148
Correct net profit			3,815
			20,945

(c) (iii) and (v) did not affect profit

Per text

32.5

(a)

Thomas Keynes

Statement of Corrected Net Loss/Profit

	Reduce profit £	Increase profit £	£
Net loss per draft accounts			2,800
Corrections			
1 Reduce repairs		2,500	
Increase depreciation	250		
2 Decrease bank interest and charges		1,400	
Increase insurances	600		
3 Increase motor expenses	500		
4 Decrease purchases		1,200	
5 Increase sales		5,000	
6 Decrease rent payable		850	
7 No effect			
8 Increase bad debts	3,800		
Decrease provision for doubtful debts (W1)		700	
Increase provision for discounts (W2)	1,026		
	6,176	11,650	
Net effect of adjustments (profit)			5,474
Corrected net profit			2,674

W1 *Decrease in provision for doubtful debts*

	£
Debtors	57,800
Bad debts	3,800
	54,000
5%	2,700
Actual	3,400
Reduce by	700

W2 *Increase in provision for discounts*

	£
Debtors net of bad debts (W1)	54,000
Less Provision for doubtful debts	2,700
	51,300
2%	1,026

(b)

Suspense

		£			£
Jan 31	(2) Bank Int./ Chgs.	1,400	Jan 31	(2) Insurance	600
	(5) Sales	5,000		(7) Sales ledger	2,500
	(5) Capital introduced	5,000		Opening balance	
	(6) Rent payable	850		(derived)	9,150
		12,250			12,250

32.7

1

Statement of Corrected Net Profit

		£	£
Net Profit per Draft Accounts			13,360

Corrections	Profit increase £	Profit decrease £
(a) No effect		
(b) Reduce purchases	7,500	
Increase depreciation		750
(c) Increase insurances		1,500
(d) Increase discounts received	650	
(e) Introduce bad debts		2,600
Reduce provision for doubtful debts (W1)	300	
Introduce provision for discounts on debtors (W2)		646
(f) No effect		
(g) No effect		
(b) Increase bank interest		1,300
Reduce rent	800	
	9,250	6,796

33.3
Considerations

(a) *Legal position re Partnership Act 1890*: Partners can agree to anything. The main thing is that of mutual agreement. The agreement can either be very formal in a partnership deed drawn up by a lawyer or else it can be evidenced in other ways.

The Act lays down the provisions for profit sharing if agreement has not been reached, written or otherwise.

(b) As Bee is not taking active part in the running of the business he could be registered as a limited partner under the 1907 Limited Partnership Act. This has the advantage that his liability is limited to the amount of capital invested by him; he can lose that but his personal possessions cannot be taken to pay any debts of the firm.

As Bee is a 'sleeping partner' you will have to decide whether his reward should be in the form of a fixed amount, or should vary according to the profits made. In this context you should also bear in mind whether or not he would suffer a share of losses if they occurred.

If he was to have a fixed amount, irrespective as to whether profits had been made or not then the question arises as to the amount required. This is obviously a more risky investment than, say, government securities. He therefore would naturally expect to get a higher return.

Bee would probably feel aggrieved if the profits rose sharply, but he was still limited to the amounts already described. There could be an arrangement for extra payments if the profits exceeded a given figure.

(c) Cee is the expert conducting the operations of the business. He will consequently expect a major share of the profits.

One possibility would be to give him a salary, similar to his current salary, before dividing whatever profits then remain.

Dee is making himself available, as well as bringing in some capital. Because of this active involvement he will affect the profits made. It would seem appropriate to give him a salary commensurate with such work, plus a share of the profits.

(d) *Interest on capital*: Whatever is decided about profit-sharing, it would seem appropriate for each of the partners to be given interest on their capitals before sharing the balance of the profits.

Net increase	2,454
Corrected net profit	15,814

W1 *Reduce provision for doubtful debts*

	£
Debtors	36,600
Bad debts	2,600
	34,000
5% Provision	1,700
Existing provision	2,000
Reduction	300

W2 *Introduce provision for discounts on debtors*

	£
Debtors net of bad debts (W1)	34,000
Less Bad debt provision	1,700
	32,300
2% Provision	646

2

(a) Suspense

Capital Introduced	12,000	(c)	Insurance	1,500
		(f)	Purchases ledger A/c	1,000
		(g)	Sales ledger A/c	2,250
Drawings	12,000		Opening balance (derived)	19,250
	24,000			24,000

33.1

Rooster and Scarecrow

Profit and Loss Appropriation Account for the year ended 31 December 1998

Net profit			60,000
Less: Salaries: Rooster	20,000		
Scarecrow	18,000	38,000	
Interest on capital:			
Rooster	5,000		
Scarecrow	3,000	8,000	
			46,000
			14,000
Balance of profits shared:			
Rooster ½	7,000		
Scarecrow ½	7,000	14,000	

Current Accounts (dates omitted)

	Rooster	Scarecrow		Rooster	Scarecrow
Drawings	2,000	3,000	Salaries	20,000	18,000
			Interest on capital	5,000	3,000
Balances c/d	30,000	25,000	Share of profits	7,000	7,000
	32,000	28,000		32,000	28,000

33.5

Mendez and Marshall
Trading and Profit and Loss Account for the year ended 30 June 1998

Sales			123,650
Less Cost of goods sold:			
Opening stock		41,979	
Add Purchases		85,416	
		127,395	
Less Closing stock		56,340	71,055
Gross profit			52,595
Add Reduction in provision for bad debts			80
			52,675
Less Salaries and wages (£18,917 + £200)			19,117
Office expenses (£2,416 + £96)			2,512
Carriage outwards			1,288
Discounts allowed			115
Bad debts			503
Loan interest			4,000
Depreciation: Fixtures		770	
Buildings		1,000	1,770
			29,305
Net profit			23,370
Add Interest on drawings:			
Mendez		180	
Marshall		120	300
			23,670
Less Interest on capitals:			
Mendez	3,500		
Marshall	2,950	6,450	
Salary: Mendez		800	
			7,250
			16,420
Balance of profits shared:			
Mendez		8,210	
Marshall		8,210	16,420

Mendez and Marshall
Balance Sheet as at 30 June 1998

	Cost	Depc'n	Net
Fixed assets			
Buildings	75,000	26,000	49,000
Fixtures	11,000	4,070	6,930
	86,000	30,070	55,930
Current assets			
Stock		56,340	
Debtors	16,243		
Less Provision for bad debts	320	15,923	
Bank		677	
		72,940	
Less Current liabilities			
Creditors	11,150		
Expenses owing	296	11,446	
Working capital			61,494
			117,424
Financed by			
Capitals: Mendez		35,000	
Marshall		29,500	64,500

	Mendez	Marshall	Net
Current accounts			
Balance at start of year	1,306	298	
Add Interest on capital	3,500	2,950	
Add Salary	800		
Add Balance of profit	8,210	8,210	
	13,816	11,458	
Less Drawings	6,400	5,650	
Less Interest on drawings	180	120	
	7,236	5,688	12,924
			77,424
Loan from J King			40,000
			117,424

33.7

(a)

Henson and Pierce

Trading and Profit and Loss Account for the year ended 31st March, 1998

	£	£	£
Sales			680,000
Cost of sales			
Opening Stock		65,000	
Purchases W1		477,000	
		542,000	
Closing Stock		72,000	470,000
Gross profit			210,000
Add discount received			8,460
			218,460
Expenses			
Wages		86,000	
Motor expenses		15,600	
Light and heat		9,100	
Telephone and postage		6,100	
Rent and rates		4,750	
Insurances (£9,350 + £1,500 accrual)		10,850	
General expenses (£7,400 + £1,200 accrual)		8,600	
Bad debts		4,700	
Provision for doubtful debts W2		1,900	
Depreciation W3		8,000	155,600
Net profit			62,860
Interest on capital – Henson	9,500		
– Pierce	5,000	14,500	
Salary – Henson		8,000	
Balance of profit to be shared equally		40,360	
Current account – Henson		20,180	
– Pierce		20,180	
		40,360	

(b)

Henson and Pierce

Balance Sheet as at 31st March, 1998

		Cost	Depreciation	Net
		£	£	£
Fixed assets				
Premises		120,000	–	120,000
Vehicles		34,000	13,600	20,400
Equipment		12,000	3,600	8,400
		166,000	17,200	148,800
Current assets				
Stock			72,000	
Debtors	W2		38,000	
Less provision for doubtful debts	W2		1,900	36,100
				108,100
Current liabilities				
Bank			12,900	
Creditors			69,400	
Accrued expenses			2,700	
			85,000	
Net current assets				23,100
				171,900
Capital accounts				
Henson	W4		95,000	
Pierce			50,000	145,000
Current accounts				
Henson			18,900	
Pierce			8,000	26,900
				171,900

Workings

			£
W1	*Purchases*		
	Per trial balance		482,000
	Less Henson's drawings		5,000
			477,000

33.8
(a) *Trading and Profit and Loss Account for the year ended 30 September 19X0*

Brick and Stone

Sales			322,100
Less Returns inwards			2,100
			320,000
Less Cost of goods sold			
Opening stock		23,000	
Purchases (208,200 − 1,000)	207,200		
Carriage inwards	1,700		
	208,900		
Less Returns outwards	6,100		
		202,800	
		225,800	
Less Closing stock		32,000	
			193,800
Gross profit			126,200
Less Establishment Expenses:			
Rent and rates (10,300 − 600)	9,700		
Heat and light	8,700		
Depreciation: Fixtures	2,600	21,000	
Administrative Expenses:			
Staff salaries	36,100		
Telephone (2,900 + 400)	3,300		
Printing, stationery and postages	3,500	42,900	
Sales and distribution expenses:			
Motor expenses	5,620		
Carriage outwards	2,400		
Depreciation: Motors	9,200	17,220	
Financial expenses:			
Discounts allowable	950		
Loan interest	250		
	1,200		
Less Discounts receivable	370	830	
			81,950
Net profit			44,250
Less Salary: Stone		6,000	
Balance of profits shared:			
Brick ⅗		22,950	
Stone ⅖		15,300	
		38,250	44,250

W2 *Debtors and provision for doubtful debts*

	£
Debtors per trial balance	42,700
Less bad debts written off	4,700
	38,000

Provision = £38,000 × 5% = 1,900

W3 *Depreciation*

		£
Vehicles	£34,000 × 20%	6,800
Equipment	£12,000 × 10%	1,200
		8,000

W4 *Current accounts*

	Henson	Pierce	Total
Balance at start of year	5,720	−2,180	3,540
Share of profit	20,180	20,180	40,360
Interest on capital	9,500	5,000	14,500
Salary	8,000	–	8,000
Drawings (W5)	−24,500	−15,000	−39,500
	18,900	8,000	26,900

W5 *Henson's Drawings*

	£
Per Trial Balance	19,500
Add Purchases	5,000
	24,500

(b)

Brick and Stone
Balance Sheet as at 30 September 19X0

Fixed assets	Cost	Depn	Net
Fixtures and fittings	26,000	13,800	12,200
Vehicles	46,000	34,200	11,800
	72,000	48,000	24,000

Current assets			
Stock		32,000	
Debtors (9,300 – 300)		9,000	
Prepayments		600	
Bank		7,700	
		49,300	

Less Current liabilities			
Creditors	8,400		
Accrued expenses	400		
		8,800	
			40,500
			64,500

Financed by:			
Capitals:	Brick (33,000 – 10,000)	23,000	
	Stone	17,000	
			40,000

Current accounts:	Brick	Stone
Balances 1.10.19X9	3,600	2,400
Salary		6,000
Loan interest	250	
Share of profits	22,950	15,300
	26,800	23,700
Less Drawings	24,000	11,000
Goods for own use		1,000
	2,800	11,700

	14,500
	54,500
Loan from Brick	10,000
	64,500

34.1

(a)

Balance Sheet as at 1 January 1999

Goodwill	12,000
Other assets	14,000
	26,000

Capitals	X (6,000 + 6,000)	12,000
	Y (4,800 + 4,500)	9,300
	Z (3,200 + 1,500)	4,700
		26,000

(b) Goodwill Workings

		Before			After		Loss or Gain		Action needed	
X	4/8	6,000		3/10	3,600	Loss	2,400	Credit X	2,400
Y	3/8	4,500		5/10	6,000	Gain	1,500	Debit Y	1,500
Z	1/8	1,500		2/10	2,400	Gain	900	Debit Z	900
		12,000			12,000				

Balance Sheet as at 1 January 1999

Net assets	14,000

Capitals	X (6,000 + 2,400)	8,400
	Y (4,800 – 1,500)	3,300
	Z (3,200 – 900)	2,300
		14,000

34.3

The senior partner's objection is a correct response. The money does not belong to the new partner once it has been paid.

This is because a new partner becomes an owner of part of the business, and this includes a part of the goodwill. This payment is specifically for that part of the goodwill. The goodwill was created by previous partners, and this is where the new partner buys his share from them. The £10,000 will be credited to the old partners in their old profit-sharing ratio.

If C, the new partner has paid £10,000 for one-fifth of the goodwill, then total goodwill is £50,000. Should the business be sold at a future date, and the goodwill realise £50,000, then C would receive one-fifth of the proceeds, i.e. £10,000 thus getting his money back. This illustrates the fairness of the accounting treatment of his original payment for goodwill. If anything had been credited to his account from this original payment for goodwill then he would have received that in addition. Obviously this would be unfair.

34.5

(a) Stone, Pebble & Brick trading as Bigtime Building Supply Company
Profit and Loss Account for the year ended 31 March 19X0

	Apl–Dec	Jan–Mar
Net profit per accounts	27,225	9,075
Less Interest on Stone's loan	–	385
	27,225	8,690
Interest on capitals: Stone		250
Pebble		200
Brick		125
Salary: Brick		2,125
Balance of profits shared:		
Stone ⅓ 9,075 ½ 2,995		
Pebble ⅓ 9,075 3/10 1,797		
Brick ⅓ 9,075 2/10 1,198		
	27,225	8,690

(b) Capitals

	Stone	Pebble	Brick		Stone	Pebble	Brick
Goodwill adjustment		2,000	6,000	Balances b/d	26,000	18,000	16,000
Transfer to loan	14,000			Goodwill adjustment (see note)	8,000		
Balances c/d	20,000	16,000	10,000				
	34,000	18,000	16,000		34,000	18,000	16,000

Current Accounts

	Stone	Pebble	Brick		Stone	Pebble	Brick
Drawings	8,200	9,600	7,200	Interest on capital	250	200	125
Balances c/d	4,120	1,472	5,323	Salary			2,125
				Share of profits			
				Apl–Dec	9,075	9,075	9,075
				Jan–Mar	2,995	1,797	1,198
	12,320	11,072	12,523		12,320	11,072	12,523

Note: Goodwill:

	Value of goodwill taken over	Elimination of goodwill	Net effect
Stone	30,000	22,000	8,000 Cr
Pebble	20,000	22,000	2,000 Dr
Brick	16,000	22,000	6,000 Dr
	66,000	66,000	–

34.6

(a) Adjusted Profit

		£
Profit for the year (per balance sheet)		10,000
(1) Increase in cost of sales due to reduction in realisable value of stocks (£1,200 – £300)		-900
(2) Reduction in purchases due to Apple's drawings		300
Adjusted profit		9,400

(b) Division of Adjusted Profit

		£
Adjusted profit (above)		9,400
Appropriations		
Interest on capital		
Apple	10% × 4,000	400
Pear	10% × 10,000	1,000
Orange	10% × 2,000	200
		1,600
Profit available for distribution		7,800
Share of Profits (to Current Accounts)		
Apple	3/6	3,900
Pear	2/6	2,600
Orange	1/6	1,300
		7,800

(c) Current Accounts

	Apple	Pear	Orange		Apple	Pear	Orange
Balance b/d		600		Balance b/d	2,050		800
Drawings	300	9,000		Interest	400	1,000	200
Bank		4,000		Profit Share	3,900	2,600	1,300
Loan				Capital		10,000	
Balance c/d	6,050		2,300				
	6,350	13,600	2,300		6,350	13,600	2,300
				Balance b/d	6,050		2,300

Bank

Balance b/d	1,200	Current Account – Pear	4,000
Capital – Lemon	10,000	Balance c/d	7,200
	11,200		11,200

(d) Apple, Orange and Lemon
Revised Balance Sheet as at 31st March, 1998

Fixed Assets	Cost	Depreciation	Net
Premises	20,000	2,000	18,000
Vehicles	11,000	4,600	6,400
	31,000	6,600	24,400

Current Assets

Stock (£12,000 – £900)	11,100	
Debtors	10,600	
Bank	7,200	
	28,900	

Current Liabilities

Creditors	12,400	
Loan – Pear	9,000	
		21,400
Net current assets		7,500
Net assets		31,900

Represented by
Capital Accounts

Apple		4,000
Orange		2,000
Lemon		10,000
		16,000

Current Accounts

Apple	6,050	
Orange	2,300	
Lemon	—	
		8,350
		24,350
Long-term loan		7,550
		31,900

35.1

(a)

Buildings

Balance b/d	8,000	Balance c/d	9,500
Revaluation: Increase	9,500		
	17,500		17,500

Vehicles

Balance b/d	3,550	Revaluation: Reduction	950
		Balance c/d	2,600
	3,550		3,550

Stock

Balance b/d	2,040	Revaluation: Reduction	150
		Balance c/d	1,890
	2,040		2,040

Office Fittings

Balance b/d	1,310	Revaluation: Reduction	220
		Balance c/d	1,090
	1,310		1,310

Revaluation

Vehicles	950	Buildings	9,500
Stock	150		
Office fittings	220		
Profit on revaluation			
Hughes	4,090		
Allen	2,454		
Elliott	1,636		
	8,180		
	9,500		9,500

Capitals

	Hughes	Allen	Elliott		Hughes	Allen	Elliott
Balances c/d	13,650	8,874	6,476	Balances b/d	9,560	6,420	4,840
				Profit on Revaluation	4,090	2,454	1,636
	13,650	8,874	6,476		13,650	8,874	6,476

(b) *Balance Sheet as at 31 December 1998*

Fixed assets

Buildings at valuation		17,500
Vehicles at valuation		2,600
Office Fittings at valuation		1,090
		21,190

Current assets

Stock at valuation	1,890	
Debtors	4,530	
Bank	1,390	
		7,810
		29,000

Capitals:

Hughes		13,650
Allen		8,874
Elliott		6,476
		29,000

35.3

(a)

Revaluation*

	£		£
Premises	90,000	Premises	120,000
Plant	37,000	Plant	35,000
Stock	62,379	Stock	54,179
Provision doubtful debts	3,000		
Profit on revaluation			
Alan 3/6	8,400		
Bob 2/6	5,600		
Charles 1/6	2,800	16,800	
	209,179		209,179

* Just the net increases/decreases could have been recorded. Either method is acceptable.

Goodwill

	£		£
Capitals: Alan 3/6	21,000	Goodwill cancelled	
Bob 2/6	14,000	Capitals: Alan 3/7	18,000
Charles 1/6	7,000	Bob 2/7	12,000
		Don 2/7	12,000
	42,000		42,000

Capitals

	Alan	Bob	Charles	Don		Alan	Bob	Charles	Don
Goodwill	18,000	12,000	–	12,000	Balances b/d	85,000	65,000	35,000	–
Retirement			42,000		Goodwill	21,000	14,000	7,000	–
Cash	21,000			67,000	Cash				79,000
Balances b/d	67,000	67,000							
	106,000	79,000	42,000	79,000		106,000	79,000	42,000	79,000

Current Accounts

	Alan	Bob	Charles	Don		Alan	Bob	Charles	Don
Retirement		2,509	7,478		Balance b/d	3,714		4,678	
Cash	9,023			3,091	Profit on revaluation	8,400	5,600	2,800	
Balances c/d	3,091	3,091			Cash				3,091
	12,114	5,600	7,478	3,091		12,114	5,600	7,478	3,091

Charles: Retirement

	£		£
Car	3,900	Capital	42,000
Cash	53,578	Current	7,478
Balance c/d	20,000	Loan	28,000
	77,478		77,478

Bank

	£		£
Don: Capital	79,000	Balance b/d	4,200
Don: Current	3,091	Retirement – Charles	53,578
Balance c/d	5,710	Repaid Alan – Capital	21,000
		Current	9,023
	87,801		87,801

(b) Balance Sheet (summarised):

Fixed assets total 168,100 + Current assets 86,919 – Current liabilities 24,746 = 230,273.

Capitals 67,000 each × 3 + Current accounts 3,091 × 3 = Total 230,273.

35.4

(a)

Tom, Gerry and Mary

Profit and Loss Appropriation Account
for the Year Ended 31st March, 1998

	£	£	£
Profit for the year			16,000
Appropriations			
Interest on Capital			
Tom (15% × £4,000)	600		
Gerry (15% × £8,000)	1,200		
Mary (15% × £4,000)	600	2,400	
Salaries			
Tom	2,000		
Gerry	2,000		
Mary	2,000	6,000	
Unappropriated profits			7,600

Shared between the partners as follows:

Tom ½	3,800	
Gerry ¼	1,900	
Mary ¼	1,900	
	7,600	

(b)

Revaluation

	£		£
Debtors (decrease)	1,000	Stock (increase)	4,000
Capital A/c – profit on revaluation			
Tom ½	1,500		
Gerry ¼	750		
Mary ¼	750		
	4,000		4,000

(c)

Capital Accounts

	Tom	Gerry	Mary	Ann		Tom	Gerry	Mary	Ann
Balance c/d	16,000	17,000	10,000	13,000	Bal b/d	4,000	8,000	4,000	–
					Bank	–	–	–	10,000
					Goodwill	12,000	9,000	6,000	3,000
	16,000	17,000	10,000	13,000		16,000	17,000	10,000	13,000

Current Accounts

	Tom	Gerry	Mary	Ann		Tom	Gerry	Mary	Ann
Balance b/d	–	1,000	–	–	Bal b/d	2,000	–	3,000	–
					Reval'n	1,500	750	750	–
					Salaries	2,000	2,000	2,000	–
					Interest	600	1,200	600	–
Balance c/d	9,900	4,850	8,250	–	Profit	3,800	1,900	1,900	–
	9,900	5,850	8,250			9,900	5,850	8,250	
					Bal b/d	9,900	4,850	8,250	

(d)

Tom, Gerry, Mary and Ann
Balance Sheet as at 31st March, 1998 (Revised)

	Cost	Depreciation	Net
Fixed Assets			
Furniture and fittings	25,000	15,000	10,000
Vehicles	12,000	6,000	6,000
	37,000	21,000	16,000
Goodwill			30,000
			46,000
Current Assets			
Stock		18,000	
Debtors		7,000	
Bank (£12,000 + £10,000)		22,000	
		47,000	
Current Liabilities			
Creditors		10,000	
Net Current Assets			37,000
Net Assets			83,000
Represented by:			
Capital Accounts			
Tom		16,000	
Gerry		17,000	
Mary		10,000	
Ann		13,000	56,000
Current Accounts			
Tom		9,900	
Gerry		4,850	
Mary		8,250	23,000
			79,000
Long-term Loan			4,000
			83,000

36.1

S W and M
Appropriation Account for the year ended 31 December 1998

Net profit			25,200
Salaries: W		3,000	
M		1,000	4,000
Interest on capital			
S		600	
W		400	
M		200	1,200
			20,000
Balance of profits			
S 2/5		8,000	
W 2/5		8,000	
M 1/5		4,000	
			20,000

36.3

Realisation

Buildings	800	Cash: Debtors	2,700
Tools and fixtures	850	Buildings	400
Debtors	2,800	Tools etc.	950
Cash: Expenses	100	Discounts	200
		Loss on realisation:	
		Moore	150
		Stephens	150
	4,550		4,550

Capital Accounts

	Moore	Stephens		Moore	Stephens
Loss on realisation	150	150	Balance b/d	2,000	1,500
Cash	1,850	1,350			
	2,000	1,500		2,000	1,500

Cash

Balance b/d	1,800	Expenses realisation	100
Debtors	2,700	Creditors	2,550
Buildings	400	Capitals: Moore	1,850
Tools	950	Stephens	1,350
	5,850		5,850

36.4

(a)

Realisation Account

Fixed Assets		Bank (sundry assets*)	54,600
Premises	50,000		
Furniture and fittings	12,500	*Capital accounts*	
Vehicle	6,800	Mary – furniture and fittings	12,500
Stock	5,400	Anne – vehicle	5,000
Debtors	5,300	Loss on realisation – Capital A/c	
		Ann ⁵/₁₀	4,700
		Mary ³/₁₀	2,820
Bank – dissolution expenses	1,500	Joan ²/₁₀	1,880
	81,500		81,500

* Premises 45,000 + Debtors 5,000 + Stock 4,600 = 54,600

(b)

Bank

Balance b/d	2,100	Realisation – dissolution exp.	1,500
Realisation	54,600	Creditors and bank loan	6,800
Anne	11,760	Capital a/c – Anne	42,300
Mary	8,820	Capital a/c – Mary	26,680
	77,280		77,280

(c)

Current and Capital Accounts

	Anne	Mary	Joan		Anne	Mary	Joan
Balance b/d	–	–	18,700	Balance b/d	52,000	42,000	–
Furniture and fittings	–	12,500	–	Bank (Joan's deficiency)	–	–	20,580
Vehicle	5,000	–	–				
Loss on real.	4,700	2,820	1,880				
Bank	42,300	26,680	–				
	52,000	42,000	20,580		52,000	42,000	20,580

36.8

(a) (i)

Amis, Lodge & Pym

Trading and Profit and Loss Account for the year ended 31 March 19X8

Sales			404,500
Less Cost of goods sold:			
Opening stock		30,000	
Add Purchases		225,000	
Add Carriage inwards		4,000	
		259,000	
Less Closing stock		35,000	224,000
Gross profit			180,500
Add Bank interest		750	
Discounts received		4,530	5,280
			185,780
Less Office expenses (30,400 + 405)		30,805	
Rent, rates, light and heat (8,800 – 1,500)		7,300	
Carriage outwards		12,000	
Discounts allowed		10,000	
Provision for bad debts		295	
Depreciation: Motor		15,000	
Plant		20,000	95,400
Net profit			90,380
Add Interest on current accounts and drawings:			
Amis		1,000	
Lodge		900	
Pym		720	2,620
			93,000
Less Salary – Pym		13,000	
Interest on capitals: Amis	8,000		
Lodge	1,500		
Pym	500	10,000	23,000
			70,000
Balance on profit shared:			
Amis 50%		35,000	
Lodge 30%		21,000	
Pym 20%		14,000	70,000

36.12

(a)

Lock, Stock and Barrel
Profit and Loss Account for the six months ended 1 February 19X7

Sales of completed houses		280,000
Less Costs of completing houses		
Houses in course of construction at start	115,000	
Materials used	35,750	
Land used (75,000 × 1/3)	25,000	
Wages and subcontractors	78,000	253,750
Gross profit		26,250
Less Administration salaries	17,250	
General expenses	12,500	
Depreciation: Freehold land	300	
Plant and equipment (6/12 × 10%)	7,500	
Vehicles (25% × 6/12)	4,500	42,050
Net loss		15,800
Shared: Lock 40%	6,320	
Stock 30%	4,740	
Barrel 30%	4,740	15,800

Capitals

	Lock	Stock	Barrel		Lock	Stock	Barrel
Drawings	6,000	5,000	4,000	Balances b/d	52,000	26,000	4,000
Loss shared	6,320	4,740	4,740	Balance c/d			4,740
Balances c/d	39,680	16,260	8,740				8,740
	52,000	26,000	8,740		52,000	26,000	

(a)(ii) *Current Accounts*

	Amis	Lodge	Pym		Amis	Lodge	Pym
Balances b/d	1,000	500	400	Salary		500	13,000
Drawings	25,000	22,000	15,000	Interest on Capital	8,000	1,500	500
Interest on drawings	1,000	900	720	Balance of Profits	35,000	21,000	14,000
Transfer to capital	16,000		11,380	Transfer to Capital		900	
	43,000	23,400	27,500		43,000	23,400	27,500

(b)(i) *Realisation*

Motors (80,000 − 35,000)		45,000	Discount on creditors		500
Plant (100,000 − 56,600)		43,400	Amis: Motor		5,000
Debtors (14,300 − 715)		13,585	Bank: Debtors		12,985
Stock		35,000	Fowles Ltd (75,000 + 63,500)		138,500
Profit on realisation					
Amis 50%	10,000				
Lodge 30%	6,000				
Pym 20%	4,000	20,000			
		156,985			156,985

(b)(ii) *Bank*

Balance b/d	4,900	Office expenses	405
		Creditors	16,000
Realisation: Debtors	12,985	Capital: Amis	76,000
Rent rebate	1,500		
Fowles Ltd	63,500		
Capitals: Lodge	4,900		
Pym	4,620		
	92,405		92,405

(b)(iii) *Capitals*

	Amis	Lodge	Pym		Amis	Lodge	Pym
Current a/c		900		Balances b/d	80,000	15,000	5,000
Fowles Ltd	25,000	25,000	25,000	Current a/c	16,000		11,380
Realisation:				Profit on real.	10,000	6,000	4,000
Motor	5,000			Bank		4,900	4,620
Bank	76,000						
	106,000	25,900	25,000		106,000	25,900	25,000

Lock, Stock and Barrel
Balance Sheet as at 1 February 19X7

	Cost	Depreciation	Net
Fixed tangible assets			
Freehold land and buildings	20,000	3,300	16,700
Plant and equipment	150,000	89,500	60,500
Vehicles	36,000	27,500	8,500
	206,000	120,300	85,700
Current assets			
Stock of land for building		50,000	
Stocks of materials		7,500	
Debtors for completed houses		35,000	
		92,500	
Less Current liabilities			
Trade creditors		52,250	
Bank overdraft		75,250	
		127,500	(35,000)
Working capital			50,700
Net assets			
Financed by:			
Capitals: Lock			39,680
Stock			16,260
Barrel			(5,240)
			50,700

(b) Amounts distributable to partners

On 28 February there was only (6,200 + 7,000 + 72,500 – 75,250) 10,450: there was nowhere near enough to pay off the creditors, and so payment to partners could not be made.

On 30 April we treat it as though no more cash will be received.

First Distribution

	Lock	Stock	Barrel
Capital balances before dissolution	39,680	16,260	(5,240)
Loss if no further assets realised (85,700 + 92,500 – 6,000 – 6,200 – 7,000 – 72,500 – 35,000 – 50,000) = 1,500 –			
Loss shared in profit/loss ratios	(600)	(450)	(450)
Cars taken over	(2,000)	(2,000)	(2,000)
	37,080	13,810	(7,690)
Barrel's deficiency shared profit/loss ratio	4,394	3,296	7,690
Paid to partners	32,686	10,514	–

Second and Final Distribution

	Lock	Stock	Barrel
Capital balances before dissolution	39,680	16,260	(5,240)
Profit finally ascertained			
100,000 – 1,500 = 98,500 Shared	39,400	29,550	29,550
	79,080	45,810	24,310
Less Distribution and cars	34,686	12,514	2,000
Final distribution (100,000)	44,394	33,296	22,310

38.1

Chang Ltd
Trading and Profit and Loss Account for the year ended 31 December 1998

Sales			316,810
Less Cost of goods sold			
Opening Stock		25,689	
Add Purchases		201,698	
		227,387	
Less Closing Stock		29,142	198,245
Gross profit			118,565
Less expenses			
Wages (£54,207 + £581)		54,788	
Rent (£4,300 – £300)		4,000	
Lighting		1,549	
Bad debts (£748 + £77)		825	
General expenses		32,168	
Depreciation: Machinery		5,500	98,830
Net profit			19,735
Add Unappropriated profits from last year			34,280
			54,015
Less Proposed dividend			10,000
Unappropriated profits carried to next year			44,015

Chang Ltd
Balance Sheet as at 31 December 1998

Fixed assets		
Premises		65,000
Machinery	55,000	
Less Depreciation	21,300	33,700
		98,700
Current assets		
Stock		29,142
Debtors	21,784	
Less Provision	938	20,846
Prepayments		300
Bank		23,101
		73,389
Less Current liabilities		
Proposed dividend	10,000	
Creditors	17,493	
Expenses owing	581	28,074
		45,315
		144,015
Financed by:		
Authorised and issued capital		100,000
Profit and loss account		44,015
		144,015

38.3

T Howe Ltd
Trading and Profit and Loss Account for the year ended 31 December 1998

Sales			135,486
Less Cost of goods sold			
Opening stock		40,360	
Add Purchases		72,360	
Add Carriage inwards		1,570	
		114,290	
Less Closing stock		52,360	61,930
Gross profit			73,556
Less Expenses			
Salaries		18,310	
Rates and occupancy		4,515	
Carriage outwards		1,390	
Office expenses		3,212	
Sundry expenses		1,896	
Depreciation: Buildings		5,000	
Equipment		9,000	
Directors' remuneration		9,500	52,823
Net profit			20,733
Add Unappropriated profits from last year			15,286
			36,019
Less Appropriations			
Proposed dividend		10,000	
General reserve		1,800	11,800
Unappropriated profits carried to next year			24,219

T Howe Ltd
Balance Sheet as at 31 December 1998

	Cost	Depreciation	Net
Fixed assets			
Buildings	100,000	37,000	63,000
Equipment	45,000	25,000	20,000
	145,000	62,000	83,000
Current assets			
Stock		52,360	
Debtors		18,910	
Bank		6,723	
		77,993	
Less Current liabilities			
Creditors	12,304		
Expenses owing	470		
Proposed dividend	10,000	22,774	
			55,219
			138,219
Financed by:			
Share capital: authorised and issued			100,000
General reserve		14,000	
Profit and loss account		24,219	38,219
			138,219

38.5

Rulers plc
(a)   Profit and Loss Account for the year ended 31 December 19X0

	£'000	£'000
Sales		3,500
Less Cost of sales		2,100
Gross profit		1,400
Add: Discounts received	7	
Reduction in provision for bad debts	1	8
		1,408
Less Expenses:		
Operating expenses	900	
Debenture interest	10	
Bad debts	5	
Bank charges	2	
Discounts allowed	8	
Depreciation	60	985
Net profit		423
Add Retained profits from last year		400
		823
Less Appropriations:		
Capital redemption reserve	100	
Preference share dividend	10	110
Retained profits carried forward to next year		713

38.6

(a) See Chapter 11.

(b) The historical cost convention does not make the going concern unnecessary. Several instances illustrate this:

  (i) Fixed assets are depreciated over the useful life of the assets. This presupposes that the business will continue to operate during the years of assumed useful life.

  (ii) Prepayments also assume that the benefits available in the future will be able to be claimed, because the business is expected to continue.

  (iii) Stocks are valued also on the basis that we will dispose of them during the future ordinary running of the business.

  (iv) The accruals concept itself assumes that the business is to continue.

All of this shows that the two concepts complement each other.

(c) A shareholder wants accounts so that he can decide what to do with his shareholding, whether he should sell his shares or hold on to them.

To enable him to decide upon his actions, he would really like to know what is going to happen in the future. To help him in this he also would like information which shows him what happened in the past. Ideally therefore he would like both types of report, those on the past and on the future.

If he had a choice, the logical choice would be to receive a report on the future providing that it could be relied on.

38.7

Extract 1

(a) The amount paid for goodwill.

(b) The excess represents share premium.

(c) Equity shares generally means ordinary shares.

(d) That although issued in 19X6 a dividend will not be paid in that year. The first year that dividends *could* be paid is 19X7.

Extract 2

(e) (i) A rate of 8% per annum interest will be paid on them, irrespective of whether profits are made or not.

  (ii) These are the years within which the debentures could be redeemed, if the company so wished.

(f) (i) This is the rate per annum at which preference dividends will be paid, subject to there being sufficient distributable profits.

  (ii) That the shares could be bought back by the company.

(g) Probably because there was currently a lower interest rate prevailing at the time of redemption and the company took advantage of it.

(h) Large amounts of both fixed interest and fixed dividend funds have resulted in a raising of the gearing.

Balance Sheet as at 31 December 19X0

	£'000	£'000	£'000
Fixed assets			
Land at valuation			230
Plant and machinery at cost		550	
Less Depreciation to date		310	240
			470
Current assets			
Stocks		600	
Debtors, less provision (*see note*)		495	
VAT receivable		150	
Bank (*see note*)		148	
		1,393	
Current liabilities			
Preference dividend	10		
Debenture interest	10		
Creditors	200	220	
Net current assets			1,173
			1,643
Long-term liabilities			
10% Debentures			100
			1,543

	£'000	£'000
Capital and reserves		
Called-up share capital		500
Share premium account		200
Other reserves		
Capital redemption reserve	100	
Revaluation reserve	30	
Profit and loss account	713	843
		1,543

Notes:

Debtors, per balances			550
Less Standing order		50	
Bad debt provision		5	55
			495
Bank, per balances			200
Add Standing order receipt			50
			250
Less Bank charges		2	
Redemption of preference shares		100	102
			148

(b) VAT. As the company is zero rated, VAT is not added to the value of sales and charged to customers. On the other hand VAT paid is reclaimable from the Revenue Commissioners. The £150 debit balance is the VAT paid which is reclaimable, and is therefore a debtor (current asset).

(i) Debenture interest gets charged before arriving at net profit. Dividends are an appropriation of profits.

(k) Shareholders are owners and help decide appropriations. Debenture holders are external lenders and interest expense has to be paid.

38.8

(a) This is incorrect. The tax portion has to be counted as part of the total cost, which is made up of debenture interest paid plus tax. Holding back payment will merely see legal action taken by the Revenue Commissioners to collect the tax.

(b) This cannot be done. The repainting of the exterior does not improve or enhance the original value of the premises. It cannot therefore be treated as capital expenditure.

(c) This is not feasible. Only the profit on the sale of the old machinery, found by deducting net book value from sales proceeds, can be so credited to the profit and loss account. The remainder is a capital receipt and should be treated as such.

(d) This is an incorrect view. Although some of the general reserve could, if circumstances allowed it, be transferred back to the profit and loss account, it could not be shown as affecting the operating profit for 19X3. This is because the reserve was built up over the years before 19X3.

(e) This is not feasible. The share capital has to be maintained at nominal value as per the Companies Act. A share premium cannot be created in this fashion, and even if it could, it would still have to be credited to *share premium account* and not the profit and loss account.

(f) Incorrect. Although the premises could be revalued the credit for the increase has to be to a Capital Reserve account. This cannot then be transferred to the credit of the profit and loss account.

41.1

Application and Allotment

Ordinary share capital	45,000	Bank	20,000
		Bank	25,000
	45,000		45,000

Ordinary Share Capital

Forfeited shares	800	Application and allotment	45,000
		First call	30,000
Balance c/d	120,000	Second call	45,000
		D Regan	800
	120,800		120,800

First Call

Ordinary share capital	30,000	Bank	29,800
		Forfeited shares	200
	30,000		30,000

Second Call

Ordinary share capital	45,000	Bank	44,700
		Forfeited shares	300
	45,000		45,000

Forfeited Shares

First call	200	Ordinary share capital	800
Second call	300		
D Regan	80		
Transfer to share premium	220		
	800		800

Balance Sheet

Bank		120,220
Ordinary share capital		120,000
Share premium		220
		120,220

Bank

Application	20,000	Balance c/d	120,220
Allotment (30,000 less excess applications 5,000)	25,000		
First call (119,200 × 0.25)	29,800		
Second call (119,200 × 0.375)	44,700		
D Regan (800 × 0.9)	720		
	120,220		120,220

D Regan

Ordinary share capital	800	Bank	720
		Forfeited shares	80
	800		800

41.2

Bank

Application (32,600 × 0.50)	16,300	Application and allotment: Refund of application monies	1,300
Allotment (20,000 × 1.50 less excess application monies 5,000)	25,000	Balance c/d	100,160
First call (19,900 × 2)	39,800		
Second call (19,880 × 2)	19,880		
B Mills (120 × 4)	480		
	101,460		101,460

Application and Allotment

Bank: Refunds	1,300	Bank	16,300
Ordinary share capital	40,000	Bank	25,000
	41,300		41,300

First Call Account

Ordinary share capital	40,000	Bank	39,800
		Forfeited shares	200
	40,000		40,000

Second Call Account

Ordinary share capital	20,000	Bank	19,880
		Forfeited shares	120
	20,000		20,000

Ordinary Share Capital

Forfeited shares	600	Application and allotment	40,000
Balance c/d	100,000	First call	40,000
		Second call	20,000
		B Mills	600
	100,600		100,600

Forfeited Shares

First call	200	Ordinary share capital	600
Second call	120		
B Mills	120		
Transfer to share premium	160		
	600		600

B Mills

Ordinary share capital	600	Bank	480
		Forfeited shares	120
	600		600

41.3
(a)

Cosy Fires Ltd

Application and allotment

Cash: Return of unsuccessful applications 5,000 × 0.60		3,000	Cash application for 65,000 × 0.60	39,000
Share capital: Due on application and allotment: 40,000 × 0.70		28,000	Cash: Balance due on allotment (see workings)*	1,975
Share premium: 40,000 × 0.25		10,000	Balance c/d: Due from allottee in respect of 500 shares:	
			500 × 0.35 = 175	
			Less o/paid on application	
			250 × 0.60 = 150	
				25
		41,000		41,000

Share Capital

Forfeited shares: Amount called on shares forfeited: 500 × 0.70	350	Balance b/d	75,000
Balance c/d	115,000	Application and allotment	28,000
		Call	11,850
		Forfeited shares	500
	115,350		115,350

Share Premium

Balance c/d	10,375	Application and allotment	10,000
		Forfeited shares	375
	10,375		10,375

Forfeited Shares

Application and allotment	25	Share capital	350
Share capital	500	Cash: 500 × 1.10 per share	550
Share premium	375		
	900		900

Call

Share capital 39,500 × 0.30	11,850	Cash	11,850

Share Capital

Forfeited shares		5,000	Balance b/d		500,000
Balance c/d		1,000,000	Application and allotment		250,000
			First and final call		250,000
			Forfeited shares		5,000
		1,005,000			1,005,000

First and Final Call

Share capital	250,000	Cash		247,500
		Forfeited shares		2,500
	250,000			250,000

Forfeited Shares

First and final call	2,500	Share capital	5,000
Share capital	5,000	Cash	4,500
Share premium	2,000		
	9,500		9,500

JJ Ltd

42.1 *Cash Flow Statement for year ended 31 December 1998*

Net cash flow from operating activities		
Net profit before tax		2,408
Add Depreciation	1,015	
Decrease in stock	116	
Less Decrease in creditors	(218)	
Increase in debtors	(105)	
		3,216
Net cash outflow on servicing finance – dividends paid		(500)
Taxation: tax paid		(856)
Capital expenditure and financial investments:		
Payment to acquire fixed assets		(2,520)
Financing		–
Reduction in cash		(660)
Note: Balance at bank at 1 January		544
Net cash outflow		(660)
Bank overdraft at 31 December		(116)

(b) *Balance Sheet as at 31 May 19X7*

Share capital			
Authorised: 160,000 ordinary shares of £1 each			160,000
Issued and fully paid: 115,000 ordinary shares of £1 each			115,000
Capital reserve:			
Share premium			10,375
Workings: Due on application 0.60 × 40,000		24,000	
Due on allotment 0.35 × 40,000		14,000	38,000
Received on application: 0.60 × 65,000		39,000	
Less Refunded 5,000 × 0.60		3,000	36,000
Balance due on allotment			2,000
Less Amount due on			
application and allotment 500 × 0.95		475	
Received on application 750 × 0.60		450	25
			1,975

41.5

M Ltd
Cash

Application and allotment (750,000 × 85p)	637,500	Application and allotment (Refund 125,000 × 85p)	106,250
Application and allotment (500,000 × 25p – overpaid 125,000 × 85p)	18,750		
First and final call (495,000 × 50p)	247,500		
Forfeited shares (5,000 × 90p)	4,500		

Application and Allotment

Share capital	250,000	Cash	637,500
Share premium	300,000	Cash	18,750
Cash	106,250		
	656,250		656,250

Share Premium

Balance c/d	302,000	Application and allotment	300,000
		Forfeited shares	2,000
	302,000		302,000

42.3

NITE Ltd
Cash Flow Statement for year ended 31 March 1998

	£000	£000
Net cash flow from operating activities		
Operating profit	15	
Depreciation charges	20	
Profit on sale of fixed assets	(7)	
Increase in stocks	(8)	
Reduction in debtors	6	
Increase in creditors	20	46
Capital expenditure and financial investments:		
Additions to fixed assets	(60)	
Sale of fixed assets	22	(38)
Financing:		
Issue of ordinary shares at a premium	30	
Repayment of 8% debentures	(30)	
Net cash inflow during the year		8

	31.3.1998	31.3.1997
Cash at bank	24	22
Cash	9	3
	33	25

Net increase in cash balances 8

42.4

(a)

Nimmo Limited
Cash Flow Statement for year ended 31 December 19X9

	£000	£000	£000
Net cash inflow from operating activities			
Operating profit		20,400	
Depreciation charged		5,050	
Loss on sale of fixed assets (5,500 − (3,800 + 1,000))		700	
Increase in stocks		(10,000)	
Increase in trade debtors		(18,100)	
Increase in prepayments		(100)	
Increase in trade creditors		4,000	
Increase in accruals		200	
Net cash inflow from operating activities			2,150
Net cash outflow in servicing finance:			
Dividends paid			(5,100)
Taxation paid			(3,200)
Capital expenditure and financial investments:			
Purchase of fixed assets		(11,800)	
Sale of fixed assets		1,000	
Net cash outflow from capital expenditure and financial investments			(10,800)
Financing:			
Issue of debenture stock			150
Net cash outflow in the period			(16,800)
Cash at bank and in hand 31.12.19X8		£600	
Overdraft at bank and cash			
in hand 31.12.19X9		(£16,200)	
Net reduction in cash balances			(16,800)

(b) The cash flow statement for the year to 31 December 19X9 indicates that the increase in trade debtors of £18,100,000 was the single largest outflow figure in the analysis. However, the increase in stocks £10,000,000 and prepayments £100,000 together with dividends £5,100,000 and investment in fixed assets £10,800,000 collectively came to a larger amount. It could also be argued that the inflow side of the cash balance may have fallen short of expectations. In essence all the items on the cash flow statement have contributed to the change in the balance at the year end.

42.5

A Trader

Cash Flow Statement for the year ended 30th June 1998

	Ref	£	£
Operating activities			
Net cash inflow from operating activities	Note 1		35,200
Capital expenditure and financial investments			
Payments to acquire tangible fixed assets	W2	−52,000	
Receipts from the sale of investments	(i)	900	
Receipts from the sale of tangible fixed assets	(ii)	6,400	
Net cash outflow from capital expenditure and financial investments			−44,700
Financing			
Proprietor's Drawings	(iii)	−14,000	
Net cash outflow from financing	Note 4		−14,000
Decrease in cash	Notes 2 & 3		−23,500

Notes to the Cash Flow Statement

1 *Reconciliation of operating profit per the profit and loss account to net cash inflow from operating activities*

			£
Operating profit**			27,000
Depreciation charges		W1	21,500
Profit on sale of tangible fixed assets		(ii)	−1,400
Loss on sale of investments		W3	100
Increase in stocks	(£60,000 − £32,500)		−27,500
Increase in debtors***	(£26,500 − £17,000)		−9,500
Increase in trade creditors	(£45,000 − £20,000)		25,000
Net cash inflow from operating activities			35,200

** Change in capital = £131,500 − £118,500 = £13,000 + £14,000
    Drawings = £27,000
*** Including prepayments

2 *Analysis of changes in cash during the year*

		£
Balance at start of year	Note 3	6,000
Net cash outflow		−23,500
Balance at end of year	Note 3	−17,500

3 *Analysis of the balances of cash as shown in the balance sheet*

	1998	1997	Change
	£	£	£
Cash at bank and in hand	0	6,000	−6,000
Bank overdrafts	−17,500	0	−17,500
	−17,500	6,000	−23,500

4 *Analysis of changes in financing during the year*

		Capital
Balance at start of year		118,500
Cash outflow from financing		−14,000
Profit for the year (** above)		27,000
Balance at end of year		131,500

Workings

W1 *Depreciation charges*

		Machinery
Aggregate depreciation at start of year	(ii)	−58,000
Aggregate depreciation at end of year		72,500
Aggregate depreciation on disposals		7,000
		21,500

W2 *Payments to acquire tangible fixed assets*

		Machinery
Cost as at start of year		−120,000
Cost as at end of year		160,000
Disposal at cost	(ii)	12,000
		52,000

W3 *Loss on the sale of investments*

Book value as at start of year	(i)	1,000
Book value as at end of year		Nil
Book value of investments sold		1,000
Proceeds		−900
Loss on sale		100

Short of Cash Ltd

42.6 Cash Flow Statement for the year ended 30th June 1998

	Ref.	£	£
Operating activities			
Net cash inflow from operating activities	Note 1		16,000
Returns on investments and servicing of finance			
Interest paid		-11,000	
Interest received		2,000	
Dividends received		6,000	
Net cash outflow from returns on investments and servicing of finance			-3,000
Taxation			
Corporation tax paid	W1		-15,000
Capital expenditure and financial investments			
Payments to acquire tangible fixed assets	W2	-135,000	
Payments to acquire investments	W3	-80,000	
Receipts from the sale of tangible fixed assets	W4	4,000	
Net cash outflow from capital expenditure and financial investments			-211,000
Financing			
Receipts from the issue of ordinary share capital	W5	50,000	
Receipts from the issue of a loan	W6	3,000	
Net cash inflow from financing	Note 4		53,000
Decrease in cash	Notes 2 & 3		-160,000

Notes to the Cash Flow Statement

1 *Reconciliation of operating profit per the profit and loss account to net cash inflow from operating activities*

Operating loss (-£18,000 + £11,000 - £2,000 - £6,000)	-15,000
Depreciation charges (£60,000 + £20,000)	80,000
Profit on sale of tangible fixed assets	-4,000
Increase in stocks (£70,000 - £30,000)	-40,000
Increase in trade debtors (£190,000 - £180,000)	-10,000
Increase in trade creditors (£135,000 - £130,000)	5,000
Net cash inflow from operating activities	16,000

2 *Analysis of changes in cash during the year*

Balance at start of year	Note 3	20,000
Net cash outflow		-160,000
Balance at end of year	Note 3	-140,000

3 *Analysis of the balances of cash*

	1998	1997	Change
	£	£	£
Cash at bank	Nil	20,000	-20,000
Bank overdraft	-140,000	Nil	-140,000
	-140,000	20,000	-160,000

4 *Analysis of changes in financing during the year*

	Share capital	Long-term loans	Total
Balance at start of year	200,000	175,000	375,000
Cash inflow from financing	50,000	3,000	53,000
Balance at end of year	250,000	178,000	428,000

Workings to Support the Cash Flow Statement

W1 Corporation tax paid | | £
Amount owed at start of year		15,000
Charge in this year's Profit and Loss Account		2,000
Amount owed at end of year		17,000
Paid during the year		-2,000
		15,000

W2 Payments to acquire tangible fixed assets

Land	
Cost as at start of year	-200,000
Cost as at end of year	250,000
Purchases	50,000

Buildings	
Cost as at start of year	-270,000
Cost as at end of year	275,000
Purchases	5,000

Plant and Equipment	
Cost as at start of year	-100,000
Cost as at end of year	150,000
Disposal at cost	30,000
Purchases	80,000
	135,000

W3 Payments to Acquire Investments

Balance as at start of year	40,000
Balance as at end of year	120,000
	80,000

W4 Receipts from the sale of tangible fixed assets

	Plant and equipment
Original cost	30,000
Aggregate depreciation (fully depreciated per note)	-30,000
NBV at time of sale	Nil
Profit on sale (per profit and loss account)	4,000
	4,000

W5 Receipts from the issue of ordinary share capital

Balance as at start of year	-200,000
Balance as at end of year	250,000
	50,000

W6 Receipts from issue of a loan

Balance as at start of year	-175,000
Balance as at end of year	178,000
	3,000

Revalue Ltd

42.9 Cash Flow Statement for the year ended 30th June 1998

	Ref.	£	£
Operating activities			
Net cash inflow from operating activities	Note 1		33,920
Returns on investments and servicing of finance			
Interest paid		-6,000	
Interest received		1,000	
Dividends received		5,000	
Net cash flow from returns on investments and servicing of finance			0
Taxation			
Corporation tax paid	W6		-12,500
Capital expenditure and financial investments			
Payments to acquire tangible fixed assets	W5	-69,400	
Receipts from the sale of tangible fixed assets	W3	81,200	
Receipts from the sale of investments	W2	3,500	
Net cash inflow from capital expenditure and financial investments			15,260
Financing			
Gross receipts from the issue of ordinary share capital	W4	105,500	
Repayment of loan		-200,000	
Net cash outflow from financing	Note 4		-94,500
Decrease in cash	Notes 2 & 3		57,820

Notes to the Cash Flow Statement

1 Reconciliation of operating profit per the profit and loss account to net cash inflow from operating activities

Operating profit	W1	61,960
Depreciation charges		46,600
Profit on sale of tangible fixed assets		-3,500
Profit on sale of investments		-22,860
Increase in stocks	(£174,240 - £132,900)	-41,340
Increase in debtors	(£93,180 - £83,020)	-10,160
Increase in trade creditors	(£37,440 - £34,220)	3,220
Net cash inflow from operating activities		33,920

2 Analysis of changes in cash during the year

		£
Balance as at start of year	Note 3	21,460
Net cash outflow	Note 3	-57,820
Balance at end of year		-36,360

3 Analysis of the balances of cash as shown in the balance sheet

	1998 £	1997 £	Change £
Cash at bank	0	21,460	-21,460
Bank overdraft	-36,360	0	-36,360
	-36,360	21,460	-57,820

4 Analysis of changes in financing during the year

	Share capital	Share premium	Long-term loans
Balance at start of year	200,000	25,000	252,000
Cash inflow/(outflow) from financing	60,000	45,500	-200,000
Balance at end of year	260,000	70,500	52,000

Workings to Support the Cash Flow Statement

W1 Depreciation charges

	£
Freehold buildings (per profit and loss account)	7,000
Plant and equipment (per profit and loss account)	39,600
	46,600

W2 Receipts from the sale of tangible fixed assets

Plant and equipment:

Original cost	10,620
Aggregate depreciation	-10,620
NBV at time of sale	Nil
Profit on sale (per profit and loss account)	3,500
Proceeds	3,500

W3 Receipts from the sale of investments

Book value as at start of year	58,340
Book value as at end of year	Nil
Book value of investments sold	58,340
Profit on sale (per profit and loss account)	22,860
Proceeds	81,200

W4 Gross receipts from the issue of ordinary share capital

	Share capital	Share premium	Total £
Balance as at start of year	-200,000	-25,000	-225,000
Balance as at end of year	260,000	70,500	330,500
Proceeds (Nominal value + premium)			105,500

W5 Payments to acquire tangible fixed assets

Land

Valuation as at start of year	-100,000	
Valuation as at end of year	134,500	
Increase in valuation		34,500
Capital reserve as at start of year	-70,000	
Capital reserve as at end of year	104,500	
Increase in capital reserve		34,500
Purchases/sales		Nil

Buildings

Cost as at start of year	-170,000	
Cost as at end of year	175,000	
Purchases		5,000

Plant and equipment

Cost as at start of year	-210,560	
Cost as at end of year	264,380	
Disposal at cost	10,620	
Purchases		64,440
		69,440

W6 Total payments to acquire tangible fixed assets

Corporation tax paid	14,500
Amount owed at start of year	16,000
Charge in this year's profit and loss account	30,500
Amount owed at end of year	-18,000
Paid during the year	12,500

43.1

(a)

(i) Gross profit as % of sales

$$\text{Store A} \quad \frac{20,000}{80,000} \times \frac{100}{1} = 25\% \qquad \text{Store B} \quad \frac{24,000}{120,000} \times \frac{100}{1} = 20\%$$

(ii) Net profit as % of sales

$$\frac{10,000}{80,000} \times \frac{100}{1} = 12.5\% \qquad \frac{15,000}{120,000} \times \frac{100}{1} = 12.5\%$$

(iii) Expenses as % of sales

$$\frac{10,000}{80,000} \times \frac{100}{1} = 12.5\% \qquad \frac{9,000}{120,000} \times \frac{100}{1} = 7.5\%$$

(iv) Stockturn

$$\frac{60,000}{(25,000 + 15,000) \div 2} = 3 \text{ times} \qquad \frac{96,000}{(22,500 + 17,500) \div 2} = 4.8 \text{ times}$$

(v) Rate of return

$$\frac{10,000}{(38,000+42,000)\div 2} \times \frac{100}{1} = 25\% \qquad \frac{15,000}{(36,000+44,000)\div 2} \times \frac{100}{1} = 37.5\%$$

(vi) Current ratio

$$\frac{45,000}{5,000} = 9 \qquad \frac{40,000}{10,000} = 4$$

(vii) Acid test ratio

$$\frac{30,000}{5,000} = 6 \qquad \frac{22,500}{10,000} = 2.25$$

(viii) Credit given to Debtors

$$\frac{25,000}{80,000} \times 12 = 3.75\,\text{months} \qquad \frac{20,000}{120,000} \times 12 = 2 \text{ months}$$

(ix) Credit taken from Creditors

$$\frac{5,000}{50,000} \times 12 = 1.2 \text{ months} \qquad \frac{10,000}{91,000} \times 12 = 1.3 \text{ months approx.}$$

(b) Business B is the most profitable, both in terms of actual net profits £15,000 compared to £10,000, but also in terms of capital employed, B has managed to achieve a return of £37.50 for every £100 invested, i.e. 37.5%. A has managed a lower return of 25%. Reasons – possibly only – as not until you know more about the business could you give a definite answer.

(i) Possibly managed to sell far more merchandise because of lower prices, i.e. took only 20% margin as compared with A's 25% margin.

(ii) Maybe more efficient use of mechanised means in the business. Note he has more equipment, and perhaps as a consequence kept other expenses down to 6,000 as compared with A's 9,000.

(iii) Did not have as much stock lying idle. Turned over stock 4.8 times in the year as compared with 3 for A.

(iv) A's current ratio of 9 is far greater than normally needed. B kept it down to 4. A therefore had too much money lying idle and not earning anything.

(v) Following on from (iv) the Acid Test ratio for A also higher than necessary.

(vi) Part of the reasons for (iv) and (v) is that A waited (on average) 3.75 months to be paid by his customers. B managed to collect them on a 2 months' average. Money represented by debts is money lying idle.

(vii) A also paid his creditors quicker than did B, but not by much.
Put all these factors together, and it is obvious that B is running his business far more efficiently, and is more profitable as a consequence.

43.4

1 *Gross Profit Ratio*

= (Gross Profit * 100) / Sales

Year 1: £152,900 * 100 / £505,000 = 30.3%
Year 2: £172,750 * 100 / £385,000 = 44.9%

The ratio has increased from 30.3% to 44.9%. Possible explanations are:

(i) Changes in the types of goods sold, where some lines carry different rates of gross profit than others.

(ii) Increase in the selling price of goods without a proportionate increase in the cost price.

(iii) Elimination of inefficiencies and factors such as theft which would reduce the profit margin.

2 *Stock Turnover*

= Cost of Sales / Average Stock   (Cost of Sales = Sales less Gross Profit)

Year 1: £352,100 / £84,000 = 4.2 times
Year 2: £212,250 / £85,000 = 2.5 times

In the first year the average stock was turned over 4.2 times. This has deteriorated to 2.5 times in the second year. This has happened because although sales and purchases have fallen considerably stock levels have remained relatively constant. It may well be possible to reduce stock levels if this reduction is likely to be permanent.

3 *Working Capital Ratio*

= Current Assets : Current Liabilities

Year 1: £180,000 : £174,000 = 1.04 : 1
Year 2: £142,000 : £59,000 = 2.41 : 1

Current Assets were roughly equal to current Liabilities at the end of year 1. However, Mr Giles might have difficulty paying his liabilities on time, depending on how quickly his current assets could be turned into cash. His position at the end of year 2 appears comfortable, with Current Assets equal to 2.41 times Current Liabilities.

4 *Acid Test Ratio*

= Current Assets less Stock : Current Liabilities

Year 1: £94,000 : £174,000 = 0.54 : 1
Year 2: £58,000 : £59,000 = 0.98 : 1

At the end of year 1 quick assets (those readily convertible into cash) amount to only 54% of current liabilities. If the current liabilities are required to be paid promptly Mr Giles would not be able to meet these in full. At the end of year 2 quick assets approximately equalled current liabilities and he should then have been in a position to meet the total liabilities.

them even if it collected all of its debtors very quickly. If some of the company's sales were for cash this would help the situation as it would be able to convert stocks into cash without first converting them into debtors and then waiting an average of 65.7 days to receive cash. At a minimum the company will have to pay its VAT liability and at least some of its trade creditors within the next month and may require additional financing in order to do so if it has already used all of its overdraft facility.

The long-term liquidity position of Appliances Ltd is also quite poor. It is financed by a Long-term Loan which is more than the net assets of the business. Repayments of the interest on, and the principal amount of, this loan will reduce the firm's ability to pay its other commitments in the short term.

In terms of gearing (in this case Long-term Loan / Ordinary Share Capital + Revenue Reserves + Long-term Loan) it can be seen that the long-term loan represents 52.7% of the company's total financing, thereby exceeding the shareholders' funds. This level of gearing is not necessarily a problem, but in this case, coupled with the poor short-term liquidity position, needs to be addressed urgently. It would be inadvisable, and probably not possible, for the company to raise more loans.

(c) From the ratios calculated above it may be seen that the average number of debtors days outstanding is 65.7 days. The rate of stock turnover for the year is 4.4 times and 6.9 times for Small and Large electrical goods respectively. This low rate of stock turnover coupled with a long period of credit given to debtors indicates that a large amount of money is tied up in Working Capital. The company should take steps to increase its rate of stock turnover and to tighten its credit policy in order to release funds to finance current and long-term liabilities.

The company would also benefit from an injection of share capital.

Ultimately, the company needs to improve profitability. As the electrical business is competitive it may not be possible to raise prices without a large fall in sales volume. Therefore, profitability must be improved by reducing costs and/or changing the sales mix in favour of 'small' electrical goods which generate a gross margin of 26.67% versus only 11.43% from 'large' electrical goods.

---

5 *Period of Credit Given*

= (Debtors * 365) / Sales

Year 1: ($£94,000 * 365$) / $£505,000$ = 68 days
Year 2: ($£58,000 * 365$) / $£385,000$ = 55 days

The average period of credit given to customers has decreased from 68 days to 55 days. This ratio reflects the time taken by customers to pay and should approximate to the credit terms allowed by the business. The situation has improved and, viewed in conjunction with the fall in sales, this would suggest that Mr Giles has been more selective in deciding who he sells goods on credit to.

43.6

(a) (i) *Gross Profit Percentage* = Gross Profit × 100 / Sales
Small Electrical Goods: = 8,000 × 100 / 30,000 = 26.67%
Large Electrical Goods: = 8,000 × 100 / 70,000 = 11.43%

(ii) *Stock Turnover* = Cost of Sales / Average Stock
Small Electrical Goods: = 22,000 / [(4,000 + 6,000) / 2] = 4.4 times
Large Electrical Goods: = 62,000 / [(10,000 + 8,000) / 2] = 6.89 times

(iii) *Current Ratio* = Current Assets : Current Liabilities = 32,000 : 40,000 = 0.8 :1

(iv) *Liquid (or Acid Test) Ratio* = Current Assets less Stock : Current Liabilities = (32,000 − 14,000) : 40,000 = 0.45 :1

(v) *Debtors Days Outstanding* = Trade Debtors × 365 / Credit Sales = 18,000 × 365 / 100,000 = 65.7 Days

It is assumed that 'Debtors' includes only Trade Debtors and that all sales are on credit.

(vi) *Creditors Days Outstanding* = Trade Creditors × 365 / Credit Purchases = 12,000 × 365 / 84,000 = 52.14 Days

It is assumed that all purchases are on credit.

(b) Appliances Ltd has a very poor liquidity position at present. Its current ratio is only 0.8 : 1. This indicates that the company may have an inadequate amount of working capital available to meet payments due in the short term.

The acid test (quick) ratio at 0.45 : 1 is also quite low. This ratio attempts to eliminate some of the disadvantages of the current ratio by concentrating on strictly liquid assets. It is based on the assumption that stocks will not be converted into cash quickly enough in order to pay creditors. It is obvious here that Appliances Ltd does not have sufficient liquid assets to pay its immediate to short-term liabilities.

If the company was to come under short-term pressure from creditors (including VAT due and bank overdraft) it would have difficulty in paying

43.7

(a)

Joan Street

Trading and Profit and Loss Account for the year ended 31 March 19X8

Sales		(W3)	240,000
Cost of sales			
Opening Stock	21,000		
Add Purchases	(W6)	174,000	
	(W7)	195,000	
Less Closing stock		15,000	
		(W1)	180,000
Gross profit		(W2)	60,000
Sundry expenses		(W5)	38,400
Net profit		(W4)	21,600

Balance Sheet as at 31 March 19X8

Fixed assets		(W9)	108,000
Current assets			
Stock		(W8)	15,000
Debtors		(W15)	24,000
Bank		(W14)	9,000
		(W14)	48,000
Less Current liabilities		(W14)	12,000
Working capital		(W13)	36,000
		(W12)	144,000
Financed by:			
Capital:			
Balance at start of year		(W11)	122,400
Add Net profit		(W10)	21,600
			144,000

Workings (could possibly find alternatives)

(W1) As average stock 21,000 + 15,000 ÷ 2 = 18,000 and stock turnover is 10, this means that cost of sales = 18,000 × 10 = 180,000

(W2) As gross profit is 25% of sales, it must therefore be 33⅓% of cost of sales.

(W3) As (W1) is 180,000 & (W2) is 60,000 therefore sales = (W1) + (W2) = 240,000

(W4) Net profit = 9% of sales = 21,600

(W5) Missing figure, found by arithmetical deduction

(W6) & (W7) Missing figures – found by arithmetical deduction

(W8) $\dfrac{\text{Debtors (?)} \times 365}{\text{Sales}} = 36\frac{1}{2}$, i.e.

$\dfrac{? \times 365}{240,000} = 36\frac{1}{2}$, by arithmetic

debtors = 24,000. Proof $\dfrac{24,000 \times 365}{240,000} = 36\frac{1}{2}$

(W9) 45% × 240,000 = 108,000

(W10) Knowing that net profit 21,600 is 15% of W10, so W10 = 21,600 × 100/15 = 144,000

(W11) Missing figure.

(W12) & (W13) Put in after (W11)

(W14) If working capital ratio is 4, it means a factor of current assets 4, current liabilities 1 = working capital 3. As (W13) is 36,000, current assets therefore

4/3 × 36,000 = 48,000 and current liabilities
1/3 × 36,000 = 12,000

(W15) Is new missing figure.

(b) Question limited to two favourable and two unfavourable aspects (four given here for reader's benefit)
Favourable: Stock turnover, liquidity, working capital, net profit on sales
Unfavourable: Gross profit to sales, debtors collection, return on capital employed, turnover to net capital employed.

(c) Drawbacks (more than two listed for reader's benefit)
(i) No access to trends over recent years.
(ii) No future plans etc. given.
(iii) Each business is often somewhat different.
(iv) Size of businesses not known.

43.9

(a)

(i) Current ratio: by dividing current assets by current liabilities.

(ii) Quick assets ratio: by dividing current assets less stock by current liabilities.

(iii) Return on capital employed (ROCE): can have more than one meaning. One in common use is net profit divided by capital plus long-term liabilities (e.g. loans), and shown as a percentage.

(iv) Return on owner's equity (ROOE): net profit divided by capital, shown as a percentage.

(v) Debtors turnover: Sales divided by average debtors, expressed in days or months.

(vi) Creditors turnover: Purchases divided by average creditors, expressed in days or months.

(vii) Gross profit percentage: Gross profit divided by sales, expressed as a percentage.

(viii) Net percentage: Net profit divided by sales.

(ix) Stock turnover: Cost of goods sold, divided by average stock, expressed in days.

(b) (This part of the question tests your ability to be able to deduce some conclusions from the information given. You have to use your imagination.)

First, an assumption, we do not know relative sizes of these two businesses. We will assume that they are approximately of the same size.

A has a higher current ratio, 2 to 1.5, but the quick assets ratio shows a much greater disparity; 1.7 to 0.7. As stock is not included in quick assets ratio, it can be deduced that B has relatively greater stocks. Expected also from these ratios is that A has high amounts of debtors, this being seen because debtors turnover is 3 times as great for A than for B.

The return on owner's equity (ROOE) is much greater for A than for B, 30% to 18%, but the ROCE for A is not that much different than for B; 20% to 17%. This shows that A has far more in long-term borrowings than B. The ROCE indicates that A is somewhat more efficient than B, but not by a considerable amount.

Gross profit percentage is far greater for A than B, but net profit percentage is the same. Obviously A has extremely high operating expenses relative to its sales.

The last ratio shows that stock in A lies unsold for twice as long a period as for B.

A summary of the above shows that A has lower stocks, greater debtors, sells at a slower rate, and has high operating expenses. B has greater stocks, sells its goods much quicker but at lower prices as shown by the gross profit percentage.

All the evidence points to A being a firm which gives emphasis to personal service to its customers. B on the other hand emphasises cheap prices and high turnover, with not as much concentration on personal service.

43.11

(There is no set answer. In addition, as a large number of points could be mentioned, the examiner cannot expect every aspect to be covered.)

The main points which could be covered are:

(i) The accounts are for last year, whereas in fact the bank is more interested in what might happen to the firm in the future.

(ii) The accounts are usually prepared on a historic cost basis. These therefore do not reflect current values.

(iii) The bank manager would want a cash budget to be drawn up for the ensuing periods. This would give the manager an indication as to whether or not the business will be able to meet its commitments as they fall due.

(iv) The bank manager wants to ensure that bank charges and interest can be paid promptly, also that a bank loan or overdraft will be able to be paid off. He will want to see that these commitments can still be met if the business has to cease operations. This means that the saleable value of assets on cessation, rather than the cost of them, is of much more interest to the bank manager.

To say that the accounts are 'not good enough' is misleading. What the manager is saying is that the accounts do not provide him with what he would really like to know. One could argue that there should be other types of final accounts drawn up in addition to those drawn up on a historic basis.

43.12

(a) The basis on which accounts are prepared is that of an 'accruals basis'. By this it is meant that the recognition of revenue and expenditure takes place not at the point when cash is received or paid out, but instead is at the point when the revenue is earned or the expenditure is incurred.

To establish the point of recognition of a sale, several criteria are necessary:

(i) The product, or the service, must have been supplied to the customer.

(ii) The buyer must have indicated his willingness to pay for the product or services and has accepted liability.

(iii) A monetary value of the goods or services must have been agreed to by the buyer.

(iv) Ownership of the goods must have passed to the buyer.

(a) This cannot be recognised as a sale. It does not comply with any of the four criteria above.

(b) This also cannot be recognised as a sale. Neither criteria (i) nor (iv) have been covered.

(c) If this was a cash sale, all the above criteria would probably be achieved on delivery, and therefore it could be appropriate to recognise the sale.

If it was a credit sale, if the invoice was sent with the goods and a delivery note stating satisfaction by the customer is signed by him, then it would also probably be appropriate to recognise the sale.

(d) Usually takes place after the four criteria have been satisfied. If so, the sales should be recognised.

(e) In the case of cash sales this would be the point of recognition.

In the case of credit sales it would depend on whether or not criteria (a) (i) and (iv) had also been satisfied.

(f) This would only influence recognition of sales if there was serious doubt about the ability of customer to pay his debts.

43.13

Obviously there is no set answer to this question. However, the following may well be typical.

(a) If the business is going to carry on operating, then the going concern concept comes into operation. Consequently, fixed assets are valued at cost, less depreciation to date. Stocks will be valued at lower of cost or net realisable value. The 'net realisable value' will be that based on the business realising stock through normal operations.

(b) Should the business be deemed as a case for cessation, then the going concern concept could not be used. The values on fixed assets and stocks will be their disposal values. This should be affected by whether or not the business could be sold as a whole or whether it would have to be broken up. Similarly, figures would be affected by whether or not assets had to be sold off very quickly at low prices, or sold only when reasonable prices could be achieved.

It is not only the balance sheet that would be affected, as the profit and loss account would reflect the changes in values.

43.14

(a) See Chapter 11

(b) Various illustrations are possible, but the following are examples.

(i) Apportionment of expenses between one period and another. For instance, very rarely would very small stocks of stationery be valued at the year end. This means that the stationery gets charged against one year's profits whereas in fact it may not all have been used up in that year.

(ii) Items expensed instead of being capitalised. Small items which are, in theory, capital expenditure will often be charged up to an expense account.

(iii) The value of assets approximated, instead of being measured with absolute precision.

(c) (i) An illustration could be made under (b) (iii). A stock of oil could well be estimated, the true figure, if known, might be one or two litres out. The cost of precise measurement would probably not be worth the benefit of having such information.

(ii) What is material in one company may not be material in another.

43.15

No set answer. Question is of a general nature rather than being specific. A variety of answers is therefore acceptable.

The examiner might expect to see the following covered. (This is not a model answer):

(a) Different reports needed by different outside parties, as they have to meet different requirements. Might find they therefore include:

(i) for bankers – accounts based on 'break-up' value of the assets if they have to be sold off to repay loans or overdrafts.

(ii) for investors – to include how business has fared against budgets set for that year to see how successful business is at meeting targets.

(iii) for employees – include details of number of employees, wages and salaries paid, effect on pension funds.

(iv) for local community – to include reports showing amounts spent on pollution control, etc.

And any similar instances.

(b) The characteristics of useful information have been stated in the Corporate Report 1975, and the accounting reports should be measured against this.

(c) Presentation (additional) in form of pie charts, bar charts, etc., as these are often more easily understood by readers.

43.16

(a) Accountants follow the realisation concept when deciding when to recognise revenue on any particular transaction. This states that profit is normally regarded as being earned at the time when the goods or services are passed to the customer and he incurs liability for them. For a service business it means when the services have been performed.

(b) The stage at which revenue is recognised could be either F or G. The normal rule is that the goods have been despatched, not delivered. For instance the goods may be shipped to Australia and take several weeks to get there. Exactly where this fits in with F or G in the question cannot be stipulated without further information.

(c) If F is accepted as point of recognition, then £130 will be gross profit. If G is accepted as point of recognition the gross profit recognised will be £120.

(d) The argument that can be advanced is to take the prudence concept to its final conclusion, in that the debtor should pay for the goods before the profit can be recognised.

Until H is reached there is always the possibility that the goods will not be paid for, or might be returned because of faults in the goods.

(e) If the goods are almost certain to be sold, it could give a better picture of the progress of the firm up to a particular point in time, if profit could be recognised in successive amounts at stages B, C and D.

43.17

(a) A 'provision' is an amount written off or retained by way of providing for depreciation, renewals or diminution in value of assets; or retained by way of providing for any known liability of which the amount cannot be determined with 'substantial' accuracy. This therefore covers such items as provisions for

depreciation. A 'liability' is an amount owing which can be determined with substantial accuracy.

Sometimes, therefore, the difference between a provision and a liability hinges around what is meant by 'substantial' accuracy. Rent owing at the end of the financial year would normally be known with precision, this would obviously be a liability. Legal charges for a court case which as been heard, but for which the lawyers have not yet submitted their bill, would be a provision.

Accrued expenses are those accruing from one day to another, but not paid at the year end. Such items as rates, electricity, telephone charges, will come under this heading.

Creditors are persons to whom money is owed for goods and services.

Reserves consist of either undistributed profits, or else sums that have been allocated originally from such profits or have been created to comply with the law. An example of the first kind is a *general reserve*, whilst a *share premium account* comes under the second heading.

Provisions, accrued expenses and creditors would all be taken into account before calculating net profit. Reserves do not interfere with the calculation of net profit, as they are appropriations of profit or in the case of capital reserves do not pass through the profit and loss account.

(b) (i) Provision made for £21,000. Charge to profit and loss and show in balance sheet under current liabilities.

(ii) Accrued expenses, $2/12 \times £6,000 = £1,000$. Charge against profit and loss account and show as current liability in balance sheet.

(iii) Creditor £2,500. Bring into purchases in trading account and show as current liability in balance sheet.

(iv) Reserve £5,000. Debit to profit and loss appropriation account as plant replacement reserve, and show in balance sheet under *reserves*.

43.18

(a) *The bank*

The bank will be interested in two main aspects. The first is the ability to repay the loan as and when it falls due. The second is the ability to pay interest on the due dates.

Mr Whitehall

He will be interested in the expected return on his investment. This means that recent performance of the company and its plans will be important to him. In addition the possible capital growth of his investment would be desirable.

(b) *Note:* More than four ratios for the bank are given, but you should give four only as your answer.

Bank
Long-term ability to repay loan

(i) Members equity/total assets
(ii) Loan capital/Members equity
(iii) Total liabilities/Members equity
(iv) Operating profit/Loan interest.

Short-term liquidity

(i) Liquid assets/Current liabilities.
(ii) Current assets/Current liabilities.

Mr Whitehall
Return on investment

(i) Price per share/Earnings per share.
(ii) Trends of (i) for past few years.
(iii) Net profit – preference dividend/ordinary dividend.
(iv) Trends of (iii) for past few years.

44.4

1 A, C, E.
2 A, C, E.
3 E
4 D, F (assuming current assets exceed current liabilities)
5 No Effect.

44.6

(a) $= \dfrac{0.1}{1.5} = 6.7\%$

(b) $= \dfrac{15,000}{100,000} = £0.15$ per share

(c) $= \dfrac{1.5}{0.15} = 10.0$

44.8

Selection of five from:

Current ratio 1.89:1; Acid test ratio 0.78:1 (Note only bank and debtor balances included) Gross profit/Sales 33⅓% Net profit/Sales (no tax assumed) 13.3%. Net operating profit/Capital employed:

$$\frac{20 + \text{Debenture interest } 3}{200} = 11.5\%$$

Net profit/Owners equity $\dfrac{20}{140} = 14.3\%$ Stock turnover $\dfrac{100}{30} = 3.3$ times.

45.8

(a) Profit and Loss Accounts for the year to 31 March 19X8

	Chan plc	Ling plc	Wong plc
	£000	£000	£000
Operating profit	300	300	300
Interest payable	–	–	(10)
Profit on ordinary activities before tax	300	300	290
Taxation (30%)	(90)	(90)	(87)
Profit on ordinary activities after tax	210	210	203
Dividends Preference	–	(20)	(30)
Ordinary	(100)	(60)	(40)
	(100)	(80)	(70)
Retained profit for the year	£110	£130	£133

(b) (i) Earnings per share

	Chan plc	Ling plc	Wong plc

$$\text{Earnings per share} = \frac{\text{Net profit after tax and preference dividend}}{\text{Number of ordinary shares in issue}}$$

Chan plc $= \dfrac{210}{500} = 42p$

Ling plc $= \dfrac{210 - 20}{300} = 63.3p$

Wong plc $= \dfrac{203 - 30}{200} = 86.5p$

(ii) Price/earnings ratio $= \dfrac{\text{Market price of ordinary shares}}{\text{Earnings per share}}$

Chan plc $= \dfrac{840}{42} = 20$

Ling plc $= \dfrac{950}{63.3} = 15$

Wong plc $= \dfrac{1{,}038}{86.5} = 12$

(iii) Gearing ratio $= \dfrac{\text{Loan capital + preference shares} \times 100}{\text{Shareholders' funds}}$

Chan plc $=$ Nil

Ling plc $= \dfrac{200}{300 + 100 + 130} \times 100 = 37.7\%$

Wong plc $= \dfrac{300 + 100}{200 + 100 + 133} \times 100 = 92.4\%$

(c) A gearing ratio expresses the relationship that exists between total borrowings (that is, preference share capital and long-term loans), and the total amount of ordinary shareholders' funds. It should be noted that other definitions of gearing are possible and are sometimes used.

Any company with a gearing ratio of, say, 70% would be considered to be high geared, whilst a company with a gearing ratio of, say, 20% would be low geared.

Gearing is an important matter to consider when investing in ordinary shares in a particular company. A *high*-geared company means that a high proportion of the

---

Sales/Fixed assets $\dfrac{150}{120} = 1.3$ times. Days Sales in Debtors = 122.

Net worth/Total assets $\dfrac{140}{290} = 48.3\%$ Fixed assets/Net worth $\dfrac{120}{140} = 85.7\%$

Coverage of fixed charges $\dfrac{20 + 3}{3} = 7.7$ times.

44.10

Current ratios (1) 2.4:1 (2) 2.4:1
Acid test ratio (1) 1.2:1 (2) 1.2:1
Gross profit/Sales (1) 21.3 (2) 20.3
Net profit/Sales (1) 5% (2) 4.5%
Operating profit/Capital employed:

(1) $\dfrac{30{,}000}{200{,}000} = 15\%$ (2) $\dfrac{38{,}000}{294{,}000} = 12.9\%$

Net profit/Owners equity:

(1) $\dfrac{30{,}000}{200{,}000} = 15\%$ (2) $\dfrac{34{,}000}{234{,}000} = 14.5\%$

Stock turn (using year-end figures)

(1) $\dfrac{472}{120} = 3.9$ times (2) $\dfrac{596}{188} = 3.2$ times

Sales/Fixed assets (1) $\dfrac{600}{60} = 10$ times (2) $\dfrac{748}{80} = 93$ times

Collection period for debtors (1) = 60.8 days (2) = 80 days

Net worth/Total assets (1) $\dfrac{200}{300} = 0.67$ (2) $\dfrac{234}{446} = 0.52$

Coverage of fixed charges.

(1) n/a (2) $\dfrac{38{,}000}{4{,}000} = 9.5$ times

45.9

(a) (i) Forecast Profit and Loss Appropriation Accounts

	19X6	19X7	19X8
	£000	£000	£000
Forecast profits	1,800	500	2,200
Less Corporation tax (30%)	540	150	660
	1,260	350	1,540
Less Dividends proposed	1,260	350	1,540

Balance sheet extracts

	19X6	19X7	19X8
Shareholders' equity			
Issued ordinary shares of £1 each fully paid	6,000	6,000	6,000
Share premium account	1,000	1,000	1,000
Retained profits	1,650	1,650	1,650
	8,650	8,650	8,650
Current liabilities			
Dividends proposed	1,260	35	1,540

(a) (ii) Forecast Profit and Loss Appropriation Accounts

	19X6	19X7	19X8
	£000	£000	£000
Forecast profits	1,800	500	2,200
Less interest (12% × £2m)	240	240	240
	1,560	260	1,960
Less Corporation tax (30%)	468	78	588
	1,092	182	1,372
Less Dividends proposed	1,092	182	1,372

Balance sheet extracts

	19X6	19X7	19X8
Shareholders' equity			
Issued ordinary shares of £1 each full paid	5,000	5,000	5,000
Retained profits	1,650	1,650	1,650
	6,650	6,650	6,650
Deferred liabilities			
12% debentures	2,000	2,000	2,000
Current liabilities			
Dividend proposed	1,092	182	1,372

(b) (i)

If planned expansion is financed by a share issue, the forecast return on shareholders' equity for the next three years will be:

19X6	1,260/8,650 × 100	=	14.6%
19X7	350/8,650 × 100	=	4.0%
19X8	1,540/8,650 × 100	=	17.8%

company's earnings are committed to paying either interest on any debenture stock and/or dividends on any preference share capital *before* an ordinary dividend can be declared. If a company is low geared, then a high proportion of the company's earnings can be paid out as ordinary dividends.

Chan plc has not issued any long-term loans or any preference share capital. Gearing does not, therefore, apply to this company, and all of the earnings may be paid out to the ordinary shareholders.

Ling plc is a relatively low-geared company. It has no debenture stock, and only a small proportion of its earnings are committed to paying its preference shareholders. The balance may then all be declared as an ordinary dividend.

Wong plc is an extremely high-geared company. A high proportion of borrowings (in this case consisting of both debenture stock and preference share capital), means that a high proportion of its earnings has to be set aside for both its debenture holders and its preference shareholders before any ordinary dividend can be declared. As a result, if the profits of the company are low, no ordinary dividend may be payable.

If profits are rising a high-geared company may not be a particularly risky company in which to purchase some ordinary shares, but the reverse may apply if profits are falling.

For the year to 31 March 19X8, Chan, Ling and Wong's operating profit is identical. Wong is committed to paying interest on its debenture stock (which is allowable against tax), and both Ling and Wong have to pay a preference dividend (which is *not* allowable against tax).

In deciding whether to invest in any of the three companies, there are a great many other factors to be considered, including future prospects of all three companies. However, when profits are fluctuating an ordinary shareholder is more likely to receive a higher return by investing in Chan rather than by investing in either Ling or Wong. Similarly, an ordinary shareholder can expect a higher return by investing in Wong.

Based on the limited amount of information given in the question, therefore, an investor considering purchasing ordinary shares in only one of these three companies would be recommended to buy shares in Chan plc.

It should be noted that if profits were *increasing*, an investor would be recommended to buy shares firstly in Wong, then in Ling and finally in Chan. The earnings per share in both Ling and Wong are far higher than in Chan, so there is a much greater chance of an increase in the ordinary dividend, but this is not necessarily the case if profits are falling or fluctuating.

(ii) If planned expansion is financed by a debenture issue, the forecast return on shareholders' equity for the next three years will be:

19X6	$1,092/6,650 \times 100$	=	16.4%
19X7	$182/6,650 \times 100$	=	2.7%
19X8	$1,372/6,650 \times 100$	=	20.6%

Note: All the above figures are, of course, net of tax and should be grossed by a factor of 100/70 if comparison with gross interest rates is to be made (on the assumption of 30% tax rate).

(c) The return on shareholders' equity for the year ended 30 September 19X5 was $600/6,620 \times 100 = 91\%$, and it could have been 9.5% if full distribution of the year's profit had been made. To have the return fluctuate between 2.7% and 20.6%, as it will do if the planned expansion is financed by the debenture issue, will surely unnerve all but the most sturdy shareholders. Such a violent swing from year to year will confuse, confound and alarm anyone looking at the shares as an investment.

To finance the planned expansion by a share issue does not improve matters greatly, as it will be seen that the return will still fluctuate between 4.0% and 17.8%. But since we are told that the industry is 'subject to marked variations in consumer demand' it does seem more appropriate to use share capital (by definition risk-bearing) rather than a debenture. The poor profits forecast for 19X7 suggest that it would not take much of a variation from the expected results to show no profit at all, and were this to occur, is there not a possibility that the debenture holders could not be paid their due interest? Failure to pay debenture interest on time would bring in a receiver (assuming the debentures were secured); his function would then be to collect not only the unpaid interest but the capital as well, as failure to pay interest would be a breach in the conditions under which the debenture was issued.

If shareholders are to miss a year's dividends as a result of there being no profits for distribution, the directors can expect a stormy annual general meeting, but that is far less dangerous than the entry of a receiver.

In practice, of course, it is unusual for a company to pay out all profits as dividends, and since shareholders will pay more attention usually to the level of dividends paid than to profits earned, it would make better financial sense if the 19X6 dividend were maintained at or slightly above the 19X5 level, enabling an addition to be made to retained profits. This in turn would enable a fund to be built up to supplement current profits for dividends and/or to redeem the debentures.

The all-shares or all-debentures choice is also an unrealistic one. Although there is much to be said for a broad share base to support what is obviously a risky business, it could make better sense to raise part of the required £2,000,000 by shares and part by debentures. A restrained dividend policy coupled with the use of the (probably enlarged) depreciation charge arising after the expansion had taken place could enable a debenture redemption programme to be established over the course of the next few years.

45.11

(a) (i) Shareholders

	19X6	19X7
Earnings per share (EPS)	$\dfrac{9,520}{39,680} = 24\text{p}$	$\dfrac{11,660}{39,680} = 29.4\text{p}$
Dividend cover	$\dfrac{9,520}{2,240} = 4.25$ times	$\dfrac{11,660}{2,400} = 4.86$ times

(ii) Trade creditors

	19X6	19X7
Current ratio	$\dfrac{92,447}{36,862} = 2.5$	$\dfrac{99,615}{42,475} = 2.3$
Acid test	$\dfrac{40,210 + 12,092}{39,862} = 1.4{:}1$	$\dfrac{43,370 + 5,790}{42,475} = 1.2$

(iii) Internal management
Debtor ratio/sales*
*assumed credit sales

	19X6	19X7
	$\dfrac{40,210}{486,300} \times 52 = 4.3$ weeks	$\dfrac{43,370}{583,900} \times 52 = 3.9$

Return on capital employed

	19X6	19X7
(before tax)	$\dfrac{15,254}{40,740} = 37.4\%$	$\dfrac{18,686}{50,000} = 37.4\%$

(b) Shareholders
EPS. An increase of 5.4p per share has occurred. This was due to an increase in profit without any increase in share capital.

Dividend cover. Increased by 0.6 times because increase in profit not fully reflected in dividends.

Trade creditors
Current ratio. This has fallen but only marginally and it still appears to be quite sound.

Acid test. This has also fallen, but still seems to be quite reasonable.

Internal management
Debtor ratio. There appears to have been an increase in the efficiency of our credit control. Return on capital employed. This has stayed the same for each of the two years. The increase in capital employed has seen a proportional increase in profits.

45.13
To the Board of G plc
From AN Other, Accountant
Subject: *Potential acquisition of either of companies A Ltd and B Ltd as subsidiaries in the machine tool manufacturing sector. Financial performances assessed.*

As instructed by you I have investigated the financial performances of these two companies to assist in the evaluation of them as potential acquisitions.

It should be borne in mind that financial ratio analysis is only partial information. There are many other factors which will need to be borne in mind before a decision can be taken.

The calculations of the various ratios are given as an appendix.

Profitability

While the main interest to the board is what G plc could obtain in profitability from A Ltd and B Ltd, all I can comment on at present is the current profitability enjoyed by these two companies.

Here the most important ratio is that of ROCE (Return on Capital Employed). A's ROCE is 27.2% as compared with B's 15.6%.

The great difference in ROCE can be explained by reference to the secondary ratios of profit and asset utilisation. Both ratios are in A's favour. The profit ratios are A 34%: B 20%. The asset utilisation ratios are A 0.9%: B 0.6 showing that A is utilising its assets 50% better than B. It is the effect of these two ratios that give the ROCE for each company.

The very low working capital employed by A Ltd very much affects the asset utilisation ratio. How far such a low working capital is representative of that throughout the whole year is impossible to say.

Liquidity

It would not be sensible to draw final conclusion as to the liquidity positions of the two companies based on the balance sheet figures. As a balance sheet is based at one point in time it can sometimes be misleading, as a reading of figures over a period would be more appropriate.

A Ltd does appear to have a short-term liquidity problem, as the current assets only just cover current liabilities. The 'quick' or 'acid test ratio' on the face of it appears to be very inadequate at 0.6.

By contrast, B Ltd with a current ratio of 1.4 and a 'quick ratio' of 1.0 would appear to be reasonably liquid.

However, much more light is shed on the position of the companies when the debtor's collection period is examined. A collects its debts with a credit period of 9 weeks. In the case of B Ltd this rises to an astonishing 36.7 weeks. Why is this so? It could be due simply to very poor credit control by B Ltd. Such a long credit period casts considerable doubt on the real worth of the debtors. There is a high probability that many of them may prove difficult to collect. It might be that B Ltd, in order to maintain sales, has lowered its requirements as to the credit-worthiness of its customers. If the credit period were reduced to a normal one for the industry it might be found that many of the customers might go elsewhere.

The problem with debtors in the case of B Ltd is also carried on to stock. In the case of A Ltd the stock turnover is 4.3 falling to 2.8 in B Ltd. There could be a danger that B Ltd has stock increasing simply because it is finding it difficult to sell its products.

Capital gearing

A Ltd is far more highly geared than B Ltd. 93.6% as compared with 14.1%. A comparison with this particular industry by means of inter-firm comparison should be undertaken.

Limitations of ratio analysis

You should bear in mind the following limitations of the analysis undertaken:

(i) One year's accounts are insufficient for proper analysis to be undertaken. The analysis of trends, taken from say five years' accounts would give a better insight.

(ii) Differences in accounting policies between A Ltd and B Ltd will affect comparisons.

(iii) The use of historical costs brings about many distortions.

(iv) The use of industry inter-firm comparisons would make the ratios more capable of being interpreted.

(v) The plans of the companies for the future expressed in their budgets would be of more interest than past figures.

Conclusions

Depending on the price which would have to be paid for acquisition, I would suggest that A Ltd is the company most suitable for takeover.

AN Other
Accountant

Appendix

	A Ltd	B Ltd
(i) Return on capital employed		
$\dfrac{\text{Profits before interest and tax}}{\text{Capital employed}}$	$\dfrac{211}{775} = 27.2\%$	$\dfrac{88}{565} = 15.6\%$
(ii) Assets utilisation ratios		
Total assets turnover: $\dfrac{\text{Turnover}}{\text{Total assets}}$	$\dfrac{985}{1{,}140} = 0.9$	$\dfrac{560}{990} = 0.6$
Fixed assets turnover: $\dfrac{\text{Turnover}}{\text{Fixed assets}}$	$\dfrac{985}{765} = 1.3$	$\dfrac{560}{410} = 1.4$
Working capital turnover: $\dfrac{\text{Turnover}}{\text{Working capital}}$	$\dfrac{985}{10} = 98.5$	$\dfrac{560}{155} = 3.6$

(iii) Profitability ratios

Gross profit %	Gross profit / Turnover	$\dfrac{335}{985}$ = 34%	$\dfrac{163}{560}$ = 29%
Profit before taxation and interest as % turnover		$\dfrac{211}{985}$ = 21%	$\dfrac{88}{560}$ = 16%

(iv) Liquidity ratios

Current ratio:	Current assets / Current liabilities	$\dfrac{375}{365}$ = 1.0	$\dfrac{580}{425}$ = 1.4
Acid test or 'quick ratio'	Current assets – stock / Current liabilities	$\dfrac{220}{365}$ = 0.6	$\dfrac{440}{425}$ = 1.0
Debtor ratio:	Trade debtors × 52 / Credit sales	$\dfrac{170}{985}$ × 52 = 9.0 wks	$\dfrac{395}{560}$ × 52 = 36.7 wks

(v) Capital structure

Gearing ratio:	Long-term borrowing / Shareholders' funds	$\dfrac{220}{555}$ × 100 = 93.6%	$\dfrac{70}{495}$ × 100 = 14
Proprietary ratio:	Shareholders' funds / Tangible assets	$\dfrac{555}{1,140}$ = 0.5	$\dfrac{495}{990}$ = 0.5

46.1

R Stubbs

Trading Account for the year ended 31 December

Sales			60,000
Opening stock	(D)	9,872	
Purchases	(C)	50,748	
		60,620	
Closing stock		12,620	
Cost of goods sold	(B)	48,000	
Gross profit	(A)	12,000	

Missing figures found in following order (A) to (D).
(A) Mark-up is 25%. Therefore Margin is 20%. Sales are 60,000 so Margin is 20% × 60,000 = 12,000 Gross Profit.
+(A) = 60,000. Therefore (B) + 12,000 = 60,000 and accordingly is 48,000.
(B) – 12,620 = 48,000. Therefore (C) is 60,620
(C) + 9,872 = 60,620. Therefore (D) is 50,748

46.3

(a) We know that $\dfrac{\text{Cost of Goods Sold}}{\text{Average Stock}}$ = Rate of Turnover

substituting $\dfrac{x}{12,600}$ = 7

x = Cost of Goods Sold = 88,200.

(b) If margin is 33⅓% then mark-up will be 50%. Gross Profit is therefore 50% of 88,200 = 44,100.
(c) Turnover is (a) + (b) = 88,200 + 44,100 = 132,300.
(d) 66⅔% × 44,100 = 29,400.
(e) Gross Profit – Expenses = Net Profit = 14,700.

46.5

B Arkwright

Statement of Affairs as at 31 December

	£	£	£
Fixed assets			
Van at cost		2,800	
Less Depreciation		550	
			2,250
Current assets			
Stock	3,950		
Debtors	4,970		
Prepaid expenses	170		
Bank	2,564		
Cash	55		
		11,709	
Less Current liabilities			
Trade creditors	1,030		
Expenses owing	470		
		1,500	
Working capital			10,209
			12,459
Capital			10,000
Cash introduced	(C)		
Add Net profit	(B)		
Less Drawings	(A)		
			5,673

Missing figures (A) (B) and (C) deduced in that order. (A) to balance is £12,459, thus (B) has to be £18,132 and (C) becomes £8,132.

46.7

(a)

William Brook

Trading and Profit and Loss Account for the year ended 31st December, 1998

		£
Sales		161,000
Cost of Sales	W4	72,000
Gross Profit	W2	89,000
Less		
Administration Costs	45,000	
Selling Expenses	15,000	
Financial Expenses	8,000	68,000
Net Profit		21,000

(b)

William Brook

Balance Sheet as at 31st December, 1998

	£	£
Current Assets		
Stock	8,000	
Debtors	24,000	
Bank	21,000	53,000
Current Liabilities		
Trade Creditors	15,000	
		38,000
Financed By:		
Capital	W3	38,000

Workings

W1	Cash Received from Debtors	164,000
	Lodgements	27,000
	Capital Introduced	137,000

W2	Cost of Sales	
	Opening Stock	Nil
	Purchases	80,000
	– Closing Stock	–8,000
		72,000

W3 Capital

Capital			
Drawings	10,000	Bank	27,000
Balance c/d	38,000	Profit	21,000
	48,000		48,000

Debtors Control

	£		
Credit Sales (derived)	161,000	Bank (W1)	137,000
		Balance c/d	24,000
	161,000		161,000

Creditors Control

		Bank	65,000
Balance c/d	80,000	Credit Purchases (derived)	15,000
		Cash	80,000
	80,000		80,000

W4

W5

46.9

Workings:

Purchases	Bank	29,487	Sales	Lodged	37,936
	Cash	2,994		Cash	9,630
		32,481			47,566
– Creditors at 1 January		5,624	– Debtors at 1 January		9,031
		26,857			38,535
+ Creditors at 31 December		7,389	+ Debtors at 31 December		8,624
Purchases for the year		34,246	Sales for the year		47,159

Opening Capital:

	£	£
Bank	405	
Stock	13,862	
Debtors	9,031	
Rates prepaid	210	
Fixtures	2,500	26,008
Less Creditors	5,624	
Rent owing	150	5,774
		20,234

Kelly

Trading and Profit and Loss Account for the year ended 31 December

		£
Sales		47,159
Less Cost of goods sold:		
Opening stock	13,862	
Add Purchases	34,246	
	48,108	
Less Closing stock	15,144	32,964
Gross Profit		14,195
Less Expenses:		
Wages	5,472	
Rent (1,650 – 150)	1,500	
Rates (890 + 210 – 225)	875	
Sundry expenses	375	
Depreciation: Fixtures	250	8,472
Net Profit		5,723

W4 *Cost of Goods Destroyed*
Cost of Sales = Opening Stock + Purchases – Closing Stock.
Therefore, Closing Stock = Opening Stock + Profit – Cost of Sales.
= 46,000 + 254,500 – 256,000
= £44,500
but £3,500 stock was on hand on 14th July.
Therefore, Stock destroyed = £44,500 – £3,500 = £41,000

46.13

John McCarthy
Capital as at 31st December, 1997

(a)

Capital = Assets less Liabilities	£
Assets	
Premises	109,680
Van (£12,000 – £4,800)	7,200
Fittings	6,500
Stock	26,500
Debtors	8,000
Rates	120
Bank	5,300
	163,300
Liabilities	
Creditors	48,800
	114,500

(b)

John McCarthy
Profit and Loss Account for the year ended 31st December, 1998

		£
Sales		220,000
Cost of Sales		174,000
Gross Profit		46,000
Expenses		
Depreciation	W3	4,400
Rates	W4	600
Wages		10,900
Delivery expenses		3,200
Fuel, light and heat		1,200
Sundry expenses (£12,000 cash withdrawals – £7,300 for personal use)	W4	4,700
		25,000
Net Profit		21,000

Kelly
Balance Sheet as at 31st December

Fixed assets			
Fixtures at valuation		2,500	
Less Depreciation		250	2,250
Current Assets			
Stock		15,144	
Debtors		8,624	
Prepayments		225	
		23,993	
Less Current liabilities			
Trade creditors	7,389		
Bank overdraft	602		
Working capital		7,991	16,002
			18,252
Capital			
Balance at 1 January			20,234
Add Net profit			5,723
			25,957
Less Drawings (1,164 + 6,541)			7,705
			18,252

46.11
W1 *Sales*

Debtors Control

Balance b/d	55,000	Bank	225,000
Credit Sales	230,000	Balance c/d	60,000
	285,000		285,000

Credit Sales	230,000
Cash Sales	90,000
Total	£320,000

W2 *Purchases*

Creditors Control

Bank	263,500	Balance b/d	48,000
Balance c/d	39,000	Purchases	254,500
	302,500		302,500

W3 *Cost of Sales*

Sales (W1)	320,000
Gross Margin 20%	–64,000
Cost of Sales	256,000

John McCarthy
Balance Sheet as at 31st December, 1998

	£	£
Fixed Assets		
Premises		109,680
Van		9,600
Fittings [£6,500 – (10% of £8,000)]		5,700
		124,980
Current assets		
Bank – current account	5,440	
Bank – deposit account	10,000	
Stock	30,100	
Debtors	11,300	
Prepayments	180	57,020
Current liabilities		
Creditors	62,000	
Net current liabilities		4,980
Net assets		120,000
Represented by:		
Capital at start of year		114,500
Add Profit for the year		21,000
		135,500
Less Drawings W4		15,500
		120,000

Workings
W1 Sales

Debtors control

Balance b/d	8,000	Cash	41,700
Credit sales (derived)	45,000	Balance c/d	11,300
	53,000		53,000

Cash sales	175,000
Credit sales	45,000
	220,000

W2 Cost of Sales

Creditors Control

Bank	82,000	Balance b/d	48,800
Balance c/d	62,000	Credit purchase (derived)	95,200
	144,000		144,000

Cash purchase	90,000
Credit purchases	95,200
	185,200
Owner's drawings of stock	7,600
Net	177,600

Cost of sales	
Opening stock	26,500
Purchase	177,600
– Closing stock	30,100
	174,000

W3 Fixed assets

Fixed Assets (at Cost)

	Van	Fittings		Van	Fittings
Balance b/d	12,000	6,000			
Bank	6,000	–	Balance c/d	18,000	8,000
	18,000	8,000		18,000	8,000

Accumulated Depreciation

	Van	Fittings		Van	Fittings
			Balance b/d	4,800	1,600
Balance c/d	8,400	2,400	Profit and Loss*	3,600	800
	8,400	2,400		8,400	2,400

	Van	Fittings	Total
* Depreciation of Van = 20% (12,000 + £6,000) =	£3,600	£800	£4,400
* Depreciation of Fittings = 10% × £8,000 =			

	Van	Fittings	Total
Cost	18,000	8,000	
Accumulated depreciation	–8,400	–2,400	
Net Book Value at 31st December, 1998	9,600	5,600	10,700

Janet Lambert

(b) *Trading and Profit and Loss Account for the year ended 31 August 19X1*

	£	£
Sales (deduced – as margin is 25% = 4 × gross profit)		128,000
Opening stock	8,600	
Add Purchases	104,200	
	112,800	
Less Closing stock	16,800	
Cost of goods sold		96,000
Gross profit (33⅓% of Cost of Goods Sold)		32,000
Less Casual labour (1,200 + 6,620)	7,820	
Rent (5,040 + 300 – 420)	4,920	
Delivery costs	3,000	
Electricity (1,390 + 160 – 210)	1,340	
		17,080
Net profit		14,920

Janet Lambert

Balance Sheet as at 31 August 19X1

	£	£
Current assets		
Stock	16,800	
Debtors	4,300	
Prepayments	420	
Bank	1,650	
Cash	330	
		23,500
Less *Current liabilities*		
Creditors	8,900	
Expenses Owing	160	
		9,060
		14,440
Capital:		
Balance as at 1 September 19X0 (Working 1)		7,850
Add Net profit		14,920
		22,770
Less Drawings (Working 2)		8,330
		14,440

Workings:

(1) Capital as on 1.9.19X0. Stock 8,600 + Debtors 3,900 + Prepaid 300 + Bank 2,300 + Cash 360 = 15,460 – Creditors 7,400 – Accruals 210 = 7,850.

(2) Cash drawings. Step (A) find cash received from sales. Debtors b/f 3,900 + Sales 128,000 – Debtors c/f 4,300 = 127,600 cash received.
Step (B) find cash lodged. Balance b/f 2,300 + cash received? – payments 117,550 = balance c/d 1,650. Therefore cash lodged? = 116,900.
Now (C) draw up cash account:

W4 *Drawings*

	£
Stock	7,600
Cash Withdrawals	7,300
Personal element of Rates	200
Personal element of Fuel, Light and Heat	400
	15,500

W5 *Expenses*

Rates

Balance b/d	120	Drawings (25% × £800)	200
Bank	860	Profit and loss (75% × £800)	600
		Prepayments	180
	980		980

Wages

Bank	10,900	Profit and loss	10,900

Fuel, Light and Heat

Bank	1,600	Drawings (25% of 1,600)	400
		Profit and loss (75%)	1,200
	1,600		1,600

W6 *Closing Stock*

	£
Closing stock per question	30,100
Closing stock taken by owner	–7,600
	22,500

46.15

(a)

Creditors Control

			£
Bank	101,500	Balance b/d	7,400
Cash	1,800	Drawings: Goods	600
Balance c/d	8,900	Purchases (difference)	104,200
	112,200		112,200

Cash

Balance b/d	360	Labour		1,200
Sales receipts	127,600	Purchases		1,800
		Lodged		116,900
		Drawings (difference)		7,730
		Balance c/d		330
	127,960			127,960

(c)   Per text.

46.17   **David Denton**

Profit and Loss Account for the year ended 31 December 19X0

Work done: Credit accounts	29,863	
For cash	3,418	33,281
Less Expenses:		
Materials (9,600 − 580)	9,020	
Secretarial salary	3,000	
Rent	225	
Rates (180 − 45)	135	
Insurance (800 − 200)	600	
Electricity (1,222 + 374 estimated)	1,496	
Motor expenses	912	
General expenses (1,349 + 295)	1,644	
Loan interest (4,000 × 10% × 3⁄4)	300	
Provision for bad debts	425	
Accounting fee	250	
Amortisation of lease (650 × 3⁄4)	487	
Depreciation: Equipment	960	
Depreciation: Van	900	1,860
		20,354
Net profit		12,927

Balance Sheet as at 31 December 19X0

	Cost	Depreciation	Net
Fixed assets			
Lease	6,500	487	6,013
Equipment	4,800	960	3,840
Vehicle	3,600	900	2,700
	14,900	2,347	12,553
Current assets			
Stock		580	
Debtors	4,250		
Less Provision for bad debts	425	3,825	
Prepaid expenses (75 + 200)		275	
Bank (see workings)		6,084	
Cash		123	
		10,887	
Less Current liabilities			
Trade creditors	714		
Interest owing	300		
Accountancy fee owing	250		
Rates owing	135		
Electricity owing	374	1,773	
Working capital			9,114
			21,667
Financed by:			
Capital			
Introduced (6,500 + 3,600)			10,100
Add Net profit			12,927
			23,027
Less Drawings (4,680 + 280 + 400)			5,360
			17,667
Loan			4,000
			21,667

47.1 Uppertown Football Club
Income and Expenditure Account for the year ended 31 December 1998

		£
Income		
Collections at matches		1,650
Profit on refreshments		315
		1,965
Less Expenditure		
Rent for pitch (300 – 60)	240	
Printing and stationery (65 + 33)	98	
Secretary's expenses	144	
Repairs to equipment	46	
Groundsman's wages	520	
Miscellaneous expenses	66	
Depreciation of equipment	125	
		1,239
Surplus of income over expenditure		726

Uppertown Football Club
Balance Sheet as at 31 December 1998

Fixed assets		
Equipment	625	
Less Depreciation	125	
		500
Current Assets		
Prepayment	60	
Cash	879	
	939	
Less Current liabilities		
Expenses owing	33	
Working capital		906
		1,406
Financed by:		
Accumulated fund		
Balance at start of year (500 + 180)		680
Add Surplus of income over expenditure		726
		1,406

47.3 Barwell Bowling Club
Bar Trading Account for the year ended 31st December, 1998

		£
Sales		85,000
Cost of sales	W6	51,400
Gross profit		33,600
Bar expenses		16,600
Net profit		17,000

Barwell Bowling Club
Income and Expenditure Account for the year ended 31st December, 1998

		£	£
Income			
Subscriptions	W1		49,400
Profit on bar			17,000
Profit on competition	W2		1,500
Interest on deposit			300
			68,200
Expenditure			
Wages	W3	24,000	
Rates		1,500	
Interest on loan		3,200	
General expenses		25,500	
Depreciation	W4	2,500	
		56,700	
Surplus of Income over Expenditure			11,500

Barwell Bowling Club
Balance Sheet as at 31st December, 1998

	£	£	£
Fixed assets			
Land and Clubhouse			75,000
Equipment and Furniture	W8		14,000
			89,000
Current assets			
Bar stocks		5,600	
Subscriptions owing		2,500	
Interest receivable accrued		300	
Bank – current account		4,800	
Bank – deposit account (£3,000 opening + £2,000 transfer)		5,000	
		18,200	
Current Liabilities			
Bar Suppliers Owed	6,450		
Subscriptions	780		
Wages	1,750		
		8,980	
Net Current Assets			9,220
			98,220
Accumulated Fund			
Balance at start of year			66,720
Surplus of Income over Expenditure for year			11,500
			78,220
Long-term Loan	W5		20,000
			98,220

Workings

W1

Subscriptions			
Balance b/d (owing)	1,250	Balance b/d (prepaid)	400
Income and expenditure	49,400	Cash received	48,530
Balance c/d (prepaid)	780	Balance c/d (owing)	2,500
	51,430		51,430

W2 *Profit on competition*

	£
Competition Entries	6,700
Expenses	5,200
	1,500

W3

Wages			
Cash	23,400	Balance b/d	1,150
Balance c/d	1,750	Income and expenditure a/c (bal)	24,000
	25,150		25,150

W4 *Depreciation*

	£
Equipment and Furniture at start of year	20,000
Additions	5,000
	25,000
Depreciation @ 10%	2,500

W5 *Long-term loan*

	£
Loan balance at start of year	24,000
Repayment	4,000
Balance at end of year	20,000

W6 *Cost of sales*

	£
Opening Stock	4,600
+ Purchases W7	52,400
– Closing Stock	5,600
	51,400

W7 *Bar purchases*

Creditors Control			
Dec 31 Cash	50,150	Jan 1 Balance b/d (creditors)	4,200
Balance c/d	6,450	Bar purchases (derived)	52,400
	56,660		56,600

W8 *Equipment and furniture*

	£
NBV at start of year	11,500
Additions	5,000
	16,500
Depreciation for year (W4)	–2,500
	14,000

47.5
(a)

South Yard Football Club
Bar Trading and Profit and Loss Account
for the year ended 31st December, 1998

		£	£
Sales			56,000
Cost of Sales			
Opening stock		7,500	
Purchases	W1	39,900	
		47,400	
Closing stock		5,600	
			41,800
Gross profit			14,200
Expenses			
Bar wages		2,200	
Light and heat	W2	1,200	
Telephone	W2	325	
Insurance	W2	3,300	
Miscellaneous expenses	W2	2,700	
Depreciation	W2	425	
			10,150
Net profit			4,050

(b)

South Yard Football Club
Income and Expenditure Account for the year ended 31st December, 1998

		£	£
Income			
Members' Subscriptions	W4		7,300
Bar Profit			4,050
			11,350
Expenditure			
Light and Heat	W2	1,200	
Telephone	W2	325	
Insurances	W2	3,300	
Miscellaneous Expenses	W2	2,700	
Net Tour Cost	W5	2,000	
Depreciation	W2	425	
			9,950
Surplus of Income over Expenditure			1,400

South Yard Football Club
Balance Sheet as at 31st December, 1998

		£	£	£
Fixed Assets				
Buildings	W6			37,500
Furniture and equipment	W7			7,650
				45,150
Current assets				
Bar stock			5,600	
Insurances prepaid			1,200	
			6,800	
Current liabilities				
Bank		3,900		
Bar Supplies		2,900		
Subscriptions in advance		850		
		7,650		
Net current liabilities			850	
				44,300
Financed By:				
Accumulated Fund at start of year (W8)				42,900
Add Surplus of Income over Expenditure				1,400
Accumulated Fund at end of year				44,300

Workings
W1

Bar Purchases

		£			£
	Bank	40,100	1 Jan	Balance b/d	3,100
31 Dec	Balance	2,900		Trading account (derived)	39,900
		43,000			43,000

W2 Apportionment of expenses

	Total	Bar 50%	General 50%
	£	£	£
Light and heat	2,400	1,200	1,200
Telephone	650	325	325
Insurances (W3)	6,600	3,300	3,300
Miscellaneous expenses	5,400	2,700	2,700
Depreciation	850	425	425

W3

Insurance

		£			£
1 Jan	Balance b/d	1,400		P & L/I & E (derived)	6,600
	Bank	6,400	31 Dec	Balanced c/d	1,200
		7,800			7,800

W4

Members' Subscriptions

	£			£
Income and exp. (derived)	7,300	1 Jan	Balance b/d	750
31 Dec Balance c/d	850		Bank	7,400
	8,150			8,150

W5 Net tour cost

	£	£
Total cost		17,500
Members' contributions	7,100	
Fund raising	8,400	15,500
		2,000

W6 Buildings

	£
Book value at start of year	30,000
Additions	7,500
Book value at end of year	37,500

W7 Furniture and equipment

	£
Book value at start of year	8,500
Less depreciation	850
Book value at end of year	7,650

W8 Accumulated Fund at start of year

	£	£
Fixed Assets		
Premises		30,000
Furniture and Equipment		8,500
		38,500
Current Assets		
Bar Stock	7,500	
Insurances Prepaid	1,400	
	8,900	
Current Liabilities		
Bank	650	
Bar Suppliers	3,100	
Subscriptions in Advance	750	4,500
Net Current Assets		4,400
		42,900

47.6

The High Towers Rural Pursuits Society
Income and Expenditure Account for the year ended 31 March 19X1

Income:

Subscriptions: year to 31 March 19X0	252	
year to 31 March 19X1 (6,810 + 420)	7,230	7,482
Bank interest		82
Profit on sale of photographic equipment (*see* note 1)		3,746
		11,310

Less Expenditure:

Secretary's honorarium	300	
Stationery and postages	600	
Meeting room hire	340	
Printing Year Book	810	
Affiliation fee to National Society	180	
Advertising for new members	230	
Lecturer for rural hobbies course	460	
Depreciation – video equipment	250	
Loss on transit coach (*see* note 2)	1,040	4,210
Surplus of income over expenditure		7,100

Notes:

1 Sales 28,100 – Cost of sales (3,420 + 22,734 – 1,800) 24,354 = Profit 3,746.
2 Cost 18,000 – Depreciation 14,400 = 3,600 – Cash 2,560 = Loss 1,040.

Balance Sheet as at 31 March 19X1

Fixed assets

Land at cost		10,000
Video equipment at cost	1,200	
Less Depreciation	250	950
		10,950

Current assets

Stock of equipment	1,800	
Bank deposit	3,082	
Bank	745	
	5,627	
Less current liabilities		
Subscriptions received in advance	330	5,297
		16,247

Financed by:

Accumulated fund as at 1 April 19X0 (*see* note 3)	9,147
Add Surplus of income over expenditure	7,100
	16,247

Note 3: Coach 18,000 – Depreciation 14,400 = 3,600 + Equipment 1,200 +
Stocks 3,420 + Bank 1,347 – Subscriptions in advance 420 = 9,147.

47.8

(a)

Café operations:	£	£
Takings		4,660
Less Cost of supplies:		
Opening stock	800	
Add purchases (1,900 + 80)	1,980	
	2,780	
Less closing stock	850	1,930
		2,730
Wages		2,000
Profit		730

Sports equipment:		
Sales		900
Less cost of goods sold:		
Opening stock	1,000	
Add Purchases (1,000 × 50%)	500	
	1,500	
Less closing stock (see note)	900	600
Profit		300

Note: To find closing stock £900 is sales at 50% on cost profit so cost of sales is found to be £900. By arithmetical deduction closing stock is found to be £900.

(b)

Subscriptions

Balance b/d (owing)	60	Balance b/d (in advance)	120
		Cash: 19X9	40
Income and expenditure	1,280	19X0	1,100
		19X1	80
Balance c/d (in advance)	80	Balance c/d (owing)	80
	1,420		1,420

Life Subscriptions

Income and expenditure (11 × 20)	220	Balance b/d	1,400
		Cash	200
Balance c/d	1,380		
	1,600		1,600

Used Sports Equipment

Balance b/d (Stock)	700	Cash	14
Transferred from purchases	500	Income and expenditure	486
		Balance c/d (Stock)	700
	1,200		1,200

Notes:

1

2 B/d 1,000 + (1,000 × ½) 500 = 1,500 – sold 600 = 900

3 B/d 1,210 + receipts 6,994 – paid 7,450 = 754

(c)

Happy Tickers Sports & Social Club

Income and Expenditure Account for the year ended 31 December 19X0

Income:		
Subscriptions (1,280 + 220)	1,500	
Profit on café operations	730	
Profit on sports equipment	300	
		2,530
Less Expenditure		
Rent	1,200	
Insurance	600	
Repairs to roller (½ × 450)	225	
Sports equipment depreciation (see note 1)	486	
Depreciation of roller (½ × 200)	100	2,611
Excess of expenditure over income		81

Balance Sheet as at 31 December 19X0

Fixed assets		
Share in motor roller at cost	1,000	
Less depreciation to date	500	500
Used sports equipment at valuation		700
		1,200
Current assets		
Stock of new sports equipment (see note 2)	900	
Stock of café supplies	850	
Subscriptions owing	80	
Carefree Conveyancers: owing for expenses	225	
Prepaid expenses	350	
Cash and bank (note 3)	754	3,159
		4,359
Accumulated fund		
Balance at 1.1.19X0	2,900	
Less excess of expenditure	81	2,819
Life subscriptions		1,380
Current liabilities		
Café suppliers	80	
Subscriptions paid in advance	80	160
		4,359

(d) To most people probably the best description of the item would be as deferred income, i.e. income paid in advance for future benefits.

It could, however, be described as a liability of the club. The club in future will have to provide and finance amenities for life members, but they do not have to pay any more money for it. This is therefore the liability of the future to provide these services without further payment.

48.1

Loose Tools

1996				1996			
Jan 1	Balance b/d (value)	1,250		Dec 31	Manufacturing	994	
Dec 31	Bank	2,000		" 31	Balance c/d (value)	2,700	
" 31	Wages	275					
" 31	Materials	169					
		3,694				3,694	
1997				1997			
Jan 1	Balance b/d (value)	2,700		Dec 31	Manufacturing	1,695	
Dec 31	Bank	1,450		" 31	Balance c/d (value)	3,340	
" 31	Wages	495					
" 31	Materials	390					
		5,035				5,035	
1998				1998			
Jan 1	Balance b/d (value)	3,340		Dec 31	Bank: Refund	88	
Dec 31	Bank	1,890		" 31	Manufacturing	1,897	
" 31	Wages	145		" 31	Balance c/d (value)	3,680	
" 31	Materials	290					
		5,665				5,665	

48.2

(a) (i) Straight line

Cost £112,000 – trade in £12,000 = £100,000
Per month £100,000 ÷ 48 = 2,083.33

19X6	9 months	=	18,750
19X7	12 months	=	25,000
19X8	12 months	=	25,000
19X9	12 months	=	25,000
19X0	3 months	=	6,250
			100,000

(ii) Diminishing (Reducing) Balance:

Cost	112,000
Depreciation 19X6 (40%)	44,800
	67,200
Depreciation 19X7	26,880
	40,320
Depreciation 19X8	16,128
	24,192
Depreciation 19X9	9,677
	14,515
Depreciation 19X0	5,806
	8,709

(iii) Units of output (Total £100,000)

19X6	4,000/20,000	=	20,000
19X7	5,000/20,000	=	25,000
19X8	5,000/20,000	=	25,000
19X9	5,000/20,000	=	25,000
19X0	1,000/20,000	=	5,000

(b) (i)

Machine

Jan 1	Balance b/d	112,000	Dec 31	Assets disposal	112,000

(ii)

Provision for Depreciation

Dec 31	Assets disposal	31,250	Jan 1	Balance b/d	18,750
			Dec 31	Profit and loss	12,500
		31,250			31,250

(iii)

Assets Disposal

Dec 31	Machine	112,000	Jun 30	Bank	80,000
			Dec 31	Depreciation	31,250
			" 31	Profit and loss	750
		112,000			112,000

48.4

T Jackson
Manufacturing, Trading and Profit and Loss Accounts
for the year ended 31 December 1998

Opening stock of raw materials		18,450
Add Purchases		64,300
Add Carriage inwards		1,605
		84,355
Less Closing stock of raw materials		20,210
Cost of raw materials consumed		64,145
Direct labour		65,810
Prime cost		129,955
Factory overhead expenses		
Rent ⅔	1,800	
Fuel and power	5,920	
Depreciation: Factory machinery	8,300	16,020
		145,975
Add Opening work in progress		23,600
		169,575
Less Closing work in progress		17,390
Production cost goods completed		152,185
Sales		200,600
Less Cost of goods sold		
Opening stock of finished goods	17,470	
Add Production cost of goods completed	152,185	
	169,655	
Less Closing stock of finished goods	21,485	148,170
Gross profit		52,430
Less Expenses:		
Office salaries	16,920	
Rent ⅓	900	
Lighting and heating	5,760	
Depreciation: Office equipment	1,950	25,530
Net profit		26,900

48.5

Manufacturers Ltd
Manufacturing Account for the year ended 31st December, 1997

		£
Cost of raw materials consumed	W1	50,500
Direct labour	W2	29,000
Direct expenses	W3	8,000
Prime cost		87,500
Factory overheads	W4	45,250
Opening work in progress		6,000
Closing work in progress		−8,000
Production cost of goods completed		130,750

W1	Cost of raw materials consumed	£
	Opening stock of raw materials	8,000
	Purchases of raw materials during the year	45,000
	Carriage is charged on purchases of raw materials	2,000
	Import duty charged on purchases of raw materials	4,500
	Closing stock of raw materials	−9,000
		50,500
W2	Direct labour	
	Per question	26,000
	Accrual required for December (per note 2)	3,000
		29,000
W3	Direct expenses	
	Hire of special equipment to manufacture complex components (per question)	3,000
	Royalties on manufacturing processes (per question)	5,000
		8,000
W4	Factory overheads	
	Loose tools (£1,000 + £2,000 − £750)	2,250
	Variable overheads (per question)	11,000
	Fixed overheads (per question)	8,000
	Rent and rates [(£16,000 − £2,000 prepaid) * 50%]	7,000
	Light and heat (£4,000 * 50%)	2,000
	Depreciation of plant and machinery (per note 1 = 10% of £30,000)	3,000
	Quality control supervisor's wages (per question)	12,000
		45,250

48.6

(a)

Mr Murphy

Manufacturing Account for the year ended 31st December, 1997

	Working	£	£
Cost of raw materials consumed	1	59,000	
Direct labour		55,000	
Prime cost			114,000
Factory overhead expenses			
Manufacturing overheads		16,000	
Depreciation of machinery		10,000	
Rent [(£12,000 + £500 Accrual) @ 50%]		6,250	32,250
			146,250
Opening work in progress			7,000
Closing work in progress			−5,000
Production cost of goods completed			148,250

Mr Murphy

Profit and Loss Account for the year ended 31 December, 1997

	Working	£	£
Sales			150,000
Cost of sales	2		−147,150
Gross profit			2,850
Expenses			
Selling and distribution overheads		11,000	
Rent [(£12,000 + £500 Accrual) @ 50%]		6,250	
Increase in bad debt provision	3	1,600	
Bad debts		400	
Administration overheads		10,000	−29,250
Net loss			−26,400

(b)

Mr Murphy

Balance Sheet as at 31st December, 1997

		£ Cost	£ Deprec	£ Net
Fixed asset				
Machinery		40,000	20,000	20,000
Current assets				
Stocks	W4		17,400	
Debtors	W5		19,800	
			37,200	
Current liabilities				
Bank overdraft		39,600		
Rent accrued		500		
Creditors		17,000	−57,100	
Net current liabilities				−19,900
Net assets				100
Financed by:				
Capital				28,000
Net loss				−26,400
Drawings				−1,500
				100

Workings

W1 *Cost of raw materials consumed*

	£
Opening stock of raw materials	6,000
Purchases of raw materials	60,000
Closing stock of raw materials	−8,000
Carriage inwards	1,000
	59,000

W2 *Cost of sales*

	£
Opening stock of finished goods	3,300
Production cost of goods completed (per Mfg. A/c)	148,250
Closing stock of finished goods	−4,400
	147,150

W3 *Provision for doubtful debts*

	£
Existing provision	600
Provision adjusted to 10% of debtors i.e. 10% of £22,000	2,200
Increase	1,600

W4 *Stock*

	£
Raw materials	8,000
Work-in-progress	5,000
Finished goods	4,400
	17,400

W5 *Debtors*

	£
As per trial balance	22,000
Less provision (W3)	−2,200
	19,800

48.9
(a)

B Sharpe

Trading and Profit and Loss Account for the year ended 31st July, 1998

		£	£
Sales			971,000
Cost of Sales			
Opening stock of finished goods		125,000	
Purchases of finished goods		59,800	
Production cost of goods completed	W1	782,200	
		967,000	
Closing stock of finished goods		137,000	
			830,000
Gross profit before discount received			141,000
Discount received			4,500
Gross profit			145,500
General Overhead Expenses	W3		121,180
Net profit			24,320

(b)

B Sharpe

Balance Sheet as at 31 July, 1998

		Cost £	Depreciation £	Net £
Fixed assets				
Vehicles		48,000	*28,800	19,200
Factory machinery		80,000	*32,000	48,000
Office equipment		7,800	*2,340	5,460
		135,800	63,140	72,660
Current assets				
Stocks	W4		202,100	
Trade debtors	W5		105,300	
			307,400	
Current liabilities				
Trade creditors	W7	63,500		
Accrued expenses		6,900		
Bank		13,140		
			83,540	
Net current assets				223,860
Net assets				296,520
Capital				
Balance at start of year				298,300
Add Net Profit				24,320
				322,620
Less Drawings				26,100
				296,520

* see W8

Workings

W1 *Production cost of goods completed*

		£
Opening stock of raw materials		64,000
Purchases of raw materials		546,000
Carriage on raw materials		18,600
		628,600
Closing stock of raw materials		−56,000
Cost of raw materials consumed		572,600
Factory wages		121,000
Prime cost		693,600
Factory overhead expenses	W2	84,500
		778,100
Add opening work in progress		13,200
		791,300
Less closing work in progress		−9,100
Production cost of goods completed		782,200

W2 Factory overhead expenses

		£
Machine maintenance and repairs		21,500
Rent and rates	W6	10,500
Insurances	W6	15,500
Light heat and power	W6	21,000
Depreciation of factory machinery (£80,000 × 20%)		16,000
		84,500

W3 General overhead expenses

		£
Rent and rates	W6	2,100
Insurances	W6	3,100
Light, heat and power	W6	4,200
Motor and travelling expenses		36,000
Telephone and postage		8,900
General office expenses (£14,600 per trial balance + £3,200 accrual)		17,800
Office wages		16,400
Bank interest and charges		9,100
Accountancy charges (nil per trial balance + accrual of £2,500)		2,500
Depreciation of vehicles (£48,000 × 20%)		9,600
Depreciation of office equipment (£7,800 × 10%)		780
Bad debts written off		8,000
Provision for doubtful debts (see W5)		2,700
		121,180

W4 Stocks

	£
Raw materials	56,000
Work in progress	9,100
Finished goods	137,000
	202,100

W5 Trade debtors

	£
Per trial balance	116,000
Less bad debts written off (note 5)	8,000
	108,000
Less provision for doubtful debts @ 2.5%	2,700
	105,300

W6 Apportionment of Expenses

	£ Total	Factory 5/6	Office 1/6
Rent and Rates	12,600	10,500	2,100
Insurances (£17,400 + £1,200 Accrual)	18,600	15,500	3,100
Light, Heat and Power	25,200	21,000	4,200

W7 Trade creditors

	£
Per Trial Balance	68,000
Less Discounts Received	4,500
	63,500

W8 Accumulated Depreciation

	Cost	NBV per Trial Balance	1997/98 Charge	Cumulative Depreciation
Vehicles	48,000	28,800	*9,600	28,800
Factory machinery	80,000	64,000	**16,000	32,000
Office equipment	7,800	6,240	*780	2,340

* per W3 **per W2

48.10

(a)

Jane Seymour
Manufacturing, Trading and Profit and Loss Account for the year ended 31 July 19X6

Direct materials purchased	43,000	
Less Stock 31 July 19X6	7,000	36,000
Direct factory wages		39,000
Prime cost		75,000
Factory overhead expenses:		
Indirect factory wages	8,000	
Machinery repairs	1,600	
Rent and insurance (11,600 – 800) × 2/3	7,200	
Light and power (5,000 + 1,000) × 2/3	4,000	
Loose tools (9,000 – 5,000)	4,000	
Motor vehicle running expenses (12,000 × 1/2)	6,000	
Depreciation: Plant and machinery	6,000	
Motor vehicles (7,500 × 1/2)	3,750	40,550
		115,550
Less Work in progress 31 July 19X6		12,300
		103,250
Transfer of goods manufactured to trading account		95,000
Loss on manufacturing		8,250
Sales		170,000
Less Goods manufactured transferred	95,000	
Stock at 31 July 19X6	10,000	85,000
		85,000
Gross profit		
Less Administrative staff salaries	31,000	
Sales and distribution staff salaries	9,000	
Administrative expenses	13,000	
Rent and insurance (11,600 – 800) × 1/3	3,600	
Motor vehicle running expenses (12,000 × 1/2)	6,000	
Light and power (5,000 + 1,000) × 1/3	2,000	
Depreciation: Motors (7,500 × 1/2)	3,750	68,350
Net profit in trading		16,650
Loss on manufacturing		8,250
Overall net profit		8,400

49.1

Charnley's Department Store
Trading Account for the year ended 31 December 1998

	Electrical	Furniture	Leisure Goods
Sales	29,840	73,060	39,581
Less Cost of goods sold:			
Opening stock	6,080	17,298	14,370
Add Purchases	18,195	54,632	27,388
	24,275	71,930	41,758
Less Closing stock	7,920	16,150	22,395
	16,355	55,780	19,363
Gross profit	13,485	17,280	20,218

49.2

J Spratt
Trading and Profit and Loss Account for the year ended 31 March 1999

	A		B	
Sales		15,000		10,000
Less Cost of goods sold:				
Opening stock	250		200	
Add Purchases	11,800		8,200	
	12,050		8,400	
Less Closing stock	300	11,750	150	8,250
Gross profit		3,250		1,750
Less Expenses:				
Wages	1,000		750	
Newspapers: Delivery	150			
General office salaries	450		300	
Rates	26		104	
Fire insurance	10		40	
Lighting and air conditioning	24		96	
Repairs to premises	5		20	
Internal telephone	5		20	
Cleaning	6		24	
Accounting and audit expenses	72		48	
General office expenses	36	1,784	24	1,426
Net profit		1,466		324

(b) *Conservatism*. The valuation of stock or work in progress does not include any element of expected future profit.

Matching. All of the prepayments and accruals adjusted for are examples of matching expenses against the time period, as also are the depreciation provisions.

Going Concern. When valuing stocks and work in progress, it has been assumed that the business is going to carry on indefinitely, and that they will be sold in the normal course of business rather than being sold because of cessation of activities.

Appendix II

Suggested solutions to selected revision questions

R4.1

(a)

J Charleton
Trading and Profit and Loss Account for the year ended 31st March, 1998

	£	£	£
Sales			750,000
Cost of Sales			
Opening stock		74,000	
Purchases		465,000	
		539,000	
Closing stock		68,000	471,000
Gross profit			279,000
Add rent receivable (£12,000 – £9,000 prepayment)			3,000
			282,000
Expenses			
Wages and salaries	87,000		
Motor expenses	26,500		
Telephone and postage	8,600		
Light and heat	17,410		
Rates	6,900		
Insurances (£13,400 – £2,200 prepayment)	11,200		
Bank interest and charges (£18,950 + £5,600 accrual)	24,550		
Legal fees (W1)	2,500		
Accountancy charges	3,200		
Bad debts	5,500		
Provision for doubtful debts (W2)	1,590		
Miscellaneous expenses	12,670		
Depreciation (£8,470 + £4,200 accrual)	13,600	221,220	
Net profit		60,780	

(b)

J Charleton
Balance Sheet as at 31st March, 1998

	Cost £	Depreciation £	NBV £
Fixed assets			
Premises (W3)	237,500	Nil	237,500
Vehicles	56,000	22,400	33,600
Equipment	24,000	9,600	14,400
	317,500	32,000	285,500
Current Assets			
Stocks		68,000	
Debtors (W2)	79,500		
Provision for doubtful debts (W2)	1,590	77,910	
Sundry debtors and prepayments (W4)		4,400	
		150,310	
Current liabilities			
Bank	16,250		
Creditors	43,500		
Accrued expenses (W5)	23,800	83,550	
Net current assets			66,760
			352,260
Non-current liabilities			
Bank loan			150,000
			202,260
Capital			
Balance at start of year			162,080
Add net profit			60,780
			222,860
Deduct drawings			20,600
Balance at end of year			202,260

(b)

B Harton

Balance Sheet as at 31st December, 1998

		Cost £	Depreciation £	NBV £
Fixed assets				
Plant and equipment		40,000	*8,000	32,000
Vehicles		60,000	*24,000	36,000
Office equipment		8,000	*1,600	6,400
		108,000	33,600	74,400
Current assets				
Stocks				160,000
Debtors	W1	108,000		
Provision for doubtful debts	W1	2,700		
			105,300	
Sundry debtors and prepayments	W3		10,800	
			276,100	
Current liabilities				
Bank		34,500		
Creditors		76,000		
Accrued expenses	W4	11,300		
		121,800		
Net current assets				154,300
				228,700
Long-term liability				
Bank loan				100,000
Net assets				128,700
Capital				
Balance at start of year				165,000
Deduct: Drawings			21,800	
Personal income tax			10,000	
Net Loss			4,500	
			36,300	
Balance at end of year				128,700
* see Working 5				

Workings

W1 Debtors/provision for doubtful debts

	£
Debtors per trial balance	114,000
Deduct bad debts	6,000
Amended debtors	108,000
Provision 2.5%	2,700
Previous provision	1,500
Increase in provision	1,200

Workings

W2 Debtors/provision for doubtful debts

	£
Debtors per trial balance	85,000
Deduct bad debts	5,500
Net debtors	79,500
2% Provision	1,590

W4 Sundry debtors and prepayments

	£
Value Added Tax	2,200
Insurances	2,200
	4,400

W1 Legal fees

	£
Per trial balance	15,000
Deduct capital expenditure	12,500
	2,500

W3 Premises

	£
Per trial balance	220,000
Add legal fees – paid	12,500
– accrued	5,000
	237,500

W5 Accrued expenses

	£
Legal Fees	5,000
Rent Prepaid	9,000
Bank Interest	5,600
Miscellaneous expenses	4,200
	23,800

R4.3

(a)

B Harton

Trading and Profit and Loss Account for the year ended 31st December, 1998

	£	£
Sales		746,000
Cost of sales		
Opening stock	180,000	
Purchases	556,000	
	736,000	
Closing stock	160,000	
		576,000
Gross Profit		170,000
Add Rent receivable (£7,400 – £1,200 prepayment)		6,200
		176,200
Expenses		
Wages	68,000	
Rent and Rates (£24,000 – £6,000 Prepayment)	18,000	
Motor Expenses	16,000	
Insurances	7,600	
Telephone and postage	8,400	
Light and heat	6,200	
Bank interest and charges	12,600	
Accountancy charges (£3,500 + £1,500 accrual)	5,000	
Bad debts	6,000	
Increase in provision for doubtful debts (W1)	1,200	
Miscellaneous expenses (£12,400 + £2,300 accrual)	14,700	
Depreciation (W2)	16,800	180,700
Net loss		4,500

W2

Depreciation	£ Cost	Rate	£ Charge	NBV per TB 31.12.97	Aggregate Depreciation to 31.12.97	to 31.12.98
Plant and equipment	40,000	10%	4,000	36,000	4,000	8,000
Vehicles	60,000	20%	12,000	48,000	12,000	24,000
Office equipment	8,000	10%	800	7,200	800	1,600
			16,800			

W3 *Sundry debtors and prepayments*

	£
Value added tax receivable	4,800
Rent payable prepaid	6,000
	10,800

W4 *Accrued Expenses*

	£
PAYE/PRSI	6,300
Rent receivable prepaid	1,200
Accountancy charges	1,500
Miscellaneous expenses	2,300
	11,300

R4.5

(a)

T Hardy

Trading and Profit and Loss Account for the year ended 31st December, 1998

	£	£
Sales		610,000
Cost of sales		
Opening stock	37,200	
Purchases	385,000	
	422,200	
Closing stock	28,500	
		393,700
Gross Profit		216,300
Expenses		
Wages and salaries (W1)	77,200	
Telephone and postage (£10,700 + £1,500 accrual)	12,200	
Motor expenses (W2)	19,600	
Rent and rates (£13,240 − £2,400 prepayment)	10,840	
Light and heat	11,470	
Insurances	14,150	
Bank interest and charges (£9,100 + £800 accrual)	9,900	
Accountancy fees	2,460	
General expenses	8,190	
Bad debts	2,400	
Provision for doubtful debts (W3)	1,250	
Depreciation	11,200	
		180,860
Net profit		35,440

(b)

T Hardy

Balance Sheet as at 31st December, 1998

	£ Cost	£ Depreciation	£ NBV
Fixed assets			
Vehicles	48,000	19,200	28,800
Equipment	16,000	6,400	9,600
	64,000	25,600	38,400
Current Assets			
Stocks		28,500	
Debtors (W3)	25,000		
Provision for doubtful debts (W3)	1,250	23,750	
Sundry debtors and prepayments (W4)		4,440	
		56,690	
Current Liabilities			
Bank Overdraft	13,740		
Creditors	49,280		
Accrued expenses (W5)	4,800		
		67,820	
Net current liabilities			11,130
			27,270
Capital			
Balance at start of year			18,580
Add net profit			35,440
			54,020
Deduct drawings (W6)			26,750
Balance at end of year			27,270

Workings

W1 *Wages and salaries*

	£
Per trial balance	48,000
PAYE/PRSI paid (excluding personal income tax)	26,700
Balance PAYE/PRSI at end of year	2,500
	77,200

W2 *Motor expenses*

	£
Per trial balance	18,400
VAT credit disallowed	1,200
	19,600

R4.6

Tony Coakley

(a) *Trading and Profit and Loss Account for the year ended 31st March, 1998*

	£	£
Sales (W1)		433,700
Cost of Sales		
Stock at start of year	27,200	
Purchases (W2)	257,600	
	284,800	
Stock at end of year	29,500	
		255,300
Gross Profit		178,400
Expenses		
Wages and Salaries (W3)	55,670	
Motor Expenses	15,470	
Rent and Rates	5,950	
Telephone and Postage	2,190	
Light and Heat	4,010	
Repairs and Renewals	1,750	
Insurances (£2,460 – £660 Prepaid)	1,800	
Bank Interest and Charges (£2,140 + £660 Accrued)	2,800	
Stationery and Advertising (W4)	2,980	
Accountancy Charges (£1,570 + £550 Accrued)	2,120	
Bad Debts	4,400	
Provision for Doubtful Debts (W6)	1,175	
Depreciation	15,430	
		115,745
Net Profit		62,655

W3 *Debtors/provision for doubtful debts*

	£
Per trial balance	27,400
Deduct bad debts written off	2,400
	25,000
Provision for doubtful debts = 5% of £25,000	£1,250

W4 *Sundry debtors and prepayments*

	£
Rent and rates	2,400
VAT receivable (£3,240 per trial balance – £1,200 per note 7)	2,040
	4,440

W5 *Accrued expenses*

	£
Telephone and postage	1,500
Bank interest and charges	800
PAYE/PRSI	2,500
	4,800

W6 *Drawings*

	£
Per trial balance	18,750
Personal income tax	8,000
	26,750

(b)

Tony Coakley
Balance Sheet as at 31st March, 1998

	Cost	Depreciation	Net
	£	£	£
Fixed assets			
Vehicles	66,000	26,400	39,600
Fixtures and fittings	15,600	3,120	12,480
Office equipment	6,700	1,340	5,360
	88,300	30,860	57,440
Current assets			
Stock			29,500
Trade debtors (W5)		47,000	
Less provision for doubtful debts (W6)		1,175	45,825
Prepayments			660
			75,985
Current liabilities			
Trade creditors		43,200	
Accrued expenses (W7)		2,710	
Bank		9,410	55,320
Net current assets			20,665
Net assets			78,105
Capital			
Balance at start of year			43,450
Add net profit			62,655
			106,105
Less drawings (W8)			28,000
Balance at end of year			78,105

Workings

W1 *Sales* £
Per trial balance 510,000
Less Value Added Tax 76,300
433,700

W2 *Purchases* £
Per trial balance 310,800
Less Value Added Tax 53,200
257,600

W3 *Wages and salaries* £
Per trial balance 37,470
PAYE/PRSI paid 16,700
PAYE/PRSI due 1,500
55,670

W4 *Stationery and advertising* £
Per trial balance 3,430
Less Value Added Tax 450
2,980

W5 *Trade debtors* £
Per trial balance 51,400
Less Bad debts 4,400
47,000

W6 *Provision for doubtful debts* £
Trade debtors (W5) 47,000
Provision @ 2.5% 1,175

W7 *Accrued expenses*

	£
PAYE/PRSI	1,500
Bank interest and charges	660
Accountancy charges	550
	2,710

W8 *Drawings*

	£
Per trial balance	18,400
Add income tax paid	9,600
	28,000

Robin Limited
Statement of Revised Profit for the year ended 31st December, 1998

R6.1

(a)

	£	£
Profit per trial balance		79,000
Less: Reduction in value of stock (£25,000 – £18,000)	7,000	
Depreciation on new vehicle (£5,000 × 20%)	1,000	
Additional PAYE provision	6,000	
Debenture interest (£30,000 × 20%)	6,000	20,000
		59,000
Add: Transfer of cost of new vehicle from repairs and renewals to fixed assets		5,000
		64,000

Robin Limited
Profit and Loss Appropriation Account for the year ended 31st December, 1998

(b)

	£	£
Adjusted net profit (as per (a) above)		64,000
Less: Proposed dividends on:		
Ordinary Shares (62,500 × 5p)	3,125	
Preference Shares (£50,000 × 10%)	5,000	8,125
		55,875
Transfer to general reserve		15,000
		40,875
Retained profit at start of year		87,000
Retained profit at end of year		127,875

(c)

Robin Limited
Balance Sheet as at 31st December, 1998

	Cost	Accumulated Depreciation	Net Book Value
	£	£	£
Fixed assets			
Premises	200,000	40,000	160,000
Vehicles W1	40,000	8,000	32,000
	240,000	48,000	192,000
Current assets			
Stocks (£90,000 – £7,000)		83,000	
Debtors and prepayments		130,000	
		213,000	
Current liabilities			
Creditors and accruals W2	100,125		
Bank overdraft	33,000		
		133,125	
Net current assets			79,875
Net assets			271,875

Represented by:

Share capital		
Ordinary shares of 40p each		25,000
Preference shares of 50p each		50,000
		75,000
General reserve		39,000
Profit and loss account		127,875
		241,875
Debentures		30,000
		271,875

Workings

W1 Vehicles

	Cost	Accumulated Depreciation	Net Book Value
Per trial balance	35,000	7,000	28,000
New vehicles	5,000	1,000	4,000
	40,000	8,000	32,000

W2 Creditors and accruals

	£
Per trial balance	80,000
Additional PAYE provision	6,000
Proposed Dividends	8,125
Debenture Interest	6,000
	100,125

R6.6

Bank

Apr 1	Balance b/d	25,000	May 1 Application and allotment (W2)	6,000
May 1	Application and allotment	66,000		
Jun 1	Application and allotment	5,000		
Jul 1	First and final call	49,500	Jul 15 Balance c/d	139,500
		145,500		145,500

Application and Allotment

May 1	Bank – refund	6,000	May 1 Bank	66,000
Jun 1	Issued share capital	25,000	Jun 1 Bank	5,000
Jun 1	Issued share capital	25,000		
Jun 1	Share premium	15,000		
		71,000		71,000

First and Final Call

Jul 15	Issued share capital	50,000	Jul 1 Bank (W4)	49,500
			Jul 15 Forfeited shares	500
		50,000		50,000

Forfeited Shares

Jul 15	First and final call	500	Jul 15 Issued share capital	1,000
Jul 15	Share premium	500		
		1,000		1,000

Issued Share Capital

Jul 15	Forfeited shares (W3)	1,000	Apr 1 Balance b/d	150,000
			May 1 Application and allotment (W2)	25,000
			Jun 1 Application and allotment (W2)	25,000
Jul 15	Balance c/d	249,000	Jul 1 First and final call	50,000
		250,000		250,000

Share Premium

			Jun 1 Application and allotment (W2)	15,000
Jul 15	Balance c/d	15,500	Jul 15 Forfeited shares	500
		15,500		15,500

Workings

W1 *Premium on each share*

Amount to be called up per share = 40p + 25p + 50p	115p
Nominal Value of each share	100p
Premium per share (payable on application)	15p

W2 *Amounts payable on application and allotment*

		£	£
Application: 100,000 shares @ 40p (including 15p premium)			
Issued share capital	100,000 @ 25p	25,000	
Share premium	100,000 @ 15p	15,000	40,000
Allotment: 100,000 shares @ 25p			
Issued Share Capital	100,000 @ 25p		25,000
Total payable on application and allotment			65,000
Money received on application:			
165,000 @ 40p		66,000	
Refunded 15,000 @ 40p		6,000	60,000
Balance of allotment money due and paid June 1st			5,000

W3 *Forfeited shares*

	Number
Shares allotted in total	100,000
Net applications accepted (165,000 – 15,000)	150,000
Therefore 2 shares allotted for every 3 applied for	
Shares originally applied for by person whose shares were forfeited	1,500
Therefore shares allotted (2 for 3 basis)	1,000
Nominal value of forfeited shares (1,000 @ £1)	£1,000
Amount due for forfeited shares (1,000 @ £1.15)	£1,150
Amount received for forfeited shares (1,000 @ 65p)	£650
First and final call money not paid	£500

W4 *Amount received on first and final call*

	£
Total due: 100,000 shares @ 50p	50,000
First and final call not paid (W3)	500
	49,500

W5 *Reconciliation*

	£	£
Closing bank balance		139,500
Opening bank balance		25,000
Money received for new share issue		114,500
Closing balance on ordinary share capital account	249,000	
Opening balance on ordinary share capital account	150,000	99,000
Closing balance on Share Premium account (no opening balance)		15,500
		114,500

R7.3

(*a*) *Gross Profit Ratio*

= (Gross Profit * 100)/Sales

Year 1 = (£122,500 × 100)/£350,000 = 35%
Year 2 = (£92,000 × 100)/£460,000 = 20%

The rate of gross profit achieved in the second year shows a substantial deterioration compared to that achieved in the first year. Possible explanations would include:

(i) Price cutting to boost or maintain sales levels.
(ii) Changes in the type of goods sold where some lines earn different rates of gross profit than others.
(iii) Theft.
(iv) Increase in the cost of sales without a proportionate increase in the selling price.

The deterioration is very substantial and unless it was brought about by a deliberate policy of management, for example, drastically reducing sales price in the short term in order to compete with a rival firm, it would warrant detailed examination.

(*b*) *Stock turnover*

= Cost of sales/average stock

Cost of sales = sales – gross profit
Year 1 = £350,000 – £122,500 = £227,500
Year 2 = £460,000 – £92,000 = £368,000

Average stock = (opening stock + closing stock)/2
Year 1 = (£52,500 + £54,500)/2 = £53,500
Year 2 = (£54,500 + £80,700)/2 = £67,600

Stock turnover
Year 1 = £227,500/£53,500 = 4.25 times
Year 2 = £368,000/£67,600 = 5.44 times

In the first year the average stock was turned over 4.25 times. In the second year this improved to 5.44 times. A possible cause for the improvement is an increase in sales activity, perhaps due to the lowering of the gross profit margin seen in part (*a*).

(c) *Working capital ratio*
= Current assets : current liabilities

Year 1 = £109,700 : £55,000 = 2 : 1 (approx.)
Year 2 = £160,200 : £160,000 = 1 : 1 (approx.)

Mr Parker's current assets were approximately equal to his current liabilities at the end of year 2. However, he might have difficulty paying his liabilities on time, depending on how quickly his current assets could be converted into cash. The position at the end of year 1 with current assets equal to twice current liabilities appeared adequate.

(d) *Acid test ratio*
= Current assets excluding stock : current liabilities

Year 1 = £55,200 : £55,000 = 1 : 1 (approx.)
Year 2 = £80,700 : £160,000 = 0.5 : 1 (approx.)

The position at the end of year 2 shows that quick assets (those readily convertible into cash) amount to only half of the current liabilities. If the current liabilities are required to be paid promptly Mr Parker would not be able to meet these in full. At the end of year 1 the quick assets approximately equalled current liabilities and he should then have been in a position to meet the total liabilities.

(e) *Period of credit given*
= Debtors × 365/sales

Year 1 = (£55,200 × 365)/£350,000 = 58 days
Year 2 = (£80,700 × 365)/£460,000 = 64 days

The Period of Credit Given to debtors has increased from 58 days to 64 days.

This ratio reflects the time taken by debtors to pay and should approximate to the credit terms allowed by the business. Better terms may have been given to customers in order to boost sales. However, if the increase has not been dictated by management, steps should be taken to restore the sanctioned credit period.

R7.4

To determine the Gross Profit Rate achieved in 1999 that is comparable with that for 1998 it is necessary to make adjustments for the various factors referred to in the question.

	Sales £	*Cost of Sales* £	*Gross Profit* £
'Unadjusted' Figures	960,000	576,000	384,000
'Adjustments'			
(1) New Line	–100,000	–65,000	–35,000
(2) Obsolete Stock	–5,000	–20,000	15,000
(3) Half Price Purchases	–80,000	–20,000	–60,000
(4) Seasonal Sales	–60,000	–40,000	–20,000
(5) Damp Goods Destroyed	–	–30,000	30,000
(6) Stock from New Supplier	–50,000	–30,000	–20,000
'Adjusted' Figures	665,000	371,000	294,000

Gross Profit Rate = Gross Profit × 100/Sales
= £294,000 × 100/£665,000
= 44.2%

The 1998 Gross Profit Rate was £360,000 × 100/£720,000 = 50%

Conclusion
The factors outlined do not account for the fall in the Gross Profit Rate and further investigations are necessary.

R7.5

Puzzles Ltd
Trading and Profit and Loss Account for the year ended 31st March, 1998

Sales			1,200,000
Cost of sales			
Opening stock	W1	300,000	
+ Purchases		900,000	
		1,200,000	
– Closing stock		300,000	
			900,000
Gross profit			300,000
Expenses			
Depreciation (£600,000 × 10%)	W2	60,000	
Business expenses	W2	120,000	
			180,000
Net profit (10% of sales)			120,000

Puzzles Ltd
Balance Sheet as at 31st March 1998

		Cost	Acc. Dep.	NBV
Fixed assets (accumulated depreciation = 40% of cost)		600,000	240,000	360,000
Current Assets				
Stock	W4		300,000	
Debtors	W5		100,000	
Cash [£480,000 – (£300,000 + £100,000)]	W3		80,000	
			480,000	
Current Liabilities				
Creditors: amounts falling due within one year (CA : CL = 2 : 1)	W3		240,000	
Net current assets (fixed assets at NBV : net current assets = 1.5 : 1)				240,000
				600,000

	Authorised	Issued
Financed by:		
Ordinary share capital	400,000	280,000
Retained profit for the year		120,000
Retained profit brought forward		200,000
		320,000
		600,000

Workings

W1 Sales
Ratio of annual sales to year-end capital employed was 2 : 1

Capital employed per balance sheet = £600,000
Therefore, annual sales = £600,000 × 2 = £1,200,000

W2 Gross profit and cost of sales
Mark-up on cost = 33 1/3% or 1/3

Therefore, margin = 1/4

Margin = gross profit/sales

1/4 (sales) = gross profit
1/4 (1,200,000) = gross profit = £300,000

Cost of sales = (sales – gross profit) = £1,200,000 – £300,000 = £900,000

W3 Current assets
Net current assets = £240,000
Current ratio = 2 : 1
Therefore, current liabilities = £240,000 and current assets = £480,000

W4 Opening stock and closing stock
Stock turnover = cost of sales/average stock = 3

Cost of sales = £900,000 = 3 × average stock

Therefore, Average Stock = [(Opening Stock + Closing Stock)/2] = £300,000
£600,000 = Opening Stock + Closing Stock

But value of stock at the beginning and end of the year was the same.

Therefore, both Closing Stock and Opening Stock = £300,000

W5 Debtors
Debtors Days Outstanding at 31st March, 1990 = 30

Debtors × 360/Sales = 30

Debtors × 360/1,200,000 = 30

360 × Debtors = 36,000,000

Debtors = £100,000

R8.1
(a)
William Greene
Trading and Profit and Loss Account for the year ended 31st December, 1997

		£	£	£
Sales	W1			254,000
Cost of sales	W2			128,200
Gross profit				125,800
Expenses				
Light and heat	W3		6,450	
Motor expenses	W3		17,072	
Bank charges			2,800	
Wages	W3		50,400	
Rent	W3		12,000	
Insurance	W3		12,000	
Stationery	W5		15,940	116,662
Net profit				9,138

(b)

William Greene
Balance Sheet as at 31st December, 1997

		£	£
Current Assets			
Bank	W4	15,050	
Stock		12,000	
Stationery stock	W5	1,920	
Sundry debtors and prepayments	W6	5,500	34,470
Current Liabilities			
Accruals	W7		4,400
			30,070
			30,070
Capital	W8		30,070

Workings

W1 Sales

	£
Sales (net of cash withdrawn)	200,000
Cash withdrawn (£4,500 × 12)	54,000
	254,000

W2 Cost of sales

	£
Opening stock	Nil
Cash purchases (£1,100 × 12)	13,200
Credit purchases (£130,000 – £3,000 refunds)	127,000
	140,200
Closing stock	–12,000
	128,200

W3 Expenses

Light and Heat

Bank	8,950	Profit and loss	6,450
		Balance c/d	2,500
	8,950		8,950

Motor Expenses

Bank	18,940	Drawings (20% × £21,340)	4,268
Cash (12 × £200)	2,400	Profit and loss	17,072
	21,340		21,340

Wages, PAYE and PRSI

Bank	15,400	Profit and loss	50,400
Cash (12 × £2,800)	33,600		
Balance c/d (accrual)	1,400		
	50,400		50,400

Rent

Bank	15,000	Balance c/d (prepayment)	3,000
		Profit and loss	12,000
	15,000		15,000

Insurance

Bank	9,000	Profit and loss	12,000
Balance c/d (accrual)	3,000		
	12,000		12,000

W4 Cash and bank accounts

Bank

Cash	200,000	Purchases	130,000
Capital	30,000	Light	8,950
Refunds from creditors	3,000	Print and stationery	17,860
		Motor expenses	18,940
		Wages	15,400
		Rent	15,000
		Insurance	9,000
		Bank Charges	2,800
		Balance c/d	15,050
	233,000		233,000

Cash

Receipts from Sales	254,000	Wages (£2,800 × 12)	33,600
		Drawings (£400 × 12)	4,800
		Purchases (£1,100 × 12)	13,200
		Motor Expenses (£200 × 12)	2,400
		Bank	200,000
	254,000		254,000

W5 Stationery Stock

Print, Packaging and Stationery

Bank	17,860	Profit and loss	15,940
		Balance c/d (stock)	1,920
	17,860		17,860

W6 Sundry debtors and prepayments £

	£
Light and Heat Deposit	2,500
Rent	3,000
	5,500

W7 Accruals

	£
PAYE and PRSI	1,400
Insurance	3,000
	4,400

W8 Capital

Capital

Drawings	9,068	Bank		48,000
Balance c/d	30,070	Profit and loss		2,000
	39,138			50,000

Drawings

Motor expenses	4,268	Capital	9,068
Cash	4,800		9,068
	9,068		

R8.5

(a) (i)

Bank

Jan 1	Capital	12,000		Creditors	27,000
	Debtors	48,000		Expenses and rent	20,000
				Drawings	6,000
			Dec 31	Balance c/d	7,000
		60,000			60,000

(a) (ii)

Joe Singleton

Trading and Profit and Loss Account for the year ended 31st December, 1997

	£
Sales	50,000
Cost of sales (W4)	26,000
Gross profit	24,000
Expenses	20,000
Net profit	4,000

(a) (iii)

Joe Singleton

Balance Sheet as at 31st December, 1997

	£	£
Current Assets		
Stock	4,000	
Debtors (W1)	2,000	
Bank	7,000	13,000
Current liabilities		
Creditors (W2)		3,000
		10,000
Financed By:		
Capital (W3)		10,000

Workings

W1

Debtors Control

Credit Sales	50,000	Dec 31	Bank – receipts	48,000
			Balance c/d	2,000
	50,000			50,000

W2

Creditors Control

Bank – payments	27,000	Credit purchases	30,000
Balance c/d	3,000		
	30,000		30,000

W3

Capital

Drawings	6,000	Profit for the year	4,000
Balance c/d	10,000	Bank – capital introduced	12,000
	16,000		16,000

W4 *Cost of Sales*

Opening stock	Nil
+ Purchases	30,000
– Closing stock	4,000
	26,000

(b) The reasons why the balance per the bank account in Joe Singleton's books might be different from the bank balance according to the Bank Statement at the same date can be divided into two:

(i) Errors in the bank account or on the Bank Statements, and

(ii) Differences due to the timing of entries made by the bank or the business.

Errors in the bank account or on the Bank Statements could be:

(a) Errors made by the bank, such as a cheque for another customer charged in our account:

(b) Errors made by the business, such as a receipt or payment entered as the wrong amount.

Differences arising due to the timing of entries made by the bank or the business could be:

(a) Outstanding cheques: i.e. cheques entered in the bank account as paid but not yet presented to the bank.

(b) Outstanding lodgements: i.e. lodgements made to the bank and entered in the bank account but not yet processed by the bank.

(c) Items, payments or receipts initiated by the bank and on the Bank Statements but not yet put through the bank account.

R8.8

Ben Lewis
Profit and Loss Account for the year ended 31st March, 1998

		£	£
Sales	W3		97,500
Cost of sales	W3		55,800
Gross profit			41,700
Profit on sale of asset	W2		250
Discount received			2,100
			44,050
Wages and expenses	W5	20,500	
Bad debts		3,000	
Provision for legal claim	W4	1,400	
Discount allowed		1,200	
Depreciation	W2	7,750	
			33,850
Net profit			10,200

Ben Lewis
Balance Sheet as at 31st March, 1998

		£	£
Fixed assets			
Plant [(£18,000 + £14,000 − £9,000) − £8,000]	W2	15,000	
Premises (£40,000 − £4,000)		36,000	
			51,000
Current assets			
Stock		18,400	
Debtors	W3	15,700	
Bank	W1	1,400	
Cash on hand		400	
		35,900	
Current liabilities			
Trade creditors	W3	16,100	
Net current assets			19,800
Net assets			70,800
Represented By:			
Capital	W6		70,800

Workings

W1

Bank

Date		£	Date		£
Apr 1	Balance b/d	3,000	Mar 31	Creditors – payments	58,000
Mar 31	Fixed assets disposal	2,000	Mar 31	Fixed assets – purchases	14,000
Mar 31	Debtors – receipts	64,000	Mar 31	Wages and expenses	11,100
Mar 31	Cash – lodgements	27,000	Mar 31	Legal claim	6,400
Mar 31	Insurance proceeds	5,000	Mar 31	Cash	5,700
			Mar 31	Drawings	13,400
	Capital – Inheritance	12,000	Mar 31	Debtors – bad debt	3,000
			Mar 31	Balance c/d	1,400
		113,000			113,000
Apr 1	Balance b/d	1,400			

W2

Plant at Cost

Date		£	Date		£
Apr 1	Balance b/d	18,000	Mar 31	Disposal	9,000
Mar 31	Bank – additions	14,000	Mar 31	Balance c/d	23,000
		32,000			32,000

Disposal of Plant

Date		£	Date		£
Mar 31	Plant at cost	9,000	Mar 31	Bank (insurance)	5,000
	Profit and loss	250		Bank (scrap)	2,000
				Accumulated depreciation*	2,250
		9,250			9,250

* £9,000 × 25%

Accumulated Depreciation

Date		Plant	Premises	Date		Plant	Premises
				Apr 1	Balance b/d	4,500	2,000
Mar 31	Disposal	2,250	–	Mar 31	Profit and Loss	*5,750	**2,000
Mar 31	Balance c/d	8,000	4,000				
		10,250	4,000			10,250	4,000

* (£9,000 + £14,000) × 25% £5,750
** £40,000 × 5% £2,000

W3 *Sales and cost of sales*

Debtors Control

Date		£	Date		£
Apr 1	Balance b/d	14,000	Mar 31	Bank	64,000
Mar 31	Dishonoured cheque	3,000	Mar 31	Bad debts	3,000
			Mar 31	Discount Allowed	1,200
Mar 31	Credit sales (derived)	66,900	Mar 31	Balance c/d	15,700
		83,900			83,900
Apr 1	Balance b/d	15,700			

R8.9

(a) Crookstown Golf Club
Statement of Affairs as at 31st December, 1994

	£	£
Fixed assets		
Clubhouse	18,000	
Equipment	10,400	28,400
Current assets		
Restaurant stocks	850	
Rates prepaid	200	
Cash on hand	75	
	1,125	
Current liabilities		
Bank overdraft	1,200	
Light and heat accrued	250	
Restaurant creditors	1,600	
	3,050	
Net current liabilities		1,925
Life subscriptions fund		900
		25,575
Financed by:		
Accumulated fund (balancing figure)		25,575

(b) Crookstown Golf Club
Restaurant Trading Account for the year ended 31st December, 1995

		£	£
Sales			13,800
Less Cost of sales	W1		–8,320
Gross Profit			5,480
Less:			
Restaurant expenses		750	
Light and heat	W3	930	
Rent and rates	W3	740	
Wages and salaries of restaurant staff		3,800	6,220
Net Loss			740

Creditors Control

		£			£
Mar 31	Bank	58,000	Apr 1	Balance b/d	18,000
Mar 31	Discount received	2,100	Mar 31	Credit purchases (derived)	58,200
Mar 31	Balance c/d	16,100			
		76,200			76,200

Cash

Apr 1	Balance b/d	500	Mar 31	Wages and expenses	9,400
Mar 31	Bank	5,700	Mar 31	Bank – lodgements	27,000
Mar 31	Cash sales (derived)	30,600	Mar 31	Balance c/d	400
		36,800			36,800
Apr 1	Balance b/d	400			

Sales

	£
Credit sales (from debtors control account)	66,900
Cash Sales (per cash account)	30,600
	97,500

Cost of sales

	£
Opening stock	16,000
Purchases (per creditors control)	58,200
Closing stock	–18,400
	55,800

W4 Legal claim

Provisions (Legal Claim)

Mar 31	Bank	6,400	Apr 1	Balance b/d	5,000
			Mar 31	Profit and loss	1,400
		6,400			6,400

Bad Debts

Mar 31	Debtors	3,000	Mar 31	Profit and loss	3,000

W5 Wages and Expenses

Mar 31	Bank	11,100	Mar 31	Profit and loss	20,500
Mar 31	Cash	9,400			
		20,500			20,500

W6 Capital

Drawings

Mar 31	Bank	13,400	Mar 31	Capital	13,400

Capital

Mar 31	Drawings	13,400	Apr 1	Balance b/d	62,000
Mar 31	Balance c/d	70,800	Mar 31	Bank – inheritance	12,000
			Mar 31	Profit	10,200
		84,200			84,200
			Apr 1	Balance b/d	70,800

(c)

Crookstown Golf Club
Income and Expenditure Account for the year ended 31st December, 1995

Income	£	£
Subscriptions for 1995 – Ordinary Members (W4)		11,400
Subscriptions for 1995 – Associate Members (W4)		1,600
Life subscriptions (W5)		180
Donations received		950
Interest on deposit (£1,220 – £1,200)		20
		14,150
Expenditure		
Staff wages	8,300	
Rent and rates W3	740	
Light and heat W3	930	
Bank interest	240	
Depreciation W6	2,400	
Loss on restaurant	740	
		13,350
Surplus of income over expenditure		800

(d)

Crookstown Golf Club
Balance Sheet as at 31st December, 1995

Fixed Assets	£	£
Clubhouse		18,000
Equipment W6		9,600
		27,600
Current assets		
Bank – current account	315	
Cash on hand	40	
Subscription due	400	
Rates prepaid	320	
Restaurant stocks	930	
	2,005	
Current liabilities		
Light and heat accrued	310	
Restaurant creditors	1,400	
	1,710	
Net current assets		295
Net assets		27,895
Accumulated fund		
Balance at start of year		25,575
Add Surplus of income over expenditure		800
		26,375
Life subscriptions fund W5		1,520
		27,895

Workings

W1 Cost of sales

	£
Opening Stock	850
+ Purchases	8,400
– Closing Stock	930
	8,320

W2 Creditors Control

Dec 31	Cash/Bank	8,600	Jan 1	Balance b/d (Creditors)	1,600
Dec 31	Balance c/d	1,400		Trading A/c (purchases)	8,400
		10,000			10,000

W3 Rent and Rates

Jan 1	Balance b/d	200	Dec 31	Restaurant Trading A/c*	740
Dec 31	Cash/bank	1,600	Dec 31	Income and expenditure*	740
			Dec 31	Balance c/d	320
		1,800			1,800

Light and Heat

Dec 31	Cash/bank	1,800	Jan 1	Balance b/d	250
Dec 31	Balance c/d	310	Dec 31	Restaurant Trading A/c*	930
			Dec 31	Income and expenditure*	930
		2,110			2,110

*50% charged to the Restaurant and 50% to the rest of the club

W4 Subscriptions – Ordinary Members

Jan 1	Balance b/d	Nil	Dec 31	Cash/Bank	11,000
Dec 31	Income and Expenditure	11,400	Dec 31	Balance c/d	400
		11,400			11,400

Subscriptions – Associate Members

Jan 1	Balance b/d	Nil	Dec 31	Cash/Bank	1,600
Dec 31	Income and Expenditure	1,600	Dec 31	Balance c/d	Nil
		1,600			1,600

W5 Subscriptions – Life Members

Dec 31	Income and Expenditure	180	Jan 1	Balance b/d	900
	10% of (£1,000 + £800)				
Dec 31	Balance c/d	1,520	Dec 31	Cash/Bank	800
		1,700			1,700

W6 Depreciation

	£
NBV of Equipment at start of year	10,400
New Computer	1,600
	12,000
Depreciation @ 20%	2,400
NBV at end of year	9,600

R8.11

(a)

Make-it Ltd

Manufacturing Account for the year ended 30th September, 1996

		£	£
Cost of raw materials consumed	W1		1,647,630
Direct labour			795,157
Prime cost			2,442,787
Factory overheads	W2		403,984
Factory cost of production			2,846,771
Opening work in progress		147,300	
Closing work in progress		−137,220	10,080
Production cost of goods completed			2,856,851

Workings to Support the Manufacturing Account:

		£	£
W1	**Cost of raw materials consumed**		
	Opening stock of raw materials		92,565
	Purchases of raw materials during the year		1,618,252
	Closing Stock of Raw Materials		−63,187
			1,647,630
W2	**Factory overheads**		
	Repairs to plant		11,827
	Production Manager's salary		23,437
	Factory power		213,157
	Depreciation of plant	W7	96,122
	Light and heat	W6	18,270
	Insurance	W6	4,676
	Factory general expenses		11,925
	Rent and rates	W6	24,570
			403,984

(b)

Make-it Ltd

Trading and Profit and Loss Account for the year ended 30th September, 1996

		£	£
Sales			3,688,042
Cost of sales	W1		−2,766,183
Gross profit			921,859
Establishment expenses	W2	−30,938	
Administrative and general expenses	W3	−130,379	
Financial expenses	W4	−18,007	
Selling and distribution expenses	W5	−96,930	−276,254
Net profit for the year before taxation			645,605

Workings to Support the Trading, Profit and Loss Account:

			£
W1	**Cost of sales**		
	Opening Stock of Finished Goods		450,697
	Transfer from Manufacturing Account		2,856,851
	Closing Stock of Finished Goods		−541,365
			2,766,183
W2	**Establishment expenses**		£
	Rent and rates	W6	3,510
	Light and heat	W6	2,610
	Depreciation of office furniture	W7	24,150
	Insurance	W6	668
			30,938
W3	**Administrative and general expenses**		£
	General expenses		53,047
	Salaries		69,457
	Audit fee		7,875
			130,379
W4	**Financial expenses**		£
	Discount given for prompt settlement		25,702
	Doubtful debt provision no longer required	W8	−7,695
			18,007
W5	**Selling and distribution expenses**		£
	Sales director's salary		26,250
	Advertising		39,960
	Packaging and delivery expenses		30,720
			96,930

W6	**Apportionment of expenses**	£ 1/8 Office	£ 7/8 Factory	£ Total
	Rent and Rates	3,510	24,570	28,080
	Light and Heat	2,610	18,270	20,880
	Insurance	668	4,676	5,344
		6,788	47,516	54,304

W7 *Depreciation charge for the year*

	£
Plant and machinery: 25% of £384,487 =	96,122
Office furniture: 20% of £120,750 =	24,150
	120,272

W8 *Provision for doubtful debts*

	£
Required provision (5% of £167,400)	8,370
Existing provision	16,065
Decrease	7,695

Glossary

The following explanations of accounting and financial terms should not be regarded as being definitive – they are meant only to provide general guidance for students. Abbreviations are listed separately at the beginning of the book.

Abridged accounts: summarised financial statements prepared by 'small' or 'medium-sized' companies (as defined by the Companies (Amendment) Act, 1986) and filed in the Companies Registration Office, Parnell Square, Dublin.

Account: the place in a ledger where all of the transactions relating to any given asset, liability, expense or revenue item are recorded together. It is usually part of the double entry records. However, accounts can be used to record data outside of the double entry system and then transfer the aggregate of all of these accounts into the double entry records using a 'control account'. In the double-entry records there is a separate account for each asset and liability as well as every expense and revenue heading. Also known as 'T-account' or 'ledger account'.

Accounting bases: the methods which have been developed for expressing or applying fundamental accounting concepts to financial transactions and items, for the purpose of financial accounts. There may be more than one accounting basis for dealing with any particular item. For example, there are several methods of depreciation.

Accounting concepts: all concepts underlying accounting. See also 'Fundamental accounting concepts'.

Accounting equation: the equation, stating that Assets = Liabilities + Capital, which underlies all double-entry accounting.

Accounting period: the period for which an entity chooses to prepare its final accounts. It is usually one year but need not be. In the case of companies, Corporation Tax is assessed on the basis of a company's accounting period.

Accounting policies: the specific accounting bases selected and consistently followed by a business enterprise as being, in the opinion of the management, appropriate to its circumstances and best suited to present fairly its results and financial position.

Accounting principles: rules and conventions which ought to be followed when preparing financial statements.

Accounting records: the records, including books of original entry etc., kept by an enterprise showing details of its transactions. These records, which may be kept on paper or magnetic media, are summarised to provide information to permit final accounts to be prepared. The Companies Acts requires that a record of certain minimum details be kept and made available to auditors.

Accounting Standards Board (ASB): a UK body, formed in 1990, responsible for issuing Financial Reporting Standards (FRSs) and other pronouncements such as Financial Reporting Exposure Drafts (FREDs).

Accounting Standards Committee (ASC): the predecessor of the Accounting Standards Board (ASB) which produced Statements of Standard Accounting Practice (SSAPs) and related professional pronouncements between 1976 and 1990.

Accounts: a term generally used to mean 'final accounts', 'financial statements' or 'annual report and financial statements'.

Accrual accounting: a system of accounting, the objective of which is to show in an entity's final accounts for a period, the financial effects on that enterprise of all transactions and events which occurred during that period. An alternative to accrual accounting is the cash basis of accounting.

Accruals: expenses which have been incurred (that is, the benefit of which has been received), but which have not been paid at the end of an accounting period. They are shown as an expense in the Profit and Loss Account for the period in which they were incurred and as a current liability in the Balance Sheet as at the end of that period. Also known as 'Accrued expenses'.

Accruals concept: the fundamental accounting concept (also known as the 'matching concept') which means that profit is the difference between revenues and expenses rather than the difference between money received and money paid. The accruals concept requires a business to show, in its final accounts for a period, all expenditure incurred in that period, whether or not it has actually been paid by the end of the period. The application of the concept means that revenue and costs are accrued (that is, recognised as they are earned or incurred, not as money is paid or received), matched with one another where there is a relationship between them that allows this, and dealt with in the Profit and Loss Account of the period to which they relate.

Accrued expenses: see 'Accruals'.

Accumulated depreciation: the total amount of depreciation written off a fixed asset up to a particular time. It is shown as an expense over one or more Profit and Loss Accounts. Also known as 'Aggregate depreciation'.

Accumulated fund: the 'capital' of a non-profit organisation. (= Assets – Liabilities)

Acid test ratio: a measure of short-term liquidity calculated as the ratio of current assets, excluding stock, to current liabilities.

Activity ratios: ratios used to measure or analyse a firm's efficiency, for example, the stock turnover ratio.

Adjusted trial balance: a trial balance prepared after all 'adjusting entries' have been posted to the relevant ledger accounts.

Adjusting entries: entries made to apply the principles of accrual accounting to transactions that span more than one accounting period.

Aged analysis of debtors or creditors: a list of amounts owed, by debtors or to creditors, showing separately for each debtor/creditor, and in total, how much of the amount owed has been owed for less than one month, between one and two months, between two and three months and so on.

Aggregate depreciation: see 'Accumulated depreciation'.

Amortisation: the writing-off of an asset or liability over a period. The term is commonly used in relation to writing off goodwill or capital grants received.

Annual General Meeting (AGM): a meeting held each year which all shareholders in a company are invited to attend. The normal business of an AGM includes considering the latest set of accounts and appointing or removing directors and/or auditors.

Annual report: a report issued each year by quoted companies containing the company's latest financial statements, the Directors' Report, the Auditor's Report, the Chairman's Statement etc. Also known as the 'annual report and accounts'.

Annual return: a document which must be sent each year by companies to the Companies Registration Office. The return gives the addresses of the company's registered office, the place at which the register of members and register of debenture holders (if any) are kept, details of the company's issued share capital, indebtedness, changes in shareholders in the company and its directors and secretary. The return must be completed within sixty days of the AGM for the year to which it relates. Companies which do not make an Annual Return may face penalties. Annual Returns will not be accepted by the Companies Office unless accompanied by the relevant set of accounts.

Apportionment of costs: the division of costs between, for example, two or more departments.

Appropriation account: an addendum to the Profit and Loss Account of partnerships and companies. The appropriation account shows how profit earned is divided. In the case of partnerships the profit, after charging partners' salaries, interest on capital and other entitlements, is divided between the partners in the profit-sharing ratio. In the case of companies, profit is divided between dividends, a provision for taxation, any transfers to reserves, profit used to issue bonus shares and retained profit.

Articles of Association: the legal document which details the internal regulations for the running of a company. The Companies Acts contain a 'model' Articles of Association known as 'Table A'. All companies must have 'Articles', whether they 'adopt' Table A, with or without modifications, or write a completely original document.

Assets: resources owned by a business. Assets are shown in the Balance Sheet, unless they cannot be valued with reasonable accuracy. Assets are categorised in two different ways: (1) between fixed assets and current assets and (2) between tangible assets and intangible assets.

Asset turnover: an activity ratio that measures the efficiency with which assets are utilised to generate sales. It is calculated as sales divided by average total assets.

Audit: the independent examination of the financial statements of an enterprise by an appointed auditor in order to form a professional opinion as to whether they have been presented fairly and prepared in conformity with generally accepted accounting practice.

Auditing: the carrying out of audits or the subject concerned with the study of audits and audit practice.

Audit opinion: the conclusion arrived at by an auditor, on the basis of evidence gathered during the course of an audit, as to whether the financial statements concerned give a 'true and fair view'. The audit opinion is expressed in an 'audit report'.

Auditors: independent professionals who undertake audits and report to shareholders thereon. The fee they charge a company for an audit must be disclosed in its accounts.

Audit report: the document, prepared upon completion of an audit and addressed to shareholders, in which auditors express their audit opinion.

Authorised share capital: the maximum amount of share capital or number of shares which a company can have in issue at any given time. The amount, which can be altered by the shareholders at a general meeting, is stated in the memorandum of association and must be disclosed in the balance sheet.

Average collection period: the number of days, on average, which it takes a business to receive

payment for sales made on credit. It is a measure of efficiency and is calculated as average debtors during a period divided by credit sales for that period x 365 (or the number of days in the accounting period if the period is not a calendar year). Average debtors is usually taken to be the average of trade debtors at the beginning and end of the period, although this is not strictly correct, particularly if sales are seasonal.

Average cost method of stock valuation (AVCO): a method of stock valuation in which products sold, or in stock, are valued at their average (simple or weighted) cost.

Bad debts: amounts owed by debtors which, it is expected, will not be received. Bad debts are 'written off' (shown as an expense) in the Profit and Loss Account of the period in which they are deemed to become 'bad'.

Balance: the balance on an account (T-account or ledger account) is the difference between the total of the debit entries and the total of the credit entries in that account. The account is 'balanced' by inserting the balance on whichever side is the smaller at the date of the balancing. Balances may be either carried down (c/d) or carried forward (c/f) at the end of one accounting period (e.g. month or year) and either brought down (b/d) or brought forward (b/f) at the beginning of the next period. 'c/d' and 'b/d' rather than 'c/f' and 'b/f' are used throughout this book. Also known as 'account balance'.

Balance sheet: a financial statement showing the assets, liabilities and capital of a business at a particular point in time. It does not necessarily show assets and liabilities at their respective 'values' as the figures in the balance sheet come primarily from the Trial Balance which is simply a list of the balances on the various ledger accounts at the date of the balance sheet. The Companies (Amendment) Act, 1986 prescribes specific formats for the presentation of company Balance Sheets from which companies may choose and also prescribes that every Balance Sheet should give a true and fair view of the state of affairs of the company.

Bank reconciliation statement: a statement, prepared at the end of each period (usually a month), which explains the difference between the balance shown by a business' cash book (or bank account in the General Ledger) at a particular point in time and the balance shown on its bank statement as at the same date. Where a business has more than one account in a bank, it should have a separate account in its ledger and prepare a separate bank reconciliation statement for each one.

Bonus issue: an issue of new shares in a company to existing shareholders without the shareholders paying for them. An entry is made in the ledger crediting share capital and debiting reserves. Also known as 'Scrip issue' and 'Capitalisation issue'.

Bonus shares: shares issued to existing shareholders free of charge.

Bookkeeping: the process of recording, in books of account or on computer, the financial effect of business transactions and managing such records. The initial records of transactions (the books of original entry) are summarised periodically and the summary figures transferred into a ledger applying the principles of double entry accounting.

Book value: the book value of an asset or liability is the monetary amount shown for that asset or liability in the balance sheet. The book value of an asset is usually its acquisition cost less the accumulated depreciation on that asset. The book value of an asset is rarely the same as the amount for which that asset could be sold. Also known as 'net book value', 'carrying value' and 'written down value'.

Books of original entry: the books of account (or computer records) in which the first record of transactions is made. Examples of books of original entry include the Sales Journal (or Sales Daybook), the Purchases Journal (or Purchases Daybook), the Returns Journals (or Returns Daybooks), the Cash Book (or Cheque Payments Book and Cash Receipts Book). The double entry accounts are posted from the monthly or annual totals of these books. Also known as 'Books of Prime Entry' or 'Daybooks'.

Books of prime entry: another name for the 'Books of Original Entry' or the 'Daybooks'.

Called-up share capital: when a company issues shares it may require those who buy the shares to pay in full for them immediately or may 'call' for part-payment immediately and part later. At any point in time, a company's called-up share capital is the amount of money which it has 'called' for. Clearly, this may be less than, or equal to, either the authorised share capital (the maximum amount of share capital a company can issue) or the issued share capital (the amount of share capital actually issued) irrespective of whether payment has been 'called' or received. Money which has been 'called' but not received is known as 'calls in arrear'.

Calls in arrear: the amount of called-up share capital which has not been received.

Capital: the amount of money invested in a business by its owner(s) or accumulated by not taking out profits earned. The capital of a sole trader is the amount he/she has invested in the business plus accumulated profits to date less any withdrawals of capital (drawings) to date. The capital of a partner in a partnership business is the sum due to him/her by the partnership. This amount, however, may be shown by two separate accounts, a current account and a capital account. Therefore the balance on the capital account is not necessarily equal to the amount owed to the partner. The capital of a company is the nominal (or par) value of the shares

(of all types) issued. The accumulated profit in a company, net of dividends and other appropriations is called a 'reserve' rather than capital.

Capital employed: this term has many meanings which include the amount of money that is being used (or 'employed') in the business, the aggregate of shareholders' funds plus long-term debt and net assets.

Capital expenditure: expenditure on the purchase or improvement of (by adding value to) fixed assets. Such expenditure will be debited to one or more fixed asset accounts rather than being charged as an expense in the Profit and Loss Account in the period in which the expenditure is incurred (as is the case for 'revenue' expenditure). The fixed assets purchased or improved (except most freehold land) must then be depreciated over their expected useful economic lives.

Capital reserves: reserves, shown in the 'Capital and Reserves' or 'Financed by' section of the Balance Sheet of a company, which cannot be used for the payment of cash dividends. The two most common types of capital reserve are the share premium account, which arises because shares are issued at a price in excess of their nominal value, and a revaluation reserve, which arises because the net book value of an asset shown in the Balance Sheet is amended.

Carriage inwards: an expense item in the Profit and Loss Account of a business representing the cost, paid by the business, of transporting goods into the business. If the transport cost is paid by the supplier then the cost will appear as 'carriage outwards' in the Profit and Loss Account of the supplier.

Carriage outwards: an expense item in the Profit and Loss Account of a business representing the cost, paid by the business, of transporting goods from the business to its customers. If the transport cost is paid by the customer, and that customer is a business entity, then the cost will appear as 'carriage inwards' in the Profit and Loss Account of the customer.

Cash book: the book of original entry (whether on paper or a magnetic medium) in which all (or all except very small amounts if a separate petty cash book is kept) cash receipts and cash payments are first entered. The totals of the book will be recorded in a ledger account at periodic intervals (monthly or annually). Many businesses choose to record payments in a Cheque Payments Book and receipts in a Cash Receipts Book. A cash book will usually have analysis columns to facilitate posting to ledger accounts.

Cash discount: discount allowed to a debtor who pays within a specified period. Cash discount is shown in the Profit and Loss account as an expense. Cash discount is the same as 'settlement discount' but is not the same as 'trade discount'.

Cash equivalents: in the context of Cash Flow Statements prepared in accordance with FRS 1 cash equivalents are short-term, highly-liquid investments that will revert to cash within ninety days of the investment being made.

Cash flow statement: a historic primary financial statement that shows the cash that has come into a business and the cash that has left it during an accounting period. Cash Flow Statements are normally prepared in accordance with FRS 1. Sometimes the term is used to describe a forecast of cash flows, usually on a month-by-month or quarter-by-quarter basis.

Cash receipts book: the book of original entry in which all cash and cheques received by a business are first recorded (usually in chronological order).

Casting: adding up figures.

Chart of accounts: a listing of the titles and numbers of all accounts found in a double entry system.

Cheque payments book: the book of original entry in which details of all cheques issued by a business are first recorded (usually in cheque number order). The totals of the book are posted to the General Ledger at periodic intervals (usually monthly or annually).

Clock card: a card, on which the daily arrival and departure time of a given employee is recorded so that the total time worked by that person can be calculated for the purpose of paying him/her. There is one card for each employee who is paid by the hour and it is stamped automatically when inserted into a special 'clock'.

Closing stock: goods available for sale at the end of an accounting period. The closing stock at the end of one accounting period is the opening stock for the next accounting period.

Company: a form of business organisation which, legally, is separate and distinct from its owners. A company can therefore have rights, privileges and liabilities of its own.

Companies Acts: a term meaning all of the Acts relating to companies passed by the Dáil. The principal Acts are the Companies Acts 1963 and 1990 and the Companies (Amendment) Acts 1983, 1986 and 1990. All of the Companies Acts and Companies (Amendment) Acts are collectively known as 'the Companies Acts 1963 to 1990'.

Companies (Amendment) Act, 1986: the legislation which implemented the fourth EC Directive on Company Law. It is the principal Act governing the format, content and publication of company accounts in Ireland.

Companies Registration Office (CRO): a civil service department which maintains a file for each registered company. Companies have a legal obligation to file numerous documents with the CRO. Company files may be inspected by the public.

Compensating errors: two (or more) errors, the net effect of which, as regards the agreement of the debit and credit totals of the Trial Balance, is zero. For example, if a transaction which should be entered as debit £10 and credit £10, is accidentally entered as debit £100 and credit £100, then both the debit and credit side of the Trial Balance will be overstated by £90 but, assuming there are no other errors, the Trial Balance will still balance. It can be seen that the two separate errors of overstating the debit entries by £90 and overstating the credit entries by £90 'compensate' for each other as regards causing the Trial Balance not to balance.

Conservatism: an accounting convention meaning essentially the same thing as the Prudence Concept, that is, if the earning of revenue or profit is in any way doubtful it should not be shown in the Profit and Loss Account (until such time, that is, as it becomes certain) and provision should always be made for all known liabilities (expenses and losses) whether the amount of these is known with certainty or is a best estimate in the light of the information available. The practical effect of the convention is that assets are valued pessimistically rather than optimistically and, when faced with two or more equally acceptable alternatives, accountants should choose the one less likely to overstate assets or income.

Consistency concept: one of the fundamental accounting concepts stated in SSAP 2 which requires that similar items should normally be dealt with by a given entity in a consistent way in any particular accounting period and also from one accounting period to the next. The reason for this is to facilitate decision-makers in identifying trends. It does not mean that all entities must treat similar items in a similar way. In special cases similar items may be treated differently from one period to the next but the fact of the inconsistency must be disclosed in the accounts.

Consultative Committee of the Accountancy Bodies (CCAB): a committee through which the various accounting bodies cooperate.

Contingent liability: a potential obligation or liability, arising from transactions that have occurred on or before the balance sheet date, that may, or may not, materialise. Whether a contingent liability actually becomes a liability depends upon some future event outside of the control of the firm.

Contra entry: a double entry which is made to offset two amounts but has no net effect on the business. For example, an amount due from a debtor of a business (who is also a creditor of that business) is set off by the business against a similar amount due by the business to the creditor/debtor. Obviously, the net debtors or creditors of the business does not change as a result of these entries. A contra entry can also arise where a cash book is maintained instead of a cash account and a bank account in the ledger or where these two accounts are kept. When cash is lodged, the cash column or account must be credited and the bank column or account must be debited. As above, these two entries have no net effect on the cash/bank balances of the business.

Control account: an account, the balance on which should be the aggregate of the balances on many individual accounts in a subsidiary ledger, which is not part of the double entry system. By comparing the balance on the control account to the aggregate of the balances on the many subsidiary accounts the arithmetical accuracy of the subsidiary ledger is checked. A separate control account is usually kept for customers' (sales ledger) accounts and suppliers' (purchases ledger) accounts.

Corporation tax: the tax payable by companies on their profits.

Cost convention: an accounting convention whereby goods, services and other resources acquired are entered in the accounting records at cost.

Cost of goods available for sale: the cost of goods purchased and not yet sold which were, therefore, available for sale to customers during a particular period. It is calculated as opening stock + net purchases. Cost of goods available for sale less closing stock = cost of sales.

Cost of goods sold: see 'Cost of sales'.

Cost of sales: the cost price of the goods sold during an accounting period. The cost of sales is calculated as the value of the stock on hand at the beginning of the accounting period plus purchases during the period (and the cost of goods manufactured during the period if the business is a manufacturing firm) less the value of the stock on hand at the end of the accounting period. Also known as 'Cost of Goods Sold'.

Cost-plus: a method of determining the selling price of an item by adding a fixed percentage of its cost price to that cost. The percentage may vary for different types of goods or may vary over time. For example, a new pharmacy may decide that it is going to sell all its products at 60% above cost. However, it may later realise that its prices are not competitive and decide to sell all prescription drugs at 50% above cost and all other products at 40% above cost. The percentage added to the cost of each item is known as the 'mark-up' on that item.

Creative accounting: see 'Window-dressing'.

Credit: this term has several meanings: the credit side of a double entry ledger account or a Trial Balance is the right-hand side (income and liabilities are shown on the credit side of the Trial Balance); to sell goods or services on credit means to sell them now and hope to get paid at some future date (within the period of credit allowed).

Credit control : a term meaning all the measures and procedures put in place by a firm that trades on credit to ensure that customers pay their accounts in full and on time. These include the evaluation of a customer's credit worthiness before selling to him on credit and follow-up once the sale is made to ensure payment.

Credit note: a document sent by a business to a customer, giving details of an allowance made by the business to him in respect of goods returned by him, unsatisfactory or damaged goods received by him, goods not received by him but invoiced to him, overcharging on an invoice sent to him etc. The amount owed by a debtor will be reduced by the amount of a credit note.

Creditors: persons or businesses to whom money is owed by a business for goods and / or services supplied to it on credit. When shown in the balance sheet of a business, 'creditors' means the total amount owed by the business to its creditors.

Creditors' ledger: see 'Purchases ledger'.

Creditors settlement period: the amount of time, on average, that it takes a business to pay to its creditors the amount owed to them.

Credit transfer: an amount paid by one person or business directly into the bank account of another.

Cumulative preference shares: preference shares on which dividends due but not paid in any year(s) accumulate over time and must be paid before any dividend can be paid to ordinary shareholders. Any dividends due but unpaid will be shown as a current liability in the Balance Sheet. Arrears of dividends arise only on preference shares which are 'cumulative'; if the shares are 'non-cumulative' any dividends not paid when due do not have to be paid later.

Current account: 1. An account in a bank used for regular lodgements and payments by cheque. Frequently interest is not paid on any balance on this type of account whereas it is always paid on a deposit account. 2. In a partnership business a current account, reflecting the sum due (excluding his capital) to or by a partner arising from his share of profits/losses, is drawn up for each partner.

Current assets: cash and other assets, such as debtors and stock, which can reasonably be expected to become cash, be sold or be consumed in the normal course of business within one year from the date of the balance sheet. They should be shown in the Balance Sheet at the amount of cash they are expected to realise. Alternatively, current assets may be defined as all assets other than fixed assets.

Current liabilities: liabilities, for example, creditors, which are due to be discharged (paid) within one year from the date of the Balance Sheet.

Current ratio: a measure of liquidity calculated as the value of current assets divided by the value of current liabilities. It is often suggested that the current ratio of a healthy business should be approximately 2 : 1 i.e. current assets be twice current liabilities. However, there are many successful businesses whose current ratio is considerably less. The optimal value of the ratio will depend on many factors including the type of business, for example, whether it is a manufacturing, wholesale/retail or service organisation. Also known as the 'Working Capital Ratio'.

Daybooks: another name for the 'Books of Original Entry' or 'Books of Prime Entry'.

Declining balance method of calculating depreciation: see 'Reducing balance method of calculating depreciation'.

Debenture: strictly speaking, a debenture is a legal document evidencing a loan to a company and having clauses concerning the payment of interest, the repayment of the capital element of the loan, security etc. However, the term is commonly used to refer to the debt itself. Such a loan is normally of a large amount, given for a specified medium- to long-term and carries a fixed rate of interest.

Debenture holders: persons, businesses or, more commonly, financial institutions, who have lent money to a company where the terms and conditions of the loan are specified in a debenture document.

Debit: the debit side of a double entry ledger account or a Trial Balance is the left-hand side. Expenses and assets are shown on the debit side of the Trial Balance.

Debit note: a document sent by a business to a supplier giving details of a claim for an allowance in respect of damaged goods received, goods not received, overcharging etc. It is called a debit note as, in the books of the business, the supplier's account will be debited. In this context a debit note is really a claim for a credit note from the supplier. By convention, when the credit note is received it is entered in the books rather than the debit note having been entered when it was prepared. Clearly, if both were entered two debit entries would be made in respect of the same items. Therefore, the only function of a debit note in this context is as a record of credit notes due and a check against credit notes received. Alternatively, a debit note may be sent by a supplier to a customer if an invoice issued did not charge the full amount due because of, for example, incorrect pricing or quantities, to charge carriage or insurance etc. In this context it is essentially a supplementary invoice and many businesses choose to issue another invoice instead.

Debt: a debt is any sum due by a debtor to a creditor. 'Debt' is another word for a company's borrowings.

Debt to equity ratio: a ratio that examines the capital structure of a business by measuring the relationship between assets provided by creditors and those provided by the owners of a business.

Debtors: persons or businesses who owe money to a business for goods and / or services supplied to them on credit. When shown in the Balance Sheet of a business, under the heading of 'current assets', 'debtors' means the total amount owed to the business by its debtors, net of any 'provision' for doubtful debts (known as 'trade debtors'), plus any prepayments or other miscellaneous amounts of money receivable.

Debtors' ledger: see 'Sales ledger'.

Debtors payment period: the average time taken by credit customers to pay their debts. It is calculated as average debtors during an accounting period * 365 divided by credit sales for that period to give a result in days.

Depletion unit method of calculating depreciation: a method of depreciation applicable to 'wasting' assets such as mines or quarries. The depreciation charge for a given year is dependant on the quantity of material extracted in that year relative to the total amount available.

Depreciable assets: fixed assets which should be depreciated, i.e. all fixed assets except freehold land. Depreciable assets are shown in the Balance Sheet at their net book value, i.e. their cost (or valuation) less the total amount of depreciation charged against them up to the date of the Balance Sheet.

Depreciation: a measure of the wearing out, consumption or other loss of value of a depreciable fixed asset whether arising from use, the passage of time or obsolescence through technology and market changes. An expense should be shown in the Profit and Loss Account to reflect this. This expense, known as a depreciation charge, should be allocated to accounting periods so as to charge a fair proportion of the cost of fixed assets, less any scrap value, to each accounting period during the expected useful life of the assets. There are several methods of allocation, the principal ones being the straight line method and the reducing balance method.

Diminishing balance method of calculating depreciation: see 'Reducing balance method of calculating depreciation'.

Direct costs: costs, such as the cost of materials or labour, which can be directly identified with specific jobs, products or services.

Direct debit: a facility offered by banks which permits a creditor, with written permission from his debtor, to extract money directly from his debtor's bank account. Such transactions are usually shown on bank statements as 'DD'.

Direct method of preparing a cash flow statement: a method of preparing a Cash Flow Statement (recommended by FRS1) which gives more detailed information than the more common 'indirect' method.

Directors: individuals elected by the shareholders of a company to manage the company on their behalf.

Directors' report: a report written by the directors of a company and required by law to be sent to all shareholders with each set of financial statements. The Companies Acts prescribe that certain matters must be commented upon by the directors in their report.

Discount: see 'Cash discount', 'Trade discount', 'Discount allowed' or 'Discount received'.

Discount allowed: an allowance given by a business to any of its debtors who pay the amount they owe within a specified time.

Discount received: an allowance received by a business from any of its creditors for paying the amount it owed within a specified time.

Dishonour: when a bank dishonours a cheque it does not pay up on the cheque because the person / business which wrote the cheque (the drawer) does not have sufficient money in the particular account to meet the cheque.

Dishonoured cheque: a cheque which a bank dishonours (see above).

Dissolution of a partnership: the cessation of operations and sale of assets usually by agreement amongst the partners.

Dividend: that part of the profits of a company which is distributed to the shareholders in cash. There are two types of dividend: 1. interim dividends are those dividends paid during an accounting period; 2. final dividends are those recommended by the directors for approval by the shareholders at the Annual General Meeting.

Dividend cover: a measure of the proportion of profit which is paid in the form of dividends. For example, if a company has £100,000 profit which it could pay out as dividends but pays out only £25,000 its dividend cover is 4 times.

Dividends in arrears: dividends on cumulative preference shares that are not paid in the year they are due.

Dividend yield: a percentage measure of the return earned by a shareholder by investing in shares. It is calculated by dividing the dividend per share by the market value of the share.

Double entry: the essential principle of bookkeeping whereby every transaction must be recorded by equal debit and credit entries in the ledger accounts.

Double entry account: see 'Account'.

Double entry bookkeeping: bookkeeping by applying the double entry principle (see above). Broadly, increases in assets and decreases in liabilities and capital items are debits, and increases in liabilities and capital items and decreases in assets are credits.

Doubtful debts: amounts owed to a business by its debtors which it is unlikely to receive. An expense is shown in the Profit and Loss Account to recognise the probable loss that will be incurred as a result. Such debts remain in the ledger accounts (unlike actual bad debts) until they are declared 'bad debts' but are offset by an account with a credit balance called a 'provision for doubtful debts'.

Drawer: the drawer of a cheque is the person who writes it.

Drawings: the amount of money and/or goods taken out of a sole trader or partnership business by a proprietor for his/her own use.

Dual aspect concept or principle: the principle underlying double entry bookkeeping whereby all transactions are seen to have two aspects and thus affect two double entry accounts. This principle is not being followed when full double entry records are not kept by a business.

Earnings Per Share (EPS): an important performance measure used particularly by investment analysts. It is calculated as the profit of a company after tax (and preference share dividends, if applicable) attributable to the ordinary shareholders divided by the number of ordinary shares issued.

Earnings yield: an investment ratio calculated as earnings per share as a percentage of the market value of one share.

Entity (or business entity): a business that is treated as being distinct from its creditors, customers and owners.

Entity concept: an accounting concept, the effect of which, is that a business entity is considered as being separate from its owners and therefore, its accounts show only those transactions affecting the business and not the private transactions of the owners.

Equity: another name for the capital of the owner(s) of a business.

Error of commission: an error resulting from entering something on the correct side of the wrong double entry account. Such an error does not affect the agreement of the Trial Balance as, assuming no other errors, total debit balances will still be equal to total credit balances.

Error of omission: an error resulting from omitting to enter a transaction in the double entry accounts at all. Such an error does not affect the agreement of the Trial Balance as, assuming no other errors, total debit balances will still be equal to total credit balances.

Error of original entry: an error resulting from entering the same incorrect amount on both sides of the correct double entry account, resulting from, for example, the wrong total on a source document. Such an error does not affect the agreement of the Trial Balance as, assuming no other errors, total debit balances will still be equal to total credit balances.

Error of principle: an error resulting from entering the correct amounts on both sides of the wrong type of double entry account. Such an error does not affect the agreement of the Trial Balance as, assuming no other errors, total debit balances will still be equal to total credit balances.

Estimated useful economic life of an asset: the period of time during which a fixed asset is expected to provide benefits to the business which owns it. An estimate of the useful economic life of fixed assets (except freehold land) must be made for the purpose of calculating depreciation.

Exempted firms: firms which do not have to add VAT to the price of goods and services supplied by them and which cannot obtain a refund of VAT paid on goods and services purchased by them.

Expenditure: payment for, or obligation to pay for at some future time, an asset or a service received. If goods are purchased on credit expenditure has been incurred even though no payment has been made. Such expenditure results in a creditor being shown in the Balance Sheet until such time as the expenditure incurred is paid.

Expenses: the cost of goods and services, except the cost of sales, necessary to run a business, used up in the course of earning revenue. Expenses are debited to the Profit and Loss Account.

Extraordinary General Meeting (EGM): any general meeting of shareholders in a company except for the Annual General Meeting (AGM).

Factoring: a method for a business to improve its cash flow by 'selling' its debtors to a factoring company (a factor) which pays the business a percentage (usually between 80% and 90%) of the face value of the debtors immediately. The factoring company then becomes responsible for collecting the full debts on the due dates. Depending on the type of factoring either the business or the factor may ultimately bear the cost of bad debts.

Factory overhead costs: costs arising in a factory and related to the production of goods, but not directly traceable to the items being manufactured e.g. insurance on a factory building. Also known as Indirect Factory Costs.

Final accounts: the accounting statements which a firm produces at the end of each accounting period. Final accounts include, but need not be confined to, a Trading and Profit and Loss Account, a Balance Sheet and a Cash Flow Statement.

Final dividend: a dividend paid to shareholders after the year end when the results are known.

Financial fixed assets: fixed assets other than tangible or intangible fixed assets, such as long-term investments.

Financial Reporting Council (FRC): a UK body which oversees the setting of Financial Reporting Standards and other professional pronouncements and monitors their operation. It appoints the members of the Accounting Standards Board, the Urgent Issues Task Force and the Review Panel, ensures that they are adequately financed and guides their activities.

Financial Reporting Exposure Draft (FRED): documents issued by the Accounting Standards Board (ASB) on a specific accounting topic on which it intends to issue a Financial Reporting Standard (FRS). A FRED is essentially a 'draft' FRS.

Financial Reporting Standards (FRSs): statements issued by the Accounting Standards Board (ASB) prescribing specific ways of dealing with certain issues in accounting. For example, FRS 1 prescribes the way in which a Cash Flow Statement should be prepared. In order for a set of accounts to give a 'true and fair view' FRS' must normally be followed in their preparation.

Financial statements: the Balance Sheet, Profit and Loss Account, Cash Flow Statement, notes to all the foregoing and any other statements and notes identified in the audit report. Published annual reports of public companies are not the same as financial statements as, although the financial statements are contained in the annual report, a lot of other information may be as well. The financial statements are subject to an audit whereas the other information is not. Also known as 'Final Accounts' or simply 'Accounts'.

Financial year: the financial year of a business is any twelve month accounting period for which the business chooses to prepare its final accounts.

First-in, First-out (FIFO) method of stock valuation: a method of stock valuation in which the first goods to be received are deemed to be the first to be sold and therefore the unit cost for the first sale is the unit cost of the earliest purchase for which goods still remain in stock. This is done solely for valuation purposes – in reality the goods sold may be a mixture of several different purchases or even from the latest purchase.

Fixed assets: assets which have an expected useful life of greater than one year from the date of the Balance Sheet in which they are shown under the heading 'fixed assets', are used in the business on an ongoing basis for the purpose of earning income and are not intended for resale to customers. Examples include land, buildings, plant, machinery, vehicles (except where these are held as stock in a garage). There are three categories of fixed assets: 1. Tangible fixed assets; 2. Intangible fixed assets, and 3. Financial fixed assets. All tangible fixed assets, except freehold land, must be depreciated.

Fixed capital accounts: capital accounts which consist only of the amounts of capital actually paid into them.

Fixed costs: costs which, in the short term, remain the same at different levels of business activity.

Fluctuating capital accounts: capital accounts, the balances on which can change from one period to the next.

Folio: the number of a page in a ledger or daybook.

Folio columns: columns used for entering references to page numbers in ledgers and daybooks.

Folio numbers: reference numbers to enable transactions to be cross-referenced between ledger accounts or between a subsidiary ledger and the General Ledger.

Foreseeable future: a term which, when used in the context of the application of the Going Concern Concept, means a period of at least one year from the balance sheet date or six months from the date of the audit report, whichever is the later.

Freehold: a form of ownership (usually of land or buildings) in which the owner has absolute title for all time. The alternative to freehold is 'leasehold' meaning that the land or buildings are leased from whoever owns the freehold. Freehold land is not depreciated although freehold buildings and leasehold land are.

Fundamental accounting concepts: the broad basic assumptions which underlie the preparation of periodic financial accounts of business enterprises. The four fundamental accounting concepts, listed in SSAP 2 are the 'going concern' concept, the 'accruals' concept, the 'consistency' concept and the 'prudence' concept. In general, 'accounting convention' has the same meaning as accounting concept.

Garner v Murray rule: a rule derived from a 1904 UK legal case relating to the dissolution of partnerships. The effect of the rule is that if one partner is unable to pay a debit balance on his capital account the remaining partners will share the resulting loss in proportion to their last agreed capitals *not* in their profit / loss sharing ratios.

Gearing: the relationship between debt (or fixed interest capital) and equity in the financing structure of a business. A firm which is heavily reliant on borrowing is said to be 'highly-geared' whereas one which is financed largely by equity is said to be 'lowly-geared'.

General ledger: the book of account (probably a computer file) in which all double entry accounts are recorded. Usually, a business will also have subsidiary ledgers for individual debtors and creditors and have a single account in the General Ledger for total debtors and another for total creditors. Also known as the 'Nominal' ledger or simply 'Ledger'.

Generally Accepted Accounting Practices (GAAP): the conventions, rules and procedures that, together, constitute what is accepted accounting practice at a particular time.

Going concern concept: a fundamental accounting concept, normally adopted when preparing the accounts of a business, which assumes that the business will continue to operate for the 'foreseeable future' (at least one year after the Balance Sheet date or six months after the date of the audit report, whichever is the later) in the absence of information to the contrary. It is assumed that there is no intention, or necessity, to liquidate assets or liabilities prematurely or to curtail significantly the scale of operation. If the final accounts of a business are prepared on the going concern basis it means that assets and liabilities are valued on the assumption that the business will continue in operation for the next year. The alternative would be to assume that the business will not continue in operation for that period and value assets at what they could be sold for in the short-term and show all liabilities as current liabilities (i.e. no long-term liabilities).

Goods: the products manufactured or bought for resale or services for sale in the normal course of business. 'Goods' does not include fixed assets sold as they were not bought for the purpose of re-selling them. However, what is a fixed asset to one business may be a 'good' in another business. For example, in most businesses cars are fixed assets but in a garage they are goods as they are bought to re-sell to customers.

Goods available for sale: see 'Cost of goods available for sale'.

Goodwill: the value of a business over and above the total value of its individual net assets. This excess may arise because of, for example, the reputation of the business, the fact that it has a skilled, well-motivated workforce or loyal customers.

Gross loss: see 'Gross profit'.

Gross profit: the amount by which the 'sales' figure exceeds the 'cost of sales' figure. It is the amount of profit earned from trading before taking account of the expenses of running a business. If 'cost of sales' exceeds 'sales' then the business has incurred a Gross Loss.

Gross profit margin or ratio: see 'Profit margin'.

Historical cost: the usual basis of valuation, whereby assets are recorded at cost in financial statements. It is used because it is more objective than others and easily verifiable by an auditor. It may not be the best method in times of inflation.

Imprest: a sum of money set aside for a particular purpose, such as to pay for miscellaneous minor expenses over a period. At the end of the period the imprest is restored to its original figure by paying in the exact amount spent.

Imprest system: a system for maintaining control over small cash payments by establishing a fund at a fixed amount and periodically reimbursing the fund by the amount necessary to bring it back to that fixed amount.

Income and expenditure account: an accounting report, prepared for a non-profit organisation such as a club, society, charity or professional body, which shows both the income earned, and the expenditure incurred during a period, and the excess of one over the other.

Income tax: a tax payable by individuals, sole traders and partnerships on their income. The tax is collected from employees by means of the PAYE (pay as you earn) system.

Incomplete records: a system of keeping accounting records which does not involve double entry accounting. The records are 'incomplete' in the sense that the dual aspect of the double entry system is not adhered to when recording transactions and events. Also known as 'single entry'

Independence: the avoidance of relationships that impair or appear to impair an accountant's or auditor's objectivity.

Indirect factory costs: see 'Factory overhead costs'.

Indirect method of preparing a cash flow statement: a method of preparing a cash flow statement in accordance with FRS 1 which results in less information being shown than would be the case if the 'Direct' method, recommended by FRS 1, was used. The indirect method, although not recommended, is permitted by FRS 1.

Input credit: the amount by which a business can reduce the amount of VAT it has to pay to the Collector-General by offsetting the VAT it has been charged on purchases against the VAT which it is liable to pay on its sales.

Insolvent: a company is legally insolvent when its liabilities exceed its assets. In accounting, it is normally considered insolvent (or illiquid) when it is unable to pay its debts when they are due to be paid.

Intangible fixed assets: assets which have long-term value to a business but which, physically, do not exist. Their value is based on rights or privileges that accrue to the owner. Examples are goodwill, copyright, patents and trademarks.

Interest on capital: an amount, based on the amount of capital invested by him and the rate of interest stated in the partnership agreement, which is allowed to a partner by the partnership firm by crediting his current account.

Interest on drawings: an amount, based on the amount of drawings taken out by him and the rate of interest stated in the partnership agreement, which is charged to a partner by the partnership firm by debiting his current account.

Interim dividend: a dividend paid to shareholders during a financial year, usually after the results for the first half of the year are known.

Interim report: a financial report, required by the Stock Exchange, issued to shareholders in quoted companies half way through each financial year.

Investments: a class of asset consisting of shares or loan stock of companies, financial institutions or the government. Investments for the long-term will be shown as a financial fixed asset and those for the short-term as a current asset.

Invoice: see 'Sales invoice' or 'Purchase invoice'.

Invoice discounting: the same as factoring, except for the fact that the business remains responsible for collecting the debts itself, so its customers are not aware that a factor is involved.

Issued share capital: the amount of the authorised share capital of a company which has already been issued to shareholders.

Issued shares: shares which have been sold to shareholders.

Journal: the book of original entry for all items other than those for cash or goods. 'Journals' means the main journal and subsidiary journals such as the Sales Journal (Sales Daybook) or Purchases Journal (Purchases Daybook).

Journal entry: the double entry recording of a transaction in the Journal.

Large company: as defined by the Companies (Amendment) Act, 1986 (amended with effect from 1 January, 1994), for the purposes of the preparation and publication of accounts, a large company is a private company which, in the current year and in the immediately preceding year, cannot satisfy at least two of the following three conditions: 1) its balance sheet totals do not exceed £6m; 2) its annual turnover does not exceed £12m, and 3) its average number of employees does not exceed 250.

Last-in, First-out (LIFO) method of stock valuation: a method of stock valuation by which goods sold are deducted from stock at the unit prices of the last batch of those goods to be purchased. Therefore, stock is not valued at the most recent purchase price.

Leasehold land (or buildings): land (or buildings) leased from the owner of the freehold. It is possible to buy a leasehold interest in the property and, when this has occurred, the cost is shown on the Balance Sheet. It is then amortised (depreciated) over the length of the lease.

Leasing: a contractual arrangement in which one party (the lessee) has the use of an asset while another party (the lessor) continues to own it.

Ledger: see 'General Ledger', 'Nominal Ledger' or 'Subsidiary Ledger'.

Ledger account: see 'Account'.

Liabilities: a liability of a business is any money owed by it, so its liabilities are the total amount of money owed by it. Liabilities arise from purchasing goods and services on credit, borrowing money etc. The amounts due may be payable within twelve months of the balance sheet date (current liabilities) or after twelve months (long-term liabilities).

Limited company: companies in which the liability of individual shareholders is limited to the amount (if any) which they owe in respect of share capital they have purchased.

Limited liability: the liability of shareholders in a company is limited to any amount they have agreed to invest but have not yet paid in cash.

Limited liability company: see 'Limited company'.

Limited life: a characteristic of a partnership – any event that breaches the partnership agreement, including the admission, withdrawal or death of a partner terminates the partnership. This is not so with a company which continues to exist although existing shareholders may sell their shares or other people may become shareholders.

Limited partner: a partner whose liability is limited to the capital he has invested in a partnership firm.

Limited partnership: a form of partnership in which limited partners' liabilities are limited to their investment and in which general partners with unlimited liability operate the business.

Liquid: a business is liquid if it can easily pay its debts as they are due for payment.

Liquid assets: assets which are readily available to pay liabilities, for example, cash on hand or money in a bank account.

Liquidation: one method of 'winding up' a company, in which its assets are sold, its liabilities paid and any money remaining is distributed amongst shareholders. A liquidation may be voluntary or compulsory.

Liquidity: the aspect of the analysis of a business concerned with whether the business has the ability to pay its debts when they are due as well as cope with unexpected needs for cash and the ease with which this can be managed either using cash flow arising from trading or by the sale of assets. A business is liquid if this is easy; otherwise it is illiquid.

Liquidity ratios: ratios that attempt to indicate the ability of a business to meet its debts as they fall due, for example, the creditors settlement period, the current ratio and the acid test ratio. Liquidity ratios may be divided into long-term and short-term liquidity ratios.

Listed companies: companies whose shares are quoted on the Stock Exchange. Also known as 'quoted companies'.

Loan stock: a form of debt finance in a company which is traded on the Stock Exchange.

Long-term liabilities: debts of a business that are due to be paid more than one year after the balance

sheet date. For example, a term loan from a bank on which only interest is payable in the next year. In published company accounts long-term liabilities are shown under the heading 'creditors: amounts falling due after more than one year'.

Lower of cost and Net Realisable Value (NRV): a rule for stock valuation where each item of stock (or group of similar items) is valued at cost or NRV, whichever is the lower, and the total value of stock is the aggregate of the value (thus determined) of each item (or group of items).

Machine hour method of calculating depreciation: a method of calculating depreciation on a machine where the depreciation charge for a period is based on the number of hours the machine has been used during that period relative to its estimated useful life.

Manufacturing account: an accounting statement, prepared by manufacturing firms at the end of each accounting period, in which the cost of producing goods for that period is calculated.

Margin: see 'Profit margin'.

Market value of an asset: the amount for which an asset could be sold on a completely open market. The market value of a share in a quoted company is the price at which it is quoted on the Stock Exchange.

Mark-up: the mark-up on a product is the gross profit on it, shown as a percentage of its cost price. The average mark-up percentage, for a business as a whole, is its gross profit expressed as a percentage of its cost of sales.

Matching concept: an accounting concept, the effect of which is that revenue and costs are accrued, matched with one another insofar as their relationship can be established or justifiably assumed, and dealt with in the Profit and Loss Account of the period to which they relate. See also 'Accruals concept'.

Material: an item is material if its non-disclosure in, mis-statement in, or omission from a set of accounts would be likely to result in the accounts not giving a true and fair view.

Material error: an error in financial statements which is of such importance as to cause them not to give a true and fair view.

Materiality: an accounting convention, the effect of which, is that accountants must judge the impact on, and importance to, the financial statements, of each transaction and event to determine how it should be correctly recorded and disclosed. Accounting Standards and Financial Reporting Standards apply only to material figures. Thus, the guidance given in them does not apply to immaterial (relatively small) amounts.

Medium-sized company: as defined by the Companies (Amendment) Act, 1986 (amended with effect from 1 January, 1994), for the purposes of the pre-

paration and publication of accounts, a medium-sized company is a private company which, in the current year and in the immediately preceding year, satisfies at least two of the following three conditions: 1) its balance sheet totals do not exceed £6m; 2) its annual turnover does not exceed £12m, and 3) its average number of employees does not exceed 250.

Members of a company: shareholders in a company.

Memorandum of Association: a legal document, which every company must have, outlining its constitution, defining the scope of its powers and giving details of the conditions governing its relationship with third parties. It includes details concerning the objects of the company (i.e. what the company is entitled to do in terms of trading) and its authorised share capital.

Modified accounts: shortened versions of full financial statements. The Companies (Amendment) Act, 1986 permits small and medium-sized companies to file modified accounts instead of full accounts with the Companies Registration Office. Full accounts must always be produced for presentation to shareholders.

Money measurement concept: an accounting concept, the effect of which is, that only transactions and events capable of being measured in terms of money and whose monetary value can be assessed with reasonable objectivity are entered in the accounting records.

Net assets: total assets less liabilities. It is equivalent to equity capital. Also known as 'Net Worth'.

Net assets per share: the value of a company's net assets divided by the number of ordinary shares issued. Also known as 'Asset Value'.

Net Book Value (NBV) of an asset: the cost (or valuation) of a fixed asset less accumulated depreciation thereon. Since freehold land is not depreciated its NBV is simply its cost or valuation. Fixed assets are shown in the Balance Sheet at their NBV. Also known as 'Carrying Value', 'Written Down Value' or simply 'Book Value'.

Net current assets: the value of current assets less that of current liabilities (this will be net current liabilities if the result is negative). Also known as 'Working Capital'.

Net current liabilities: see 'Net current assets'.

Net loss: see 'Net profit'.

Net profit: gross profit (sales less cost of sales) less all expenses – if the result is positive. If the result is negative then a net loss has been incurred.

Net profit margin or ratio: see 'Profit margin'.

Net purchases: total purchases less the aggregate of purchases returns (returns outwards) and discount received.

Net sales: total sales less the aggregate of sales returns (returns inwards) and discount allowed.

Net Realisable Value (NRV) of stock: the value of stock calculated at its estimated selling price (after deducting trade discount but before deducting cash discount) less all costs yet to be incurred in marketing, selling and distributing the products (and less all costs yet to be incurred to complete the manufacture of the products in the case of work in progress). Stock must be valued at the lower of its cost and its NRV.

Net worth: see 'Net assets'.

Nominal accounts: double entry accounts in which expenses, revenue and capital are recorded.

Nominal ledger: see 'General ledger'.

Nominal value of a share: see 'Par value of a share'.

Non-cumulative preference shares: preference shares which, if the dividend due on them is not paid when due, forfeit the right to that dividend, i.e. the unpaid dividends do not accumulate.

Notes to, and forming part of, the accounts: information about a business made available with its financial statements which expands upon, or explains, data found in those statements.

Objectivity: a principle fundamental to accounting, requiring that accounting information be free from bias and be verifiable by an independent party. It is because of this principle that accountants have adopted the cost convention and formulated rules for recording financial transactions and events which, so far as is possible, do not depend upon personal judgement.

Obsolescence: the process of becoming obsolete, that is, a reduction in the estimated useful life of an asset for reasons other than deterioration. For a fixed asset, becoming obsolete means that its actual useful life is less than its estimated useful life and therefore, when the asset is sold it may still have a substantial net book value, which, in turn, means that a loss on its sale is likely as the proceeds will be relatively little.

Opening entries: the entries in the double entry records to set up a General Ledger for a business previously operating without one.

Opening stock: goods available for sale at the beginning of an accounting period. The opening stock at the beginning of an accounting period is the same as the closing stock for the previous accounting period.

Operating expenses: expenses, other than cost of sales (or cost of goods sold), that are incurred in running a business as opposed to financing it. Therefore, interest payable is not an operating expense. Dividends are an appropriation of profit, not an expense.

Ordinary share capital: that part of a company's share capital consisting of ordinary shares.

Ordinary shareholders: persons, companies or institutions who own ordinary shares.

Ordinary shares: shares which carry voting rights, the dividend on which depends on how much profit remains after debenture interest and preference dividends have been paid and how much of this the directors decide to pay out. If a company is wound-up persons who own ordinary shares in it can recoup their investment only if there is money left, when the company's assets are sold, after paying debenture holders, preference shareholders and creditors. Ordinary shares means the same as equity shares but not the same as equity capital as the latter also includes reserves.

Overcast: a column of figures is overcast if the total arrived at when they are added exceeds the correct total.

Overtrading: a business is overtrading when it is trading at a level beyond that which it can finance. If a business is very successful it may have to increase stocks to keep pace with demand and debtors may increase because of lots of credit sales. This may lead to the business owing money for stock purchased on credit but not having the cash to pay for it because it is waiting for its debtors to pay.

Owners' equity: the value of the proprietor's interest in the net assets of a business.

Paid-up share capital: that part of a company's authorised and issued share capital which has been called-up by the company and paid for in full by the shareholders.

Partnership (business): any business, other than a company, owned by two or more people.

Partnership agreement: the contractual relationship, either written or verbal, between partners usually covering details such as the way in which profit is to be shared and the relative responsibilities of various partners.

Partnership salaries: agreed amounts payable to individual partners in respect of duties undertaken by them. Partners' salaries are deducted before sharing profit between partners in their profit-sharing ratio.

Par value of a share: the arbitrary value of a share specified in the company's memorandum of association and printed on each share certificate. The number of shares issued multiplied by the par value of each share is the figure which appears in the Balance Sheet for share capital. The par value of a share bears no relationship to its market value. Its only significance is that a share cannot be issued for less than its par value. Also known as the 'nominal value of a share'.

PAYE (Pay As You Earn): a form of income tax paid by most employees. PAYE is deducted from an employee's gross pay by his/her employer.

Payee: the person to whom a cheque is paid.

Paying-in slip: a form used when lodging money into a bank account. The person lodging the money will keep part of the slip, known as the counterfoil.

Period of credit: the time within which a debtor should pay the amount owed to a creditor.

Personal accounts: double entry accounts for individual debtors and creditors.

Petty cash: an amount of cash set aside by a business for making small (petty) payments in cash to avoid having to write many cheques. It is usually kept control of by using the 'imprest system'. Any amount of cash on hand at the balance sheet date is shown as an asset.

Petty cash book: the Book of Original Entry for small payments. It usually has analysis columns. The totals of the columns at the end of each month are posted to the General Ledger. The source documents for the book are petty cash vouchers.

Petty cash voucher: a form signed by each person requesting a payment from petty cash and authorised for payment by a superior showing the date, amount and purpose of the expenditure. It is the source document for the petty cash book.

Piecemeal realisation: a method of accounting for the dissolution of a partnership which calculates how much each partner can be paid as soon as is possible without paying them more than they may ultimately be due.

Piece work: a system of paying employees in which they are paid a certain amount per item produced or job performed.

Posting: entering information, from sources such as the Books of Original Entry, into the General Ledger by means of double entry accounting.

Preference share capital: the part of a company's share capital which consists of preference shares (of all types).

Preference shareholders: persons, businesses or institutions who own preference shares.

Preference shares: shares which usually command a fixed percentage rate of dividend in priority to any dividend being paid on ordinary shares. Preference shareholders are also entitled to repayment of their investment if the company is wound up before ordinary shareholders receive any money.

Pre-incorporation profit or loss: profits or losses which arise in a business before it becomes a company. This may happen when a new business incurs legal and other expenses before it is registered in the Companies Office as a company or may be because an existing business converts from being a sole trader or a partnership to being a company.

Prepaid expenses: see 'Prepayments'.

Prepayments: expenditure on services and products (other than goods for resale) which has been paid (or shown as a creditor) in one accounting period, the benefit of which will not be received until a subsequent period. Because money has been paid there will be an entry in the Trial Balance but an adjustment must be made when preparing final accounts to ensure that only the amount of the expense relevant to the current accounting period is shown in the Profit and Loss Account (in accordance with the accruals concept) and the balance is shown as a current asset in the Balance Sheet. For example, rates paid during an accounting period ending in December up to March of the next year. Also known as 'Prepaid Expenses'.

Price Earnings (P/E) ratio: the price of a share in a company quoted on the Stock Exchange divided by its earnings per share (EPS). The ratio is of much interest to investment analysts and is given in the financial pages of the press.

Prime cost: a subtotal shown in a Manufacturing Account, being the total of direct costs i.e. direct material costs + direct labour costs + direct expenses.

Private company: a company with a share capital and between two and fifty shareholders (excluding employees and ex-employees) who are restricted in terms of who they can transfer their shares to and which cannot invite the public to subscribe for shares or loan stock in it.

Professional pronouncements: the collective term for all documents required to be followed by accountants issued by the bodies which regulate the accounting profession. These include Financial Reporting Standards and Statements of Standard Accounting Practice but exclude legislation and Stock Exchange rules.

Profitability ratios: ratios that measure a business' success (or lack of it) during an accounting period in terms of its profit.

Profit and loss account: an accounting statement in which the profit for an accounting period is calculated. It shows details of revenues and expenses for that period. Companies are required by law to prepare a Profit and Loss Account for each accounting period.

Profit margin: the profit margin on a product is the gross profit on it expressed as a percentage of its selling price. The profit margin for a business as a whole may be expressed in terms of either gross profit or net profit. Its gross profit margin (or gross profit ratio) is its gross profit as a percentage of its sales and its net profit margin (or net profit ratio) is its net profit as a percentage of its sales.

Pro-forma: pro-forma has two main meanings. 1. A pro-forma invoice is a draft invoice issued by a vendor to a customer to inform him of the amount due in respect of a transaction. If this amount is paid the goods concerned will be dispatched and a formal invoice will be issued. Sometimes a pro-forma invoice simply means that the customer

cannot (for the time being) claim the VAT shown on it. 2. A pro-forma set of accounts (or just Profit and Loss Account or Balance Sheet) means a forecast set of accounts for one or more future accounting periods.

Provisions: adjustments made at the end of an accounting period, usually to provide for costs which have accrued or liabilities which are likely or certain to be incurred and would not otherwise be included in the financial statements. A provision is 'made' by debiting the Profit and Loss Account and crediting an asset or liability account. Provisions are made for depreciation, doubtful debts, discounts on debtors etc.

Provision for bad or doubtful debts: an amount charged in the Profit and Loss Account of a firm and deducted from the figure for debtors in its Balance Sheet in accordance with the prudence concept, to allow for possible non-payment by some of the firm's current debtors. Often, the provision is a fixed percentage of debtors (say 5%). The rate is usually determined from the past experience of the business.

Provision for discounts on debtors: an amount charged in the Profit and Loss Account and deducted from the figure for debtors in the Balance Sheet to reflect the fact that some debtors, who would be entitled to a cash discount if they paid on time, might pay on time. In accordance with the accruals or matching concept the charge in the Profit and Loss Account must be shown in the same period as that in which the sales revenue is shown.

PRSI (Pay Related Social Insurance): a form of insurance required to be paid by most employees to the government. The amount paid depends on the type of employment and the amount earned. Employees are entitled to certain medical and other benefits in return.

Prudence concept: an accounting convention, the effect of which, is to ensure that profit and assets are not shown at figures higher than they should be. See also 'Conservatism'.

Public company: a term loosely used to mean either a Public Limited Company (plc) or a Quoted Company. However, care should be taken with this term as its two supposed meanings are not the same, as, while every quoted company must be a 'plc', every 'plc' need not be quoted on the Stock Exchange.

Public limited company (plc): a public limited company is a company which states in its memorandum that it is a public company, ends its name with the words 'public limited company' or the abbreviation 'plc' (or its Irish equivalent 'cpt'), has a minimum authorised share capital of £30,000 and at least seven shareholders. Sometimes referred to as simply 'public company' although this is not strictly correct (see above).

Purchase discounts: see 'Discount received'.

Purchase invoice: a document received from a vendor (seller) whenever a business purchases goods on credit. It gives details of the vendor, the business purchasing the goods, a description of the goods, the quantity being purchased, their value, the vendor's terms and conditions of sale and VAT.

Purchases: goods bought solely for the purpose of re-selling them to customers.

Purchases daybook: see 'Purchases journal'.

Purchases journal: the book of original entry in which details of all goods purchased on credit for re-sale are recorded (usually chronologically or in order of the reference numbers allocated to purchase invoices). From the Purchases Journal, entries are posted to the suppliers' accounts and, in total, to the purchases account. Also known as a 'Purchases Daybook'.

Purchases ledger: a ledger (often known as a subsidiary ledger), separate from the General Ledger with a separate account for each creditor. A single account, known as a 'Control Account' is then kept in the General Ledger for all creditors.

Purchases returns: see 'Returns outwards'.

Qualified audit report: an audit report in which the audit opinion expressed is that the financial statements, the subject of the report, may not, or do not, give a true and fair view, or have not been prepared in accordance with relevant accounting or other requirements.

Qualitative characteristics of financial information: standards for judging the quality of information that accountants provide.

Quick ratio: see 'Acid test ratio'.

Quoted companies: public limited companies (PLCs) whose shares are traded on the Stock Exchange. Also known as 'listed companies'.

Quoted investments: investments in shares or loan stock which are quoted on the Stock Exchange.

Ratio analysis: a method of analysing the financial statements of a business with a view to evaluating its liquidity, profitability etc. It involves comparisons of actual relationships between figures in financial statements (ratios) to relationships reasonably expected to exist (standards). These standards may be based on, for example, ratios for prior periods, ratios for competitors or targets set.

Real accounts: the category of double entry account used for assets with physical existence, for example, stock or fixed assets.

Realisable value of an asset: the amount for which an asset can be sold.

Realisation account: a double entry account in which the entries necessary to record the dissolution of a partnership are made.

Realisation concept: an accounting convention, the effect of which, is that profit should not be included in the Profit and Loss Account until it is reasonably certain of being earned.

Receipts and payments account: a summary of the cash book of a non-profit organisation.

Recommended Retail Price (RRP): the price at which the manufacturer of a product recommends it should be sold. Trade discount is based on RRP.

Reducing balance method of calculating depreciation: an accelerated method of calculating depreciation in which the depreciation charge is calculated by applying a fixed percentage to the carrying value or net book value (the reducing balance) of a tangible fixed asset giving rise to a depreciation charge which declines over time. Also known as the 'declining balance' or 'diminishing balance' method of calculating depreciation.

Register of members: see 'Register of Shareholders'

Register of shareholders: the record, required by law to be kept by all companies, which gives details of the names of persons owning shares in a company and the number of shares each owns. Also known as the 'Register of Members'.

Registrar of companies: the person in charge of the Companies Registration Office.

Replacement cost of stock: the amount which it would cost to purchase or manufacture the items currently in stock. According to SSAP 9 stock should not be valued at its replacement cost.

Reserves: the aggregate of Capital Reserves and Revenue Reserves.

Residual value of a fixed asset: the amount that a business expects to receive for a fixed asset when it sells it at the end of its expected useful life. Also known as 'salvage value'.

Retained earnings: means the same as 'Retained Profit'.

Retained profit: the retained profit for a particular accounting period is the profit which could be paid out in the form of dividends but is withheld in the business instead. Retained profit can also mean the accumulated retained profit of a business since it began operation.

Return on assets: a measure of profitability that shows how efficiently a business is using its assets by comparing profit to average assets owned.

Return on Capital Employed (ROCE): a measure of profitability in terms of profit expressed as a percentage of the capital used in earning it.

Return on equity: a measure of profitability which shows the amount of profit earned by a business in relation to the investment by its owners in it.

Return on investment: a profitability measure which shows the amount of profit earned by a business in relation to the total investment in it.

Returns: this term has several meanings including 1. profits or gains resulting from the ownership of assets, for example return on capital employed or returns from investments; 2. goods sent back to a vendor or received back from a customer (See 'Returns inwards' or 'Returns outwards') and 3. documents required to be submitted to some authority, for example, the annual return of a company or a tax return.

Returns inwards: goods returned to a business by its customers. Also known as 'Sales Returns'.

Returns inwards journal: the book of original entry for goods returned to a business by its customers.

Returns outwards: goods, originally purchased for resale, which are returned by a business to its suppliers. Also known as 'Purchases Returns'.

Returns outwards journal: the book of original entry for goods returned to suppliers.

Revaluation: the process of changing the amount at which a fixed asset is shown in a Balance Sheet. It usually involves increasing the book value from cost less accumulated depreciation to a figure approximating current market value. However, a revaluation can also mean reducing the book value of an asset.

Revaluation account: a double entry account used to record the profits or losses arising when assets or liabilities are re-valued in an event such as a change of partners in a partnership.

Revenue: the sales of a business plus any money coming into it from other sources such as the return it earns on its investments. It is not the same as profit.

Revenue expenditure: expenditure incurred in the day-to-day running of a business the benefit of which arises only in the current accounting period. It includes expenditure on repairing and maintaining fixed assets as distinct from capital expenditure, which is expenditure incurred in acquiring or adding value to them. Revenue expenditure is recorded by debiting expense accounts – it is not depreciated.

Revenue reserves: reserves of a company which are available for distribution as dividends. The principal revenue reserve is retained profit (shown in a Balance Sheet as the 'Profit and Loss Account').

Rights issue: an issue of new shares in a company to existing shareholders at a price below the current market price.

Sale or return: goods supplied to a business on 'sale or return' may, if not sold, be returned to the supplier without obligation. Therefore, if a business acquires goods on such terms it does not have to worry about whether it can sell them. In the books of the seller, goods sold on sale or return should be treated as stock and not as a sale until the customer has agreed to purchase and pay for them, although

they have physically left the vendor's premises before that time. In the books of the business receiving the goods, they should not be included as stock until purchase is agreed, as they do not belong to it.

Sales: the value of goods and services sold by a business to its customers, both for cash and on credit, during an accounting period.

Sales daybook: see 'Sales journal'.

Sales discounts: see 'Discount allowed'.

Sales invoice: a document which is prepared whenever a business sells goods on credit. It gives details of the vendor and the customer, the goods being sold and their value, the terms and conditions of sale and VAT.

Sales journal: the book of original entry in which details of all sales on credit of goods purchased for re-sale are recorded (usually in invoice number order). From the Sales Journal, entries are posted to the double entry records and to individual customer 'accounts' in the Debtors' (or sales) (subsidiary) Ledger. Also known as a 'Sales Daybook'.

Sales ledger: a ledger, separate from the General Ledger (often known as a subsidiary ledger) with a separate account for each debtor. A single account, known as a Control Account is then kept in the General Ledger for all debtors. Also known as a 'Debtors' Ledger'.

Sales returns: see 'Returns inwards'.

Salvage value: see 'Residual value of a fixed asset'.

Scrip issue: see 'Bonus issue'.

Settlement discount: see 'Cash discount'.

Share: see 'Shares'.

Share capital: the capital of a company which is divided into shares owned by shareholders. There are many possible meanings of share capital including 'authorised share capital' and 'issued share capital'. Share capital is stated in the Balance Sheet at its par (nominal) value.

Share certificate: a document issued to a shareholder indicating the number of shares which he/she owns.

Shareholders: persons, companies, institutions etc. who own one or more shares in one or more companies. Every shareholder will be issued with a share certificate showing the number of shares they own and their name must be recorded in the register of shareholders. Also known as 'members' of a company.

Shareholders' funds: the amount of a company's share capital and reserves 'owned' by the shareholders. It includes the share capital and equity reserves but excludes debt finance.

Share premium: when a share is issued at a price above its par (or nominal) value, the excess is known as a share premium. The total share premium is the premium on each individual share issued multiplied by the number of shares issued. This amount is credited to a share premium account.

Share premium account: a reserve account which is part of 'shareholders funds' and which is shown in the 'capital and reserves' section of the Balance Sheet. It is credited with the aggregate amount for which shares are issued in excess of their par (or nominal) value.

Shares: units of ownership of capital in a company. A company's capital may be divided into shares of different types, for example, ordinary shares and preference shares. Each share of a particular type is of equal value.

Single entry: see 'Incomplete records'.

Small company: as defined by the Companies (Amendment) Act 1986 (amended with effect from 1 January 1994), for the purposes of the preparation and publication of accounts, a small company is a private company which, in the current year and in the immediately preceding year, satisfies at least two of the following three conditions: 1. its balance sheet totals do not exceed £1.5m; 2. its annual turnover does not exceed £3m, and 3. its average number of employees does not exceed 50.

Sole trader: a business owned by one person only, rather than being owned by partners or shareholders.

Source documents: documents which are the basis for entries in a particular Book of Original Entry. For example, sales invoices are the source document for the Sales Journal.

Standing order: an instruction to a bank to make specific payments from a particular bank account at specified intervals, for example, monthly rent payments.

Statement: a term generally used to mean 'Bank Statement' or, more commonly, 'Statement of Account'.

Statement of account: a document sent out by a business at the end of each month to each of its debtors showing the amount owed at that date and its composition in terms of invoices not paid. It shows the details contained in a debtor's personal account in the business' Sales (or Debtors') Ledger (or General Ledger). Often referred to simply as 'Statement'.

Statement of affairs: a listing of assets and liabilities showing their values.

Statements of Standard Accounting Practice (SSAPs): documents prescribing particular methods of accounting for certain types of transactions. SSAPs must be followed by accountants who are members of the professional accountancy bodies who issued them (including the Institute of Chartered Accountants in Ireland (ICAI)) when preparing

financial statements intended to give a true and fair view. SSAPs are no longer being issued and will, over time, be replaced by Financial Reporting Standards issued in the UK by the Accounting Standards Board and modified, where necessary, for issue in Ireland by the Technical Committee of the ICAI.

Statutory books: the records and registers that a company is required to keep by law. They include the register of shareholders and the register of directors and secretaries.

Stock: goods purchased by a business for resale, but not yet sold, and therefore on hand and available for sale to customers. In a manufacturing business stock would consist of raw materials, work-in-progress and finished goods ready for sale.

Stock Exchange: an organised market for shares in quoted companies. Any companies whose shares are traded on the Stock Exchange must adhere to Stock Exchange regulations including, for example, publishing certain information not required by law or by Generally Accepted Accounting Practice in its annual report.

Stockturn: see 'Stock turnover'.

Stock turnover: a measure of performance or efficiency which shows the relationship between a business' sales during an accounting period and its average stock during that period in terms of what multiple of its average stock is its sales. It is calculated as the 'Cost of Sales' for an accounting period divided by the average value of goods in stock during that period.

Straight line method of calculating depreciation: a method of calculating depreciation based on the assumption that the value of a fixed asset decreases at a constant rate over time and is not dependant on any other factor, for example, usage. Therefore, the cost of a depreciable asset, less its residual value, is allocated to each accounting period (of equal length) over its estimated useful economic life in equal instalments. Often, this method is used for convenience rather than because it is felt to be the most accurate. Sometimes, if an asset is bought or sold during an accounting period it is depreciated only for the period for which it was owned rather than for the whole period.

Subsidiary ledger: a ledger separate from the General (or nominal) Ledger that contains a group of related accounts, for example, all individual debtors' accounts or all individual creditors' accounts. All of the individual accounts in the subsidiary ledger are represented by a single 'control' account in the General Ledger. The total of the balances in the Subsidiary Ledger accounts should equal the balance on the relevant control account in the General Ledger. Subsidiary ledgers are generally maintained so as to avoid entering lots of detail in the General Ledger and as an independent record of

transactions – they are usually not part of the double entry system. The Subsidiary Ledger is 'posted' from the individual lines in the Sales Journal, Purchases Journal etc. whereas the General Ledger is posted from the monthly totals in these books of original entry.

Substance over form concept: the accounting concept which gives rise to transactions being accounted for in accordance with their true substance (commercial reality) rather than their legal form. Leasing is a good example of the difference between substance and legal form. If a business leases a car from a financial institution, then, for all practical purposes, the business owns the car. However, legally the financial institution owns it. If this transaction was accounted for in accordance with the substance over form concept the leased car would be shown as a fixed asset in the business' balance sheet and would therefore be depreciated.

Sum of the digits method of calculating depreciation: a method of calculating depreciation that allocates the cost of a depreciable asset, less its residual value, over its estimated useful economic life in steadily declining amounts.

Super profit: the profit remaining after deducting an allowance for the owner's services and a charge for the use of his capital from the net profit shown in the Profit and Loss Account.

Suspense account: when a Trial Balance is prepared its totals should be equal i.e. it should 'balance'. However, if errors have been made in the double-entry records, it may not. If a Trial Balance does not balance and the errors which cause it not to balance cannot be found a suspense account (a double entry account) is opened and the difference between the debit and credit totals in the Trial Balance is entered in it, on whichever side is necessary so that when another Trial Balance is prepared including the suspense account that Trial Balance will balance.

Table A (Articles of Association): a model set of Articles of Association contained in the Companies Act, 1963. Most companies will have Articles of Association very similar to 'Table A'. The provisions of Table A apply to any company except to the extent that they are excluded by that company.

T account: see 'Account'.

Tangible fixed assets: fixed assets that have physical substance, for example, land or vehicles.

Taxable profit: the amount of profit on which tax is assessed. The taxable profit of a business is not the same as the profit calculated in its Profit and Loss Account because taxable profit is calculated under tax rules as well as accounting rules.

Tax year: the period for which both personal and business Income Tax returns must be made. Each tax year runs from the 6th of April in one year to

the 5th of April in the following year. For example, the tax year 1998/99 commenced on 6/4/98 and ended on 5/4/99.

Technical committee: a committee of the Institute of Chartered Accountants in Ireland responsible for, amongst other things, making amendments to Financial Reporting Standards issued by the Accounting Standards Board in the UK so that they can be issued as FRSs applicable in Ireland.

Time interval concept: the accounting concept which gives rise to the life of a business being arbitrarily divided up into accounting periods and final accounts being prepared at the end of each such period.

Trade creditors: the amount of the total creditors shown in a balance sheet, which relates to creditors resulting from the trading activities of the firm i.e. the purchase of goods and services on credit. The figure for trade creditors, therefore, does not include accruals or other miscellaneous creditors.

Trade debtors: the amount of the total debtors shown in a balance sheet, which relates to debtors resulting from the trading activities of the firm i.e. the sale of goods and services on credit. The figure for trade debtors, therefore, does not include prepayments or other miscellaneous debtors.

Trade discount: an amount deducted by a manufacturer or wholesaler from the Recommended Retail Price (RRP), or list price, of a product when calculating the price at which it is to be sold to a retailer to enable him to make a profit when he sells at RRP, or list price, to his customer. This is distinct from discount given to customers who pay quickly (cash discount) or discounts for large purchases etc. Sales are recorded in the Sales Journal at the net amount of the invoice i.e. after deducting trade discount.

Trading account: an account which shows the financial effects of trading and in which the gross profit earned (or gross loss incurred) for an accounting period is calculated.

Trading and profit and loss account: a combined account in which both gross profit and net profit are calculated. In the case of company accounts prepared in accordance with the Companies Acts the two accounts together are simply known as a Profit and Loss Account.

Transposition errors: errors which occur when transactions are being posted whereby the digits in the amounts involved are transposed. For example, '69' entered as '96'.

Trend analysis: a method of analysing financial statements involving comparison of the same item or ratio over two or more years to highlight a trend.

Trial balance: a list of all the balances on double entry (or ledger) accounts (and the cash book if this is used in place of ledger accounts for cash and bank)

at a particular point in time, for example, the end of an accounting period. The Trial Balance lists the name of each account, with the balance on that account opposite it in either the debit column or the credit column. The purpose of preparing a Trial Balance is to see whether the total of the debit balances equals that of the credit balances, as it should if all double-entries have been correctly made, and also to facilitate the preparation of final accounts. If the two totals are not equal there must be one or more errors in the double- entry records. Even if the totals are equal this is not conclusive proof that the double entry records are error-free as 'errors of original entry', 'errors of omission', 'errors of commission', 'errors of principle' or 'compensating errors' will not be detected.

True and fair view: the Companies Acts require that the Balance Sheet and Profit and Loss Account of a company must give a 'true and fair view'. Broadly speaking, this means that they must not contain any significant errors, must be presented in accordance with the formats prescribed in the Companies (Amendment) Act 1986 and must adhere to the requirements of Statements of Standard Accounting Practice, Financial Reporting Standards and other professional pronouncements.

Turnover: the total value of sales during an accounting period.

UITF abstract: a document issued by the Urgent Issues Task Force giving guidance on the accounting treatment of particular items in the same way as Statements of Standard Accounting Practice and Financial Reporting Standards do.

Undercast: if a column of figures, for example in a Daybook, are undercast the total arrived at is less than the correct total.

Unlimited liability: a characteristic of the partnership and sole trader forms of business organisation meaning that each partner (except limited partners) or the sole trader, is personally liable for all the debts of the business.

Unpresented cheque: a cheque which has been sent to the payee (the party to whom the cheque is payable) but has not yet been debited on the bank statement of the drawer (the party issuing the cheque) usually either because it has not been cashed or, if so, has not yet been processed by the drawer's bank.

Unqualified audit report: an audit report in which the audit opinion expressed is that the financial statements, the subject of the report, give a true and fair view and have been prepared in accordance with relevant accounting or other requirements.

Unquoted investments: investments in shares or loan stock which are not quoted on the Stock Exchange.

Urgent Issues Task Force (UITF): a subcommittee of the Accounting Standards Board (ASB) set up to provide guidance on accounting issues faster than

the ASB could issue or amend a Financial Reporting Standard.

Value Added Tax (VAT): a tax charged on the supply of most goods and services. The tax is borne by the ultimate consumer of the goods or services, not by the business selling them to that customer.

Variable costs: costs which increase or decrease in proportion to changes in the level of business activity. For example, the cost of raw materials increases or decreases in line with increases or decreases in the number of units produced.

Vendor: the vendor of a product is the seller of it.

Voucher: any document supporting transactions entered in a journal, ledger or book of original entry.

Weighted average method of stock valuation: the valuation of stock by reference to the weighted average of the costs of all items in stock.

Winding-up: the liquidation, or cessation of the life of a company, when its assets are sold and the proceeds distributed to those entitled to them.

Window-dressing: the manipulation of figures in the financial statements so as to show a business' financial performance, position and/or adaptability in a more favourable light than would be the case if such manipulation did not take place. The objective of such manipulation may be to encourage investors to invest in the business. There are illegal or fraudulent ways of manipulating figures in financial statements, though these are generally not what is meant by the term.

Working capital: the amount by which current assets exceed current liabilities. Also known as 'net current assets'.

Work in progress: work on manufacturing or processing goods, which, at a given point in time, for example, the last day of an accounting period, is incomplete or 'in progress'. An adjustment for the value of these partly-completed goods is made when preparing a manufacturing account. The value of work in progress is shown as part of the stock figure in the Balance Sheet.

Write-off: to 'write off' something means to debit (charge) it to the Profit and Loss Account. Expenses are 'written off' in the period to which they relate. Items of continuing value, for example fixed assets, because the benefits of owning them last over several accounting periods are 'written off', by means of depreciation, over the period for which they are expected to provide benefits to the firm which owns them.

Yield: the rate of return on an investment, usually expressed as a percentage. For example, dividend yield is the rate of return on an investment in shares.

Zero-rated firms: firms which do not have to add VAT to goods and services supplied by them, to others, and which receive a refund of VAT paid on goods and services purchased by them.

Index

The numbers shown after entries in the index refer to section numbers (not page numbers) within the text. For example, 'Accumulated fund, 47.5' means that reference to the Accumulated fund of a non-trading organisation will be found in Chapter 47, section 5.